ISBN 978-1-5280-4308-3
PIBN 10917614

1 MONTH OF
FREE
READING

at

www.ForgottenBooks.com

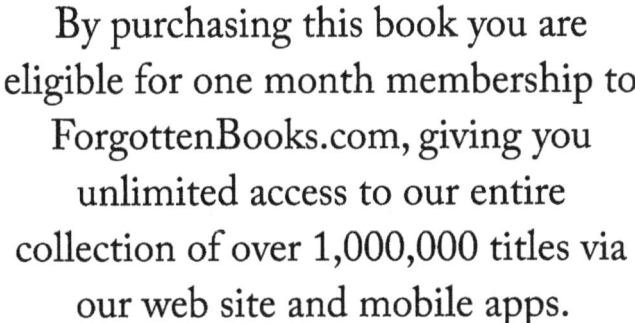

By purchasing this book you are eligible for one month membership to ForgottenBooks.com, giving you unlimited access to our entire collection of over 1,000,000 titles via our web site and mobile apps.

To claim your free month visit: www.forgottenbooks.com/free917614

REPORTS OF CASES

ARGUED AND DETERMINED

IN

The Court of King's Bench,

FROM

MICHAELMAS TERM, 1826, TO TRINITY TERM, 1827,

BOTH INCLUSIVE.

BY

JAMES DOWLING, Esq. of The Middle Temple,

AND

ARCHER RYLAND, Esq. of Gray's Inn,

BARRISTERS AT LAW.

VOL. IX.

WITH AN INDEX,

AND

TABLE OF PRINCIPAL MATTERS.

LONDON:

S. SWEET, 3, CHANCERY LANE; R. PHENEY, 17, FLEET STREET;
A. MAXWELL, 32, AND STEVENS AND SONS, 39, BELL YARD;
Law Booksellers and Publishers:
AND MILLIKEN AND SON, DUBLIN.

1831.

LONDON:

G. ROWORTH AND SONS, BELL YARD,
TEMPLE BAR.

JUDGES

COURT OF KING'S BENCH

During the period comprised in this volume.

———◆———

CHARLES Lord TENTERDEN, C. J.
Sir JOHN BAYLEY, Knt.
Sir GEORGE SOWLEY HOLROYD, Knt.
Sir JOSEPH LITTLEDALE, Knt.

———

ATTORNEYS-GENERAL.
Sir CHARLES WETHERELL, Knt.
Sir JAMES SCARLETT, Knt.

SOLICITOR-GENERAL.
Sir NICHOLAS CONYNGHAM TINDAL, Knt.

———

A

TABLE

OF THE

CASES REPORTED

IN THE NINTH VOLUME.

CASES

ARGUED AND DETERMINED

IN THE

COURT OF KING'S BENCH,

IN

MICHAELMAS TERM,

IN THE SEVENTH YEAR OF THE REIGN OF GEORGE IV.

𝕸emoranda.

DURING the last vacation, the Right Honorable *Robert*, Lord *Gifford*, Master of the Rolls, died at his house in *Whitehall Place*; and was succeeded by Sir *John Singleton Copley*, Knight, his Majesty's Attorney General.

Sir *Charles Wetherell*, Knight, his Majesty's Solicitor General, was promoted to the office of Attorney General. *Nicholas Conyngham Tindal*, of the Honorable Society of *Lincoln's Inn*, Esq. was appointed his Majesty's Solicitor General; and afterwards received the honour of Knighthood.

Monday,
6th November.

A ship sailing in 1821, for her port of destination and never arriving, but reported a few days after her departure to have foundered (crew surviving), may reasonably be presumed to be lost by perils of the seas, in the absence of any proof to the contrary; and in such case the assured on *goods* is not bound to call any of the crew, assuming them to have survived the loss of the vessel.

KOSTER *v.* REED, Bart., and another, administrators of Sir THOMAS REED.

ASSUMPSIT on a policy of insurance on goods on board the *Spanish* vessel *La Virgine della Solitudine,* at and from *Leghorn* to *Lisbon.* The first count of the declaration averred that the policy was effected by the plaintiff as agent of one *Leon Taurel;* that on the 9th *April,* 1821, the goods insured were shipped at *Leghorn,* and that the vessel sailed on that day, with the goods on board from *Leghorn* on the voyage insured, and was lost by perils of the sea. Second count, averring the loss to be by barratry of the master. Plea, non assumpsit. At the trial before *Abbott,* C. J., at the *London* adjourned sittings after last term, proof was given that the vessel sailed from *Leghorn* on the 9th *April,* 1821, with the goods in question on board, upon the voyage insured, but had never arrived at her port of destination. A witness, called on the part of the plaintiff, stated, that within a week after the vessel had sailed from *Leghorn,* he heard a report that she had sunk at sea, and that the crew had been saved. On the part of the defendant, it was objected that this evidence was insufficient to prove a loss either by perils of the sea or by barratry; and assuming that the hearsay evidence that the vessel had foundered, could be resorted to, then it was the duty of the plaintiff to produce the best, or rather the highest, evidence upon the subject, namely the crew of the vessel, or to shew that diligent efforts had been made to procure their attendance without success. The learned Judge, however, overruled the objection, and left it to the jury (who were merchants), to say, whether the circumstance of the ship never having arrived at her port of destination after the lapse of so many years, did not afford a reasonable presumption that she had foundered at sea; and he observed that, in his opinion, they might reasonably draw that conclusion from the evidence. The jury found for the plaintiff.

Barnewall now moved for a rule to shew cause why the verdict found for the plaintiff should not be set aside, and a new trial granted. It is submitted that there was not sufficient evidence to go to the jury, that the vessel was lost by perils of the sea or by barratry. The only evidence was the fact of non-arrival, and the report that the vessel had foundered at sea, her crew surviving. There was nothing to shew, in fact, that she was lost by a peril of the sea; and, if the hearsay evidence can be brought to bear upon the case, then as the crew were reported to have survived, they ought to have been called, or their absence accounted for. [*Abbott*, C. J. You must take the statement altogether; there is the fact of her non-arrival, and the report of her having foundered. There is no admissible evidence of the crew having survived, for that is merely hearsay]. But the bare fact of non-arrival is not sufficient, if there be other evidence to shew that the ship has been heard of. Here the ship was heard of, and the plaintiff ought to have gone farther, and given the highest evidence of which the case was susceptible. It may be admitted, as a general rule deducible from several cases in the books, that if a ship has been missing, and no intelligence received of her within a reasonable time after she sailed, it shall be presumed that she has foundered at sea (*a*). But here the vessel has been heard of in such a way as to afford a ground for presuming that the crew still survive. If so, then some of them ought to have been called to prove the loss averred, or at least, the plaintiff was bound to account for their absence. If it is part of the plaintiff's case to prove that the vessel was never

. (*a*) *Green* v. *Brown*, 2 Stra. 1199; *Twemlow* v. *Oswin*, 2 Camp. 85; *Houstman* v. *Thornton*, Holt. 488.   N. P. C. 242; Park on Insurance, 63; 413 Id.; 2 Marshall on Ins. 488.

heard of after her departure, and he proves that she has been heard of by means which are not admissible, namely, hearsay, then he must stand or fall by such evidence. If not, then here the jury were called upon to presume from hearsay testimony that the vessel foundered at sea, which is contrary to all the authorities upon the subject of hearsay evidence; *Williams* v. *The East India Company* (a); *Bull N. P.* 293.

ABBOTT, C. J.—The question is, whether there was sufficient evidence to be left to the jury to justify them in concluding that the ship was lost by the perils of the sea, or by the barratry of the master and mariners. Being a *Spanish* vessel, and owned by natives of that country, she sailed in the year 1821, for the port of *Lisbon*. It is admitted that she never arrived at *Lisbon*, but it is said that it was incumbent on the plaintiff to shew that she had never been heard of. That would be calling upon the plaintiff to do something like an impossibility, the fact being that she had been heard of, and was reported to have been lost. After the lapse of so long a time, it would be too much to require the plaintiff to be hunting all over *Europe*, for the purpose of endeavouring to find some of the *Spanish* seamen who navigated the vessel. In such a case as this, it would be laying down a rule, leading to great inconvenience and injustice, if the assured were bound to give any farther evidence than was produced at this trial. I think the jury might reasonably conclude from the fact that she had never been heard of for five years, that she was lost by perils of the sea.

BAYLEY, J.—It seems to me that there was sufficient evidence of a loss by perils of the sea, and that the jury drew the right conclusion. The ship sails in 1821. The plaintiff has no connexion with her or her crew; he is merely the owner of certain goods on board, which he

(a) 3 East, 192.

has insured against sea risk. From 1821, down to 1826, the ship never arrived at her destination. It is objected that the plaintiff has not called some persons connected with the ownership of the vessel, to shew that they have never heard of her. There is no legal evidence to shew that there are persons in existence connected with the ownership, who could be called; but I apprehend it was not an essential ingredient in the plaintiff's case, to shew that she had never been heard of by the owners. It is true that some of the crew may be living, and their testimony might be obtained by sending out a commission to examine them upon interrogatories, but that was all matter proper for the consideration of the jury, in forming their conclusion upon the question, whether this was a loss by perils of the sea; and I think they were fully warranted in the conclusion to which they came. It is said that the allegation being that she was lost by perils of the sea, the mere fact that she never was heard of, would not sustain that averment, for non constat, but that she may have been lost by means not insured against, and therefore, the plaintiff would not be entitled to recover; but these were all circumstances which have been presented to the consideration of the jury. The probability is, that if she was still in existence, or had been lost by other means than a peril of the sea, she would have been heard of during a period of five years. If she had been heard of, that evidence would as properly come from the defendant's side, as from the plaintiff's. The plaintiff is merely the owner of the goods; the owner of the ship is a middle man between him and the underwriter. If, then, there was any foundation for believing that there was evidence to rebut the presumption that the ship sailing on so dangerous an element, was really not lost at sea, but had arrived in safety, it was competent for the defendant to give such evidence; but in the absence of such evidence, I think the Judge at the trial was fully warranted in telling the jury, that there was sufficient primâ facie evidence to go to them, from which they might reasonably presume that the vessel was lost by the peril alleged in the declaration.

HOLROYD, J.—I am of the same opinion. I think there was sufficient primâ facie evidence, for the reasons mentioned by the Court, from which the jury might fairly draw the conclusion, that the vessel was lost by the perils of the sea.

LITTLEDALE, J., concurred.

Rule refused.

GILLBANK'S Bail.

Time allowed to add and justify bail by Habeas Corpus, where one of the bail of whom notice had been given, was taken suddenly ill.

IT is a general rule, that no additional time is allowed in bail by habeas corpus, if the bail do not come up pursuant to notice, or are rejected. In this case, however, one of the bail of whom notice had been given, had become suddenly ill, and was unable to attend. Upon an affidavit of this fact,

BAYLEY, J., allowed two days time to add and justify another bail.

Chitty, for the defendant.

SHILLITOE'S Bail.

Where time was applied for to send an affidavit of justification into the country, to amend a mistake in the jurat, the Court made the attorney pay the costs of the application.

IN this case there being a mistake in the jurat as to the names of the bail by affidavit,

R. V. *Richards* applied for time to send the papers back into the country, to have the mistake rectified.

1826.

SHILLITOE'S
Bail.

BAYLEY, J.—Let it be so, but it must be at the expense of the attorney. These applications are too frequent, from the carelessness or negligence of the attorney or his clerk. People will recollect, when they have to pay for their blunders.

Time given.

The KING v. JOHN RAWLINSON, Esq.

Tuesday,
7th November.

THIS was a rule, calling on the defendant, one of the justices of the peace for the county of *Middlesex*, to shew cause why a writ of mandamus should not issue, directed to him, commanding him to hear and determine an information exhibited before him by the surveyor of the pavements in the south-west district of the parish of *St. Pancras*, against *Robert Johnson*, a hackney-coachman, for taking his stand with his chariot in *Howland Street*, *Tottenham Court Road*, in the said district, and plying for a fare there, and thereby obstructing the public carriage way. Cause was now shewn against the rule, and the circumstances disclosed by the affidavits were these :— For more than twenty years there had been a hackney-coach stand, in *Howland Street*. Of late it had become inconvenient, in consequence of the width of the street not being sufficient for the passage of carriages to the houses of the inhabitants. The inhabitants complained to the commissioners for paving and lighting the district, and desired that the stand might be removed to some more convenient place. The commissioners acting, under the authority supposed to be vested in them, under the 12

A Paving Act authorised the commissioners to " direct and regulate" the hackney coach stands within their district ;— Held, that they might remove a hackney coach stand altogether, if it obstructed the public street.

Geo. 3, c. 69, s 36 (*a*), made an order that the stand should be removed from *Howland Street*, into a part of *Tottenham Court Road*, within the same district.   Due notice of this order was given to the coachmen plying on the stand, and they were required to remove their carriages into *Tottenham Court Road*.   With this order they refused to comply, on the ground that the commissioners had no jurisdiction to make it; and *Robert Johnson*, one of the coachmen, having taken his stand in the street, contrary to the said order, an information was exhibited against him before Mr. *Rawlinson*, to recover the penalty of the act; but the latter being of opinion that the paving commissioners had no authority to *remove* the coach stand, refused to interfere; wherefore the present application was made for a mandamus.

Scarlett and *Andrews*, against the rule, now contended that the commissioners of pavements had no authority to make the order sought to be enforced.   The 36th section of the 12 *Geo.* 3, c. 69, gives them power to " direct and regulate," the coach-stands within their district, but it does not authorise them " to alter and remove." Unless the words " direct and regulate," are tantamount " to alter and remove," it is quite clear that they have exceeded their jurisdiction in making the order in question.   The words " direct and regulate," are referrable only to the conduct of the coachmen, and the order in which the business of the stand is to be arranged, for which purpose the commissioners may give directions

(*a*) Which is in the following terms :—" And whereas hackney coachmen and hackney chairmen frequently take their stands with their coaches and chairs, in such parts of the streets so as to occasion obstructions both in the foot and carriage ways; be it therefore enacted, that from and after the passing of this act, the said commissioners, or any two or more of them, may *direct and regulate* such stands of all hackney coaches and chairs within the limits of this act, as they, in their discretion, think proper ; and if any hackney coachman or hackney chairman shall not comply with such directions and regulations, he or they shall forfeit the sum of 10s. for every such offence."

and make regulations; and it would be carrying these words beyond their fair and natural meaning, to say that they import a power to *alter and remove* the stands after they have been once established. The Hackney Coach Act, 9 *Anne*, c. 23, s. 16, gives power to the commissioners to make bye laws, which shall be binding on licensed hackneymen; and by s. 17, such bye laws are required to have the approval of the Lord Chancellor, the Lord Chief Justice of either Bench, and the Lord Chief Baron of the Exchequer, before they can be carried into effect. By virtue of the power so given, the commissioners of hackney coaches, in the year 1771, made certain bye laws, in which it was, amongst other things, ordered, " that no hackney coachmen shall stand and ply in any of the high or broad streets of the cities of *London* or *Westminster*, or suburbs thereof, being of the breadth or width of 30 feet between the posts or foot pavement on each side, or of 40 feet between the houses, where there are no posts or foot pavement, unless it be in the middle of such streets; nor shall stand in any street where it is not of the respective breadth or width before mentioned." It appears that *Howland Street* is more than 30 feet wide, and, therefore does not come within the prohibition. The power now assumed by the paving commissioners, has never hitherto been exercised by them; and, if they had supposed that they had such power, several acts of parliament which have passed to prohibit hackney coaches from standing in certain specified places, need not have been enacted. If this power exists in the commissioners, they may remove hackney coaches out of the parish of *St. Pancras* altogether; an extent of authority which the legislature certainly never could be supposed to have given them. Unless, therefore, the words " direct and regulate" are synonymous with " alter and remove," the commissioners have exceeded their jurisdiction.

Tindal, S. G., contrà. Adverting to the words of recital in the 17th section of 12 *Geo.*, 3, c. 36, it is clear that the legislature intended to give the paving commissioners the power now contended for. That section recites that " hackney coachmen and hackney chairmen frequently take their stands with their coaches and chairs in such parts of the streets, so as to occasion obstructions both in the foot and carriage ways," and then power is given to. the commissioners to " direct and regulate" *such* stands. It cannot be doubted that under the words " direct and regulate," they might remove a coach-stand from one part of a street to another; and, if so, why not from one street to another street, if within the same district ? The power of directing and regulating the coach-stands would be altogether nugatory, in many instances, if the commissioners might not change the site of coach-stands, as circumstances and public convenience might require. It is not pretended that they have any power to remove a coach-stand altogether out of the parish. If such an attempt were made, it would be such an abuse of their power as might render the commissioners criminally liable.

ABBOTT, C. J.—Looking at the whole of this clause of the act of parliament, I think the word " direct," may be taken to have been used in the sense of the word " appoint." Now, if the commissioners have power to *appoint* the situations in which hackney coachmen shall stand, that power necessarily includes the power of saying to them, " you shall not take your station here, but you may take it there." And if that be so, then I think the commissioners were justified in ordering that the hackney coachmen should not take their station, or make their stand, in any part of *Howland Street.* It seems to me, therefore, that the magistrate ought to hear the information exhibited against *Johnson* for refusing to obey the commissioners' order ; and, on that ground, the rule must be made absolute for a mandamus. With respect, however, to that part of the order which directs the coachmen to take their stand in *Tottenham Court Road*, I doubt whether the commissioners have power to send them there.

HOLROYD, J. (*a*).—Taking the recital in the clause in question, and the obstruction sworn to have been occasioned by the stand in *Howland Street*, into consideration, I think the words of the enacting part of the clause are sufficiently strong to authorise the commissioners in removing the stand, so as it shall not obstruct the public highway. The recital is, that hackney coachmen frequently take their stands with their coaches in such parts of the streets so as to occasion obstructions, and then power is given to the commissioners to direct and regulate *such* stands; that is, such stands as occasion obstructions. Now, if to remove the obstruction, it is necessary that the stand should be entirely removed, this power, as it seems to me, is necessarily incident to the power of directing and regulating such stands.

LITTLEDALE, J.—I am of the same opinion. The bye laws made by the hackney coach commissioners in 1771, enumerate a great many places in which hackney coachmen are not to ply at all. Now, the statute 9 *Anne*, c. 23, merely authorises the making of bye laws " for the good government and regulation of licensed hackney coachmen." The Paving Act is just as large in its terms, and ought to receive a liberal construction; for, otherwise, the object of the legislature in preventing obstructions, might in many instances be defeated.

Rule absolute.

(*a*) *Bayley*, J., was gone to chambers.

PIGGOTT, Clerk, *v.* BAYLEY.

In an action for not setting out tithes of hay, an immemorial custom for setting out such tithe was averred to exist " within the parish, and the limits, bounds, and titheable places thereof," and it appearing in evidence, that one township of the parish was covered by a modus for hay tithe:—Held, no variance from the custom alleged.

THIS was an action of debt on the statute 2 and 3 *Ed.* 6, c. 13, for not setting out tithes of hay in the parish of *Edgmond*, in the county of *Salop*, of which the plaintiff was rector. The second count of the declaration (upon which alone the plaintiff went), averred, that from time immemorial, there hath been within the parish of *Edgmond*, the bounds, limits, and titheable places thereof, a custom of and concerning the tithe of hay, that every eleventh cock of hay, after the grass has been mowed and cut down, and so managed, treated, and dealt with, as to be in a fit state to be carried from the ground and made into ricks, after the course of good husbandry, shall be separated, divided, and set out from the residue of the cocks, for the tithe of all the hay so mowed and cut down as aforesaid; and that defendant mowed divers, to wit, fifty acres of hay, and did not set out the tithe according to the custom aforesaid. Plea, the general issue, nil debet. At the trial before *Garrow*, B., at the last *Shrewsbury* assizes, it appeared in evidence, that the parish of *Edgmond* consisted of several distinct townships, and that in each the custom of tithing hay prevailed, as alleged in the declaration, with the exception of one township, called *Tiverton*, which was covered by a modus. Upon this fact appearing, it was objected on the part of the defendant, that the custom as alleged was not proved, and therefore, that the plaintiff must be nonsuited. The learned Judge, however, overruled the objection, and the plaintiff had a verdict, with liberty to the defendant to move to enter a nonsuit.

W. E. Taunton now moved accordingly. It was incumbent on the plaintiff to prove the custom as laid. Here the custom was laid, as being applicable to all the titheable places within the bounds and limits of the parish. Proof that it prevailed in most places in the parish was not sufficient; the evidence should have gone on to shew, that it prevailed in all. It is a general rule, that customs and prescriptions shall be proved as broadly as laid. Now here, the township of *Tiverton* is a titheable place within the parish, and that being proved to be covered by a modus, there is a fatal variance between the averment and the evidence of the custom.

ABBOTT, C. J.—I think the allegation in the declaration may be reasonably understood to apply to those places in the parish wherein the tithe of hay was usually set out in kind; and that was proved. I observe the allegation is only, that this custom prevails *within*, and not *throughout* the parish. If the allegation had been that the custom prevailed *throughout* the parish, there would have been a great deal more in the argument.

BAYLEY, J.—I also think that the fair construction of the custom, as alleged, is, that in all those parts of the parish in which hay is titheable, the manner of setting out the tenth cock is that which is averred, and if so, then the evidence fully supports the declaration. It is no answer to the construction thus put upon the custom as averred, that there is a modus existing in point of fact in one of the townships. That modus may, or may not, be good in point of law. Suppose this modus should be hereafter called in question, and proved to be bad, it seems to me, that the evidence given in this case would, if not rebutted, be sufficient to establish the custom as to that township, although a modus may now exist therein. I am, therefore, of opinion, that the allegation in this declaration is substantially proved, and that we are at liberty to construe it as applicable to those parts of the parish in which the tithe of hay is set out. To that extent the evidence fully supports the custom.

HOLROYD J.—I think that the custom, as stated, was substantially proved. It is a custom applicable to the setting out of the tithe of hay only in those parts of the parish where the hay tithes are set out. If a money payment exists in other places, they are virtually excluded from the operation of the custom; but still that will not affect the legality of the custom, as set out.

LITTLEDALE, J.—If the custom can be construed as prevailing *throughout* the parish, from the manner in which it is averred in the declaration, it is clearly not proved; *Rogers* v. *Allen* (a). I am inclined to think, that the averment must be so construed, and therefore that the variance is fatal.

Rule refused.

(a) 1 Campb. 309.

FREE, D. D. v. BURGOYNE.

PROHIBITION. Judgment had been given by this Court for a prohibition as to part of the proceedings, and for a consultation as to the rest (b). A writ of error was brought to reverse that judgment, made returnable in the Exchequer Chamber, where it was decided by this Court, that a writ of error in prohibition did not lie to the Exchequer Chamber (c), and a new writ to the House of Lords was issued and allowed.

Denman now moved to stay the proceedings upon the consultation. He produced an affidavit, stating, that after the first writ of error had been allowed, and a consultation carried down and delivered to the Judge of the Court

In prohibition, a writ of consultation sued out and delivered to the Judge of the Court below, before a writ of error allowed, is not supersedable by such writ of error; and this Court will not stay the proceedings upon it.

(b) Ante, vol. viii., 179.   (c) Ante, vol. viii., 587.

below, the plaintiff moved to stay the proceedings upon that consultation ; and that upon the motion being refused, a new writ of error had been sued out and allowed ; and contended, that this was a description of suit to which the ordinary rules of law did not apply, and that the suing out a writ of consultation, and delivering it to the Judge of the Court below, could not be deemed an executing of a writ in execution. *Sed,*

PER CURIAM.—This application comes too late. If the writ of consultation had been sued out after the writ of error had been allowed, we might have quashed it, quia improvidé emanavit. Even if the writ of consultation had been delivered to the Judge of the Court below, after the writ of error had been allowed, that might have been a misprision, of which we might have taken cognizance. Here, it is evident, upon the affidavit, that the writ of consultation had been both sued out and delivered to the Judge of the Court below, before the second writ of error, directed to the House of Lords, was allowed. The writ of consultation, therefore, was in the nature of an execution on the judgment in prohibition, and became, by its delivery to the Judge of the Court below, a writ in execution, executed. That being the case, it was not supersedable by the writ of error, and the proceedings upon it cannot be stayed.

Rule refused.

DOE, on the demise of TYNDALE, and others, *v.* HEMMING, GEORGE, and others.

THIS was an action of ejectment, to recover the possession of certain lands in the county of *Suffolk*. Plea, The attorney for the lessor of the plaintiff, in ejectment, obtained from the defendant an existing lease, to him, of the premises in question, for the purpose of preventing the defendant from setting it up as a defence to the action, and afterwards produced it at the trial, pursuant to notice from the defendant :—Held, that he had thereby admitted the validity of the lease, and that it might be read in evidence on the part of the defendant, without proof of its execution.

not guilty, and issue thereon. At the trial before *Bayley*, J., at the last *Suffolk* assizes, the lessors of the plaintiff having made out a primâ facie title, as the devisees of a Mr. *Blacknell*, heir at law of a Lady *Graves*, who was alleged to be seised in fee of the estate; the defendants called upon them to produce a lease of the same estate, which had been granted in the year 1812, by Lady *Graves*, to the defendant *George*, for a term of fourteen years, commencing in *October* 1812. The plaintiff's attorney had been entrusted with the lease, in confidence, by the defendant *George*. At the assizes, a summons was taken out by the defendant's attorney, for the plaintiff's attorney, to shew cause why he should not produce the lease, and allow a copy of it to be made. Upon that, the defendant, *George*, expressly forbade the plaintiff's attorney to give up or shew the contents of the lease; and the result of the summons was, an order for the plaintiff's attorney to give up the names of the subscribing witnesses, which he did: the lease was produced; but as the defendants were not in a situation to call the subscribing witnesses, it was objected that it could not be read. The learned Judge over-ruled the objection; the lease was read, and the plaintiff nonsuited; with liberty, however, for him to move to enter a verdict in his favour.

Storks now moved for a rule to shew cause accordingly. This lease was admitted to be read in evidence by the learned Judge at the trial, upon the authority of the cases of *Pearce* v. *Hooper* (a), and *Orr* v. *Morrice* (b), considering it as a muniment of the title of the lessors of the plaintiff. If it had been rightly so considered, it would undoubtedly have been admissible in evidence, without proof of its execution; because those cases establish the principle, that where an instrument is produced by a person who derives a beneficial interest under it, proof of its execution is dispensed with (c). But the present is distin-

(a) 3 Taunt. 60. (b) 6 J. B. Moore, 347; 3 B. & B. 139.
(c) Vide *Barnett* v. *Lynch*, ante, vol. viii. 368. 5 B. & C. 589.

guishable from both these cases. In *Pearce* v. *Hooper*, the plaintiff claimed a beneficial estate under the deed; in *Orr* v. *Morrice*, the lease was the title of the party producing it: here the lessors of the plaintiff had a title entirely independent of the lease, and which they would equally have relied on, if there had been no such instrument in existence. This case, therefore, falls within another established principle, namely, that where an adverse party, having notice to produce a written instrument, produces it accordingly at the trial, the party who calls for it is bound to call the subscribing witness to prove the execution. *Phil. Ev.* 3d ed. 396; *Gordon* v. *Secretan* (a).

ABBOTT, C. J.—I am of opinion that the nonsuit in this case was right. The lease was delivered by one of the defendants to the attorney for the lessors of the plaintiff, as a valid lease, and was received as such by him. The subsequent detention of the lease by him, and the authority he obtained from that defendant, to refuse either to deliver it up, or to exhibit its contents, could have originated but in one motive, namely, to prevent the possibility of the defendants setting up the lease as a defence to the action. The lessors of the plaintiff, therefore, intended to derive a benefit from the possession of the lease, and their conduct, through their attorney, was such as clearly admitted its validity; and upon that ground it seems to me, that this case is within the principle laid down in *Pearce* v. *Hooper*, and *Orr* v. *Morrice*, and that the lease was properly received in evidence, without proof of its execution.

The rest of the Court concurred.

Rule refused.

(a) 8 East, 548.

WINTER *v.* BARNES.

Process being returnable in *Easter,* plaintiff, in *Trinity* term, files common bail for defendant, and delivers a declaration with notice to plead. In *Trinity* vacation, judgment is signed for want of plea: —Held, that defendant was not entitled to an imparlance until *Michaelmas* term, for this rule only applies where the defendant himself is properly in Court before the declaration is delivered.

JEREMY moved for a rule nisi, to set aside the judgment signed in this case, for irregularity, with costs. The writ was returnable on *Wednesday,* after fifteen days of *Easter.* Nothing was afterwards done until the 6th of *June, in Trinity* term, when the plaintiff filed common bail for the defendant, under the statute, and, on the same day, served a declaration with notice to plead indorsed thereon. In *Trinity* vacation, the plaintiff signed judgment as for want of a plea. It was now contended that the judgment was irregularly signed, inasmuch as the defendant was entitled to an imparliamence until the present *Michaelmas* term, by reason that the plaintiff had not filed his declaration before the *essoign* day of *Trinity* term. *Sed Per*

BAYLEY, J. (*a*).—That rule applies only where the defendant is completely in Court. Had the defendant himself filed common bail or appeared, that would have been the rule of practice; but, if the plaintiff had irregularly filed common bail for the defendant, under the statute, in the term after the term of which the process was returnable, he ought to have come immediately to the Court for that irregularity. The instant the declaration was delivered, he must have known that the plaintiff had filed common bail. There were then eight remaining days in *Trinity* term, in which the defendant ought to have applied to the Court. Upon payment of costs, and bringing the money into Court, the judgment may, however, be set aside.

Rule refused.

(*a*) The only Judge in Court.

Thursday,
9th November.

LLOYD and Co. v. FRESHFIELD and another.

ASSUMPSIT for money lent to the defendants as co-partners. The first-named defendant pleaded non assumpsit, on which issue was joined. The other defendant suffered judgment by default. At the trial before *Abbott*, C. J., at the *London* adjourned sittings after last term, it appeared in evidence that the money, for which the action was brought, had been lent by the plaintiffs to one of the defendants only. Two questions were raised at the trial; first, whether the money had been lent on the partnership credit, or only on the private credit of one of the partners for his own private purposes, with the plaintiffs' knowledge; and second, whether any portion of the money had found its way into the partnership funds, and had been applied to partnership purposes, so as to make the defendant *Freshfield* liable pro tanto. The jury found their verdict for the defendant.

Where a partner borrowed money on his own private account, and subsequently applied part of it to partnership purposes:—Held, that the lender could not sue the partnership for the money so borrowed.

Brougham, now moved for a rule nisi for a new trial, on the ground that on the second point the verdict was against the evidence.

ABBOTT, C. J.—Assuming that any portion of this money found its way into the partnership funds, I by no means wish it to be understood, that if one partner borrows money on his own private credit, and afterwards applies it to the partnership uses, the lender of the money may, in consequence of such subsequent application, charge the partnership with the liability of the single partner in his private capacity. That is a doctrine to which I cannot yield; and which cannot, in my opinion, be supported in law.

BAYLEY, J., HOLROYD, J., and LITTLEDALE, J., concurred in the propriety of the verdict.

Rule refused.

Thursday,
9th November.

HARGRAVE *v.* SHEWIN and DIGBY.

In replevin for illegally distraining plaintiff's growing corn in *four* closes, the defendants avowed the distress for rent in arrear, averring that plaintiff held the closes in which, &c., at and under a certain yearly rent; to which plaintiff pleaded that he did not hold in manner and form as alleged. Upon proof that the plaintiff held the *four* closes and *two* others at the rent stated in the avowry :— Held, no variance.

THIS was an action of replevin. The declaration averred that the defendants took the growing corn of the plaintiff in *four* closes, mentioning them severally by name. Avowry by *Shewin,* and cognizance by *Digby,* alleged that the plaintiff, and two other persons, naming them, for a long space of time, to wit, &c., ending, &c., and from thence until, and at the same time when, &c., held and enjoyed an undivided moiety of the said closes, in which, &c., with the appurtenances, as tenants thereof to the defendant *Shewin,* by virtue of a certain demise thereof, theretofore made, at and under a certain yearly rent, to wit, the yearly rent of 14*l* 1*s.* 2*d.,* payable quarterly; and so justified the taking the corn for rent in arrear. Plea in bar, that the plaintiff and the other persons named in the avowry and cognizance, did not hold in manner and form as alleged in the said avowry and cognizance; and issue thereon. At the trial before *Abbott,* C. J., at the last assizes for the county of *Lincoln,* it appeared in evidence, that the plaintiff and the other persons mentioned in the avowry and cognizance, held an undivided moiety of *six* closes at the rent therein stated. It was objected that this was a fatal variance between the evidence and the avowry; but the learned Judge thought otherwise, and the defendant had a verdict, with liberty to the plaintiff to move to enter a verdict the other way.

Reader, now moved accordingly. There was a fatal variance between the evidence and the avowry. The defendants avow that the plaintiff held only *four* closes at the yearly rent of 14*l.* 1*s.* 2*d.;* and the evidence is of a demise of *six* closes. There is, therefore, a fatal variance. The defendant is bound to state the demise correctly in his pleading, *Brown* v. *Layce* (*a*). Great inconvenience may follow, if hereafter another action shall be brought between the same parties, for the judgment in this case will be an estoppel against the defendant from shewing that the rent of the six closes is more than 14*l.* 1*s.* 2*d.* Perhaps the defendants were not bound to point out precisely what closes were held by the plaintiff. It would have been sufficient to allege that the premises in question, "amongst others," were holden of the defendants, but having chosen to give a precise description of the premises, they ought to have been proved in form and manner as alleged.

ABBOTT, C. J.—There is no doubt that each of the closes demised is liable for the whole rent; and therefore, there is no incongruity in the defendants saying that the closes in which the distress was taken, were held under the whole rent payable for the six closes.

BAYLEY, J.—I think the evidence proved the allegation that the plaintiff held four closes; for those four might have been held with others under one tenancy. The rent for the whole might be taken in one close.

HOLROYD, J.—The plaintiff holds the four closes at the entire yearly rent mentioned in the declaration, and a distress might be taken for the whole rent in each close, or any part of the demised premises.

LITTLEDALE, J., concurred.

Rule refused.

(*a*) 4 Taunt. 320.

1826.

HARGRAVE
v.
SHEWIN.

HOPKINS *v.* GRAZEBROOK.

Vendor con-
tracting to sell
to vendee an
estate with a
good title,
when he has
only an equi-
table title l'im-
self, and is not
in possession,
and failing
in his contract
by the time
stipulated, is
liable to more
than *nominal
damages* for
the breach of
the contract,
in addition to
the expenses
incurred by
the purchaser.

THIS was an action for damages, in not performing a
contract for the sale of certain premises, agreed to be sold
by the defendant to the plaintiff. The declaration stated,
that the defendant caused the premises in question (situate
at *Stourbridge*, in *Worcestershire*) to be put up to sale by
auction, in *November*, 1825, subject to certain conditions,
and, amongst others, that the purchaser should immediately pay down a deposit, and should pay the residue
of the purchase money on the 25th of *March* then next
ensuing, and that, on payment thereof, he should be let
into possession, and a proper conveyance should be executed
by the vendor, who undertook to make a good title. The
declaration then averred, that the plaintiff became the
purchaser of the premises in question, paid a deposit, and
was ready to pay the remainder of the purchase money
at the time specified, and requested the defendant to make
a good title to the premises ; breach, that he did not do
so, and did not execute a proper conveyance to the plaintiff,
whereby plaintiff was deprived of all benefit, which he
might have derived from the purchase, and was put to
great expense. Other counts more general. Plea, non
assumpsit, and issue thereon. The defendant paid into
Court the sum of 22*l.* 8*s.* 8*d.*, being the amount of the
plaintiff's particulars of demand for expenses actually incurred, and also a small sum of money as nominal damages
for the breach of the contract of sale. At the trial, before
Garrow, B., at the last assizes for the county of *Worcester*,
it appeared in evidence that Messrs. *Hill* and *Co.*, of
Worcester, had contracted to sell a certain estate, consisting of a dwelling-house, stables, outhouses, yards and
other premises, situate in that city, to a Mr. *Harwood*.
Whilst the negociation for a conveyance was depending,
the defendant agreed to purchase the whole estate of
Harwood, and before the conveyance of the latter was

completed, the defendant advertised the property for sale by auction, in lots. The sale took place accordingly, and the plaintiff became the purchaser of two lots, consisting of a yard and a stable, which were contiguous to his dwelling-house, and paid the deposit money thereon in pursuance of the conditions of sale. In the mean time, some dispute arose between *Hill* and Co. and *Harwood*, and the former ultimately refused to convey the estate to the latter, and, consequently, the defendant was unable to fulfil his contract with the plaintiff, who thereupon brought the present action. The plaintiff produced some evidence to shew that, had the contract of sale been completed, the premises in question would have added materially to the convenience, and improved the value of, his own property, and, on that ground, he sought to recover substantial damages for the breach of the contract. For the defendant, it was insisted that, in the absence of all fraud on his part, the plaintiff could be entitled to no more than the nominal damages, which, together with the expenses out of pocket, had been paid into Court, and therefore, that the action must fail. The learned Judge was of opinion that the jury might, if they thought proper, give more than nominal damages; and, under his Lordship's directions, they found for the plaintiff, damages 70*l.*, with liberty, however, to the defendant, to move to enter a nonsuit.

Campbell now moved accordingly for a rule nisi to enter a nonsuit. The question is, whether the plaintiff was entitled to recover more than nominal damages, and it is submitted that he was not. It is clear that the defendant acted bonâ fide, and without fraud, and all the authorities go to shew that under such circumstances the plaintiff can only be entitled to recover nominal damages. [*Bayley* J. Is he not entitled to recover damages to the amount he proves himself to have been injured by the breach of the defendant's contract? You say here is no fraud; is it no fraud for a man to take upon himself an authority to sell an estate, and convey a good title, when he has no title himself at the time of the sale?] Upon what principle can more than nominal damages be given in a case where it is not pretended that there is any fraud? In *Sugden's Vendor and Purchaser* (a), it is said, on the authority of cases there cited, that " where a bonâ fide vendor has not a title to the estate, the Court will not in favour of the purchaser decree an impossibility, but will leave the purchaser to his remedy at law upon the articles, and although he must necessarily obtain a verdict, if he have recourse to law, yet he would obtain nominal damages only, for a purchaser is not entitled to any compensation for the fancied goodness of his bargain, which he may suppose he has lost." One of the authorities there cited, is decisive to shew that the verdict in this case cannot be supported; *Fleaureau* v. *Thornhill* (b). In that case the defendant, acting in perfect good faith, had sold an estate, and contracted to make a good title, but failed in performing his contract; whereupon the plaintiff brought an action, and recovered damages to the amount of 20*l.*, ultra the expense incurred; and upon a motion being made for a new trial, *De Grey*, C. J., said, " I think the verdict wrong in point of law. Upon a contract for a purchase, if the title proves bad, and the vendor is, without fraud, incapable of making a good one, I do not think that the purchaser can be entitled to any damages for the fancied goodness of the bargain, which he supposes he has lost;" and *Blackstone*, J., said, " These contracts are merely upon condition, frequently expressed, but always implied, that the vendor has a good title. If he has not, the return of the deposit, with interest and costs, is all that can be expected." On the, authority of this case, the defendant is entitled to have a rule nisi to enter a nonsuit.

(a) 7th Ed. 197.
(b) 2 Sir W. Bl. 1078 ; and see *Johnson* v. *Johnson*, 3 B. & P. 167.

Brig's case, Palm. 364. *Bratt.* v. *Ellis*, Sug. V. & P. 7 Ed. Appendix ; and *Jones* v. *Dyke, Id.* 8.

1826.

Hopkins
v.
Grazebrook.

Abbott, C. J.—I shall only say, that at this moment of time, I cannot give my unqualified assent to the general proposition, that when the vendor of an estate is not competent to make good a title which he has engaged to perfect, the vendee shall only recover nominal damages for the breach of contract. If it were necessary to decide that general question, I should wish to take further time for consideration. As at present advised, I only say that I do not at this moment give my assent to it. I think it unnecessary to decide that question on this occasion, because the facts of this case are perfectly distinguishable from those in *Fleaureau* v. *Thornhill.* In that case, the vendor was the only owner of the estate. An objection was made to his title; he made an offer to convey the estate with such title as he had, or to return the purchase money with interest; and the Court thought that the buyer ought to have been content with that proposition. In this case, not only no such offer was made, but none could have been made, because the vendor at the time of the sale, had no title whatever, good or bad, to the estate. The defendant, unfortunately for himself, relying upon the contract which he had made with *Harwood,* which *Harwood* had himself only become a contractor with *Hill* & Co., thought proper to put up the estate to auction before he had obtained the conveyance. I think that, before he put up the estate to be sold by auction, he ought to have taken care to inform himself that he should be in a situation to offer *some* title, if he could not make a perfect title. I do not say he was bound to go the length of offering a *good and perfect* title; far from it, because some serious inconvenience might result from laying down so broad a proposition. Here, however, the defendant had nothing at all, which he could offer in the shape of title; he chose to take upon himself the chance of offering to sale an estate, in which he had not himself a shadow of interest or title whatsoever, and therefore I think he is bound to make good to the purchaser at the auction, whatever benefit he has lost, by the breach of the defendants' undertaking.

BAYLEY, J.—The case of *Fleaureau* v. *Thornhill* is perfectly distinguishable from the present. Where a party sells that which is his own, and which he has obtained upon an understanding and belief that there is a good title to it in himself, he stands in a very different situation from the man who, for aught that appears, has never examined the title to that which he professes to sell, and who, at the most, has nothing more than an equitable interest in himself, or the right to go into a court of Equity to call upon another person to perform the contract he has entered into with him. When a man professes to sell an estate to another, he holds out that it is his own. If he holds out to the purchaser that it is his own estate—that he has derived it from his ancestors, or otherwise; the presumption on the part of the purchaser, is, that the vendor himself is satisfied with the validity of the title; and in such a case, there may be great hardship in forcing the vendor to pay damages, if it turned out ultimately that he was mistaken in his own legal rights, and had not upon accurate investigation, a legal title: but where the party professes to sell as his own, that which is not his own—and as if he had examined the title when he had not, it seems to me, that his misconduct in those particulars, subjects him to the payment of such damages to the purchaser, as a jury may think he has really sustained, by not having that which the seller contracted he should have. I therefore think that the verdict in this case ought not to be disturbed.

HOLROYD, J.—I also think that this case is very distinguishable from that in Sir *W. Blackstone's* Reports. In that case the Court thought, that inasmuch as the contract was not to make a good title absolutely; but only to sell the estate [of which the party was then actually in possession], with such title as he had, and having every reason to suppose that he should be able to make a good title; he ought not to pay any thing more than nominal damages for the breach of his contract. But here the party at the time of the sale, had no right to suppose that he had a title to the property, because there was no title conveyed to him. He chose to rely upon an agreement with a person, who was himself only endeavouring to negociate the sale of the estate to him from the original owner. Under such circumstances, I think the defendant ought to take the consequences of his own improvident contract, and that the plaintiff was entitled to such damages as the jury in their discretion thought he was entitled to receive.

LITTLEDALE, J.—I am of the same opinion.

Rule refused.

JOHN DODDS and others *v.* RICHARD EMBLETON.

CASE for damage sustained by the plaintiffs, as owners of a vessel called *The Atlantic,* in consequence of that vessel having been run down in the river *Tyne,* by a ship called *The George* (a *British* vessel), owned by the defendant, through the negligence and mismanagement of the defendant's master and crew. At the last assizes for the county of *Newcastle,* before *Park,* J., it appeared in evidence, that at the time when the accident happened which occasioned the injury complained of, there was on board the defendant's vessel, a pilot duly licensed by the Trinity-House at *Newcastle-upon-Tyne,* in pursuance of the Local Pilot Act, 41 *Geo.* 3, c. 86, s. 6, and therefore it was con-

The master of a vessel having on board a licensed pilot appointed by the Trinity-House of Newcastle-upon-Tyne, under the Local Act, 41 G. 3, c. 86, s. 6, is not entitled to the protection of the 55 section of the General Pilot Act, 6 G. 4, c. 125.

tended on the part of the defendant, that he was not liable for the damage sought to be recovered, inasmuch as he was entitled to the protection of the General Pilot Act, 6 *Geo.* 4, c. 125, s. 55. The learned Judge reserved the point, and the plaintiffs had a verdict, with liberty to the defendant to move to enter a nonsuit.

Holt, now moved accordingly. The case turns upon the two acts of parliament, 41 *Geo.* 3, c. 86, which is the *Newcastle-upon-Tyne* Trinity-House Pilot Act, and the 6 *Geo.* 4, c. 125, which is the General Pilot Act; and the question is, whether upon the construction of these two acts taken together, the defendant having a licensed pilot on board, in pursuance of the Local Act, is not within the protection of section 55 of 6 *Geo.* 4, c. 125. That section declares, " that no owner or master of any ship shall be answerable for any loss or damage which shall happen to any person from any neglect, default, incompetency, or incapacity of any licensed pilot, so long as such pilot shall be duly qualified, or so long as no qualified pilot shall have offered to take charge thereof." By the 41 *Geo.* 3, c. 86, s. 6, the Trinity-House of *Newcastle-upon-Tyne* is authorised to appoint licensed pilots for the navigation of the river *Tyne* and port of *Newcastle,* and it was proved that on the occasion in question, there was on board the defendant's vessel, a pilot duly licensed under that act. It is admitted, that the 6th section alone of the Local Act might not perhaps protect the defendant, because it may be said that it was optional whether he would take a pilot on board or not, and that the protection given by the General Pilot Act, was only given where it is compulsory to take a pilot; but, upon adverting to the 6th section of the General Pilot Act, it will be found, that the Trinity-Houses of *Hull* and *Newcastle* are to appoint pilots, under the General Pilot Act, in the same mannner as the corporation of the Trinity-House of *Deptford, Dover, Deal, Isle of Thanet, Cinque Ports,* &c.; and section 55 of the same act, affords the protection now contended for, in the words already referred to. It is true, indeed, that by section 89 (*a*), an exception is made in favour of particular jurisdictions and districts; but this is for the purpose merely of preserving their franchises, and does not take from masters of ships who receive licensed pilots on board, the protection of the 55 section, which it is submitted overrides the local act.

Abbott, C. J.—We are of opinion that the provision contained in the General Pilot Act, 6 *Geo.* 4, c. 125, s. 55, does not extend to the case of a ship having on board a pilot licensed by the *Trinity-House* of *Newcastle-upon-Tyne*, and therefore that this defendant was not protected from liability for the damage sought to be recovered in this action.

The other Judges concurred.

Rule refused (*b*).

(*a*) Which enacts, "That nothing in this act shall extend to the taking away, abridging, defeating, impeaching, or interrupting of any grants, liberties, franchises, or privileges, heretofore granted by any charters or acts of parliament to the pilots of the *Trinity-House* of *Kingston-upon-Hull*, or the *Trinity-House* of *Newcastle-upon-Tyne*, or to give any authority to the *Trinity-House* of *Deptford Strond*, within any [ports having separate jurisdiction in matters of pilotage, under any act of parliament or charter, or to alter or repeal any provisions contained in any act or acts of parliament as to pilots or pilotage, within the limits prescribed by any act or acts relating to pilotage for such ports, or to the burthen of vessels navigating to or from such ports."

(*b*) Vide, *The Attorney General* v. *Case*, 3 Price, 302.

Where *A.*
has been te-
nant of pre-
mises, and
upon his
quitting them
B. takes pos-
session, the
legal pre-
sumption, un-
til the con-
trary appears,
is, that *B.*
came in as the
assignee of
A.; and a no-
tice to quit,
served upon
B., will sus-
tain an eject-
ment against
A.

DOE, on the demise of MORRIS, *v.* WILLIAMS.

THIS was an action of ejectment, to recover the possession of certain premises, situate in the parish of *Brilley,*
in the county of *Hereford.* Plea, not guilty, and issue
thereon.   At the trial before *Burrough,* J., at the last
Herefordshire assizes, the lessor of the plaintiff proved
that he was the owner of the premises, and that the
defendant had occupied them as his tenant, and paid rent
for them down to the year 1819; that after that time the
defendant ceased to occupy the premises, and they were
occupied by one *Wellings,* his son-in-law; and that since
the occupation by *Wellings,* no rent had ever been paid
either by him or the defendant.   It also appeared, that
notice to quit had been served upon *Wellings,* but none
upon the defendant; and that, when the copy of the
declaraton in ejectment was served, the defendant entered
into a rule to come in and defend as the landlord.   It was,
thereupon, objected, that a notice to quit, served upon
another person, would not sustain the action against the
defendant; and that no notice to quit having been served
upon the defendant, the plaintiff must be nonsuited.
The learned Judge over-ruled the objection, and the plaintiff obtained a verdict, with liberty to the defendant to
move to enter a nonsuit.

O. *Russell,* now moved accordingly.   The notice to quit
served upon *Wellings* was a nullity, for there was nothing
to shew that the relation of landlord and tenant ever
existed between him and the lessor of the plaintiff.   He
had never paid rent to the lessor of the plaintiff; he had
never, in any way, recognised him as his landlord, and
therefore a notice to quit, served upon him, could not
sustain the ejectment against the present defendant.

BAYLEY, J.—Where it appears in evidence, that *A.* is

tenant, and that, upon his quitting the premises, *B.* takes possession of them, the legal presumption is, unless rebutted, that *B.* comes in as the assignee of *A.*, *Doe v. Murless* (*a*). Here there was nothing to rebut the presumption that *Wellings* took possession of the premises as the assignee of his father-in-law *Williams*, and therefore, the notice to quit was properly served on *Wellings*.

ABBOTT, C. J.—Under the circumstances of the case, as they appeared at the trial, I think the notice to quit is sufficient to maintain the action.

The other Judges concurred.

Rule refused.

(*a*) 6 M. & S. 110.

----◆----

THOMPSON and others *v.* GEORGE TRAIL, GEORGE
TRAIL the younger, and MATTHEW BROWN.

THIS was an action of trover to recover the value of ten barrels of tin, alleged to have been wrongfully converted by the defendants to their own use. Plea, the general issue, and issue thereon. At the trial before *Abbott*, C. J., at the *London* adjourned sittings after last term, it appeared in evidence that the plaintiffs were merchants in *London*, and that the defendants, *Trail* and Son, were the owners of the ship *George* and *Mary*, of which the defendant *Brown* was master and commander. On the 23d *January* last, the plaintiffs sold the ten barrels of tin in question to persons trading under the firm of *May, Alewyn,* and Co., and by their order the tin was shipped by the

Vendor ships by order of vendee, goods which by the bill of lading are consigned to a third person at a foreign port. Before the vessel sails, the vendee stops payment, and the vendor thereupon demands the goods of the captain, without tendering freight or expenses of unshipping. The captain refuses to deliver, solely on the ground that he has signed a bill of lading for the consignee:—Held, sufficient evidence of a conversion to maintain trover at the suit of the vendor.

plaintiffs on board the *George* and *Mary*. The invoice was made out to *May, Alewyn,* and Co. When the goods were delivered on board, the mate signed a receipt for them, as coming from the plaintiffs. On the 24th *January,* the captain signed the bill of lading, which stated that the goods were shipped by *May, Alewyn,* and Co., and consigned to one *Lousini,* or his assigns, at the port of *Leghorn.* Messrs. *May, Alewyn,* and Co. stopped payment on the 4th *February,* and on the 8th of that month the plaintiffs made a formal demand of the captain to have the tins unshipped and delivered up to them. No tender however was made for freight, nor any offer of compensation for the trouble of unloading the ship, and making delivery of the goods in pursuance of the demand. The cargo of the ship was then nearly complete, and the tins had been placed at the bottom of the vessel under other goods, and could not be got at without removing the superincumbent packages. The captain refused to deliver the goods, assigning no other reason than that he had signed a bill of lading for them in other persons names. The question was, whether this refusal amounted to a conversion, for the purpose of sustaining an action of trover. The learned Judge was of opinion, that it was evidence of a conversion, and under his Lordship's directions the jury found for the plaintiffs.

Campbell now moved for a rule to shew cause why the verdict found for the plaintiffs should not be set aside, and a nonsuit entered. It is submitted, that in this case there was no evidence of a conversion so as to support trover. At the time the demand was made of the delivery of the goods, the plaintiffs had no right of possession, inasmuch as the goods had been bonâ fide, delivered to the captain for him to carry them to *Leghorn.* He received them under a contract to deliver at *Leghorn,* and no where else ; and therefore his refusal to deliver in *London* is no conversion. The case of *Baldwin* v. *Cole* (a) is an authority to shew, that the party demanding must have the right to the possession, before the refusal to deliver can be considered as evidence of a conversion. So also, in *Gordon* v. *Harper* (b), it was held, that the plaintiff must have a right of possession as well as of property. Here the plaintiffs' right of possession was gone by the bailment to the captain, and as the contract entered into with him had never been rescinded, the plaintiffs were concluded quoad the right of possession. [*Bayley*, J. Do you mean to say, that they had not a right of stoppage in transitu?] They had a right to do that which would make the property in the goods revest, but they had no right to demand possession of the captain, because the goods had been delivered to him absolutely, under a contract to carry and deliver them to another person at *Leghorn*. But assuming that the plaintiffs had a right to demand possession, still they ought to have tendered the freight, and the expenses of unshipping the other goods on board in order to get at the barrels of tin. This they did not do, and. therefore the mere demand and refusal to deliver is not sufficient evidence of a conversion; because the captain had a lien upon the goods for the freight, if not for the expense to which he might be put in unshipping the goods. But having been once put on board, under the circumstances proved at the trial, the captain was not bound to deliver to the plaintiffs under any circumstances, and his refusal was no conversion. If, indeed, it had appeared. that he had delivered the tin at *Leghorn*, contrary to the orders of the consignor, that, according to *M'Combie* v. *Davies* (c), would be evidence of a conversion; but that is a different case from the present; for here the plaintiffs had no right of possession, and if they had, still they ought to have tendered the freight and expenses.

(a) 6 Mod. 212.   (b) 7 T. R. 9.   (c) 6 East, 538.

ABBOTT, C. J., delivered no opinion.

BAYLEY, J.—I am of opinion that there was evidence of a conversion in this case to go to the jury. Whether a refusal to deliver is sufficient evidence of a conversion, must depend upon the circumstances under which the refusal takes place. If my goods are on board another man's ship and I demand possession, and he answers that the goods are in such a situation, that he cannot get at them without displacing other goods, at a great inconvenience, and, therefore, he will not then deliver them, probably a jury would say that was no conversion; but if, upon demanding the delivery of goods which you have a right to demand, the party says, " I won't deliver them to you, not because I can't get at them, or because you don't pay me for the freight, but because I have signed bills of lading in another man's name," there is then reasonable ground for a jury to presume a conversion. Here goods, which are the property of the plaintiffs, are shipped on board the defendants' vessel. The persons to whom they are sold, fail; and the plaintiffs, having a right to stop in transitu, demand possession of the captain. The captain does not refuse to deliver the goods because the freight and expenses are not tendered, but because he thinks he has a right to insist upon taking them to, and delivering them at, *Leghorn*, by reason of the contract to deliver in the name of another person. That I think is evidence of a conversion; and, assuming it to have been necessary to tender the freight and expenses, it appears to me that the defendants' ground of refusal to deliver, dispensed with the necessity of making any tender of the freight and expenses.

HOLROYD, J., and LITTLEDALE, J., concurred.

Rule refused.

M‘GILLIVRAY and others, Assignees of INGLIS and anothers, Bankrupts, *v.* SIMSON.

Saturday,
November 11

ASSUMPSIT. The declaration stated, that the bankrupts, together with another person, since deceased, had carried on business with one *Edward Ellice,* under the firm of *Inglis, Ellice* and Co.; and that *Ellice* retired from the said partnership on the 30th of *April,* 1821, and the bankrupts and the now deceased partner then commenced business, under the firm of *Inglis* and Co.; that a sum of 1844*l.* 7*s.* 5*d.* was due to the defendant from the firm of *Inglis, Ellice* and Co., and a further sum of 418*l.* 4*s.* 2*d.* from the firm of *Inglis* and Co.; that the firm of *Inglis* and Co., since the death of the deceased partner, was possessed of four bills of lading, whereby a quantity of timber was delivered to them; that at the time of making the promise thereinafter mentioned, the firm of *Inglis* and Co. was insolvent, of which defendant had notice; that in consideration that *Inglis* and Co. would employ defendant as broker, to sell the timber upon commission, and would indorse and deliver the bills of lading to him, defendant undertook to account for, and pay over, the proceeds of the sale, *without deducting therefrom the sums of money, or either of them, so due to him as aforesaid.* Averment of performance, on the part of the bankrupts, before their bankruptcy, and that the timber was sold for 9,000*l.*, besides the expenses and charges upon the sale; but that defendant did not, nor would account for and, pay over the proceeds, without deducting the two sums so due to him as aforesaid; but, on the contrary, rendered an account, in which he did deduct the whole of those two sums, and refused to render any other account. Plea, non assumpsit, with notice of set-off. Issue thereon. At the trial before *Abbott,* C. J., at the *London* adjourned sittings after last term, the case was this. The plaintiffs were the assignees of *Inglis* and Co.

An agreement by a broker, that he will sell goods for his principal, and pay over the whole proceeds, without setting off a debt then due to him from his principal, is not binding upon the broker, so as to deprive him of his legal right of lien or set-off.

The partnership of *Inglis, Ellice* and Co. was dissolved
on the 30th of *April,* 1821, that firm then being indebted
to the defendant upwards of 1,800*l.* After the retirement.
of Mr. *Ellice,* who was still living, the firm of *Inglis*
and Co. became indebted to the defendant about 400*l.*
On the death of Mr. *John Inglis,* a partner in both the
firms, on the 7th of *August,* 1822, it was found that the
house was insolvent, and the creditors, among whom was
the defendant, were called together and informed of it.
In the months of *October* and *November,* 1822, the bills of
lading, in question, arrived. They were of timber, the
property of the house. The defendant, who had for many
years been employed by the house as broker, was requested to act as broker in the sale of the timber, and
was told, that he must not set off the debt due to him
from either of the firms against the proceeds, but must
render an account of the whole proceeds, and pay them
over; to which he agreed. There was, at that time, no
contemplation of a bankruptcy by the firm; but it was
intended that the business should be carried on by the
partners, under the inspection of trustees, which was done
from *August,* 1822, to *May,* 1823; and on the 29th of
May, 1823, a commission of bankruptcy issued. The
defendant sold the timber for 7,768*l.* 10*s.*, and rendered
an account, in which, after deducting the costs and
charges upon the sale, and the debts owing to himself
from both the firms, he credited the bankrupts with a
balance of 925*l.* 13*s.* 10*d.*; and which balance he had
paid into Court. This was the case on the part of the
plaintiffs. On the part of the defendant, the following
letter, sent to him by the old firm, at the time of their
dissolution, and of the establishment of the new firm, was
put in :—" *London,* 30th of *April,* 1821. Sir,—We beg
to acquaint you, that Mr. *Ellice* retires from our firm
from the present date. The business of the house will be
continued, as heretofore, by the remaining partners, *who
assume the funds, and charge themselves with the liqui-*

dation of the debts of the partnership. We remain, &c., *Inglis, Ellice* and Co."—" *A. Simson,* Esq." It was contended, on the part of the defendant, that he was entitled to set off the debts due to him from both the firms, inasmuch as the new firm had, by that letter, expressly undertaken to liquidate " the debts of the partnership," that was, of the old firm. The Lord Chief Justice was of opinion, that Mr. *Ellice,* a partner in the old firm, being still alive, the defendant could not set off, as against the assignees of the new firm, the debt owing to him from the old firm; but that he might set off the debt owing to him from the new firm, the agreement to the contrary not being, in his Lordship's opinion, binding. He, therefore, directed the jury to find a verdict for the plaintiffs, for the amount of the proceeds of the timber, after deducting the charges of the sale, the sum of 418*l.* 4*s.* 2*d.,* due to the defendant, from the new firm, and the sum paid into Court.

Gurney now moved for a rule nisi for a new trial, or to increase the verdict by the amount of 418*l.* 4*s.* 2*d.,* the sum due from the new firm to the defendant. The defendant had no right, as against the assignees, to set off the debt due to him from either of the firms. He expressly undertook, in consideration of the commission to be paid him for the sale of the timber, not to set off *either* of the debts; but to account for, and pay over, the *whole* of the proceeds. That was a promise founded upon a valuable consideration, and was, therefore, binding upon him. He entered into a special agreement, that this particular transaction should be kept distinct from all his former dealings with the bankrupts, and that the whole of the proceeds of the timber, with the exception of his own expenses and commission, should be paid over to them; he had, therefore, no right to retain any part of the money in respect of his own general balance. The transaction must have been considered as separate and distinct

from all others between the bankrupts and the defendant,
even if they had been acting for themselves only; and the
defendant's undertaking so to consider it, would, even
under those circumstances, have operated as a waiver of
his lien upon the goods, or the produce of them, for his
general balance.   But the defendant knew, at the time
when he entered into the agreement, and thereby obtained
possession of the goods, that the bankrupts were in insolvent circumstances, and that they were not acting for
themselves, but for the benefit of their creditors at large ;
and upon that ground, therefore, he could not be entitled
to a lien upon the goods to the full amount of his own
debt, to the prejudice of the rest of the creditors.

ABBOTT, C. J.—This is an action by the assignees of
bankrupts.   Their duty is a plain one.   It is to take the
account between the bankrupts, and those who are indebted to them on one hand, and have claims upon them
on the other, precisely as it stands at the time of the
bankruptcy.   This is clear from the language of the
statute, 5 *Geo.* 2, c. 30, s. 28, which is not materially
altered by the 6 *Geo.* 4, c. 16, s. 50, and which enacts,
" that where it shall appear that there has been mutual
credit given by the bankrupt and any other person, or
mutual debts between the bankrupt and any other person,
at any time before such person became a bankrupt, the
assignees shall state the account between them, and one
debt may be set against another ; and what shall appear
to be due on either side, on the balance of such account,
and on setting such debts against one another, and no
more, shall be claimed or paid on either side."   This is
clear, also, from the language of the Lord Chancellor, in
the case Ex parte *Prescott* (a).   There the petitioner was
a creditor of the bankrupt upon simple contract, and a
debtor of the bankrupt upon a bond ; and he applied to
be allowed to set off one against the other, under the

(a) 1 Atk. 230.

5 *Geo.* 2, c. 30, s. 28. The Lord Chancellor said, " I think this case is within the equity of the statute. Therefore, let it be referred to the commissioners to take the account between him and the bankrupt, and let what shall be found due from the bankrupt, at the time of the bankruptcy, be deducted out of what shall be due on the petitioner's bond, and the balance only be paid by the petitioner to the assignees." I think that case is applicable to the present; and therefore, that so far as the bankrupt laws are concerned, the defendant is clearly entitled to deduct, from the claims of the assignees, the debt owing to him from the bankrupts. Neither do I think that the agreement entered into between the bankrupts and the defendant varies the case. I do not consider such an agreement binding upon the defendant, so as to deprive him of the legal rights which he possessed, of lien and of set-off. In the case of *Cornforth* v. *Rivett* (a) this Court held that, in assumpsit for goods sold, the defendant might set off an acceptance of the plaintiff's, which had come into his hands after the delivery of the goods, although the defendant had agreed to pay for the goods in ready money.

BAYLEY, J.—I am entirely of the same opinion. It was decided by this Court, in *Eland* v. *Carr* (b), that if to a plea of set-off, the plaintiff replies that the goods, for which the action is brought, were to be paid for in ready money—such replication is bad; and the same principle was recognised and acted upon by the court of Common Pleas, in *Mayer* v. *Nias* (c).

The other Judges concurred.

Rule refused.

(a) 2 M. & S. 510. (b) 1 East, 375. (c) 8 J. B. Moore, 275. 1 Bing. 311.

Saturday,
November 11.

M'CULLOCH *v.* DAWES and another, executors of ———, deceased.

Where one of two joint executors was applied to for payment of a debt of his testator's, who had been dead 20 years, and as against whom the debt was barred by the Statute of Limitations, and said, " I believe the debt is a just one, and has never been paid. I should be happy to serve you in the matter if I could, but I cannot do any thing without the consent of the (testator's) family :"— Held, in an action against both the executors, that there was no such acknowledgment of the debt, as took the case out of the Statute of Limitations, as against them ; there being no promise, express or implied, to pay the debt.

ASSUMPSIT upon the money counts, averring promises, first by the testator in his life-time, and secondly, by the defendants, as his executors, since his death. Pleas, first, non assumpsit ; and second, the Statute of Limitations. Issues thereon. At the trial before *Abbott,* C. J., at the *London* adjourned sittings after last term, the case was this. The debt which the plaintiff sought to recover, was incurred by the testator in the year 1796. The testator died in the year 1804. The defendants were his executors, but *Dawes* had taken the most active part in the arrangement of his affairs. It was admitted that, as to the testator, the debt was barred ; the question was, whether there had been such a promise to pay it by the defendant *Dawes,* within six years of the action brought, as would be binding upon both the defendants, and take the case out of the statute. Upon this point it appeared, that shortly before the action was brought, the plaintiff called upon the defendant *Dawes,* stated his claim upon the testator's estate, and expressed a hope that the executors would see it settled. *Dawes* admitted that the debt was a just one, and that it had never been paid ; and said he should be happy to serve the plaintiff in the matter if he could, but that he could not do any thing without the consent of the (testator's) family. The Lord Chief Justice was of opinion, that this was not such a personal acknowledgment of the debt, or promise to pay it, as would take the case out of the statute, and therefore nonsuited the plaintiff.

E. Lawes, now moved to set aside the nonsuit, and for a new trial. Except for the Statute of Limitations, the defendants, as executors, were both legally liable to the payment of the plaintiff's debt : if, therefore, there is

such an acknowledgment of the debt and promise to pay it
by one, as bars the statute quoad him, and makes him
still liable, that will support the action against both.
Here, there was an express acknowledgment by *Dawes,*
that the debt was still owing, which was evidence of
a promise on his part to pay it, and his reference to
the testator's family made no difference ; because, when
he admitted the existence of the debt, his legal liability
to pay it immediately revived, and the law will imply
a promise to discharge that liability.   If so, his admission, and the implied promise arising out of it, is
binding upon his co-executor. It is clear that one of
two joint executors has power to release a debt due
to both, why then should he not have power to acknow-
ledge a debt due from both ?   In *Perry* v. *Jackson* (*a*),
Lord *Kenyon* said, " It is admitted that one partner may
do several acts to bind the interests of all : he may release as well as create a debt ; he may also, by his
acknowledgment, take a case out of the Statute of Limitations."   Now, co-executors are in the nature of partners,
for they are the joint representatives of their testator ;
therefore, the principle there laid down by Lord *Kenyon*
applies.   So, in *Jackson* v. *Fairbank* (*b*), one of two
makers of a joint and several promissory note having
become bankrupt, the payee received a dividend under his
commission, on account of the note. It was held, that the
payment of the dividend under the commission was such
an acknowledgment of the debt, as took the case out of
the Statute of Limitations, and prevented the other maker
from availing himself of the statute, in an action brought
against him for the balance due on the note : the dividend
having been paid within six years of the action brought.
So, in *Whitcomb* v. *Whiting* (*c*), an acknowledgment by
one of several makers of a joint and several promissory
note, was holden sufficient to take it out of the statute
against the others.   The authority of the last two cases,

(*a*) 4 T. R. 516   (*b*) 2 H. Bl. 340.   (*c*) Doug. 651.

has, undoubtedly, been questioned; but they have been very recently fully discussed and recognised as law by the whole court of Common Pleas, in an elaborate judgment delivered by *Best*, C. J., in the case of *Perham* v. *Raynall* (a), where it was held, after deliberation, that an acknowledgment within six years, by one of two makers of a joint and several promissory note, was sufficient to revive the debt against the other; although he had made no acknowledgment within that period, and had signed the note as a surety only.

ABBOTT, C. J.—It appeared at the trial, that the plaintiff's debt accrued in the year 1796; that the testator died in 1804; and that no claim was made in respect of the debt till a period of more than twenty years after his death. Under such circumstances payment was to be presumed, unless the contrary was clearly shewn. Perhaps that was shewn sufficiently, because one of the executors undoubtedly admitted that, so far as he knew, the money had never been paid. But the question is, whether there was such an acknowledgment of the debt by one of the executors, as raised an implied promise on behalf of himself and his co-executor to pay it, and took the case out of the Statute of Limitations as against them both. The evidence was, that *Dawes* said, he believed the debt was a just one, and had never been paid; and that he should be glad to serve the plaintiff in the matter, if he could, but that he could not do any thing without the consent of the testator's family. I was of opinion at the trial, that this was not a personal promise to pay the debt, nor even a personal acknowledgment of its existence; but a mere reference of the plaintiff to the family of the testator, with whom it lay to say whether the debt would be paid or not; and consequently, that there was nothing to take the case out of the statute against the defendants. I am of the same opinion now, and therefore I think we ought not to grant any rule.

(a) 9 J. B. Moore, 566.   2 Bing. 311.

BAYLEY, J.—I am of the same opinion. I think the nonsuit was perfectly right. The evidence scarcely amounted to an acknowledgment of the existence of the debt, but it certainly did not amount to a promise to pay it; on the contrary, the reference to the testator's family was a refusal to pay, for it was in effect saying, " I would serve you if I could—apply to the family—if they chuse to pay it, they may, but without them I can do nothing." Such language could not properly be construed into a promise to pay a debt by any individual, and much less by an executor, whose testator has been dead twenty years, and where the debt claimed is 30 years old. If executors could be bound by evidence so loose as this, their situation would be most alarming. They are bound, if possible, to resist such a claim; they have no right to waive any legal defence to such an action: and if they did, and were to pay a debt, against the recovery of which there was any legal bar, they would render themselves liable over to those who were interested in the testator's property.

HOLROYD, J.—I also think the nonsuit was right. There was no such acknowledgment of the existence of the debt, as amounted to an admission that the executor thought himself liable as such to pay it, or from which the law would imply a promise to pay; and a mere acknowledgment of the existence of a debt, unaccompanied by a promise, express or implied, to pay it, is not sufficient to take a case out of the Statute of Limitations.

LITTLEDALE, J., concurred.

Rule refused.

1826.

M'CULLOCH
v.
DAWES.

Tuesday,
November 14.

BATES *v.* PILLING and SEDDON.

Where an attorney, at the instance of a creditor, sued out process against a debtor in the county court, and the attorney's agent, after the debt and costs had been paid, but in ignorance of that fact, signed judgment, and sued out execution, and levied upon the debtor's goods, though he had never appeared:— Held, that both the creditor and his attorney were liable to the debtor, in an action of *trespass.*

THIS was an action of trespass, for breaking and entering plaintiff's dwelling-house, situate at *Furness*, in the county palatine of *Chester*, and seizing and carrying away ten pieces of broad cloth, his property. Plea, not guilty, and issue thereon. At the trial before *Warren*, C. J., and *Jervis*, J., at the last assizes for *Chester*, the facts of the case were these. *Pilling*, one of the defendants, who was a manufacturer at *Manchester*, had employed the other defendant. *Seddon*, who was an attorney at the same place, to recover for him a debt of 2*l*. 5*s*., owing to him from the plaintiff. *Seddon*, after making several unsuccessful applications for payment to the plaintiff, in the early part of *March*, 1825, instructed his agent at *Chester*, to commence legal proceedings against the plaintiff. Process, returnable on the 29th *March*, was served upon the plaintiff on the 25th, and on that same day, the plaintiff called upon *Seddon* at *Manchester*, and paid him 5*l*. for the debt and costs. On the 29th, *Seddon* wrote to his agent at *Chester*, informing him that the debt and costs had been paid, but before the letter reached *Chester*, his agent had signed judgment, taken out execution, and put the writ into the hands of a sheriff's officer, who made a levy upon the goods mentioned in the declaration, on the 31st *March*. It was objected, on the part of the defendants, that upon this evidence neither of them was liable to an action of *trespass*, for that even if *Seddon* had been guilty of negligence in not countermanding the proceedings, still he was not a trespasser, and was liable only in an action *on the case*. The learned Judges overruled the objection, but reserved the point, and the plaintiff had a verdict with nominal damages, with liberty to the defendants to move to enter a nonsuit.

Campbell, for the defendant *Seddon*, now moved accordingly. *Seddon* was not liable in this form of action; he was not a trespasser himself, nor was the trespass complained of committed under his authority. All that he did was, to direct his agent to sue out process; and even if he was guilty of negligence in not countermanding the process in time to prevent the seizure, still he could only be liable in an action on the case. His agent, unquestionably, was irregular in the course he pursued, because he ought to have proceeded by summons, attachment, and distress infinite, *Com. Dig.* tit. *County*, C. 9; whereas, he signed judgment, and sued out execution, before the defendant had appeared; both which were void. *Williams* v. *Lord Bagot* (a). *Seddon* could only be bound by the acts of his agent, so far as he had given that agent authority to act for him, and as he never authorised his agent to arrest the plaintiff, he was not answerable for his misconduct in that respect. It was, indeed, decided in *Barker* v. *Braham* (b), that an action of trespass would lie against the attorney, as well as against the client, for suing out an illegal ca. sa. against a defendant, and causing him to be imprisoned thereon; but there, the attorney conducted the whole of the business himself, sued out the ca. sa. in his own person, and delivered it personally to the sheriff's officer, with orders to execute it immediately: here, *Seddon* neither sued out the writ himself, nor knew of its being sued out; so that the cases are perfectly distinguishable.

Chitty, for the defendant, *Pilling.* The arguments urged on behalf of *Seddon,* have still more weight as applied to *Pilling. Pilling* did not know that the debt and costs had been paid, so that he was not even guilty of negligence. The process under which he acted was regular and well founded in its inception, and as a mere agent, he was perfectly justified in proceeding, until he received a countermand. [*Bayley,* J. *Pilling,* by his agent, signed judgment, and took out execution, against a party who

(a) Antr, vol. v., 719; 3 B. & C. 772.   (b) 3 Wils. 368; 2 Bl. R. 866.

had never appeared, and that, after the debt and costs had been paid to his principal]. That was in effect the act of the Court, not of *Pilling* ; and he cannot be responsible for the error of the Court, in regulating their practice. [*Bayley,* J. Signing judgment was no act of the Court, but an act done by *Pilling* himself, and for which he ought to be responsible]. Evidence of suing out a writ, and arresting a party, after the debt has been paid, will not maintain an action, unless actual malice is averred and proved ; *Schubel* v. *Fairbain* (a) ; *Gibson* v. *Chaters* (b). An act done under a writ of execution, is not the subject of an action of trespass ; for the writ is similar to a magistrate's warrant, and a party acting under a warrant, although improperly granted by the magistrate, is not liable to an action of trespass. 3 Esp. 96. No obligation was imposed upon either of the defendants, of preventing the arrests, after the debt and costs had been paid, nor can any action be maintained for such a nonfeasance. *Page* v. *Wiple* (c).

ABBOTT, C. J.—In the cases cited for the defendants, the parties in the suits were merely passive : here, *Pilling* was active in the transaction ; and that makes all the difference. *Pilling* was the plaintiff in the suit below, and was clearly answerable for the acts of *Seddon* his attorney ; and *Seddon* was as clearly answerable for the acts of his agent ; for he and his agent must be considered as one and the same person. Then, *Pilling* has signed judgment and sued out execution after the debt and costs were paid ; and *Barker* v. *Braham* is a decisive authority to shew, that both he and his attorney are trespassers, and liable in the present action.

The rest of the Court concurred.

Rule refused.

(a) 1 B. & P. 388.   (b) 2 B. & P. 129.   (c) 3 East, 341.

KINDER and another, Assignees of SYKES, a Bankrupt, *v.* BUTTERWORTH.

Tuesday, November 14.

THIS was an action of assumpsit for money had and received by the defendant to the use of the plaintiffs as assignees. Plea, non-assumpsit, and issue thereon. At the trial before *Abbott*, C. J., at the *London* adjourned sittings after *Trinity* term, 1825, the plaintiff obtained a verdict for 849*l.* 19*s.* 8*d.*, which was taken as the aggregate of the sums received from the bankrupt by the defendant, subsequent to the act of bankruptcy, not arising from the sale of goods consigned by the bankrupt to the defendant, subject to correction by an arbitrator, if necessary. In the ensuing term, a rule was applied for, to set aside the verdict, when the Court ordered the facts to be stated in the following case:

Thomas Sykes, the bankrupt, carried on the business of a clothier, at *Bath Easton*, in *Somersetshire*, and employed the defendant as his broker in *London*. The factorage commenced in *June*, 1822, and continued down to the date of the commission of bankruptcy, namely, 26th *June*, 1823; during which time there was an open account between *Sykes* and the defendant. *Sykes* was in the habit of accepting bills, payable at the defendant's house; and the defendant was in the habit of advancing cash to *Sykes*, and on his account, in taking up such bills, and otherwise, and of accepting bills for *Sykes*'s accommodation, on the credit of goods in his possession as factor. In his general account with *Sykes*, the defendant debited *Sykes* with the cash so advanced, and with such acceptances, when paid; and he credited *Sykes* with the proceeds of the goods sold, and with monies received on his account, and also with bills received on his account, and when he received the same, without waiting until the same became due. On 1st *February*, 1823, *Sykes* committed an act of bankruptcy, unknown to the defendant; and he

Assignees may recover from the factor of a bankrupt, all monies received by him from the bankrupt within two months before the issuing of the commission; and the factor cannot set off debts incurred by the bankrupt to him within the same time, although the factor has acted bona fide, and in ignorance of the act of bankruptcy. Note; that this applies only to commissions issued before the passing of 6 G. 4, c. 16; by s. 50 of which, the law upon this subject is materially altered.

continued to carry on business until 6th *May*, 1823.
On 1st *February*, 1823, the balance of the said general
account, on the face thereof, was 45*l.* 16*s.* 5*d.* in favour of
Sykes: although the actual cash balance was 217*l.* 14*s.* 7*d.*
in favour of the defendant; and the defendant was then
under acceptances for *Sykes*, to the amount of 991*l.* 14*s.* 6*d.*,
which were then in circulation; and the defendant then
had in his possession a quantity of cloth belonging to
Sykes, and consigned by him to the defendant for sale, as
factor. On 18th *April,* 1823, *Sykes* appeared, on the
face of the aforesaid account, to be indebted to the defendant in the sum of 590*l.* 9*s.* 11*d.*; but the actual cash
balance in favour of the defendant, was 944*l.* 9*s.* 11*d.*,
and the defendant was under acceptances for *Sykes* to
the amount of 1,633*l.* 4*s.* 2*d.*; and the defendant then
also held a quantity of cloth belonging to *Sykes*, consigned to the defendant for sale, as factor; which goods
were insufficient to repay him such balance and such
acceptances. On 26th *April,* 1823, *Sykes* appeared, on
the face of the aforesaid account, to be indebted to the
defendant in the sum of 877*l.* 7*s.* 7*d.*; but the actual
cash balance in favour of the defendant, was then 1,294*l.*
8*s.* 11*d.*, and the defendant was then under acceptances
for *Sykes* to the amount of 1,658*l.* 18*s.*; and the defendant
then also held a quantity of cloth belonging to *Sykes*,
and consigned to the defendant for sale, as factor. All
the sums sought to be recovered by the plaintiffs in this
action, were paid to the defendant in cash and bills, in
May, 1823; and the particulars of the sums, constituting
the sum of 849*l.* 19*s.* 8*d.*, for which the verdict was
taken, were as follows:—A cheque, being the balance of
a bill for 273*l.* 14*s.*, accepted by the defendant for the
accommodation of *Sykes*, 36*l.* 1*s.* 2*d.*; another cheque, in
part proceeds of a like bill for 300*l.*, 200*l.*; a cheque for
goods, 213*l.* 18*s.* 6*d.*; a cheque for cash, 400*l.* The
defendant paid on the 3rd *May*, by the direction of *Sykes*,
the sum of 252*l.* 7*s.*, on his account, namely, 190*l.* on

taking up a bill for that amount, drawn by *Cazenove* on, and accepted by *Sykes*, and made payable at the defendant's house; and 62*l.* 7*s.*, for a debt owing by *Sykes* to *Lewin* and Co. On 26th *June*, 1823, the date of the commission of bankruptcy, the balance on the face of the said account was 391*l.* 2*s.* 2*d.* in favour of *Sykes*; but the actual cash balance at that time was 1,118*l.* 3*s.* 10*d.* in favour of the defendant, and the defendant was under acceptances for *Sykes* to a large amount; and the defendant then also had in his possession a quantity of cloth belonging to *Sykes*, and consigned to the defendant for sale, as factor, which the defendant afterwards sold; and upon making up the account to the time of the trial, the defendant appeared a creditor of *Sykes* for the sum of 391*l.* 8*s.* 6*d.*, after giving credit for all the sums recovered in this action; but in making such balance, the defendant took credit for 870*l.* 4*s.* 10*d.*, being the amount of two bills of exchange drawn by *Sykes*, and accepted by the defendant for his accommodation, in favour of *Richard Edmonds*, which bills the defendant, before the same became due, had notice not to pay, on the ground of the original consideration for the same being usurious, as the plaintiffs still insist the same to be; but which usury the said *Richard Edmonds* and the defendant dispute.

Campbell, for the plaintiffs. The sums of money sought to be recovered by the plaintiffs in this action, consisted of payments made by the bankrupt to the defendant within two months before the commission issued. Those monies, therefore, clearly belonged to the plaintiffs, as the assignees of the bankrupt; for he had no power to pay them away; they were not payments made in the ordinary course of business; and they are not protected by any statute. The plaintiffs, consequently, are entitled to retain the verdict found in their favour.

F. Pollock, contrà. The bankrupt's estate was not in a

worse condition when the commission was sued out, than it was when the act of bankruptcy was committed. That is apparent, from the account kept between the bankrupt and the defendant; and the assignees cannot affirm some of the dealings between the bankrupt and the defendant, and repudiate others: they must abide by the account, as it stands, altogether. They are not at liberty to take one side of the account, which may be in favour of the bankrupt, and to reject the other, which may be against him; neither is it competent for them to select that period which they may deem most advantageous to the bankrupt's estate, for the commencement of their claim. The accounts between the parties were continually fluctuating; and, finally, the balance due to the defendant increased. In an action of trover, the assignees might recover goods delivered under similar circumstances; but they cannot, by disaffirming some of the bankrupt's transactions, and affirming others, entitle themselves to maintain an action of assumpsit for money so paid. Two of the sums included in the verdict were parts of the proceeds of bills accepted by the defendant for the bankrupt; those bills the defendant has already been called upon to pay, and if he is now compelled to refund the money he has received from the bankrupt on account of them, he will, pro tanto, be paying the same bills twice over, which will be a great hardship upon him. The bankrupt's estate was, upon the whole, benefited by these dealings with the defendant. In all the cases of this kind, where the doctrine of relation has been relied on, the question was raised by an action of trover. Here, by declaring in assumpsit, the assignees have in part approved the bankrupt's dealings. In an action of trover, the question of mutual credit could not, of course, be raised; but in the present form of action it clearly may. [*Bayley*, J. At the utmost, that can only be up to the time of the act of bankruptcy]. In *Smith* v. *Hodgson* (a), it was held, that if the assignees bring

(a) 4 T. R. 211.

assumpsit, they affirm the contract, and the defendant, if a creditor of the bankrupt, may set off his debt. *Copland* v. *Stein* (a), will be cited on the other side as a decision to the contrary; but that case cannot affect the general principle, because there it was expressly agreed between the parties, to waive any objection to the form of action. In *Ashley* v. *Kell* (b), it was held, that though under 2 *Geo.* 2, c. 30, the future effects of a bankrupt, against whom two commissions had issued, were liable to be seized for the benefit of the creditors; yet, the bankrupt had in the mean time such a property in them, as enabled him to transact and sell to a bonâ fide purchaser; and *Dowton* v. *Ritchie* (c), *Coles* v. *Wright* (d), and *Cash* v. *Young* (e), are all cases tending to confirm the validity of transactions had bonâ fide with the bankrupt, while he was ostensibly carrying on his business. Now, it is quite evident that the defendant in this case, was throughout acting bonâ fide, because, between the date of the act of bankruptcy and of the commission, he became a creditor to a large amount. As to one of the sums included in the verdict, namely, the checque for 200*l.*, that appears, upon the case, to have been money produced by the discounting a bill which the defendant had accepted for the accommodation of the bankrupt; consequently, that 200*l.* never can by possibility have been the property either of the bankrupt or his assignees, and cannot be recovered in this action.

Campbell, in reply. The general question as to the right of assignees to recover money paid by a bankrupt to an acceptor of bills, for the purpose of meeting those bills when due, was decided in the case of *Tamplin* v. *Diggins* (f), which is expressly in point with the present case. There the defendants had accepted bills for the accommo-

(a) 8 T. R. 199.   (e) Ante, vol. iii., 652.   2 B. &
(b) 2 Str. 1207.   C. 413.
(c) Ambler. 630.   (f) 2 Camp. 212.
(d) 4 Taunt. 198.

E 2

dation of a trader. He, after committing an act of bankruptcy, but before a commission was sued out, lodged
money with the defendants, for the purpose of taking up
the bills, which did not become due until after the commission was sued out, and were then paid by the defendants. It was held, that the defendants were bound to
refund this money to the assignees, and that they were
not entitled to a set-off under the 5 *Geo.* 2, c. 30, nor
were protected by the 19 *Geo.* 2, c. 32, as having received
the money in the ordinary course of business. The
plaintiffs, therefore, are entitled to retain the verdict for
all the items included in it, for they are all payments
made by the bankrupt to the defendant, within two
months before the issuing of the commission, and are not
protected by the 46 *Geo.* 3, c. 135, s. 3. The law upon
that particular point has been altered by the 6 *Geo.* 4,
c. 16, s. 50, which gives a right of set-off in cases of
mutual credits, up to the time of the issuing of the commission; but that alteration does not affect the present
case, because these transactions took place before the
passing of the new statute.

ABBOTT, C. J.—I am of opinion that the plaintiffs are
entitled to retain their verdict for the full amount of
849*l*. 19*s*. 8*d*. I cannot agree that the assignees are
affirming some, and disaffirming others, of the transactions
between the bankrupt and the defendant; on the contrary,
it appears to me, upon the facts stated in the special case,
that they have disaffirmed all the acts of the bankrupt, so
far as by law they might. Neither do I consider that the
form of action at all varies this case; because, if the
assignees might have maintained trover for the checque
itself in the hands of the defendant, they may equally
maintain assumpsit for the proceeds of the checque in his
hands. It has been urged upon us, as an argument
in favour of the defendant, that the bankrupt's estate was
not in a worse condition at the time when the commission

1826.

KINDER
v.
BUTTER-
WORTH.

issued, than it was at the time when the act of bankruptcy was committed; but no authority has been cited
shewing that we ought to take that fact into consideration,
and, therefore, I am of opinion, that it must be laid
entirely out of the case. It is clear, according to the
decision in *Tamplin v. Diggins*, that if all these monies
had been paid by the bankrupt to the defendant at one
time, they might all have been recovered; and I do not
see that the circumstance of their having been paid at
different times, makes any real difference. The bill for
200*l.*, as far as appears, was entirely under the control of
the bankrupt, before it was paid to the defendant; it was,
therefore, his property, and became the property of his
assignees: the placing it in the hands of the defendant
was the bankrupt's own voluntary act. If, when the bill
was accepted by the defendant, there had been an express
undertaking by the bankrupt, that the defendant should
receive that portion of the proceeds, the case, with respect
to that bill, might have required a different consideration;
but it is clear that the fact was not so: therefore that bill
cannot be distinguished from the other items of the demand. The doctrine of relation in bankruptcy has, undoubtedly, in some particular cases, operated with some
degree of hardship and severity; but that must be the
consequence of all general rules: and, for the future, the
evil has been remedied. The present case, however, stands
upon the law as it was previous to the recent act of parliament, and we are bound to decide it according to the
law, without any regard to the hardships which may
result from our decision.

The other Judges concurred.

Judgment for the plaintiffs.

SHAW and others, Assignees of E. HOWARD and J. GIBBS, Bankrupts, *v.* DARTNALL.

Tuesday, November 14.

Where the agents for the grantor and grantee of an annuity rendered accounts to the latter, crediting him with instalments upon the annuity as "not yet received," and debiting him with commission and receipt stamps; and also other accounts crediting him with instalments as actually received, and debiting him with commission and receipt stamps; but, afterwards, with the knowledge and consent of the grantee, debited him with the same instalments, as not having been paid, which, in fact, they had not; and the agent afterwards became bankrupt:—Held, that his assignees were entitled to withdraw those sums from the credit side of the grantee's account with the bankrupt.

THIS action was brought to recover the sum of 846*l.* 19*s.* 1*d.*, being an alleged balance of monies advanced by the bankrupts to, or on the account of, the defendant. At the trial, before *Abbott*, C. J., at the *London* adjourned sittings after *Hilary* term, 1825, a verdict was found for the plaintiffs, subject to the award of a Barrister, who afterwards made his award, as follows :—

The bankrupts were employed by the defendant, to purchase annuities for him. All payments and receipts on account of such annuities passed through their hands, and they charged a commission of two and a half per cent. upon the annuities which they received for the defendant. The bankrupts were the agents for many other grantees of annuities, and also for some of the grantors. They kept their accounts in ledgers, wherein, in every case, whether concerned for the grantee alone, or for both the grantee and grantor, they opened an account in the names of both, and entered, on the credit side of the accounts of the grantees, and on the debit side of the accounts of the respective grantors, the instalments of the annuities from time to time; but not always at the precise periods when they became due. To the grantees of annuities the bankrupts also delivered pass-books, which pass-books generally contained a copy of the grantee's account in the ledger, varying only as to the receipts ; the pass-book being balanced at the time it was left with the bankrupts, and no notice whatever being taken of any balance that might have been previously struck in the ledger. An account was kept in the bankrupts' ledger, in the manner described, of the annuities which the defendant had purchased, with but one exception; and a pass-book was in like manner delivered to the defendant, and made up from time to time from the ledger, but varying from it in some particulars, which will be mentioned hereafter. No accounts were settled between the bankrupts and the defendant, except by the making up of the pass-book, and striking balances therein in the manner above mentioned. Acts of bankruptcy were committed by *Howard* and *Gibbs*, on the 10th of *January*, 1821. The commission was dated the 22nd of *August*, in the same year. The alleged balance of 846*l.* 19*s.* 1*d.*, which the plaintiffs sought to recover, arose upon the account stated in this pass-book, by withdrawing from the credit side certain instalments of annuities granted to the defendant by *Henry Michael Goold*, the Marquis *Wellesley*, and the Duke of *Marlborough*, which instalments had never been received by the bankrupts from the grantors of those annuities.

The circumstances respecting these annuities, are as follow :—

First, in respect of *Goold*'s annuity. Prior to the year 1815, *Goold* had granted several annuities to different persons, for whom the bankrupts were agents ; and the accounts of such annuities were entered in the ledger of the bankrupts in the manner before described. In some of these annuities the bankrupt *Howard* was a trustee, and in others, the bankrupt *Gibbs*. These annuities were secured on certain estates belonging to *Goold*, in *Ireland*, of which estates the bankrupts, prior to 1815, had been appointed receivers. The rents of the estates in *Ireland*, were not sufficient to discharge the annuities secured thereon prior to 1815. In *January*, 1815, the defendant, through the agency of the bankrupts, became the purchaser of an annuity from *Goold*, of 216*l.*, the consideration money for which was 1,400*l.* This annuity was secured on *Goold*'s estates in *Ireland*. An account was opened in the ledger of the bankrupts, in the names of the grantor and grantee; and from the time such annuity was granted, down to the 4th of *May*, 1820, the grantor is regularly debited, and the grantee credited, with this

annuity, from time to time, though not always at the precise periods at which it became due. The grantee was
regularly debited with a commission of two and a half per
cent., and stamps for receipts, upon every credit that was
given to him for the annuity. Balances were, from time
to time, struck in the ledger and the pass-book, after the
defendant was credited with the instalments of this annuity. The pass-book, made up by the bankrupts, and
delivered to the defendant, contains all the items, both on
the credit and debit side of the grantee's account in the
ledger, though not exactly corresponding as to dates; but
with this distinction as to the last item on the credit side,
on the 4th of *May*, 1820, the entry in the pass-book was
as follows :—" *May*, 4, 1820. By *H. M. Goold*, one
year's annuity, due 11th *January* last (not yet received),
144*l.*" In the ledger, the words " not yet received," are
omitted. In both the pass-book and the ledger, the
defendant is debited with the commission on this sum.
Statements of the arrears of the annuity were delivered
by the bankrupts to the grantor, after the instalments had
been credited to the grantee in the bankrupts' ledger and
pass-book. In 1817, *Goold* took the benefit of the Insolvent Act, prior to which the usual notice was given to the
defendant, as one of the creditors. The plaintiffs sought
to withdraw from the credit side of the defendant's account in the ledger and pass-book, all the instalments of
this annuity with which he had been credited from the
time it had been granted; withdrawing, at the same time,
from the debit side of the account, all the charges for
commission and stamps with which he had been debited
at the time such instalments had been credited. The
bankrupts had not received from *Goold*, or his estate,
any of the sums of money, with which they had credited
the defendant on account of this annuity.

Second, in respect of the Marquis *Wellesley's* annuity. The bankrupts received the instalments of an
annuity of 151*l.*, which had been granted to the defendant,

by the Marquis *Wellesley*, in the year 1812. The account of this annuity was kept in the bankrupts' ledger in the names of the grantor and grantee, and the grantee was regularly credited, and the grantor debited, with the instalments of the annuity. The grantee was also debited with a commission of two and a half per cent., and receipt stamps, upon all instalments with which he was credited. The pass-book, in respect of this annuity, contained the same debits and credits as the ledger. In the pass-book, on the debit side, under the date of the 4th of *May*, 1820, there was the following entry, contained also in the ledger :— " To Marquis *Wellesley*, one and a quarter year's annuity, due 7th *September*, 1818, 188*l.* 15*s.* ;" and on the credit side, the following entry, also contained in the ledger :—" By commission returned on 188*l.* 15*s.*, 4*l.* 17*s.* 4*d.*" These were the last items of any description, either on the debit or credit side of the pass-book. A balance was then struck, making the defendant a debtor, to the amount of 338*l.* 14*s.* 1*d.* Of this sum of 188*l.* 15*s.*, being the amount of five quarterly payments of Lord *Wellesley*'s annuity, so carried to the debit of the defendant's account, the defendant had been credited with one quarter in *June*, 1816, and debited with the commission and stamps thereon ; he had been credited with one half-yearly payment in *April*, 1818, and debited at the same time with commission and stamps thereon ; and he was credited with the remaining half-yearly payment in *November*, 1818, and debited at the same time with commission and stamps. A balance was struck in the pass-book, after the entry of each of these credits. The bankrupts had not received this sum of 188*l.* 15*s.*, from the grantor of the annuity. The instalments of this annuity, with which the defendant had been credited prior to 1816, had been received by the bankrupts from the Marquis *Wellesley*. On the 17th *July*, 1821, the defendant filed a bill against the Marquis *Wellesley*, in the court of Chancery, in *Ireland*, in which bill he claimed, as due to him from the

Marquis *Wellesley*, on the 7th of *September*, 1820, twelve quarterly payments of this annuity of 151*l.*; and in an affidavit made by the defendant in the same cause, in the court of Chancery in *Ireland*, on the 15th of *March*, 1822, the defendant swears, that on the 7th of *September*, 1820, twelve quarterly payments of this annuity were due and owing to him from the Marquis *Wellesley*. The plaintiffs sought in this action to withdraw from the credit of the defendant's account, this sum of 188*l.* 15*s.*, after deducting therefrom the commission and stamps, with which the defendant had been debited.

Third, in respect of the Duke of *Marlborough's* annuity. In *January*, 1818, the defendant, through the agency of the bankrupts, became the purchaser of an annuity of 200*l.* from the Duke of *Marlborough*, the consideration money for which was 1,200*l.* An account was opened in the ledger of the bankrupts, in the names of the grantor and grantee. In the pass-book, the defendant is debited on the 10th of *January*, 1818, with the purchase money, 1,200*l.*; and on the 16th of *June*, 1818, with the insurance of the Duke of *Marlborough's* life, 58*l.* 12*s.* 3*d.* Both these items are entered in the bankrupts' ledger, but the ledger contains no further entries as respects this annuity. In the pass-book, the defendant is credited on the 21st of *August*, 1816, with one half-yearly payment of this annuity, due 10th *July*, 100*l.*, and is debited on the same date with commission of two and a half per cent. on this sum, and receipt stamps. On the same date, after this entry, a balance is struck in the pass-book. Under the date of the 13th of *November*, 1818, the same half-yearly payment of 100*l.* is carried to the debit side of the defendant's account; and the commission thereon, and stamps, under the same date, are placed to his credit. On the same date, after this entry, a balance was struck in the pass-book. The pass-book contains a few entries, on the debit and credit side, after those of the 13th of *November*, 1818. A balance was struck on the 19th of

March, 1819; and on the 4th of *May*, 1820, a balance is again struck, making the defendant a debtor, to the amount of 238*l*. 14*s*. 11*d*. This balance is the last entry of any description in the pass-book. The bankrupts did not receive from the Duke of *Marlborough*, the half-year's annuity of 100*l*., with which they originally credited the defendant. The plaintiffs sought to withdraw this sum from the credit side of the account, after allowing for the commission and stamps, with which the bankrupts had debited the defendant, on account of this instalment.

The arbitrator awarded, that a verdict should be entered for the defendant, and a rule having been obtained for setting aside the award, and for entering a verdict for the plaintiffs, for such sum as the Court should direct, the Court directed the facts, as above, to be stated in a special case.

Scarlett for the plaintiffs. With respect to *Goold's* annuity, it must be admitted that the plaintiffs are bound by the decision in the recent case of *Shaw* v. *Picton* (a), and cannot recover any of the sums for which the bankrupts have given the defendant credit in account, as actually received by them. That decision, however, will not apply to the sum of 144*l*., which the bankrupts have entered in the pass-book as " not yet received ;" and that sum the plaintiffs are clearly entitled to recover. With respect to that sum, the defendant had express notice that it had never been paid by *Goold*, or received by the bankrupts; there was nothing to mislead him on the subject ; for the charge for commission was evidently made in expectation that the money would be paid when due, to be deducted if that expectation was not realised. With respect to the Marquis *Wellesley's* annuity, the plaintiffs are also clearly entitled to recover the sum of 188*l*. 15*s*. The bankrupts had at first credited the defendant's account with that sum, as money received by them for him

(a) Ante, vol. vii., 201. 4 B. & C. 715.

in payment of that annuity; but they afterwards debited him with the same sum in the pass-book, and he saw and returned the pass-book containing that entry to his debit, without making any objection: besides, he actually proceeded against the Marquis *Wellesley* for the recovery of that very sum, and made an affidavit stating that that sum was due and owing to him from the Marquis. Having so done, he has admitted the bankrupts' account to be correct in that respect, and he must remain bound by that admission. With respect to the Duke of *Marlborough's* annuity, the same observation applies. In *August,* 1818, 100*l.*, a half-year's annuity, was carried to the defendant's credit. In the following *November*, it was placed to his debit; and three successive balances were afterwards struck, in which that sum always remained on the debit side of his account, without any remonstrance or objection on his part.

Taddy, Serjt. contrà. The bankrupts were not mere agents; they were agents acting upon a del credere commission: they, therefore, guaranteed the payment of the annuities. The moment an instalment became due from the grantor, it constituted a debt from the bankrupts to the grantee; and the relation of debtor and creditor having thus been formed between the bankrupts and the grantee, could not be dissolved by any particular mode of keeping the accounts between them. That such was the relative situation of these parties, is plain from the facts stated upon the award, for the bankrupts purchased the annuities for the grantee, and made a charge for commission and receipt stamps upon the half-yearly instalments; admitting thereby, that they had actually received the money, or that they were to be answerable for it to the grantee, as much as if they had actually received it. [*Bayley*, J. If that had been the case, the bankrupts would have credited the defendant with the instalments on the precise days on which they became due]. Still, even if the bankrupts were mere agents, the plaintiffs are not entitled to withdraw these sums from the credit side of the account. The decision upon one part of the case of *Shaw* v. *Picton* (a), goes far to shew. that the sum of 144*l.*, upon *Goold's* annuity, is not recoverable. There the agents for the grantor and grantee of an annuity rendered an account to the latter, in which they gave him credit for instalments due from the former, stating at the same time, that the money had *not* then been received. They, however, allowed the grantee to draw upon them for the amount. In about twelve months afterwards, they became bankrupt, without having apprised the grantee in the interval that the instalments still remained unpaid by the grantor, who had become insolvent. It was held, that the money so advanced to the grantee was not recoverable back by the assignees of the agents. Now, the present appears as strong a case in favour of the grantee as the one just cited. It does not appear, here, when the words " not yet received," were inserted in the pass book; and in the ledger, the sum stood placed to the defendant's credit for an interval of several months, without any intimation being given to him that the money had not really been paid. Neither ought the instalments upon the Marquis *Wellesley*'s and the Duke of *Marlborough*'s annuities, to be held recoverable by the assignees. They were in the first instance carried by the bankrupts to the defendant's credit, as monies received by them on his account; while they stood to his credit in their books, a balance was struck: and the relative situation of the parties, in legal effect, then became the same, as if that balance had been actually paid over by the bankrupts to the defendant, which if it had been; it is clear that neither the bankrupts, nor their assignees, could have recovered it back. [*Bayley*, J. Upon the same principle, when the defendant was informed that the money had

(a) Ante, vol. vii., 201.

in payment of that annuity; but they afterwards debited him with the same sum in the pass-book, and he saw and returned the pass-book containing that entry to his debit, without making any objection: besides, he actually proceeded against the Marquis *Wellesley* for the recovery of that very sum, and made an affidavit stating that that sum was due and owing to him from the Marquis. Having so done, he has admitted the bankrupts' account to be correct in that respect, and he must remain bound by that admission. With respect to the Duke of *Marlborough's* annuity, the same observation applies. In *August*, 1818, 100*l*., a half-year's annuity, was carried to the defendant's credit. In the following *November*, it was placed to his debit; and three successive balances were afterwards struck, in which that sum always remained on the debit side of his account, without any remonstrance or objection on his part.

Taddy, Serjt. contrà. The bankrupts were not mere agents; they were agents acting upon a del credere commission: they, therefore, guaranteed the payment of the annuities. The moment an instalment became due from the grantor, it constituted a debt from the bankrupts to the grantee; and the relation of debtor and creditor having thus been formed between the bankrupts and the grantee, could not be dissolved by any particular mode of keeping the accounts between them. That such was the relative situation of these parties, is plain from the facts stated upon the award, for the bankrupts purchased the annuities for the grantee, and made a charge for commission and receipt stamps upon the half-yearly instalments; admitting thereby, that they had actually received the money, or that they were to be answerable for it to the grantee, as much as if they had actually received it. [*Bayley*, J. If that had been the case, the bankrupts would have credited the defendant with the instalments on the precise days on which they became due]. Still, even if the bankrupts were mere agents, the plaintiffs are not entitled to withdraw these sums from the credit side of the account. The decision upon one part of the case of *Shaw* v. *Picton* (a), goes far to shew that the sum of 144*l*., upon *Goold's* annuity, is not recoverable. There the agents for the grantor and grantee of an annuity rendered an account to the latter, in which they gave him credit for instalments due from the former, stating at the same time, that the money had *not* then been received. They, however, allowed the grantee to draw upon them for the amount. In about twelve months afterwards, they became bankrupt, without having apprised the grantee in the interval that the instalments still remained unpaid by the grantor, who had become insolvent. It was held, that the money so advanced to the grantee was not recoverable back by the assignees of the agents. Now, the present appears as strong a case in favour of the grantee as the one just cited. It does not appear, here, when the words " not yet received," were inserted in the pass book; and in the ledger, the sum stood placed to the defendant's credit for an interval of several months, without any intimation being given to him that the money had not really been paid. Neither ought the instalments upon the Marquis *Wellesley's* and the Duke of *Marlborough's* annuities, to be held recoverable by the assignees. They were in the first instance carried by the bankrupts to the defendant's credit, as monies received by them on his account; while they stood to his credit in their books, a balance was struck: and the relative situation of the parties, in legal effect, then became the same, as if that balance had been actually paid over by the bankrupts to the defendant, which if it had been; it is clear that neither the bankrupts, nor their assignees, could have recovered it back. [*Bayley*, J. Upon the same principle, when the defendant was informed that the money had

(a) Ante, vol. vii., 201.

agents for the defendant in these transactions; that they were agents acting under a del credere commission; in short, that they were guarantees; but looking at the whole of these entries, I cannot bring my mind to that conclusion. If the bankrupts guaranteed the payments of the annuities, why did the defendant consent to the return of the 100*l.*? Why did he sue the Marquis *Wellesley* for the arrears of his annuity, and make affidavit that *he* was indebted to him in respect of it? And why did the bankrupts enter the instalment upon *Goold's* annuity as *not yet received*, and the defendant submit to that entry? Taking these facts into consideration, and looking at all the entries, the conclusion to which my mind is brought, is, not that the bankrupts guaranteed the payment of the instalments, but that they wished, and laboured, from time to time, to induce the defendant to believe that the instalments had been regularly paid, in order that he might continue his dealings with them. Upon the whole, therefore, I am of opinion, that the plaintiffs are entitled to withdraw from the credit side of the defendant's account with the bankrupts, the three sums which I have before specified, and no others, namely, 144*l.* in respect of *Goold's* annuity, 151*l.* in respect of the Marquis *Wellesley's* annuity, and 100*l.* in respect of the Duke of *Marlborough's* annuity.

The other Judges concurred.

Judgment for the plaintiffs accordingly.

Ex parte MARY ANN MARTIN.

A WRIT of Habeas Corpus, for bringing up the body of *Mary Ann Martin*, from the House of Correction, at *Petworth*, in *Sussex*, had been obtained, upon an affidavit stating the following facts. Upon a complaint, made by the clerk of the guardians of the poor of the city of *Chichester*, that the prisoner, a single woman, had been delivered of a bastard child, which was likely to become chargeable to the parish of *Pancras*, within that city, she was taken before a single justice of the peace, to be examined respecting the father of the child. She refused to answer any questions, or to give any information, and persisting in this resolution, was committed, by the same justice, to the House of Correction, at *Petworth*. The child had not, in fact, become chargeable. The return to the writ was now read. It set out the warrant under which the prisoner had been committed, which was in these words. " Whereas information and complaint have been made unto me, one of his majesty's justices, &c., by *A. B.*, clerk to the guardians of the poor of the city of *Chichester*, that *Mary Ann Martin*, of the parish of *Pancras*, in the county aforesaid, single woman, hath lately been delivered of a bastard child in the said parish, which said child was likely to become chargeable to the said parish, and that she the said *Mary Ann Martin* had refused, and did refuse, to appear before one of his majesty's justices of the peace for the said county, to be examined touching the father of the said child. And whereas the said *Mary Ann Martin*, having appeared before me pursuant to my summons, hath shewn no cause why she should not be examined touching the father of the said bastard child, but hath refused, and doth refuse, to be examined," &c. The warrant concluded by requiring the keeper of the House of Correction to receive *Mary Ann Martin* into his custody, and her safely keep,

One magistrate has no power to commit a single woman for refusing to be examined respecting the father of her bastard child.

until she should submit to be examined touching the
father of the said bastard child. It was signed by one
magistrate only.

Campbell now moved, that the prisoner should be discharged out of custody.

O. Russell shewed cause. Three objections have been
raised to this commitment. First, that one justice only
had no jurisdiction to commit. Second, that the prisoner
was not compellable to answer inquiries respecting the
father of the child. And, third, that the clerk to the
guardians to the poor was not the proper person to make
the complaint. First, as to the jurisdiction, which involves the first two of these objections. In providing for
the maintenance of a bastard child, there are three pro-
gressive measures to be adopted; first, to secure the
apprehension of the father; second, to make an order of
filiation upon him; and third, to enforce that order; and
the proceedings, in the present case, were taken with reference to the first of those measures, namely, the apprehension of the father of the child. The statute which
applies to this case, and the only one, is the 6 *Geo.* 2,
c. 31. The first section of that statute enacts that " if any
single woman shall be delivered of a bastard child, which
shall be chargeable, or likely to become chargeable, to any
parish, &c., and shall, in an examination to be taken in
writing, upon oath, before any one or more justice or justices of the peace, &c., charge any person with having
gotten her with child, it shall and may be lawful to and
for such justice or justices, upon application made, &c.,
to issue out their warrant or warrants, for the immediate
apprehending such person so charged," &c. Now, as
that section expressly gives to one magistrate the power of
taking the examination of the woman, it must, by necessary implication, give him the power also of summoning
her before him, and compelling her to undergo the

examination; because the one, without the other, would be wholly nugatory. The fourth section of the same statute provides, " that it shall not be lawful for any justice or justices of the peace to send for any woman whatsoever before she shall be delivered, and one month after, in order to her being examined concerning her pregnancy, or supposed pregnancy, or to compel any woman, before she shall be delivered, to answer any questions relating to her pregnancy." That clearly shews the legislature to have intended, that after the delivery of the woman, one justice should have the power, which it withholds from him before her delivery. *Rex* v. *Ravenstone* (a), seems an authority directly in support of the present argument. There the mother of a bastard child had been examined, under the 6 *Geo.* 2, c. 31, before one magistrate, and had deposed upon oath to the father; she afterwards died; and her examination was held to be admissible evidence upon a question of settlement. Undoubtedly, where the object of the examination is to make an order of filiation, the examination is a judicial act, and must be taken before two justices; *Rex* v. *Beard* (b), *Rex* v. *West* (c); but that is a very different proceeding from the present. It was also held, in *Billings* v. *Prinn* (d), that two justices must be present, at the same time and place, when a woman is examined, and committed for not filiating a bastard child; but there the proceedings were under a different statute, the 7 *J.* 1, c. 4, which expressly gives the power of commitment to " *the justices* of the peace." If one justice has power to examine, he must, incidentally and necessarily, have power to compel the party to answer, and to commit upon refusal; as is the case with respect to a pauper who refuses to be examined touching his settlement; *Rex* v. *Jackson* (e). That case is analogous to the present, and the same reasons and principles apply to

(a) 5 T. R. 373.
(b) 2 Salk. 478.
(c) 6 Mod. 180.

(d) 2 Bl. R. 1017.
(e) 1 T. R. 653.

both. It was there held, that when the pauper is examined, if he refuses to answer proper questions put to him
in the course of his examination, the justices may commit
him, until he shall answer; " for," said the Court, " as
they have a right to examine him touching his settlement,
it would only be a shadow of a right, unless they have a
power likewise of enforcing that examination, by committing the pauper for refusing to be examined." Secondly, the clerk to the guardians of the poor of the parish
was the proper, or at least a competent person, to make
the complaint; *Rex* v. *St. Martyr* (a); where it was held,
that where parishes are united under the 22 *Geo.* 3, c. 83,
the guardian thereby appointed is substituted in the
overseer's place; and one who is *de facto* such, being so
received and acknowledged by the parish, though not
legally appointed, is competent to apply, in that character,
to a justice of the peace, to take the examination of a
single woman, pregnant with child, in order to filiate the
bastard.

Campbell, contrà. *Billings* v. *Prinn* is decisive to shew,
that the magistrate had no jurisdiction in this case.
There the woman was committed for refusing to filiate
her bastard child. It was assumed that the commitment
had been made, under either the 18 *Eliz.*, c. 3, or the
7 *J.* 1, c. 4, for it was not even contended that it would have
been good under the 6 *Geo.* 2, c. 31; and yet there a commitment, where the woman had been examined separately by
two magistrates, and the warrant signed separately by two,
was held to be bad. The latter statute gives no power
whatever to the magistrate, it merely authorises him to
act upon the voluntary declaration of the woman, that is,
when she comes before him of her own accord, and charges
some person as the father of the child. This point has
been repeatedly conceded as settled. In *Weller* v. *Toke* (b),

(a) 13 East, 55.   (b) 9 East, 364.

which was an action against *one* magistrate for committing a woman for refusing to filiate a bastard child, it was admitted, that the magistrate had no power to commit; it was admitted, that he was liable to an action for having committed; and the only point contested on his behalf, and which the Court decided in his favour was, that he was entitled to notice of action, under the 24 *Geo.* 2, c. 44. Secondly, the clerk to the guardian of the poor had no authority to make the complaint; it could only be made by the guardian himself. Thirdly, the warrant itself is defective, for it does not state that the child was chargeable, or likely to become chargeable, or even that it was living, at the time when the complaint was made.

Abbott, C. J.—I am clearly of opinion, that one magistrate had no jurisdiction to compel this woman to be examined touching the father of her child. The statute 18 *Eliz.*, c. 3, has always been considered as virtually giving a power of that nature to two or more magistrates; but the question here is, whether any such power is incidentally given by the statute, 6 *Geo.* 2, c. 31, to one magistrate. Now, the first section of that statute enacts, that " if any single woman shall be delivered of a bastard child, which shall be chargeable, or likely to become chargeable to any parish, &c.; and shall, in an examination to be taken in writing upon oath before any one or more justice or justices of the peace of any county, &c., *charge* (that is, if the woman shall charge) any person with having gotten her with child, it shall be lawful for such justice or justices to cause him to be apprehended." Now, it is by no means necessary to infer from that enactment, that it was intended to give one magistrate the power of compelling the woman to be examined, because that power had been previously given to two magistrates: and the authorising one magistrate to act, where a woman voluntarily comes before him, and charges a person as the father of her illegitimate child, is very different from empowering him to compel her to answer questions, and so to force her to make such a charge. Then, does the fourth section remove the difficulty? I think not. That merely provides, that no woman shall be sent for by any justice or justices, in order to her being examined, or compelled to answer any questions, before she is delivered, and one month after. That is a merely negative provision, and if an affirmative is to be implied from it, then, at least, the warrant ought to have shewn, that the requisites of that provision had been complied with, by stating that the woman had been delivered one month before she was sent for to be examined. This commitment, therefore, is illegal, and the woman must be discharged.

The other Judges concurred.

Prisoner discharged.

The KING v. The INHABITANTS of WARMINSTER.

A hiring, for an indefinite period, at six shillings a week for the winter, and nine shillings a week for the summer, is not a yearly hiring, and a year's service under it will not confer a settlement.

TWO justices, by their order, removed *William Mould,* his wife and children, from the parish of *Heytsbury* to the parish of *Warminster,* both in the county of *Wilts;* and the sessions, on appeal, confirmed the order, subject to the opinion of this Court upon the following case :—

The pauper was born a bastard, in the parish of *Font Hill Gifford,* in the county of *Wilts.* When about 25 years of age, he hired himself to Mr. *John Thring,* a solicitor at *Warminster,* as gardener. At the time of the hiring, Mr. *Thring* asked the pauper what he should give him *a week.* The pauper asked 20*l. a year* wages, which Mr. *Thring* refused to give, but said he would give 6*s.* a week for the winter, and 9*s.* a week for the summer, which the pauper agreed to take. He was to be in Mr. *Thring's* house.

Under this hiring the pauper served more than a year, living in the house. He and his master then came to a fresh agreement for weekly wages, without board; and about a week afterwards Mr. *Thring*, upon detecting some irregularities among his servants, discharged the pauper without notice. Mr. *Thring* made at the time, in a book kept for that purpose, entries of the several facts as they occurred, which were as follows:—" *William Mould:* agreed with him, as a gardener, into house, at 6*s.* a week in the winter, and 9*s.* a week in the summer. Came *Monday*, 2d *November*, 1818. Agreed with him, 6th *November*, 1819 (which was a *Saturday*), to give him 8*s.* a week in winter, and 9*s.* in summer. —4th *July*, 1820, went out of house, as labourer, at 18*s.* a week, and left my service shortly after." During the service under the first hiring, the pauper, on one occasion, gave his master a month's notice of his intention to quit; but the notice was not acted upon. The wages were accounted for weekly; but were paid occasionally, as they were wanted, and applied for, by the pauper. The question for the consideration of the Court was, whether there was a hiring for a year, in *Warminster*, or not.

Bingham, in support of the order of sessions. This was a general hiring; not for any definite period of time: it was, therefore, in contemplation of law, a yearly hiring, and the pauper, having served a year under it, gained a settlement. The master was a gentleman of that rank in life in which the ordinary mode of hiring servants is by the year, and it is not to be supposed that a person in his station would allow a weekly servant to live in his house. The agreement for one rate of wages in the summer, and another in the winter, shews that it was the intention of both parties that the service should continue for a year; and the fact of a month's warning having once been given, though it was not acted upon, affords a strong presumption that the original contract was for a yearly hiring. Then, the mere circumstance of the wages being accounted for weekly will not rebut that presumption, and the contract stands as one for an indefinite, that is, a yearly hiring.

Merewether, contrà, having referred to *Rex* v. *Dedham* (a), *Rex* v. *Pucklechurch* (b), *Rex* v. *Dodderkill* (c), and *Rex* v. *Lambeth* (d), was stopped by the Court.

ABBOTT, C. J.—The cases referred to are all directly in point; but independently of any authorities, it is perfectly clear, from the facts of this case, that the master never intended to hire the pauper for a year. He first asks the pauper what he shall give him *a week*—the pauper asks 20*l. a year*: the master refuses to give those wages, and finally agrees with the pauper for *weekly* wages. Under those circumstances, it is impossible to suppose that any thing but a weekly hiring was intended.

The rest of the Court concurred.

Order of Sessions quashed.

(a) Burr. S. C. 653.   (c) 3 M. & S. 243.
(b) 5 East, 382.   (d) 4 M. & S. 315.

The KING v. The INHABITANTS of KENARDINGTON.

A person
coming into a
parish as *a
servant*, and
during his ser-
vitude renting
a tenement
[*without re-
siding thereon*]
of 10*l.* value,
gains a settle-
ment under
13 and 14
Car. 2, c. 12.

BY an order of two justices, *William Knight* and *Sarah* his wife, and their eight children, were removed from *Kenardington* to *Ulcomb*, both in the county of *Kent*. On appeal, the sessions quashed the order, subject to the opinion of this Court upon the following case :—

The pauper *W. Knight*, when about sixteen years of age, hired himself for a year to *T. Knight*, at the wages of four guineas. He served the year in the parish of *Ulcomb*,

dwelling in his master's house there, and received his
wages. He afterwards, and about 22 years ago, married
Sarah his wife; and having about four years after his
marriage removed to *Kenardington*, he entered into a
contract with *Joseph Stead*, a farmer there, to serve him
as a labourer upon his farm, at the wages of 16s. a week,
to have his wheat at 6s. a bushel, butter at 1s. a pound,
and a small house of his master's, situate on his master's
farm, rent free to live in. He entered into the service, and
continued in it under these terms for three years; and
between *Christmas* and *Lady-day*, in the third year of
his service with *Stead*, the pauper, with two other persons,
hired of *Joseph Boon* seven acres and a quarter of land in
the parish of *Kenardington*, at the price and of the value
of 25l. 7s. 6d., being 3l. 10s. per acre, and at the same time
he, on his own account, took an acre of land in the same
parish of *Joseph Boon*, at the price and value of 50s.
The seven-acre piece was cultivated and cropped with
potatoes, and the expenses and the rent for the same were
paid equally by the pauper and his two partners; but the
one-acre piece was cultivated and cropped with potatoes
by and at the sole expense of, and rent for the same was
paid by, the pauper alone; thereby making his renting
in the parish of *Kenardington*, at one time, 10l. 19s. 2d.;
and these two parcels of land were held together by the
pauper, and by the pauper and his partners, six months.
The pauper at no time resided on any part of the land
taken of *Joseph Boon*, but resided in the small house of
his master's, on his master's farm, as his servant. At
the end of the three years, he quitted *Stead's* employment,
and at the same time left his house.

Bolland and *Brodrick*, in support of the order of sessions.
The question in this case is, whether, in order to gain a
settlement by renting a tenement of 10l. annual value, it is
necessary, according to the sound construction of the
statute, 13 and 14 *Car.* 2, c. 12, that the party should

reside on the tenement. If this be the true construction of that statute, then it will come to this, that if a man rents a field in a parish, of the annual value of 10*l.*, but does not dwell upon it, he gains no settlement. Now if that be so, it will introduce a new principle in settlement law, never thought of before. It is true, that in *Rex* v. *Bardwell* (a), and *Rex* v. *Shipdham* (b), the Court seemed inclined to think, that unless the pauper resided on the tenement, the words of the statute " coming to settle," were not satisfied. Those cases were, however, determined without sufficient consideration of the language of the statute, and of prior solemn decisions to the contrary. Until those cases were decided, the fact of the pauper actually residing on the tenement never formed an ingredient in the settlement, it being always deemed sufficient if the party resided in the parish where the tenement was situated (c). Upon this principle, the cases of *Rex* v. *Winster* (d), and *Rex* v. *All Saints, Derby* (e), proceeded. In *Rex* v. *Benniworth* (f), which was argued before all the Judges of this Court, the cases of *Rex* v. *Bardwell* and *Rex* v. *Shipdham*, appear to have been re-considered ; and the Court, adverting to the inconvenience of unsettling what had been considered a rule of law for so many years (whether rightly or wrongly), felt themselves bound to adhere to the principle of the prior decisions, which held that a residence on the tenement was not necessary to confer a settlement.

(a) Ante, vol. iii., 369. 2 B. & C. 161.

(b) Ib. 384.

(c) See *Rex* v. *Butler*, Burr. S. C. 107 ; *Rex* v. *Sowton*, Id. 125 ; *Rex* v. *Shenston*, Id. 474 ; *Rex* v. *Llandrerras*, Id. 571 ; *Rex* v. *Old Arlesford*, 1 T. R. 358 ; *Rex* v. *Melkridge*, Id. 598 ; *Rex* v. *Whixley*, Id. 137 ; *Rex* v. *Stoke*, 2 Id. 451 ; *Rex* v. *Knigh-* ton, 2 Id. 48 ; *Rex* v. *Piddletrent-hide*, 3 Id. 772 ; *Rex* v. *Brampton*, 4 Id. 348 ; *Rex* v. *Tolpuddle*, 4 Id. 671 ; *Rex* v. *Houghton Le Spring*, 1 East, 247 ; *Rex* v. *Cherry Willingham*, Ante, vol. iii., 13.

(d) 3 M. & S. 276.

(e) 5 M. & S. 90.

(f) Ante, vol. iv, 355. 2 B. & C. 775.

Nolan, and *D. Pollock*, contrá. The question is, whether a person who has been hired as a servant, and living in a parish in the character of a servant, can, by taking a tenement of 10*l.*, upon which he never resides during his servitude, gain a settlement by renting a tenement in that parish by force of the statute, 13 and 14 *Car.* 2, c. 12? If this question had depended upon the words of the statute alone, without regard to decisions, it is quite clear, that under the circumstances of this case, the pauper could not have gained a settlement. It is submitted, that the true construction of that statute requires that the party should come to settle and reside upon a tenement in the charac‐ter of a *tenant*. Now here, if the pauper came to settle at all, it was in the character of servant, and he never resided as tenant. The cases of *Rex* v. *Bardwell* and *Rex* v. *Ship‐dham*, were rightly decided; upon the sound distinction between a person coming into a parish in the character of a servant, and coming to settle upon a tenement in the character of tenant. Here, the pauper comes merely as a servant in the first instance into the parish, and during the whole time of his occupation of the tenement, he still con‐tinues in the character of a servant. [*Bayley*, J. Suppose a man comes into a parish and takes a tenement of 2*l.* a year, and six years afterwards he takes a 10*l.* tenement, can you say that he does not come to settle in a 10*l.* tene‐ment, because he originally came to settle upon a 2*l.* tene‐ment?] Certainly not, inasmuch as he originally came to settle in the character of *tenant*, although he did not rent to a sufficient value in order to gain a settlement; but by afterwards taking a tenement of the requisite value, and residing upon it for 40 days, he would acquire a set‐tlement. [*Bayley*, J. Suppose a man comes originally into a parish in the character of servant, and quitting the service, takes a 10*l.* tenement in the same parish, would he thereby gain a settlement?] Certainly, by changing his character from servant to that of tenant, he would then be considered as coming to settle within the meaning of the statute, and would gain a settlement, provided he resided on the tenement.

BAYLEY, J.—I am of opinion, that the sessions did right in quashing the order of removal form *Kenardington* to *Ulcomb*, inasmuch as it appears to me, that a settlement was gained by the pauper in the former parish. The ground on which it is now argued, that a settlement was not gained in the parish of *Kenardington*, is, that although the pauper rented a tenement of more than the value of 10*l.*, yet, as he did not reside upon any part of it, but resided with a master, and as the character of servant continued at the time he took the tenement, he could not be considered as coming to settle within the meaning of the statute. In *Rex* v. *Bardwell*, there certainly fell an expression from Mr. Justice *Best* and myself, intimating a much stronger stress upon the words " coming to settle," than upon further consideration of the 13 and 14 *Car.* 2, I think we ought to have given. The case of *Rex* v. *Shipdham* was decided upon the same principle. When *Rex* v. *Benniworth* came before the Court, time was taken to consider of the question, because the Court was pressed with the decisions in *Rex* v. *Bardwell* and *Rex* v. *Shipdham*; and they accordingly reconsidered those two cases. Although I do not find that my Lord Chief Justice, in giving his judgment in *Rex* v. *Benniworth*, points out this particular question, yet it is quite certain, that the Court took time to reconsider the former cases; and certainly, if the doctrine in *Rex* v. *Bardwell* and *Rex* v. *Shipdham* was right, the Court could not have come to the conclusion that they did in *Rex* v. *Benniworth*. The statute of 13 and 14 *Car.* 2, recites, that poor persons are not restrained from going from one parish to another, and therefore do endeavour to settle themselves in those parishes where there is the best stock, the largest commons, or wastes to build cottages, and the most woods for them to burn and destroy; and when they have consumed it, then to another parish, and

at last become rogues and vagabonds, to the great dis-
couragement of parishes to provide stock, where it is liable
to be devoured by strangers; and therefore, it is enacted,
"that any such person or persons coming so to settle as
aforesaid, in any tenement under the yearly value of 10*l*.,"
may be removed to their last legal settlement. Therefore,
the language of the statute is not confined to persons
coming *generally* to settle on a tenement under 10*l*. a year,
but coming to settle *as aforesaid*; *i. e.*, persons shifting
about from parish to parish, and coming to abide in a
parish merely because there is the best stock, the largest
commons or waste, and the most woods for them to burn
and destroy. I had known by experience, that the decisions in *Rex* v. *Piddletrenthide, Rex* v. *Minster*, and
others, had [particularly in part of the country with which
I am well acquainted] produced great inconvenience between master and servant, and that masters were deterred
from granting certain privileges to their servants, such as
the feed of a cow, and the run of sheep [which contributed very much to the comfort of the servants] from an
apprehension that by so doing, they would be conferring
a settlement upon their servants, and entailing burthens on
the parish. Perhaps, with a knowledge of this on my
mind at the time, I was more inclined to lay hold of the
distinction which occurred to me in *Rex* v. *Bardwell*, than
upon consideration I ought to have done. When we come
to look at former decisions, it is quite clear that the
paupers did not reside upon any part of that which constituted the tenement of 10*l*. value. That was the case
in *Rex* v. *Minster*. There the servant stipulated for a
house to reside in, and the feed of two cows upon his
master's farm. He held the house, not in the character
of tenant, and, therefore, it constituted no part of the
tenement; but the feed of the two cows, on his master's
farm, being of the value of 10*l*., he was held to have
gained a settlement; and yet, he did not reside upon any
thing which constituted a part of the tenement, inasmuch

as he resided in the house in the character of servant. In *Rex* v. *Sutton Saint Edmonds* (a), the pauper was hired as a labourer in husbandry, to serve a farmer, under an agreement that he was to have yearly wages, and his master either to provide him two cows, or provide himself with two, and feed them on his master's farm. The pauper lived in a cottage on his master's farm, but the occupation of the cottage was incidental to the service. The cows were fed during the summer in the master's pasture, and in the winter, in the master's straw yard, with hay grown upon the farm. The pasture and the hay feeding were, respectively, worth five guineas a year; and the Court held, that the pauper gained no settlement, inasmuch as the contract was not, that the cows were to be pasture fed, but otherwise, if such had been the agreement; which shews, that if the Court thought residence upon the tenement necessary, that would have been a decisive objection, without going into the other parts of the case. In *Rex* v. *Benniworth*, the pauper had, according to agreement, a house and garden, a rood of potatoe land, and the keep of a cow on his master's land. The cow was instead of so much money for wages. After some time the pauper's cow failed in milk, on which account, through the kindness of his master and not in consequence of any bargain, the pauper had, in the place of the former cow, two heifers, kept for him by his master, on his master's land, about eleven months. The potatoe land and keep of two heifers were, together, of the value of 10*l.* per annum and upwards; but the potatoe land and keep of one cow were below that value. In that case the pauper gained a settlement by renting a tenement, and renting only, for he did not reside upon any part of what he rented, and by renting that which he took during the time he had the character of servant impressed upon him. That case, therefore, is in point with this, because, here the pauper had the

(a) Ante, vol. ii., 800. 1 B & C. 536.

character of servant impressed upon him at the time he took that which makes the tenement amount to the full value of 10*l.* It can make no difference, whether the pauper took the whole, or only part of the tenement at the period the service commenced. Here, he certainly took the whole during the continuance of the service. I consider *Rex* v. *Benniworth* as establishing this position, namely, that renting a tenement of 10*l.* a year will confer a settlement, although the party does not reside upon the tenement; and, certainly, that case has corrected an erroneous judgment, which I had formed in the cases of *Rex* v. *Bardwell* and *Rex* v. *Shipdham.* I am, therefore, of opinion, that a settlement was gained in the parish of *Kenardington,* and that the order of sessions must be confirmed.

LITTLEDALE, J. (*a*).—I am of the same opinion. I think that, according to the sound construction of the 13 and 14 *Car.* 2, it is not necessary for the party to reside upon the tenement in order to gain a settlement. The only doubt is, whether the words in the act " coming to *settle*" necessarily mean coming to *reside* upon the tenement; and I think, that considering the way in which the word *settle* is introduced, it does not at all imply the necessity of actual residence upon the tenement. The act speaks of persons coming to settle themselves in parishes where there is the best stock of provisions, &c.; and as the object of the act was to prevent persons of small means from coming into parishes, if a man could afford to pay 10*l.* a year for a tenement, it would be perfectly immaterial whether he did or did not actually reside upon the tenement. It would make no difference, as to the probability of his being burthensome to the parish, whether he rents house and land together or separately, or whether he resides upon the tenement. The question in these cases is, as to the party's ability, and whether he is a fit person, on account of apparent property, to remain in the

(*a*) HOLROYD, J., was in the Bail-Court.

parish. But then, it is contended by Mr. *Nolan* and Mr. *Pollock*, that the party must come to settle in the character of tenant. I find no words in the act which impose that qualification. The act certainly does not look to it. I see no reason why a man, who comes originally into a parish in the character of servant, may not, during his servitude, take a 10*l.* tenement, and so gain a settlement, though he does not reside upon it. He is, in my opinion, as much within the protection of the act, as if he came originally into the parish in the character of tenant. It seems to me, that *Rex* v. *Benniworth* has properly corrected the decisions in *Rex* v. *Bardwell* and *Rex* v. *Shipdham*, which were determined without full consideration of the language of the act and the previous authorities.

Order confirmed.

The KING v. The INHABITANTS of CRAYFORD.

Where a
person hired a
house at 12*l.*
a-year for a
whole year,
paid rent for a
whole year,
and died three
days before
the year ex-
pired, but his
corpse re-
mained in the
house until
after the year
expired :—
Held, that he
gained no
settlement
under 59 *G.* 3,
c. 50, which
could be com-
municated to
his wife and
children.

BY an order of two justices, dated 22nd *November*, 1826, *Sarah Stone*, widow of *Thomas Stone*, and their six children, were removed from *Bexley* to *Crayford*, both in the county of *Kent*. The sessions on appeal confirmed the order, subject to the opinion of this Court on the following case :—

In the month of *September*, 1824, *Thomas Stone*, the pauper's husband, was settled in the parish of *Crayford*. At *Michaelmas* in the same year, he hired a house situated in the parish of *Bexley*, for a year, at the rent, and of the annual value of 12*l.* He took possession of the house on *Michaelmas-day*, the 29th *September*, 1824, and continued to live in the same, till the 26th *September*, 1825, when he died. His body remained in the house till the 30th of the same month, when it was buried. The rent for the first three quarters of a year was paid by him, and for the last quarter, ending on the 29th *September*, 1825, by his widow, the pauper. The pauper continued in the house till she was removed under the order, and paid the rent thereof up to 25th *December*, 1825. The question is, whether the pauper and her children, under the above circumstances, were entitled to settlements in the parish of *Bexley*.

D. Pollock, in support of the order of sessions. The pauper and her children are not entitled to settlements in the parish of *Bexley*. This question depends upon the words of the *59 Geo.* 3, c. 50, which requires, not only that the tenement shall be hired for 10*l.* a-year at the least, for the term of one whole year, but that the tenement shall be occupied, and the rent for the same actually paid, for the term of one whole year at the least " *by the person hiring the same.*" Now one condition here has completely failed, namely, that the pauper's husband, who was the person hiring the house, did not occupy it for the term of one whole year at the least, inasmuch as he died three days before the year was out.

Bolland, contrà, contended, that as the rent had been paid for the whole year out of the husband's assets, that was sufficient, coupled with the remaining of his corpse in the house, under the circumstances mentioned in the case, until after the year had expired, to confer a settlement ; those words which require that there shall be an occupation of the tenement, *by the person hiring the same,* ought to receive a liberal construction, especially as all the other conditions of the act were in this case complied with. [*Bayley*, J. In this case you rely upon a derivative settlement. Can you derive a settlement from a person who was not in existence at the time the settlement is supposed to have been gained ?] Certainly, if the husband did not gain a settlement in *Bexley* during his life, none can be derived from him by his widow, in that parish.

BAYLEY, J.—I believe, that in all these cases, it is by far the safest rule to go by the language of the act of parliament. The words of this statute are, that " no person shall acquire a settlement by reason of his or her dwelling for forty days in any tenement rented by such person, unless such tenement shall consist of a house or building, being a separate and distinct dwelling-house or building, or of land, or both, bonâ fide hired by such person, at and for the sum of 10l. a year at the least, for the term of one whole year; nor unless such house or building shall be held, and such land occupied, and the rent for the same actually paid, for the term of one whole year at the least, *by the person hiring the same.*" The settlement, therefore, is to be gained by the person who has hired the tenement, and occupied it for one whole year. Here the husband may have hired, but he has not occupied the house for a whole year, inasmuch as he expired three days before the end of the year; and assuming that the wife occupied, and paid the rent for a year, still she is not the person who hired the house. This certainly is a very critical case, and perhaps if it had been foreseen by the legislature at the time of passing the act, some provision would have been made to meet it. Adhering, however, to the language of the statute, we must say, that no settlement was gained either by the husband or the wife.

LITTLEDALE, J. (a).—I am of the same opinion. It cannot be said that the pauper resided for a year, because he died three days short of it, although his corpse remained in the house the usual time before interment : and therefore, he cannot be said to have gained a settlement which he could communicate to his children.

Order of Sessions confirmed,

(a) HOLROYD, J., was in the Bail-Court.

HOLLOWAY and PADWICK *v.* BERKELEY.

TROVER for six horses. Plea, not guilty, and issue thereon. At the trial before *Littledale*, J., at the *Hants* summer assizes, 1825, the plaintiffs obtained a verdict, with nominal damages, subject to the opinion of the Court upon the following case :—

The plaintiffs are the executors of the last will and testament of one *George Haselar Andrews*, deceased. The defendant was, at the time of the death of the said *G. H. Andrews*, and from thence hitherto, and still is, the lord of the manor of *Bosham*, in the county of *Sussex*. The horses in question were the property of the said *G. H. Andrews*, at the time of his death, and had been seized and taken by the defendant as and for heriots, as hereinafter mentioned. Within the manor of *Bosham* there are, and from time immemorial have been, divers customary tenement , called and known by the name and description of *Boardland* tenements, demised and demisable by copy of the court rolls of the said manor, by the lord of the manor, or by his steward of the court thereof for the time being, in fee simple or otherwise, according to the custom of the manor; and by the custom of the manor, there is payable to the lord, on the death of any tenant of any of the copyhold tenements called *Boardland*, who shall die seised thereof, as and for a heriot in respect of each of the said copyhold tenements, the best beast of the said tenant, at the time of his death. In the year 1812, one *John Andrews* died seised in his demesne as of fee, of six copyhold tenements of *Boardland*; and, upon his death, there happened to the lord of the manor, according to the custom of the said manor, for heriots, in respect of the said six several copyhold tenements, the six best beasts of him the said *J. Andrews*, that is to say, one for each of the said several tenements. Previously to his death, *J. Andrews* had surrendered the

The creation of a tenancy in common in a copyhold tenement held by heriot custom, entitles the lord to a heriot from each of the tenants in common ; but if the several tenancies are re-united in the same person, the lord is entitled to one heriot only.

G 2

said several tenements to such uses as should be declared by his last will and testament; and, after such surrender, he, by his will, dated the 16th of *April*, 1812, gave and devised the said six copyhold tenements to [his two sons, *J. H. Andrews* and *J. Andrews*, and their heirs for ever, as tenants in common and not as joint tenants. At a court, holden for the said manor, on the 29th of *August*, 1812, *G. H. Andrews* was admitted to one undivided moiety, or half-part or share, the whole into two equal parts or shares to be divided, of and in the said six copyhold tenements, to have and to hold to him, the said *G. H. Andrews*, and his heirs, by copy of court-roll, according to the form and effect of the last will and testament of *J. Andrews*, deceased, and according to the custom of the manor, by the apportioned yearly rents, heriots, suits of court, and other services, therefore formerly due and of right accustomed; and, at the same court, *J. Andrews* was, in like manner and form, admitted to the other undivided moiety of the said six copyhold tenements. At a court, holden for the manor, on the 22nd of *February*, 1818, *J. Andrews*, for a valuable consideration paid to him by *G. H. Andrews*, duly surrendered into the hands of the lord, his undivided moiety of and in the said several tenements, to the use and behoof of *G. H. Andrews*, and his heirs for ever, according to the custom of the manor; and at the same court, *G. H. Andrews* prayed to be, and was admitted, tenant of and to the said moieties, lands, tenements and premises so surrendered, to have and to hold unto him, the said *G. H. Andrews*, and his heirs, by copy of court-roll, according to the custom of the manor, by the yearly rents, heriots, suit of court, and other services, therefore formerly due and of right accustomed. *G. H. Andrews* died in the year 1824, seised of the said several tenements as aforesaid, whereupon the defendant, then being the lord of the manor of *Bosham*, claimed to be entitled to, and seized and took, twelve horses, as and being the twelve best beasts which

were of *G. H. Andrews*, at the time of his death, as
heriots for and in respect of the said several tenements.
The action was brought to recover the value of six of the
said twelve horses, being the six which were marked, and
agreed upon between the plaintiffs and the defendant,
upon the seizure thereof as aforesaid, as being the inferior
beasts; and the question for the opinion of the Court
was, whether the defendant, as such lord, was entitled to
twelve, or only to six heriots, in respect of the said several
tenements, whereof *G. H. Andrews* died seised as aforesaid.

Carter, for the plaintiffs. The two leading decisions
upon this subject are of a conflicting nature. The first
is *Attree* v. *Scutt* (a), which will be relied upon for the
defendant; the second is *Garland* v. *Jekyll* (b), which is
an express authority for the plaintiff. With respect to
the former of those cases, in the first place it is not strictly
applicable to the present, because, the question there was
with respect to fines payable on admittance to copyholds;
and, in the second place, it was founded entirely upon the
authority of a case in *Fitzherbert* (c), which, it seems
hardly too much to say, has in recent times been thought
not to be law. It is there said, " if my tenant, who
holds of me by heriot, aliene parcel of the land to another, each of them is chargeable to me with a heriot, for
it is entire; and if the tenant purchase the land again,
yet if I were seised of the heriot by another man, I shall
have of him, the tenant, for each portion a heriot." That
is quoted by Lord *Ellenborough*, in his judgment in *Attree*
v. *Scutt*, who adds, that he cannot see any distinction
between a case where the land is occupied in severalty,
and where there has been an entire tenement holden by
several persons in common; it will be contended, therefore, that the law respecting heriots was treated in that case

(a) 6 East, 476.   (b) 9 J. B. Moore, 502; 2 Bing. 273.
(c) Fitz. Abr. *Heriot*, Pl. 1.

as settled, and that the present must be governed by it. Independently, however, of the argument, that the case in *Fitzherbert* is not law, it is by no means an authority for saying, that several heriots are demandable in this case. Heriots are, in their nature, personal: they are paid in respect of the estate held by the lord of the tenant; they are not a charge upon the land itself. They are presumed to have originated in some contract or agreement made between the lord and his tenant, at the time of his parcelling out his estates to different individuals; and then, if by the subsequent act of the tenant several tenements were created, several heriots might properly become payable; and that is the only case to which the doctrine of *Fitzherbert* appears at all strictly applicable. Where " a tenant, holding by heriot, alienes *parcel of the land* to another," each may be properly " chargeable with a heriot," because the effect of that alienation is to create several distinct copyhold tenements; and " if the tenant purchase the land again," several heriots may still be payable, because that re-purchase would not have the effect of re-uniting those distinct tenements. But that is not the presnt case, because here there never was any actual separation of the tenements; therefore, the results which would properly follow there, cannot arise here. With respect to Lord *Ellenborough's* opinion, that there would be no distinction between the case where the land is held in severalty, and where it his held by several in common ; it does not seem to be warranted by the authority upon which he grounds it, nor consistent with the reason. of the thing : for, when several tenements become re-united in one person, it is not easy to suggest upon what principle the lord should be entitled to more than the one heriot, which he received when the whole tenement was granted originally. If these arguments are well founded, *Garland* v. *Jekyll* (a) appears a decision founded upon principle, and is a direct authority in favour of the plaintiff.

(a) 9 J. B. Moore, 502 ; 2 Bing. 273.

Merewether, contrà. The defendant relies upon the
decision in *Attree* v. *Scutt* (a), which proceeded upon
principles long established and well understood in the law
of copyholds, and which are these :—First, that the lord
cannot, by any act of his, prejudice the rights of his
tenant, *Lane's* case (b) ; second, that the tenant cannot,
by any act of his, prejudice the rights of his lord, *Kite*
and *Queinton's* case (c) ; and third, that where the interest
has been severed by the act of the tenant, and distinct
tenements created, in respect of which several heriots
become payable to the lord, the tenant cannot, by afterwards rejoining the interest, and re-uniting the tenements,
destroy the lord's right to such several heriots, *Bruerton's*
case (d). The judgment of this Court, in *Attree* v. *Scutt,*
founded upon these principles, has been overruled by the
court of Common Pleas, in *Garland* v. *Jekyll,* upon grounds
which it is necessary to examine into. The first and principal ground assigned by *Best,* C. J., for the judgment in
that case was, that this Court had been misled by the passage
quoted from *Fitzherbert.* His Lordship is reported to have
delivered himself upon the point thus" (e) : " It is clear
that there is some great mistake as to that case. It was
a loose note, probably the decision of a Judge at Nisi
Prius. It will not be found in any one book of authority ;
for if it had, it would have been cited in *Brooke's* or
Rolle's Abridgment, or in *Viner* or *Comyns* ; but it is in
none of these, and is only to be found in *Kitchin on
Courts,* and in a way that shews that it was greatly mistaken by *Fitzherbert.* *Kitchin* refers to him, and thought
it was not an authority. He makes the tenants in common, while they continue in common, pay several heriots ;
but he goes no further. His words are, ' if my tenant,
which holds of me by a heriot, alienes parcel of his land
to another, every one of them shall pay a heriot, for

1826.

HOLLOWAY
v.
BERKELEY.

(a) 6 East, 476.
(b) 2 Rep. 17.
(c) 4 Rep. 25.

(d) 6 Rep. 1.
(e) 9 J. B. Moore, 553.

that it is entire' (a) ; there the passage stops, there is not a word implying, that if they are again united, they shall pay more than one heriot; and he refers to *Fitzherbert* only, and not to the Year Books." His Lordship had previously observed, that *Fizherbert* could not mean to refer to the Year Books, because the case was supposed to have occurred in the 34 *Edward* 3, and the Year Books of *Edward* 3, stopped at the 30th year of that reign, and did not begin again till the 38th. So that there was no Year Book of the 34 *Edward* 3. Now, it is true, that in the printed copies of the Year Books now extant, there is the chasm pointed out by *Best*, C. J., but there may have been many MS. notes of the cases decided in the interval; for there are other chasms in the Year Books : and of the cases decided during one of them, namely, from 10 to 18 *Edward* 3, there is now extant, in the *Inner Temple* library, a MS. report. The case, however, is to be found in several books of authority. In *Statham's* Abridgment, the first that was published, many of the cases decided between the 30th and 38th *Edward* 3, are given, and among them is the case in question, stated verbatim the same as in *Fitzherbert* (b). In *Comyn's* Digest, the passage is mentioned thus :—" If tenant by heriot service aliènes parcel, the heriot shall be multiplied ; *Fitzherbert, Heriot,* 1. And if the lord be seised of a heriot by the alienee, it continues, though the tenant re-purchase this parcel" (c). So in *Kitchin,* the whole passage is given, though not in the page referred to by *Best,* C. J.; for he says, " if my tenant who holds from me aliene parcels of his lands to others, every one of them will owe to me a heriot; for that is entire; and though the tenant purchase the land again, I shall have two heriots from him. And *Fitzherbert* says, that was the opinion of *Wildby* and *Shard,*" and he refers also to *Statham* (d). Lord *Coke* refers to the same passage, in *Bruerton's*

(a) Kitchin on Courts, 268.   (c) Com. Dig. Copyholder. K. 19
(b) Stath. Abr. tit. Heriot.   (d) Kitchin on Courts, 269.

case (*a*), where he says, " and no difference as to this purpose between entire services annual, as suit, a hawk, &c., and not annual, as homage, fealty, &c. ; and as to heriot, vide 34 *Ed.* 3, *Heriot*, 1 ; and in *Talbot's* case (*b*), where he says, " also they cited the book in 34 *Ed.* 3, *Heriot*, 1 ; where it is held, that if my tenant, who holds of me by a heriot, alienes parcel of his land to another, each of them is chargeable to me of a heriot, because it is entire ; and although the tenant purchases the land again, &c., I shall have of him, for each portion, a heriot :" and it is cited by *Scroggs*, in his book upon Courts Leet, with a reference to the two cases last mentioned (*c*). Again, *Best*, C. J., in his judgment in *Garland* v. *Jekyll* (*d*), cites this dictum of Lord *Coke's*:—" If two several copyholders join in a grant of their copyhold by one copy ; or if one copyholder having several copyholds, granteth them by one copy ; yet the grantee shall pay several fines, for they shall enure as several grants : but if two joint tenants, two tenants in common, or tenant for life and he in the remainder, join in the grant of a copyhold, one fine only is due, and it shall enure as one grant only" (*e*). Now, that dictum must be allowed to be correct as it respects joint tenants, and tenant for life and remainder man, but there is no authority in support of it as it respects tenants in common ; and the case referred to in the margin, in 4 Rep. 27 b, certainly furnishes no such authority. But the passage cited by Lord *Ellenborough* in *Attree* v. *Scutt* (*f*), from a case in *Plowden*, *Browning* v. *Beston* (*g*), is an authority the other way, for there it is said, " if two tenants in common grant a rent of 20*s*. out of their land, it shall enure as several grants ; and in *Perkins*, sec. 207, it is laid down, " that if two tenants in common of a close of land lease the

---

(*a*) 6 Rep. 1.   (*e*) Co. Copyh. S. 56, p. 162.
(*b*) 8 Rep. 104 b.   (*f*) 6 East, 476.
(*c*) Scroggs on Courts Leet, 157.   (*g*) 1 Plowd. 140.
(*d*) 9 J. B. Moore, 548.

same, it shall take effect as several leases." There is no real distinction between a severance of title and a severance of estate. In each case the tenant holds by a separate copy of court roll; and that is the title, and regulates the respective rights of the lord, and of the tenant, in each.

Curter, in reply. The lord will not be prejudiced by the Court holding that only one heriot is payable in this case, because he will be precisely in the same situation as he was when the copyhold tenement was originally granted. He had only one heriot then; and though he may have received more occasionally in the interval, still if he receives one now, he has no reasonable cause of complaint. The dictum of Lord *Coke,* in his Copyholder, does not require the support of the case referred to; and the former part of it clearly shews, that he was then keeping in mind the distinction between a severance of title and a severance of estate.

The case was argued before the three Puisne Judges at the sittings in *Banc* after last term; judgment was now delivered by

BAYLEY, J.—The question in this case was, whether two heriots were payable upon death, in respect of what had formerly been six copyhold tenements. They were held of the manor of *Bosham.* By the custom of that manor, there is payable to the lord, on the death of any tenant of any of the copyhold tenements called *Boardland,* dying seised thereof, as and for a heriot in respect of each of the said copyhold tenements, the tenant's best beast. In *April,* 1812, *John Andrews* died seised of these tenements, having previously surrendered them to the use of his will, and having devised them to his two sons, *George Haselar Andrews* and *James Andrews,* as tenants in common, in fee. In *August,* 1812, the two sons were respectively admitted to undivided moieties; and in *February,* 1818, *James Andrews* surrendered his moiety to *George Haselar Andrews*, who was admitted thereto. There never, therefore, was any dying seised while the moieties were in different ownerships; no heriots ever became payable for separate moieties; and there was no instance in which the heriots were, in fact, multiplied. In 1824, *George Haselar Andrews* died seised, and upon his death the lord seized two beasts in respect of each of the six copyhold tenements, and for the seizure of six, that is, all but one on each tenement, the action was brought. The question, therefore, in substance, is, whether upon a tenancy in common, the share of each tenant constitutes *a distinct tenement*; or, whether, notwithstanding *the distinct estates* of both tenants in common, the copyhold does not still remain *one entire tenement*. The custom, which is against common right, and to be construed strictly, gives a heriot in respect of each *tenement* of which the copyholder dies seised. It is not in respect of each *estate* in a copyhold tenement of which the tenant dies seised, but in respect of each *tenement*. In the case of heriot service, or heriot custom, the law multiplies the heriot in two cases: one, where the tenement is actually divided, *and converted into two or more separate tenements*; the other, where the tenement is left entire, but different persons have distinct undivided estates therein. Before the statute of *Quia Emptores*, if a tenant in fee, who held under certain services, aliened part of his land in fee, without the lord's assent, the lord might, nevertheless, distrain, either upon the land sold, or upon the land retained, for the whole of his services; and the lord was entitled to consider the whole tenement as if it remained entire: 10 *H.* 7, 10 pl. 26; *Co. Litt.* 43 a; and because this statute did not bind the king, the same continued in the king's case, notwithstanding this statute; *Plowden,* 240. But in ordinary cases, since the statute, any *freehold* tenant may subdivide his tenement and aliene part, and such of his services as are divisible will be liable to be apportioned, and such of his services as are entire will be multiplied; but the alienee will, in such case, hold his portion as an entire, independent tenement: his portion will be liable to the apportioned proportion only of the divisible services; and the residue will also be held as an entire, independent tenement, liable only to its apportioned proportion of the divisible services. For instance:—if *C.* has 300 acres of freehold land at 15*l.* rent, fealty, homage, and heriot, and he alienes 100 acres to *A.*, 100 acres to *B.*, and retains 100 acres to himself, and each 100 acres is of the same value; *A.* will hold 100 acres at 5*l.* rent, fealty, homage, and heriot, and *B.* and *C.*, respectively, will do the same, and each will hold his proportion as a separate, independent tenement. The tenements of *A.*, *B.*, and *C.*, respectively, will no longer be liable to the 15*l.* rent, but to the 5*l.* only; and it is not necessary in this case to say, whether, by the union of three tenements in one person, the 15*l.* rent would be revived, and extend over the whole estate, or whether the three tenements would continue each a distinct tenement, liable to its 5*l.* only. If a copyhold tenant can subdivide his tenement in the same manner, the same consequences will follow. But, will the creation of a tenancy in common have the same effect of producing, even for a time, separate tenements? Where the tenement is subdivided, each tenant holds his share in severalty, and it is subject to nothing but its own services. In the case of a tenancy in common, the tenancy is divided; none of the tenants in common, be there what number there may, knows his own in severalty; the services, which, in case of division would be divisible, remain entire, and the whole land is liable to all the services. In case of copyholds, they are not within the statutes of partition; *Rowden* v. *Maltster* (a), Co. Copyh. s. 54, Com. Dig. Copyh. (O); and the reason is, because *the alteration of the tenure,* without the lord's assent, may redound to the lord's pre-

(a) Cro. Car. 44.

judice. How will the tenure be altered, except by splitting into two or more separate tenements, what before was an entire tenement? In his comment upon the second chapter of the statute of *Quia Emptores*, Lord *Coke* takes the distinction between the alienee of the distinct parcel of a freehold tenement, and the creation of a tenancy in common. That branch of the statute provides, "that if a freeman sell any part of his lands or tenements, the feoffee shall hold immediately of the chief lord, and shall be forthwith charged with the services for so much as belongs, or ought to belong, to the chief lord for that parcel, *particula illa*, according to the quantity of the land or tenement sold. And so, in this case, the same part of the services shall remain to the chief lord, to be taken by the hands of the feoffee, for the which he ought to be attendant upon, and answerable to the chief lord, according to the quantity of land or tenement sold, for the parcel of the services so due." This provision is the foundation of apportionment in these cases; rent, where that is one of the services, not being apportionable at common law; 3 Vin. Abr. *Apportionment*, pl. 1. Note. Upon that part of this clause which relates to the holding part of the chief lord, and at a proportion of the services, Lord *Coke's* comment is this; "particula illa (for which he is to be charged), is to be understood of a part in severalty, and not in common; and therefore, it is holden, that if the tenant make a feoffment in fee of the moiety or third part of the tenancy, that such a feoffee is not within the purview of this statute: for a moiety, or third part, pro indiviso, is not particula, for that word implieth a part in severalty" (a). The same doctrine may be found in 6 Rep. 1 b; in *Plowden*, 240; and in *Fitzherbert*, N. B., 162 d; and the meaning of it is very distinctly explained in *Brooke's* Abridgment, *Tenures*, pl. 64, from 29 *Henry* 8th, which Lord *Coke* cites:—"A man makes feoffment of a moiety of his land. The feoffee shall hold of the lord by the entire services, by which the

(a) 2 Inst. 503.

entire land was held before; for the statute, tenendo pro particulâ, has not taken place here, for a moiety is not particula; and there is a contrariety between one or two acres in certain, and a third part, or the like, which extends through the part and the whole." This is a clear authority to shew, that in the case of freehold lands, which are within the statute of *Quia Emptores*, the creation of a tenancy in common leaves the services entire, and consequently, must leave entire the tenement also; and if that is the case in freeholds, à fortiori, must it be the case in copyholds? In *Coke*'s Copyholder, s. 56, p. 130, cited in 6 *Viner*'s Abridgment, 105, there is an authority in the case of copyholds upon this very point; for there Lord *Coke*, after noticing, that "if several copyholders join in a grant of their copyholds by one copy, or if one copyholder having several copyholds, grant them by one copy, yet the grantee shall pay several fines, for they shall enure as several grants:" adds, "but if two joint tenants, two tenants in common, or tenant for life and he in remainder, join in the grant of a copyhold, one fine only is due, and it shall enure as one grant only." And *Kitchin*, 245, is nearly to the same purpose:—"Also, if tenant for life and he in remainder or reversion, join in a surrender to one, and his heirs, he, to whose use the surrender is made, shall pay but one fine; for it is but one admittance and not several, and one surrender and not several; and there is but one tenant admitted. The same law, where two joint tenants, two tenants in common or coparceners, surrender to one, and his heirs, there shall be paid but one fine." These authorities appear to us to establish a plain distinction between the alienation of an entire part, and the creation of a tenancy in common; and to shew, that though the former may split one tenement into several, the latter cannot. It is to be observed also, that the former, the alienation of an entire part, must always be the act of the owner in fee of the whole; so that whoever feels the consequences, must claim through the person by whose act

they were occasioned ; whereas the owner of a part of the
tenement only, that is, one of several joint tenants, or one
of several parceners, may create a tenancy in common ;
and if a tenancy in common would create a division into
distinct tenements, every division would increase the number of tenements in arithmetical progression. Dividing the
whole six times into moieties, which would be allowing
something less than one division in every century since
the commencement of legal memory, would make what
was originally one tenement, sixty four; and dividing it
six times into three shares, would make it 729; and we
might then have in pleading, what I apprehend has never
hitherto been seen, a statement that a party was seised in
fee at the will of the lord, according to the custom of the
manor, of 729 undivided parts of certain copyhold lands,
the whole into 729 parts to be divided. Such an anomaly
will, I hope, never be seen ; but whatever may have been
at any time the number of tenants in common of what was
originally one copyhold tenement, when all the interests
are again vested in one person, he may consider himself as
seised, not of so many undivided portions of the land, but
of one entire estate and tenement as sole proprietor. If
this is the true view of the effect of a tenancy in common,
and the proper light in which the question in this case
ought to be considered, it will not be necessary to occupy
much time in noticing the authorities that were relied on
in the argument. The authority from *Fitzherbert* is a case,
not of the creation of a tenancy in common, but of the
severance of an estate into distinct parcels, and the alienation of one of those parcels to others ; and if we are correct in supposing that the creation of a tenancy in common
in what was previously an entire tenement, will not destroy
the entirety of the tenement, it is immaterial to consider
what would be the effect of severing a tenement into
distinct parcels. It does not appear from *Fitzherbert*,
whether that was the case of a freehold or a copyhold

tenement; but it has been frequently noticed in subsequent cases, in 6 Rep., 1; 8 Rep., 105; *Palmer*, 342; *Kitchin on Copyholds*, 269; and Com. Dig. *Copyhold*, (K). 19; and it is a satisfaction to us, that we are not required for the decision of this case to impeach it. The question, whether it is fairly impeachable or not, we shall leave as it stood before: whether it is a right or wrong decision, we consider a matter still open to discussion. In *Attree* v. *Scutt*, it may be difficult to collect from the report, whether there was not a severance of the tenements, so as to allot to one tenement what had previously been parcel of another; but the judgment of the Court appears to have proceeded on the ground, that the creation of a tenancy in common, though there was no division or severance of the property, created distinct and separate tenements; and in that respect we think that decision wrong, and that it has been properly corrected by the subsequent case of *Garland* v. *Jekyll*. That was the case of a creation of a tenancy in common; and upon the principle that the creation of a tenancy in common leaves the tenement entire, we think the decision in that case right, and an authority for us here. It is not necessary for us to say what our opinion would have been, if that had been a case in which there was an actual severance and division of a tenement into distinct and separate parcels, so as to have given to separate holders separate properties in severalty; and we cautiously abstain from saying any thing on that point. For these reasons, we are of opinion that the plaintiff is entitled to judgment.

Judgment for the Plaintiff.

The KING v. CORNELIUS CALLANAN.

1826.

INDICTMENT for perjury, in an affidavit made in this Court, in support of a rule for setting aside the judgment in a suit brought against the defendant by one *Stevens*, the prosecutor, stated, that defendant, on, &c., at, &c., came before *F. J. Chell*, gentleman, and then and there was duly sworn, and did take his corporal oath, &c., before the said *F. J. Chell*, he the said *F. J. Chell*, then and there having sufficient and competent power and authority to administer the said oath to the said defendant in that behalf, and the said defendant, being so sworn as aforesaid, falsely, maliciously, wilfully and corruptly did then and there, before the said *F. J. Chell, as such commissioner as aforesaid*, depose, swear, and make affidavit in writing, amongst other things, in substance and to the effect following, that is to say, &c. The indictment then set out various matters deposed to. In one part it stated, that the defendant, in his affidavit, speaking of a mortgage and warrant of attorney, deposed that they were for " securing the sum of 250*l.*;" and, in another part of it, set out a particular fact as simply deposed to by the defendant in his affidavit, contradicting the fact, and assigning perjury thereon. At the trial, before *Abbott*, C. J., at the *London* adjourned sittings, after last *Easter* term, it was proved that Mr. *Chell*, before whom the affidavit was sworn, was a commissioner duly appointed for taking affidavits in the court of Kings's Bench; but, upon producing the affidavit, it appeared that the defendant had deposed, that the mortgage and warrant of attorney were " for securing *the repayment* of the sum of 250*l.*;" and that he had not simply deposed to the particular fact stated in the indictment, but had added certain reasons accounting for that fact. It was thereupon objected, first, that the indictment was bad for not sufficiently describing the official character and authority of the person before whom the affidavit was

In an indictment for perjury it is sufficient to state that the person who administered the oath had competent authority to do so, without setting out the nature of his authority. If an indictment assigns perjury upon several parts of an affidavit, and sets them out as continuous, though other matters, not set out, intervene in the affidavit; this is not a fatal variance.

stated to have been sworn; and second, that there was a fatal variance between the indictment and the affidavit, in the two particulars above pointed out. The Lord Chief Justice overruled both objections, and the defendant was found guilty. The defendant being now brought up for judgment,

Scarlett moved for a rule in the alternative, either for a new trial or to arrest the judgment. First, the indictment is bad, for not shewing that the person by whom the oath was administered, was an officer duly authorised to administer it. It states, that the defendant made the affidavit " before the said *F. J. Chell*, as such commissioner as aforesaid;" but it contains no previous averment that Mr. *Chell* was a commissioner authorised to take affidavits in this Court. Now, though the statute 23 *Geo.* 2, c. 11, removes the necessity of setting out the commission of the officer before whom the affidavit is made, it still leaves it incumbent to shew the nature of his office, and to aver, affirmatively and not inferentially, that he is a person duly authorised to administer an oath. Secondly, there were two fatal variances between the affidavit produced in evidence and that set out upon the record. The omission, in the indictment, of the words " the repayment of" in the affidavit was material; for the " securing the sum of 250*l.*," and the " securing the repayment of the sum of 250*l.*," are two very distinct things. The omission in the indictment of the reasons detailed in the affidavit for the deposing to a particular fact, was material also, because the fact itself might assume an extremely different character, as stated, with or without certain reasons explaining it. If the whole of the affidavit was not set out, at least it ought to have been stated that " in one part thereof the defendant deposed, so and so, and in another part thereof, so and so." Such omissions as these would clearly be fatal either in a declaration or an indictment for a libel; *Tabart* v. *Tipper* (a); and in an

(a) 1 Camp. 350.

indictment for perjury, which is a yet more serious offence, at least equal precision ought to be required.

ABBOTT, C. J.,—I am of opinion that there is no ground for granting a rule, either for arresting the judgment, or for a new trial, in this case. The statute 23 Geo. 2, c. 11, provides that in every indictment for perjury it shall be sufficient to set forth the substance of the offence charged, and by what Court, or before whom, the oath was taken, averring such Court or person to have a competent authority to administer the same, together with the proper averment to falsify the matter wherein the perjury is assigned, without setting forth the bill, &c., or any part of any proceeding other than as aforesaid, and without setting forth the commission or authority of the Court or person before whom the perjury was committed. Now, if the indictment in this case has set forth all that is required by that statute, that is an answer to both these objections; and, I am of opinion that it has; for it sets forth the substance of the affidavit, and the person before whom the affidavit was sworn, and it avers that that person had competent authority to administer the oath. The object of the statute was, to remove the difficulties which had previously arisen out of the averments and matters usually set forth in indictments for perjury; therefore, we ought not to extend the operation of its language, so as to require more than we see it was the intention of the legislature to require. The averment, that the person who administered the oath had competent authority to do so, is sufficient, for this reason, that at the trial the prosecutor cannot support that averment without proving the situation of the person administering the oath, and the nature of his authority. It seems to me, that it is sufficient if the indictment contains the name of the person, or the title of the Court, before whom the defendant was sworn, and, therefore, that there is nothing in the first objection. As to the second, it has been decided that in indictments for perjury it is sufficient to state the substance and effect of the false oath, which is stated here; though in declarations or indictments for libel more precision is necessary. *Rex* v. *Solomon* (a), is a case in point, and very much resembling the present. There the perjury was alleged to have been committed by the defendant as a witness in a civil action, and it appeared that the evidence given on that trial by the defendant, contained all the matter charged as perjury, but other statements, not varying the sense, intervened between the matters set; but in the indictment the evidence appeared to have been given continuously. I was of opinion that there was no fatal variance there, and I see no reason for being of a different opinion now.

The other Judges concurred.

Rule refused.

(a) 1 Ry. & M. 252.

DOE, on the several demises of GEORGE CATES the elder, and others, v. The REV. W. SOMERVILLE and others.

A lease, by
a rector, of
his glebe lands
and other
rectorial pro-
perty, made
between the
years 1803
and 1816,
while the sta-
tute 13 *Eliz.*
c. 20, continu-
ed repealed,
is valid.
A person
who held
THIS was an action of ejectment, brought by the lessors of the plaintiff, against the defendants, who were the occupiers of the parsonage houses and glebe lands, belonging to the rectory of *Bedworth*, and vicarage of *Meriden*, respectively, in the county of *Warwick*. At the trial, before *Hullock*, B., at the *Warwickshire Lent* assizes, 1826, a verdict was found for the plaintiff, subject to the opinion of this Court, as to the plaintiff's right to recover the whole, or any part of the premises in question, upon the following case.

The Hon. and Rev. *Edward Finch* became rector of the rectory of *Bedworth*, in the county of *Warwick*, on the 13th of *April*, 1816, on a vacancy by a resignation of the last incumbent; and he became vicar of the vicarage of *Meriden*, in the same county, on the 29th of *March*, in the same year, on a vacancy by the death of the last incumbent; and being such rector and vicar, by a certain indenture, dated the 20th of *December*, 1816, in consideration of 600*l.*, granted for his life to Mr. *George Cates*, an annuity of 100*l.*, charged upon the abovementioned rectory of *Bedworth* and vicarage of *Meriden*, with the usual powers of distress and entry in case of the said annuity being in arrear; and for better securing the said annuity, and in consideration of 10*s.*, the said *Edward Finch* did, by the said indenture, grant, bargain, sell, and demise unto *William Hicks*, his executors, administrators and assigns, all and singular the said rectory of *Bedworth* and vicarage of *Meriden*, in the said county of *Warwick*, and all the glebe lands, messuages or tenements, tithes, tenths, oblations, obventions, profits and emoluments, arising from the said rectory and vicarage, habendum, to the said *William Hicks*, his executors, &c., for and during the term of 100 years, thence next ensuing, *if the said Edward Finch should so long live, and his interest therein continue so long*, at a peppercorn rent. Upon trust for better securing the due payment of the said annuity, and all costs, &c., by the ways and means therein mentioned; and upon further trust, that, until the said annuity should be in arrear by the time therein mentioned, and also, when and as often as all arrears of the said annuity and the said costs, &c., should be raised, or fully satisfied and paid, to permit and suffer the said *Edward Finch*, his executors, administrators or assigns, to receive and take the rents, oblations, produce and profits of the said rectory, vicarage, glebe lands, messuages, tithes, tenths, emoluments and appurtenances, to and for his and their own use and benefit; and to pay the surplus, after paying the annuity and costs, to the said *Edward Finch*, or his appointees. The said *William Hicks* died on or about the 26th of *December*, 1819, leaving *Edward Jones* and *George Hicks*, two of the lessors of the plaintiff, his executors. Ten writs, of fieri facias, on judgments in debt, entered up in, or as of, *Trinity* term, 1819, at the suit of various creditors of the said *Edward Finch*, having been, on the 26th of *June*, in the same year, issued against him, and directed to the sheriff of *Warwickshire*; and the sheriff having thereupon returned nulla bona, and that the said *Edward Finch* was a beneficed clerk, having no lay fee, ten writs of levari facias de bonis ecclesiasticos, were, on the 3rd of *July*, 1819, issued, directed to the then bishop of *Litchfield* and *Coventry*, within whose diocese, the rectory of *Bedworth* and the vicarage of *Meriden*, are situated, who, upon receipt of those writs, granted to W. *Mott*, Esq., sequestrations, dated, respectively, the 8th of *July*, 1819, of the rents, tithes, oblations, obventions, fruits, issues, and rights, and other ecclesiastical goods of the said *Edward Finch*, belonging to the said rectory and vicarage; by the first of which sequestrations the sequestrator was empowered to levy, sue for and receive, and to dispose of the rents, tithes, &c., to the end that thereout the charges of duty and serving the cures in the churches, and throughout the parishes of *Bedworth* and *Meriden* aforesaid, by ministers to be nominated or approved by the bishop for the time being, with such stipend as he should appoint for so doing, and all other burthens, ordinary or extraordinary, incumbent on the said rectory and vicarages, and on the said *Edward Finch*, as rector and vicar thereof, might be, in the first place, paid and discharged by the said sequestrator, and the remainder rendered to *William Little*, *John Woodcock* the elder, and *John Woodcock* the younger, the creditors named in the first writ of levari facias, for the debt and damages in the said writ mentioned: provided, that the said sequestrator should, during the sequestration, render to the bishop a true account of what he should receive and discharge in that behalf. All the sequestrations bear the same date, and are in the same form, except that those issued after the first are made subject to the prior ones. A witness stated that he had, since 1822, received the rents of the tenants of the premises belonging to the vicarage of *Meriden*, and paid them over to the sequestrator. The Rev. *Henry Bellairs*, curate of *Bedworth*, and the Rev. *William Somerville*, curate of *Meriden*, two of the defendants, are in the respective occupation of the parsonage houses of the said rectory and vicarage, and of lands adjoining thereto. The other defendants are tenants of premises belonging either to the rectory or the vicarage, : and some of them, namely, The *Coventry* Canal Company, *Joseph Cox, Joseph Chilwell, William Jenkins, Thomas Kelly, James Smith, John Sparrow, John Paxford Shaw, John Worrand* and *Elizabeth Wheatley*, occupied the premises in their possession, as tenants to the former incumbent, *previously* to Mr. *Finch's* becoming rector and vicar, and have since continued in such occupation. Mr. *Finch* was living at the island of *Mauritius*, in the year 1824.

Goulburn, for the lessors of the plaintiff. Two objections were raised at the trial to the right of the lessors of the plaintiff to recover, and will probably be relied on now, first that the lease was void under the statute 13 *Eliz.* c. 20, and second, that a notice to quit ought to have been given to such of the defendants as were tenants to the former incumbent. First, the lease is valid. The 13 *Eliz.* c. 20, which rendered void all charges of benefices with cure with any pension, &c., was repealed by the 44 *Geo.* 3, c. 84; it was re-enacted, for some purposes, by the 57 *Geo.* 3, c. 99, which was passed in the year 1817; but this lease was made in the year 1816, therefore it was made while the 13 *Eliz.* c. 20 was inoperative, and, consequently, is a valid lease. The legal estate in the premises, therefore, is in *Edward Jones* and *George Hicks,* the executors of *William Hicks,* the trustee of the term for securing the annuity : *White* v. *the Bishop of Peterborough* (a), *Silver* v. *the Bishop of Norwich* (b). Even if the statute of *Elizabeth* applied to this case, the lease would be good during the life of the incumbent, both as against him and all claiming under him ; for " though leases contrary to this act are declared void, yet they are good against the lessor during his life ; for the act was intended for the benefit of the successor only, and no man shall make an advantage of his own wrong." That is the doctrine laid down by Mr. Justice *Blackstone* (c), and the same position is advanced by Lord *Coke* (d), and was acted upon in several cases mentioned in the *Lincoln College* case (e). Second, no notice to quit was necessary. The case, certainly, finds that some of the defendants were tenants to the former incumbent, but their tenancies were determined by the death of the former incumbent, and though they afterwards continued to occupy the premises, there is nothing to shew that they were ever recognised by Mr. *Finch* as his tenants, or that any thing was done by either of the parties to constitute the relation of landlord and tenant between them.

Holbech, contrà. The authorities are, undoubtedly, strong to shew that a lease by a rector is good, during his life, against him, and all who claim under him ; though, in one of the old cases, *Revell* v. *Hart* (f), the point was doubted, and in a modern case, *Frogmorton* v. *Scott* (g), it was held, that a rector might recover in ejectment against his lessee, on the ground that the lease was void for his own non-residence. The question, however, in this case is, whether the lessors of the plaintiff are entitled to recover against these defendants. Their object is to sweep

(a) 3 Swanst. 109.
(b) 3 Swanst. 111, in Notis.
(c) 2 Bl. Comm. 321.
(d) Cq. Litt. 45, a.

(e) 3 Rep. 59, b.
(f) Gouldsb. 139.
(g) 2 East, 467.

away the entire possessions of the church, and to grasp for their own benefit the whole profits of the rectory, without leaving any fund as a provision for the service of the cure. But that they cannot be allowed to do; *Errington* v. *Howard* (a). There the rector, who received an annual stipend in lieu of tithes, had assigned it by way of mortgage. A creditor afterwards obtained a judgment, and a sequestration of the stipend thereon. The Master of the Rolls held, that the mortgage creditor was to be preferred before the judgment creditor, but without prejudice to an annual sum of 50*l.*, which had been allowed by the ordinary as a provision for the service of the cure. In this case, if the bishop had sequestered, independently of any writ of fieri facias, in order to provide for the service of the cure, this ejectment could not possibly have been maintained. At all events, this action is not maintainable against those defendants who were tenants to the former incumbent. They have, ever since his death, continued in the occupation of the same premises, and therefore, it must be presumed, in the absence of proof to the contrary, that they have occupied as tenants to Mr. *Finch*, the new incumbent. At least they are tenants by sufferance, and not trespassers, and if so they cannot be ejected without a notice to quit.

The case was argued in the course of last term, when the Court took time for consideration. Judgment was now, in the absence of the Lord Chief Justice, delivered by

BAYLEY J., who having recapitulated the facts of the case, thus proceeded. Upon the first point made in this case, we are of opinion, that the legal estate of the premises in question vested in the lessors of the plaintiff, *Edward Jones* and *George Hicks*, as executors of *William Hicks*, the trustee of the term granted by Mr. *Finch*, for securing the annuity, by the indenture of the 20th *December*, 1816. Unfortunately, the statute 13 *Eliz.* c. 20, had

(a) Ambler. 485.

been repealed by the 43 *Geo.* 3, c. 84, and the 57 *Geo.* 3, c. 99, had not been passed when that indenture was made; so that there was no statute in existence at the time which affected the validity of the grant, and the grant was consequently good during the incumbency of the grantor. Upon the second point, we are of opinion, that those defendants who were in possession of the premises, as tenants, before the commencement of Mr. *Finch's* incumbency, were entitled to a notice to quit. The occupiers of the *Bedworth* premises had been in possession eight months, and the occupiers of the *Meriden* premises nine months, between the date of Mr. *Finch's* induction, and the date of the grant of the annuity, without being disturbed; and after that lapse of time, we think Mr. *Finch* must be presumed to have recognised them as his tenants, and to have assented to the continuance of their tenancies upon the same terms as before; and that therefore, *he* could not dispossess them without giving them notice to quit, and if he could not, it follows that no person claiming under him could. Our judgment, therefore, is, that the verdict is to be entered for all the defendants who come under that description; and as respects all the other defendants, that it must be entered for the plaintiff. The question as to the authority of the bishop to place curates in the parsonage houses, under the sequestrations, does not properly arise in the case, because there is no evidence that the present curates were placed in the houses by the bishop, or that they had been nominated or approved by him, pursuant to the terms of the sequestrations.

Judgment accordingly.

NORTON, Gent., one, &c., v. MOSELEY.

F. POLLOCK, on a former day, had obtained a rule, calling upon the plaintiff to shew cause, why the bail-bond given in this cause should not be delivered up to be cancelled, the defendant having been discharged under the Insolvent Debtors' Act, 1 *Geo.*, 4, c. 119, from the debt for which the plaintiff had arrested him.

D. F. Jones, and *Abraham*, shewed cause, and contended, upon the authority of *Done* v. *Smith* (a), that a distinction was to be taken between the case where the party was in actual custody, and where he had given bail; that in the former case, the Court had authority under the statute to discharge the defendant, but that in the latter, they had no power to interfere. *Sed per*

BAYLEY, J. I am not convinced by the case cited, nor do I see the propriety of the distinction contended for. I think the Court is equally authorised to interfere, whether the party is in actual custody, or in virtual custody only, having executed a bail-bond. In the latter case, special bail to the action must be put in, and then the bail may at any time render the principal. When rendered, it is clear, that the Court would interfere to discharge him; and I see no reason why they should wait till he has undergone that inconvenience, instead of interfering in the first instance.

Rule absolute.

Where a defendant is arrested for a debt, in respect of which he has been discharged under the Insolvent Act, and gives a bail-bond, the Court will order the bail-bond to be delivered up to be cancelled.

(a) Ante, vol. iii., 600.

FOSTER and others, Assignees of FOWLER, a Bankrupt,
v. FRAMPTON.

Where goods are ordered to be delivered to a consignee at a particular place, the transitus, generally speaking, continues until they are delivered to him at that place; but if he postpones, or changes the place of delivery, or does any act equivalent to the taking possession of the goods, the transitus is at an end. Where a consignee ordered goods to be delivered to him at his own warehouse, and upon their arrival at the warehouse of the carrier, took samples of them to his own warehouse, and left the bulk for his own convenience, at the carriers, and became bankrupt :— Held, that the transitus was at an end, that the possession of the goods had vested in the consignee, and that his assignees were entitled to recover them from the consignor, who had stopped them in the hands of the carrier.

TROVER for a quantity of sugar. Plea, not guilty, and issue thereon. At the trial before *Abbott*, C. J., at the last *London* sittings in the present term, the case was this. The plaintiffs were the assignees of *Fowler*, a bankrupt, who had been a grocer at *Birmingham*. The defendants were wholesale grocers in *London*. In *August*, 1825, the defendants, by the bankrupt's order, sent him a quantity of sugar by *Corbett*, the *Birmingham* carrier. The sugar arrived at *Corbett*'s wharf on the 5th of *September*, and on the following day, *Corbett* gave the bankrupt notice of its arrival, when the latter removed a small quantity of the sugar, and samples of the whole, to his own premises, but desired that the bulk might remain at *Corbett*'s, until he fetched it away. The bankrupt was in the habit of keeping his large heavy goods at *Corbett*'s, and fetching them away as he wanted them. There was a running quarterly account between *Corbett* and the bankrupt; but the latter might have had the sugar away without paying for the carriage. On the 4th of *October*, *Fowler* committed an act of bankruptcy, the sugar being then still remaining on *Corbett*'s premises; and on the 12th, the defendants gave *Corbett* notice not to part with the sugar to any one but them: and finally, *Corbett*, on being indemnified by the defendants, re-delivered the sugar to them. Upon these facts, the Lord Chief Justice was of opinion, that the transitus was at an end when the goods arrived at *Corbett*'s wharf, for the bankrupt; and that, independently of that, the taking of a part of the sugar, and of samples of the whole, by the bankrupt to his own premises, amounted, in point of law, to a delivery of the whole to him: he, therefore, directed the jury to find a verdict for the plaintiffs.

Gurney now moved for a rule nisi for a new trial. The goods never reached the place of their destination, which was the bankrupt's shop; therefore, the transitus was never at an end. So long as they were in the course of transit to the bankrupt, the defendants had a right to stop them; and they were in such course of transit, so long as they continued in the possession of the carrier. This case differs from all those in which it has been held, that the transitus was terminated by the delivery of the goods to the carrier or agent of the vendee. In *Richardson* v. *Goss* (a), the decision turned upon the question, whether the contract between the parties had been rescinded or not. It was said by *Chambre*, J., in that case, that if a person were in the habit of using the warehouse of a wharfinger as his own, and made that the repository of his goods, *and disposed of them there*, the journey would be considered at an end, when the goods arrived at such warehouse; but that observation does not apply to the present case, because, here, the bankrupt did not use *Corbett*'s warehouse as his own, still less did he dispose of his goods there. So, with respect to the delivery of the sugar, this case differs from those in which it has been held, that a delivery of a part constituted in point of law, a delivery of the whole. In *Slubey* v. *Hayward* (b), it was held, that a delivery of part of the goods to the vendee of the consignee, amounted to a delivery of the whole; but there the goods had been actually sold by the consignee, and a part of them delivered to the purchaser: therefore, the rights of a third person had intervened there, but here the question remains between the original parties.

BAYLEY, J. (c). I am opinion that the transitus of the goods was at an end in this case, and that there was in point of law a complete delivery of them to the bankrupt. The general rule is, that if a man orders goods, to be sent to him at a particular place, the transitus con-

1826.

FOSTER
v.
FRAMPTON.

(a) 3 B. & P. 119.   (b) 2 H. Bl. 504.   (c) *Abbott*, C. J., was absent.

tinues until they are delivered to him at that place. But that extends only to transactions in the ordinary course of business, for if the consignee before the goods have arrived at their original place of destination, postpones the delivery, or changes the place of destination, or does any act equivalent to the taking possession of them, the transitus is at end. Here the original place of destination was the bankrupt's shop, and but for his interference the transitus would have continued until they arrived there; but he prevented their arriving there; he changed the place of destination, and in effect took possession of them at *Corbett's* premises, for he took samples from thence to his own shop, and desired that the bulk might remain at *Corbett's*, until he fetched it away. From that moment *Corbett* ceased to be the carrier of the bankrupt, and became his warehouseman, and the goods were as much in the possession of the bankrupt, as if he had actually removed them to his own shop. In *Richardson* v. *Goss* (a), *Richardson*, the vendor, shipped goods at *Newcastle* for *London* to the order of *Wilson*. The goods arrived at a wharf in *London*, where *Wilson* usually landed goods, and kept them until it suited him to fetch them away. *Richardson* finding that *Wilson* was insolvent, demanded the goods of the wharfinger, at the same time tendering him his charges and expenses; but the wharfinger refused to deliver them, except upon payment of a general balance due to him from *Wilson* for wharfage. *Chambre*, J., said, that if a person is in the habit of using the warehouse of a wharfinger as his own, and makes that the repository of his goods, and disposes of them there, the journey must be considered as at an end, when the goods arrive at that warehouse; and a similar opinion was expressed by Lord *Alvanley* in a subsequent case of *Scott* v. *Pettitt* (b). Here, the bankrupt was in the habit of using the warehouse of the wharfinger as his own, and of making it the repository of his goods, and did so on this particular occasion; and therefore I consider

(a) 3 B. & P. 119.   (b) 3 B. & P. 469.

the transitus to have been at an end, and the goods
to have reached the possession of the bankrupt, the
moment he took samples of them to his own shop, and
desired the bulk to be kept for him at *Corbett's*.

HOLROYD, J.—I am of the same opinion. The possession of the goods had completely vested in the bankrupt.
The transitus was at an end as soon as the bankrupt
treated the goods as his own, which he did by taking
samples of them to his own shop, and desiring the bulk to
be kept at *Corbett's*. From that moment *Corbett* ceased
to be a carrier, and became a mere baillie.

LITTLEDALE, J.—I am of the same opinion also. The
taking samples of the sugar was a complete act of ownership by the bankrupt, and the possession vested in him,
and the transitus was at an end from that moment.

Rule refused.

The KING v. The JUSTICES of SUFFOLK.

TWO justices had made an order for stopping up
an unnecessary footway in the county of *Suffolk*. The
notices described the footway as situate within the parish
of *Nowton*, and within an extra parochial place in the hundred of *Thingoe*, both in the county of *Suffolk*, and as commonly known by the name of *Hencote Lane*. They were
signed by the chief constables of the hundred of *Thingoe*,
but they were served upon the justices by one of the
clerks to the acting magistrates of that hundred. The
order was not appealed against, but the sessions being of
opinion that the notices ought to have been served as well
signed by the chief constables, or one of them, refused
to enrol the order. A rule nisi having been obtained for a
mandamus commanding the sessions to enrol the order,

Where no-
tices of hold-
ing a special
sessions for
stopping up a
footway, were
signed by the
chief con-
stables, and
served by a
person acting
under their
authority upon
the justices:—
Held, that the
notices were
given by the
chief con-
stables, within
the meaning
of the 13 *G*. 3,
c. 78, s. 62,
and regular.

Biggs Andrews now shewed cause, and contended that the service of the notices was irregular. The statute 13 *Geo.* 3, c. 78, s. 62, required that the notices of holding a special sessions for the purpose of stopping up a highway, should be given to the justices by the high constable, or other proper officer ; and *Rex* v. *The Justices of Surrey* (a), was an express authority to shew that where such notices were served upon the justices by the magistrates' clerk, and not by the high constable, the proceeding was irregular. The word *given* in the statute must be taken to mean *served*, and as the notices here were served by the magistrate's clerk, and not by the high constable, they were clearly irregular.

Alderson, contrà. The provision in the act of parliament that the notices shall be *given* by the high constable, must have reference to the party who *signs* and issues the notices, and not to the party who is the mere hand to *serve* or deliver them. Here, the notices were signed and issued by the proper officer, and it was perfectly immaterial by whom they were served. Having been signed by the high constable, and served upon the justices by some person, no matter whom, under his authority, they have been duly *given* within the meaning of the statute.

HOLROYD, J.—It seems to me that the notices having been signed by the chief constables, and served, by a person acting under their authority, upon the magistrates, have been given by them, within the meaning of the statute. The order, therefore, ought to have been inrolled and the rule for a mandamus must be made absolute.

LITTLEDALE, J., concurred.

Rule absolute (b).

(a) Ante, vol. vii. 857.   (b) *Abbott*, C. J., and *Bayley*, J., were absent.

BUCKERIDGE *v.* FLIGHT.—(In error).

1826.

THIS was an action of covenant on an annuity deed, to which the defendant below pleaded various pleas. The fourth (upon which the question arose), stated, that although plaintiff, within thirty days after the execution of the indenture mentioned in the declaration by certain persons (in the plea mentioned), caused a memorial thereof, and of certain other instruments and assurances for granting and securing the said annuity, to be enrolled in the high court of Chancery as follows :—(memorial set out). Yet defendant, in fact, saith, that he did not execute the indenture in the declaration mentioned, until long after the enrolment of the above-mentioned memorial; to wit, on, &c. And defendant further saith, that no memorial whatsoever of the indenture was enrolled in the high court of Chancery, within thirty days after the execution of the indenture by the defendant, according to the directions of the statute 53 *Geo.* 3, c. 161. The fifth plea stated, that although plaintiff, within thirty days after the execution of the indenture, caused a memorial to be enrolled as follows :—(setting forth the memorial, from which it appeared, that, in the column for the names of witnesses, " *A. B.* and *C. D.*" were mentioned as witnesses, without stating any parties whose execution of the deed they attested); yet defendant saith, that he did not execute the indenture in the memorial and declaration mentioned in the presence of *A. B.* and *C. D.*, as in the last-mentioned memorial is mentioned. Replication to the fourth plea; that a memorial of the indenture in the declaration mentioned was, within thirty days after the execution thereof, to wit, &c., duly enrolled, as follows :—(setting forth the memorial with a prout patet). And plaintiff further saith, that the memorial did and does duly contain the date of the indenture, the names of all the parties, and of all the

An annuity deed need not be executed before the memorial thereof is enrolled, if the memorial be enrolled within 30 days from the *date* mentioned in the annuity deed.

In the memorial of an annuity deed, it is sufficient to set forth all the names of the subscribing witnesses, without specifying which party's execution the witnesses respectively attested.

witnesses thereto, and of the person for whose life such annuity was granted, and of the person by whom the same was to be beneficially received, and the pecuniary considerations for the granting of the same, and the annual sum to be paid, as required by the statute. Demurrer to the fifth plea, assigning for cause, that the averment in the plea that the defendant did not execute the deed in the presence of *A. B.* and *C. D.*, is irrelevant and immaterial. Joinder in demurrer. Rejoinder to the replication to the fourth plea, that defendant did not execute the indenture until long after the memorial was enrolled. Surre-joinder, that during the whole of the thirty days next after the execution of the indenture by the defendant, the memorial in the replication mentioned remained, and still remains enrolled in Chancery. Demurrer, assigning for cause, that the plaintiff hath not traversed the allegation in the rejoinder. Joinder in demurrer. Judgment having been given by the court of Common Pleas for the plaintiff below, a writ of error was brought by the defendant below, which was now argued by

Tindal, S. G., for the plaintiff in error. Two questions arise in this case : first, whether it is a material averment that the party did not execute the indenture in the presence of the witnesses named in the memorial ; and second, whether the memorial ought to be enrolled after the execution of the deed by the party who is sought to be charged with the payment of the annuity. First, it is contended, that it is a material averment, that the defendant did not execute in the presence of these witnesses ; and this argument is supported by the words of the Annuity Act itself. The 53 *Geo.* 3, c. 141, s. 2, requires that the memorial should state the date of the instrument whereby the annuity is secured, the nature of the instrument, the names of the parties, and the names of the witnesses ; and therefore it is a material allegation, that the annuity deed was not executed by the defendant in the presence of

the persons whose names are put into the deed as witnesses.
The old statute, 17 *Geo.* 3, c. 36, is couched in similar
terms, quoad the provision recited from the 53 *Geo.* 3.
The Court has always been in the habit of giving a strict
construction to these statutes, in order to give full effect
to the purpose for which they were enacted, namely, the
prevention of frauds. In *Hart* v. *Lovelace* (a), where
an annuity was secured by various instruments, the execution of which was witnessed by different persons, and
the memorial stated those instruments, and that the execution of them was attested by *A.*, *B.*, *C.*, &c., or some of
them (naming the several persons who had attested the
execution of the several instruments), this was held to be
insufficient. [*Bayley*, J. Suppose there are twenty
parties to a deed, and there are twenty witnesses to the
execution; would it not be sufficient to allege, that the
deed was executed in the presence of those twenty witnesses, without saying which was the attesting witness
to each executing party?] It is not necessary to deny
that. The point is, that here is an allegation that the
party did not execute in the presence of the witnesses
named in the memorial, which is a material allegation. If such an allegation be necessary with respect to
other parties, certainly it is much more necessary in the
case of a party who is to be charged with the payment of
the annuity, and who has a real and substantial interest in
the transaction. Here it is stated generally, in the memorial, that the instrument was executed in the presence
of *A. B.* and *C. D.*; from which it is to be inferred, that
all the parties executed in the presence of those persons.
If, therefore, the fact were otherwise, then the memorial is
calculated to mislead; which it was the object of the legislature to guard against. This point turns solely upon the
words of the statute. Then, secondly, as to the enrolment of the deed, the statute requires that, within thirty
days after the execution of the deed, the memorial of the

(a) 6 T. R., 441.

i 2

date of the deed shall be enrolled. The *date*, as it respects the party executing, is the *delivery* of the deed. Now if the defendant was not a party to the deed until the execution, then the memorial of the execution is false, and does not comply with the provisions of the statute. [*Abbott*, C. J. Does not the provision in the statute mean *the date expressed in the deed?*] If there is any difficulty, it arises from the manner in which the statute itself is expressed. This deed not being executed until three months after the memorial is enrolled, can it be said, that the defendant was a party to it at the time it was enrolled? On the other side it may be said, that it will be extremely difficult in some cases to enrol a memorial at all, if this objection could prevail. The objection, however, might in this case have been avoided, by causing a second memorial to be enrolled. Here the instrument had not become a deed at the time the memorial was enrolled; and a party cannot enroll a deed in anticipation that it will be executed.

Chitty, contrà. In this case there is no averment that the plaintiff in error executed the deed in the presence of any witnesses; and as it cannot be assumed that he did so, it follows that the memorial is sufficient. All that the statute requires, is, that the memorial should state the deed whereby the annuity is secured, and the names of all the witnesses thereto. This provision has been complied with, and it was not necessary to specify whose signatures they witnessed; *Orton* v. *Knight* (a). Secondly, it was not necessary to enroll the memorial within thirty days next after the execution of the deed; all that was necessary, was, that it should be enrolled within thirty days next after the *date* expressed in the deed. If this were not so, the greatest inconvenience might follow; for it might happen that if thirty days elapsed before the execution of the deed by all the parties, the grant of the annuity would become actually inoperative. There is nothing in the

(a) 3 Bos. & Pul. 153.

statute to authorise the enrolment of several memorials; and therefore, the mode of avoiding the difficulty, suggested on the other side, would be of no avail. The object of the legislature was to give publicity to the transaction. Here the transaction was made sufficiently public by the means resorted to; and consequently, there is no ground for disturbing the judgment of the Court below.

ABBOTT, C. J.—I am of opinion, that the judgment of the Court below must be affirmed. The question arises upon the construction of an act of parliament, which was made for the protection of miners, and others, against frauds which might be practised against them, by persons taking undue advantage of their necessities; but inasmuch as the effect of the act, when its provisions are not complied with, is to defeat deeds solemnly executed, we are not at liberty, in our construction, to go beyond that which the legislature itself states to be an express ground for defeating a solemn deed. The present question arises upon the sufficiency of the memorial. On a view of that instrument, and referring to the clause of the act of parliament which requires a memorial, it appears to me, that the memorial in this case does contain all that is required by the legislature. The memorial should be a memorial, not of the transaction, but of the instrument whereby the annuity is granted and secured; and when you look to the form of the instrument given in the schedule to the act, you find a column headed, "Date of the instrument." The date there, means the day expressed in the instrument itself, and not the day on which it is executed. In cases where there are several parties, it frequently happens that they severally execute on different days; and that shews that the date must mean the date of the instrument. The act also requires, that the memorial shall express the names of all the parties to the deed. It is contended, that no person can be a party to a deed, until he has executed it. It is true, that, until that time, he is not to be a party chargeable ; but still a person may be a party to a deed, though not chargeable until he has executed ; and I take the expression, " party to the deed," as used in the statute, to mean all those who, upon reading the instrument, are *therein expressed* to be made parties to it. I think the same construction is to be given to the expression, " all the witnesses thereto." That is, all the witnesses who have attested the instrument, shall be mentioned in the memorial. This point was decided on the former act, in the case of *Orton* v. *Knight :* in which it was held, that you need not specify in the memorial, the particular person whose execution each witness respectively attested. That was certainly a very strong case, for there the memorial professed to specify and set out that the instrument had been attested by three particular witnesses, when only two, in fact, had attested ; and yet the memorial was held to be sufficient, because all the witnesses in the deed were mentioned. Here, also, all the witnesses are set out in the memorial, whose names are mentioned in the deed. It appears, that the present defendant, who became a surety, had not executed the deed at the time when the memorial was enrolled ; and if he had afterwards executed in the presence of a subscribing witness, not being one of those who attested the other signatures, a second memorial might have been necessary. But we must now take it, that there was no person attesting the execution by the defendant, for no person of that description appears to be named in the instrument itself ; and if there had, it must have been stated in distinct terms, in compliance with the statute. If the legislature had meant to require that the execution of an annuity deed by every person to be charged therewith, should be in the presence of a witness, there should have been a separate and distinct clause to that effect. There is such a clause, with regard to the person who is beneficially interested. In that case, the name of the party is to be inserted both in the deed and in the memorial. It seems to me, therefore, that if it had been intended to require that the execution should be attested by a witness, that would have been specifically provided for in the act. As it is not, the memorial does contain every thing on the face of it, which the statute makes requisite; and it appears to me to be immaterial to inquire whether the memorial was enrolled before or after the execution, for that does not affect the nature of the instrument.

BAYLEY, J.—I think that the enrolment of the memorial before the deed was executed, answered every purpose for which the legislature thought an enrolment necessary. The great object of the act in this respect, was to enable the grantor of an annuity, by referring to the memorial, to see on what terms the annuity was granted. If an annuity deed be enrolled within the time specified, and the enrolment contains the date of the instrument, and the other particulars pointed out by the statute, all the information which the legislature intended that the party should have, will be given, whether the deed has, or has not at that time been executed by all the parties. I agree to this, that if it is afterwards executed by some other person, or in consequence of a mistake in the execution, or from other circumstances, it becomes necessary to make an addition to the memorial, that addition must be made within thirty days; but if no such addition be made, then, I think, that the original enrolment would be good and valid, although the execution of the deed was subsequent. The other objection, as to the names of the subscribing witnesses, struck me at first as being entitled to more weight; for if the execution by various persons be attested by various witnesses, and they are all inserted, without shewing whose execution they respectively attest, that might be applied to purposes of concealment. But when I look to the act of parliament, and to the form of the schedule, which points out in what manner you are to specify the different things which the act requires, I think that the entry of the names of the witnesses in the manner here exhibited, is quite sufficient. The case of *Orton* v. *Knight*, is an extremely strong authority upon this point; but it has been recognised and acted upon by Lord Chief Justice *Gibbs*, in the subsequent case of *Brown* v. *Rose* (a).

HOLROYD, J., and LITTLEDALE, J., concurred.

Judgment affirmed.

(a) 6 Taunt. 124.   1 Marsh. 478.

The KING v. WILLIAM FOWKE, Esq.

UPON an appeal of *W. Fowke*, Esq. to the *Northumberland* Quarter Sessions, against a certain rate or assessment for the relief of the poor of the township of *Tynemouth*, in that county; the sessions ordered the rate to be confirmed, subject to the opinion of this Court, on the following case :—

Mr. *Fowke* is the proprietor and occupier of a certain lighthouse, called *Tynemouth Castle Lighthouse*, in the township of *Tynemouth*, and is entitled to certain tolls, payable in respect thereof, and the light therefrom, under, and by virtue of, certain letters patent under the great seal, bearing date at *Westminster*, 30th *June*, 7 *Car.* 2 (to wit), the sum of twelve pence of and for every ship, belonging to any of the king's subjects, passing by the said lighthouse, and belonging or trading to the ports of *Newcastle* and *Sunderland*, or either of them, or the creeks and members of the same; and three shillings for every ship of or belonging to any foreigner or stranger, coming or passing by the said lighthouse: and Mr. *Fowke* is also entitled to additional light duties, under, and by virtue of, an act of parliament, made and passed in the 40 *Geo.* 3, intituled, "An Act for improving the *Tynemouth Castle* Lighthouse, and for authorising additional Light Duties in respect of such Improvement." The alterations in the said lighthouse have been made, in conformity to the said act. The lighthouse in the township of *Tynemouth,* and the tolls or duties arising to Mr. *Fowke,* are payable in respect of vessels passing the lighthouse, and receiving the benefit thereof. Of the entire number of the vessels thus paying toll, thirty-seven thirty-eighth parts do not come within the township of *Tynemouth,* but pass the lighthouse, and so incur the toll when sailing upon their course in the *German* ocean, or when entering from the main sea, into parts of the river *Tyne,* and port of *Newcastle,* belonging to other townships. The remaining thirty-eighth part of the vessels paying toll, do come within the township of *Tynemouth,* and receive their loading there. The tolls received in respect of such last-mentioned vessels, do not equal in amount the expense of maintaining the light and managing the lighthouse, the whole of which expenses are incurred within the township of *Tynemouth.* The tolls or duties paid in respect of ships arriving at, or sailing from, the said port of *Newcastle-upon-Tyne,* including the tolls or duties paid by the ships receiving their loading in the said township of *Tynemouth,* are collected at the custom-house, in the parish of *All Saints,* in the town and county of *Newcastle-upon-Tyne,* by a person appointed by Mr. *Fowke* for that purpose, and the tolls or duties paid in respect of ships sailing from other coasting ports, are collected at the ports from whence they sail, if they clear at the custom-house there, to a port beyond *Tynemouth* lighthouse; if to a port short of *Tynemouth,* no tolls or duties are payable by them in the first instance; but if they afterwards extend their voyage to *Newcastle,* or beyond the lighthouse, then the toll or duty is paid at the port of their arrival. Some of the tolls collected at the coasting ports, are remitted to the person who collects them at *Newcastle*; and others are accounted for, in the first instance, to Mr. *Fowke*; but neither does Mr. *Fowke*, nor do any of the receivers of the said tolls or duties, reside within the township of *Tynemouth*. The township of *Tynemouth* maintains its own poor, and Mr. *Fowke*, the appellant, is rated as follows :—" *William Fowke*, Esquire, lighthouse, five hundred pounds." If the lighthouse should be let by the appellant without the tolls, it would be worth six pounds a-year, to be rented by a third person. If let together with the tolls, it would be worth 500*l.* a-year, to be rented by a third person. The questions for the opinion of the court of King's Bench are :— First, whether the rent that would be given on a demise of all the tolls, together with the lighthouse, ought to be taken as the rateable value of the lighthouse. If so, the order of sessions to be confirmed. Secondly, whether the rent that would be given for any portion of the said tolls, ought to be added to that which would be given for the lighthouse alone, in estimating the rateable value of the said lighthouse ; if not, the assessment on the present appellant in respect of such lighthouse, to be reduced to six pounds. Thirdly, whether the rent that would be given for the tolls paid by ships coming within the township of *Tynemouth*, such tolls being less in amount than the expenses incurred within that township on account of the said lighthouse, ought to be added to the rent that would be given for the lighthouse alone, in estimating the rateable value of the said lighthouse ; if so, the assessment on the present appellant, to be reduced to 29*l.* 3*s.* 9*d.*

Parke and *Ingham*, in support of the rate, contended that the privilege of having the light, being identified with the lighthouse itself, must be considered as giving an additional value to the building, and on that ground rateable to the extent of the increased value. They endeavoured to distinguish this case from *Rex* v. *Coke* (a), and relied upon *Rex* v. *Rebowe* (b), *Rex* v. *Tynemouth* (c), *Rex* v. *St. Nicholas, Leicester* (d), *Rex* v. *Payne* (e), *Rex* v. *The New River Company* (f), and *Rex* v. *The Birmingham Gas-light and Coke Company* (g).

Brougham, and *E. Alderson,* contra, after citing and relying upon *Rex* v. *Coke* as a decisive authority, to shew that the lighthouse was not rateable in respect of the light communicated from it to ships at sea, were stopped by the Court.

BAYLEY, J. (h).—I cannot distinguish this case from *Rex* v. *Coke.* There the Court decided, that a lighthouse is rateable only as a house, and that if any body resided in it, the occupier was to be rated as a housekeeper, and that the value of the tolls ought not to be included. Upon what principle was that case so decided? Because the value of the tolls arose not from the building, nor from any thing of necessity connected with it, but from the power of communicating light from the building to ships which are at sea. Here the light is the thing for which the whole payment of the tolls is made, and I think that if the act of parliament mentioned in this case makes any distinction between this case and *Rex* v. *Coke*, it affords an additional reason why this lighthouse should not be burthened with a poor rate, because that act shews that the legislature considered it as being a public benefit, to be compensated for by a public charge. If a toll is to be levied upon the proprietors of all ships passing the lighthouse, in proportion to the benefit which they receive therefrom, the profits of the proprietor of the lighthouse will be

(a) Ante, vol. viii. 666.   5 B. & C. 797.

(b) 1 Const. 115. Bott. 142.

(c) 12 East, 46.

(d) Cald. 262.

(e) 4 T. R. 543.

(f) 1 M. & S. 507.

(g) Ante, vol. ii. 735. 1 B. & C. 506.

(h) *Abbott,* C. J., had left the Court, to hold Nisi Prius sittings, and *Holroyd,* J., was gone to chambers.

diminished, if you take from him in the shape of poor rate part of that which is contributed by the proprietors of the ships, and therefore in order to enable him to keep up his light, he must of necessity require a larger contribution from the ship-owners, which would be contrary to public policy, and the provisions of the act of parliament. *Rex v. Coke*, establishes that a lighthouse is properly exempted from poor rates, the conveyance of light from the building being nothing more than a mode of carrying on a species of trade ; and on the authority of that case, I think the rate upon the tolls, as a part of the profits of this light-house, must be quashed.

LITTLEDALE, J.—I am of the same opinion, for the reasons given by my brother *Bayley*, and I do not think it necessary to enter more fully into the grounds of our decision.

> Order of sessions quashed for insufficiency, and the rate ordered to be sent back to be amended, by reducing the charge made and assessed, to the sum of six pounds.

MOORE v. STOCKWELL.

Where a defendant was arrested upon a latitat made returnable in vacation, and after the return day took out a summons for time to put in bail:—Held, that this waived the irregularity.

THIS was a rule calling on the plaintiff to shew cause why the latitat sued out against the defendant should not be set aside for irregularity, and why the bail-bond should not be delivered up to be cancelled, and why the proceedings thereon should not be stayed in the meantime. The alleged irregularity was, that there was a mistake in the writ, which rendered it void ; namely, that it was made returnable " on *Thursday* next after the end of *Trinity* term," which was in vacation.

Follett now shewed cause on an affidavit stating, that after the return-day of the writ, the defendant took out a summons for time to put in special bail, to which the plaintiff consented, and that the defendant having neglected to put in bail accordingly, the plaintiff took an assignment of the bail-bond and proceeded upon it. This, he contended, was a waiver of the irregularity; for the defendant, by taking out a summons for time to put in bail, allowed the plaintiff to incur further expense.

Platt, contrà, insisted that the writ was altogether void, and not merely irregular, being made returnable in vacation; and he cited *Kenworthy* v. *Peppiatt* (a).

ABBOTT, C. J.—This was merely an irregularity, which we think was cured by the defendant taking out a summons for time to put in bail.

The other Judges concurred.

Rule discharged.

(a) 4 B. & A. 288.

HAM v. GREGG.

THIS was a rule nisi for judgment as in case of a nonsuit. It appeared from the affidavits, that issue was joined in last *Easter* term, and notice of trial given for the *London* sittings after the term. The cause not coming on for trial at those sittings, it was made a remanet to the sittings after *Trinity* term, when the plaintiff declined entering the record with the Marshal, on the ground of the absence of a material witness. The question now was, whether the defendant was entitled to move for judgment as in case of a nonsuit.

Merewether contended, that the delay in not trying at the sittings after *Easter* term, having been occasioned by the act of the Court, in making it a remanet, and not by the act of the plaintiff, the defendant was not entitled to

A town cause was entered for trial, and notice given for the sittings after Easter term. At those sittings it was made a remanet to the sittings after Trinity term, and the plaintiff having neglected to proceed to trial at those sittings:—Held, that the defendant was entitled to move for judgment as in case of a nonsuit.

move for judgment as in case of a nonsuit, and that this circumstance differed the case from *Gadd* v. *Bennett* (a).

Campbell, contrà, relied upon the unqualified terms of the rule laid down in *Gadd* v. *Bennett*, which decided in general terms, that judgment as in case of a nonsuit may be moved for after a cause has been made a remanet in *London* or *Middlesex*.

ABBOTT, C. J.—The rule as to *London* and *Middlesex* causes, varies from that in country causes at the assizes; where a cause is made a remanet in *London* or *Middlesex*, it is not re-entered at the subsequent sittings, nor is any fresh notice of trial necessary, but it comes on as a matter of course at the subsequent sittings. This is not so with respect to country causes. Here the cause was made a remanet at the *Easter London* sittings, and the plaintiff having neglected to proceed to trial pursuant to his prior notice, at the sittings after *Trinity* term, I think the defendant is entitled to move for judgment as in case of a nonsuit.

The other Judges concurred.

The rule was, however, discharged upon a
peremptory undertaking.

(a) 2 B. & A. 709.

———◆———

J. CARNE and others *v.* W. LEGH, Esq.

SCARLETT, on a former day, obtained a rule calling on the plaintiffs to shew cause why the proceedings in this action should not be stayed without payment of costs, on

Therefore, where a plaintiff brought two actions against two joint contractors for the same debt, the Court set aside the proceedings *without* costs in one action, the debt and costs in the other having been paid.

the ground, that the plaintiffs had received the debt and costs in a separate action, brought by them against another party, jointly liable with the defendant, and why the plaintiffs should not pay the costs of the application.

Marryat now shewed cause upon an affidavit, stating that the two actions were brought to recover a debt due to the plaintiffs from the "*Wheal Concord* Mining Company ;" that the deponent believed that the defendants in both actions were members of the said company, but had refused to admit that fact, and therefore the two actions became necessary. He likened this to the case of several actions being brought against all the parties to a bill of exchange.

Scarlett, (with whom was *R. N. Clarke*), contrà, was stopped by the Court.

ABBOTT, C, J.—I am of opinion, that this rule must be made absolute. The plaintiffs might have sued the defendant jointly or separately, leaving him in the latter case to plead in abatement if he thought proper, but they had no right to bring separate actions against several members of the same company. This is not at all analogous to the case of several actions brought against the different parties to a bill of exchange, for there the parties are all severally liable ; here the partners in the company are only jointly liable, and if sued separately, might plead in abatement.

BAYLEY, J., HOLROYD, J., and LITTLEDALE, J., concurred.

Rule absolute.

The KING *v.* The INHABITANTS of TONBRIDGE.

Where a pauper took a house at the annual rent of 8*l.* from *Lady-day* to *Michaelmas* 1821, and then took another house from *Michaelmas* 1821 to *Lady-day* 1822 at the annual rent of 9*l.*, and during the whole of both periods was the tenant of a piece of garden ground at the rent of 2*l.* 2*s.*, but had agreed with a third person that they should share the expense and the profits equally of cultivating the garden ground, and the partner paid half the rent to the pauper, but the latter paid the whole to the landlord:— Held, that no settlement was gained by operation of the 59 *G.* 3, c. 50.

BY an order of two Justices, *John Hazell* and *Mary* his wife, were removed from *Tonbridge* to *Lamberhurst*, both in the county of *Kent.* On appeal, the sessions quashed the order, subject to the opinion of this Court on the following case :—

Upon the hearing of the appeal, it was proved on the part of the parish of *Tonbridge*, that the paupers, *John Hazell* and *Mary* his wife, had been removed in 1812, from the parish of *Frant* to the parish of *Lamberhurst*, under an order of removal, against which no appeal had been prosecuted. On the part of the appellant parish, it was proved that the pauper *John Hazell*, about *Michaelmas* 1816, took a cottage situate in the parish of *Tonbridge*, of one *Douch*, for a year, at the yearly rent, and of the value of 8*l.* 10*s.* At *Michaelmas* 1817, he made a fresh agreement for the cottage for one year, at the annual rent of 8*l.*, and continued to hold and occupy it from that time until *Michaelmas* 1821, paying a rent of 8*l.* per annum only for it, from *Michaelmas* 1817. At *Lady-day* 1821, he took a garden, also situate in the parish of *Tonbridge*, for a year, at the yearly rent, and of the value of 2*l.* 2*s.* He agreed with one *William Maynard*, that they should share the expenses and profits arising from the cultivation of the garden. *Maynard* paid to *Hazell* half of the rent, but the latter paid the whole rent to the landlord, who was not (to the knowledge of *Hazell*) aware of the partnership. The garden was thus occupied for a year, until *Lady-day* 1822, and the rent paid for the whole year. At *Michaelmas* 1821, *Hazell* having quitted *Douch's* house, took a house situate in the parish of *Tonbridge*, of one *Lawrence*, for a year, at the yearly rent of 9*l.*, and he occupied it from that time until his removal in 1825, and paid the rent for it during the whole time. The question for the opinion of the Court is, whether the pauper gained a settlement by renting a tenement, by operation of the statute 59 *Geo.* 3, c. 50.

At the sittings after *Trinity* term, the case was argued by *Bolland*, and *D. Pollock*, in support of the order of sessions, and by *Marsham*, against it.

In support of the order of sessions it was contended, on the authority of *Rex* v. *North Collingham* (a), that by operation of the 59 *Geo.* 3, c. 50, a settlement might be gained under different holdings, and that even where there was an under-letting of part of the tenement, as in this case, that circumstance made no difference. In this case it was clear that the pauper was tenant of the whole garden ; and if so, then he rented a tenement consisting of a house, or building, and of land, from *Lady-day*, 1821, to *Michaelmas*, 1821, of the annual value of 10*l.* 2*s.*; and of the annual value of 11*l.* 2*s.*, from *Michaelmas*, 1821, to *Lady-day*, 1822.

Contrà, it was argued, that this case was distinguishable from *Rex* v. *North Collingham*, by reason that, in that case, the pauper held the house or building for *the whole year*, during which he occupied the land. Here there was no period of a year during which the pauper held the house ; and if so, then no settlement was gained by operation of the statute 59 *Geo.* 3, c. 50. By that statute, in order to gain a settlement, the tenement must consist of a house or building, held for a year, or of land occupied for a year, or of both. If it consists of both, the house and the land must be held, and the land occupied for a year. Here, though the land was occupied for a year, there was no concurrent holding of the house for the same year. But even supposing this to be no objection, still the house and land together, were not of the annual value of 10*l.*, and that takes the case out of the statute ; for here the house occupied by the pauper from *Lady-day* to *Michaelmas*, 1821, was only of the annual

(a) Ante, vol. ii. 743. 1 B. & C. 578.

value of 8*l.*, and the moiety of the garden, jointly occupied with *Maynard*, was no more than of the annual value
of one guinea; so that, in either way of viewing the case,
no settlement was gained.

The *Court* took time to consider of the case, and judgment was now delivered by

BAYLEY, J.—This was a settlement question between
the parishes of *Tonbridge* and *Lamberhurst*, depending on
the 59 *Geo.* 3, c. 50. The facts were these :—The pauper
was removed to *Lamberhurst* in 1812, and there was no
appeal. In 1816 he took a cottage in *Tonbridge*, at 8*l.*
10*s.* per 'annum; but in 1817 the rent was reduced to 8*l.*
He continued in that cottage till *Michaelmas*, 1821. At
Lady-day preceding (in 1821), he took a garden at 2*l.* 2*s.*
a-year; but he agreed with one *Maynard*, that the expense and profits should be shared between them. The
garden was occupied a year, and the rent paid. At
Michaelmas, 1821, when he quitted the house at 8*l.* a-year,
he entered upon another at the yearly rent of 9*l.*, which he
occupied till 1825. So that from *Lady-day*,1821, to the *Michaelmas* following, he had the garden and the 8*l.* house, and
from *Michaelmas*, 1821, to *Lady-day*, 1822, he had the garden and the 9*l.* house; and it is only from *Lady-day*,1821,
to *Lady-day*, 1822, that there is any pretence for saying he
had 10*l.* a-year. By 59 *Geo.* 3, c. 50 (which operated
from 2d *July*, 1819), no settlement shall be gained by
dwelling 40 days in any tenement rented, unless such
tenement consist of a house or building in the parish or
township, being a separate and distinct dwelling-house or
building, or of land there, or of both, bonà fide hired at
10*l.* a-year, for a whole year; nor unless such house or
building shall be held, and the land occupied, and the
rent for the same actually paid, for one whole year at the
least, by the person hiring the same. One of the requisites, therefore, under that statute, in the case of land, was,

1826.

The King
v.
The
Inhabitants
of
Tonbridge.

that it should be occupied by the person hiring it for one whole year at the least. A distinction is made in that statute between houses and buildings on the one hand, and land on the other; and though this distinction is removed by the 6 *Geo.* 4, as to settlements subsequent to the period from which that statute operates, it must still be attended to in cases of previous settlements. By the 59 *Geo.* 3, c. 50, it was required, in case of a house, or building, that it should be *held* for a year by the person hiring it; in the case of land, that he should *occupy.* In the case of houses and buildings, therefore, so as the tenure subsisted, it was, in this respect, before the statute of 6 *Geo.* 4, c. 57, sufficient; so that under-letting a part of a house or building would not have prevented a settlement; and that point was accordingly so decided in *Rex* v. *North Collingham* (a), which was cited in the argument. But in the case of lands, the person hiring was to *occupy* for the year. Did the pauper, then, occupy the garden for the whole year? It is stated in the case, that though the pauper took the garden, it was agreed between him and *Maynard,* that they should share the expense and profit. It is also stated, that *Maynard* paid the pauper half the rent, and that the garden was thus occupied. It is not in terms stated that there was a joint occupation; but as *Maynard* was entitled to participate in the occupation, we think it must be taken that he did, and if so, the pauper cannot be considered as occupying more than a moiety of the garden. Unless the garden was separately occupied by the pauper the whole year, no settlement was gained. We are therefore of opinion, that there was no settlement in *Tonbridge,* that the settlement in *Lamberhurst* remained, and that the order of sessions, which quashed the removal to *Lamberhurst,* on the ground of a settlement in *Tonbridge,* cannot be supported.

Order of Sessions quashed.

(a) Ante, vol. ii., 743. 1 B. & C., 578.

The KING v. The INHABITANTS of CARSHALTON.

A person hiring and occupying a 10l. tenement for more than a year, and after his death, the rent is paid out of the proceeds of the sale of his effects, gains no settlement either under the 59 Geo. 3, c. 50, or the 6 Geo. 4, c. 57.

BY an order of two justices, *Charlotte Long*, widow, and her two children, were removed from *Carshalton* to *Wandsworth*, both in the county of *Surrey*. On appeal, the sessions quashed the order, subject to the opinion of this Court, on the following case :—

Thomas Long, the husband of the pauper, who was previously settled by apprenticeship in the parish of *Wandsworth*, at *Lady-day*, 1824, came with his family to reside in a house in the parish of *Carshalton*, which he had hired of his father-in-law, *Daniel Tarling*, by the year, at the rent of 14l. He put his own furniture into the house, and continued to reside there until *July*, 1825, when he died in possession. During his lifetime, no more than the sum of 25s. was paid by him on account of the rent. His widow, after his death, continued to reside in the house in question, until the month of *September* following, when *Daniel Tarling*, the landlord, put a distress into the premises, under which he seized the furniture and goods which had been put in by *Thomas Long*, and the same were afterwards sold and purchased by the said *Daniel Tarling*, for the sum of 12l. 15s., upon which the following receipt was given :—"Received from Mr. *Savage* of *Tooting*, on advance of goods, the sum of 12l. 15s., for balance of rent due from Mr. *Thomas Long*, to *Midsummer*, 1825. *Daniel Tarling*."

Barnewall, in support of the order of sessions. The pauper is entitled to a derivative settlement from her husband, either under the 59 *Geo.* 3, c. 59, or by the old statute, 13 and 14 *Car.* 2, which became pro tanto revived in the interval between the passing of the 53 *Geo.* 3, c. 50, and the 6 *Geo.* 4, c. 57. First, under the 59 *Geo.* 3, c. 50, the pauper's husband clearly rented and occupied a house of 10l. a year, for more than the term of one whole year, namely, from *Lady-day*, 1824, to *July*, 1825, when he died in possession. The question then is, whether the circumstances of the rent not having been paid during his lifetime, prevents the completion of the settlement. It is submitted, that the remainder of the rent having been paid by the money arising from the sale of his effects after his death, reasonably satisfies the provision of the statute, which requires, that the rent shall be paid for one whole year. Suppose the pauper had given a promissory note for the rent, which did not become due until after his death, and it was then paid by his administrator out of his effects, would not that be sufficient to satisfy the statute ? But, secondly, there was a residence on the tenement by the pauper's husband for 40 days, in the interval between the 59 *Geo.* 3, and the 6 *Geo.* 4, c. 57, such as would gain him a settlement under the statute 12 and 13 *Car.* 2, which became revived during that period. The statute 6 *Geo.* 4, c. 57, which received the royal assent on the 22d *June*, 1825, recites the 59 *Geo.* 3, c. 50, and then repeals that statute, without making any provision for such cases as might arise in the interval between the passing of the two acts. The statute 59 *Geo.* 3' operated pro tanto as a repeal of the 13 and 14 *Car.* 2, which conferred a settlement by a residence of forty days on a 10*l.* tenement. In *Com. Dig.* tit. *Parliament*, (R) 9, it is laid down, that " an act which repeals a statute by which another was repealed, will be a reviver of the statute which was repealed"; and Lord *Coke* says (a), the old law becomes thereby revived, as if the mere repealing statute had never been passed. It follows therefore in this instance, that as the pauper resided for forty days on a 10*l.* tenement in the interval between the two statutes alluded to, he gained a settlement under the 12 and 13 *Car.* 2, which thus became revived. [*Bayley*, J. See the extent to which that argument might be pushed. Suppose by a statute of *Elizabeth* it was made felony without benefit of clergy, to

(a) 12 Rep. 8.

steal to the value of 40s. in a shop ; that by the 10th
Geo. 3, the same offence was made clergyable, and that by
the 20th Geo. 3, the 10th Geo. 3, was repealed, then according to your argument, an offence of that description, '
which was committed between the passing of the two latter acts, but not brought to trial till after the repealing act
passed, would be an offence not clergyable?] Still, the
Court would be bound to act upon the law as it then
stood. Assuming that this case comes within the operation
of the 6 Geo. 4, c. 57, then it is clear that the facts found
would establish the settlement according to the provisions
of that act. The year's rent did not become due until the
25th September, 1825, and the statute 6 Geo. 4, passed in
June, 1825. That statute only requires that the rent shall
be paid for the term of one whole year at the least, and
does not say that it shall be paid by the party renting the
house. Here, then, as the rent was in fact paid out of the
pauper's assets, though not in his life-time, the provisions
of the statute, which was in force when the rent became
due, were substantially complied with.

Thesiger, contrà. It is submitted, that the order of
sessions must be quashed. This, it is to be remembered, is
a question of derivative settlement, and therefore, unless
the pauper's husband had actually gained a settlement in
the parish of Carshalton at the time of his death, the order
cannot be supported. The question depends upon the
construction to be given to the 59 Geo. 3, c. 50. By that
statute, three things must concur before a settlement can
be gained under it, by renting a tenement. First, the
tenement must be of the value of 10l. at the least;
second, it must be occupied for one whole year ; and
third, there must be the payment of 10l. at the least, for a
year, " by the person hiring the same." The first two
requisites had been complied with by the pauper's husband before his death ; but not the third. Payment of
the rent out of his effects after his death, is not sufficient,

because it must be a payment by the person hiring the tenement. If, indeed, the distress had been made before the pauper's death, then it might be admitted, that the statute would have been substantially complied with. After his death, the effects on the premises became the property of some other person, and therefore it cannot be said that it was a payment out of the proceeds of his goods. The question is, whether the pauper had, in fact, personally complied with all the requisites of the statute before his death. It is clear that he had not, and therefore there is an end to this, as a derivative settlement. . If the argument on the other side could prevail, it would come to this, that a man may gain a posthumous settlement, which would be rather a new proposition in settlement law. If the pauper did not gain the settlement before death, he did not afterwards. At the time of his death, the settlement was inchoate; and the payment of the rent out of his effects afterwards, cannot perfect the settlement by relation back to the time when he was alive. This is a much weaker case than *Rex* v. *Ampthill* (a), where, though the rent was actually paid by the pauper himself, yet, inasmuch as it was not paid until he was removed to another parish, the Court held, that still he did not gain a settlement, the rent being paid when it was too late. Then, as to the second point, the effect of the 6 *Geo.* 4, was not absolutely to repeal the 59 *Geo.* 3. All that it did was to let in the old law, from the time of the repeal. If that statute were absolutely repealed, the effect would be to annul all acts done, and destroy every right acquired under it. But assuming the argument on the other side upon this point to have any weight, still on this occasion it is wholly irrelevant, because the 6 *Geo* 4, c. 57, received the royal assent on the 22nd *June*, three months before the rent was paid, and therefore, according to *Rex* v. *St. Mary-le-bone* (b), no settlement could be gained, inasmuch as it was incomplete at the time the statute came into operation.

(a) Ante, vol. iv. 447.   2 B. & C. 847.   (b) 4 D. & A. 681.

ABBOTT, C. J.—I am of opinion, that the order of sessions must be quashed. The question is, whether the pauper had a derivative settlement from her husband; or in other words, whether the husband had acquired a settlement in *Carshalton* at the time of his death. I think he had not, whether we consider the 59 *Geo.* 3, or the 6 *Geo.* 4, as the governing law. It is true he occupied the tenement for more than a year, but he died before the rent of 10*l.* was paid *by him,* which is the language of the 59 *Geo.* 3; nor was there any payment of one whole year's rent, as required by the 6 *Geo.* 4, *at the time of his death;* and I think that the subsequent payment by means of the sale of his goods, is not sufficient to satisfy the requisites of that statute. Therefore, whichever statute is to be considered as the governing law, he had acquired no settlement in *Carshalton,* which he could communicate to his wife.

BAYLEY, J., HOLROYD, J., and LITTLEDALE, J., concurred.

Order of Sessions quashed.

DOE, on the demise of JANE SMYTH, *v.* Sir GEORGE HENRY SMYTH, Bart.

A devisee of lands refused to take them under the will, but claimed to be entitled to them as heir at law:—Held, that this was no disclaimer, and that he might afterwards recover possession of the land as devisee. *Quære,* whether a disclaimer of devised lands may be by parol.

THIS was an action of ejectment, brought to recover the possession of the freehold part of a messuage, farm, lands and premises, in the parishes of *Elmswell* and *Norton,* in the county of *Suffolk.* The declaration contained two demises, one on the 2nd of *March,* 1814; the other on the 2nd of *February,* 1824. Plea, not guilty, and issue thereon. The cause was tried before *Gaselee,* J., at the *Suffolk* summer assizes, 1824, when, by the direction of the learned Judge, a verdict was found for the plaintiff, with liberty to the defendant to move to set aside that verdict, and enter one for himself; and the court of King's Bench, on that motion being made, directed the following case to be stated for their opinion.

Ann Brand, being seised in fee of the estate in question, on the 7th of *October*, 1813, duly executed her last will, which contained a devise in the following words:—" I give and bequeath to Miss *Jane Smyth*, of *Ogle Street, London*, all that messuage, farm, lands and hereditaments, situate at *Elmswell*, or in any other parish in the county of *Suffolk*, during the term of her life, keeping the said estate in good repair. I also give to the said Miss *Jane Smyth* the sum of 500*l.*, for the purpose of discharging the fines and other fees, on her admission to the copyhold part of the said estate. I also give to the said Miss *Jane Smyth* all my books, and Sir *Henry Smyth's* miniature picture: and from and after her decease, I give and devise the said messuage, farm, lands and hereditaments, situate in *Elmswell*, or in any other parish in the county of *Suffolk*, unto Sir *Henry Smyth*, of *Bee Church*, in *Essex*, and his heirs." The testatrix died in *March*, 1814, without revoking her said will, and the lessor of the plaintiff and the defendant are the devisees therein named; the latter by the name of Sir *Henry Smyth*. Shortly after the death of the testatrix, the Rev. *Charles Cooke*, who was one of her executors, called upon the lessor of the plaintiff, for the purpose of paying her the said legacy of 500*l.*, when she refused to receive the same; and she had not received it at the time of the trial. Early in 1815, and three or four times afterwards in the course of that year, and once in the next, Mr. *Serjeant*, the attorney of the defendant, by his desire, called upon the lessor of the plaintiff, upon the subject of the devise. She claimed the estate as heir at law to Sir *Henry Smyth*, and on all these occasions declared she would never accept any benefit under Mrs. *Brand's* will; and on one of them she said, she knew there was a legacy to enable her to take up the copyhold, but nothing should induce her to accept that legacy. On one occasion, Mr. *Serjeant* shewed her a pedigree to convince her she was *not*, but that the defendant *was*, the heir at law; she said the pedigree was wrong, but did not point out where; and upon Mr. *Serjeant* telling her that the copyhold might be seized by the lady of the manor; that the defendant would not suffer the estate to go to ruin for want of a landlord; and that, if she persisted in refusing to take it up, she must not blame him for any proceedings he might institute; she replied, he might do as he pleased, but she was determined not to take any benefit under Mrs. *Brand's* will. On Mr. *Serjeant's* last visit, he proposed to her, on the part of Sir *George Henry Smyth*, that if she did not chuse to take the estate, and would permit him to do it, he would account to her for all the profits, and give her security. She answered, she would take nothing under the will; that she had already been kept out of all that estate, and all that Mrs. *Brand* had given to Mrs. *Vincent*, since the death of Sir. *Henry Smyth*; that she should claim the whole of the property under that title, and should have nothing to do with Mrs. *Brand;* and that she considered it an insult. Part of the estate in question is freehold, and part copyhold; and the largest and most valuable part is copyhold. On the 9th of *May*, 1814, at a general court baron held for the manor of *Elmswell*, a presentment was made of the death of the testatrix, and a proclamation for any person claiming the copyhold part of the estate to come in. A second similar proclamation was made on the 8th of *November*, 1814; and a third on the 6th of *March*, 1815. No person having appeared on any of those occasions, on the 12th of *December*, 1815, the copyhold lands were seized by the bailiff of the manor, and an eject ment was brought against the tenants in possession by the lady of the manor. There was no defence to the ejectment, and the lady of the manor took possession of the

copyhold land, and retained it from that time to the time
of the trial, and received the rents. All the tenants in
possession were served with declarations in ejectment.
In *Trinity* term, 1823, the defendant caused declarations
in ejectment to be served on the tenants of the estate,
containing two demises by him; the first on the 2nd of
March, 1814; the second on the 17th of *March*, 1817.
Judgment passed by default, and the defendant obtained
possession by a writ of habere facias possessionem on the
12th of *January*, 1824. The jury found a refusal on the
part of the lessor of the plaintiff to take under the will,
and an assertion of title by her from the death of Sir
Henry Smyth, but that she had taken no steps to obtain
possession under that title.

Storks, for the plaintiff. Two propositions are relied
upon in behalf of the lessor of the plaintiff:—first, that
there has been, in point of fact, no waiver of the devise to
her; and second, that even if there has, still such a
waiver, being by parol only, does not amount, in point of
law, to a disclaimer, so as to destroy her right to sue.
First, the facts do not by any means prove a waiver. It is
clear, that the lessor of the plaintiff, though she knew
she was devisee, thought she was entitled to the estate as
heir at law; therefore, she did not intend wholly to
abandon the estate, but to claim a larger interest, and
under a superior title, than that which the will gave her.
No case has gone the length of establishing that such an act
was a waiver, or that a party who mistakes his legal rights,
and acts under that mistake, is not at liberty afterwards to
correct his error, and to avail himself of his better information. Second, even if a complete parol waiver has
been proved in fact, that does not deprive the devisee of
her right in law. The only case upon this point, which
can be adduced in favour of the defendant, is that of
Townson v. *Tickell*(a); but there the decision of the

(a) 3 B. & A. 31.

Court amounted to no more than that a disclaimer by deed was sufficient, though one of the learned Judges certainly expressed a doubt, whether a disclaimer by deed was necessary. It was held in *Thompson* v. *Leach* (a), that if tenant for life surrenders by deed to him in remainder, the estate is in the latter without proof of assent, and that by devise the estate is in the devisee immediately. The lessor of the plaintiff, therefore, had the freehold interest vested in her, immediately upon the death of the devisor; and by the Statute of Frauds, that interest could not pass from her except by a note in writing. The rule of law, indeed, was the same before the passing of that statute. In *Co. Litt.* 111 a, it is said, that "in the case of a devise by will of land, whereof the devisor is seised in fee, the freehold or interest in law is in the devisee before he doth enter;" and in 111 b, that lands ought not to be transferred from one to another, but by solemn livery of seisin, matter of record, or sufficient writing:—and *Butler* and *Baker's* case (b) is a direct authority to shew, that if the estate once vested in the lessor of the plaintiff by the devise, it could not be devested out of her by parol.

Dover, contrà. The defendant is in possession; and the lessor of the plaintiff must recover, if at all, upon the strength of her own title. The fact of the waiver has been found by the Jury, therefore it is now too late to discuss that question; but if not, the fact of the refusal is abundantly proved, for the lessor of the plaintiff repeatedly refused to have any thing to do with the will, or the estate devised by it; never received any of the rents or profits; and permitted the defendant to pursue his action of ejectment without opposition. But the law of the case is as clearly in favour of the defendant, as the facts. The only modern case in which the question has arisen, is that already cited, of *Townson* v. *Tickell.* It was there fully discussed and considered, and the whole Court expressed a

(a) 2 Ventr. 198.   (b) 3 Rep. 26.

decided opinion, that a disclaimer by deed was sufficient. But *Holroyd, J.*, went further, and gave it as his opinion, that unless some strong authority was produced, the Court could not hold that a party was bound to disclaim by deed ; and he cited *Bonefaut* v. *Greenfield* (a), in support of that opinion. In *Thompson* v. *Leach, Ventris, J.*, said, "a man cannot have an estate put upon him against his will" (b), so that he must have considered the surrender merely as an offer, presumed to be accepted only until the contrary appeared ; and he said not a word about the necessity of a disclaimer by deed. In *Smith* v. *Wheeler*, Lord *Hale* said, " *Crooke*," one of two trustees, "is a good lessor, for the other trustee's disagreement makes the estate wholly his." In *Brooke's Abridgment*, tit. *Waiver des choses*, pl. 1, it is said, "if there be a devise to one for life, remainder to another in fee, and the devisee for life waive the devise, the remainder man may enter ;" and it is not said that the waiver must be by deed. In *Sheppard's Touchstone*, 452, tit. *Testament*, it is said, "if one devise his land to another in fee simple, fee tail, for life or years, and the devisee, after the death of the testator, doth refuse and waive the estate devised to him, in this case and by this means the devise is become void. And it seems a verbal waiver is sufficient in this case." The argument respecting the Statute of Frauds does not apply, because that assumes the estate to have vested in the lessor of the plaintiff, which is denied on the part of the defendant: the estate was offered to the devisee, and the law would have presumed an acceptance of the offer, unless the contrary had appeared ; but the contrary did appear, for the Jury have found that she refused the estate, and the cases shew that such refusal need not be by deed.

The case was argued in the course of last term, when the Court took time for consideration. Judgment was now delivered by

(a) 1 Leon. 60. Cro. Eliz. 80. (b) 2 Ventr. 206.

BAYLEY, J., who, after recapitulating the facts of the case, thus proceeded. Upon these facts, we are of opinion that the lessor of the plaintiff is entitled to recover. By presumption of law, a devised interest vests in the devisee before entry ; *Co. Litt.* 111 a. Undoubtedly a devisee cannot be compelled to accept the interest devised to him, but may by some mode renounce or disclaim it ; and the interest so renounced or disclaimed will descend to the heir, or pass to the remainder man. Whether such renunciation or disclaimer must be by deed, or may be by parol, we do not think it necessary in the present case to decide, because we are clearly of opinion that, whatever be the form adopted, there must be an express and unequivocal disclaimer of any estate in the land. Here there was no disclaimer of any estate in the land, but merely of benefit under the will, accompanied on every occasion by an assertion of a right to the land by a superior title. In that respect the lessor of the plaintiff acted under a mistake, of which, though slowly and reluctantly, she has at length become convinced. No case similar to the present has been offered to our notice, nor do we believe any such can be found ; and in the absence of any authority upon the subject, we are of opinion that the lessor of the plaintiff is not precluded from availing herself of her improved judgment, and taking the land as devisee under the will. The verdict, therefore, must stand.

Judgment for the Plaintiff.

The KING v. THOMAS MUTTERSHAW HUBBALL Esq.

QUO WARRANTO information against the defendant for usurping the office of a Justice of the Peace within the borough of *Stafford*. The plea set out a charter of 12 *Jac.* 1, by which that king granted that the corporation of *Stafford* should consist of a mayor, ten aldermen, and ten capital burgesses; that the mayor, aldermen, and others of the common-council of the borough for the time being, or the greater part of them, of whom the mayor for the time being was to be one, should have full power to chuse and nominate within the borough two of the aldermen of the borough for the time being, to be the Justices within the borough for one whole year. The plea then stated the acceptance of the charter by the corporation, and that on the charter day in 1825, the then mayor, and divers to wit, six of the aldermen, and divers, to wit, six others of the common council of the borough, to wit, six of the capital burgesses of the borough for the time being, they being the major part of the mayor, aldermen, and capital burgesses of the borough, did, within the borough, chuse and nominate the defendant, being one of the aldermen of the borough for the time being, to be one of the Justices of the Peace within the borough, for one whole year then next following; and that he after he was so nominated and chosen, took the requisite oath, and was thereupon duly admitted into, and did take upon himself the office of Justice of the Peace within the borough, &c.,

Quo warranto information for usurping the office of Justice within the borough of S. Plea that defendant was elected at a corporate meeting where a majority of the aldermen and capital burgesses were present. Replication, that at the supposed election, five capital burgesses (naming them) and no others, were present, and that they were not the major part of the capital burgesses. Rejoinder, that at the election, besides the five capital burgesses named in the replication, there were present

K. and T., being then capital burgesses, and that the five capital burgesses named in the replication, together with K. and T., were the major part of the capital burgesses. Sur-rejoinder that K. and T., before the election of the defendant, had been elected, admitted into, and exercised the office of aldermen, and at the election of the defendant were present as aldermen, and that before the defendant's election two other persons were elected, and admitted as capital burgesses in the room and stead of K. and T. Rebutter that at the election of K. and T. as aldermen of the borough, the major part of the aldermen were not assembled, and that after the election of K. and T., and before the election of the defendant as Justice, and whilst K. and T. exercised the office of aldermen, quo warranto informations were filed against them, and judgment of ouster given, with a denial that K. and T. ever were aldermen : —Held, on demurrer, that K. and T. were not good capital burgesses, though they had been ousted from the office of aldermen, and judgment for the Crown.

and by that warrant exercised the office. To this plea there were several replications, but the points discussed at bar, and decided by the Court, arose upon the demurrer to the pleadings following upon the sixth replication. That replication alleged, that at the supposed election of the defendant in the pleas mentioned, the following persons and no others were present, and attended as capital burgesses of the borough, viz: *J. Shaw, J. Griffin, J. Marsh, E. Worsey,* and *J. Rogers;* and that the said persons who so attended and were present as capital burgesses at the said supposed election of the defendant, were not the major part of the capital burgesses of the borough; and this, &c. Rejoinder, that at the said election of the defendant, the said *J. Shaw, J. Griffin, J. Marsh, E. Worsey,* and *J. Rogers,* being capital burgesses of the borough, attended and were present as in the replication mentioned; and that over and above and besides the said five last mentioned burgesses, *E. Knight,* and *R. Turnock,* being then capital burgesses of the borough, attended and were present at the same election, and that the said five capital burgesses of the borough who so attended and were present at that election, and the said *E. Knight,* and *R. Turnock,* so then being capital burgesses of the borough, were the major part of the capital burgesses of the borough. And this, &c. Surre-joinder that *Knight* and *Turnock,* before the supposed election of the defendant, were respectively elected and chosen aldermen of the borough, and had taken their corporal oath as aldermen of the borough, and had been admitted into the office of aldermen of the borough; and that *Knight* and *Turnock* had from thence hitherto exercised the office of aldermen of the borough, and at the supposed election of the defendant, attended and were present as aldermen of the borough; and that after the said election of *Knight* and *Turnock* as aldermen, as aforesaid, and before the supposed election of the defendant, two other persons, to wit, *J. Hawthorn,* and *J. Rogers,* were elected and chosen capital burgesses, and took their corporal oath, and were admitted as capital burgesses of the borough, in the room and stead of Knight and Turnock. And this, &c. Rebutter, that at the time of the supposed election of Knight to be alderman of the borough, the major part of the aldermen of the borough were not assembled or present, nor did meet, and that the supposed election of Knight to be such alderman, took place without the major part of the aldermen of the borough having assembled, or met, or having been present thereat; and that after the supposed election of Knight to be such alderman, and before the election of the defendant, and whilst Knight exercised the said office of alderman, under a colour of his supposed election, and not otherwise, to wit, in Michaelmas term in the 6 Geo. 4, a certain information in the nature of a quo warranto, was duly exhibited against Knight, charging that he, on the 2d of October, 2 Geo. 4, did use and exercise without any legal warrant the office of an alderman of the borough, &c. And thereupon, that Knight, in Hilary term, in the 6 and 7 Geo. 4, in the year of our lord 1825, having heard the said information read, disclaimed the office in the information specified, and could not deny that he had usurped upon our lord the King the said office, and confessed and acknowledged the said usurpation, in manner and form as in the said information above alleged; and thereupon it was adjudged that the said Knight should not further intermeddle with, or concern himself in or about the said office, but that he should be absolutely prejudged and excluded from using or exercising the same. The rebutter then stated a similar information and a judgment of ouster against Turnock, and then traversed that Knight and Turnock ever were elected and chosen aldermen. And this, &c. Demurrer to the rebutter, and joinder in demurrer.

The case was argued by Campbell, for the crown, and R. Bayly, for the defendant. The authorities cited were, Rex v. Miller (a), Rex v. The Mayor of York (b),

(a) 6 T. R. 268.   (b) 5 T. R. 66.

Lane v. *Allwood* (a), *Rex* v. *Bower* (b), and *Rex.* v. *Hughes* (c).

ABBOTT, C. J.—I am of opinion that judgment must be given for the crown upon the demurrer to the rebutter. The defendant alleges, in his plea, that he was chosen a justice of the peace for the borough of *Stafford*, at an assembly where a majority of the aldermen and capital burgesses attended. The relator, in one of his replications, denies that the major part of the capital burgesses were present, and if he had done no more, the question now raised upon demurrer would have arisen upon the evidence. But he goes further, and in his sixth replication states, that five persons by name, and no others, were present as capital burgesses at the election of the defendant, and that five persons were not the major part of the capital burgesses of the borough. Now, as five are certainly not a majority of ten, it may be said that this is an argumentative replication. But if the defendant had intended to insist that it was bad on that ground, he ought to have demurred specially. He does not do so; but goes on and endeavours to shew, that more than five persons did attend as capital burgesses; and for that purpose he alleges, by way of rejoinder, that at the election of the defendant, the five capital burgesses, named in the replication, attended, and that over and above and besides those five, *Edward Knight*, and *Robert Turnock*, being also capital burgesses, attended and were present, and that the five capital burgesses named in the replication, and *Knight* and *Turnock*, so then being capital burgesses, were the major part of the capital burgesses of the borough. In answer to that, the relator states in his sur-rejoinder, that, before the election of the defendant, these two persons had been elected, admitted to, and exercised the office of aldermen, and that they, at the supposed election of the defendant, attended, and were present as aldermen; and

(a) Yelv. 132.   (c) Ante, vol. viii., 708.
(b) Ante, vol. ii., 761.

that after the election of these two persons to the office of aldermen, and before the supposed election of the defendant, two other persons were elected and admitted as capital burgesses in the room of *Knight* and *Turnock*. It may be said, that this sur-rejoinder is also argumentative; but the defendant, in order to take advantage of that objection, ought to have demurred specially. Instead of that, he endeavours to shew by his rebutter, that at the time of his election, *Knight* and *Turnock* were not aldermen, but capital burgesses; for in the rebutter he states, that in *Michaelmas* term, 1825, judgment of ouster was obtained against them in an information in the nature of quo warranto, which charged that they, in *October*, 1822, usurped the office of aldermen; and then it concludes with a traverse of the fact, that *Knight* and *Turnock* ever were chosen aldermen. It is insisted, that the legal effect of that judgment of ouster was to throw them back upon their office of capital burgesses, inasmuch as they had been improperly elected aldermen. Now, that is the very point which was decided in the late case of *Rex* v. *Hughes*, and decided in the negative by my three learned brothers; and no reasonable mind can doubt the propriety of that decision. It was there decided, that these two persons having accepted and been sworn into the office of aldermen, and their places, as capital burgesses, filled up by other persons, it was impossible to contend that they were to be still deemed capital burgesses, but must be taken to be aldermen. It appears to me, therefore, that upon this part of the pleadings, judgment must be given for the crown.

BAYLEY, J., HOLROYD, J., and LITTLEDALE J., concurred.

Judgment for the crown.

GOOM v. AFLALO.

THIS was an action of assumpsit, brought by the plaintiff against the defendant, for refusing to deliver a quantity of *Barbary* gum, pursuant to a contract of sale,
alleged to have been entered into with the plaintiff, by a
Mr. *Virgo*, as the broker of the plaintiff and defendant.
Plea, non assumpsit, and issue thereon. At the trial
before *Abbott*, C. J., at the *London* adjourned sittings,
after last *Hilary* term, a verdict was found for the plaintiff; and afterwards, upon a motion being made for a new
trial, the Court directed the facts to be stated for their
opinion in the following case.

Mr. *Virgo*, as the broker of the defendant, and with his
authority, agreed with the plaintiff, that the defendant
should sell and deliver to him 170 serons of *Barbary* gum,
at the price of 55s. per cwt. The broker thereupon wrote
in his broker's book, the terms of the contract, as follows :—

"*London*, 23d *February*, 1825.

Sold, for account of Mr. *Aflalo*, to Mr. *S. T. Goom*,
170 serons of *Barbary* gum, subject to approval of quality
to-morrow, per the *Mogadore*, lying in the *London* docks,
at 55s. per cwt., in bond ; customary allowance for tare
and draft ; two and a half per cent. discount for cash in
fourteen days, or four months' credit. The gum remaining
in the seller's name at the docks."

The entry in the broker's book was not signed by the
broker, or any other person. Between nine and ten
o'clock at night of the said 23d *February*, the broker sent
to the plaintiff and the defendant, respectively, paper
writings, commonly called bought and sold notes, copied
from the entry in his book, and signed by him. Between
nine and ten o'clock in the morning of the 24th *February*,
the defendant objected to, and returned the sold note to

the broker, and wholly refused to deliver the gum ; whereupon this action was brought.

Law, for the plaintiff. The question in this case is, whether the bought and sold notes, signed by the broker, and delivered by him to the parties, constituted a sufficient note or memorandum of the bargain, signed by an agent duly authorised, within the meaning of the Statute of Frauds, 29 *Car.* 2, c. 3, s. 17; or whether the signature of the broker to the entry in his book, was necessary, in order to make the contract binding upon the parties. It was decided in *Simon* v. *Motivos* (a), and that decision was recognised and confirmed in *Hinde* v. *Whitehouse* (b), that the broker is the duly authorised agent of both the contracting parties ; and it was ruled by Lord *Kenyon*, in *Rucker* v. *Cammeyer* (c), and by *Gibbs*, C. J., in *Cumming* v. *Roebuck* (d), that the bought and sold notes signed by the broker, were a sufficient memorandum of the bargain. In the latter case, *Gibbs*, C. J., observed, that an opinion had been somewhere expressed, that the entry in the broker's book, signed by him, was the only proper evidence of the contract, but added, that it had been over-ruled. The case to which the learned Judge alluded, was doubtless that of *Heyman* v. *Neale* (e). There the broker signed the entry in his book, and afterwards sent bought and sold notes to the parties. It was contended on the part of the defendant, that the bought and sold notes were delivered for the approval of the parties, and that until that approval was given, there was no binding contract. Lord *Ellenborough* said, that the entry made and signed by the broker, was alone the binding contract, and that the bought and sold notes were merely copies of that entry, which would be binding of itself, even if no such notes were ever sent to the parties. That judgment, however,

(a) 3 Burr. 1921. 1 Bl. Rep.   (c) 1 Esp. 105.
599.   (d) Holt's N. P. C. 172.
(b) 7 East, 558.   (e) 2 Camp. 337.

must be taken to have been formed with reference to the particular facts of that individual case, and will not therefore govern the present case, because there is this material distinction between the two—that there the entry in the broker's book was signed by the broker, whereas, here it is not signed by him or any other person.   In the subsequent case of *Powell* v. *Divett* (a), the entry in the broker's book was not signed by him. The plaintiff produced a note signed by the broker, but as that appeared to have been altered, it was considered not admissible in evidence, and the plaintiff was nonsuited ; but the nonsuit proceeded entirely upon that ground, and it was not contended that the note, if it had remained unaltered, would not have been good evidence of the contract. And in the very recent case of *Grant* v. *Fletcher* (b), *Abbott*, C. J., is reported to have said, that if the bought and sold notes had both been similar, and both been signed by the broker, they would probably have been binding, although the memorandum of the contract in the broker's book, had not been signed.

Chitty, contrà. The first question is, which was intended by the broker to be the original memorandum of the contract—the entry in his book, or the bought and sold notes. If the entry in the broker's book was intended to be the original memorandum of the contract, that was the best and only evidence of the contract, and the bought and sold notes were inadmissible : and then as the entry in the broker's book was not signed, it was not binding, and was inadmissible also, so that there was in reality no evidence of the contract at all. The case of *Powell* v. *Divett*, was decided entirely upon the ground of fraud, and therefore it forms no authority for the present case, one way or the other. But *Heyman* v. *Neale* (c), is decisive in favour of the defendant, for there Lord *Ellen-*

(a) 15 East, 29.   C. 436.
(b) Ante, vol. viii., 59.   5 B. &   (c) 2 Camp. 337.

borough said, " after the broker has entered the contract in his book, neither party can recede from it. The bought and sold note is not sent on approbation, nor does it constitute the contract. The entry made and signed by the broker, is alone the binding contract." It must be admitted, that in *Cumming* v. *Roebuck* (a), *Gibbs*, C. J., mentioned that doctrine of Lord *Ellenborough's*, as having been over-ruled; but the case to which he must have alluded, *Dickinson* v. *Lilwall* (b), does not go that length. There the broker made no entry in his book, but merely signed and delivered to the parties bought and sold notes. It was contended, on the authority of *Hinde* v. *Whitehouse* (c), that they were insufficient, but Lord *Ellenborough* said, " that case does not go the length of deciding, that where *no entry* is made in the broker's book, the bought and sold notes may not be sufficient to satisfy the statute." Now here there was an entry in the broker's book, though it was not signed by the broker; therefore, there is a material distinction between the two cases.

The case was argued on a former day in this term, when the Court took time for consideration. Judgment was now delivered by

BAYLEY, J.—It is found by the special case, that *Virgo*, the broker, was authorised by the defendant to sell the gum; that he contracted for the sale of it to the plaintiff; that he made an entry of the contract in his broker's book, but did not sign the entry; and that he afterwards sent to each of the parties a copy of the entry, signed by himself. The objection to the validity of the contract, is the want of the broker's signature to the entry in his book. It is plain that the contract was made in such a manner as rendered it binding upon the defendant within the provisions of the Statute of Frauds, and it can only be

(a) Holt's N. P. C. 172.   (c) 7 East, 558.
(b) 1 Stark. Rep. 128.

held invalid, therefore, upon the ground of some usage or custom of merchants, which the Court may recognise as part of the common law. The special case, however, does not find the existence of any such usage or custom. In the cases bearing upon this subject, a signed entry in the broker's book, and similar signed notes delivered to the parties, are mentioned as forming a binding contract; and the entry is spoken of as the original, and the notes as copies. There is not, however, any express decision that a binding contract may not be made by notes properly signed, where the entry in the broker's book is not signed; and in one case, *Gibbs*, C. J., is reported to have said, that a supposed decision of that kind had been over-ruled. Under these circumstances, we cannot say that the custom on which the defendant relies, has ever been adopted by the Courts, as part of the law of merchants. The strong expressions which Judges have used as to the duty of brokers, to sign the entries in their books, will not suffice for such a purpose; nor will the obligation supposed to be laid upon them when licensed to practise in the city of *London*. In some countries brokers are established under municipal regulations, by which punctuality and integrity in their dealings are insured. A regulation compelling them to sign the entries in their books, would, undoubtedly, be one mode of insuring these, and might in some cases be highly useful, as furnishing evidence of the contract. We are all of opinion, that a broker ought to sign the entry in his book, and that every prudent and careful broker will do so. But if we were to say that the signature of the broker was essential to the validity of the contract, we should be going further than the Courts have as yet gone, and might be laying down a rule calculated to produce inconvenience, because we should make the validity of the contract dependent upon the private act of an individual, of which the contracting parties would be ignorant, and by which a fraudulent or negligent man would have it in his power to render the contract valid or

invalid at his pleasure. For these reasons, we are of opinion that the plaintiff is entitled to retain his verdict.

Judgment for the plaintiff.

A. M. Bidgood v. Davies and another.

DOWLING on a former day obtained a rule calling on
the plaintiff to shew cause why the bail bond given by the
defendant, *Jeremiah Davies*, should not be delivered up
to be cancelled upon filing common bail, on the ground
that he was privileged from arrest by virtue of his appointment, as one of the yeomen-warders of the tower
of *London*. The affidavits in support of the rule stated,
that on the 5th *February*, 1819, the defendant was duly
appointed one of his majesty's yeomen, or warders of the
tower, by virtue of a warrant under the hand and seal
of the lieutenant of the tower (a); that on the 21st

Where a
yeoman
warder of the
tower of
London was
arrested, and
put in special
bail, and
thereby ob-
tained his
liberation, the
Court refused
to decide on
motion, his
right to be
exempt from
arrest, even
though thes
terms of hi
warrant gave
him that pri-
vilege.

(a) The warrant was in the following terms :—" *W. L.*, Esq., a
general of his majesty's forces,
lieutenant of his majesty's.tower,
London, &c. &c. &c.

Jeremiah Davies,

By virtue of the power and authority given unto me by his majesty, I do hereby, in the absence
of the constable, constitute, ordain, and appoint you *J. D.*, a
yeoman, waiter, or warder of the
tower of *London*, you behaving
yourself as becometh a loyal and
faithful subject and servant to his
majesty, his lawful heirs and successors, according to the trust reposed in you. To which end and
purpose, I do hereby signify and declare that you *J.D.*, have taken the

usual and accustomed oath of a
yeoman-warder. You are to receive the wages and fees incident
to the office or place of a yeoman-
warder, and to enjoy all other
duties, profits, emoluments, and
commodities, with all ancient privileges to the same belonging or
anywise appertaining. Amongst
divers others, you are superseded
from arrests. You may not be
restrained of your liberty or detained prisoner without leave first
had and obtained from me. You
are likewise exempt from bearing
any parish office, as churchwarden,
collector, constable, scavenger, or
the like. Neither are you chargeable with any kind of taxes or
payments, (except in Court only),

1826.

BIDGOOD
v.
DAVIES.

October last, he was arrested at the suit of the plaintiff, by the sheriff of *Middlesex*; that on being arrested, he produced his appointment to the sheriff's officer, and claimed to be released by virtue thereof, but that the officer refused to discharge him; that since defendant's appointment he had from time to time, until the present time, discharged the duties, and received the emoluments arising from the office; that the pay of a yeoman-warder of the tower is 21*l.* per annum, which pay he had since the time of his appointment received, and did now receive; that the duties of the office require a constant daily attendance in the tower of *London*, as occasions arise which are signified by the lieutenant; that as such yeoman-warder, defendant was required to attend half-yearly musters, and had attended such musters accordingly; that he was obliged to be in daily and hourly readiness to attend on his majesty's person to the House of Lords, at the royal castle and palace of *Windsor*, at *Carlton Palace*, and wheresoever his majesty might please to command his presence; that he was subject to military discipline, and liable to divers pains and penalties in case of non-attendance to or neglect of his several duties in the tower;

as other his majesty's servants are. You are not to be empannelled on juries, or give your attendance at assizes or sessions. Neither are you to watch, or ward, or pay for doing those duties, with divers other privileges not herein particularly mentioned, which as his majesty's servant you may justly pretend to enjoy, which said place of yeoman-waiter or warder of the tower, together with all profits, commodities, emoluments, and privileges above specified and thereunto belonging, you are to hold, possess, and enjoy, for and during the royal will and pleasure of our sovereign lord the king. And I do hereby require all persons whom these presents shall or may concern, that they do take notice hereof, and commit no act or thing whatsoever, that may any way infringe or violate the privileges of you the said *J. D.*, as they tender his majesty's service, and will answer the contrary at their peril. Given under my hand and seal of the tower, this 5*th* day of *February*, in the 59 *Geo.* 3, *A. D.* 1819.

(Signed)　　*W. L.*　　(*L.S.*)
General Lieutenant of the Tower.

By the Lieutenant's command,.

　　J. H. Ebrington,
　　　Major commander

that it was the special duty of yeomen-warders to keep in safe custody all state prisoners committed to the tower; that on a late occasion, when *Thistlewood* and other prisoners were committed to the tower on charges of high treason, defendant with other yeomen-warders had the charge of the safe keeping of those persons during a period of six weeks, day and night; that on divers other occasions since his appointment, defendant had discharged the duties of his office when called upon so to do; that amongst other duties to which he was liable in rotation with other yeomen-warders, was that of keeping nightly watch and guarding the gates of the tower; that when on duty, defendant could not leave the tower without the leave and licence of the lieutenant or other superior officer in command; that when not on duty he could not change at any time, for any period or for any purpose or business whatsoever, his place of residence (which was registered with the proper officer at the tower), without first giving notice thereof; that whenever private business might require him to leave his residence, even for the shortest period, he was under the necessity of specifying to what place he was going, in order that he might give his speedy attendance at the tower in case of any exigency arising; that upon defendant being arrested, he took out a summons before the Lord Chief Justice for the purpose of obtaining his discharge; that upon that occasion the Lord Chief Justice expressed some doubt as to the propriety of granting an order, and referred the defendant to the Court, whereupon defendant gave a bail bond. The affidavits in answer to the application, stated, that at the time the defendant was arrested, the officer told him that the plaintiff did not wish to have him taken into custody, and would be satisfied if he entered a common appearance, but that the defendant refused to do this, and insisted upon his privilege from arrest, whereupon the officer took him into custody, but offered to take him to his own attorney's office to execute a bail bond, which he declined doing.

Scarlett now shewed cause, and contended, that as the defendant was not now in actual custody, and as the king's service was in no degree prejudiced by his arrest, the Court would not, in this summary manner, propound any opinion as to the privilege which the defendant claimed, but would leave him to sue out his writ of privilege, as in the case of *Luntley* v. *Battyne* (a). The Court stopped him, and called upon

Tindal, S. G., *Dowling*, and *Chitty*, contrà. This case is distinguishable from *Luntley* v. *Battyne*, and *Tapley* v. *Battyne* (b), because there the privilege claimed was doubtful, and the defendant was not a servant in ordinary with fee. Here the privilege is clearly expressed in the very terms of the defendant's warrant, and he is a servant in ordinary with fee. The defendant actually discharges the duties of the office in person, and it is not an honorary privilege. It is true that the privilege of being free from arrest, is for the king's service, and not for the advantage of the private individual; but this defendant is precisely in the situation of a domestic servant of the king, and may be called upon at a moment's notice to attend his majesty's person, on state as well as other occasions. If, therefore, the freedom from arrest is to be allowed in any case, this is the very case in which it ought to receive the sanction of the Court. The defendant's is not a mere honorary office; he is in constant attendance at a royal palace; he is paid and clad by his majesty, and is to all intents and purposes the king's domestic servant. In *Batson* v. *M'Clean* (c), it was held, that no arrest can take place in the tower; but in that case there was no warrant granted for the immunity of the defendant from arrest. Here the defendant is exempted by the terms of the warrant, and the Court observed in that case, "yeomen-warders are exempted from arrest, but then they are expressly exempted by the terms of their warrant." They

(a) 2 B. & A. 234.   (b) Ante, vol. i. 79.   (c) 2 Chitty, 48.

cited *Pegge's Curialia*, 76 ; *Sard* v. *Forrest (a)*, *Tidd's Practice*, 8th Ed. 192, 193.

ABBOTT, C. J.—If this person were actually in custody, so that his majesty would be likely to lose the benefit of his services if they were required ; or if the party himself was likely to incur a forfeiture of his office by reason of his being prevented from discharging the duties of the office, there might be some ground for contending that the Court should decide the question of privilege on motion ; but it appears that the defendant is not in custody. When he was arrested, he was informed that if he would put in common bail, not special bail, the plaintiff would be satisfied ; but no, he did not think proper to do so, he chose to put in special bail ; and he said he would insist upon his privilege. Under these circumstances, I think we shall best exercise our discretion in forbearing to decide the question of privilege upon motion, and leaving the defendant to the ordinary legal mode in which such questions are decided, namely, by bringing his writ of privilege, if he thinks that the privilege can be so enforced (*b*).

HOLROYD, J., and LITTLEDALE, J., concurred.

(*a*) Ante, vol. ii., 250. 1 B. &   (*b*) *Bayley*, J., was gone to
C. 139.   chambers.

FEARNE *v.* WILSON.

THIS was a rule calling on the defendant's attorney to shew cause why his bill of costs should not be referred to the Master for taxation. It was admitted, that all the items in the bill, except one, were not taxable, and the

To attending a defendant to a lock-up-house, filling up a bail-bond, and obtaining his release, is a taxable item in an attorney's bill, as a charge at law within the statute, 2 Geo, 3, c. 23, s. 23.

question was, whether that one did not draw all the others after it. The item was as follows :—

"Yourself ats Fearne; same ats Burwash, 13th *December*, 1825. Attending you and your bail at *Radford's* Lock-up-house, in *Carey Street*, and obtaining your release on guaranteeing the responsibility of your bail, and filling up the bonds. Engaged one hour and a half, 1*l.* 1*s.*"

R. Bayly shewed cause against the rule. The item in question does not make the attorney's bill taxable, inasmuch as it is not a charge for any thing done at law or in equity, within the meaning of the statute 2 *Geo.* 2, c. 23, s. 23. This is not a charge in a cause, nor is it for any thing done in order to the commencement or defence of a suit at law or equity. The case of *Burton v. Chatterton* (a), is in principle decisive of this. In that case it was decided, that a charge for preparing an affidavit of a petitioning creditor's debt, and bond to the Chancellor, in order to the suing out a commission of bankruptcy, was not a taxable item in an attorney's bill within the meaning of the statute, it appearing that the affidavit had not been sworn, nor had the commission issued. The Nisi Prius case of *Sanderson* v. *Brown* (b), will be cited on the other side, as an authority to shew that an attorney's bill, containing a charge for preparing a warrant of attorney, with a view to business to be done in court, was taxable; but in *Burton* v. *Chatterton*, the authority of that case was doubted. Here it does not appear that the attorney, whose bill is sought to be taxed, was an attorney in any suit whatever, and, therefore, there is no pretence for saying that his bill is taxable. All that the attorney did was, to fill up the bail bond, which was no part of his business to do, but properly belonged to the sheriff's officer.

Lawes, contrà. From the very terms of the item, it cannot be doubted, that the attorney was acting in that character

(a) 3 B. & A. 486.   (b) 4 Campbell, 68.

when he appeared for the defendant, and did what was necessary for his liberation, iu a case in which a suit had been commenced against him. If so, then the statute comes into operation. It is not necessary that the charge should be for costs in a cause actually at issue. The statute is to receive a liberal interpretation in favour of the party to be charged, inasmuch as the only regular mode in which an attorney's bill can be taxed, is, by referring it to the officer of the Court, to judge of its reasonableness. But the case of *Winter* v. *Payne* (a), is an authority in point. There it was held, that an item, charging a client with drawing and engrossing an affidavit of debt, in order to hold a person to bail, and attending to get the deponent sworn thereto, rendered the bill subject to taxation. In *Exparte Prickett* (b), a dedimus potestatem, charged in an attorney's bill, was held to be sufficient to render the whole taxable, though the remaining charges were for business, as a conveyancer. And in the late case of *Wilson* v. *Gutteridge* (c), where a bill consisted merely of a charge for drawing a warrant of attorney, and attending a defendant respecting it, the Court ordered it to be referred to taxation, and at the same time observed, that independently of the statute, they still retained the power, and had constantly exercised the right, at common law, of directing taxation of any attorney's bill.

ABBOTT, C. J.—Attending to the provisions of the statute, the question is, whether this item comes within the words " fees, charges and disbursements, at law or equity." Is this a charge at law? It certainly is a charge for something done by the attorney in the progress of a suit. The defendant is arrested and taken to a lock-up-house. The attorney is sent for, and he does what is requisite to obtain his client's liberation. He fills up the bail-bond, and gives a guaranty for the sufficiency of the

(a) 6 T. R. 645.
(b) 1 N. R. 266.

(c) Ante, vol. iv., 736. 3 B. & C. 157.

bail. It is said to be no part of the duty of an attorney to fill up a bail-bond, and that the duty properly belongs to the sheriff's officer; but if an attorney, being sent for by his client, chuses to fill the bond up, and thinks it right to make a charge for what he has done, and make a profit of it, I think we must consider him (as he does himself) as acting in the character of an attorney, and therefore, that his bill is taxable. The attorney clearly considers himself as acting in the character of attorney, from the very terms in which the charge is made.

The other Judges concurred.

Rule absolute (a).

(a) Vide *Anonymous*, 2 Chit. Rep. 155. *Weld* v. *Crawford*, 2 Stark. 538. *Collins* v. *Nicholson*, 2 Taunt. 321. *Lee* v. *Wilson* Chit 63. *Nuttall* v. *Marr*, ante, vol. iii. 33. Tidd., 8 Ed. 328, et seq., and 1 Archbold's Prac. 29 & 31.

The KING *v.* The INHABITANTS of ST. MARGARET'S, KING'S LYNN.

A shoe-maker pro-posed to the mother of a pauper, a boy, to take him to learn his business. The boy was to serve four years, was to board and lodge with his mother, and was to have half what he earned. The mother consented, and the boy served four years upon those terms. No indentures were executed, *on account of the poverty of the mother*; and no premium was paid :— Held, that this was not a contract of hiring and service, but a defective contract of apprenticeship, and that the pauper gained no settlement by service under it.

TWO Justices for the county of *Norfolk*, by order, removed *John Cotton*, *Sarah* his wife, and their five children, from the parish of *St. Margaret's* in *King's Lynn*, to the parish of *Wolferton*. The sessions, on appeal, quashed the order, subject to the opinion of this Court upon the following case.

It was proved that one *Hoadley*, a shoemaker, a friend of the pauper's mother's family; applied to her, and offered, if she would agree to his proposal, that he would take her son, then a boy, to learn his business ; but there were no indentures on account of her poverty ; the pauper was to

MICHAELMAS TERM, SEVENTH GEO. IV. · 161

1826.

The King
v.
The
Inhabitants
of St. Mar-
garet's,
King's Lynn.

serve for four years, to board and lodge with his mother in St. *Margaret's*, in *Lynn*, and to have half what he earned. The pauper entered upon this service; worked in the shop with the apprentices; did not stay with his master on a *Sunday*, and was not required to do any work but in the shop. The pauper continued in the service four years, boarding and lodging in *St. Margaret's, Lynn.* Some time after entering upon the service, *Hoadley* sent the following writing by the pauper to his mother, which was neither stamped nor signed:—" An agreement drawn up between Mrs. *Cotton* and *Thomas Hoadley*, that the said *Thomas Hoadley*, is to find her son, *John Cotton*, work for four years, and he is to have half what he earns all the four years; and Mrs. *Cotton* to find her son *John Cotton* every thing else during the four years." The Court of Quarter Sessions, considering the pauper gained a settlement by hiring and service, quashed the Order of Removal.

Alderson, in support of the order of sessions. This is a contract of hiring and service, and not a defective contract of apprenticeship. The terms of the agreement clearly shew that the parties intended to create the relation of master and servant, and not the relation of master and apprentice. The undertaking by *Hoadley* to find the pauper work for four years, is of itself a contract of hiring and service. The agreement to teach the pauper the business, does not constitute him an apprentice. The instruction may have been given as a partial remuneration for service, without creating an apprenticeship; *Rex* v. *Little Bolton* (a); and a settlement may be gained as an hired servant, although the object of the agreement and service be to learn a trade, *Rex* v. *Hitcham* (b). The fact that no premium was paid in this case, is of itself almost conclusive to shew that no apprenticeship was intended. *Rex* v.

(a) Cald. 367. 2, Bott. 221.   (b) Burr. S. C. 489.
pl. 264.

1826

The KING
v.
The
INHABITANTS
of ST. MAR-
GARET'S,
KING'S LYNN.

Bilborough (a), and *Rex* v. *St. Mary Kidwelly* (b), were cases extremely similar to the present in all their circumstances, except that in each of them a premium was paid, and it was held in both that the contract was one of defective apprenticeship: but in *Rex* v. *Burbach* (c), where no premium was paid, and where the facts in other respects resembled the facts of this case, the contract was held to be one of hiring and service.

· *Marryat* and *Manning*, contrà. The contract in this case is, both in intention, and in terms, a defective contract of apprenticeship. In *Rex* v. *Little Bolton* (d), nothing was said from which an apprenticeship could be implied; and in *Rex* v. *Eccleston* (e), Lord *Ellenborough* declared that he was not convinced by the reasoning of that case, and that if the point was new, he should think otherwise; and "that where the contract was, that the master should teach the other, a trade, and the latter was to do nothing ulterior the employment in that trade, it was a contract *apprendre*, in the true sense of the word." The true criterion is, whether the contract is that the one party shall teach, and the other learn a trade; *Rex* v. *Rainham* (f), *Rex* v. *Mountsorrell* (g); and in the former of those cases, Lord *Kenyon* said, " no technical words are necessary to constitute the relation of master and apprentice, nor is it necessary that there should be any premium given to the master." The contract here, was for the master to teach, and the pauper to learn, a trade, and that contract would have been perfected by the execution of an indenture, except for the poverty of the mother.

BAYLEY, J.—It seems to me, that the contract in this

(a) 1 B. & A. 115.

(b) Ante, vol. iv., 309. 2 B. & C. 750.

(c) 1 M. & S. 370.

(d) Cald. 367. 2 Bott. 221. pl. 264.

(e) 2 East, 298.

(f) 1 East, 531.

(g) 2 M. &. S. 460.

1826.

The King
v.
The
Inhabitants
of St. Mar-
garet's
King's Lynn.

case was a defective contract of apprenticeship, and not a contract of hiring and service. Every case of this nature must be determined with reference to its own peculiar circumstances. Where it appears from all the circumstances that the parties at the time of making the contract intended to create the relation of master and apprentice, the contract must be construed as one of apprenticeship, and then if it is a defective apprenticeship, no settlement can be gained by service under it. Where, on the other hand, it appears that the parties intended to create the relation of master and servant, the contract must be construed as one of hiring and service, and a settlement will be gained by service under it.. The payment of a premium is cogent evidence to show that an apprenticeship was intended; but it is not conclusive, and much less is the absence of a premium, evidence to shew that a contract of hiring and service was intended. The written agreement, in this case, not having been signed or stamped, must be laid entirely out of consideration, and the original verbal contract, between the master and the pauper's mother, must alone be looked to as evidence of the real intention of the parties. The proposal, and consequently the purpose of the master, was to teach the pauper his trade; and the pauper was to serve him four years for that purpose, was to have half of what he earned, and was to board and lodge with his mother. No indentures were executed, on account of the poverty of the mother, but the very fact that the execution of indentures was thought of, though not realised, shews clearly that the parties did not contemplate the mere relation of master and servant, but did contemplate the relation of master and apprentice. The case of *Rex* v. *Little Bolton* (a), certainly comes very near the present. There the pauper proposed to the master, who was a weaver, to teach him to work counterpanes. The object of the pauper, therefore, was to be

(a) Cald. 367.   2 Bott. 221. pl. 264.

1826.

The King
v.
The
Inhabitants
of St. Mar-
garet's
King's Lynn.

taught a trade, but the master agreed to teach him only upon the condition that he should work for a given period. In many cases, the object of the party hiring himself is to learn a particular trade, and the instruction which he receives, is given as a partial remuneration for his services. In *Rex* v. *Burbach* (a) it was agreed, that the pauper should work for two years, and have what he earned, allowing his master so much per week for teaching him. The Court held that to be a contract of hiring and service, but upon the ground, that there was nothing to shew that the parties had intended to create the relation of master and apprentice. Here the relation of master and apprentice was evidently contemplated, and indentures would have been executed but for the poverty of the pauper's mother; and on that ground I am of opinion that the contract here was a defective contract of apprenticeship, the service under which conferred no settlement. The order of sessions, therefore, must be quashed.

HOLROYD, J.—I am of the same opinion. I think the intention of the parties, in this case, was to create the relation of master and apprentice; or, at least, that there is not evidence to justify us in saying, that they intended to create the relation of master and servant. The case states that the master, a shoemaker, applied to the pauper's mother, and offered her, *if she would agree to his proposal,* to take her son, then a boy, to learn his business. The proposal was to teach, and the mother was to consider whether she would accept that proposal. The condition upon which the master proposed to teach the pauper was, that the pauper should serve four years; and the purpose for which the pauper was to serve four years was, that he might learn the business. Under such circumstances I think the sessions were not warranted in finding that the relation of master and servant existed in this case, or that the pauper served in the character of servant, and not of

(a) 1 M. & S. 370.

1826.

The KING
v.
The
INHABITANTS
of St. MAR-
GARET'S
KING'S LYNN.

apprentice; for the mere fact of service is not enough to constitute the relation of master and servant.

LITTLEDALE, J., concurred.

Order of sessions quashed.

———◆———

SOPHIA NYE, spinster, HENRY NYE and CHARLES NYE, infants, by the said SOPHIA NYE, their mother and next friend v. MOSELEY.

HIS Honor, the Vice Chancellor, sent the following case for the opinion of this Court :— ˊ

In the year 1808, *Sophia Nye* became the servant of *John Moseley*, and continued to live in his family in the capacity of cook, until the year 1812. *John Moseley* was at the time of *Sophia Nye's* becoming his servant, and has ever since continued to be, a married man, living with his wife, but had at the time aforesaid, ceased to have sexual intercourse with his wife, by medical advice. In the course of the year 1810, a cohabitation took place between *John Moseley* and *Sophia Nye,* previously to which, *Sophia Nye* had always conducted herself with propriety and morality, and she continued to live in *John Moseley's* family, and to cohabit with him until the year 1812, when he provided and fitted up a cottage for her in the neighbourhood of his residence, and she removed to, and resided at such cottage, and cohabited with him there until the year 1816. In the course of such cohabitation, *Sophia Nye* was delivered of one child, and was at the determination thereof, in a state of pregnancy, and has since been delivered of another child. In 1816, *John Moseley* determined such cohabitation, and at the time of determining such cohabitation, he executed a bond to the said *Sophia Nye,* conditioned for the payment of an annuity of

Where a married woman living with his wife, cohabited with a single woman, who knew that he was married, and at the termination of the illicit intercourse, gave her a bond to secure the payment of annuity for the support of herself and two children, the offspring of their cohabitation :—Held, that an action at law might be maintained on the bond to recover the arrears of the annuity.

100*l.* to her, for the term of her natural life, and for the payment of 500*l.* each to the said children at his death. The annuity is unpaid for one year. The question for the opinion of this Court is, whether the circumstances of the case afforded to *John Moseley* a good ground of defence at law, to an action brought by *Sophia Nye* against him, upon the bond to recover the arrears of the annuity.

Storks for the plaintiff. The question sent by the Vice Chancellor for the opinion of this Court, must be answered in the negative. If otherwise, it can only be on the ground, that a married man is not bound in law to make any provision for a woman whom he has seduced and cohabited with, whilst the matrimonial contract subsisted between him and another woman. To lay down so general a proposition, would be productive of the most serious consequences, violating the dictates of humanity, contrary to good policy, and in opposition to the principle of decided cases. It is to be observed, that the consideration for the bond in this case, is *past* cohabitation, and on that general ground it may be upheld, according to the cases of *Walker* v. *Perkins* (a), *Turner* v. *Vaughan* (b), and *Lady Con's* case (c). The general rule undoubtedly is, that if the consideration be for a future state of concubinage, it would be void; but where the illicit connexion has ceased, the rule is otherwise. The question then is, whether the circumstances of the defendant being a married man at the time of the illicit cohabitation, and that the woman knew that fact, take this case out of the general rule. Probably it will be insisted on the other side, that it does, and reliance will be placed upon the case of *Priest* v. *Parrott* (d), as an authority in point; but it does not appear from the circumstances of that case, as reported, whether the bond was given in consideration of a future immoral intercourse. Here that circumstance is expressly

(a) 3 Burr. 1568.   (c) 3 Peere Wms. 339.
(b) 2 Wils. 339.   (d) 2 Ves. 160.

negatived, for the bond was not given until after the connexion had ceased.   It cannot be denied, that the motive for giving this bond was praiseworthy, namely, to make some compensation to the woman for the injury she had sustained by his means ; and shall it be said, that a man, under any circumstances, shall be prohibited from repairing the wrong that he has committed?   The case of *Annandale* v. *Harris* (a), goes in principle the whole length of the argument.   In that case, the Marquis of *Annandale* had seduced a virtuous woman, and had a child by her. He gave her a written obligation to pay her a sum of 2000*l*. after his death, to enable her to purchase an annuity for her and the child for their lives, and a court of Equity compelled the performance of the contract. Certainly it does not appear from the report of that case, that the Marquis was a married man at the time of the seduction, but there Lord *Hardwicke* said, " if a man does mislead an innocent woman, it is both reason and justice that he should make her a reparation."   The case of *Spicer* v. *Hayward* (b), is however an authority expressly in point.   In that case, the plaintiff being a married man, during the marriage, seduced his wife's sister, by whom he had several children.   For the purpose of providing for her and the children, he executed several money bonds, and these bonds being put in suit, he filed a bill of injunction to restrain proceedings, and suggested that the bonds were given without any valid consideration, but the Court, after argument, dismissed the bill with costs.   Public policy, and the interests of morality suggest the propriety of enforcing bonds given under such circumstances, because if they could not be enforced, an inducement would be thereby held out to the parties to continue the same vicious course of life, instead of returning to the paths of decency and virtue.   On the principle that this bond was given after the cohabitation had ceased, it is contended, that it may be enforced in a court of Law, even though

1826.

Nye
v.
MOSELEY.

(a) 2 Peere Wms. 422.   (b) Chan. Prec. 114.

the cohabitation took place whilst the obligor was a married man.

Lovatt, contrà. The circumstances stated in the case afford the defendant a good defence to an action at law upon the bond to recover the arrears of the annuity. The fact that the obligor was a married man, and known to be such by the obligee, during the cohabitation, renders the bond absolutely void. This is not a mere voluntary bond, which it is not denied would be valid either at law or in equity. It is conceded on the other side, and cannot indeed be denied, that a bond, the consideration for which is *future* cohabitation, would be void; but upon what principle is that doctrine founded? Because of the tendency which such bonds have to encourage vice and profligacy. But if a bond be given during the continuance of the cohabitation, it is equally objectionable on the same ground: for it cannot be denied that the continuance of the illicit intercourse, must form part of the consideration. It is perhaps now too late to contend, that a bond given by a single man in consideration of past cohabitation would be void; but if that question were now res integra, it may be doubted whether the contrary proposition could be upheld, for in such cases, it must be conceded, that the very hope of obtaining such a bond, holds out an inducement to continue the illicit intercourse between the parties, and on that ground the instrument would be void. But why are such bonds allowed to be enforced? Because the sum secured is treated in the nature of a voluntary compensation for the supposed injury done to the woman. The injury has reference, not to her seduction, because on that ground she personally would have no remedy; but to the supposition that she had sacrificed her chastity under a promise of marriage, which had been broken. As between single persons, able to contract the relation of marriage, that principle is consentaneous with reason and justice, but it altogether fails, when one of the parties at the time of the cohabitation, and the giving of the bond, is already married, with the knowledge of the other. The cases cited on the other side certainly do not bear out the argument which has been urged, for they are all distinguishable from this, and indeed no case is to be found in the books which goes the length contended for; and that is a cogent reason against the validity of such a bond. In *Spicer* v. *Hayward,* the Court refused to interfere, because both parties were equally criminal. No argument in favour of the plaintiff can be derived from *Annandale* v. *Harris,* because it is clear from the report of that case in 3 *Bro. P. C.* 445, that the Marquis was unmarried during the cohabitation; and Lord *Hardwicke,* in taking notice of that case in *Priest* v. *Parrott,* observes, "that the commerce was wholly after the death of the Marquis's first wife, and before his second marriage." From this observation it must be collected, that that learned Judge was of opinion, that the fact of a man's being married, with knowledge on the part of the obligee of the bond, rendered it absolutely void. This is the view taken of that case in *Matthews* v. *L——e* (a), and *Hunt* v. *Maunsell* (b). There being no authority, nor any principle to be collected in any reported case, tending to support a bond given under the circumstances here found, it is submitted that judgment must be given for the defendant. At the conclusion of the argument,

BAYLEY, J. (c), observed :—There can be no doubt that a bond given by a single man to a single woman, as premium *pudicitiæ,* at the time when he ceases the immoral intercourse, is binding upon the obligor. Undoubtedly, in such a case, the woman has been guilty of fornication; but that is as immoral as adultery, and both offences may be punished in the Ecclesiastical Court. Adultery cer-

(a) 1 Madd. 258.
(b) 1 Dow. P. C. 211.

(c) *Abbott,* C. J., was gone to Guildhall.

tainly is a greater offence than fornication ; but it is very difficult for a Court of law to distinguish precisely the different degrees of immorality which shall avoid an instrument of this nature. It being once established that a bond given to secure a provision to a woman who has lived with a man in a state of fornication, is valid, the present inclination of my mind is, that we ought not to hold that a bond given to a woman who has lived with a man in a state of adultery, is void, because in the one case, the woman has been guilty of a greater degree of immorality than in the other. The case of *Priest* v. *Parrot*, is not an authority to shew that such a bond may not be enforced at law. All that it decides, is, that the bill should be dismissed, and this may have been on the ground that the bond might be enforced in a court of Law. If, indeed, the decree had been that the bond should be delivered up to be cancelled, it would have been a strong authority for the defendant in this case.

The following certificate was afterwards sent into Chancery.

This case has been argued before us by counsel. We have considered it, and are of opinion, that the circumstances of this case do not afford a good ground of defence at law to an action by the said *Sophia Nye*, against the said *John Moseley*, upon the said bond, to recover the arrears of the said annuity.

J. BAYLEY.

G. S. HOLROYD.

J. LITTLEDALE.

1826.

TODD and others *v.* MAXFIELD.

THIS was an action of debt upon a judgment recovered in this Court in *Hilary* term, 4 *Geo.* 4, in an action of assumpsit. Plea, that the defendant had become bankrupt, and obtained his certificate, and that the cause of action upon which the judgment was recovered, accrued to the plaintiff before the defendant became bankrupt. Replication, after setting out all the proceedings in the former action, that defendant obtained his certificate before the trial of that cause, and did not before the judgment was recovered, plead the certificate to that action. Demurrer to the replication, and joinder in demurrer. When the case was called on for argument, the Court expressed so strong an opinion in favour of the plaintiffs, that

Comyn, for the defendant, prayed leave to withdraw the demurrer, which the Court granted upon payment of costs.

F. Pollock, now prayed judgment for the plaintiffs, upon an affidavit stating that the costs had been taxed, but had not been paid by the defendant.

PER CURIAM. Then let judgment be entered for the plaintiffs.

Judgment for the plaintiffs.

If a bankrupt is sued upon a cause of action arising before his bankruptcy, and obtains his certificate pending the suit, he must plead it puis darrein continuance; and if he does not, and judgment is obtained, and an action upon that judgment brought, against him, he cannot plead his certificate to that action.

The KING v. MUSSON.

Where the magistrates of a borough had exclusive jurisdiction within the borough, but concurrent jurisdiction with the county magistrates over the liberties of the borough: —Held, that for offences committed within the liberties, they might commit to the county gaol, and try the prisoners at the borough sessions.

THIS was an indictment against the defendant, as keeper of the gaol for the county of *Leicester*, for a misdemeanour, in refusing to deliver up to *John Brooks*, one of the constables of the borough of *Leicester*, and the liberties thereof, pursuant to an order of the court of Quarter Sessions of the said borough and liberties, then sitting, one *Mary Lovett*, then in the defendant's custody in the said gaol, for the purpose of the said *Mary Lovett* being conveyed by the said *John Brooks* to the said court of Quarter Sessions of the said borough and liberties, there to take her trial upon a bill of indictment for felony found against her. Plea, not guilty. At the trial before *Holroyd*, J., at the last summer assizes for *Leicestershire*, a verdict was taken for the crown, subject to the opinion of this Court, upon a case similar to that stated in *Rex* v. *Arnos* (a), with the following exceptions.

The borough of *Leicester* at present extends into six parishes, namely, *St. Martin's*, *St. Nicholas*, *All Saints*, *St. Margaret's*, *St. Mary's*, and *St. Leonard's*. Of these, the first three are wholly comprised within the ancient limits of the borough, over which the borough magistrates have exclusive jurisdiction. The latter three are situate, partly within the liberties of the borough, and over the parts so situate, the borough and county magistrates have concurrent jurisdiction. Jurisdiction over those parts was given to the borough by a charter of queen *Elizabeth*, which contained a saving to all persons of such privileges, pre-eminences, and jurisdictions, as they had before the granting of the charter. The felony for which *Mary Lovett* was indicted, was alleged to have been committed in that part of the parish of *St. Margaret*, which is subject to this concurrent jurisdiction. There is a rate in the

(a) 2 B. & A. 533.

nature of a county rate for those parts of the borough over which the borough magistrates have exclusive jurisdiction. The inhabitants of those parts do not contribute to the general county rate, but the inhabitants of the liberties contribute to that rate, and not to the borough rate.

Goulburn, for the crown, having referred to the case of *Rex* v. *Amos* (a), as decisive of the present, was stopped by the Court.

Reader, for the defendant, contended that the present case was distinguishable from that of *Rex* v. *Amos* in two particulars : first, because if the borough magistrates had power at their sessions to try offences committed within the liberties, and for which the parties charged had been committed to the county gaol, they would thereby necessarily oust the county magistrates of their jurisdiction, inasmuch as the latter had no right to attend and act at the borough sessions, where the borough magistrates had exclusive jurisdiction. That such an effect would be contrary to the saving clause in the charter of queen *Elizabeth,* which expressly reserved to the county magistrates their pre-eminences, privileges, and jurisdictions, one of which was, that before the granting of the charter, they had the exclusive right of trying persons charged with the commission of felonies within the county. And that in *Rex* v. *Amos,* no such difficulty arose, because there the borough magistrates had no exclusive jurisdiction. Second, that if the borough magistrates had authority to try prisoners under such circumstances, they would also have the power of ordering the allowance of the expenses of prosecutions, both for felonies and misdemeanours, out of the general county rate, over which, as they did not in any degree contribute to it, it would be exceedingly unjust that they should have any such power.

(a) 2 B. & A. 533.

PER CURIAM.—*Rex* v. *Amos* (a), decided that the borough magistrates, in cases where their jurisdiction was concurrent with that of the county magistrates, had a right to commit to the county gaol, and to order the prisoner to be brought before them for trial at their borough sessions. There is no substantial distinction between that case and the present, consequently we can do no other than come to the same decision here. The verdict, therefore, must stand.

Judgment for the crown.

(a) 2 B. & A. 533.

The KING v. WILLIAM HENRY ELLIS.

If several acts of felonious taking property, are so connected as to form one transaction, evidence of each taking may be received against the prisoner, so as to establish the specific felony charged in the indictment.
Affidavits are not admissible to aggravate punishment upon a conviction for felony, even though the record be removed into this court.

INDICTMENT against the prisoner for feloniously stealing six pieces of the current coin of this realm, called shillings, the property of *Susan Newman*. Second count, laid the property in *S. Newman*, and her nine children, naming them. Third count, charged the prisoner with feloniously stealing six pieces of the current coin of the realm, called sixpences, the property of *Susan Newman*; and the fourth count laid the property in the sixpences to be in *S. Newman*, and her nine children, naming them. This indictment was found at the gaol delivery, in and for the city of *Exeter*, and upon a suggestion made by the prisoner, supported by affidavits, that he could not have a fair and impartial trial at *Exeter*, by reason of prejudicial statements published respecting his case in the *Exeter* newspapers, it was afterwards removed into this court by certiorari; whereupon an order was made that a jury to try the indictment should be impannelled from the body of the county of *Devon*. At the last summer assizes for the said county, the prisoner was accordingly tried before

Littledale, J., on the Nisi Prius side, and found guilty. In support of the indictment, the facts proved were these :— The prisoner had been shopman in the employment of the prosecutrix, a general dealer, at *Exeter*. Suspicion being entertained of his honesty, on the 5th *September*, 1825, one of the sons of the prosecutrix, put seven shillings, and one half crown, and one sixpence, all marked in a particular manner into the shop till, in which there was no other silver at that time. The prisoner was then watched by the prosecutrix's son, who went in and out of the shop at different times, looking occasionally into the till, whilst customers came into the shop and purchased goods. When the till was first examined by the prosecutrix's son, it contained eleven and sixpence. After that he received one shilling from a customer and placed it in the till. Another customer soon afterwards paid one shilling to the prisoner, who was seen to go with it to the till, to put his hand into the till, and withdraw it clenched. He then left the counter, and was observed to raise his hand, clenched, to one of his waistcoat pockets. The till was examined again by the prosecutrix's son, and he found only 11*s.* 6*d.* instead of 13*s.* 6*d.*, which ought to have been there. The counsel for the prosecution was then proceeding to examine the witness to other acts of taking money from the till, when *Wilde*, Serjeant, for the prisoner, contended the prosecutrix must make her election, and confine herself to evidence of one felony, and ought not to be permitted to prove cumulative felonies. The learned Judge, after consulting with *Gaselee*, J., the other Judge of assize, over-ruled the objection, and allowed the prosecutrix's son to prove several takings by the prisoner. He proved that upon each of several inspections of the till after the prisoner had opened it, he found a less sum than he expected to find. On one occasion there was 8*s.* 6*d.* in the till, and he observed that most of that money was marked. He then put in 1*s.* 6*d.* more, and upon examining the till again he found only 6*s.* 6*d.* A constable was then sent for, and on searching the prisoner's person, there were 14s. 6d. found in his waist-coat pocket. Six of the shillings were part of the money marked by the prosecutrix's son, and placed by him in the till that morning.

C. F. Williams for the prosecution said, he relied upon the taking of the 3s. 6d. after the witness had added 1s. 6d. to the 8s. 6d, which was then in the till, and desired that the learned Judge would exclude from the consideration of the Jury the other takings; which was done accordingly. The Jury found the prisoner guilty.

Praed, on the fourth day of this term (the prisoner being present and placed at the bar), moved for a rule nisi for a new trial, on the ground that the learned Judge had improperly received evidence of more than one felony, the effect of which was to prejudice the prisoner; for, although at the conclusion of the case the counsel for the crown desired the attention of the jury to be confined to one act of taking, yet, as other acts of taking had been previously proved, the minds of the jury must, necessarily, have been biassed against the prisoner by such evidence, when they came to consider of their verdict.

ABBOTT, C. J.—There may be several counts in an indictment, each professing to charge the prisoner with a distinct and separate felony; and in such case it is usual for the Judge to confine the prosecutor to evidence of one single act of felony, in order that the prisoner may not be entangled in his defence; but where the act charged is of itself multifarious, and it becomes necessary to go through the whole of the evidence, in order to arrive at the truth, I think the Judge at the trial has a right to receive such evidence as he in his discretion may think proper for the ends of justice. The course of proceeding at a trial of this nature is entirely a matter of discretion in the Judge; and it can be no ground for granting a new trial, that he has exercised that discretion in a way which may be thought prejudicial to the prisoner. If we should lay down the rule so strictly as is contended for, it might lead to very serious consequences, for it might tend to the exclusion of evidence, in many cases essential to the ends of justice. It very often becomes necessary to go through a mass of evidence, in order to enable the Judge to fix upon that which establishes distinct proof of a specific crime. However, although we are of opinion that no rule ought now to be taken, yet if when the prisoner is brought up for judgment, and the learned Judge's report is read, it should occur to us that any injustice has been done towards the prisoner, he shall have the benefit of our opinion.

The prisoner was then remanded, and on a subsequent day he was brought up for judgment, when the Judge's report having been read,

Chitty and *Praed*, renewed the application, and contended; first, that inasmuch as each act of taking money from the till was a distinct felony, the evidence of any more than one act was inadmissible on the trial of the prisoner, because of its tendency to distract his attention, and confound him in his defence, and also of the effect it was likely to have on the mind of the Jury to his prejudice; and secondly, that if all the marked money was taken at one time, then the offence amounted only to embezzlement, which was different from that with which he was charged; and therefore, in either view of the case, the prosecutrix ought to have been put to her election, and not allowed to go into evidence of any more than one taking. They cited 1 East's P. C. 354, 519. *Rex* v. *Wylie* (a), *Rex* v. *Millard* (b), *Rex* v. *Taylor* (c), and *Rex* v. *Ball* (d).

(a) 1 N. R. 92. 2 Leach C.C. 983.   (c) R. & R. C. C. 63. 3 Bos. &
(b) R. & R. C. C. 245.   P. 596. 2 Leach C. C. 974.
        (d) R. & R. C. C. 132. 1 Camp. 324.

1826.

The KING

v.

ELLIS.

C. F. Williams, and *Coleridge,* for the Crown, were stopped by the Court.

BAYLEY, J. (*a*).—I am of opinion that it was in the discretion of the Judge to confine the prosecutrix to the proof of one felony, or to allow her to give evidence of other acts which were all tending to one entire transaction, and to shew that in fact but one felony was committed. Generally speaking, where an indictment contains charges of different unconnected felonies, the rule is to confine the prosecutor to one specific charge, in order that the prisoner may not be embarrassed in his defence; but where there are several felonies connected together, forming parts of one entire transaction, then one may be evidence to shew the character of the other. It seems to me, that all the evidence admitted in this case, had a tendency to shew that the prisoner was guilty of the felony in question. The evidence objected to, was in fact, nothing more than the history of the state of the till from the time when the marked money was put into it, until the period when it was found in the possession of the prisoner. Early in the morning the prosecutrix's son puts into the till seven shillings, a half-crown, and a sixpence, marked in a particular manner. He afterwards sees the prisoner go to the till, and then ascertains what is the state of the till. Unless he had done so, he could not tell whether the prisoner had abstracted any of the marked money at that time. The subsequent examinations of the till, only went to shew a history of the state of it; and if that particular question had been pointed out to the attention of the Court, probably the prisoner's counsel would have acceded to it. Inasmuch, therefore, as the whole of the evidence only went to give an account of the state of the drawer, until the ultimate period of the prisoner's detection, (and with that view it was absolutely necessary), I think

(*a*) *Abbott,* C. J., was absent.

there was nothing unfair towards the prisoner, in allowing the evidence to be received, and consequently that there is no ground for the present application.

HOLROYD, J.—I am of the same opinion. In the case of *Rex* v. *Egerton* (a), where the prisoner was indicted for robbing the prosecutor of a coat, the robbery having been committed by the prisoner's threatening to charge the prosecutor with an unnatural crime, I received evidence of a second ineffectual attempt to obtain a 1*l*. note from the prosecutor by similar threats, but reserved the point for the consideration of the Judges, and they were of opinion that the evidence was admissible to shew that the prisoner was guilty of the prior offence.

LITTLEDALE, J., concurred.

Rule refused.

N.B. The counsel for the prosecution tendered affidavits in aggravation of punishment; but the Court was clearly of opinion that in cases of felony such a mode of proceeding was not allowable. In cases of misdemeanour the rule was otherwise.

The COURT sentenced the prisoner to be transported for seven years.

(a) R. & R. C. C. 375.

GENERAL RULE.

KING'S BENCH PRISON,

MICHAELMAS TERM, 7 G. 4, 1826.

WHEREAS in and by a Rule of this Court, made *Monday* next after the *Octave of the Purification of the Blessed Virgin Mary,* in the 57th year of his late Majesty, King *George* the Third: It was "Ordered, that not more than three prisoners be suffered to lodge in one room in the King's Bench Prison at the same time, until the number of prisoners within the prison shall exceed 540, and not more than four when they exceed that number, until they exceed 700." It is hereby further Ordered, that not more than five prisoners shall be suffered to lodge in one room in the King's Bench Prison at the same time, until the whole number of prisoners within the prison shall exceed 900.

· BY THE COURT.

CASES

ARGUED AND DETERMINED

IN THE

◣ *COURT OF KING'S BENCH,*

IN

HILARY TERM,

IN THE SEVENTH AND EIGHTH YEARS OF THE REIGN OF GEORGE IV.

The KING *v.* SLYTHE.

1827.

*Tuesday,
January 23.*

THIS was a rule calling upon the defendant to shew cause why an information in the nature of *quo warranto* should not be filed against him, for usurping the office of free burgess of the borough of *Ipswich.* The rule was granted upon the affidavit of one *Clark,* setting forth the following facts:—According to the prevailing charter of the borough of *Ipswich* there are two bailiffs, elected annually on the 8th of *September,* for the good government of the town. It has always been the custom for the old bailiffs to preside as returning officers at the court holden on the 8th *September,* for the election of the new bailiffs and other officers. At a court holden on the 8th *September,* 1824, *A.* and *B.,* the old bailiffs, presided as bailiffs and returning officers, and *Seckamp* and *Hammond* were elected bailiffs. In *Easter* term, 1825, informations in the nature of *quo warranto* were filed against *Seckamp* and *Hammond,* and in

A corporator who has voted at an election of corporate officers, is not a competent relator to impeach that election, on the ground of an objection to the presiding officer; at least without shewing that he was ignorant of the objection when he voted at the election.

Trinity term, 1825, they disclaimed, and judgment of ouster was signed against them. On the 14th *June*, 1825, a *mandamus* issued to the bailiffs, burgesses, &c., of the borough, commanding them to assemble on the 21st July then next, and elect bailiffs. At that meeting *Batley*, a common-councilman, *C.* and *D.*, two of the portmen, and several other burgesses, attended, and *Seckamp* and *Hammond* were elected bailiffs. *Batley* presided at that meeting, and *Seckamp* and *Hammond* were sworn in before him. By the immemorial custom of the borough the portmen take precedence of the common-councilmen at all corporate meetings. At the court holden on the 8th *September*, 1825, *Seckamp* and *Hammond* presided, and were re-elected bailiffs for the following year. In *Michaelmas* term, 1825, rules for *quo warranto* informations against *Seckamp* and *Hammond* were made absolute, but were not further proceeded in, and they continued to execute the office of bailiffs for the entire year. At a court holden before them on the 15th *June*, 1826, *Slythe* (the defendant) was admitted and sworn a freeman. The affidavits on the other side merely stated that *Clark* (the relator) voted at the election of bailiffs in *September*, 1825, when *Seckamp* and *Hammond* presided.

Campbell (with whom was *Patteson*) shewed cause. The objection intended to be raised against the defendant's title is, that *Seckamp* and *Hammond*, the persons before whom he was admitted and sworn, were not *de jure* the bailiffs of the borough, not having been legally elected to that office. In the first place, *Clark*, the present relator, is not competent to raise that objection, because, as he was present and voted at their election, he cannot now impeach it, either directly as against themselves, or collaterally by impugning the title of a burgess admitted and sworn before them. *Rex* v. *Trevenen* (a). (Here the Court stopped him.)

(a) 2 B. & A. 339.

Adam, contrà. The general rule, as laid down in the case cited, that a corporator who has concurred in an election is estopped from afterwards impeaching it, cannot be denied; but it does not apply to this case. Rules for *quo warranto* informations have already been made absolute against *Seckamp* and *Hammond,* so that the relator here is not originating a measure to disturb the peace of the borough, which it is the object of the rule to preserve, but is merely following up, and rendering more effectual and complete, that which the Court has already done. There is nothing to shew that he knew of any objection to *Seckamp* and *Hammond* at the time of the election of bailiffs in September, 1825, and his concurrence in that election having been *bonâ fide,* and in ignorance of its invalidity, ought not to operate to his prejudice now.

1827.

The KING
v.
SLYTHE.

In the two following cases a similar question being raised, the Court reserved their opinion upon this, until they had heard the arguments upon those.

The KING *v.* LANE.
The KING *v.* COBBOLD.

SIMILAR rules had been obtained against these defendants, the bailiffs of the same borough. They had been elected at a court holden on 8th September, 1826, at which *Seckamp* and *Hammond* presided. One *Monk* was the relator in these cases. The objection raised against the title of the defendants was, that they had been elected before *Seckamp* and *Hammond,* and that the latter were not good presiding officers. It appeared in these, as in the former case, that the relator had attended and voted at the election in *September,* 1825.

A corporator who has voted at an election of corporate officers, is not a competent relator to impeach that election on the ground of an objection to the presiding officer; *at least* without shewing that he was ignorant of the objection when he voted at the election.

Campbell and *Patteson,* against the rule, were stopped by the Court.

Tindal, S. G., and *Alderson,* in support of the rule. The title of *Seckamp* and *Hammond* was faulty from the beginning. The objection to it arose at their election in *July*, 1825, at a meeting assembled together in obedience to a *mandamus* from this Court. *Batley* presided at that meeting, and he was a common councilman, who had no power or authority to preside or act as returning officer on the occasion. But there is nothing to shew that *Monk*, the present relator, attended the meeting called in pursuance of the *mandamus*, or took any part in that election; nor does it appear that when he concurred in the subsequent election of *Seckamp* and *Hammond* in *September* 1825, he knew of the objection previously existing against them. It should, therefore, seem, upon the principle acted upon in *Rex* v. *Morris* (a), that his concurrence in that second election does not estop him from coming forward as a relator on the present occasion.

ABBOTT, C. J.—It is a general rule of corporation law, that a corporator is estopped from coming forward as a relator to impeach a title conferred by an election in which he has concurred, or the titles of those mediately or immediately claiming through that election. In the cases cited, *Rex* v. *Morris* and *Rex* v. *Trevenen*, the point now relied upon was considered, and some importance does appear to have been attached to the question whether the person coming forward as a relator were or were not cognizant of the particulars of the case at the time when he voted at the former election. In many cases, however, it would be impossible to ascertain whether the relator had acted with knowledge or in ignorance of the particular facts, and to allow such an inquiry to be made in every instance, would, as it seems to me, be productive of great inconvenience, without any corresponding advantage. I think every corporator may fairly be presumed to be cognizant of circumstances which have recently occurred in the corporation to which he belongs; at least until he shews the contrary.

(a) 3 East, 213.

The relators in these cases both concurred in the last election of *Seckamp* and *Hammond;* and the question is whether we shall allow them thus indirectly to raise the question of the validity of that election. It has been contended that they did not concur in the prior election, and perhaps they did not; but still it must be presumed, the contrary not being shewn, that they were cognizant of the circumstances under which it took place. For these reasons, I am of opinion that these relators are estopped, and, therefore, that these rules must be discharged. But as I feel anxious to prevent any misunderstanding upon this point, I think it right to add, that if a party should concur in an election, in honest ignorance of some circumstance rendering that election void, and should afterwards come before the Court and shew that such an objection exists, that it came to his knowledge after the election, and that it is a matter deserving of inquiry; I would by no means have it inferred from the present decision that such a party ought not to be heard.

LITTLEDALE, J.—Concurred (*a*).

Rules discharged (*b*).

(*a*) *Bayley,* J. was gone to chambers, and *Holroyd,* J. was absent through indisposition.

(*b*) Afterwards, in the course of this term, similar rules against *Lane* and *Cobbold,* obtained by relators to whom there was no objection, came on for argument. The only point made was, that the affidavits were insufficient for not stating positively, that the defendants exercised the offices which they were charged with usurping; the allegation being that the deponents *had been informed and believed* that they exercised those offices. The objection, however, was overruled, the Court being of opinion, upon the authority of *Rex v Harwood,* 2 East, 177, that these affidavits, uncontradicted, were sufficient. These rules, therefore, were made absolute. And see *Rex v. Slythe, post.*

1827.

BOVILL and another, Assignees of the estate and effects of ANSTICE and THORNHILL, Bankrupts, *v.* HAMMOND.

*Thursday,
January* 25.

Three ship-brokers agreed in writing with a ship-owner to freight his vessel at a certain commission, dividing profits of commission. One of the brokers alone paid and received money on account of the ship, and delivered to the owners an account charging a liquidated sum for commission. The owner acquiesced in the accuracy of the account, but objected to the charge for commission, being too much, but which the broker retained in his hands. There was no adjustment of accounts between the brokers: Held, that money had and received would not lie by the two brokers against the third, for their share of the commission.

THIS was an action of assumpsit for money had and received by the defendant, to the use of the plaintiffs, as assignees. Plea, non-assumpsit. At the trial before *Abbott*, C. J. at the sittings in *London* after last Michaelmas term, it appeared in evidence, that before, the transaction in question, the bankrupts carried on business in partnership as ship brokers, and that the defendant carried on the like business on his own account. In *February*, 1826, the bankrupts and the defendant signed a written agreement with the owners of a vessel called the *Earl of Liverpool*, then bound for *Van Dieman's Land*, by which they undertook to procure freight and passengers for the ship on her outward voyage, charging a certain commission, of which the bankrupts were to receive one-half and the defendant the other. Both parties exerted themselves to procure a cargo for the vessel, the defendant making all disbursements and receiving all monies due on account of the ship. After the ship was freighted and despatched, the defendant sent in an account to the owners, of disbursements, &c., amounting to 1300*l.* and charging five per cent. commission on the business, making 65*l.* The owners admitted the correctness of the account, but objected to settle it, inasmuch as the defendant, as they alleged, charged 5*l.* too much for commission. It appeared that the defendant had retained in his hands sufficient to cover the amount of all disbursements, and the full amount of commission claimed. During the lading of the ship, *Anstice* and *Thornhill* had become bankrupts. Amongst other objections taken at the trial was, that the agreement entered into between the bankrupts and the defendant made them partners *quoad* this transaction, and consequently that no action could be maintained at law, the account being unadjusted. The learned judge upon this objection directed a nonsuit, but saved the point for the consideration of the Court.

Gurney now moved for a rule to shew cause why the nonsuit should not be set aside, and a verdict entered for the plaintiffs for 30*l.* This cannot be said to be a partnership transaction, in which accounts remain to be settled. Here the defendant has been reimbursed by the owners of the ship the whole amount of the monies he had ever expended, and has received for commission all that was ever expected to be paid. The account delivered was not an account between *Anstice, Thornhill* and *Hammond,* but a demand which *Hammond* made upon the ship. There were no other accounts between the bankrupts and *Hammond.* There is a liquidated sum received by the defendant on account of the agreement for commission on the freight, and of that sum the bankrupts are entitled to receive one-half. The disputed sum of 5*l.* was between the defendant and the owners, but for the moiety of the 60*l.* the plaintiffs are clearly entitled to maintain this action. It would be extremely hard to drive the plaintiffs into equity to settle an account which is clearly liquidated.

ABBOTT, C.J.—I think we ought not to grant a rule in this case. The general rule with respect to partnerships is, that an account between partners, whether general, or in a particular transaction, such as this is, cannot be taken at law. If the partners themselves had settled the amount *inter se,* and struck a balance, that would make a difference. In the present case the partners have not settled the account as between themselves. The only ground upon which this case could be distinguished from an ordinary case of partnership is this, that here the payments have been made, and the money received, by the same person. That certainly is a circumstance which would render an account between themselves less necessary, than where one partner had paid and received one sum, and another partner another; but still I am of opinion, that as there was no account taken and settled between these partners, no action at law can be maintained by the plaintiffs against the defendant. To hold otherwise, would be breaking down a general rule of law, and introducing nice distinctions, which I think it is proper, as far as possible, to avoid. I am, therefore, of opinion, that the nonsuit was right.

BAYLEY, J.—There is so much of doubt in this case, that I should have been better satisfied if the rule were granted. In this case the business was to be done for a compensation to be paid to *Anstice, Thornhill* and *Hammond.* In the course of the business disbursements are made solely by *Hammond ;* he renders an account of them to the owners of the ship, and at the same time claims against them the sum of 65*l.*, due for commission, which, if it was wholly allowed, would ultimately have been to be divided between him and *Anstice* and *Thornhill.* The owners of the ship, as I understand, acquiesed in the accuracy of the account, with the exception of the sum of 65*l.* retained for commission, which they insist ought to be reduced to 60*l.* Now I think that when the defendant got that sum of money into his possession for the joint benefit of himself and the present plaintiffs, all other partnership matters being entirely at an end, and the sum in dispute being reduced to that single item, and that only, the policy of the law of partnership does not require that the plaintiffs should go into a Court of Equity to take an account, when all that the defendant can be called upon to account for, is one moiety of a liquidated sum of 60*l.* This strikes me to be the reason and justice of the case.

LITTLEDALE, J. (a)—In the present case neither the plaintiffs as assignees, nor the bankrupts as partners, appear ever to have agreed to the account settled between the defendant and the ship-owners. If two persons engage jointly in a particular business, and one is the hand both to pay and receive, and if the form of the account shews that he has received so much money on account of the other, I

(a) *Holroyd,* J. was absent.

agree that in that case, an action at law might be maintained for money had and received. That, however, is not the case here. There is here no settlement of account, even as between the defendant and the ship-owners; for after all there is a sum of 5*l.* in dispute; and, therefore, I think no action at law can be maintained. I should regret breaking in upon a general rule of law, where it appears that the account is not assented to by all parties. The rule is, that an action at law cannot be maintained by one partner against another, unless the account be adjusted between them some way or other.

Rule refused.

Campbell for the defendant.

STRONG and others *v.* HART and others.

ASSUMPSIT for the freight of a cargo of fish from *St. John's, Newfoundland,* to *Bilboa,* in *Spain.* Plea, *non assumpsit,* and issue thereon. At the trial before *Abbott,* C. J., at the *London* adjourned sittings after last term, the case was this. The plaintiffs were merchants at *Poole,* and owners, with one *Allen,* since dead, who was also captain, of the brig *Atlantic.* The defendants were merchants in *London.* The cargo was originally consigned to *Page* and *Noble,* the defendants' agents, at *Oporto,* and bills of lading were signed by the captain, making the cargo deliverable at *Oporto* to *Page* and *Noble,* or their assigns, he or they paying freight for the same at the rate therein specified. The captain had orders from the defendants to follow the directions of *Page* and *Noble,* and a higher freight was to be paid if the ship was sent to a second port to deliver. When the captain arrived with the ship and cargo at *Oporto, Page* and *Noble,* considering the market there unfavourable,

The captain and co-owner of a ship signed bills of lading making the cargo deliverable to the consignees, or their assigns, he or they paying freight. He delivered the cargo to the consignees, and took a bill for the freight, which was dishonoured. In an action against the consignors for the freight:— Held, first, that the jury were rightly directed to find for the

defendants, if they thought the captain took the bill as a matter of preference and convenience to himself; and, secondly, that it lay upon the plaintiffs to prove that he took it from necessity, if the fact were so.

directed him to proceed to *Bilboa,* and to place the cargo under the care of *Acha Basozabel* & Co. there. He accordingly proceeded to *Bilboa,* placed the cargo under the care of *Acha Basozabel* & Co., demanded his freight from them, and received from them a bill of exchange for the amount, drawn by them upon *Domingo de Agaste,* their agent in *London.* It did not clearly appear whether the captain demanded payment of the freight in cash, and took the bill to accommodate *Acha Basozabel* & Co.; or whether he took the bill as a matter of choice, and as more convenient to himself. The captain remitted the bill to his co-owners in a letter, stating that he should return to *Newfoundland* for another freight, instead of returning to *England.* The bill was presented for acceptance to the drawer, by whom it was accepted. Before the bill became due, *Acha Basozabel* & Co. stopped payment, whereupon one of the plaintiffs wrote to the defendants, among other matters, as follows:—" You have no doubt been informed that *Acha Basozabel* & Co., of *Bilboa,* have suspended their payments. I hold a bill of their drawing, on *Domingo Agaste,* and accepted by him; will you have the goodness to say your opinion as to his respectability?" To this the defendants replied as follows :—" We have heard of *Acha* & Co.'s failure, and we fancy their agent here, Mr. *Agaste,* will be materially affected by their stoppage, but we hope he may be good for your bill, if not a large one." The bill was dishonoured when due, and the plaintiffs gave no notice of the dishonour either to the drawers or the defendants, but commenced this action. It was contended on the part of the defendants, that the bill having been received by the captain under such circumstances, amounted to payment of the freight; that the cargo being, by the tenor of the bill of lading, deliverable to " *Page* and *Noble,* or their assigns, he or they paying freight for the same," the captain was bound to hold the cargo until the freight was paid; that the whole transaction shewed that the captain had taken the bill as payment, and for his own convenience; and that neither he nor his co-owners contemplated looking to the defendants for payment of the freight until the parties to the bill had failed; and that, at all events, the plaintiffs were bound to have given the defendants notice of the dishonour of the bill. For the plaintiffs, on the other hand, it was insisted, that the defendants could not rely upon the bill as amounting to a payment of the freight, without proving distinctly that *Acha* & Co. had tendered payment of the freight in cash, and that the captain had taken the bill as a matter of preference, for his own convenience; that he was not bound to hold the cargo until the freight was paid; that the defendants, not being parties to the bill, and having no remedy over upon it, were not entitled to have notice of its dishonour; and that, even if they were so entitled, the letter written to them by the plaintiffs, announcing the failure of *Acha* & Co., amounted to such notice. The Lord Chief Justice was of opinion that the captain was not bound to hold the cargo until the freight was paid, and that the plaintiffs were not bound to give the defendants notice of the dishonour of the bill; but he left it to the jury, as a question of fact, to say, whether the captain took the bill as a matter of preference, and for his own convenience, without demanding payment in cash; or whether he took it for the accommodation of *Acha* & Co., and because he could not obtain payment in cash: directing them, if they were of the former opinion, to find for the defendants, and if of the latter, for the plaintiffs. The jury found for the defendants.

Tindal, S. G. now moved for a rule *nisi* for a new trial, upon the ground of misdirection by the learned judge. He cited *Marsh* v. *Pedder* (a) as an authority, to shew that the

(a) 4 Camp. 257, the abstract of which is thus given:—" *Where there is a charterparty* covenanting for payment of freight on a right and true delivery of the goods at a foreign port, the freighter is not discharged by the master there taking from the freighter's agent, who was furnished with funds to pay him the freight, a bill of exchange upon a third person, by whom it is accepted, if the bill is not duly honoured, although the agent fail with the amount of the freight in his hands, unless the master had the offer of a cash payment, and preferred the bill for his own convenience."

captain, by taking the bill in payment of the freight, could not discharge the consignors from their liability, unless it was proved distinctly that he had been offered payment of the freight in cash, and had taken the bill as a matter of preference; and contended that the *onus* of proving the fact lay on the defendants, who had given no evidence upon the subject. He also referred to *Tapley* v. *Martens* (a) as an analogous case, where it was held, that the taking of a bill from a consignee in payment of freight, which bill turned out to be of no value, did not release the consignor from his liability to pay the freight.

ABBOTT, C. J.—I think the present case is distinguishable from that of *Marsh* v. *Pedder*. In that case there was a charterparty under seal, binding the charterers to the payment of the freight. Here there was no charterparty, and the goods were, by the terms of the bill of lading, made deliverable " to *Page* and *Noble*, or their assigns, *he or they paying freight* for the same." But there are other peculiarities about this case. Before the bill became due, one of the plaintiffs, in a letter to the defendants, communicated the fact of *Acha* & Co. having stopped payment, stated that he held a bill drawn by them upon and accepted by *Agaste*, and requested the defendants to give him their opinion whether it was probable the bill would be paid. That letter was answered by the defendants, stating that the failure of *Acha* & Co. would probably greatly affect *Agaste*, but expressing an opinion that the bill, if not a large one, would probably be paid. Now that correspondence shewed pretty clearly, that the plaintiffs did not, at that time, entertain the idea of looking to the defendants as liable to the payment of the freight, in the event of the bill being dishonoured. Again, the captain, who it must be remembered

(a) 8 T. R. 451, the abstract of which is this:—" *A.* wishing to send goods to *B.* at *X.*, employed *C.* to carry them and deliver them to *B.*, and engaged to pay *C.* for the freight. *C.* on delivering them according to the order, took a bill of exchange from *B.* drawn on *A.*, which was never paid: Held, that *A.* was liable to pay the amount of the freight to *C.*, notwithstanding the bill of exchange.

was a co-owner with the plaintiffs, remitted the bill to them in a letter, stating that he should not return to *England*, but should make another voyage to *Newfoundland*, with the hope of obtaining another freight from thence; which was very strong evidence, in my opinion, to shew that he had taken the bill, not because he could not obtain cash, but as a matter of preference, and for his own convenience. The jury took this view of the case, and I think properly; and upon that ground, as well as upon the ground that the peculiar circumstances of this case take it out of the general rule laid down in *Marsh* v. *Pedder*, I think the verdict was right. With respect to the other case cited, that has no bearing upon the present, because the bill there taken was drawn upon the very party who originally agreed to pay the freight.

BAYLEY, J.—I think the general rule laid down in *Marsh* v. *Pedder* does not apply to the present case. Where the captain of a ship is left to obtain payment of the freight in the best mode he can, and can obtain no mode of payment except a bill of exchange, he has no option; he must take the bill. But if he can obtain a better mode of payment, and still takes the bill, he has an option, which he must be presumed to have exercised, and he is bound by taking the bill. The correspondence adverted to by my Lord Chief Justice fully authorized him in leaving it to the jury to say, whether the captain took the bill from necessity, or from choice, and, looking at the evidence altogether, I see no reason to be dissatisfied with the conclusion at which the jury arrived on that subject. If the contrary was the fact, and the captain took the bill because he could obtain no other mode of payment, the *onus probandi* in that respect clearly lay upon the plaintiffs, and not on the defendants.

LITTLEDALE, J. concurred.(a)

Rule refused.

(a) *Holroyd*, J. was absent.

ROGERS *v.* BRODERIP, Esq.

Saturday,
January 27.

The 2 *Geo.* 3,
c. 28, which
gives addi-
tional protec-
tion to justices
in cases of ac-
tions brought
against them
for any thing
done *in pur-*
suance of that
act, but which
does not re-
quire notice of
action, does
not deprive
them of their
right to the
notice re-
quired by the
24 *Geo.* 2, c.
44, which re-
quires notice
in cases of ac-
tions brought
against jus-
tices for any
thing done *in*
execution of
their office.
Therefore,
where in an
action against
a magistrate,
under the 2
Geo. 3, c. 28,
the plaintiff
proved service
of a notice not
perfectly con-
formable with
the requisites
of the 24 *Geo.*
2, c. 44, and
was thereupon
nonsuited :—
Held, that the
nonsuit was
right.

THIS was an action brought against the defendant, one
of the magistrates of the *Thames Police Office,* in respect
of an alleged wrongful act committed by him as such
magistrate, under the statute, 2 *Geo.* 3, c. 28, commonly called the *Bum Boat Act* (*a*). The jurisdiction
given by that statute is confined to the four counties of
Middlesex, Essex, Surrey, and *Kent.* It enacts, that if any
action shall be commenced against any justice of the peace
for any thing done in pursuance of that act, the same shall
be laid in *London* or *Middlesex,* and not elsewhere; that
every such action shall be commenced within six months
next after the cause of action accrued; that if any such
action shall be commenced in any other place, or after the
expiration of six months from the time when the cause of
action accrued, the jury shall find a verdict for the defendant; and that in every such action, wherein the defendant obtains judgment, he shall have treble costs. But
the act does not any where require that any notice of action
shall be given to a justice of the peace previous to the
commencement thereof. At the trial before *Abbott,* C. J.
at the adjourned *Middlesex* sittings after last term, the plaintiff put in evidence a notice which had been served upon
the defendant, and which was framed in pursuance of the
directions of the statute, 24 *Geo.* 2, c. 44, s. 1 (*b*), except

(*a*) Continued and amended by
the subsequent statutes, 1 & 2 *Geo.*
4, c. 118; 3 *Geo.* 4, c. 55; and
6 *Geo.* 4, c. 21.

(*b*) Which enacts, that " no writ
shall be sued out against, nor any
copy of any process at the suit of a
subject shall be served on, any justice of the peace for any thing by
him done in the execution of his
office, until notice in writing of
such intended writ or process shall
have been delivered to him, or left

at the usual place of his abode, by
the attorney or agent for the party
who intends to sue, at least one
calendar month before the suing
out or serving the same, in which
notice shall be clearly and explicitly contained the cause of action;
on the back of which notice shall
be indorsed the name of such attorney, with the place of his abode,
who shall be entitled to the fee of
twenty shillings for preparing and
serving such notice."

that the name and place of abode of the plaintiff's attorney
were not indorsed upon the back of it; whereupon it being
objected that proof of service of a notice of action was
necessary under s. 3 of that statute (*a*), and that the notice
given in evidence was insufficient, the Lord Chief Justice
was of opinion that the objection was fatal, and accordingly
directed a nonsuit.

Chitty now moved for a rule *nisi* to set aside the nonsuit,
and for a new trial. If the present action had been founded
on the statute, 24 *Geo.* 2, c. 44, which specifically requires
notice, it must be admitted that it could not be maintained,
because the notice produced did not comply with all the
requisites of that act (*b*).   But this action is founded upon
a subsequent and different act of parliament, by the provisions of which it must be regulated independently of and
without reference to the prior statute. The 2 *Geo.* 3, c. 28,
upon which this action is brought, provides and specifies
the form and mode according to which actions commenced
against justices of the peace, for acts done in pursuance of
that statute, shall be conducted, and makes no mention of
any notice; clearly, therefore, warranting the inference that
no notice was intended to be required. It gives peculiar
privileges to the magistrate in the case of his obtaining a
verdict, and throws an extensive protection round him; and
it would not be just to increase those privileges and enlarge

(*a*) Which enacts, that " no such
plaintiff shall recover any verdict
against any justice of the peace,
where the action is grounded on
any act of the defendant as such
justice of the peace, unless it is
proved upon the trial that such
notice was given; but in default
thereof, such justice of the peace
shall recover a verdict and costs."

(*b*) Vide *Lovelace* v. *Curry*, 7

T. R. 631. *Sabin* v. *De Burgh*, 2
Camp. 196. *Strickland* v. *Ward*,
7 T. R. 631, in notis. *Weller* v.
Toke, 9 East, 364. *Taylor* v. *Fenwick*, 7 T. R. 635, cited by *Lawrence*, J. *Osborn* v. *Gough*, 3 Bos.
& Pul. 551. *Prestidge* v. *Woodman*, ante, Vol. II. 43. *Morgan*
v. *Palmer*, *ante*, Vol. IV. 283. *James*
v. *Swift*, *ante*, Vol. VI. 625. *Gim-
bert* v. *Coyney*, 1 M'Clel. & Y. 469.

that protection, by incorporating with this the provisions of a prior and distinct act of parliament. The act in question may be considered as a local act, for its operation is confined to four counties; and its operation cannot be extended by incorporating with it the general act, 24 *Geo.* 2, c. 44, which was passed for more general purposes, and was made, to a certain degree, *alio intuitu.* The plaintiff was not bound to prove any notice at all, and if so, he ought not to be prejudiced by proving one, which under other circumstances would have been defective, and fatal to the action.

ABBOTT, C. J.—It is quite clear that the plaintiff and his legal advisers were of opinion that a notice of action was necessary in this case; and it is equally clear, and indeed admitted, that the notice served upon the defendant was informal and defective. I think the plaintiff was right in his notion of the law, but he has, unfortunately for himself, been guilty of a fatal error in his attempt to comply with the requisites of the law. The terms of the statute, 24 *Geo.* 2, c. 44, s. 1, are as general and comprehensive as language could make them; for it requires a previous notice of every action commenced against any justice of the peace, *not* for any thing done by him *in pursuance of that act,* but for any thing done by him *in the execution of his office:* rendering the notice necessary, therefore, in any action against a justice of the peace, upon whatever statute that action may be founded. Then upon what general principle, or upon what particular provision in either of these acts of parliament, can it be contended that the notice required by the one is not necessary in an action founded on the other? I can see no ground for the argument in either point of view, nor any reason why the privileges and protection given to the magistrate by one statute, should deprive him of those which were previously given him by another. I am, therefore, of opinion that the plaintiff was properly nonsuited, and that there is no pretence for granting the present application.

The other judges concurred.

Rule refused (a).

(a) Vide *Lewis* v. *Smith*, Holt's N. P. C. 27. *Stringer* v. *Martyr*, 6 Esp. N. P. C. 134. *Bird* v. *Gunston*, 2 Chit. Rep. 459. *Briggs* v. *Evelyn*, 2 H. Bl. 114. *Bax* v. *Jones*, 5 Price, 168. *Mayhew* v. *Locke*, 2 Marsh. 377; 7 Taunt. 63, S. C. *Stears* v. *Smith*, 6 Esp. N. P. C. 138. *Weston* v. *Fournier*, 14 East, 491. *Ex parte Martin, ante,* 65. *Parton* v. *Williams*, 3 Barn. & Ald. 331. *Smith* v. *Wiltshire*, 5 J. B. Moore, 332. *Nestor* v. *Newcomb, ante,* Vol. IV. 476. 776; 3 B. & C. 159.

GOLDSTEIN v. E. FOSS.

THIS was an action for a libel. The declaration contained four counts. The first count stated, by way of inducement, that the plaintiff, before the time when, &c., was a person of good name, fame, &c., and had for many years carried on business as a merchant, in partnership with one *Castle*, and had never, until the publication of the libel hereinafter mentioned, been suspected of swindling or cheating, and then proceeded as follows:—" And whereas also, before the time when, &c., divers persons had been associated together under the name and description of ' The Society of Guardians for the Protection of Trade against Swindlers and Sharpers;' and the defendant, under colour and pretence of being the secretary of the said society, had from time to time published, and was accustomed to publish, certain printed reports, for the purpose of denoting and signifying to the members of the said society, the names of such persons as were deemed and considered swindlers and sharpers, and improper persons to be proposed and balloted

Saturday, January 27.

Where a declaration for a libel concerning the plaintiff set out the following matter, " Society of Guardians for the Protection of Trade against Swindlers and Sharpers, &c. I (defendant) am directed to inform you that G. (plaintiff) is reported to this society as improper to be proposed to be balloted for as a member thereof," (meaning that plaintiff was a swindler and sharper, and

an improper person to be a member of the said society) :—Held, after verdict, that the innuendo was not warranted by the libel, and that the words themselves were not actionable, for want of a proper colloquium.

for as members of the said society, to wit, at, &c. Yet the said defendant, well knowing the premises, but contriving, &c., on, &c., did compose, print and publish, and cause and procure to be composed, printed and published in a certain printed paper, a certain false, scandalous, malicious and defamatory libel, containing, among other things, the false and scandalous, malicious and libellous matter following, of and concerning the said plaintiff, in the way of his trade and business: that is to say, " No. 10. Correspondence; 1825. Society of Guardians for the Protection of Trade against Swindlers and Sharpers; *Richard Clarke*, Esq. Chamberlain of *London*, President; *George Bridges*, Esq. Alderman and M.P., Vice President; Messrs. W. *Praed* and Co. Bankers, Treasurers; I (meaning the said defendant) am directed to inform you, that the persons undernamed, or using the firms of *Goldstein*, (meaning the plaintiff,) *Castles* and *Co.*, 51, *Mark Lane*, and *Benjamin Foster Baker, Hackney Road*, are reported to this society as improper to be proposed to be balloted for as members thereof," *(thereby then and there meaning that the said plaintiff was a swindler and sharper, and an improper person to be a member of the said society.)* The three other counts were more general, leaving out the introductory averment as to the objects of the society, and the character and proceedings of the defendant. Plea, the general issue. At the trial before *Abbott*, C. J., at the Sittings in *Westminster* after last *Hilary* Term, the plaintiff had a verdict with 100*l.* damages. In *Easter* Term last,

Campbell obtained a rule nisi to arrest the judgment, on the ground that there was no count in the declaration which would support the verdict. The first count, which was the least objectionable, was ill, for two reasons; first, that the colloquium or introductory averment was not connected with the statement of the alleged libel, so as to authorise a meaning beyond the ordinary acceptation of the words, and therefore the innuendo affixed to the libel was not warranted;

and, secondly, the matter *per se* was not libellous. As to the other counts they were clearly bad for want of an induce-ment. He cited *Barham's* case (a); *Holt* v. *Scholfield* (b), and *Hawkes* v. *Hawkey* (c).

Brougham and *Chitty* (with whom were *Scarlett* and *F. Pollock*) now shewed cause, and contended that upon the whole declaration there was sufficient in the first count to connect the colloquium or introductory matter with the state-ment of the libel, and consequently to authorise the innu-endo which accompanied the words. It must be understood that the society mentioned in the libel is the same as that described in the colloquium, and if the innuendo is rejected as surplusage, as it may be, *Roberts* v. *Camden* (d), there will be no ambiguity; *Tuchin's* case (e). Admitting the col-loquium and statement of the libel not to be sufficiently connected, still the innuendo was warranted in order to remove ambiguity, and the finding of the jury established the truth of the innuendo, *Coles* v. *Haveland* (f). At all events the libel, as the declaration alleges, being published of the plaintiff in the way of his business, is actionable without an innuendo, and therefore the verdict may be sus-tained. The words must be understood in their popular sense, that in which all mankind must understand them, *Woolnoth* v. *Meadows* (g), and it is impossible to say that the statement contained in this libel has not an injurious effect upon the plaintiff's character, considering the object and proceedings of the society, of which he is announced to be an unfit person to become a member. The jury have put this interpretation upon the libel, and their finding is well warranted.

Campbell (with whom were *Gurney* and *Bolland*) contrà,

(a) 4 Co. Rep. 20 a.   (e) St. Tr. 1095.
(b) 6 T. R. 691.   (f) Cro. Eliz. 250.
(c) 8 East, 427.   (g) 5 East, 463.
(d) 9 East, 93.

admitted that if the introductory part of the declaration were connected with the subsequent statement of the libel, the innuendo might have been justified, on the authority of *Hawkes* v. *Hawkey* (a), but that is not so, for here the innuendo refers to the *said* society. What society? The introductory matter speaks of a society, and so does the libel. Then it is clear that there is no connexion between these parts of the declaration. If so, the innuendo is not authorised, because its object is to extend the meaning of the words, and not merely to explain an ambiguity, which is the proper office of an innuendo. In *Coles* v. *Haveland* there was probably something in the introductory part of the declaration to justify the innuendo. The declaration is not set out in the report. As the innuendo here is not warranted, then the only question is, whether the matter charged as libellous is *per se* actionable. It is quite clear that it will not bear the meaning imputed to it by the innuendo; and if it is reconciled with an innocent interpretation, the verdict cannot be supported. The plaintiff may be an unfit person to be a member of the society in question, but that unfitness might arise from many circumstances, without any reflection upon his character for morality, or his honesty as a tradesman. Standing alone, therefore, the matter is not actionable, and as the innuendo is not warranted by the import of the statement, the judgment must be arrested.

ABBOTT, C. J.—The first question which presents itself for our consideration is, whether the matter published by the defendant is, upon this record, connected with the introductory averment in which it is alleged that there existed a society for the protection of trade against swindlers and sharpers, and that the defendant, as secretary of the society, was in the habit of publishing printed reports for the purpose of denoting and signifying to the members the names of such persons as were deemed and considered

(a) 8 East, 427.

swindlers and sharpers. If the matter published by the defendant were sufficiently connected with the introductory averment, I should have no doubt that the action was maintainable, but upon looking at the record, it does not appear to me that they are connected. The introduction stands by itself, without any reference being had to what is afterwards set out as libellous. After setting out the introductory averments, the pleader goes on to allege that the defendant, intending to injure the plaintiff, composed and published of and concerning him in a certain printed paper a certain false and defamatory libel, of and concerning the plaintiff in the way of his trade and business. There is not here one word of reference to the previous introduction. The declaration then proceeds to set out the libellous matter, at the close of which there is this innuendo: " thereby then and there meaning that the said plaintiff was a swindler and a sharper, and an improper person to be a member of the *said* society." Now the introduction mentions a society, and the libel itself also mentions a society. I think it is impossible, therefore, to construe the *said society*, mentioned in the innuendo, to be the society mentioned in the introductory averment. The more natural meaning of the innuendo, is to refer the words " *said society*," to the society mentioned in the libel itself, as the last antecedent to that mentioned in the introduction. This is, I think, the proper construction of this part of the record. Then comes to be considered the question whether the publication itself, in its natural sense, having no regard to any introductory matter, or to any thing but what is to be collected from the paper itself, is libellous. The paper itself is in these words: " No. 10. Correspondence; 1825. Society of Guardians for the Protection of Trade against Swindlers and Sharpers; *Richard Clark*, Esq., Chamberlain of *London*, President; *George Bridges*, Esq., Alderman and M.P., Vice-President; Messrs. *W. Praed*, and Co., Bankers, Treasurers; I am directed to inform you, that the persons under-named, or using the firms of *Gold-*

stein, *Castles*, and Co., 51, *Mark Lane*, are reported to
this society as improper to be proposed to be balloted for
as members thereof." Then the pleader thinks fit to introduce this allegation by way of innuendo, " thereby then and
there meaning that the said plaintiff was a swindler and
sharper, and an improper person to be a member of the
said society." It appears to me, however, as by no means
following, that because a man may be an improper person
to be proposed as a member of a society for the protection
of trade and commerce against swindlers and sharpers, he
is himself a swindler and sharper. There may be many
reasons which may render a person unfit to be a member
of such a society, although he is not a swindler, and, therefore, it appears to me, that the innuendo is not warranted
by the libel. It comes then to the simple question, whether
independently of all introductory averment of innuendo, the
natural import of the publication itself is actionable. There
may be so many reasons why a person may be improper to
be balloted for as a member of this society, without casting
any injurious reflections upon him whatever, that I can by
no means say that the words of this publication are necessarily libellous. There may have been rules of this society
arbitrarily fixed, requiring the members to be of a certain
particular class or description of persons, excluding others
of another class, without any imputation whatever upon
those who belong to the latter. I can very easily conceive
this to be the case. Thinking, therefore, that the statement
that this plaintiff was an improper person to be a member
of this society, may be reconcilable with an innoxious reason, and referable to fixed arbitrary rules of the society, I
am of opinion that this action is not maintainable.

BAYLEY, J.—I am of the same opinion. The objection
being on the record, it is open to the plaintiff to take the
opinion of a court of error upon it. If the libel, as stated
in the record, had been connected with the introductory
part of the declaration, that the defendant was in the habit

1827.

GOLDSTEIN
v.
Foss.

of publishing the names of those persons who were sharpers and swindlers and improper to be proposed as members of the society, I should have thought there was something to warrant the innuendo, which is connected with the matter complained of; but, when the rest of the count is looked at, there is nothing to connect them, nor any thing to justify the innuendo. The office of an innuendo is to explain what was previously mentioned, but not to extend its meaning. If an allegation is general, you are not at liberty to confine it to the particular species falling within the genus. There is one case in the books extremely applicable to this. In *Peake* v. *Oldham* (a), the words were, "I am thoroughly convinced that you are *guilty*," (meaning guilty of the death of D. D.) " and rather than you should go without a *hangman*, I will *hang* you." In that case there was nothing previously to shew that D. D. had been murdered, but Lord *Mansfield* said the word *guilty* implied a malicious intent, and could be applied only to something which is universally allowed to be a crime, and that the remaining words shewed what species of death the defendant meant, and, therefore, in themselves, manifestly imputed a charge of murder. Now, in the present case, the words themselves cannot by any construction support the innuendo, there being nothing to connect them with the previous introductory averment. The case of *Hawkes* v. *Hawkey* (b), is strictly in point to shew that words not in themselves actionable, cannot be made so by an innuendo referring them to a particular species of offence. The words in this case are capable of the most innocent interpretation, and as they cannot be made actionable by innuendo without doing violence to their natural meaning, I think the judgment ought to be arrested.

LITTLEDALE, J. (c).—I am of the same opinion upon both points. First, I think there is nothing to connect the

(a) Cowp. 275.   (b) 8 East, 427.   (c) *Holroyd*, J., was absent.

alleged libel with the introductory averment; and secondly, the words themselves are not actionable, and cannot be made so by the innuendo, which extends their meaning beyond what they fairly import.

.Rule absolute.

The KING v. The Justices of the NORTH RIDING of YORKSHIRE.

Where a *cer-tiorari* was granted on the application of two parties, and one of them died before the matter came on for argument, the Court heard the case notwithstanding.

The petty sessions have no jurisdiction to allow the accounts of the surveyor of highways under 13 *Geo.* 3, c. 78, s. 48, where the parties have been before one justice, who had not gone into the accounts, but referred the case to the petty sessions.

ON shewing cause against a rule *nisi*, obtained last term, for a *certiorari* to bring up an order of petty sessions, for allowing the accounts of the surveyors of the highways of the township of *Fylingdales*, in the parish of *Whitby*, in the North Riding of *Yorkshire*, in order that the same might be quashed for want of jurisdiction in the justices, it appeared from the affidavits, that on the 13th *October* last there had been a parish meeting, at which the surveyor of the highways accounts were submitted. After investigating them, it was agreed by the vestry, that the surveyor should go before a single magistrate next day, to have his accounts verified, pursuant to the Highway Act, 13 *Geo.* 3, c. 78, s. 48. On the following day the surveyor attended before a single magistrate, but omitted to take with him the assessments; whereupon two of the rated inhabitants of the township, named *Edmund Cook* and *Alexander Blunt*, objected that the magistrate, without the assessments, could not verify the accounts. The magistrate yielded to this objection, and desired the parties to attend at the petty sessions, appointed to be holden next day at *Whitby*. All the parties attended accordingly, when *Cook* objected that the petty sessions had no jurisdiction to investigate the matter, the accounts not having been previously examined by one justice, according to the statute. The petty sessions, however, allowed the accounts. The present application was originally made at the instance of *Cook* and *Blunt*, but since the rule was granted *Cook* had died.

Brodrick now objected, that as *Cook* had since died, the application must fall to the ground, the Court not having competent parties before it, who would be responsible for costs, in the event of the rule being discharged; *sed*

Per curiam.—We think *Alexander Blunt* is a good applicant, and we shall hear the case.

Brodrick then shewed cause. The question is, whether under the 48th section of the Act sufficient was done before the single magistrate, in order to give the petty sessions jurisdiction. This application was granted on the authority of *Rex* v. *The Justices of Somersetshire* (a), which would seem to support it; but as this is a mere formal objection, the Court will not look very astutely into it, where the substance of the act was complied with. Now here the surveyor's accounts were actually submitted to the vestry and approved of, and the parties went before the single justice to have them verified as a mere matter of form, but by mere accident the assessments were not produced. This was a compliance with the substance of the act, so as to give the petty sessions jurisdiction. There having been an objection made before the single justice, it was competent to him to refer the accounts to the petty sessions, *Rex* v. *Mitchell*(b), for examination and allowance. In *Rex* v. *The Justices of West Riding, Yorkshire* (c), *Buller*, J. says, " The appointment to go before the justice is to be made with the consent of the inhabitants and of the surveyor; and if they all consent at first to go to the petty sessions, instead of going before the magistrate, I doubt whether any of the parties can afterwards object to it. The justices at the petty sessions have the same power over the surveyor's accounts that one justice has." [*Bayley*, J. But the petty sessions have not jurisdiction, where the parties have been before the single justice, but who has not gone into the accounts

(a) *Ante*, Vol. VI. 469. 5 B. & C. 816.   (b) 5 T. R. 701.   (c) 5 T. R. 632.

for want of materials; the justices in this case were under that difficulty. *Abbott*, C. J. If you agree amongst yourselves to go at once before the petty sessions, instead of the single justice, then the observation of *Buller*, J. is applicable.] There can be no sensible reason for going before the single justice, if the accounts are afterwards only allowed by the petty sessions. Here the parties, in fact, went before a single justice, and he referred the matter to the petty sessions.

ABBOTT, C. J.—We are not called upon to give any opinion as to the reasonableness of the objection in this particular case, but to determine whether that was done, which is declared to be necessary by the legislature. These guards and securities against improper practices have been deemed wise and necessary by parliament. The act requires that the accounts shall in the first place be submitted to a single justice, and then to the petty sessions, if there be any objection to the allowance. Here the single justice had no means of exercising his judgment as to the correctness of the accounts, the assessments not having been produced, and therefore it appears to me, that the petty sessions had no jurisdiction under the circumstances of this case.

BAYLEY, J. and LITTLEDALE, J.(*a*) concurred.

Rule absolute for quashing the order of petty session.

(*a*) *Holroyd*, J. was absent.

1827.

C. FINLEY *v.* GARDNER.
J. DAVIS *v.* GARDNER.
J. COLE *v.* GARDNER.

Monday,
January 29.

STORKS, in last Michaelmas Term, obtained rules to shew cause why the judgments in these cases should not be set aside, and the grants of certain annuities, and the deeds securing the same, delivered up to be cancelled; and why the same, together with the warrants of attorney upon which the said judgments were founded, should not be declared null and void on the ground of usury.

It appeared from the affidavits, that the defendant being desirous of raising the sum of 3000*l.* by way of annuity, applied in the month of February, 1818, to one *White* for that purpose, and stated what he wanted. *White* applied to one *C. Dufour*, a money broker, and the latter introduced him to one *Thomas* as a monied man, who could command the sum required. *Thomas* said he could raise the sum that *Gardner* wanted for an annuity of 430*l.*, but that his charge was 10*l.* per cent. for law expenses, and that 5*l.* per cent. would be required by way of commission to pay *Dufour* for his agency in the transaction. Upon being informed that the defendant's income amounted only to 200*l.*, which was an allowance from his father, *Thomas* further stipulated, as a condition upon which the money should be advanced, that one year's amount of the annuity should be paid by the defendant in advance, and deposited in one of the *Cambridge* banks in the name of *White*, who was to draw it out in quarterly sums, and remit the money to *Thomas*. The defendant, *Gardner*, being made acquainted with these terms acceded to them. On the 7th of March, 1818, deeds were executed by him for securing, during his life, five annuities to the following persons, and for the following sums, viz.:—55*l.* to *J. Davis*, in consideration of 375*l.*; 50*l.* to *J. Coles*, consideration, 350*l.*; 75*l.* to *C. Fin-*

The marginal note reads: Where the grantor of an annuity, in pursuance of an agreement with the broker, received the whole consideration money, and immediately afterwards returned 15*l.* per cent. for law expenses and brokerage, and the amount of one year's annuity, which was deposited in a bank and drawn out quarterly to pay the annuitants:—Held, that this was an illegal retainer of part of the consideration money, within the meaning of 53 *Geo.* 3, c. 141, ‚. 6, and after the lapse of eight years the Court set aside the annuity on paying principal and interest on the money advanced, together with reasonable expenses, although the

annuitants were not directly privy to the retainer, and although one of them was dead before the application made.

ley, consideration, 525l.; 150l. to S. Hicks, consideration, 1050l.; and 100l. to G. Millerett, consideration, 700l. At the same time the defendant gave warrants of attorney to confess judgments to the several grantees of these annuities, for securing the same. Thomas then paid the defendant the full sum of 3000l. in Bank notes, and immediately afterwards, in pursuance of the before-mentioned agreement, the latter paid 300l. to Thomas for his charge of 10l. per cent. for law charges; 150l. to Dufour for his agency in the transaction, at 5l. per cent., and deposited 430l. with White to pay the said several annuities for one year. This latter sum was lodged by him at a Cambridge Bank, and drawn out from time to time to pay the annuities as they became due. In order to account for the lateness of the present application, the defendant's affidavit stated that until his father's death, about two months before, he had no means of repaying the money advanced or discharging the annuities. On the part of the grantees of the first two annuities, it was sworn that they were not privy to the agreement for returning any part of the consideration, nor were they aware that any part of the money had been in fact returned to Thomas. With respect to Cole's annuity, it was sworn that he was since dead, and that the party now entitled had purchased it for valuable consideration. It further appeared, that, down to the year 1824, the annuities had been regularly paid.

Curwood, Comyn, and Barstow now shewed cause. This application is now too late. The grantor has acquiesced in the payment of these annuities for six years, without any objection, and therefore, on the authority of Ex parte Maxwell (a), the Court will not interfere, there appearing to be no objection on the face of the memorials. Assuming that there may have been something objectionable as to the terms in which these annuities were negociated, still unless the grantees can be affected with privity, they ought not to

(a) 2 East, 85.

be damnified. The annuitants retained no part of the consideration money, nor were they aware of the terms on which the negociation took place. In the case of *Cole's* annuity, the greatest hardship and injustice would be worked if that were set aside. That party is dead, and a *bonâ fide* purchaser for valuable consideration is now entitled to receive it. This, at all events, cannot be considered as a fraudulent retainer, contemplated by the 53 *Geo.* 3, c. 141, s. 6; *Barber* v. *Gamson* (a). The retainer must be by the party to be benefited by it. Here the annuitants derive no benefit from the transaction beyond what they were entitled to by law, and it would be extremely hard to bind them by the acts of *Thomas*, who, assuming that he was their agent, still he has exceeded his authority in retaining part of the consideration money.

Storks, in support of the rule, contended that this case came within the operation of the 6th section of the statute, which enacts that if the consideration money, or any part of it be retained, on pretence of answering the future payments of the annuity, or on any other pretence, it shall be lawful for the Court to order the deeds to be delivered up to be cancelled, &c. Now these words are very general, and clearly include the present case, for here there is an express retainer of 430*l.* to pay the amount of the first year's annuities. *White* must be considered as the agent of the grantees of the annuities, and the cases of *Williamson* v. *Goold* (b), and *Gorton* v. *Champneys* (c), are authorities to shew that under circumstances like the present the Court will set aside these annuities, upon the grantor's paying what shall be found to be due for principal and interest at 5*l.* per cent.

ABBOTT, C. J.—I am of opinion that this rule must be

(a) 4 B. & A. 28.   (c) 8 J.B. Moore, 302; 1 Bing.
(b) 8 J. B. Moore, 109; 1   287.
Bing. 234.

1827.

FINLEY
v.
GARDNER.

made absolute, on the terms of paying each of the annuitants his principal and interest at 5*l.* per cent. in proportion
to the sums which each has advanced, together with the
reasonable expense of preparing the deeds and securities,
and procuring the annuity, and the costs of this application
to be taxed by the master. It is quite clear that this is a
case within the 6th section of the statute, the sum of 430*l.*
having been retained out of the consideration money to pay
the first year's annuity, and the cases in the *Common Pleas*
shew that it makes no difference that the annuitants are not
privy to the retainer.

BAYLEY, J.—I am of the same opinion on the authority
of *Williamson* v. *Goold* and *Gorton* v. *Champneys.*

LITTLEDALE, J. (*a*).—It is clear that this case is within
the policy as well as the terms of the act. By the agreement the defendant was to deposit 430*l.* in a *Cambridge*
bank, which was to be drawn out by instalments as the
annuities became due; which is the same thing as if the
whole money was to be paid at once to the annuitants, for
the grantor was deprived of the benefit of the money so retained; and I think it makes no difference that the annuitants themselves did not know of the arrangement, inasmuch
as I consider the annuity broker as their agent.

Rule absolute on the terms above mentioned.

(*a*) *Holroyd,* J. was absent.

———◆———

Monday,
January 29.

Three several
appeals in-
volving the

The KING *v.* The JUSTICES of WORCESTERSHIRE.

ON shewing cause against a rule *nisi* obtained last term,
for a *mandamus* to the Justices of the county of *Worcester,*
same facts, and the same questions of law, having been entered for hearing at sessions,
and the appellants having agreed that the decision of the Court on one should bind the
other cases, and the sessions having by a majority of justices decided with the respondent in the first :—Held, that the Court would not compel the sessions to hear the other
cases, although the justices had granted a case, but not upon any doubt of their own as
to the propriety of their decision.

commanding them to enter continuances and hear two appeals against an order made by commissioners under a local turnpike act, it appeared from the affidavits, that at the last sessions three several appeals, founded upon the same facts and depending upon the same question of law, had been entered for hearing and trial. It was agreed by the counsel on both sides, that the decision of the sessions in one of the cases should be binding upon the parties in the other two. The first case was fully argued and discussed upon the merits, and the question of law decided by a majority of the justices in favour of the respondent. The counsel for the appellants in the other cases then pressed the justices to grant a case for the opinion of this Court in the other appeals, inasmuch as the writ of *certiorari* was expressly taken away by the turnpike act. The sessions, at the importunity of the counsel, granted a case, but expressly declared that they had no doubt whatever upon the subject, and therefore decided in favour of the respondents in the other cases.

W. O. Russell, on shewing cause, was stopped by the Court.

Scarlett and *Carter,* in support of the rule, contended that the appellants in the other cases had a right to be heard, it appearing that the justices below were not unanimous in their opinion, and had in fact granted a case for the opinion of this Court. The reason for this application was stronger, when it appeared that the *certiorari* was taken away by the statute.

ABBOTT, C. J.—I am of opinion that this rule ought to be discharged. If it had appeared that there was an understanding between the bench and the bar, that the matter of law involved in the first case was to have been submitted to the judgment of this Court, and that the magistrates had come to a decision *pro formâ* amongst themselves with that view, I should have thought we ought to make the

rule absolute, and direct a hearing of the other two cases;
but upon looking at the affidavits, nothing of that kind appears.   The affidavits in answer to the rule state distinctly
that the merits of all the cases were alike, that precisely
the same question of law was involved, and that it was
agreed that the decision of one was to be binding in all.
It appears that the sessions decided generally upon the
whole case in favour of the respondent in the first appeal,
confirming the order of the commissioners.   The justices do
not appear to have expressed any doubt either upon the law
or the facts of the case, but at the importunity of the appellant's counsel in the other appeals a special case is
granted.   Now we know that the Quarter Sessions do
sometimes, in deference to gentlemen at the bar, grant
cases for the opinion of this Court where they themselves
entertain no doubt whatever upon the point in consideration.   Here the magistrates have actually heard and determined a case upon the understanding that their decision
shall be final in two other appeals.   Can we then call upon
them to rehear a case which they have already determined?
It is urged that they have in fact granted a case, which implies a doubt of the propriety of their decision.   Suppose,
however, no case had been granted; if upon the hearing
of the first appeal, and after a long discussion upon the law
and facts involved, the sessions had determined the case,
could they with any propriety have been called upon to hear
the other cases, upon a supposition that they would change
their opinion?   I cannot think that such a course could with
propriety have been adopted.   The sessions having decided
the first case, after mature deliberation, and it having
been agreed by the parties that that decision should be
final in the other appeals, and a case having been granted
merely at the importunity of counsel, I think we ought not
to require the justices to go into the matter again.

BAYLEY, J.—It is stated that the three cases stood
exactly on the same footing; and I collect from the affida-

vits, that there was a difference of opinion on the bench, on some points, although the majority of the justices agreed in disallowing the appeal on the principal point at issue. I do not find it suggested that there was any difference of opinion upon the substantial question raised by the appeal. If that had appeared, I should have thought the magistrates ought to hear the other two cases; or if it had appeared that the appellants in the other cases had foreborne to press for a hearing of their cases, under an expectation and belief that the point would be brought under the considertion of this Court, I should have been inclined to make this rule absolute; but inasmuch as it appears that all the cases were exactly the same in facts and circumstances, and the same question of law being applicable to each, I am disposed to concur with my Lord Chief Justice (but not without some doubts on my mind) in opinion that we ought not to send these cases to be reheard at sessions. I certainly entertain doubts upon it.

LITTLEDALE, J. (a)—I am decidedly of opinion that this rule ought to be discharged. All the cases were exactly similar in circumstances, and the same question was involved. It was agreed that two should abide the event of one. That one was fully discussed and considered, and a majority of the Court having determined its merits, I think we ought not to compel the sessions to hear the other cases.

Rule discharged.

(a) *Holroyd*, J. was absent.

———◆———

1827.

Monday,
January 29.

ROLFE *v.* PECKHAM.

It is no ground
for setting
aside service-
able process
that the initials
instead of the
full Christian
names of a
defendant are
introduced.

IN this case the defendant had been served with a *lutitat*,
describing him by the initials only of his Christian name,
" *J. W. Peckham*," and on a former day *Comyn* obtained a
rule *nisi* to set aside the bill of *Middlesex* for this irregularity.

Chitty now shewed cause and contended, that this being
merely serviceable process, the same strictness was not required as in bailable process.

Comyn, in support of the rule, cited *Tomlin* v. *Preston*
and *Gill* (*a*), where it was held, that in this respect there
was no distinction between bailable and serviceable process.

ABBOTT, C. J.—It is settled, that where the Christian
names of a defendant are omitted in a bailable *latitat*, the
Court will, on motion, set it aside for irregularity; but we
think that ought not to be so in the case of serviceable process. The party may plead in abatement, if he thinks fit.

Rule dischaiged.

(*a*) 1 Chit. Rep. 397.

———————◆———————

Monday,
January 29.

Exparte The TRUSTEES OF THE RUGBY CHARITY.

Mandamus re-
fused to the
Trustees of the
Rugby Charity
to compel the
payment of in-
creased alms
to claimants
on the funds,

BROUGHAM moved for a rule calling upon the Trustees
of the *Rugby Charity* to shew cause why a *mandamus*
should not issue, commanding them to pay an increased
weekly allowance of alms to certain persons, claimants upon
the charity. The Trustees of the *Rugby Charity* were
made a corporation by the statute 17 *Geo.* 3, c. 71. The

although the applicants were at an advanced age, and would probably be dead before
relief could be had in Chancery.

object of the application was to compel the payment of 7s. instead of 5s. weekly to these persons. If it should be said, that this was not the proper Court to apply to, these persons would be without remedy, for one being 80 years of age and the other 95, it was probable that they would be dead before any relief could be afforded in Chancery. In support of the motion he cited *Rex* v. *Windham*(a), as an authority in principle warranting the application. The affidavit stated, that the Trustees had a large surplus fund, applicable to the purposes of the charity.

ABBOTT, C. J.—These are matters which this Court cannot inquire into.

Rule refused.

(a) Cowp. 377.

BLOXHAM and another, Assignees of H. and S. FOURDRINIER and another, Bankrupts, v. ELSEE.

CASE for infringing a patent for making paper. The defendant pleaded the general issue, not guilty. At the trial before *Abbott*, C. J. at the sittings in *London* after *Michaelmas* term, 1825, the case was this:—" In *April*, 1801, his Majesty granted letters-patent to a Mr. *Gamble* for making paper of greater length and width than had been known in this country, by means of a machine which had been invented by *M. Didot*, a *French* paper-maker. The letters-patent, which were given in evidence, recited that *Gamble* had, by his petition to the King, represented that

Where an Act of Parliament secured to certain persons, for a further term, the benefit arising from a patent for making a machine, with a proviso, that it should become void, if they should transfer or assign their in-

terest therein to any persons *exceeding the number of five*; and two of the patentees became bankrupt:—Held, that the assignment of their interests to their assignees for the benefit of creditors, though the number exceeded twenty, was not within the proviso.

A patent being granted upon a specification, that the machine was capable of performing all the operations necessary to the perfection of the proposed invention; and it appearing that a second patent was taken out for improvements necessary to the efficient operation of the original machine:—Held, that the consideration of the first patent having failed, both patents were void.

Quære.—Whether a patent, in which an alien enemy has an interest, can be supported.

he was in possession of a machine for making paper in single sheets, without seam or joining, from one to twelve feet and upwards in width, and from one to forty-five feet and upwards in length, the method of making which machine had been communicated to him by *Didot*, then residing in *France*, with whom he was connected, and that he conceived the same would be of great public utility, and that the same was new in this kingdom, and had not been practised therein by any other person whomsoever to the best of his knowledge and belief; his late Majesty thereby granted to *Gamble*, his executors, administrators, and assigns, the sole privilege of making, using, exercising, and vending the said invention for fourteen years. It appeared also, that by other letters-patent, dated the 7th of *June*, 1803, reciting that *Gamble* had, by his petition, represented to the King, that he, in consequence of a further communication made to him by *Didot*, with whom he was connected, was in possession of certain improvements on, and additions to, a machine for making paper in single sheets, without seam or joining, from one to twelve feet and upwards in width, and from one to forty-five feet and upwards in length, being the machine for which he had obtained the letters-patent dated the 20th of *April*, 1801; that such improvements and additions would not only make the said machine more perfect and complete, but by far more useful to the public than it was in its then present state; that the same so improved was new in this kingdom, and had not with such additions and improvements been practised therein by any person to the best of his knowledge and belief; his late Majesty did, by the last-mentioned letters-patent, grant to *Gamble*, his executors, administrators, and assigns, the sole privilege of making, using, exercising, and vending his said invention for the term of fourteen years from the date of the last-mentioned letters-patent. In *January*, 1807, *Gamble* assigned all his right, title, and interest in these several patents to the bankrupts, paper-makers in *London*. By an act of parliament, 47 *Geo.* 3, reciting that the bank-

rupts and *Gamble* had made, used, and continued to make
use of the said improved machine in a very extensive trade,
in part whereof the bankrupts and *Gamble* were jointly
concerned as co-partners, and that they had incurred great
expense in consequence thereof, it was enacted that the sole
privilege, right and authority of making, using and vending
the said improved machine, within the United Kingdom of
Great Britain and *Ireland*, and in his late Majesty's colo-
nies and plantations abroad, should, from and after the
passing of that act, be, and the same was thereby declared
to be, vested in the bankrupts and *Gamble*, their executors,
administrators and assigns, for and during the term of fifteen
years from thenceforth next ensuing, being an addition of
about seven years to the term granted by the said letters-
patent. By sect. 6, it was enacted, that every objection
which might have been made to the validity of the said
letters-patent, and to the sufficiency of the specifications
enrolled as aforesaid, should be of the like force and effect
in law, in any action or suit brought by virtue of that act, as
such objections respectively would have been if that act had
not been passed, and if also the specifications to be enrolled,
as required by that act, had been enrolled, instead of the
former specifications respectively, except only as to the ex-
tension of the said privileges for the further term of years
thereby granted. By sect. 7 of the same act, it was provided, that the bankrupts and *Gamble*, their executors, administrators and assigns, or any person or persons who
should at any time during the said term of fifteen years have
or claim any right, title or interest, in law or equity, in or to
the power, privilege or authority of the sole making, using
and vending the said improved machine, should make any
transfer or assignment, or pretended transfer or assignment,
of the said liberty or privilege thereby vested in the bankrupts and *Gamble*, their executors, administrators and assigns, or any share or shares of the benefit or profits thereof,
or should declare any trusts thereof to or for any number of
persons *exceeding the number of five*, or should divide the

benefit of the liberty or privileges thereby vested in the
bankrupts and *Gamble*, their executors, administrators and
assigns, into any number of shares exceeding the number of
five, or should do or procure to be done any act whatsoever
during such time as such person or persons should have any
right or title either in law or equity, which should be contrary to the true intent or meaning of an act of the 6 *Geo.* 1,
c. 18, s. 19; or in case the said power, privilege, or authority should at any time become vested in or in trust for
more than the number of five persons or their representatives at any one time, otherwise than by devise or succession,
(reckoning executors and administrators as and for the single
persons they represent as to such interest, as they are or shall
be entitled to in right of such their testators or testator),
then and in every of the said cases all liberties and advantages whatsoever thereby vested in the bankrupts and
Gamble, their executors, administrators and assigns, should
utterly cease, determine and become void, any thing therein
contained to the contrary thereof notwithstanding. In *November*, 1810, a commission of bankrupt was sued out
against Messrs. *Fourdrinier*, under which they were declared bankrupts, and the plaintiffs chosen as assignees of
their estate and effects. More than twenty creditors proved
debts against the bankrupt's estate under the commission.
Proof being given that the defendant had infringed the
patent, several objections were taken to the plaintiff's right
of recovery. First, it was objected that the original letters-
patent were void, inasmuch as *Gamble* appeared to be
merely a trustee for *Didot*, who in 1801 was an alien
enemy, and, consequently, a fraud had been committed
against the crown. Secondly, that the property in the patent
having become vested in the assignees of the bankrupts in
trust for more than five creditors, the interest of the patentees
in the invention had utterly ceased and determined by the
express declaration of the 7th section of the act of parliament. Thirdly, that there was a variance between the first
and the second patents, for by that in 1801, the machine

1827.

BLOXHAM
v.
ELSEE.

then invented was so constructed as to be capable of making paper of one definite width only, whereas it was described as capable of making paper of different widths, but the new machine, for which the second patent was taken out, was requisite to produce paper of different widths, and, consequently, as the second was founded on the first, both were void. The Lord Chief Justice gave no opinion upon the first and third objections, but was clearly of opinion upon the second, that the assignment under the commission of bankrupt against Messrs. *Fourdrinier*, was not within the meaning of the act of parliament, and this objection was over-ruled; he, however, reserved these and several other objections for the consideration of the Court. As a question of fact he left it for the jury to determine whether the machine for which the first patent was granted, was capable of producing useful paper, and the jury found for the plaintiffs.

Scarlett, in last *Hilary* term, moved for a new trial on the grounds reserved at the trial, upon all of which a rule *nisi* was granted, except upon the last above-mentioned; in support of which it was contended, that as the interest in the patent had become devested by reason of the patentees' bankruptcy and assignment for the benefit of more than five creditors, no action could be maintained. The assignment under the bankruptcy for the benefit of more than five creditors is clearly an infraction of the 7th section of the act of the 47 *Geo.* 3. It cannot be contended that the assignees are the representatives of the bankrupts within the meaning of this clause, for the *representatives* therein mentioned clearly mean executors or administrators. The assignees here are representatives of the creditors and not of the bankrupts, and therefore there is a violation of the proviso contained in the act.

ABBOTT, C. J.—I am clearly of opinion that the proviso can be construed only as applying to acts of the parties, by which the interest in the patent shall be devested, and does not apply to an assignment by operation of law, which is the effect of a commission of bankrupt. The assignees represent the bankrupts by operation of law, and therefore a transfer of the interest in the patent to assignees is not, in my opinion, within the meaning of the clause.

BAYLEY, J., HOLROYD, J., and LITTLEDALE, J., were of the same opinion.

Tindal, S. G. Marryat, Gurney, and *Curwood,* shewed cause against the rule, and applied themselves to the grounds on which the rule *nisi* had been granted. First, assuming that *Didot,* as an alien enemy, had an interest in this patent, still the patent is not absolutely void on that ground; at the utmost it is only voidable on inquisition found, *Attorney General v. Weedon* (a). It may have been that the crown granted a license to *Didot,* in which case there would be nothing objectionable in his having an interest in this patent. Secondly, there is no ground for maintaining that the first patent was void, because the second was necessary to give effect to the improvements subsequently introduced into the machinery. The recital in the first patent did not import that paper of different widths was to be made by one and the same machine, but that a machine might be constructed capable of making paper of any width between one and twelve feet. It was unnecessary to shew that the machine mentioned in the first patent was in fact capable of making paper of different widths. (They then proceeded to argue the other objections, but as the Court gave no opinion upon them, it is unnecessary to report them.)

Scarlett, in support of the second objection, contended, on the authority of *Rex v. Arkwright* (b), that a patent for a machine is void, if the machine will not answer the purpose for which it is intended without some addition, adjust-

(a) Parker, 267. (b) Cited in 8 Taunt. 399.

ment or alteration, which the mechanic who makes it must introduce of his own invention, in order to make it work. Now here it was clearly in evidence, that the machine described in the first patent was incapable of making paper of different widths, without the help of the machinery described in the second patent, and therefore both patents are void. Then *Didot* being an alien enemy at the time the first patent was granted, and having clearly an interest in it, the patent was void, on the general maxim of law, that where the crown is deceived in making its grant, the grant is void.

Cur. adv. vult.

. Abbott, C. J., now delivered judgment.—It appears to us that one of the objections which has been taken in this case is valid and must prevail, and consequently it is not necessary to give any opinion upon the others. By the patent it appears that the patentee had represented to His Majesty that he was in possession of *a* machine for making paper in single sheets, without seam or joining, from one to twelve feet or upwards wide, and from one to forty-five feet and upwards in length. Upon this representation the patent is granted. The consideration of the grant is the invention of a machine for making paper in sheets of width and length varying within the limits designated. If any material part of the representation was not true, the consideration has failed in part, and the grant is consequently void, and a defendant in an action for infringing the patent has a right to say that it is so. Now it appears to me to be impossible to say that both width and length are not important parts of this representation. It may be, that if the representation had mentioned length only, a patent would have been granted for the invention, which (in its improved state at least) is eminently useful, in a very important manufacture, as saving both time and labour in a very considerable degree. But although we may think this probable, we are not at liberty to pronounce judicially that it would have been so.

We must therefore see, as it seems to me, whether the representation was true. It has been contended, in support of the patent, that the recital does not import that paper of different widths was to be made by one and the same machine, but may mean only that the width might be obtained by different machines, each adapted and constructed to the extent required. I think, however, that this construction of the recital cannot be allowed; for it is a very different thing whether a manufacturer must supply himself with several different machines, or with one only, capable alone of accomplishing all the purposes to be obtained by many. And if the width is not to be considered material, the length cannot be so considered, and then the representation will only be that he has invented machines, by the use of several of which, paper of various widths and lengths may be made without seam or joining; and this will be at variance with all the specifications, which plainly shew that whatever was to be done, was to be done by one and the same machine. Then if the representation be, (as I think it is,) that paper of various widths may be obtained by one and the same machine, I must look to the evidence to discover whether the patentee was possessed of a machine, or of the invention of a machine, capable of accomplishing this object; and unfortunately the evidence shews that he was not. I say unfortunately, because it is to be lamented that the advantage of great ingenuity, labour, anxiety and expense, should be lost to those who have bestowed them. The patentee was at the time possessed of one machine, and one only, and this adapted to one degree of width and one degree only; and he was not then possessed of any method by which different degrees might be manufactured by that machine or by any other. I think it may be admitted, that by subsequent improvements and discoveries, a machine was obtained capable of making paper of width varying within certain limits, though probably not extending to more than half the width mentioned in the patent. The specification enrolled under the act of parliament appears suffi-

ciently to describe such a machine, and a mode of adjusting
it to different degrees of width within the limits of its own
breadth, but I incline to think that the representation contained in the second patent does not. Certainly the first
specification is confined to one width only. This is obvious
from the evidence of Mr. *Donkin*, a scientific witness, who
was examined on the trial. Then can the last specification
be taken to furnish an answer to the objection? Now
taking the construction of the act of parliament most favourably, as substituting the last specification in the place and
stead of the former specifications, so as to remove all the
formal objections to them, to which the latter is not open,
still it cannot operate so far retrospectively as to enable the
patentee to say that he possessed in 1801, or had then discovered or invented, a machine which it appears that he did
not possess, and had not invented or discovered until a
much later date. If the first machine had been capable of
working at different degrees of width, though clumsily and
imperfectly, the latter machine would have been an improvement of it; but as the first, whether considered as actually
existing or in theory, was wholly incapable of this, the latter
machine does not in this respect furnish an improvement of
anything previously existing, but an addition of some new
matter not existing or known at the date of the first patent,
and which nevertheless is therein represented as existing or
known, and which cannot but be considered an important
part of the representation then made, and of the consideration of the grant. If the first grant was void, the subsequent grants by the patent and by the statute must fall to
the ground, as having nothing to support them. I think
myself compelled, therefore, to yield to this objection, and
to hold that the rule for a new trial should be made absolute.
If, however, the law in this respect should not be, in the
opinion of my learned brothers, that which I own it has
appeared to me to be, still there must be a new trial, because the question ought to have been left to the jury,
whether the machine, as originally constructed, was capable,

in every state, of doing that which the patentee professed it should do, namely, of making paper of different widths. I may say, that I did not leave that question to the jury, because it appeared to me to be clear upon the evidence that the machine, as originally constructed, would not make paper of different widths. I do not think it necessary to give any opinion on the point about the alien.

Rule absolute for a new trial.

---

*Thursday,
February* 8.

A constable having a warrant authorizing the seizure of certain specified goods alleged to have been stolen, seized those goods and others not specified in the warrant. The latter goods were not likely to furnish evidence of the identity of the former: Held, that he was liable in an action of trespass, though a copy of the warrant had not been demanded of him pursuant to 24 *Geo.* 2, c. 44, s. 6.

CROZIER *v.* CUNDY and others.

TRESPASS for breaking and entering plaintiff's dwelling-house, and seizing and taking away his goods. There was a second count for seizing and taking away the goods only. Plea, not guilty, and issue thereon. At the trial before *Best*, C. J. at the *Derbyshire* Spring Assizes, 1826, it was proved on the part of the plaintiff that the defendants had entered the plaintiff's house, had searched it, and had seized and carried away 100lbs. weight of cotton, two cases in which it was packed, a tin pan, and a hair sieve. In answer to this case, it was proved on the part of the defendants, that the cotton and the cases were the property of the defendant *Cundy*, from whom they had been stolen ; that the defendants, one of whom was a constable and the others his assistants, had entered the house under the authority of a search-warrant granted by a magistrate, which was produced in evidence, and which empowered them to search the house for 100lbs. weight of cotton; that finding the cotton packed in cases they carried it away in them ; and that they also carried away the tin pan and the hair sieve, because the defendant *Cundy* claimed them as his property. It was admitted that the plaintiff had not demanded a copy of the search-warrant. The Lord Chief Justice was of opinion that under the 24 *Geo.* 2, c. 44, s. 6, the plaintiff was bound to demand a copy of the search-warrant, and that not having done so he could not maintain the action. The plaintiff, therefore, was nonsuited, with liberty to move to enter a verdict for one shilling damages.

Clarke having in *Easter* term last obtained a rule *nisi* accordingly,

Reader now shewed cause. The statute provides that no action shall be brought against any constable for anything done in obedience to any warrant, until demand has been made of a copy of such warrant. The cotton was seized in obedience to the warrant, for it was specifically mentioned in it, and the only question is whether, under the circumstances, the seizure of the other articles was not a thing done in obedience to the warrant. Though the constable was not commanded by the terms of the warrant to seize any other goods than the cotton, still he was not restrained from so doing, if those other goods appeared to him to have been stolen, and if their detention was likely to prove useful in the investigation of the felony mentioned in the warrant. In *Price* v. *Messenger* (*a*), where the warrant was to seize " stolen sugar," not describing it particularly, and the constable seized sugar which turned out not to have been stolen, he was held to be within the protection of the statute. There he must have been considered as acting, virtually, in obedience to the warrant,—and here, upon the same principle, the defendants must be considered as having seized all the goods in obedience to the warrant, and therefore to be within the protection of the statute.

Clarke, contrá, was stopped by the Court.

ABBOTT, C. J.—By the warrant which was produced in evidence, the constable was authorised to seize certain articles therein specified. Unfortunately for him he also seized

(*a*) 2 B. & P. 158; 3 Esp. 96.   subject see Chitty's Statutes, 649,
For the other decisions upon this   in notis.

some other articles not specified in the warrant. If those articles had from their nature been likely to furnish evidence of the identity of the articles stolen and mentioned in the warrant, I should have been inclined to assent to Mr. *Reader's* argument, and to think that there might have been reasonable ground for seizing them, though not mentioned in the warrant. But it cannot be contended that the tin pan and the hair sieve were articles likely to furnish such evidence, and therefore I am of opinion that the nonsuit cannot be supported. It will be collected from the mode in which I have expressed myself, that I am anxious to prevent the supposition that a constable who seizes goods not specified in the warrant under which he acts is invariably and necessarily a trespasser : neither the act of parliament, nor our present decision, justifies such a supposition. The verdict must be entered for the plaintiff for one shilling damages ; but it must be entered on the second count, which charges only the seizure of the goods.

The other Judges concurred.

Rule absolute.

The KING v. SLYTHE.

Friday,
February 9.
The title of a
person having
an inchoate
right to be ad-
mitted a free
burgess of a
borough can-
not be im-
peached on
the ground of
a defect of
title in the
officer by
whom he was admitted.

THIS was a similar case to the preceding one of *Rex v. Slythe* (a), with these exceptions : There was no objection to the competency of the relator. His affidavit stated only that he *had been informed and believed* that the defendant exercised the office of free burgess of the borough. The defendant's affidavit shewed that he had an inchoate right, by birth, to be admitted a freeman at the time when he was admitted and sworn before *Seckamp* and *Hammond*.

The affidavit of a relator in a motion for a *quo warranto,* that he "has been informed and believes" that the defendant exercises the office which he is charged with usurping, is sufficient.

(a) *Ante,* p. 181.

1827.

The King
v.
Slythe.

Campbell and *Patteson* shewed cause. First, the relator's affidavit is bad, for not alleging positively that the defendant exercises the office which he is charged with usurping. It states only that he *has been informed and believes* that the defendant exercises the office. That is far too loose an averment. It is irregular to charge a party with a misdemeanor in such dubious terms. The charge ought to be clear and positive, as it easily may be; for there can be no difficulty in ascertaining such a fact. In this respect an information in the nature of *quo warranto* resembles a criminal information; they both impute to the defendant an offence, and ought both to be framed in clear and positive language. [*Holroyd*, J. A *quo warranto* information is not a criminal proceeding. It was, I believe, once held by Lord *Kenyon*(a), that the affirmation of a Quaker was admissible in support of an application for a *quo warranto* information; which could not have been the case if the proceeding had been one of a criminal nature. A criminal information is very different; that is, strictly speaking, a criminal proceeding, and the charge must be clearly and positively stated; but the same degree of precision is not necessary in a case like this, which is substantially a civil proceeding.] Secondly, the persons before whom the defendant was admitted were bailiffs *de facto*, and that is enough to give

(a) The case here alluded to by the learned Judge does not appear to have been reported, but was once before mentioned by him, in his judgment in the case Ex parte *Gellibrand*, H. T. 3 Geo. 4, *ante*, Vol. I. 124, in these terms:—" I remember a case before Lord *Kenyon*, where an application was made for a *quo warranto* upon the affirmation of a Quaker, which proceeding is in its form criminal, though in substance civil, and according to my recollection, that noble and learned Judge said, that the rule to try the admissibility of a Quaker as a witness was, whether the object was criminal, though the form was civil, and upon that principle he held that the affirmation was admissible, the object being only criminal in form, but civil in substance. According to my recollection he drew that distinction." See the authorities upon this subject collected in the case above cited, and in *Skipp* v. *Harwood*, Willes, 292, (b).

him a perfect title. He had by birth an inchoate right of admission, and that cannot be invalidated by the circumstance of the officers before whom he was admitted having a defective title. No case can be found in which the admission of a freeman has been set aside upon the ground of a defect of title in the presiding officer; and the Court will not now for the first time entertain such a question, the probable effect of which would be to impeach the titles of many hundreds of freemen in different corporations throughout the kingdom. The admitting and swearing the defendant by the bailiffs was not a voluntary act on their parts; in so doing, they acted as merely ministerial officers; and if they had refused to do so, this Court, upon being satisfied that the defendant had an inchoate right of admission, would have issued a *mandamus* to compel them to admit him, without inquiring whether they were bailiffs *de jure* or *de facto* only. What return could the bailiffs possibly have made to such a *mandamus?* Clearly none. There are many analogous cases shewing that the defendant's admission is good. All acts which an officer is compellable to do are valid, though done by an officer *de facto. Rex* v. *The Corporation of Shrewsbury* (a). A lord of a manor, who is in by disseisin, may admit to a copyhold estate. *Chudleigh's* case (b), *Brown's* case (c). A mayor *de facto* may bind a corporation by his voluntary concurrence in corporate acts; *Knight* v. *The Corporation of Wells* (d); *à fortiori*, his acts are binding where they are compulsory and ministerial, as in the present instance.

Adam and *Alderson*, contrà. First, the affidavit of the defendant having exercised his office is sufficiently certain. Information and belief might not be admissible if they went to affect the validity of the title; but where they refer only to the exercise of the office they are sufficient, especially

(a) Cas. *temp.* Hard. 150.   (c) 4 Co. Rep. 24 a.
(b) 1 Co. Rep. 140 b.   (d) 1 Lutw. 519.

where they are uncontradicted. *Rex* v. *Harwood* (a). Secondly, the arguments urged to induce the Court to refuse this application, namely, the novelty and importance of the question, are the very grounds upon which the rule ought to be made absolute. It is said, that the Court would grant a *mandamus* to compel the admission of a person who shewed an inchoate right to the office of a free burgess. That may be true, and yet it by no means follows that they ought not to grant leave to file a *quo warranto* information against the same person, for in either case they would act upon colourable grounds only; and where a *mandamus* is sent, all questions of law remain open to discussion upon the return. Where a *mandamus* is applied for, the titles of the parties to whom it is directed are necessarily admitted; and it is not competent for them to raise any objection on that point themselves. It has been assumed that the admission of a free burgess is a compulsory and ministerial act, and may, therefore, be performed by persons who are officers *de facto;* but there is no proof that it is so: and, at all events, it is the duty of the presiding officer on such occasions to ascertain that the party claiming to be admitted is entitled to the privilege he claims.

ABBOTT, C. J.—It seems to me, upon the authority of the case of *Rex* v. *Harwood*, that the affidavit respecting the defendant's exercising the office of free burgess is sufficient, being, as it is, uncontradicted by the other side, and not affecting the validity of the title to that office. But, upon the other point raised in this case, I am of opinion, that this rule must be discharged. The application is for a *quo warranto* information, and was made solely upon the ground that the defendant was admitted and sworn into his office of free burgess before persons who were incompetent to admit him, they not being good presiding officers. *Primâ facie*, that is a valid objection to the defendant's title. The answer to it is, that the defendant had an inchoate right to

(a) 2 East, 177.

singular the premises, did bargain, sell, assign, transfer, set over and confirm to plaintiff all the share and interest of him *J. Brymer*, of, in and to all and singular the debts, sum and sums of money whatsoever, then due and owing to them, plaintiff and *J. Brymer*, under, or by virtue, or in consequence of the same several contracts, or otherwise; and all bonds, bills and notes relating to the said contracts, debts and sums of money, or any of them, or any part thereof; and of and in all and singular other the monies, goods, chattels, stock and effects whatsoever and wheresoever thereof, or belonging to them, plaintiff and *J. Brymer*, as such copartners respectively, and all the right, title and interest, property, claim and demand whatsoever of him, *J. Brymer*, of, in, to, from, out, or in respect of the premises; to have and to hold to plaintiff, as and for his own proper monies and effects, absolutely. Covenants and breaches were then set out. Pleas, *non est factum*, and other special pleas (*a*). At the trial before *Abbott*, C. J., at the *London* adjourned sittings after last *Trinity* term, the deed set out in the declaration being produced in evidence was found to bear the ordinary deed stamp only. It was objected on the part of the defendants, that according to the 48 *G.* 3, c. 149, schedule, part 1, title *conveyance*, (the stamp act in force at the time the deed bore date,) it ought to have borne an *ad valorem* stamp upon the 50,000*l.*, the consideration paid by the plaintiff for *J. Brymer's* share of the partnership property, which would have been 500*l.*; and the Lord Chief Justice being of that opinion directed a nonsuit. In *Michaelmas* term a rule *nisi* for setting aside the nonsuit, and for a new trial, having been obtained,

Denman, C. S., *Manning*, and *Brodrick*, now shewed cause. This rule was granted upon the authority of the case of *Lyburn* v. *Warrington* (*b*), but that was very distinguishable from the present case. There, nothing that

---

(*a*) The question before the Court turning entirely upon the amount of the stamp requisite for the deed, it is unnecessary to set out the pleadings more at length.

(*b*) 1 Stark. N. P. C. 162.

could be fairly called *property* was assigned; the consideration was paid for the goodwill of a trade, and for the privilege of carrying it on upon particular premises, for a certain
number of years. In this case the deed itself speaks of
property, and its language throughout shews that valuable
property was assigned, for it states that *J. Brymer sold* his
share and interest in *goods* and *chattels, stock* and *effects*, to
the plaintiff. Here, therefore, there is a *sale of property*
within the express words of the act of parliament, which
imposes an *ad valorem* duty " upon the *sale* of any lands,
tenements, rents, annuities, *or other property*, real or personal, heritable or moveable, or of any *title, right, interest,
or claim*, unto, out of, or upon any lands, tenements, rents,
annuities, *or other property*." This deed therefore required
the *ad valorem* stamp, and being defective in that respect,
the nonsuit was right.

Tindal, S. G., *Scarlett, Marryat* and *J. Evans*, contrà.
The act of parliament does not extend to this deed. In the
first place, there was no *sale* at all in this case. In the
second place, the *property* assigned was not of a description
contemplated by the statute. First, this was a deed of dissolution of partnership, and the real object seems to have
been merely a settlement of accounts between the partners
upon their separation. There was no sale; the parties did
not stand in the relative situation of vendor and vendee.
There was hardly what can be termed an assignment; it
was more properly speaking a release. Suppose the
agreement had been that upon the dissolution of the partnership, the plaintiff should receive and realize all the out-
standing debts and property, and should pay over a moiety
of the proceeds to *Brymer;* that could not properly have
been called a sale; and yet that was in substance the arrangement made between the parties to this deed. It was
a mere calculation that the retiring partner was entitled to
50,000*l.*, and an agreement to pay him that sum at once,
instead of the more inconvenient course of paying him from

time to time, as the funds were got in. Secondly, it is clear, from the case of *Warren* v. *Howe* (a), that the statute is not to be construed as extending to every species of property, and certainly not to the species of property referred to by this deed; and *Denn* v. *Diamond* (b) is another authority to the same effect. [*Bayley*, J. The first of those cases was merely an assignment as security for a smaller sum; and in the other there was nothing paid to the assignor.] *Coates* v. *Perry* (c) and *Lyburn* v. *Warrington* (d) are also strong authorities in favour of the present plaintiff.

ABBOTT, C. J.—If the decision in *Warren* v. *Howe* (a) is correct, and I am not prepared to say that it is not, this rule must be made absolute, for it is impossible to distinguish that case, in principle, from the present. As at present advised, we are all of opinion that the subject-matter of this contract was not *property* within the meaning of the act of parliament. The case, therefore, must go to a new trial, and the parties will then have the opportunity, if they please, to raise the question again in such a shape as to obtain a more solemn decision upon the point.

Rule absolute.

(a) *Ante*, Vol. III. 494; 2 B. & C. 281.

(b) *Ante*, Vol. VI. 328; 4 B. & C. 243.

(c) 3 B. & B. 48.

(d) 1 Stark. N. P. C. 162.

The KING v. The Rev. SAMUEL DAVIES, Clerk.

Friday,
February 9.
Mandamus lies
to a minister
to restore a
parish-clerk
removed by
him without
just cause.

THIS was a rule calling upon the defendant, the perpetual curate of the parish of *Oystermouth*, in the county of *Glamorgan*, to shew cause why a writ of *mandamus* should not issue, directed to him, commanding him to restore one *John* And the Court will not judge of the justice of the cause of removal upon the *ex parte* statement of the minister; he must state it in his return to the *mandamus*, and give the clerk an opportunity of answering it.

Tovey to the place and office of parish-clerk and sexton of the church of *Oystermouth.*

The affidavit of *John Tovey,* upon which the rule had been obtained, stated, that he had been appointed parish-clerk and sexton in the time of the predecessor of Mr. *Davies,* and had continued in that office until he was removed by Mr. *Davies* appointing another in his stead.

The affidavits in opposition to the rule imputed to *Tovey* misconduct and inefficiency in his office; that he had refused to attend funerals; had demanded extortionate fees; had left the church before divine service was concluded; was in the habit of cursing and swearing; and had behaved disrespectfully to Mr. *Davies;* and that he could neither read nor sing correctly. They also stated that the bishop of the diocese had been informed, and approved, of *Tovey's* removal. There was no statement that any formal charge had ever been preferred against *Tovey* in his presence, so as to afford him an opportunity of defending his conduct.

Taunton and *Russell* shewed cause. *Rex* v. *Warren* (a) is an authority to shew that the defendant, as incumbent of the parish, had power to remove the parish-clerk, provided he had sufficient grounds for the removal. It will hardly be contended that the affidavits produced on the part of the defendant do not shew such grounds, especially as the removal founded upon them was approved of by the bishop of the diocese. Under such circumstances this Court will not interfere by granting the writ prayed for.

Maule, contrà. The facts adduced in answer to this rule will not warrant the Court in discharging it. *Rex* v. *Warren* (a) is an express authority for granting the *mandamus* in this case. It was there decided that a *mandamus* will lie to restore a parish-clerk, removed without sufficient cause. Lord *Mansfield,* on the case first coming on, said,

(a) Cowper, 370.

the clerk has his office only during his good behaviour. But though the minister may have a power of removing him on a good and sufficient cause, he can never be the sole judge and remove him at pleasure, without being subject to the control of this Court. And *Aston*, J., said, as long as the clerk behaves himself well, he has a good right and title to continue in his office. Therefore if the clergyman has any just cause for removing him, he should state it to the Court. And afterwards, on the decision of the case, Lord *Mansfield* said, a parish-clerk is a temporal officer, and the minister must shew ground for turning him out. And the rule for a *mandamus* to restore the clerk was made absolute, on the ground that the minister had not shewn sufficient cause for removing him. Upon all the principles laid down in that case, this rule must be made absolute. Here the minister has been the sole judge, and has removed at pleasure; and he has not stated to the Court any just cause for the removal. Even if the objections raised to the clerk were sufficient in themselves, still he has never been allowed the opportunity of answering them; and the bishop's acquiescence in the removal cannot vary the case, because that was obtained by an *ex parte* statement, which is not before the Court, and which the clerk had not the means of hearing and refuting.

ABBOTT, C. J.—I am of opinion that the discharge of this officer has been made in too hasty and summary a manner, and therefore that the rule for a *mandamus* to restore him ought to be made absolute. It does not appear that the charges against him have ever been made in form, or in such a mode as to draw his attention to them, or to give him an opportunity of defending himself against them. If Mr. *Davies* has good and sufficient grounds for the removal, he may state them in his return to the writ, and *Tovey* will then have the opportunity of answering them.

The other Judges concurred.

Rule absolute.

1827.

The KING v. EVETT.

AN inquisition taken before one of the coroners for the county of *Bucks*, touching the death of one *Elizabeth Baldwin*, was removed into this Court by *certiorari*, being in the following words:—

"Inquisition taken at *Wolverton*, in the county of *Bucks*, on, &c., before *James Burnham*, one of the coroners for the said county, on view of the body of *Elizabeth Baldwin*, an infant then and there lying dead, upon the oaths of the several persons under-written, and whose seals are affixed, who, being duly sworn, say, that the said *Elizabeth Baldwin*, on, &c., at the parish and in the county. aforesaid, being crossing the king's highway in the said parish, it so happened accidentally, casually, and by misfortune, that the said *Elizabeth Baldwin*, in the attempt to cross such road, was suddenly forced to and against the ground by the leaders of a certain coach called the *Tally ho*, which was passing through such parish, by means whereof she was so much bruised, and otherwise injured, as to occasion her death, as to languish for the space of 57 hours, and then she died. And so the jurors aforesaid, upon their oath do say and present, that *Elizabeth Baldwin* in manner and by the means aforesaid came to her death, and not otherwise, and that the said coach and horses were moving to the death of her, the said *Elizabeth Baldwin*, and are of the value of 80*l.*, the property and in the possession of *Humphry Evett*, *William Gilbert*, and Company."

This inquisition was signed and sealed by the coroner and the jurors, but several of the jurors signed the initials only of their christian names. A *venire* issued to the defendant *Evett*, upon which he appeared, and demurred to the inquisition.

The demurrer was argued in the course of last term by

Campbell in support of the demurrer, who contended that the inquisition was bad on three grounds:—First, for not

---

Saturday,
February 10.

A coroner's inquisition can be amended in matters of *form only.* Omitting the name of the place where the death happened, or the body was found; omitting the names of the jurors in the body of the inquisition; inserting their christian names by initials or abbreviations; stating the death to have been caused by horses, the property of *A., B., & Co.,* they being in fact the property of *A.* and *B.* only; are all defects of *substance,* which cannot be supplied by amendment, and for which an inquisition may be quashed.

setting out the names of the jurors in the body of the inquisition; secondly, for not stating where the death happened, nor where the body was found; and thirdly, for not
stating the cause of the death with sufficient certainty.
First, the names of the jurors ought to have been inserted
in the body of the inquisition. As it is, the Court have not
the means of knowing the real names of the jurors at all,
either from the body or the foot of the inquisition, for several
of them have signed with the initials only of their christian
names; but their names ought to be disclosed fully and
correctly, at least at the foot, if not in the body of the inquisition; in either point of view, this, therefore, is a fatal
objection (*a*). Secondly, the inquisition ought to state that
the death took place, and that the body was lying within
the county of *Bucks*. Without these statements there is
nothing to shew that the coroner had jurisdiction. An inquisition ought to be as certain as an indictment. At common law, if a mortal wound was inflicted in one county, and
the death happened in another, it was formerly matter of doubt
in which the offender ought to be indicted; and though
this has been remedied, first by the 2 & 3 *Edw.* 6, c. 24,
and subsequently by the 7 *G.* 4, c. 64, and 9 *G.* 4, c. 31,
and the party may now be tried in that county in which the
death happens, still, an indictment must shew with certainty
which that county is, and an inquisition must do the same.
Here, for all that appears, the deceased may have received
the injury in *Buckinghamshire*, and have died in some other

(*a*) "Care should be taken to
insert the names of the jurors accurately; for if there be a variance
between the names of the jurors in
the caption, and those in the attestation, it will be fatal. *Rex* v.
Huggins, 3 C. & P. 414." Jervis
on Coroners, 252. An inquisition
must be signed by all the jurors as
well as the coroner. *Rex* v. *The
Justices of Norfolk*, 1 East, P. C.

383. If the names of the jurors
be not set out in the caption of a
coroner's inquisition, and the inquisition be not signed by the jurors
with their names at length, the inquisition is bad. Per *Parke*, J. in
Rex v. *Bowen, Monmouth* Lent Assizes, 1829, 3 C. & P. 602. If some
of the jurors sign with their marks,
such marks ought to be verified by
an attestation. *Id. ibid.*

county, and in that respect the inquisition is bad for uncertainty. Thirdly, the cause of the death is very obscurely
and insufficiently described. It is not averred that the
bruises and injuries received by the deceased were mortal;
but such an averment is indispensably necessary, *Regina* v.
Clerk (a). There is nothing to explain what is meant by
" the leaders of the coach," and the Court cannot be
expected either to construe or adopt the cant phrases of
the day. The word " leaders" does not of necessity mean
horses; and if it did, there is no averment that at the time
when the accident happened, they were attached to and
drawing the coach; there is, therefore, no fact stated to
warrant the conclusion that either the horses or the coach
were moving to the death.

Chitty, contrà. The same certainty is not required in an
inquisition like the present as in an indictment. If it were
an inquisition of blood, for the purpose of punishment and
the advancement of justice, it might be different; but here
the only object is the enforcement of a deodand. First,
there seems no good reason for requiring that the names of
the jurors shall appear in the body of the inquisition. The
practice has always been to insert them at the foot of the
inquisition only, (since they have been inserted at all, for
formerly inquisitions were only sealed); and if the names
are there given in such a shape, although abbreviated, that
the persons of the jurors can be ascertained, every reasonable requisite seems to be satisfied. Secondly, the Court
will presume, as well upon general principle, as from the
facts stated, that the death happened, or that the body was
found, in the county where the inquisition was held, and

(a) 1 Salk, 377. " The wound
or bruise must be alleged to be
mortal, whereof the party died;
and an omission in this respect cannot be supplied by the allegation
contained in the conclusion of the
inquisition, which is at all times
necessary, that the deceased died
in consequence of the violence inflicted upon him. 2 Hale, P. C.
186; 2 Haw. P. C., c. 23, s. 82,
83." Jervis on Coroners, 269.

consequently that the coroner had jurisdiction. It is stated that the body was there viewed, and that the injury was there received; and if the coroner had not jurisdiction there, the defendant should have pleaded that fact instead of demurring. Thirdly, the cause of the death is stated in a manner sufficiently certain and intelligible. It is impossible to read the statement in the inquisition without understanding that the death was caused by the leading horses of the coach, and that they were at the time drawing the coach. Though the Court cannot be called upon to construe cant phrases, yet neither can they be called upon to say that they do not understand those ordinary expressions in general use, which they must, and do, in common with the rest of mankind, perfectly understand. Moreover, this and the first objection are objections merely of form, and are, therefore, not grounds of general demurrer.

The Court did not deliver any judgment, but as their opinion seemed to be strongly against the inquisition,

Chitty, on a former day in this term, obtained a rule *nisi* for a *venire facias* to bring the coroner into Court, for the purpose of amending the inquisition by inserting the name of the place where the death happened, and the christian names of the jurors, and by erasing the words " and Company," so as to leave the finding of the property in *Evett* and *Gilbert* only. The rule was obtained upon the coroner's affidavit, which set out the names of the jurors at length, and averred that they were the same persons who signed the inquisition, and before whom it was taken, as also that the coach and horses belonged to *Evett* and *Gilbert*, and that the coroner, believing them to be in partnership with others, had for that reason inserted the words, " and company."

Campbell now shewed cause. The proposed amendments cannot be allowed. They would not lead to the advancement of justice, which is the only object for which amendments are in general allowed; the only object to be gained by these, is the power of enforcing payment of a deodand.   Besides, the application here is to amend matters of substance, which cannot be done (a).   No case can be cited in which an inquisition, defective in matter of substance, has been allowed to be amended.   Lord Chief Baron *Comyns* lays down the rule, and says, that "*if an inquisition finds the substance*, though defective in form, it may be amended" (b).   All the other cases bearing upon the point are to the same effect. He cited *Rex* v. *Saloway* (c), and *Rex* v. *Glover* (d).   He was then stopped by the Court.

Chitty, contrà.   This application is founded upon the affidavit of the coroner, and is not altogether new, for there are instances in which similar amendments have been made in the Crown Office.   [*Abbott*, C. J. The statement as to the property in the coach and horses is the finding of the jury.   How can we, or the coroner by our order, have authority to alter that?]   An amendment of a precisely similar nature has been made.   In a case of *Rex* v. *Williams* and *Bellamy*, 15 *G.* 3, it appears by the record of the inquisition filed in the Crown Office, that the death was caused by a fall from a cart, which the inquisition originally stated to be the property of " Messrs. *Williams* and Company, of *Stratford*, in the county of *Essex*, calico-printers;" and by an order of *Yates*, J., that was afterwards altered to " *Stephen Williams* and *Clement Bellamy*, of the *Poultry*, *London*, linen drapers."   [*Abbott*, C. J. We do not know the contents of the affidavit upon which that was done.] There are several cases mentioned in *Rolle's Abridgement*,

(a) " An inquisition, which is *good in substance*, but defective in form, may be amended. 1 Sid. 225, 259 ; 3 Mod. 101 ; 1 Saund. 356 ; 1 Keb. 907 ; 1 Haw. P. C.,

c. 27, s. 15." Jervis on Coroners, 280.
   (b) Com. Dig. tit. *Officer*. (G.12.)
   (c) 3 Mod. 101.
   (d) 1 Sid. 259.

in which the sheriff has amended the names of jurors in the panel after verdict(a); in *Rex* v. *Atkinson*(b), it was held that the caption of an indictment might be amended by inserting the names of the grand jurors; and in *Rex* v. *Harrison* (c), it is said, that an inquest may be amended in all points except the matter of the verdict.

ABBOTT, C. J.—This inquisition is defective in several respects, and we are asked to supply the defects by amendments. The inquisition does not state where the death happened, nor where the body was found; it does not set out the names of the jurors in the body, nor is it subscribed with their christian names at length at the foot. In all these particulars, we are asked to allow of amendments. Now it is essential for the purpose of originating the jurisdiction of the coroner, that the inqusition should state where the death happened, and where the body was found; these, therefore, are defects in substance, not in form merely; and we should be going further than this Court has ever yet gone, if we were to allow amendments of such a nature. They are not required for the advancement of justice, and that is the only purpose for which, generally speaking, amendments are allowed. But in addition to this, we are asked to alter the finding of the jury with respect to the ownership of the coach and horses by which the death was occasioned. If this were an indictment found by a grand jury at the assizes, in which the Court has power to amend matters of form, but not of substance, such an alteration as this clearly could not be made; neither can it be made in this inquisition. The present rule, therefore, must be discharged.

The other Judges concurring,

Rule discharged.

(a) 1 Rol. Abr. 196. tit. *Amendment*, (B.)

(b) 4 East, 176, n. And see

Rex v. *Aylett*, and *Rex* v. *Darley. Ibid.*

(c) 1 Sid. 225.

Campbell then moved that the inquisition might be quashed for the defects before mentioned, and,

1827.

The KING
v.
EVETT.

, *Per Curiam,*

Inquisition quashed.

━━━◆━━━

CHECCHI and Wife *v.* POWELL and others.

*Monday,
February 12.*

THIS was an action by husband and wife for money lent by the wife before her marriage. Notice of trial had been given and countermanded, and a rule for judgment as in case of a nonsuit thereupon obtained. The wife had died after the notice of trial given.

Russell shewed cause. The action being for money lent by the wife before her marriage, and the wife having died after notice of trial given, the action has abated, and is at an end. The debt was a *chose in action,* never reduced into possession by the husband. Now the husband cannot recover the *chose in action* of the wife, unless he does reduce it into possession in her lifetime. Upon her death, it passes to her personal representative. Lord *Coke* lays down the law upon the point most clearly. He says, " the marriage is an absolute gift of all chattels personal of the wife in possession in her own right, whether the husband survive the wife or no; but if they be in action, as debts by obligation, contract, or otherwise, the husband shall not have them unless he and his wife recover them." (*a*) *Beamond* v. *Long* (*b*) shews that the bringing an action is not sufficient to change the property, unless judgment is obtained before the wife dies; for the Court there said, " if judgment be recovered, and the wife die, there the husband may have a *scire facias* to execute that judgment; for the debt being recovered, the husband, after the death of the wife, shall have it." *Woodyear* v. *Gresham* (*c*) is another authority to the same effect.

Where husband and wife sue for money lent by the wife while sole, and the wife dies pending the suit, the suit abates, and the defendant cannot have judgment as in case of a nonsuit.

(*a*) Co. Litt. 351 b.   (*b*) Cro. Car. 227.   (*c*) Carth. 415.

Halcomb, contrà. The husband may release or assign the *chose in action* of the wife during her lifetime, and it will pass to his assignees in the event of his bankruptcy. It is only a technical rule which requires her name to be joined where an action is brought. The action in this case was properly commenced, and the husband has done all that in him lay to reduce the debt into possession while his wife was living. Then, as he has been guilty of no laches, the Court will allow him to enter upon the record a suggestion of the death of his wife, and to proceed with the action. If the money was due to the wife, the husband is at all events entitled to recover it; for he has a right to sue out letters of administration under the statute 29 *Car. 2,* c. 3, s. 25.

ABBOTT, C. J.—There is no question before the Court respecting an equitable assignment of the wife's *chose in action,* or the effect of the bankruptcy of the husband. The doctrine laid down by Lord *Coke,* in Co. Litt. 351 b., has always been received in *Westminster Hall* as good law. Then, in this case, as the debt was never recovered during the lifetime of the wife, it has never vested in the husband, and he cannot go on with this action. He may have another mode of enforcing his claim as his wife's personal representative, but he clearly cannot proceed with this suit. The rule, therefore, must be discharged.

The other Judges concurred.

Rule discharged.

1827.

Monday,
February 12.

FAREWELL, Administratrix, *v.* DICKENSON.

DEBT for rent. The declaration alleged a demise of " a messuage, land, and premises, with the appurtenances." At the trial before *Bayley, J.*, at the last *Middlesex* sittings in the present term, the plaintiff, in order to prove the amount of rent due, produced an agreement between the defendant and the intestate, in which the premises demised were described as " a messuage or tenement, stable, and out-buildings, with the cottage, garden, land, and appurtenances belonging thereto, *together with the furniture, utensils* and *implements.*" The learned Judge was of opinion that the agreement was an entire contract for the rent of the house and the furniture, and, therefore, that the variance was fatal. He consequently directed a nonsuit, but gave the plaintiff leave to move to set aside the nonsuit, and to enter a verdict for 120*l.*

In a declaration in debt for rent, an averment of a demise of " a messuage, land, and premises, with the appurtenances," is well supported by proof of a demise of " a messuage, &c. together with the furniture, utensils and implements."

Rowe, on a former day, moved accordingly, and obtained a rule *nisi.* He cited *Spencer's* case (a), *Emott* v. *Cole* (b), *Newman* v. *Anderson* (c), and *Walsh* v. *Pemberton* (d), and relied upon those cases as authorities to shew that the whole rent in this case issued out of the land, and no portion of it out of the furniture, and, therefore, that the demise was well laid as a demise of the house only, and that there was no fatal variance.

Chitty now shewed cause. The declaration describes the demise as one of real property only; the agreement shews that it comprised both real and personal property: that is a fatal variance. The word " appurtenances" in the declaration, appended as it is to real property, will not include personal effects. It may be true that the rent issues principally out of the realty, but that will not cure the

(a) 5 Co. Rep. 17.   (c) 2 New. Rep. 224.
(b) Cro. Eliz. 255.   (d) Selw. N. P. 616, 6th ed.

variance; for the "furniture" is no part of the realty, and the rent must be considered as issuing in part out of the furniture. The agreement was an entire contract for all the property demised at one rent; the whole property vested in the tenant by the demise: and if the furniture had not formed a part of the property demised, the lease would have been of less value, and the rent of smaller amount.

Rowe, contrà, was stopped by the Court.

ABBOTT, C. J.—The furniture is undoubtedly one of the things demised, and that is not mentioned in the declaration. But, in point of law, the rent issued out of the land demised, and not out of the furniture; therefore it was sufficient for the plaintiff to allege and prove a demise of the land out of which the rent which she claimed issued. The consequence is, that there is no variance, that the nonsuit was wrong, and that the rule for entering a verdict for the plaintiff must be made absolute.

The other Judges concurred.

Rule absolute (*a*).

(*a*) "As a rent could not issue out of an incorporeal hereditament, so, it was held, that it could not be reserved out of a mere personal chattel; and that a covenant for payment of it would not bind the assignee. *Spencer's* case, 5 Co. Rep. 17. Upon which ground it was much doubted, whether rent reserved upon a lease of land with stock upon it, or on the de-mise of a ready-furnished house or lodgings, could be distrained for, as the greater part of the rent must be considered as paid for the goods; but it has been determined that it can, because, in contemplation of law, the whole rent issues out of the land or premises demised. *Newman* v. *Anderson,* 2 New Rep. 224." *Bradby on Distresses,* 26. And see *id.* 103.

GENERAL RULES.

HILARY TERM, 7 & 8 *Geo.* 4, 1827.

1. WHEREAS much vexation and expense have been occasioned to defendants in informations in the nature of Quo Warranto, by the practise of raising issues upon various matters distinct from the ground on which the information was granted by the Court:

Now, for providing a remedy in this behalf, it is ordered, that from henceforth the objections intended to be made to the title of the defendant shall be specified in the rule to shew cause, and that no objection, not so specified, shall be raised by the prosecutor on the pleadings, without the special leave of the Court, or of some Judge thereof.

2. It is ordered, that no officer of the King's Bench prison, or any of the persons employed by the Marshal therein, in the management or superintendence of the prison or prisoners, shall either directly or indirectly be concerned in selling any article to, or doing any work for, any of the prisoners; and that the Marshal shall remove from his place every such officer or person aforesaid who shall be guilty of violating this Rule, pursuant to the Rule of this Court of *Michaelmas* term, in the 58th year of his late Majesty.

WAGSTAFFE *v.* BOARDMAN (*a*).

In an action by the indorsee against the indorser of a bill of exchange, evidence of an acknowledgement of an existing debt and of a promise to pay by the defendant, is admissible and sufficient to support a count upon an account stated.

ASSUMPSIT by the indorsee against the indorser of a bill of exchange, with the usual money counts, and a count upon an account stated. At the trial before *Hullock*, B. at the last Assizes for the county of *Lancaster*, there appearing to be a fatal variance between the bill itself and the description of it in the declaration, it was admitted that the plaintiff could not recover upon the counts setting out the bill. It was then proposed to give evidence of an admission of the debt by the defendant, coupled with a promise to pay, which, it was contended, would entitle the plaintiff to recover upon the count upon an account stated. The learned Judge was of opinion that the evidence was not admissible, and nonsuited the plaintiff. In *Michaelmas* term last, a rule *nisi* for a new trial having been obtained,

Starkie now shewed cause. The evidence was properly rejected. The plaintiff had no cause of action except upon the bill of exchange, and it was to that instrument the acknowledgment referred. There is no case to be found in which it has been held that such evidence would support a count upon an account stated, under such circumstances and between such parties as the present. *Knowles* v. *Mitchell* (*b*), *Leaper* v. *Tatton* (*c*), and *Highmore* v. *Primrose* (*d*), will probably be cited on the other side; but in all those cases there was an original debt, there was a privity of contract between the parties, and the defendant was primarily liable. Here there was no original debt from the defendant to the plaintiff, there was no privity of contract between them, the defendant was not an original party to

(*a*) The three puisne Judges of this Court sat, as on former occasions, from *Tuesday* the 13th, to *Thursday* the 22d of *February* inclusive; and from *Monday* the 30th of *April*, to *Tuesday* the 1st of *May* inclusive; during which periods this and the following cases were decided.

(*b*) 13 East, 249.
(*c*) 16 East, 420.
(*d*) 5 M. & S. 65.

the bill, nor primarily liable to the plaintiff. The only
dealing between these parties was constructively by the
custom of merchants upon the bill, and therefore the plaintiff could rely only upon the bill to support his claim
against the defendant.

D. F. Jones, contrà, was stopped by the Court.

BAYLEY, J.—I am of opinion that the evidence tendered
and rejected in this case should have been received, and,
therefore, that there ought to be a new trial. Evidence of
an existing debt is sufficient to support a count upon an account stated. The circumstance of the defendant in this instance not being an original party to the bill makes no difference, for his indorsement of the bill created a debt from
him to the indorsee. Besides, his acknowledgment of an
existing debt, and his promise to pay it, created a privity of
contract between him and the plaintiff, independently of the
bill, and was good evidence to support the count upon an
account stated. The rule for a new trial, therefore, must
be made absolute.

HOLROYD, J. and LITTLEDALE, J. concurred.

Rule absolute.

————◆————

HOBSON and another *v.* MIDDLETON.

DECLARATION in covenant, that by a certain indenture
made between *William Thomas Hislop*, of the first part;
defendant, *Middleton*, of the second part; and plaintiffs,
executors of *Samuel Hobson*, of the third part; defendant,
for the consideration therein mentioned, did, according to

A covenant
that defendant
has not *per-
mitted or suf-
fered* to be
done any act
whereby an
estate was en-
cumbered, is not broken by his *consenting* to an act which he *could not prevent*.
It is a general rule in pleading that an equivocal expression shall be construed against
the party using it; but if the other party pleads over, it shall be construed in that sense
which will support the previous pleadings.

his estate, right and interest in the premises thereinafter mentioned, but not by way of warranty or covenant for title, or further, or otherwise, bargain, sell, and demise; and *W. T. Hislop* did grant, bargain, sell, demise, ratify, and confirm unto plaintiffs, certain premises in the indenture particularly described, to hold to plaintiffs for 500 years. And defendant covenanted with plaintiffs, that he had not, at any time or times theretofore, made, done, or committed, or executed, or knowingly or willingly *permitted or suffered* any act, deed, matter, or thing whatsoever, whereby, or by reason or means whereof the premises thereinbefore mentioned and intended to be thereby granted and demised, or any part thereof, were, could, should, or might be impeached, charged, encumbered, or affected in title, charge, estate, or otherwise howsoever. Breach, that defendant had, before the time of making the indenture, made, done, and executed certain acts and deeds, whereby the premises were impeachable, charged, encumbered, and affected in title, charge, and estate; that is to say, that defendant heretofore and before the making of the covenant, by a certain conveyance or assurance, parted with and conveyed his right, title, estate and interest in the premises to one *Joseph Scholes*. Second breach, that defendant, before the making of the indenture, had made, done, committed, and executed, and knowingly and willingly *permitted and suffered to be done*, certain other acts, deeds, matters, and things, whereby, and by reason whereof, the premises were impeachable, charged, encumbered, and affected in title, charge, and estate; that is to say, that defendant heretofore and before the making of the indenture, did execute a certain deed or indenture, between *W. T. Hislop*, of the first part; defendant, of the second part; one *Joseph Scholes*, of the third part; and one *Edwin Ford*, of the fourth part; and did *suffer and permit W. T. Hislop* to execute the indenture; whereby the premises were impeachable, charged, encumbered and affected in title, charge and estate. Pleas, first, the general issue. Second, that long before and at the

time of making the conveyance to *Joseph Scholes* in the
declaration mentioned, one *Robert Tudor* was seised in his
demesne as of fee of and in the premises in the declaration
mentioned; and being so seised, by indenture bearing date
25th *March*, 1813, made between *Robert Tudor*, of the first
part; *W. T. Hislop*, of the second part; and defendant, of
the third part; *Robert Tudor*, for the money therein mentioned, did bargain, sell, alien, release, and confirm the premises (then in the actual possession of *W. T. Hislop* and
defendant) to *W. T. Hislop* and defendant, their heirs and
assigns, to hold to *W. T. Hislop* and defendant, their heirs
and assigns, to the use and behoof of *W. T. Hislop* and his
assigns, during the term of his natural life; and from and
after the determination of the estate, by any means in his
life-time, to the use of defendant, his executors, &c. during
the natural life of *W. T. Hislop*, in trust for *W. T. Hislop*
and his assigns, and to be conveyed and disposed of as he or
they should direct or appoint; and from and after the determination of the estate so limited to defendant, to the only
proper use and behoof of *W. T. Hislop*, his heirs and
assigns for ever. That defendant was, at the time of
making the conveyance to *Joseph Scholes*, as in the declaration mentioned, possessed of such estate and interest in the
premises as in this plea above stated, and of no other estate
or interest whatever in the same; and being so possessed of
such estate and interest in the premises, and having no other
or greater estate or interest in the premises, defendant did
afterwards, and before the making the indenture in the declaration mentioned, part with and convey his right, title,
estate and interest in the premises to *Joseph Scholes*, in
manner and form as in the declaration mentioned, without
this, that by the conveyance to *Joseph Scholes* of the right,
title, estate and interest of defendant in the premises, the
hereditaments and premises in the declaration mentioned
were impeachable, charged, encumbered or affected in title,
charge or estate, in manner and form as plaintiffs have in their
declaration in that behalf alleged; concluding with a verification. The fifth plea was similar, only omitting the traverse.

To the second breach defendant pleaded, secondly, that nothing passed by the indenture in that breach mentioned, whereby the premises were impeachable, &c. concluding with a verification. Sixth plea, as to so much of the second breach as related to *permitting and suffering Hislop* to execute, that defendant, protesting that he did not permit or suffer *Hislop* to execute the indenture in that breach mentioned, *could not prevent* his executing it; concluding with a verification. Demurrer to the second and fifth pleas to the first breach, and joinder in demurrer. Replication to the second plea to the second breach, that an interest did pass by the indenture in that breach mentioned, whereby the premises were impeachable, &c. concluding to the country. To the sixth plea to the second breach, that *Hislop* executed the indenture *with the consent* of defendant; concluding with a verification. Demurrer to the replication to the second plea to the second breach, assigning for causes, that it was not stated in that replication what interest passed by the indenture, by which the premises, or any part thereof, could be impeachable, &c., nor was it shewn from whom or which of the parties to the indenture any interest in the premises passed; and that the replication did not deny or take any certain issue upon any fact alleged in the second plea, but disclosed new matter to the Court, and should have concluded with a verification, and not to the country. General demurrer to the replication to the sixth plea to the second breach. Joinder in demurrer.

Parke, in support of the demurrer to the pleas. The second plea to the first breach is clearly bad. It states what interest the defendant had at the time of the execution of the conveyance to *Scholes;* admits that that interest passed to *Scholes* by that conveyance; and then traverses that the estate was thereby encumbered. But the effect of the conveyance is matter of law, and is, therefore, not the subject of traverse, to be sent to a jury. The fifth plea is equally bad with the second, because, although it omits the traverse, it admits matters which amount to a breach of the covenant. It shews that the defendant had the legal estate in remainder after the determination of *Hislop's* life estate by any means in his life-time. Now that, although in trust for *Hislop* and his assigns, was nevertheless a vested estate in the defendant; and if he conveyed it for a valuable consideration, without notice of the trust, *Scholes* would hold the estate discharged of the trust; and even if the defendant conveyed with notice of the trust, so that *Scholes* might in equity be declared a trustee for the plaintiff, still that would have the effect of forcing a new trustee upon the plaintiff. [*Bayley*, J. That is entirely matter for a court of equity, we cannot take notice that *Scholes* would be declared a trustee.] The conveyance, in either point of view, was clearly a breach of the covenant. The second breach is different. [*Holroyd*, J. How is it shewn on the part of the plaintiff that the defendant could have prevented *Hislop* from executing the indenture?] Perhaps he could not prevent him, but that is immaterial; he suffered him to execute, and that was a breach of the covenant. If the defendant had objected to the conveyance, or had even not consented to or joined in it, *non constat* that the purchaser would have accepted it; and if so, his consent, as alleged in the replication to the sixth plea to the second breach, was a breach of the covenant. [*Holroyd*, J. The words " permit and suffer" in the covenant must be construed strictly; I think you cannot support the second breach.] At any rate the pleas to the first breach are bad, and so far the plaintiff is clearly entitled to judgment.

Wightman, contrà. The defendant was merely a trustee for *Hislop*, therefore the conveyance by him was not an encumbrance upon the estate within the meaning of the covenants. It must be admitted that the defendant had a vested estate in remainder after the determination of *Hislop's* life estate, but until such determination the conveyance by the defendant could not operate as an encumbrance; and *Hislop's* life estate is, by construction of law, greater than the term for 500 years. [*Bayley*, J. It seems to me impossible to say that there was not an encumbrance. The conveyance to *Scholes* was a conveyance of part of the estate; *Scholes* took a vested interest under it; that clearly establishes the first breach.] The second breach is more material. Now that does not state from whom the conveyance proceeded, nor what interest passed under it; and the replication to the sixth plea is equally vague and uncertain. The plaintiff was bound to shew that some interest passed from some person, capable of operating as an encumbrance upon the estate. [*Holroyd*, J. I think the plaintiff has shewn as much as it was in his power to shew. He states by his declaration, that by the indenture executed by the defendant, and by *Hislop* by the defendant's permission, the estate was encumbered and affected in title. To that the defendant might have pleaded that the estate was not encumbered, instead of which he has pleaded that no interest passed; having done that, and the indenture being within his knowledge, it became his duty to shew the nature of it.] Then if the plea is bad, the Court will look back to the first fault, which is the plaintiff's, in the assignment of the breach; for that leaves it equivocal whether the estate was or was not encumbered by means of the execution of the indenture by the defendant and *Hislop*. [*Holroyd*, J. The defendant should have demurred to the declaration. The language of the breach is equivocal and informal no doubt; but the defendant has cured that informality by pleading over.] If the language of the breach is equivocal, it ought to be construed against the plaintiff, the party using it. [*Bayley*, J. That is the general rule in pleading undoubtedly; but where the opposite party pleads over, he cures the fault, because he admits that the equivocal expression is to be taken in the sense which will support the previous pleading. *Avery* v. *Hoole* (a)]. At any rate the sixth plea to the second breach is good, namely, that the defendant could not prevent *Hislop* from executing the conveyance; and the replication that *Hislop* executed it with the consent of the defendant is no answer, for the defendant's

(a) 2 Cowp. 825.

consenting to an act which he was unable to prevent was perfectly immaterial. The words " permit and suffer" in the covenant must be taken as applying to such acts only as the defendant could prevent; and his consenting to *Hislop's* execution, which he could not prevent, did no harm, and was no breach of the covenant.

Parke, in reply. *Consenting* is *permitting and suffering* within the fair meaning of these covenants. The words " permit and suffer" are not to be construed strictly, at least not so strictly as to confine their operation to acts over which the covenantor has a control. In *The Mayor of Liverpool* v. *Tomlinson* (*a*), where the proper construction of those words in a covenant were matter of consideration, *Bayley*, J. said, " It is said that the defendant could not prevent, and therefore cannot be said to have permitted or suffered the doing of the act. But he might have prevented it by a proper arrangement, or, at least, he ought to have taken that into consideration before he bound himself by such a covenant." And in *Butler* v. *Swinnerton* (*b*), a very extensive meaning was assigned by the Court to the words " privity and procurement."

BAYLEY, J.—I am of opinion that the plaintiff is entitled to recover on the first breach, and to judgment on the demurrer to the replication to the second plea to the second breach; but that the defendant is entitled to judgment on the sixth plea to the second breach. The traverse in the second plea to the first breach is mere matter of law; that plea, therefore, is clearly bad. The fifth plea to the first breach omits the traverse, but sets out all the facts set out in the inducement to the second plea. Those facts make it appear very clearly, that the defendant had a vested interest in the premises, a legal estate which was to take effect whenever *Hislop's* life estate should be determined, during his life. Now that interest and estate the defendant has

(*a*) *Ante,* Vol. VII. 562.　　(*b*) Cro. Jac. 656.

conveyed away, and has thereby been guilty of a breach of his covenant; for we cannot look to the trusts which might attach upon the estate in the hands of a purchaser, nor take into consideration the chance or the amount of the damage, however slight or nominal. Then comes the second breach. That alleges, " that the defendant, before the making of the indenture in the declaration mentioned, did execute a certain deed or indenture, between *Hislop,* the defendant, *Scholes* and *Ford,* and did *suffer and permit Hislop* to execute it, *whereby* the premises were encumbered and affected in title." The second plea to that breach is, " that nothing passed by that indenture *whereby* the premises were encumbered or affected in title." The replication to that plea is, " that an interest did pass by that indenture, *whereby* the premises were encumbered and affected in title." To that replication there is a special demurrer, " that it does not state what interest passed by the indenture, nor from whom it passed." Now with respect to the nature of the interest, that was a matter necessarily more within the knowledge of the defendant, therefore I do not consider that it was incumbent on the plaintiff to set that out. The consideration of the other branch of this demurrer, namely, the person from whom the interest passed, brings us back to the breach. The import of the word *whereby* there used is certainly equivocal. It may mean that the premises were encumbered and affected in title by the deed itself; or it may mean that the execution of the deed by the defendant, and his permitting and suffering *Hislop* to execute it, produced the encumbrance. If by the word *whereby* the deed alone is meant, the breach is bad; if it applies to the execution by the defendant and his suffering *Hislop* to execute, the breach is good. Now although, as was suggested during the argument, both by my brother *Holroyd* and myself, the general rule in pleading is, that an equivocal expression shall be construed against the party using it; still, if the other party pleads over, he thereby admits that the expression is used in that sense which will support the previous pleading, and so cures the informality (a). In this case, the defendant by pleading over that nothing passed by the deed *whereby* the premises were encumbered or affected in title, must mean that nothing passed by the execution of the deed by the defendant and *Hislop*. Now the replication puts that question in issue, therefore it seems to me that the replication is good, and that our judgment upon the demurrer to that replication must be for the plaintiff. Then comes the sixth plea to the second breach. That is pleaded to so much of that breach as relates to the defendant " permitting and suffering" *Hislop* to execute the deed in that breach mentioned, and it states that the defendant could not prevent *Hislop* from executing. The replication to that plea is, that *Hislop* executed the deed with the consent of the defendant; and then the question is, whether that *consent* is a *permitting and suffering* so as to constitute a breach of the covenant. Now the words " suffering and permitting" are not co-extensive in their import with the words " knowing of and being privy to;" they mean only that the defendant will not concur in any act over which he has the control, or which he has the power to prevent. As regards his own execution of the deed, the defendant admits the breach; as regards the residue, he says he could not prevent it: and if " permitting and suffering" applies only to that which he could prevent, as I think it does, it follows that his consent in this case was not a breach of the covenant. It was suggested in the course of the argument, that the defendant's non-consent might have prevented the execution of the deed, inasmuch as without his consent the purchaser might perhaps have refused to accept the conveyance; but as the plaintiff has not thought proper to raise that point by his replication, the Court cannot raise it for him.

HOLROYD, J. concurred.

(a) Vide *Avery* v. *Hoole*, 2 Cowp. 285; *ante*, p. 254.

1827.

Hobson
v.
Middleton.

Littledale, J. was sitting at the Old Bailey.

Judgment for the plaintiff on the demurrer to the second and fifth pleas to the first breach, and on the demurrer to the replication to the second plea to the second breach; and for the defendant on the demurrer to the replication to the sixth plea to the second breach.

———◆———

Corbett v. Packington, Bart.

A count stating "that plaintiff, at the request of defendant, caused to be delivered to defendant divers pigs, to be taken care of by defend^ant for plaintiff, for reward to defendant, and, in consideration thereof, defendant undertook and agreed with plaintiff to take care of the pigs, and to re-deliver them on request," is a count in assumpsit, and cannot be joined with counts in case.

Case for negligently keeping plaintiff's pigs, whereby they were lost. The first and third counts of the declaration were properly framed in *case*. The fourth count was in *trover*. The second count was in the following form:—

"That plaintiff, at the like request of defendant, had caused to be delivered to defendant divers other pigs, to be taken care of by defendant for plaintiff, for reward to him, defendant, in that behalf, and, *in consideration thereof*, he, defendant, *undertook*, and then and there *agreed* with plaintiff, to take due and proper care of the last-mentioned pigs, *and to re-deliver* the same to plaintiff when defendant should be thereto afterwards requested; and although defendant was afterwards, to wit, on, &c. requested by plaintiff to re-deliver the same to plaintiff, yet defendant, not regarding his duty in that behalf, did not, when so requested, re-deliver them; but, on the contrary, by and through his carelessness, the last-mentioned pigs became wholly lost to plaintiff."

Plea, the general issue, not guilty, and issue thereon. At the trial before *Garrow*, B., at the *Worcestershire* Summer Assizes, 1826, the plaintiff obtained a verdict. In *Michaelmas* term last a rule *nisi* was granted for arresting the judgment, on the ground of a misjoinder of counts, the second count being, as it was contended, framed in *assumpsit*.

Peake, Serj. now shewed cause. It will not be disputed that the first, third, and fourth counts in this declaration are properly framed in case, but it will be contended that the second count shews a cause of action arising *ex contractu;* that it is, in short, framed in assumpsit, and therefore cannot be joined with the other counts. According to the old practice, a plaintiff might declare in case for all the causes of action for which it is now customary to declare in assumpsit; and properly so: for the distinction between the two forms of action is, when rightly considered, scarcely more than ideal. Against carriers, as one instance, it was formerly usual to declare in case; the practice now is, to declare in assumpsit; but either form of action is clearly maintainable. So, in this case, either case or assumpsit would clearly lie upon the facts disclosed in the declaration, and if so, there seems to be no valid objection against joining counts in both in the same declaration. But the second count in this declaration is not framed in assumpsit. There is nothing stated in it shewing a cause of action necessarily arising *ex contractu.* The facts which it states raise a duty without any promise; and if that duty has been violated, either by the wilful act, or by the negligence of the defendant, a cause of action arises which is properly *ex delicto,* and not *ex contractu.* [*Bayley,* J. The second count alleges that the defendant undertook and agreed; surely that is very like assumpsit.] But it does not allege that he promised, and the words " undertook and agreed," standing by themselves, imply only a duty cast upon the defendant. Even if those words can be held to amount to an allegation of a promise, still the count merely states that the defendant promised to do that which he was legally liable to do; and that will support a cause of action *ex delicto.* There are cases in the books which go far to support this argument. *Brown* v. *Dixon* (a) is in point. The first count in that case was in trover for a dog. The second

1827.

CORBETT
v.
PACKINGTON.

(1) 1 T. R. 274.

stated that the plaintiff, at the defendant's request, had de-livered a dog to the defendant, to be returned at a reason-able time, but that the defendant did not return the dog, but carried it to places unknown to the plaintiff, and de-tained it, until, through his carelessness, the dog was lost. Upon special demurrer to the declaration, upon the ground that the second count was framed in assumpsit, the Court held the declaration good. And *Buller*, J. said, " Perhaps the rule of judging whether two counts can be joined, by considering whether the same judgment can be given on both, is not true in its extent; but by adding another re-quisite, it is universally true: for wherever the same plea may be pleaded, and the same judgment given on two counts, they may be joined in the same declaration." And again, " Assumpsit and tort cannot be joined together, be-cause the pleas to both are not the same; but the whole of this is case: the same plea of not guilty goes to the whole declaration, and the Court may give the same judgment on the whole." Now the rule there laid down applies here. The count objected to in that case, as being framed in as-sumpsit, can scarcely be distinguished from the second count in the present case; how then can it be said, that the plea of not guilty might not be properly pleaded, as in fact it has been, to the whole of this declaration, or that the same judgment might not be pronounced upon the whole declaration? And if not, there is no misjoinder. *Judin* v. *Samuel*(a), is an authority to the same effect. It was there held by the Court of Common Pleas, that a count stating, that the plaintiff had delivered a note to the defend-ant to get it discounted, or to account to the plaintiff for the money raised upon it, and that the defendant received the money for that purpose, but intending to defraud the plaintiff had not, though requested, accounted with him, was laid in tort, (whether formal or not in its frame,) and not in assumpsit; and that it was no ground of general de-

(a) 1 New Rep. 43.

1827.

CORBETT
v.
PACKINGTON.

murrer that it was joined with a count in assumpsit. And that decision was afterwards confirmed by the Court of King's Bench on a writ of error (*a*). *Govett* v. *Rudnidge*(*b*) involves the same principle. There, in an action against three defendants, the plaintiff declared, that they had the loading of a hogshead, his property, for certain reward to be paid to one of them, and for certain other reward to the others, and that the defendants so negligently conducted themselves in the loading, that the hogshead was damaged: it was held, that the gist of the action was the tort, and not the contract out of which it arose; and therefore, that on plea of not guilty, the two being acquitted, judgment might be had against the third, who was found guilty. So in *Brotherton* v. *Wood*(*c*), in the Exchequer Chamber, where the subject was fully discussed, and all the cases bearing upon it carefully examined, it was held that proof of contract was not necessary to support an action against a common carrier; that he may be sued in an action on the case for the injury as arising *ex delicto*; and that such an action is not necessarily to be considered *quasi ex contractu*, or to be founded on contract. In all the cases that will be cited on the other side, a contract was necessary in order to originate a cause of action, because without it there was no plain legal obligation bearing upon the defendant; here the defendant is charged as a common baillee, and there is such an obligation shewn, independently of any contract at all. In *Orton* v. *Butler*(*d*) the demurrer was to the particular count, and not to the whole declaration for a misjoinder of counts; and the count was held bad because the cause of action was the non-payment of money, which cannot properly be considered as a cause of action *ex delicto*. [*Bayley*, J. Might not your second count be well joined with other counts framed confessedly in assumpsit? *Littledale*, J. And would not a plea, that the defendant did not

(*a*) *Samuel* v. *Judin*, 6 East, 333.   (*d*) 5 B. & A. 652; 1 D. & R.
(*b*) 3 East, 62.   282.
(*c*) 6 Moore, 141; 9 Price, 408.

undertake and agree *modo et formâ*, be a good plea to such a declaration?] It is submitted, not. The word *agree* will not constitute assumpsit, without the word *promise*. In *Coggs* v. *Bernard* (a), a count containing the word *undertook* was held good as laid in tort, and *undertook* is a much stronger term than *agreed*; here the word agreed may be rejected as surplusage. [*Littledale*, J. In *Mountford* v. *Horton* (b) it was held, that the word agreed implied a promise, without any averment of mutual promises.] There the count was clearly framed in assumpsit, and the whole cause of action arose out of a contract. Here there is a cause of action arising out of a duty, without any contract at all.

Taunton, contrà. The case of *Orton* v. *Butler* (c) is material on the present occasion, not as a decision expressly in point, but as containing the solemnly pronounced opinion of the Court, as to the importance of adhering to the forms of action provided by the law for particular cases. If those forms are to be adhered to, the present case is at once decided by that of *Mountford* v. *Horton*, for it was there held that the word *agreed* was equivalent to the word *promised*. It follows, that the second count in this declaration, which contains the word *agreed*, and shews a sufficient consideration for the agreement, is a count in assumpsit, and might well be joined with counts expressly adapted to that form of action. The Court, therefore, cannot hold that this count can be joined with counts in case, without either overruling the case of *Mountford* v. *Horton* on the one hand, or incurring the charge of inconsistency on the other. But independently of any cases, this count, by the whole of its language, approves itself a count in assumpsit, and not in case. Reward is to be paid to the defendant; that implies a contract. In consideration thereof he under-

(a) 2 Ld. Raym. 909.   (c) 5 B. & A. 652; 1 D. & R.
(b) 2 New Rep. 62.   282.

takes and agrees to redeliver; that implies a contract. It is impossible to say that such a count is any other than a count in assumpsit; and if so, it cannot be joined with counts in case, and this rule must be made absolute.

BAYLEY, J.—I cannot but regret the effect of our deciding in favour of this objection, which is merely technical, and quite beside the justice of the case; but it appears to me that the objection is fatal, and therefore we have no alternative: we must make the rule for arresting the judgment absolute. It has been properly admitted that counts in tort and in assumpsit cannot be joined in the same declaration; and the only question, therefore, is, whether the second count of this declaration is framed in the one form of action or the other. It has been urged in argument that the count in question is not a count in assumpsit, because it does not allege that the defendant *promised*, and because it states only a duty on the part of the defendant, which the law would impose without any promise. Now it was certainly held in the case of *Lea* v. *Welch* (a), that a count was not good in assumpsit which did not allege a promise by the defendant. But in that case it was not stated that the defendant either undertook or agreed; here both those words are inserted, and the case of *Mountford* v. *Horton* (b), which I think a sensible decision, goes the whole length of proving that those words amount to a promise. This count, therefore, is in form in assumpsit. It was then argued, that as the alleged agreement was only to perform that which was a common law duty, it was unnecessary to resort to any promise, and therefore it might be rejected, and the count be still considered as a count in tort. Now the only common law duty of the defendant was to take care of the pigs delivered to him until the plaintiff should come and fetch them away; but this count goes beyond

(a) 2 Ld. Raym. 1516; 2 Stra. 743.   (b) 2 New Rep. 62.

that, for it alleges that the defendant, in consideration of reward to be paid to him, undertook and agreed to take care of the pigs, *and to redeliver them to the plaintiff on request ;* and the breach is that he did not redeliver them on request. Now that lays upon the defendant a duty beyond his common law obligation, namely, the duty to redeliver, which arose entirely and exclusively out of the agreement. In *Coggs* v. *Bernard* (a), the declaration undoubtedly. contained the word undertook, but there was no consideration for a promise shewn, and the plea was not guilty. The declaration consisted of one count only, and no question of misjoinder could arise. It was held to be a count in tort, and I think properly so, because one essential ingredient in a contract, namely, a consideration, was wanting. Here the count shews both a promise and a sufficient consideration to support that promise; it is therefore clearly a count in assumpsit, and cannot be joined with counts in tort. It might, perhaps, be not impossible so to frame a count charging only a common law duty, that it might be joined with other counts either in tort or assumpsit; but it is not necessary to express any decided opinion upon that point. For the reasons I have already given, I am of opinion that the judgment in this case must be arrested.

HOLROYD, J.—I concur in thinking that the judgment in this case must be arrested. The objection is of an ungracious nature, and I at one time entertained a hope that it might be surmounted by considering the count as disclosing merely a common law obligation, although arising out of a contract, as in the case of *Mast* v. *Goodson* (b). But this count, unfortunately, discloses an undertaking which goes far beyond the defendant's common law obligation; for it shews not only that the defendant was to do that for which the pigs were delivered to him, namely, to take care of them, but that he was to redeliver them when

(a) 2 Ld. Raym. 909.   (b) 3 Wils. 348.

requested, and the breach is more properly speaking a breach of the undertaking to redeliver, than it is of the common law obligation to take care of the pigs. In *Must* v. *Goodson* (a), the plaintiff's right arose *ex contractu;* but the obstruction to that right, for which the action was brought, arose *ex delicto :* which cannot be said of the breach in the second count in this case. In *Beson* v. *Sandford* (b), it was held that the action for not safely carrying the goods was not *ex delicto*, but *quasi ex contractu,* and that a non-feasance could not be treated as *delictum,* so as to make the action maintainable against two of four joint owners of the vessel.

LITTLEDALE, J.—I am clearly of opinion that the second count in this declaration is framed in assumpsit, and was therefore improperly joined with the count in trover. It possesses all the real requisites of a count in assumpsit, except that the word *agreed* is substituted for the word *promised.* But agreeing is equivalent to promising; that was decided in the case of *Mountford* v. *Horton* (c), and I think the decision right. *Coggs* v. *Bernard* (d), and the other cases of that class, are quite different from the present, for there, although the word undertook occurred in the declaration, it was inserted merely as inducement; here it is introduced as a substantial allegation, after the inducement, which is the delivery of the pigs. Besides, this count would be bad in itself as a count in tort, for in that case the whole extent of the defendant's duty would have been to take care of the pigs; but the undertaking goes further, and is to redeliver: therefore it is larger than the purpose for which the pigs were delivered. Suppose the parties had entered into a written agreement in the terms of this count, it could not have been contended that a breach of it

(a) 3 Wils. 348.   (c) 2 New Rep. 62.
(b) 2 Salk. 440.   (d) 2 Ld. Raym. 909.

might have been laid in tort; it would be as reasonable to lay in tort a breach of an agreement to convey a house or land. For these reasons I concur in the opinion that the judgment in this case must be arrested.

Rule absolute to arrest the judgment.

The COMPANY of PROPRIETORS of the STAFFORDSHIRE and WORCESTERSHIRE CANAL NAVIGATION v. HALLEN, Gent., one, &c.

In an action by a canal company, bound by act of parliament to keep the banks of the canal in good repair, against the owner of adjoining land for excavating his land, whereby the banks fell in, the plaintiffs cannot recover without shewing that the banks were in good repair when they fell in.

CASE against the defendant for digging clay-pits in his field adjoining to the bank and towing-path of the canal of the plaintiffs, in consequence of which the bank sunk down, and the towing-path was rendered unsafe, and the plaintiffs incurred great expense in repairing the damage. Plea, not guilty, and issue thereon. At the trial before *Garrow*, B. at the *Worcestershire* Summer Assizes, 1826, the case was this :—The plaintiffs were a company established by the statute 6 *Geo.* 3, for making and maintaining the *Worcestershire* and *Staffordshire* Canal. The defendant was the owner of land in the parish of *Kidderminster*, in the county of *Worcester*, contiguous and next adjoining to the canal. The defendant, in the year 1825, had caused clay-pits to be dug in his own land, in the direction of and near to the bank of the canal, to the extent of fifty-five feet, without causing any injury to the bank. He then caused a clay-pit to be dug beyond the fifty-five feet, but at the same distance from the bank, and in July, 1825, the part of the bank next adjoining to that last clay-pit gave way. It appeared in evidence that the part of the bank which fell in was composed of sand, and that it had not been sufficiently puddled, so as to keep the water from oozing through and injuring the bank ; but it also appeared that the bank would not have given way if the pit had not been dug in the adjoining land.

One clause of the canal act provided that the company

should at their own charges divide and separate, and keep constantly divided and separated, the towing-paths on each side of the canal and navigable trenches or passages, or such part or parts thereof as should be found necessary by the commissioners, with a sufficient post and rail, hedge, ditch, trench, *bank*, or other fence sufficient to keep in sheep and other cattle, to be set and made on the lands or grounds which should be purchased by, conveyed to, or vested in them, from the lands or grounds adjoining to such towing-paths, and should at their own cost from to time maintain and support the towing-paths, and the posts, rails, hedges, ditches, trenches, *banks*, and other fences so set up and made as aforesaid, and also should, at their own charges, make and set up gates, bridges and stiles over the hedges and fences, and all such gates, stiles, bridges, arches, and other conveniences so to be made, should from time to time be supported, maintained, and kept in sufficient repair by the company. Another clause of the act provided, that nothing in the act contained should extend to defeat, prejudice, or affect the right of any lord of any manor, common, or waste grounds, or of any owner of any lands in, upon, or through which the said canal, towing-paths, wharfs, quays, &c. or any of them, should be made, to the mines, minerals, or quarries, or to the salt-springs, brine, or rock-salt, lying or being within or under the lands to be set out or made use of for such canal, &c., or any of them ; but all such mines, minerals, quarries, &c., were thereby reserved to the lords of such manors, common, or waste grounds, or such owners of such lands respectively, subject to the conditions and restrictions therein contained, to take and carry away to their own use, such mines, minerals, and quarries, not thereby injuring the canal.

It was pressed upon the jury by the counsel for the defendant, that the bank was not in a proper state of repair at the time when it gave way ; that as the canal act required the company to keep the banks in repair, the owners of adjoining lands were entitled to presume that they were so kept, and to work their lands to such an extent as they might do without injury to the banks if they were in proper repair; that the defendant had, at all events, a right to dig as much clay from his own land as he might have dug without injury to the plaintiffs, if their bank had been in good repair; that if he had dug no more in this instance, and the bank gave way in consequence of his digging to that extent only, the damage was occasioned not by any wrongful act of the defendant, but by the breach of duty of the plaintiffs in neglecting to repair the bank; and that, consequently, the plaintiffs were not entitled to recover for any injury resulting to them by means of the defendant's digging clay upon his own land, if that injury would not have resulted provided they had performed their duty in keeping the bank in repair.

The learned Judge left one question only to the jury, namely, whether the bank had given way in consequence of the defendant's having dug the clay-pits, directing them, if they were of opinion in the affirmative, to find a verdict for the plaintiffs. The jury found a verdict for the plaintiffs. In *Michaelmas* term last a rule nisi for a new trial was obtained, on the ground that the learned Judge ought to have left it to the jury to say, whether the bank would have given way if it had been in a proper state of repair.

Russell and *Holroyd* now shewed cause. The case was properly put to the jury. In leaving to them the question whether the injury to the bank was occasioned by the defendant's digging the clay-pits, the learned Judge did also, in effect, though not in express words, leave to them the other question, whether the injury would not have happened if the bank had been in proper repair. But the latter question, as pressed on the part of the defendant, did not arise in the case. The act of parliament requires only that the banks of the canal shall be kept in such a state of repair as will render them adequate to the public purposes for which it was intended, such as the towing of barges, and a free navigation. Now, it has never been pretended that the bank in question was not in a state of repair adequate for those purposes, up to the time when the defendant by excavating the soil upon which the bank rested, weakened and destroyed it; the plaintiffs, therefore, have not been guilty of any breach of duty, and the injury complained of has been occasioned entirely by the wrongful act of the defendant. It follows, that the action is maintainable; that the verdict is right; and that this rule ought to be discharged.

Campbell and *R. V. Richards*, contrà, were stopped by the Court.

BAYLEY, J.—I am of opinion that this case was not properly presented to the jury. I think it should have been presented to their consideration, as a question of fact, whether there was, at the time when the alleged cause of complaint arose, such a bank on the side of the canal, as the act of parliament required that the company should make, and as the proprietors of the adjoining lands were justified in assuming that they had made. Before the passing of the act of parliament, the latter were at liberty to work their lands in any way they might think fit, provided they did not thereby injure the lands of their neighbours in their then existing state. The defendant, therefore, until the act passed, would have had an undoubted right to dig in his soil the clay-pits, the digging of which forms the ground of complaint in the present action. Now the act of parliament, authorising the plaintiffs to make a canal, introduces a species of property which, with reference to the proprietors of adjoining lands, may be considered as in some respects dangerous. But it provides that the company, who are to have the benefit of the canal, shall make and support its banks, and shall keep them in sufficient repair. It is incumbent upon them, therefore, to make good and proper banks, by which I understand, banks adequate to keep the water within its channel, not only while the adjoining lands shall continue in the state in which they were when the canal was made, but also, when they may be applied to any of those purposes to which they might have been applied by the proprietors before the canal was made. One of the modes of keeping good and proper banks, is by what is termed puddling the banks; and when the bank is composed of sand, as in this case, the effect of puddling is to render that impervious to the water, which is otherwise by its nature pervious to it. That being so, it was certainly a question proper to be decided by the jury, whether this bank, with reference to the materials of which it was composed, was a good and proper bank, and calculated to keep in such a body of water; and if it was a good and proper bank with reference to the materials of which it was composed, it then became a question for the consideration of the jury, whether effectual guards were adopted for the purpose of preventing the water from oozing out of its channel, and getting into and moistening, and thereby injuring, the adjoining bank. The oozing of the water through the bank might not have the effect of injuring the canal, so long as the land beyond the bank and the bank itself were on the same level. But when the land beyond the bank was lowered by digging, as in this case, the pressure of the water might cause it to ooze through, and by degrees remove the bank, in consequence of its being deprived of that support which it formerly received from the land on the other side. I am, for these reasons, of opinion that this case should be sent down to another jury, for the purpose of ascertaining, not merely whether the bank would have stood if the clay-pits had not been dug, (for upon that point I entertain no doubt,) but for the purpose of presenting to the consideration of the jury the second question, namely, whether the bank of the canal was such a bank, with reference to the materials of which it was composed, and the nature of the adjoining lands, and the rights of ownership thereon, as the proprietors of those lands were entitled to expect, and the company were bound to make and maintain : in other words, whether any injury would have resulted to the bank from the act of the defendant, if the bank itself had been in good and proper repair.

HOLROYD, J.—I am of the same opinion. The company had no right upon the land on which the bank stood, except under the act of parliament, and upon the terms which that act of parliament imposes on them. It has been contended that the act of parliament requires only that the bank shall be in such a state of repair as will render it adequate for all those public purposes for which it was intended. But the act of parliament not only gives the company a right of ownership over the banks on the side of the canal adjoining lands belonging to other proprietors, but also imposes upon them the obligation of keeping the banks in proper repair ; which, I think, must be considered as an obligation to keep the banks in repair, not merely for their own benefit, and the purposes of the canal of which they are the proprietors, but for the benefit of those other individuals who have rights which are in some degree invaded by the powers given by the act of parliament to the company, and which otherwise the proprietor of the land in question would have had. If the act of parliament had never been passed, and the canal had never been made, the defendant would have had a right to excavate his land to any extent he pleased. And, in my opinion, he has still the same right, and the company cannot complain of the injury they have sustained, because they have omitted to do that which they were bound to do for the purpose of maintaining their right in the canal. They hold the bank upon the express condition of keeping it in repair. If they do not keep it in repair, then they are invading the rights of other persons, without performing the condition imposed upon them by the act of parliament. The falling in of the bank might not have happened if the defendant had not dug the clay-pits ; but still, if it would not have happened if the bank had been in good repair, the company have no cause of action. It was their duty to

1827.

STAFFORD
CANAL Co.
v.
HALLEN.

keep the bank in good repair, and if the damage has happened from their not performing that duty, or would not have happened if they had performed that duty, I am clearly of opinion that they can maintain no action for it. Upon this view, I think there ought to be a new trial in this case, because there was some evidence upon this point, (I do not say to what extent,) which ought to have been, but was not, left to the consideration of the jury.

LITTLEDALE, J. concurred.

Rule absolute.

TARLING *v.* BAXTER.

Defendant agreed to sell to plaintiff a stack of hay for 145*l.*, to be paid for in one month, and to be allowed to stand on defendant's premises for three months. Plaintiff stipulated that the hay should not be cut till paid for. The hay was accidentally burned on defendant's premises:—Held, that there was a contract for an immediate sale, by which the property in the hay vested immediately in plaintiff, and that he having paid for the hay, could not recover back the price from defendant.

ASSUMPSIT, for money paid by the plaintiff to the use of the defendant, with a count for money had and received, and the other common counts. Plea, non-assumpsit, with a notice of set-off for goods sold and delivered, and goods bargained and sold. At the trial before *Abbott*, C. J. at the *London* adjourned Sittings after *Hilary* Term, 1826, the plaintiff obtained a verdict for 145*l.*, subject to the opinion of this Court upon the following case:—

On the 4th of *January*, 1825, the plaintiff bought of the defendant a stack of hay belonging to the defendant, and then standing in a field belonging to the defendant's brother. The note signed by the defendant, and delivered to the plaintiff, was in these words:—" I have this day agreed to sell *James Tarling* a stack of hay, standing in *Canonbury Field, Islington*, at the sum of 145*l.*, the same to be paid on the 4th day of *February* next, and to be allowed to stand on the premises until the 1st day of *May* next." And the following note was signed by the plaintiff, and delivered to the defendant:—" I have this day agreed to buy of Mr. *John Baxter*, a stack of hay, standing in *Canonbury Field, Islington*, at the sum of 145*l.*, the same to be paid on the 4th day of *February* next, and to be allowed to stand on the premises until the 1st day of *May* next, *the same hay* *not to be cut till paid for. January* 4th, 1825." At the meeting at which the notes were signed, but after the signature thereof, the defendant said to the plaintiff, " You will particularly oblige me by giving me a bill for the amount of the hay." The plaintiff rather objected. The defendant's brother, *S. Baxter,* on the 8th of the same month of *January,* took a bill of exchange for 145*l.* to the plaintiff, drawn upon him by the defendant, payable one month after date, which the plaintiff accepted. The defendant afterwards indorsed it to *George Baxter,* and the plaintiff paid it to one *Taylor,* the holder, when it became due. The stack of hay remained on the same field entire until the 20th of *January,* 1825, when it was accidentally wholly consumed by fire, without any fault or neglect of either party.

A few days after the fire, the plaintiff applied to the defendant, to know what he meant to do when the bill became due. The defendant said, " I have paid it away, and you must take it up to be sure; I have nothing to do with it: why did you not remove the hay?" The plaintiff said, " I could not; there was a memorandum that it should not be removed until the bill was paid: would you have suffered it to be removed?" The defendant said, " Certainly not." The defendant's set-off was for the price of the hay, agreed to be sold as aforesaid. The question for the opinion of the Court was, whether the plaintiff, under the circumstances, was entitled to recover the sum of 145*l.*, or any part thereof.

Chitty, for the plaintiff. The plaintiff is entitled to recover for the whole amount, for the loss, under the circumstances of this case, must fall upon the defendant. The two contracts, as exhibited by the bought and sold notes, are different; the one containing a stipulation not to be found in the other, that the hay was not to be cut until paid for. [*Bayley,* J. Your argument, therefore, will be, that there is no one sufficient contract in writing, to satisfy the statute of frauds.] Certainly; and the case of *Grant* v. *Fletcher* (a) is an authority in point. There a broker employed to effect a sale of goods for his principal made a verbal contract with the vendee, and after entering it into his own book without signing it, delivered a bought and sold note to the vendor and vendee respectively, each paper differing in its terms: and it was held that there was no memorandum in writing of the contract to bind either, under the statute of frauds. [*Bayley*, J. The two notes varied much more there than they do here. Besides, there the notes were signed by the broker, in the absence of the parties, and each received one different from the other, though both supposed that they received the same; here the notes were signed by the parties themselves in the presence of each other, and by assenting to the insertion in one of them of the condition that the hay was not to be cut till paid for, they made that the binding contract. *Holroyd*, J. These two notes do not contradict each other. They make together a valid contract, under which, as it seems to me, the property in the hay passed immediately to the buyer, who has paid for the hay, and must bear the loss.] The whole question in the case is, whether the property passed or not. There was no absolute sale, but only an agreement for a sale. At all events, it was a sale upon credit, and the buyer was not entitled to have possession of the hay until the credit expired; therefore the property did not vest in him until the credit expired. [*Holroyd*, J. It is laid down in Com. Dig., title, *Agreement* (B. 3), " that if a sale be of goods for such a price, and a day of payment limited, the contract will be good, and the property altered by the sale, though the money be not paid;" and R. 10 *H*. 7, 8 a, 14 *H*. 8, 20 a, and *Dyer*, 30 a, are cited. Also, " If *A*. sell a horse to *B*., upon condition that he pay 20*l*. at *Christmas*, and afterwards sell it to *D*., the sale to *D*. is void, though *B*. afterwards do not pay;" and Plowd. Com.

(a) 8 D. & R. 59; 5 B. & C. 436.

432 b, is cited; and the reason there assigned is, that at the time of the second contract *A*. had no interest nor property in, nor possession of the horse, nor any thing but a condition, and therefore the second contract was merely void.] It is true that in *Noy's Maxims*, p. 88, it is laid down, that " if I sell my horse for money, I may keep him until I am paid, but I cannot have an action of debt until he be delivered; yet the property in the horse is by the bargain in the bargainee or buyer: but if he presently tender me my money, and I refuse it, he may take the horse, or have an action of detinue." But that is evidently said with reference to a ready money bargain, and therefore does not apply to the present case. *Goodall* v. *Skelton*(a) is in point. There *A*. agreed to sell goods to *B*., who paid a certain sum of money as earnest; the goods were packed in cloths furnished by *B*. and deposited in a building belonging to *A*., until *B*. should send for them; but *A*. declared at the time that they should not be carried away until he was paid: and it was held, that there was no delivery to *B*., and that *A*. could not maintain an action for goods sold and delivered. So here, the hay was to remain in the possession of the seller, and was not to be cut till paid for, and the buyer did not go the length of making any payment as earnest upon the bargain. For the same reason this case is distinguishable from that of *Hinde* v. *Whitehouse*(b), where it was held, that the property in sugars, deposited in the king's warehouse, passed to the buyer by the contract of sale and delivery of a sample, though the duties were not paid. The present case resembles more that of *Tempest* v. *Fitzgerald* (c). There, *A*. agreed to purchase a horse for ready money from *B*., and to fetch him away on a given day. Two days before that day *A*. rode the horse, and gave directions as to his exercise and future treatment, but requested that he might remain in *B*.'s possession for a further time, at the expiration of which he promised to fetch him

(a) 2 H. Bla. 316.   (b) 7 East, 558.   (c) 3 B. & A. 680.

away, and pay the price; to which *B.* assented. The horse died before *A.* paid the price or fetched him away. It was held, that there was no acceptance of the horse, so as to make the bargain executed within the meaning of the statute of frauds.

Comyn, contrà, was stopped by the Court.　·　·　·

BAYLEY, J.—There is no doubt about the principle of law which applies to this case; it is perfectly clear that the loss must be borne by the party in whom the property was vested at the time of its destruction by fire. The question, therefore, is, in whom was the property in this hay vested at that time? By the contract note delivered to the plaintiff, the defendant agreed to *sell* to the plaintiff a stack of hay, standing in *Canonbury Field,* for the sum of 145*l.,* the same to be paid for on the 4th day of *February* next, and to be allowed to stand on the premises until the 1st day of *May* next. That was a contract for an immediate sale; it was not prospective. Then in whom did the property by virtue of that contract vest? The right of property and the right of possession are distinct. The right of property may be in one person, and the right of possession in another. The vendor may have a lien upon the goods he has sold— a qualified right to retain possession of them until the price is paid—while the property in them may be in the vendee. If, therefore, it was the intention of the parties in this case, that the vendee should by virtue of the contract immediately acquire a right of property in the hay, and the vendor a right of property in the price, the fact that the hay was not to be paid for until a future period, and that it was not to be cut until it was paid for, makes no difference. The settled rule of law is, that where there is an immediate sale, and nothing remains to be done by the vendor as between him and the vendee, the property in the thing sold vests in the vendee, and then all the consequences resulting from the vesting of the property follow, one of which is that if the goods are lost or destroyed, the loss must be borne by the vendee. In this case the buyer's contract note imports an immediate, perfect, absolute agreement of sale, and I think the true construction of the contract is, that the parties intended an immediate sale; and if that is so, it follows that the property in the hay vested in the vendee, and that he must bear the loss. I am, therefore, of opinion, that the defendant is entitled to judgment of nonsuit.

Holroyd, J.—I am also of opinion that there was an immediate and not prospective sale of the hay in this case, though coupled with a stipulation on the part of the vendee, that he would not cut it until a future period. It is a rule in every case of a sale of goods, that if nothing remains to be done on the part of the seller, as between him and the buyer, before the goods are to be delivered, the property in the goods passes immediately to the buyer, and the property in the price to the seller; but that if any thing remains to be done on the part of the seller, the property does not pass until that has been done. In this case, therefore, I am of opinion, not only that the property in the hay passed immediately to the buyer by virtue of the contract, but also that the seller thereby immediately acquired a property in the price agreed to be paid for the hay, although the payment was not to be made, or the hay to be cut, until a future period. Then the property in the hay having passed to the buyer, and the hay having been accidentally destroyed before the day of payment, the buyer must bear the loss.

Littledale, J.—There was an absolute agreement on the 4th of *January* for the sale and purchase of the hay, to be paid for in a month. According to the seller's contract note, the buyer might have cut and removed the hay immediately. By the buyer's contract note it was stipulated that he should not cut the hay until it was paid for. But the property in the hay had already passed to him by the first contract of sale, and all that he did afterwards was to waive his right to the immediate possession. Then the property having passed to the buyer, the loss must fall on him.

Judgment of nonsuit (a).

(a) See *Simmons v. Swift*, 8 D. & R. 693, and the cases there collected.

The THAMES TUNNEL COMPANY v. SHELDON.

By the *Thames Tunnel Act,* 5 G. 4, c. 156, s. 23, it was enacted, " that the persons who had *subscribed,* or should thereafter *subscribe or advance money* towards making the tunnel, should pay the sums by them *subscribed* at the time and place, and in the manner directed by the company, and in case any such subscribers should neglect to pay, the company were empowered to sue for and recover the money. By

THIS was an action brought to recover the sum of 80*l.*, being the amount of two calls of 5*l.* each on eight shares in the capital stock of the said company. At the trial before *Abbott,* C. J., at the *London* adjourned Sittings after *Michaelmas* Term, 1826, the plaintiffs obtained a verdict, subject to the opinion of this Court upon the following case :—

Early in the year 1824 it was proposed to construct a tunnel under the river *Thames,* near *Bermondsey,* and a subscription was accordingly opened for that purpose, to be divided into shares of 50*l.* each, upon which a deposit of 2*l.* per share was required to be paid in advance, for and towards the expenses of applying to parliament for an act to incorporate the company, and carrying the intended work into execution. The defendant applied for eight shares in the intended capital of the company, and that number of shares was set against his name accordingly; and he then gave a check on Messrs. *Dorien & Co.,* his bankers, for 16*l.,* being the before-mentioned deposit of 2*l.* on each of

s. 91, reciting that the probable expenses would amount to 160,000*l.*, and that more than four-fifth parts of such expenses had already been *subscribed* by several persons under a contract, binding them, their heirs, &c., for payment of the sums so *subscribed* by them, it was enacted, that the whole 160,000*l.* should be *subscribed* in like manner, before the act should be put in force :—Held, that the word *subscriber* in the act meant only those who had stipulated to pay, and not those who had paid money, and that a person whose name was inserted in the act, and who had paid a deposit on shares, but who had not signed the contract, was not a SUBSCRIBER within the act, nor liable to be sued by the company.

the eight shares, which check was duly paid upon being presented, and took a receipt for such deposits. Application was afterwards made to parliament in the session of 1824, when an act, 5 *G*. 4, c. 126, passed for incorporating the company, and enabling them to execute the tunnel and other necessary works, and the name of the defendant was inserted in the act as one of the company. The capital authorised to be raised by the company was 200,000*l*. By s. 91 of the act, after reciting that the probable expenses would, according to the estimate thereof, amount to 160,000*l.*, and that the sum of 141,000*l.*, being more than four-fifth parts of such expenses, had already been subscribed for defraying such expenses, by several persons under a contract binding them, their heirs, executors, and administrators for payment of the several sums so subscribed by them respectively, it was enacted, that the whole of the said sum of 160,000*l.* should be subscribed in like manner, before any of the powers and provisions given by that act should be put in force(*a*). A petition was pre-

---

· (*a*) Certain other sections of the act were referred to, the substance of which it is deemed advisable to insert here:—

Sect. 1 recited, that the persons thereinafter named were willing and desirous, at their own expense, to make and maintain a tunnel, and enacted, that certain persons, naming them, and among them the defendant, together with such other person or persons as then were or thereafter should become possessed of any share in the undertaking, or had agreed to subscribe for the same, and their successors, executors, &c., should be a body politic and corporate for making the tunnel.

Sect. 2 authorised the company to raise and contribute among themselves a competent sum, not

exceeding 200,000*l.*, such sum to be divided into shares of 50*l.* each, and such shares were thereby *vested in* the several persons so subscribing, &c., proportionably to the several sums they should raise and contribute.

Sect. 3 enacted that the shares should be deemed to be personal estate.

Sect. 4 enacted that any person who should, by virtue of the act, have subscribed, or undertaken, for two or more shares in the undertaking, should have a vote or votes as therein mentioned.

Sect. 23 enacted that the respective persons who had subscribed, or who should thereafter subscribe *or advance* any money towards making and maintaining the tunnel, should, and they were

sented to the House of Commons, praying for leave to bring in a bill for the purposes proposed by the subscription, which the clerk to the company stated at the trial he had reason to believe was not signed by the defendant.

The contract mentioned in s. 91 of the act was signed to the extent of more than the sum of 160,000*l*., before any proceedings were taken in execution of the act. Before the passing of the act, the contract was left at the company's office for the signatures of the subscribers, but was not signed by the defendant, although his name was mentioned at the foot of it as a subscriber for eight shares, and a space left opposite to each subscriber's name for his signature and seal thereto. A short time after the act of parliament had passed, when the company were procuring additional signatures and seals to the contract for completing the said amount of 160,000*l*., the defendant, on being then applied to, refused to execute the contract, alleging that he had sold his shares in the concern; but no evidence of the sale of such shares was given by the defendant, nor did the defendant give any evidence whatever at the trial.

The works authorised by the act being in progress, the calls for which this action was brought became necessary. They were made and duly advertised. Notice of them respectively was given to the defendant, from whom they were severally demanded, but neither of them has been paid.

D. Pollock, for the plaintiffs. The defendant is liable in this action as a subscriber for, or proprietor of, shares in the undertaking, within the meaning of the act of parliament. The words " subscriber" and " proprietor" are used

thereby required to pay the sums by them respectively *subscribed*, at such times, and in such manner as should be directed by the directors; and in case any such *subscribers* should neglect to pay the same, at the time and place, and in the manner so required for that purpose, the company or their directors were thereby empowered to sue for and recover the same.

And sect 32 enacted that, after a call made, no share should be transferred until such call should have been paid.

synonimously in several parts of the act of parliament. The defendant is clearly one of the persons mentioned in the first section, and there described as willing and desirous, at their own expense, to make and maintain the tunnel. There is no decided case to be found which closely resembles the present; the only one which bears at all upon it is that of *The Bristol and Taunton Canal Company* v. *Amos*(b), where it was held, that the register book of that company was evidence, in an action brought by them for calls, of the defendant being the proprietor of the number of shares therein affixed to his name. Here the defendant's name was inserted in the act, and that is equivalent to its insertion in the register book of the company, as in that case. [*Bayley*, J. His name might be inserted in the act without his knowledge or authority; the case finds that the defendant did not sign the contract mentioned in the ninety-first section of the act.] It was not necessary that he should; he was previously liable as a subscriber. The act evidently contemplates two classes of subscribers; first, those who merely subscribed for shares in the undertaking; and secondly, those who, in compliance with the requisition of the ninety-first section, which was introduced entirely for the benefit of the public, consented to bind themselves and their legal representatives by a contract deed. The general subscribers were to be to the extent of 200,000*l.*, the special subscribers were to be to the extent of 140,000*l.* only. By the third section of the act the shares are declared to be personal estate, and by the thirty-second section the subscribers, upon paying up all calls then due, may sell and transfer their shares, and upon the transfers being registered the sellers are to be for the future entirely exonerated from all calls in respect of those shares. But the subscribers who executed the deed would not be so exonerated, for if the purchasers of their shares made default in payment of future calls, they would be liable under the deed to make

(a) 1 M. & S. 569.

good the money. Therefore, if no one who has not executed the deed is a subscriber within the meaning of the act, the provision in the thirty-second section becomes wholly inoperative. The word " subscribe" in the act cannot properly be confined to the signing of the deed, because by the twenty-third section those persons " who have subscribed, or shall hereafter subscribe or advance money," are required to pay the calls. The defendant, therefore, having subscribed money by paying a deposit upon shares, became a proprietor of the shares when the company was incorporated, although he had not signed the deed. He would have had a right to claim the shares if they had been profitable, and he ought not to be permitted to withdraw from them because they are at a discount. It would be unjust to those who have continued subscribers, *honâ fide*, for the purpose of completing the tunnel, that the funds upon which they relied for assistance, and had a right to rely, because the parties had "subscribed" in the very words of the act, should now be withdrawn, merely because those parties had not signed the deed. The real object of the ninety-first section seems to have been merely to prevent the possibility of the work being abandoned after it had been commenced; and not to enable the original subscribers to continue proprietors, or not, at their pleasure, by declining to sign the contract deed.

Patteson, contrà, was stopped by the Court.

BAYLEY, J.—This action is founded upon the twenty-third section of the act of parliament, and the question is, whether the defendant has, or has not, brought himself within that section, because if he has not, the action cannot be supported. Now the words of that section are, " that the respective persons who have subscribed, or who shall hereafter subscribe *or* advance any money for or towards making and maintaining the said tunnel, shall, and are hereby required to pay the sums by them respectively *subscribed*,

at such times, and in such manner as shall be directed by
the directors; and in case any of such *subscribers* shall neglect to pay the same at the time and place, and in manner
so required for that purpose, the said company or their directors are hereby empowered to sue for and recover the
same." The case, therefore, turns upon the meaning of
the word *subscriber*, and the question is, whether or not the
defendant has become a subscriber to this undertaking
within the meaning of that term, as used in the act of parliament. Before the defendant can be made liable, it must
be made out that he has subscribed, and subscribed money.
Then what is meant by the word *subscribe* there used?
Does it mean actual payment? That is one meaning of
the word. If I actually contribute a sum of money towards
a particular object, I may be said to subscribe that sum; or
if, without paying any money, I sign my name binding myself to contribute, 1 may be termed a subscriber for that
amount of money which I, by so signing, state that I mean
to contribute. In which of these two senses is the word
"subscribe" used in this section? Does it apply to those
persons who have actually advanced money, or to those who
have stipulated to advance money hereafter? Looking at
the whole of the section, I feel satisfied that it applies, not
to those who have actually made a payment, but to those
who have stipulated that they will make a payment; for the
latter part of the section provides, that if any of the *subscribers* neglect to pay, the company may sue for and recover
the money: which must, of necessity, mean money which
they have bound themselves to pay, but have not paid.
The word *subscribed* is evidently used in the same sense in
the ninety-first section. That recites, that the probable expenses of making the tunnel will amount to the sum of
160,000*l.*, and that the sum of 141,000*l.*, being more than
four fifth parts of such expenses, had already been *subscribed* for defraying such expenses, by several persons,
under a contract, binding them, their heirs, executors, and
administrators for *payment* of the several sums so *subscribed*

by them respectively. The word *subscribed* in that recital
must clearly allude to persons who have bound themselves
by a contract to pay hereafter, and not to those who have
actually made advances. It then enacts, that the whole of
the said sum of 160,000*l.* shall be *subscribed in like manner,*
before any of the powers and provisions given by that act
shall be put in force; which must also mean, not that the
money shall be actually paid, but that names to that amount
and for that purpose shall be put down. It is clear, therefore, that in both these sections the word *subscribed* means,
not a payment, but a pledge to pay, and applies to persons
who sign their names to a contract by which they bind
themselves to contribute to the extent of the number of
shares for which they sign. It has been suggested in argument, that the act of parliament contemplates two sets of
subscribers, distinguishing those to the extent of 140,000*l.*
from those beyond that sum; and shewing that the former
are to sign the contract, and to bind themselves and their
legal representatives, and that the latter are not bound to
incur that obligation. If such a distinction had been contemplated, it might reasonably be expected to have been
clearly pointed out, but no such distinction can be found.
The object of the legislature is perfectly plain. A sum of
200,000*l.* is to be raised, and is to be applied to the purposes mentioned in the recital of the ninety-first section.
An estimate of the expense is to be laid before the legislature, and four-fifths of that estimated amount are to be subscribed before the act shall be put in force, as a security to
the subscribers that there is an available fund to that extent;
but when that sum is subscribed, as a further amount may
be required, power is given to raise money beyond that
sum. I consider the true construction of the act of parliament to be this:—Every original proprietor, whether named
in the act of parliament or not, is to stand upon precisely
the same footing. He is not to be bound to subscribe because he is named in the act; he is ultimately to decide
whether, and to what extent, he chuses to become a sub-

scriber. When he contributes so much money in the first instance for so many shares, he thereby specifies the number of shares for which he then proposes to become a subscriber, and he may be guilty of a breach of faith if he does not afterwards subscribe for that number of shares; but that, according to the provisions of the act of parliament, is to be matter of subsequent arrangement. By the second section the company are authorised to raise and contribute among themselves a sum not exceeding 200,000*l*., such sum to be divided into shares of 50*l*. each, and such shares to be vested in the several persons so subscribing, and their successors, proportionably to the several sums they shall raise and contribute. The fourth section enacts, that any person who shall, by virtue of the act, have subscribed or undertaken for two or more shares, shall have so many votes. That seems to me to contemplate, not that the parties are actually bound unless they have signed the previous subscription, but that they shall be at liberty, if they have not so signed, to arrange the extent to which each shall contribute and have shares. For who can be considered as having subscribed by virtue of the act, except those who have signed the contract specified in the ninety-first section? There are no other subscribers alluded to in any other part of the act, and that section implies that there has been a subscription of 140,000*l*. only, and not beyond that amount. The meaning must be, that if any person who shall by virtue of the act, that is, by virtue of having been one of the subscribers to the amount of 140,000*l*., be said to have subscribed or undertaken for two or more shares, then he shall have so many votes. I think the true construction of the statute is, that no man is to be deemed a subscriber by advancing money towards the expenses of the act, unless he also signs the contract mentioned in the ninety-first section, which is to describe the number of shares he has subscribed for. A man who advances money towards obtaining an act of parliament, ought to have a *locus pænitentiæ* when the act is passed. He may approve of the scheme generally, but he may disapprove of some of the particular provisions in the act. For these reasons I am of opinion that the defendant is not a subscriber within the meaning of the twenty-third section of this act, and therefore that this action is not maintainable.

HOLROYD, J. and LITTLEDALE, J. concurred.

Judgment for the defendant.

———◆———

CROWTHER *v.* WENTWORTH.

An indenture, releasing one annuity, and granting another, is well described in the memorial as a " grant of an annuity," within 53 *Geo.* 3, c. 141, s. 2.

COVENANT upon an annuity deed; breach, non-payment of the annuity. The deed, as set out upon oyer, was an indenture dated 14th *December*, 1822, made between *H. Wentworth* of the first part, *A. Payne* of the second part, *J. Wentworth* of the third part, *W. Harris* of the fourth part, and *W. Crowther* of the fifth part. It recited that *Payne*, on the 6th *March*, 1822, had contracted and agreed with *Crowther* for the sale to him, *Crowther*, of an annuity of 60*l.* during the life of him, *Payne*, in consideration of 495*l.* then paid by *Crowther*; that for securing the payment of the annuity *Payne* executed a warrant of attorney, on which judgment had been entered up; that it was further agreed that the premises comprised in the thereinafter recited indenture of lease should be a security for the payment of the annuity; that *Payne* and *Wentworth* had been in partnership as millers, and on 25th *November* then last had agreed to dissolve the partnership, on condition that *Wentworth* should advance to *Payne* 500*l.*, and pay all partnership debts, in consideration of which *Payne* was to assign the leasehold premises to *Wentworth*, subject to the payment of the annuity to *Crowther*, and one other annuity of 41*l.* to *Harris*; that *Payne* did assign to *Wentworth* the premises comprised in the lease, subject to the payment of

those two annuities, and that in consideration of a release given by *Harris* to *Payne* of the annuity of 41*l.*, and for other considerations, *Wentworth* granted to *Harris* during the life of *Wentworth* an annuity of 100*l.*, to be issuing out of the leasehold premises, and for that purpose assigned the same to *Harris*, charged with the payment of that annuity; that all arrears of the annuity of 60*l.* had been duly paid to *Crowther*, and that in further pursuance of the agreement of 25th *November*, *Crowther* had, at the request of *Wentworth*, consented to release *Payne* from the annuity of 60*l.*, upon *Wentworth*'s granting to *Crowther* an annuity of equal value in lieu thereof, and that *Wentworth* having contracted with *Crowther* to grant a further annuity of 135*l.*, in consideration of 1,000*l.* then agreed to be advanced by *Crowther* to *Wentworth*, it was agreed between *Crowther* and *Wentworth* that the two annuities should be consolidated into one annuity of 195*l.*, to be granted by *Wentworth* to *Crowther* for the life of the former; that *J. Wentworth* had agreed to join with his brother, *H. Wentworth*, as his surety for securing the payment of the annuity of 195*l.*, and that thereupon *J. Wentworth* and *H. Wentworth* had executed a warrant of attorney to confess judgment against them, and each of them, for the sum of 3,000*l.*, with a defeazance; and, that it had been also agreed between the parties, that the annuity of 195*l.* should be further secured by such covenants as were thereinafter contained. After this recital, the indenture stated, that in pursuance and part performance of the agreement on the part of *Crowther*, and in consideration of the premises, and particularly of the annuity of 195*l.* during the life of *H. Wentworth*, to be granted and secured in the manner therein-before expressed, and in lieu of the annuity of 60*l.* granted to him, *Crowther*, and intended to be thereby released; and in consideration of the sum of ten shillings paid by *Payne* to *Crowther* before the sealing and delivery of that indenture, *he, Crowther, released, and for ever quitted claim unto Payne of all that annuity of 60l. so granted by Crowther to Payne, and all arrears and future* *payments thereof.* And in further performance of the afore-said agreement, and in consideration of the release therein-before made by *Crowther* to *Payne* of the annuity of 60*l.*, and also in consideration of 1,000*l.* paid by *Crowther* to *Wentworth*, he, *Wentworth*, gave, granted, and confirmed unto *Crowther* one annuity of 195*l.*, for the life of him, *Wentworth*, to be paid by equal quarterly payments therein mentioned. Covenant by *Wentworth* to pay the annuity on the days therein mentioned. Pleas; first, that no memorial of the indenture, containing a description of the nature of the instrument by which the annuity was granted, was en-rolled in the High Court of Chancery, according to the directions of 53 *Geo.* 3, whereby the indenture was null and void; second, that no memorial of the indenture, containing the true pecuniary considerations for granting the annuity, was enrolled in the High Court of Chancery, according to the direction of the act, whereby the indenture was null and void. Replication; to the first plea, that a memorial of the indenture was, within thirty days after the execution thereof, duly enrolled in the High Court of Chancery, in pursuance of the statute in that case made and provided. The memorial was then set out. In the column headed " Nature of the instrument," there were the words " Grant of annuity," and " Warrant of attorney to confess judgment." Averment, that the memorial contained the date of the indenture, the names of all the parties and witnesses thereto, and of the person and persons for whose life and lives the annuity was granted, and of the person and persons by whom the same was to be beneficially received, the pecuniary consideration and con-siderations for granting the same, and the annual sum and sums to be paid, in manner and form as in and by the statute in that case made and provided is required, as by the said enrolment remaining of record in the High Court of Chan-cery more fully appeared. Similar replication to the second plea. Demurrer to the replication, and joinder in demurrer.

J. Evans, in support of the demurrer. The instrument

by which the annuity was granted is described in the memorial merely as a "grant of annuity." That is no description at all of its "nature," which the statute requires, and therefore the memorial is bad. The instrument is not even described as an indenture, nor does it appear from the memorial, that besides the grant of one annuity it contained a release of another. In this respect also the memorial is bad. The grant of an annuity may be by various instruments, and therefore the law requires strictness and precision in the description. By the 53 Geo. 3, c. 141, s. 2, the memorial is to be enrolled in the High Court of Chancery "in the form or to the effect following." The form is given in the schedule to the act, and comprises several columns, one of which is headed "Nature of the instrument," and in which are specified two species of deeds by which annuities may be granted, namely, "lease and release," and "bond in penalty." It was, therefore, clearly intended by the legislature that the memorial should contain a correct description of the nature of the deed by which the annuity was granted; and as an annuity may be granted by either of the deeds mentioned in the schedule, it follows that the word "grant" alone is no description of the nature of the deed by which the annuity was granted, within the meaning of the legislature. The Court have always construed this statute strictly, and held that they have no discretionary power to mitigate the severity of its provisions. In *Ex parte Mackreth* (a), where the memorial of an annuity, registered under the former statute of 17 Geo. 3, c. 26, stated that the bond, warrant of attorney, indenture and deed-poll, given to secure the annuity, were witnessed by *four* persons, and it appeared that *three* of those instruments were attested by *two* persons only, the Court felt themselves bound to give effect to the provisions of the act of parliament, and they set aside the annuity (b). In *Davidson* v. *Gill* (c), it was held, that an order of jus-

(a) 2 East, 568.
(b) And see *Darwin* v. *Lincoln*, 5 B.& A. 444; *Smith* v. *Pritchard*, 5 B. & A. 717; 1 D. & R. 374;

Cheek v. *Jefferies*, 3 D. & R. 185; 2 B. & C. 1.
(c) 1 East, 64.

tices, made under 13 *Geo.* 3, c. 78, s. 19, for stopping up an old footway, and setting out a new one, must follow the form prescribed in the schedule annexed to the act, and set forth the length and breadth of the new footway. And in *Willey* v. *Cawthorne* (a), it was held, that a memorial, under the annuity act, of a bond, stating that *A.* and *B. severally* became bound, was not sufficient in law, the bond being *joint* as well as *several*.

F. Pollock, contrà. The recent case of *Butler* v. *Capell* (b), is a complete answer to this objection. There the memorial of an annuity granted under the 53 *Geo.* 3, c. 141, described the instrument by which the annuity was secured as " an *assignment* of certain hereditaments," whereas it appeared that in fact the instrument was an *under-lease,* and it was held that the instrument was sufficiently described in popular language, and that the requisites of the statute, therefore, were satisfied. And *Abbott,* C. J., in delivering judgment, made these observations :—" All that is required in the memorial is, that the nature of the instrument shall be stated. In the column of the schedule, under the head ' Nature of instrument,' are given examples of the manner in which the instrument is to be described, namely, ' Indenture of lease and release,' ' Bond in penalty of 1200*l.,*' ' Warrant of attorney to confess judgment on the same bond.' It seems to me, therefore, that we are to understand the words ' Nature of instrument,' as meaning such a description of it as would be understood, in the common and popular sense of mankind, as applicable to it." (Here the Court stopped him.)

BAYLEY, J.—I am of opinion that the memorial in this case is sufficient. The question turns upon the construction of the 53 *Geo.* 3, c. 141, which was passed for the purpose of remedying the inconveniences which had been complained of as resulting from some of the decisions upon the former

(a) 1 East, 398.　　　　(b) 3 D. & R. 485; 2 B. & C. 251.

statute, 17 *Geo.* 3, c. 26. By the fifth section of the 53 *Geo.* 3, c. 141, the grantor is empowered to enforce the delivery of a copy of the original deed, and he may thereby obtain full information of the transaction, provided the description furnished him under the second section enables him to apply for such copy. The question, therefore, is, what does the second section require as the description to be furnished? Now it enacts "that a memorial of the date of every deed, of the names of all the parties and of all the witnesses, of the persons for whose lives the annuity is granted, and of the persons by whom the same is to be beneficially received, the considerations for granting the same, and the annual sums to be paid, shall be enrolled in the High Court of Chancery, in the form or to the effect following, with such alterations therein as the nature and circumstances of any particular case reasonably may require." The form or schedule is then given. It contains eight columns. The first is headed, "Date of instrument." The second is headed, "Nature of instrument," and under those words three examples are given, namely, "Indenture of lease and release," "Bond in penalty of 1200*l.*," "Warrant of attorney to confess judgment on the same bond." It has been argued, in effect, that by the *nature* of the instrument the legislature meant its *contents;* but that is clearly not so: for how could either of the examples given in the schedule possibly furnish to any individual any information of the contents of the deed? None of the descriptions there given would convey to any person reading them any information beyond the mere technical nature of the instrument. Then does not this memorial accurately describe the technical nature of the deed? The word here used is *grant;* and I think the deed set out on oyer operates as a grant of an annuity, and that the word *grant* is an adequate description of the nature of the instrument within the meaning of the act of parliament. From the other columns of the memorial the grantor may ascertain all the other particulars; the names of the parties —the names of the witnesses—and the names of the persons for whose lives the annuity is granted,—and thus furnished, he will be in a situation to demand a copy of the deed itself, under the fifth section, and to see whether he has a copy of the deed described in the memorial or not. For these reasons I am of opinion that the nature of the instrument is properly described in this memorial, that every thing has been done that the act of parliament requires, and, consequently, that the judgment of the Court ought to be for the plaintiff.

HOLROYD, J.—I am of the same opinion. It is clearly not necessary to state the *contents* of the instrument in the memorial, nor do I consider it necessary to describe its *nature*, except by reference to the other columns. It has been contended that as the deed in question contained the release of another annuity, that circumstance should have been stated in the memorial; but that appears to me quite unnecessary, because the only reason for requiring the nature of the deed to be described in the memorial seems to be, that the grantor of the annuity may know what to inquire for at the register office, and of what to demand a copy. The statute is in some degree a penal one, for it avoids the security; it ought not, therefore, to be construed too largely. Neither do I consider it any ground of objection that the deed is not described as an indenture. The so describing it would make no difference in its operation; and if the word *indenture* were a material part of the description, the effect would be to prevent the party from having recourse to any other instrument. I think the nature of the instrument is properly described in the memorial, and that the requisites of the act of parliament have been complied with.

LITTLEDALE, J.—I am entirely of the same opinion. It seems to me that the nature of the instrument is most properly described in the memorial by the word *grant*, and that no other term could have been used equally suitable to the particular case. An annuity is a thing lying in grant, and the word grant is the proper technical description of that species of instrument by which an incorporeal hereditament is conveyed.

1827.

CROWTHER
v.
WENTWORTH.

Judgment for the plaintiff.

———◆———

ROHDE and others *v.* THWAITES.

ASSUMPSIT. The declaration stated, that on the 3d *December*, 1825, defendant bargained for and bought of plaintiffs, and plaintiffs, at request of defendant, sold to him certain goods, to wit, twenty hogsheads of sugar, at 56*s*. 6*d*. per cwt., to be delivered by plaintiffs to defendant upon request, and to be paid for at the expiration of two months then following; and in consideration thereof, and that plaintiffs, at like request of defendant, had undertaken and faithfully promised defendant to deliver the goods to him, defendant undertook and faithfully promised plaintiffs to accept the goods when requested, and to pay plaintiffs for the same at the expiration of the said credit. Averment, that the price of the goods amounted to a certain sum, to wit, &c., and that although plaintiffs had always been ready and willing to deliver the goods to defendant, and requested him to accept the same, and although the credit had expired, yet defendant did not, nor would, when so requested, or at any time before or afterwards, accept the goods, or pay plaintiffs, or either of them, for the same, but refused so to do. *Indebitatus* count for goods bargained and sold. The defendant suffered judgment to go by default. Upon the execution of the writ of inquiry, the plaintiffs adduced evidence establishing a contract for the sale of twenty hogsheads of sugar, at 56*s*. 6*d*. per cwt., made on the 3d *December*, 1825; but it did not appear that there was a sufficient note in writing of the contract to satisfy the statute of frauds. The plaintiffs on that day had, in bulk on the floor of their warehouse, a quantity of sugar, much more than sufficient to fill twenty hogsheads, and the defendant

A. agreed, by parol, to sell to *B.* 20 hogsheads of sugar out of a larger quantity which he had in bulk. *A.* filled 4 hogsheads, and delivered them to *B.* who accepted them. *A.* afterwards filled 16 other hogsheads, and requested *B.* to fetch them away, who promised to do so:—Held, that the property in the 16 hogsheads thereby passed to *B.*; that his acceptance of the 4 was an acceptance of part of the 20, within the exception in 29 *Car.* 2, c. 3, s. 17; and that *A.* might recover the value of the whole from *B.* in an action for goods bargained and sold.

had seen it there in that state immediately before he made the contract in question. On the 10th of *December*, the plaintiffs filled up and delivered to the defendant four hogsheads, which he accepted, and in a few days afterwards they filled up the remaining sixteen hogsheads, and sent notice to the defendant that they were ready, and that they expected him to fetch them away, which he promised to do as soon as he could. The sixteen hogsheads were not weighed until *February*, 1826, when the plaintiffs delivered a bill of parcels to the defendant. The plaintiffs added to their bulk of sugar from time to time, as they effected sales of it, and it was not distinctly proved whether the sixteen hogsheads were filled with the same sugar that the defendant had seen in the warehouse on the day he made the contract; but it was proved that the four hogsheads delivered to the defendant, and accepted by him, were filled with that sugar. It was admitted that as the defendant had accepted the four hogsheads, there was sufficient evidence of a *sale* to that extent; but it was contended, that as no contract in writing sufficient to satisfy the statute of frauds had been proved, there was no evidence of any *sale* of the sixteen hogsheads, and, therefore, that the plaintiffs could only recover for the four hogsheads which had been actually delivered. The jury, under the direction of the under-sheriff, found a verdict for the amount of the whole twenty hogsheads.

Hutchinson, in *Trinity* term last, obtained a rule *nisi* for setting aside the inquisition, against which,

F. Pollock now shewed cause. First, the defendant having allowed judgment to go by default has thereby admitted the whole contract alleged in the declaration, therefore, the plaintiffs are entitled to recover for the full amount of the damage sustained by the breach of that contract. Secondly, by accepting four hogsheads of the sugar, the defendant has brought the case within the exception of the seventeenth section of the statute of frauds; for here the buyer has accepted part of the goods sold and actually received the same. Thirdly, there has been an acceptance of the whole; for when the sixteen hogsheads were filled, and notice was sent to the defendant that they were ready, and that he was expected to fetch them away, he promised to do so as soon as he could; that was tantamount to an actual delivery and acceptance.

Hutchinson, contrà. The suffering judgment to go by default does not amount to an admission in full of the claim set up by the declaration. Undoubtedly, when a defendant suffers judgment to go by default, he admits the cause of action, that is, he admits generally the plaintiff's right to recover *something* upon the contract stated in the declaration; and in this case, the defendant admits the plaintiffs' right to recover to the extent of the value of the four hogsheads which were actually delivered and accepted, but no more. The statute of frauds is not satisfied by the facts proved in this case; nor is the case brought within the exception in the seventeenth section. That section enacts, "that no contract for the sale of any goods for the price of 10*l.* or upwards shall be allowed to be good, except the buyer shall accept part of the goods so sold, and actually receive the same." Now in this case it cannot be said that the defendant accepted the four hogsheads, "part of" the twenty hogsheads "so sold," for no specific twenty hogsheads were sold or agreed to be sold, but the plaintiffs were to be at liberty to select from a large bulk in their warehouse a quantity of sugar sufficient to fill twenty hogsheads. At the time when the four hogsheads were delivered to the defendant and accepted by him, the quantity of sugar necessary for filling the other sixteen hogsheads had not been separated from the bulk. The four, therefore, did not constitute a part of the twenty, nor was an acceptance of the four an acceptance of part of the goods sold, within the meaning of the exception in the statute. That being so, and there being no sufficient note in writing of any contract of sale, the property in the sixteen hogsheads never passed to the defendant, and as the plaintiffs found their claim upon a bargain *and sale*, they can, upon this declaration, recover no more than the value of the four hogsheads which were sold to the defendant, *and were accepted by him*. In order to recover the value of the sixteen hogsheads, the plaintiffs ought to have declared specially, that in consideration that the plaintiffs would sell, the defendant promised to accept them.

BAYLEY, J.—Where a man sells part of a large quantity of goods, and the option is in him to select the part from the whole, he cannot, until he has made that selection, maintain an action for goods bargained and sold. But as soon as he selects part, and appropriates it for the benefit of the vendee, the property in the part so selected and appropriated passes to the vendee, although the vendor is not bound to part with the possession until the price is paid. In this case there was a bargain, whereby the defendant agreed to buy twenty hogsheads of sugar, to be prepared or filled up by the plaintiffs. Four of the twenty hogsheads were actually delivered to the defendant and accepted by him; so that as to them there is no question. But with respect to the sixteen it is insisted, that as there was no note or memorandum in writing of a contract sufficient to satisfy the statute of frauds, there was no valid sale of them; and that as the plaintiffs in their declaration have described their claim as founded upon a bargain *and sale*, they can recover, in this action, for no more than the four hogsheads which were actually delivered to the defendant and accepted by him; that in order to recover for the other sixteen hogsheads, they ought to have declared specially, that in consideration that the plaintiffs would sell, the defendant agreed to accept them. On the other hand, it is contended there was an entire contract for the sale of twenty hogsheads, and that the defendant's acceptance of four was an acceptance of part of the goods sold, within the meaning and operation of the exception in the seventeenth section of the statute of

1827.

ROHDE
v.
THWAITES.

frauds. Now it appears that the plaintiffs did in point of fact appropriate sixteen hogsheads for the benefit of the defendant; that they communicated to the defendant that they had so appropriated them, and requested him to fetch them away, and that he adopted that act of the plaintiffs, and said that he would fetch them away as soon as he could. I am of opinion that by means of that appropriation so made by the plaintiffs, and assented to by the defendant, the property in the sixteen hogsheads of sugar passed to the vendee; and that being so, the plaintiffs are entitled to recover the full value of the twenty hogsheads of sugar under the count for goods bargained and sold. It seems to me, therefore, that the rule for setting aside this writ of inquiry ought to be discharged.

HOLROYD, J.—I am of the same opinion. The sugars bargained for were part of a larger parcel, and the vendors were to select them for the vendee. The plaintiffs did select them, and upon that being communicated to the defendant, he promised to fetch them away. That was equivalent to an actual acceptance of the sixteen hogsheads by the defendant, and by that acceptance the property in the sugars passed to him, subject to the plaintiffs' lien for the price. If the sugars had afterwards been destroyed by fire, the defendant must have borne the loss (a). The selection of the sixteen hogsheads by the plaintiffs, adopted as it was by the defendant, converted that which was previously only an agreement for a sale into an actual sale, and vested the property in them in the defendant; therefore, the plaintiffs are entitled to recover for the whole under the count for goods bargained and sold.

LITTLEDALE, J. concurred.

Rule discharged.

(a) See *Tarling* v. *Baxter, ante,* 272.

1827.

JAMES HAUGHTON LANGSTON *v.* Sir CHARLES MORICE
POLE, Bart., HAUGHTON FARMER OKEOVER, MARIA
SARAH LANGSTON, CHARLES BARTER the elder, and
ELIZABETH CATHERINE his wife, and CHARLES BARTER
the younger, an infant, by his guardian.

J. L. devised to his son *J. H. L.* for life; remainder to trustees to preserve contingent remainders; remainder to the *second*, third, fourth, fifth, and *all and every other* the son and sons of his said son *J. H. L.* in tail male, according to seniority of age and priority of birth. There was no limitation to the *first* son of *J. H. L.* The declaration of the trust contained a provision to raise money for the daughters of *J. H. L.* on failure of issue male of his body; and the will also provided that in case *J. H. L.* should have any child or children other than and except an eldest or only son, then *J. H. L.* might raise money for portions:—Held, that the *first* son of *J. H. L.* took no estate under the will.

THE Master of the Rolls sent the following case for the opinion of this Court:—

John Langston, late of *Sarsden House, Oxfordshire*, Esq., now deceased, by his will, dated 28th *July*, 1801, gave and devised all his freehold and copyhold manors, messuages, farms, lands, tenements, tithes, and hereditaments, in the counties of *Oxford* and *Middlesex*, or elsewhere in *England*, with their appurtenances, (except as therein mentioned,) unto and to the use of his son *James Haughton Langston*, and his assigns during his life, without impeachment of waste; remainder to the use of trustees and their heirs during the life of the said *James Haughton Langston*, in trust to preserve contingent remainders; remainder to the use of the *second*, third, fourth, fifth, *and all and every other* the son and sons of his (the said testator's) said son *James Haughton Langston*, lawfully to be begotten, severally, successively, and in remainder one after another, as they and every of them should be in seniority of age and priority of birth, and the several and respective heirs male of the body and bodies of all and every such son and sons lawfully issuing, the elder of such sons, and the heirs male of his body, to be always preferred and to take before the younger of such son and sons, and the heirs male of his and their body and bodies issuing; remainder to his, testator's second and other sons successively in tail male; remainder to the use of other trustees for the term of 500 years, upon certain trusts thereinafter mentioned; remainder to the use of the *first*, second, third, fourth, fifth, and all and every other the daughter and daughters of his said son *James Haughton*

Langston, successively, in tail general; remainder to the use of other trustees for the term of 99 years upon the trusts thereinafter mentioned; remainder to the use of testator's eldest daughter, *Maria Sarah Langston*, and her assigns, for life, without impeachment of waste; remainder to the use of trustees during the life of the said *Maria Sarah Langston*, upon trust to preserve contingent remainders; remainder to the use of the *first*, second, third, fourth, fifth, and all and every other the son and sons of testator's said daughter, successively, in tail male; remainder to other trustees for the term of 600 years upon the trusts thereinafter mentioned; remainder to the use of the *first*, second, third, fourth, fifth, and all and every other the daughter and daughters of the said *Maria Sarah Langston*, successively, in tail general; and for default of such issue, like remainders with like attendant terms to the use of testator's daughters, *Elizabeth Catherine Langston, Caroline Langston, Agatha Maria Sophia Langston, Henrietta Maria Langston*, and their issue respectively; remainder to the testator's sixth and other daughters thereafter to be born, successively, in tail general; remainder to the use of other trustees for the term of 1500 years, upon the trusts thereinafter mentioned; remainder to the use of testator's sister, *Sarah*, the wife of *Peter Cazalet*, Esq., in fee. And the said testator did by his said will declare, that the said term of 500 years was upon trust that the trustees thereof, *in case there should be no son of the body of his said son James Haughton Langston*, should by mortgage or sale of the premises comprised in the said term, raise money for additional portions and for maintenance, as therein mentioned. And the said testator did by his said will declare, that the said term of 99 years was upon trust, that the trustees thereof, *in case there should be no son of the body of his said son James Haughton Langston*, should levy and raise such sum and sums of money for portions as therein mentioned. And the said testator did by his said will declare, that the said term of 600 years was upon trust that the trustees thereof, *in case there should be no son of the body of his said son James Haughton Langston*, should raise such sum and sums of money for portions as therein mentioned. And the said testator did by his said will declare, that the said term of 700 years was upon trust that the trustees thereof, *in case there should be no son or daughter of the said James Haughton Langston*, should raise such sum and sums of money for portions, as therein mentioned. And the said testator did by his said will declare, that the said term of 800 years was upon trust that the trustees thereof, *in case there should be no son of the said James Haughton Langston*, should raise such sum and sums of money for portions as therein mentioned. And the said testator did by his said will declare, that the said term of 900 years was upon trust that the trustees thereof, *in case there should be no son of the said James Haughton Langston*, should raise such sum and sums of money for portions as therein . mentioned. And the said testator did by his said will declare, that the said term of 1000 years was upon trust that the trustees thereof, *in case there should be no son of the said James Haughton Langston*, should raise such sum and sums of money for portions as therein mentioned. And the said testator did by his said will declare, that the said term of 1500 years was upon trust that the trustees thereof, *in case there should be no son of the said James Haughton Langston*, should levy and raise such sum and sums of money as therein mentioned for the purposes therein also mentioned. And in the said testator's will is contained a power or proviso, authorising his, the said testator's, said son, *James Haughton Langston*, from time to time, during his life, *in case there should be any child or children of his, the said James Haughton Langston's body lawfully begotten, other than and except an eldest or only son*, to charge portions as therein mentioned. And in the said will is contained a proviso, that *in case the said testator's said son, James Haughton Langston, should die under the age of 21 years, and there should be no son or daughter of his*

*body living at his decease; or being such, if all such sons
should die under* 21 *years of age,* and all such daughters
should die under that age and unmarried; then the trustees
of the said will should be possessed of certain stocks or
funds therein mentioned, upon the trusts therein contained.

The said *John Langston,* the testator, departed this life
in *February,* 1812, leaving the said *James Haughton Langston,* his only son and heir-at-law, (then a minor,) and
several daughters, him surviving, having previously made
three codicils to his said will, the last of which bears date
in *December,* 1811, but none of them making the least
variation, or in any manner affecting the above mentioned
limitations of his real estates.

The said *James Haughton Langston* attained the age of
21 years in *May,* 1817, and since that time intermarried,
and has issue by his wife two sons, viz. *Henry Langston,*
his eldest and first born son, and *Edward Langston,* his
second born son.

The question for the opinion of the Court was, whether
Henry Langston, the *first* son of the testator's son, *James
Haughton Langston,* took any estate under the said tes-
tator's will.

Shadwell, for the plaintiff. The eldest son of *James
Haughton Langston,* the testator's eldest son, took an
estate tail in remainder under the will. The Court must
look at the whole will, in order to arrive at the true construction of any particular part of it. The limitation to the
sons of the testator's eldest son contains express words of
gift, and a sufficient description of the persons meant to
take, among whom it is clear from the whole of the will
that the eldest son was intended to be included. In the
specific enumeration of the second and other sons, the *first*
undoubtedly is omitted; but the subsequent general words
supply that omission, for they are " *all* and *every other* son
and sons." Those words must have been intended to comprehend all sons, whether previously enumerated or not;

and, taken in their ordinary grammatical sense, they do in point of fact comprehend *all* the sons; which they could not do unless they included the first, though omitted in the enumeration. [*Bayley*, J. Is it not one rule of construction that where a specific enumeration begins with inferior persons, subsequent general words will not include superiors? It is so with respect to acts of parliament; (*a*) does not the rule apply here?] It is submitted that it does not. The principle upon which it applies to statutes is, that such a construction is consistent with the intention of the legislature (*b*); here such a construction is inconsistent with the evident intention of the testator. His intention clearly was that the eldest son should take, for there are no words expressly providing that he shall not take. [*Bayley*, J. Perhaps the strongest way in which you can put your argument is to say that this limitation consists of two clauses. But even then, the second, third, fourth, and fifth sons would take first under the first clause, and the first, sixth, and other sons would take afterwards under the second clause.] In answer to that difficulty it may be observed that the order of the limitations is not the only criterion for the true construction of the will, and that the Court may transpose the two clauses in this case, in order to effectuate the intention of the testator. There is not one other limitation in the will, numerous as they are, in which the first child, whether son or daughter, *is* not expressly mentioned; that shews that it was omitted in this limitation merely by mistake. If there had been a first son born and

---

(*a*) " A statute, which treats of things or persons of an inferior rank, cannot by any *general words* be extended to those of a superior. So a statute (13 *Eliz.* c. 10.) treating of ' deans, prebendaries, parsons, vicars, and others having spiritual promotion,' is held not to extend to bishops, though they have spiritual promotion, deans being the highest persons named, and bishops being of a still higher order."2 *Bla. Comm.* 88, 18 Ed.; *Archbishop of Canterbury's case*, 2 *Co. Rep.* 46.

(*b*) Professor *Christian*, in his note to the above passage in the Commentaries, takes the same view, and says, " This construction must be presumed to be most conformable to the intention of the legislature."

no other, this limitation would fail altogether, if the first son does not take under it. In one of the provisoes of the will, the testator in express terms anticipates the existence of an eldest son, which seems to be unaccountable, unless he intended such eldest son to take under the will. The present case is very similar to that of *Doe,* d. *Le Chevalier* v. *Hathwaite* (a). There *A.* devised to *S. D.* for life, remainder to his first, second, third, fourth, fifth, sixth, and other sons, in tail male, according to seniority of age and priority of birth, remainder to his first, &c., and other daughters in tail general; remainder to *G. H.* the eldest son of *J. H.,* for life, remainder in strict settlement to his first and other sons in tail male, and first and other daughters in tail general; with like limitations as to *S. D.;* remainder to *S. H.,* the second son of *J. H.* for life, remainder to his first and other sons and daughters in strict settlement; remainder to *J. H.* the third son of *J. H.* for life, remainder to his first and other sons and daughters in strict settlement, with similar limitations. *J. H.* was the second son, and *S. H.* the third. It was held, that *S. H.* being rightly named, was entitled to take, although wrongly described in the will as being the second son of *J. H.* [*Bayley,* J. There was a palpable misdescription of the devisee in that case.] Which was matter of mistake, and, therefore, held not to vitiate. Here there is a palpable mistake also, in the omission of the word *first,* which ought not to defeat the limitation, especially as it is clear from other parts of the will that the first son was intended to take.

Horne, contrà. It lies upon the plaintiff to prove the

(a) 2 Moore, 304, the marginal note of which report is copied into the text. *S. C.,* not *S. P.,* 3 B. & A. 632. The marginal note of the latter report describes the devise nearly in the same terms as the former, but concludes thus:— "Held, that evidence of the state of the testator's family, and other circumstances, was admissible to shew whether he had mistaken the name of the devisee or not; and that, upon such evidence being given, the jury might find the fact whether the mistake of the testator was in the name or the description of the devisee."

affirmative of the question propounded by the case. He must shew that the will contains a devise to the eldest son. But the will contains no such devise. It does contain a devise to the second and other succeeding sons; but it studiously avoids any devise to the first son. The limitation in question is the first that occurs in the will, and the eldest son would doubtless have been named there, if the testator had intended to name him at all. But he is never named in the will, at least as a devisee, for the allusion in the proviso to an eldest or only son is with a wholly different view. It is said that the omission was unintentional, and that the testator intended to make, and seems to have thought that he had made, provision for the first son. But he has not made such provision, and the Court cannot make it for him. The Court cannot make a will for the testator either in whole or in part; nor introduce into the will the name of a devisee not inserted by the testator, which they are asked to do to day; for that would be, in part, to make a will for him. The case cited on the other side is very distinguishable from the present. There the testator had made a palpable mistake in the description of a person whom he had named in his will, and evidently intended to take under it. Here the eldest son is entirely omitted in the first limitation, and the mention of the first son in all the other limitations rather tends to the presumption that the omission in the first was not accidental or unintentional.

Shadwell, in reply. No answer has been given to the argument originally advanced on the part of the plaintiff, namely, that the first limitation contains a devise to *all* sons, necessarily, therefore, including the first. Giving to the words " all and every other son and sons" their natural and ordinary import, they as clearly and necessarily include the first as the sixth, for neither of them is specifically mentioned. [*Littledale*, J. " All and every other" may have been meant to apply only to sons born after the fifth, and may have been introduced merely to prevent the neces-

sity of enumerating one by one all the sons that might by
possibility be born.] It seems a narrow mode of construction to limit words so very large and general to persons
inferior in order of birth to those previously specified. The
statute 13 *Eliz.* c. 10, which is given in the books as an
instance of the rule of construction mentioned by the Court,
does not contain the words " *all and every* other," but
merely the word " others"(a), which is a very important
distinction, and removes the applicability of the rule to this
case. Unless the word "all" is erased from the will, it is
impossible to say that the first son is not included as well
as the sixth, who it is admitted is included.

The Court took time to consider of the case, and afterwards sent the following certificate to the Master of the
Rolls :—

" This case has been argued before us by counsel. We
have considered it, and are of opinion that the said *Henry
Langston,* the first son of the said *James Haughton Langston,* did not take any estate under the said will.

J. BAILEY.

G. S. HOLROYD.

J. LITTLEDALE (b)."

1827.

LANGSTON
v.
POLE.

(a) *Ante,* 302, (a).

(b) Upon receiving this certificate, the then Master of the Rolls,
Sir *John Leach,* who had succeeded
Lord *Gifford,* by whom the case
was sent to this Court, directed a
case to be sent for the opinion of
the Court of Common Pleas, " whether *Henry Langston,* the first son
of the testator's son *James Haughton Langston,* took any *and what*
estate under the said testator's
will;" and the Judges of that Court
certified that they were of opinion,
" that the said *Henry Langston,*
the first son of the said testator's

son *James Haughton Langston,*
took an estate in tail male under
the said will, expectant on the decease of his father the said *James
Haughton Langston.*" The case
sent to the Court of Common Pleas
set forth the will much more fully
than it was set out in the case sent
to this Court. See the variations
between the two as pointed out in
Langston v. *Pole,* 1 Tamlyn's Chancery Cases, 128; see also the report of the case in the Court of
Common Pleas, 5 Bingh. 228.
Upon receiving the latter certificate, the Master of the Rolls,

principally, it should seem, for the purpose of enabling the parties to carry the cause to the House of Lords, (See 1 Tamlyn's Chancery Cases, 133,) came to an immediate decision upon the case, adopting the opinion of the Court of Common Pleas. The cause is now (*June*, 1830) before the House of Lords.

Friday,
January 26.

A debtor appointing a time and place to meet and pay his creditor, and failing to keep the appointment, must be presumed, in the absence of evidence to the contrary, to have absented himself with intent to delay his creditor, and thereby commits an act of bankruptcy; and in an action by a bankrupt against his assignees to try the validity of the commission, the plaintiff must give evidence to rebut the presumption, or he cannot maintain the action.

WIDGER *v.* BROWNING and another (*a*).

TROVER, by a bankrupt against his assignees. At the trial before *Abbott,* C. J. at the *London* adjourned sittings after last term, the only question was, whether the bankrupt, who had brought this action to try the validity of his commission, had committed an act of bankruptcy. It appeared that in 1823 a creditor met the plaintiff at *Exeter,* and pressed him for payment of his debt. The plaintiff said he could not pay then, but promised to meet the creditor at the *Globe* Inn the same evening. The creditor waited at the *Globe* Inn all that evening, and the whole of the next day, but the plaintiff never came. He then went to the inn usually frequented by the plaintiff, but could not find him there. The plaintiff produced no evidence to shew why he had broken the appointment. The Lord Chief Justice intimated that he should leave it to the jury to say whether, in the absence of any other explanation of the plaintiff's conduct in breaking his appointment, they believed his motive was to delay his creditor, adding, that if the jury should be of that opinion, he considered an act of bankruptcy would be made out. Upon this suggestion, the plaintiff's counsel submitted to a nonsuit.

Scarlett now moved for a rule *nisi* for a new trial. The learned Judge's direction to the jury, for it may be considered such in effect, was erroneous in point of law. The mere circumstance of a debtor failing to keep an appointment for the payment of a debt does not amount to an

(*a*) This case was decided before the full Court in *Hilary* term, on the day it bears date.

act of bankruptcy, unless there is also evidence to shew that his intent is to delay his creditor. That was expressly decided in the recent case of *Tucker* v. *Jones* (a), and the observations of *Best*, C. J. in that case, shew that the decision was founded in reason, and that it ought to govern the present case. His lordship said, "The intent to delay a creditor, (which is proof of fraud or insolvency,) is the essence of the act of bankruptcy, which this person is supposed to have committed. There was not even *primâ facie* evidence of such an intent. It was only proved that he made an appointment with a creditor to meet him, and that he did not keep that appointment. If a jury could, without more evidence, presume that he broke his engagement to delay his creditor, there are very few in the commercial world that could be assured they were not bankrupts. It has been insisted that this proof was sufficient to call on the other side to shew that something had occurred to prevent the supposed bankrupt from keeping his engagement, and so rebut the inference of an intention to delay a creditor. An inference must be raised before it can be required that it should be rebutted. When once a man has committed an act of bankruptcy, he cannot be relieved from it until he has discharged every debt which he then owed. A docket might be struck against him when it was too late to trust to his own memory, much less to prove by witnesses what had induced him not to keep his appointment; and thus he and his family might be ruined by a circumstance that had been occasioned by forgetfulness, accident, or necessity." Here there was no evidence whatever to shew that the plaintiff had failed in keeping his appointment with any intent to delay the creditor.

PER CURIAM.—The question of intent, in a case and under circumstances like the present, is a question of fact within the province of the jury to decide. A creditor, with

(a) 2 Bingh. 2; S. C. nom. *Toleman* v. *Jones*, 9 Moore, 24.

whom such an appointment is made, cannot be supposed to know, or, consequently, to have the means of proving, what particular circumstance had occurred to prevent the debtor from keeping his engagement. But that is within the knowledge of the debtor, and it is incumbent, therefore, on him to prove it, and thereby to rebut the inference which, in the absence of such proof, a jury may think proper to draw. Where no explanation is given, it is difficult to imagine what inference a jury can draw from the fact of the debtor breaking such an appointment, but one, namely, that he neglected to keep the appointment because he intended to avoid paying, or in other words, to delay, the creditor with whom he made it. The direction in this case, therefore, was correct, and the rule prayed for cannot be granted.

Rule refused.

·1827.

The KING v. The BRISTOL DOCK COMPANY.

Saturday,
February 3.

MANDAMUS to the defendants to compel them to make certain alterations and amendments in the sewers of the City of *Bristol.* The writ, after reciting part of the statute 43 *Geo.* 3, c. 140, by which the defendants were empowered to make a floating dock, &c., proceeded as follows :— " And it was in and by the said act further enacted, 'that it should and might be lawful for the directors of the said company, at the charge of the company, and they were thereby authorised and required, to form and complete a common sewer from a certain place called *Castle Pill,* through *Bread Street* and *Avon Street,* or the streets or lands adjoining, or near adjoining, thereto, into the river *Avon,* above a certain dam directed by the said act to be made at *Temple Meads,* and also to form and complete collateral sewers leading thereto, and to alter the then present sewers of the said city of *Bristol,* so and in such manner that the greater part of the sewage there discharged into the river *Avon* above *Bristol Bridge* might be carried off, and not permitted to mix with the water in the floating harbour, and also, to alter and reconstruct all or any of the sewers of the said city at the mouths thereof, so and in such manner that the sewers might be discharged considerably under the surface of the water in the said floating harbour; and also to make such other alterations and amendments in the sewers of the said city as might or should be necessary in consequence of the floating of the said harbour:' And whereas we have been given to understand in our court before us, that by virtue and in pursuance of the said act and of certain other acts of parliament made and passed

The return to a mandamus denying the matters of the writ with a *protestando,* is ill.

An act of parliament authorised the *Bristol* Dock Company to make a floating harbour, and required them to make a common sewer in a certain direction, and also to alter and reconstruct all or any of the sewers of *Bristol* at the mouths, so that they might be discharged considerably under the surface of the water in the harbour, and also to make such " *other alterations and amendments*" in the sewers as should be necessary in consequence of the floating harbour. The sewers constructed under

the water of the floating harbour became a nuisance to the neighbourhood :—Held, that mandamus would lie to compel the company under the words, " other alterations and amendments," to construct a new sewer, without carrying it under the floating harbour, even at the expense of purchasing land adjacent. A mandamus " to make such alterations and amendments in the sewers as were necessary in consequence of the floating of the harbour" is sufficiently specific, the mode of remedying the evil being left by parliament to the discretion of the company.

respectively for altering and amending the same, and extending the powers and provisions thereof, the said floating
harbour in the said first mentioned act has been made:
And whereas we have also been given to understand in our
said Court before us, that in consequence of the floating
of the said harbour, as by the said act is mentioned and
directed, divers noxious and unwholesome smells and
stenches have been for a long time past and still are
emitted and sent forth from the sewage discharged into the
said floating harbour, and from the waters dammed up
therein, and the air there hath thereby become and still is
greatly corrupted and infected, and that divers alterations
and amendments in the sewers of the said city of *Bristol*
have become and still are necessary in consequence of the
floating of the said harbour, and that application hath been
made to you, the said company, by and on behalf of divers
of our liege subjects inhabiting and dwelling within the said
city, and near to the said floating harbour, to make such
alterations and amendments in the sewers of the said city as
have so become and are necessary, in consequence of the
floating of the said harbour, as aforesaid, but that you, the
said company, well knowing the premises, but not regarding your duty in this behalf, have altogether neglected and
refused, and still do neglect and refuse to make any such
alterations and amendments as aforesaid, in contempt of us,
and to the great discomfort, prejudice, and inconvenience
of divers of our said subjects inhabiting and dwelling within
the said city, and near to the said floating harbour as aforesaid: And whereas they have humbly besought us that a fit
and speedy remedy may be provided in this respect, we,
being willing that due and speedy justice should be done
in the premises as it is reasonable, do command you, the
said *Bristol* Dock Company, that you do without delay
make and cause to be made all such alterations and amendments in the sewers of the said city as have become and
are necessary, in consequence of the floating of the said
harbour, or that you shew us cause to the contrary thereof," &c.

To the above writ the following return was made by the
defendants: " We, the *Bristol* Dock Company, most
humbly certify to our Lord the King, that after the passing
of the said Acts of Parliament, and before the issuing of
the said writ, we did in due manner form and complete the
said common sewer from the said place called *Castle Pill,*
through *Bread Street* and *Avon Street,* in the streets and
lands adjoining, or near adjoining thereto, into the river *Avon*
above the said dam, directed by the said first-mentioned act
to be made at *Temple Meads,* and did form and complete
collateral sewers leading thereto, and did then alter the
then present sewers of the said city of *Bristol,* so and in
such manner that the greater part of the sewage, at the time
of passing the said first-mentioned act of parliament, discharged into the river *Avon* above *Bristol Bridge* might be
and was, and is carried off, and not permitted to mix with
the water in the floating harbour ; and also did alter and
reconstruct part of the sewers of the said city at the mouths
thereof, as was requisite and necessary to be done in that
behalf, so and in such manner that the sewers might be, and
were, and are discharged considerably under the surface of
the water in the said floating harbour ; and protesting that
no other alteration or amendment in the sewers of the said
city, according to the true intent and meaning of the said
statute, hath become, or at the time of issuing the said writ
was, or hath been since, or now is necessary, in consequence
of the floating of the said harbour ; nevertheless we do
further make answer and certify to our Lord the King, that
so long as the said sewers, so altered and reconstructed as
aforesaid, shall continue to be discharged under the surface
of the water in the said floating harbour according to the
directions of the said statute, neither the nuisances in the
writ of our Lord the King mentioned, nor any other grievance arising in consequence of the floating of the said harbour can be removed, or in any manner remedied by any
alteration or amendment whatsoever of the same sewers, or
of any other sewers whatsoever of the said city. And we

do further certify and inform our Lord the King, that if the same nuisances, or any other grievance arising in consequence of the floating of the said harbour can be removed or remedied by any other means of sewage, it can only be by forming and completing new sewers to be conducted to and discharged at some other and different place or places than under the surface of the water of the said floating harbour; and we do further certify and inform our Lord the King that all the powers and authorities given to us by the said statute, or by any other of the statutes in this behalf made and provided, to enter upon any lands and tenements of others the subjects of our Lord the King, for the purpose of constructing, forming, and completing, any new sewer or sewers, long before the issuing of the said writ of our Lord the King, had by virtue of the said statutes ceased and determined, and that we had not before the issuing of the said writ, nor have we now, any lands nor any lawful power or authority to obtain and have any lands by, through, or under which any new sewer, for the purpose aforesaid, could or can be made, formed, and completed."

W. O. Russell for the crown. The return to this writ of mandamus is bad on the face of it, and a peremptory mandamus must go. It is argumentative and evasive. It does not state any matters of fact explicitly and distinctly in answer to the writ; nor does it admit or deny that the alterations and amendments in the sewers are necessary in consequence of the floating harbour. In *Bac. Abr. Mandamus* (I), it is said, that " the return to a mandamus must be certain to every respect; therefore it is said not to be sufficient to offer such matter, as the party may falsify in an action, but also such matter must be alleged that the Court may be able to judge of it, and determine whether the party's conduct be agreeable to law or not." In *Rex* v. *Lyme Regis* (a), *Buller*, J., in speaking of the requisites of a return to a writ of mandamus, says, " I agree that in

(a) Doug. 158.

these returns, the same certainty is required as in indictments, or returns to writs of habeas corpus." Now here the return is so uncertain on the face of it, that the Court cannot judge and dispose of the matter. In the first place it begins with a *protestando* which is a mode of drawing up a return to a mandamus quite unprecedented. If this were intended as an admission that certain repairs are necessary, still, it being indirect, it is sufficient to vitiate the return, which requires every matter to be stated in the most unqualified manner. Again, the return proceeds to state, " *that so long* as the said sewers so altered and reconstructed as aforesaid, shall continue to be discharged under the surface of the water in the said floating harbour, according to the directions of the said statute, neither the nuisances mentioned in the writ, nor any other grievance arising, &c. in consequence of the floating harbour can be removed, or in any manner remedied by any alteration or amendment whatsoever of the *same* sewers," &c. This is no more than a conditional allegation, which is insufficient. It does not shew that the nuisance can be abated only by discharging them under the surface of the floating harbour. The nuisance, however, is in fact admitted, and also that alterations in the floating dock are necessary. But then it is averred in substance, that, supposing it to be true that the nuisance does exist to the extent complained of, still the company cannot be called upon to abate it, so long as the *same* sewers exist. That argument, however, cannot avail the defendants when reference is had to the act of 43 *Geo.* 3, c. 140, s. 37, by which it will appear that they are bound to make the alterations required. That section, after requiring the company to make certain alterations in the sewers of *Bristol,* enacts, " and also to make such other *alterations and amendments* in the sewers of the said city as may or shall be necessary in consequence of the floating of the said harbour." It is clear, according to the authority of *Rex* v. *Hall* (a), that the words " alterations and amend-

(a) 2 D. & R. 241.   1 B. & C. 136.

ments" include the making of new sewers if necessary. In that case, *Abbott*, C. J., said, " the true meaning of particular words in acts of parliament is to be found not so much in a strict etymological propriety of language, nor in popular usage, as in the subject-matter of the occasion in which they are used, as connected with the object which is sought to be attained." If, then, new sewers be necessary to remedy this nuisance, the company have power to make them by force of these words, inasmuch as " alterations and improvements" comprehend those measures which are requisite to the sewage of the city. The object of the act was to guard the inhabitants against the introduction of a nuisance by means of the floating harbour. It never could have been intended that the health and comfort of the citizens were to suffer for the benefit of the company's interests. The allegation in the return that the company " have not now any lands nor any lawful power or authority to obtain and have any lands by, through, or under which any new sewer for the purpose aforesaid could or can be made, formed, and completed," is no answer to the mandamus or any excuse for not obeying it, inasmuch as it is not essentially necessary that they should have the soil and freehold in the lands for all the purposes contemplated by the act of parliament. This principle is fully recognized and enforced by the cases of *Hollis* v. *Goldfinch* (a), and *Earl of Portmore* v. *Bunn* (b). Suppose the sewers under the floating harbour were presented as a nuisance, would it be an answer to the presentment that the company were unable to enter into the harbour and make a sewer that would remedy the evil? Surely not. If the defendants bring a public nuisance into the populous city of *Bristol*, it is incumbent on them to find a remedy, even if it cast upon them the obligation of purchasing lands for this purpose. In form as well as in substance the return is insufficient, and a peremptory mandamus ought to go.

(a) 2 D. & R. 316; 1 B. & C. 205. (b) 2 D. & R. 145; 1 B. & C. 694.

Maule, contrà. First, the return is good in point of form 1827.
and substance; and, secondly, the mandamus is itself bad.
As to the objection to the return that it neither admits nor
denies that alterations are necessary, that is not tenable,
because the return at least shews an exclusion of a conclusion, which it is competent for the defendants to do.
[*Bayley*, J. Provided you be not concluded by the statute.]
This objection is mere matter of form. The rules of pleading do not apply to returns to writs of mandamus. [*Abbott*, C. J. Do you mean to say that a protestation is an
assertion?] The word *protesting* here may be taken as
synonimous with alleging. Protesting is an earnest assertion, and amounts to a positive denial. Assuming this not
to be so, still the return may be bad as to part, and good as
to the rest. It is no objection to such a return that it does
not afford a sufficient answer to all the parts of the writ.
Though it may be shocking to the ears of a pleader to
plead *double*, yet the return to a mandamus may be double,
Rex v. *the Mayor of Cambridge* (a). If part of the return
be good and part bad, the bad part does not hurt that
which is good. However, the real question in this case is,
whether any thing which has been suggested to be necessary to be done in consequence of the floating harbour,
falls within the scope of the words " other alterations and
amendments." Now it is denied that these words comprehend the making of new sewers, not specifically pointed
out by the statute. Whatever sewers are to be made
must be conformably to the directions of the act. The act
throughout specifically points out what sewers shall be
made, and work to be done. In the very clause in question
(37th), upon which the argument is founded on the other
side, the direction and termini of the new sewers thereby
authorised to be made are particularly pointed out, so that
the sewage shall be discharged under the floating harbour.
This does not give the defendants any power to take the
sewers in another direction from that pointed out. Ad-

The King
v.
The Bristol
Dock Co.

(a) 2 T. R. 456.

mitting that so forced a construction could be put on this act, still the defendants have no power to purchase lands. [*Abbott*, C. J. I see there is a clause in the act which limits the clause giving a power of *compulsory* sale; but there is nothing to shew that the defendants might not purchase all lands necessary for this purpose.] Still it lies upon the other side to point out what land the company have a right to take and do the thing required of them. [*Abbott*, C. J. That brings the case back again to the construction of that one sentence in the 37th section, " and also to make such other *alterations and amendments* in the sewers of the said city as may or shall be necessary in consequence of the floating of the said harbour."] Then the writ of mandamus itself is bad, and must be quashed, whatever may be the defect of the return. It alleges that noxious smells, &c. arise from the damming up of the water, and that certain alterations and amendments of the sewers have become necessary in consequence of the making of the floating harbour; but it does not say that these alterations and amendments have become necessary in consequence of the noxious smells. It says that something is necessary to be done, but it does not point out what. The company are at a loss to conjecture from the writ what alterations and amendments are necessary. No request to do particular specified work is set forth, and therefore the writ itself must be quashed for uncertainty.

ABBOTT, C.J.—I am of opinion that this return must be quashed, and that a peremptory mandamus must be awarded. I shall first dispose of the writ itself, for if that be bad in form or substance, then the sufficiency of the return will not call for consideration. The writ begins by reciting the act of parliament under which the floating harbour was made; and then states that his Majesty has been given to understand that the floating harbour has been made, and that in consequence of the floating of the said harbour divers noxious and unwholesome smells have been and still are emitted from the sewage discharged into the said floating harbour, and that the air there hath thereby become corrupted, and that divers alterations and amendments in the sewers of the city of *Bristol* have become necessary in consequence of the floating of the harbour; that the Dock Company have been requested to make such alterations and amendments as have so become necessary, but have neglected to do so; and then the writ commands them to make such alterations and amendments. Two objections have been made to this writ, first, that although it recites that noxious and unwholesome smells are sent forth from the sewage discharged under the floating harbour dammed up, and that divers alterations are necessary, it does not say that the alterations are necessary in consequence of the sewage being discharged into the harbour. Certainly there is no direct allegation as to that, but I think the writ uses language so plain that no man can misunderstand it. The second objection is, that the application to the corporation to make alterations does not specify what particular works are required to be done to remedy this nuisance, and that the writ itself is equally uncertain, which it is. I am of opinion, however, that such specification was not necessary, nor even proper, to be made, because the act of parliament gives the power to the company to do what is necessary, and leaves them to judge in the first instance what is necessary, and other persons have no right to deprive them of the exercise of that discretion. It appears to me, therefore, that the writ is perfectly sufficient, and is in form adapted to the case laid before the Court. The next question is, whether the return to the writ is sufficient. Most undoubtedly it is perfectly informal; but on a great question of this kind I should be unwilling to determine it on a mere matter of form. I prefer the consideration of the question upon the substance rather than the form. The substantial and indeed the only question raised upon the return is, as to the true construction and meaning of the 37th section of the 43 *Geo.* 3, c. 140, for the latter part of the return relating

to the ceasing of the powers given to the company certainly
is not warranted by the act. The 43d section applies only
to the purchase of lands, and the return does not say that
the thing required cannot be done without purchasing.
Then what is the true construction of the 37th section?
By this enactment (passing by that which does not relate to
the question now before us,) I find that it is made lawful
for the company, and they are authorised and required, to
alter and reconstruct all or any of the sewers of the city at
the mouths thereof so and in such manner that the sewers
may be discharged considerably under the surface of the
water in the floating harbour; "and also to make such other
alterations and amendments in the sewers as may or shall be
necessary in consequence of the floating of the said harbour." It is contended that the company, by making the
sewers to be discharged under the surface of the water in
the floating harbour have done all that this act requires them
to do, and that they cannot be compelled to do more, notwithstanding the power of making such other alterations
and amendments in the sewers as may become necessary in
consequence of the floating of the harbour. Now if that
be so, then the latter part of the clause would become useless and inoperative. Another consequence may also arise;
namely, that the legislature must be presumed to have given
the company power to stop the course of the rivers *Avon*
and *Frome,* and to keep out the tide; and to have provided
that if the air should be thereby rendered so corrupt as to
prove unwholesome to all the neighbourhood, still the nuisance must be allowed to exist. To suppose that the legislature intended to give such a power, is to suppose something so outrageous and so absurd, that we cannot for a
moment imagine it to have been within their contemplation. We must, therefore, give the act such a construction
(taking it altogether) as shall exclude such a supposition,
and prevent it from doing that which it must be admitted
would be so highly prejudicial to the health of the public.
It has been urged also that the sewers are at all events to

be discharged into the floating harbour; but the direction,
that if they are taken into the floating harbour the mouths
shall be carried considerably under the surface of the water,
is quite consistent with a power to carry them elsewhere if
necessary. I am clearly of opinion that the construction
I have put upon the act is the true one,—that the writ is
sufficient, and the return bad, and consequently that a peremptory mandamus must be awarded.

BAYLEY, J.—I am of the same opinion. For the reasons given by my Lord Chief Justice, I think the writ is
sufficiently certain to call the attention of the defendants to
their duty and to the obligations of the statute. The question then is, whether the return to it is sufficiently certain,
and whether the defendants have given a legal ground of
excuse for not obeying it. I think, according to the authorities cited, that it is not sufficiently certain in point of
form. It is argumentative and inconclusive, and averring
no certain matter upon which the Court can decide. Is it
good in substance, though not in form? I think not. This
depends upon the effect of the act of parliament. The
strongest argument in favour of the return is, that the
company are supposed to be compelled to alter the sewers
so that they should be discharged under the surface of the
waters in the floating harbour. Looking at the context of
the act, I do not think that any such result necessarily flows
from it. I take it that by the rule of construction applicable
to acts of parliament, if there are several words importing
power, authority, and obligation at the commencement of
a clause containing several branches, it is not necessary that
each of those words should be applied to each of the different branches of the clause. It may be construed reddendo
singula singulis, the words giving power and authority may
be applicable to some branches, those of obligation to
others. Apply this rule of construction to the act in question. By the 37th section it is enacted, " that it shall and
may be lawful for the said directors, and they are hereby

authorised and required to form a new common sewer," in a certain direction. To this certainly the words of obligation apply,—they are *required* to do it. It then proceeds: " And also to alter and reconstruct *all or any* the sewers of the city at the mouths, so and in such manner that the sewers may be discharged under the surface of the floating harbour." Who ever heard of such an *obligation* attached to the duty of altering or reconstructing all or some—all or any? This is obviously left to their discretion. They have *authority* to do it, provided they so alter the construction of the sewers, that they may be discharged under the surface of the water. Then follows the most important part of the section: " And also to make such other alterations and amendments in the sewers of the said city as may or shall be necessary in consequence of the floating of the said harbour." Now it cannot reasonably be supposed that the legislature meant to leave it in the discretion of the dock company to do or leave undone such things as were necessary, or that they imposed the obligation without giving power to perform it. To this part of the clause, therefore, both the words of authority and those of obligation are applicable. It is said that they have no power to go upon another person's land to make the necessary alterations and amendments, and as they have no land of their own, they are not compellable to make the alterations and amendments. It is not essential that they should have land of their own, nor that they should have the power to go upon other people's land; but there is nothing to prevent them from buying land from other persons to enable them to make a proper sewage. They do not state that they have no funds for this purpose, nor that they *cannot* make the alterations. All they say is, that *so long* as the sewage is discharged under the floating harbour, they cannot remove the nuisance. It may be that the company have no power, under the act, to use the lands of other persons; but having regard to the language of the 37th section, they must purchase out of their own funds the means, which they have the power of

1827.

The King
v.
The Bristol
Dock Co.

applying according to their own undertaking, and which they are required to do, namely, of making all necessary amendments and alterations in the sewage in order to abate the alleged nuisance.

HOLROYD, J.—I am of the same opinion. The return resolves itself into the construction to be put upon the 37th clause of the act. I had some doubts during the argument, but I am now satisfied upon further consideration, and upon the grounds likewise stated by the Court, that the return is insufficient. The doubt I had was whether in consequence of the wording of the clause the company were not bound to discharge the whole of the sewage into the floating harbour. I think, however, that the power and authority given vest a discretion in the company as to which sewers shall be discharged into the harbour, and that the words of the obligation as to discharging them under the surface of the water are satisfied by applying them to those sewers. With respect to the writ itself, I think the observations made by my Lord Chief Justice remove all doubt upon that point.

Scarlett (who was with *Maule*,) suggested that the owners of the adjoining land might not chuse to sell for the purpose of enabling the defendants to comply with the decision of the Court.

ABBOTT, C. J.—It is a general rule that where an act of parliament gives a power of doing a particular act, and possession of land is essential for the purposes of executing it, the party to whom the power is given may use it for the purpose.

> Return quashed, and a peremptory mandamus ordered to issue; or an information, if the defendants refused to obey the mandate.

The KING v. The Inhabitants of HOLSWORTHY.

A militia-man hired himself for a year, and served a year under such hiring. It did not appear that at the time of the hiring he told his master that he was a militia-man: —Held, that he gained no settlement.

BY an order of two justices F. H. *Trim*, his wife and child, were removed from the parish of *Thornbury* to the parish of *Holsworthy*, both in the county of *Devon*. On appeal, the Court of Quarter Sessions confirmed the order, subject to the opinion of this Court upon the following case : —

In the month of *May*, 1819, the pauper, being a single man, was enrolled as a substitute in the *South Devon* Militia as a private to serve for the space of five years; and in *June*, 1822, while he was still a member of the corps, being at *Plymouth*, he offered himself as a recruit to one *George M'Gie*, a private in the fifteenth regiment of infantry, who paid him a shilling for enlisting money, and took him to a serjeant of the regiment, and he was, after inspection by the surgeon, sworn in before the mayor of *Plymouth*, as a recruit in that regiment for unlimited service. At the time of receiving the shilling from *M'Gie*, he informed him that he belonged to the *South Devon* militia, and was by him told not to mention it. He did not mention it, either to the serjeant, the surgeon, or the commanding officer of the regiment. For this offence he was subsequently tried, convicted, and imprisoned. In *February*, 1823, he, being still a single man, hired himself for a year to one *Penwarden*, in the parish of *Holsworthy*, and performed a year's service in that parish under that hiring. The question for the opinion of the Court is, whether by such hiring and service he gained any settlement in that parish.

Crowder, in support of the order of sessions. The question in this case is, whether the pauper, at the time when he hired himself to *Penwarden* was *sui juris*, and capable of entering into a valid contract to serve for a year. Now he was not at that time legally a soldier in the army, because he belonged to the militia when he enlisted, and his enlistment, consequently, was void (a); he must, therefore, be considered, with reference to this case, merely as a militia-man. Then as a militia-man he was sufficiently *sui juris* to be capable of making a valid contract to serve for a year, and having served for a year under such a contract, he has thereby acquired a settlement; *Rex* v. *Westerleigh* (b), *Rex* v. *Winckcomb* (c). But it will be said, first, that the pauper was not *sui juris* to contract at all.; and, secondly, that if he could contract at all, the hiring must necessarily be either exceptive or fraudulent. Upon the first point, *Rex* v. *Norton-juxta-Kempsey* (d) will be cited as shewing that a militia-man, being subject at any moment to be called out to discharge his public duty, cannot bind himself to serve a master for a year. But that case only decided that a *deserter* from the king's marine service cannot gain a settlement under a hiring and service for a year, not being *sui juris*, or competent lawfully to hire himself within the statute 3 W. & M. c. 11. s. 7; a decision which does not at all affect the present case, because there the pauper having deserted from the marine service had been guilty of an offence against the law, and every moment of his continuance in the master's service was an illegal act. In *Rex* v. *Beaulieu* (e), indeed, an invalided soldier at a depôt, who, in pursuance of an order from government, had leave of absence upon agreeing to relinquish his pay for the time, which leave was renewed from time to time, was held, by Lord Ellenborough, C. J., and Le Blanc, J., not to gain a settlement by hiring and service for a year, not being *sui juris* lawfully to hire himself within the statute; though before the hiring the mistress applied to the commanding officer at the depôt to know if he might hire himself for a year, and was told that he might, and during the year's service he received no pay, and was never called upon, or performed any military duty. The Court, however, were

(a) See the statute 42 *Geo.* 3, c. 90, s. 64. (d) 9 East, 207.
(b) Barr. S. C. 166. (e) 3 M. & S. 229.
(c) Dougl. 391.

not unanimous in the decision of that case, for *Bayley*, J., was of opinion that the hiring and service were sufficient, inasmuch as there was a lawful hiring for a year, although a conditional one. That case, therefore, cannot be considered as one of any great authority. The distinction there taken by *Bayley*, J., seems to be a sound one. Every person is *sui juris*, for the purpose of acquiring a settlement, who is capable of lawfully hiring himself for a year. It is not necessary that he should at all events be liable to complete his year's service. In this respect a militia-man and an apprentice stand in very different situations. An apprentice cannot lawfully hire himself, because he has already contracted to be absolutely subject to his master's control during the whole term of his apprenticeship; but a militia-man has not so contracted, but is free for the whole year, excepting only such part of it as is mentioned in the acts of parliament, and for which he may be called upon to devote himself to military service. Then, if the pauper in this case was sufficiently *sui juris* to contract, secondly, the hiring was neither exceptive nor fraudulent. The case does not state whether *Penwarden* was or was not informed that the pauper was a militia-man; but that circumstance, which ever way assumed, did not make the hiring exceptive. If nothing was said about the militia, the hiring was not an exceptive, but an absolute hiring for a year, by a person capable of contracting, and followed by a year's service: and in that case a settlement was gained. If the pauper's enrolment in the militia was mentioned, the hiring was not an exceptive but a conditional hiring within the distinction laid down in *Rex* v. *Byker* (a), and the condition not having

(a) 3 D. & R. 330; 2 B. & C. 114; by *Bayley*, J., in the following terms :—" Where the bargain is originally made for an entire year, and terms are introduced indicating a continuance of the relation of master and servant during the whole year, but there is also a provision, that in a given event it shall be in the power of either party to suspend or terminate the service for a part of the year; still, if the service is in fact performed during the whole year, and neither party avails himself of the condition, a settlement is gain-

been acted upon, in that case also a settlement was gained. But it will be said, that it must be assumed in this case that the pauper did not communicate the fact of his enrolment in the militia, that the concealment of such a fact was a fraud, and consequently that the hiring was fraudulent, and did not confer a settlement. The answer to that argument is, that fraud can never be presumed; it must always be expressly found: *The Chancellor of the University of Oxford's case* (a), *Bennet* v. *Clough* (b), *Rex* v. *Twyning* (c), *Williams* v. *The East India Company* (d), *Rex* v. *Fillongley* (e), *Rex* v. *Llanbedergoch* (f), *Rex* v. *Weston* (g), *Rex* v. *Newnham* (h); the fact of the concealment, therefore, which is to raise the presumption of fraud, cannot be assumed; on all general principles, indeed, the contrary is to be assumed, and that being done, there is a good conditional hiring, and a good service under it to confer a settlement. If the Court entertain any doubt upon this point, they will at least think it right to remit the case to the sessions, to have the fact expressly found one way or the other.

Fraser and *Coleridge*, contrà, were stopped by the Court.

BAYLEY, J.—I think this case admits of no doubt. Upon the question, whether a militia-man may or may not acquire a settlement by serving for a whole year under a yearly hiring, where, at the time of making the contract, he communicates to the person with whom he is contracting the fact that he is in the militia, and that he is liable to be

ed. For this purpose, a conditional hiring is the same as an absolute hiring, if the condition is not acted upon. But where by the terms of the bargain, the relation of master and servant will not subsist during a whole year, without some further arrangement being made between the parties, the hiring is exceptive; and therefore, where the agreement is to exclude days or hours from

the service, that is an exceptive hiring." 3 D. & R. 336.

(a) 10 Co. Rep. 56 a;
(b) 1 B. & A. 461.
(c) 2 B. & A. 386.
(d) 3 East, 192.
(e) 2 T. R. 709.
(f) 7 T. R. 105.
(g) Burr. S. C. 166.
(h) Burr. S. C. 756.

called out during the year, I shall give no decided opinion, because I do not deem it necessary for the proper disposal of the present case. If a master chuses to engage a servant subject to the risk of his being called away from his service to perform duty as a militia-man during the year, I do not see that there is anything illegal in such an arrangement: such a hiring may be considered a conditional hiring, and if the servant is not called out during the year, and the condition therefore is not acted upon, service under such a hiring may perhaps confer a settlement. But is that the kind of contract stated in the present case? Far from it. The contract here is one by which the master stipulates to have, and the servant undertakes to give, an entire unbroken year's service. There is no condition or qualification whatever in this contract: if there had been any, it probably would, and certainly ought to have been stated in the case: it cannot be assumed. I do not presume fraud in this case, for the law never presumes fraud; and, besides, the non-communication by the pauper of the fact that he belonged to the militia may have arisen quite innocently, from his considering it altogether immaterial, from inadvertence, or from various circumstances unconnected with a fraudulent motive. Without, therefore, breaking in upon any case in which it has been decided that a militia-man, who in his contract of hiring stipulates for the time that he may be called out to perform his duty in the militia, may gain a settlement by a whole year's service under such hiring, I confine myself to the expression of my opinion, that the pauper in this case not having communicated to the party whom he agreed to serve for a whole year that he was in the militia, cannot be said to have lawfully hired himself for a whole year, within the meaning of the statute 3 *W. & M.* c. 11, s. 7, and, therefore, that he acquired no settlement in the parish of *Holsworthy.*

Holroyd, J.—I concur with my brother *Bayley* in the view which he has taken of this case. It cannot be assumed, because it is not stated in the case, that the pauper, at the time when he made the contract with his master, communicated to him the fact of his being in the militia; on the contrary, we must deal with the case as if no such communication was made. I think the present case comes within the principle laid down by Lord *Ellenborough* in that of *Rex* v. *Norton-juxta-Kempsey* (a). He there says, "A variety of cases have occured which have decided the question in the case of an apprentice; and this, not on the ground of its being an excepted case, or as standing upon any occult efficacy in the indenture of apprenticeship; but on the broad principle, that one who has contracted a relation which disables him from serving any other without the consent of his first master is not *sui juris,* and cannot lawfully bind himself to serve such second master so as to gain a settlement by serving for a year under such second contract. In reason and principle it cannot make any difference whether he be originally bound by a contract of apprenticeship or by any other contract equally obligatory upon him, which disables him from binding himself to serve a second master." It is said that the present case is distinguishable from that, inasmuch as the militia not having been called out during the year, there has been a year's service under a conditional hiring. But that question does not arise; the objection here is, that the pauper was not capable of making a contract so as to give the master a control over his services during the whole year. As the pauper did not communicate to his master that he had entered into a contract to serve in the militia, I am of opinion that this must be considered not as a conditional, but as an absolute hiring for a year, and if so, it is clear that the pauper was not capable of making an unconditional contract to serve for a whole year. I am therefore of opinion, that the pauper in this case was not lawfully hired

(a) 9 East, 209.

into the parish of *Holsworthy* for one whole year within the meaning of the statute 3 *W. & M.* c. 11, s. 7.

LITTLEDALE, J. concurred.

Order of Sessions quashed.

———◆———

The KING v. JOHN ATTWOOD, Esq. and others.

The owner and occupier of a coal mine is rateable at the sum for which the mine would let, without reference to the expense incurred in making the mine productive.

The lessee and occupier of a coal-mine is rateable at the sum which he pays as rent or royalty for it, without reference to the expense incurred in planting or improving the mine.

ON the 29th day of *March*, 1825, the churchwardens and overseers of the poor of the parish of *Rowley Regis*, in the county of *Stafford*, made a rate for the relief of the poor, in which the above named *John Attwood* was assessed as owner and occupier, and *Thomas Devey Wightwick, John Jones* and *Joseph Fereday*, and *Josiah Parkes*, were assessed as lessees and occupiers of certain coal mines then at work. The rate was in the following form :

Occupiers.	Owners.	Species of Property.	Annual Value.	Rate at 10d. in the Pound.
			£.　s.　d.	£.　s.　d.
J. Attwood, Esq.	J. Attwood, Esq.	Coal-mine at work	428　9　0	17 17　0¼
J. D. Wightwick	T. & J. Moore	Ditto	785 14　0	32 14　9
J. Jones and J. Fereday	Sir H. St. Paul	Ditto	100 12　0	4　3 10
Josiah Parkes	Joseph Line	Ditto	95 13　0	3 19　8

On appeal to the *Midsummer* general quarter sessions for the county of *Stafford*, the rate was confirmed, subject to the opinion of this Court upon the following case:

The appellant, *John Attwood*, was the owner and occupier of the coal mine upon which the above rate upon him was made, (which mine is situate in the parish of *Rowley Regis*, in the county of *Stafford*,) and had expended upwards of £10,000 in planting the mine and setting it to work. The mine had been at work one year and a quarter. The value of the whole of the coals which had then been raised from the mine did not exceed £5,000. The full value of the annual produce of the mine in question, after deducting the current expenses of working the same, amounted to the sum of £428. 9s. Upon that amount the appellant was rated.

The appellant, *T. D. Wightwick*, had been for five months prior to the said 29th day of *March*, 1825, lessee of the coal mine upon which the rate upon him was made, and which is situate in the said parish of *Rowley Regis;* and during the five months that he had been lessee he had paid £785. 14s. in royalties for coals raised; he had also expended in the purchase of the lease, and in setting the mines to work, £5,020. During the five months that he had occupied the mine, he had raised coals to the amount of £3,825. 2s. 8d. The appellant, *T. D. Wightwick,* was rated upon the sum paid for royalties, the sum of £785. 14s. being considered by the respondents as the annual value of the royalties paid by him.

The appellants, *John Jones* and *Joseph Fereday*, were the lessees of the coal mines upon which the rate upon them was made, and which are situate in the said parish of *Rowley Regis*. Sir *Horace St. Paul,* the owner and lessee of the mines, sunk the pits and made preparations requisite for working the mines, and then let them to the appellants, Messrs. *Jones* and *Fereday,* at a certain fixed royalty, not a specific proportion of the amount of sales; £492. 12s. 8½d. was the amount of royalties paid to the lessor during the last year. The appellants had expended £600 in permanent erections on these mines. The appellants, Messrs. *Jones* and *Fereday,* were rated upon the supposed amount of the annual sums paid for royalties.

The appellant, *Josiah Parkes,* had been eight years lessee of the mine upon which the rate upon him was made, and which is situate in the said parish of *Rowley Regis,* and had expended £2,500 in planting the mine and setting it to work. During the last year he had raised coals to the value of £2,500, and during that period had paid £585 in royalties, and was rated upon the supposed amount of the annual sums paid for royalties.

The questions for the consideration of the Court are, first, whether, under all the circumstances of the case, Mr. *Attwood* was properly rated at the sum of £438. 9s. in respect of the said coal mine, such sum being the full value of the annual produce of the mine after deducting the current expenses of working the same; and secondly, whether the said *J. D. Wightwick, John Jones* and *Joseph Fereday,* and *Josiah Parkes,* were rateable in respect of the said coal mines to the full amount of the sums paid for royalties upon the coals raised from such mines.

Campbell, Shutt, and *Holroyd,* in support of the order of sessions. Two objections will be made to this rate. It will be said, first, that the assessment should have been made upon the interest only of the annual value of the produce of the mines, and not upon the full annual value itself; and, secondly, that the assessment should have been made after deducting the expenses of planting the mines and setting them to work. To the first of these objections, the statute 43 *Eliz.* c. 2, s. 1, is a decisive answer, because that authorises the " taxation of every occupier of coal mines" to the relief of the poor, which can only mean that every such occupier shall be taxed in respect of the annual value of his mine. Now while the mine is in the occupation of the owner, the annual value of it is the coal raised, and upon the full amount of the coal raised, therefore, the occupier is to be rated, whether he derives a profit from the mine or not. When the mine is in the occupation of a lessee, the annual value of it is the rent or royalty which he pays, and therefore he is to be rated upon the full amount of such rent or royalty, so long as he continues to work the mine. These propositions will be found fully supported by the cases *Rex* v. *Parrott* (a) and *Rex* v. *Bedworth* (b). Then, the argument in support of the second

(a) 5 T. R. 593, where it was held that the lessee of a coal mine is liable to be rated to the relief of the poor, though he derives no profit from the mine.

(b) 8 East, 387, where it was

objection must go the length of contending that no rate can ever be assessed upon a coal mine until the whole expense of planting it and setting it to work has been recouped, because no proportion of that expense can by possibility be selected as the proper amount to be deducted before the rate is made. It has been laid down as a general rule of law applicable to this subject, that every person is to be rated according to the present value of his estate, whether that value has or has not been increased by his own improvements, *Rex* v. *Mast* (a). If a house is built, it is rateable as soon as occupied; if a canal is cut, the whole produce of the tolls is rateable as soon as it is realized; and the principle is the same whether the subject-matter of the rate is in the hands of the owner or of an occupier. In *Rex* v. *The Hull Dock Company* (b), it was decided that the company were rateable in respect of their annual income, minus their annual outgoings, and that the rent, after deducting the outgoings, is the proper criterion of value. The value is to be calculated, deducting only the fair annual expenses necessary to render the property productive (c); and " it is not enough in those cases" (where an exemption is claimed for property as unproductive), " to shew that the expenses laid out in any particular year absorbed the profits of that year ; for the benefit of such expenses may be derived in future years, as is often the case with improvement of farms. If valuable land in the neighbourhood of a town be covered with buildings in one year, the expenses of that year would probably exceed its profits, but the lands would not cease to be rateable on that account (d)." The

held, that where a coal mine becoming unproductive ceases to be worked, the lessee is no longer liable to be rated for it to the relief of the poor, although he be still bound by his covenant to pay the rent reserved to his landlord : *aliter*, where the mine itself is productive, although it be worked to a loss by the lessee, after deducting the proportion of the gross value of the produce reserved to the owner.

(a) 6 T. R. 154.

(b) 5 D. & R. 359; 3 B. & C. 516.

(c) 1 Nol. P. L. 202, 3d. ed.

(d) Per Lord *Ellenborough*, in *Rex* v. *Agar*, 14 East, 264.

same principle seems to be deducible from the case of *Rex* v. *Mirfield* (a), where it was decided that saleable underwoods were rateable annually, though they might not be cut down more than once in twenty-one years; and that a fair mode of rating them was by estimating their value according to the annual rent for which they would let under a lease for a term sufficient to cover their intended growth. In this case the lessees of the mines pay a certain proportion of the value of the produce as rent or royalty, and upon that amount they are clearly rateable. As to Mr. *Attwood*, who is both owner and occupier of his mine, he makes a certain clear profit after deducting his expenses; that would be the amount of rent or royalty coming to him if the mine were in the hands of a lessee, and upon that amount, therefore, he is clearly rateable.

Tindal, S. G., *Russell*, and *Whateley*, contrà. The appellants, in common with other occupiers of property of the same nature, have been led to entertain doubts whether the principle upon which coal mines have hitherto been rated is a just and correct principle, and their main object on the present occasion is to obtain the opinion of this Court, upon that (to them) most important question. It does seem that the mode of rating coal mines has never yet been sufficiently well considered. All the other species of property enumerated in the statute of *Elizabeth*, as subject-matters of rating, are permanent in their nature; those, therefore, are properly rated upon their full annual value, because that value is returned in perpetuity in the shape of an annual income. But the produce of a coal mine is of a different character; the coal is the capital; it is the soil and freehold; and the money realized by the sale of it must be considered as the purchase-money received upon the sale of a part of the estate; therefore the rate ought to be calculated, not upon the entire sum produced by the sale of the coals, but upon the interest of that sum only. In the

(a) 10 East, 219.

present case the rate is imposed, in effect, upon *capital*, not upon *income*, and in that respect is clearly unjust; for, " deductions for expenses of labour and *capital* necessary to render the subject productive, should be considered as drawbacks upon the profit" (a). The only cases to be found in the books upon the subject of rating coal mines, are the two which have been already cited, of *Rex* v. *Parrott* (b) and *Rex* v. *Bedworth* (c); but the point now submitted to the Court was not discussed in either of them, nor was the attention of the Court called to the important fact, that the subject-matter of the rate was substantially part of the realty, constantly diminishing and never renewable, and therefore in a limited time certain to be exhausted. Independently of this point, it is submitted that Mr. *Attwood* was not liable to be rated at all. He had never been recouped the money which he had expended in planting the mine and setting it to work, therefore the mine had never become *really* productive. Now it was decided in *Rex* v. *Bedworth,* that when a coal mine ceases to be productive, it ceases to be rateable; and it seems impossible to find any sound distinction between a mine which has ceased to be productive of profit, and one that has never produced any profit at all. In *Rex* v. *Dursly* (d), it was held that stock in trade was not rateable, because it was not proved to be productive of profit; and Lord *Kenyon* seems to have considered that the sole question necessary to determine its rateability was, " whether or not it produced a profit, or was liable to incumbrances equal to the value of the property itself (e)": a principle applicable to the present case. At all events, Mr. *Attwood* is assessed too highly in proportion to the other appellants. He is rated upon the full value of the annual produce of his mine, which includes both the landlord's and the tenant's profit; to that extent the rate clearly cannot be supported; it can

(a) 1 Nolan's P. L. 198, 3d ed.   (d) 6 T. R. 53.
(b) 5 T. R. 593.   (e) 1 Nol. P. L. 193, 3d ed.
(c) 8 East, 387.

only, at the utmost, be good to the extent of the estimated value of the property to let. With respect to the other appellants, the rate upon them is made upon the full annual rents or royalties which they pay, which, with reference to property of this peculiar description, cannot be supported. The owner of the mine must be considered as the seller of part of his estate; the lessee, consequently, must be regarded as the purchaser, and the rent or royalty as the purchase money; and then it follows that the rate should not be on the rent or royalty itself, but upon the sum for which the mine would let, subject to such rent or royalty.

Abbott, C. J.—We are unanimously and clearly of opinion that the owner and occupier of a coal mine ought to be rated at such sum as the mine would let for to a tenant, and no more; as far as that point is applicable therefore, the rate must be amended. With respect to the other points raised in argument, one was, that the rate ought not to be imposed upon the coals produced, because the coals are part of the realty. It is, confessedly, the first time that such a proposition has ever been submitted to a court of justice, although many coal mines in various parts of the country have for many years been constantly rated; and I have no hesitation in saying, that the arguments in support of it are as untenable as the proposition itself is new. Coal mines are expressly made rateable by the act of parliament, and if they are to be rated at all, they can only be rated for that which they produce, namely, coals. A coal mine in time becomes exhausted, so does a slate quarry and a clay pit; yet in the latter instances the rate has always been imposed upon the slate or the clay produced. The other point made was, that the rate ought not to be imposed until the expense of planting the mine and setting it to work had been recouped. I confess I can discover no difference between money expended in bringing a mine into a productive state, and money expended in building a house and making it habitable; and if a house is liable to be rated as soon as it is built and occupied, as it is, I can see no reason why a coal mine should not be liable to be rated also as soon as it is set to work and produces coals, although it may happen that the owner proves unfortunate in his speculations, and never recovers the expense of preparing the mine for working. I take the law to be clear, that when the tenant of a mine expends money in making it more productive, he stands in the same situation as the tenant of a farm or a house who expends money in making improvements, and is equally liable to be rated upon the improved value.

The other Judges concurred.

> Order of Sessions quashed as to the rate upon Mr. *Attwood*, and confirmed as to the rate upon the other appellants (*a*).

(*a*) Vide *Rex* v. *Lord Granville*, 9 B. & C. 188; 4 M. & R. 169.

Mitchell, Clerk, *v.* Fordham.

REPLEVIN for seizing plaintiff's goods. Avowry by defendant, as overseer of the poor of the parish of *Kelshall*, in the county of *Hertford*, that before the passing of an act of parliament after mentioned, the rector of the parish was entitled to certain great and small tithes arising in the parish; that by an act of parliament passed in the 35th year of *Geo.* 3, for inclosing lands in the parish of *Kelshall*, it was, among other things, enacted, that a certain yearly corn rent, *free from all taxes and other deductions whatsoever, except the land tax*, should be issuing and payable from and out of the lands and grounds thereby intended to be divided and allotted, and the old inclosures, (except as therein excepted,) to the rector of the parish for the time being, and should be payable by the respective proprietors

A corn rent given to the rector in lieu of tithes, payable "free from all taxes and other deductions whatsoever, except the land tax," is exempt from payment of poor rates.

of the said lands and grounds in the proportions and at the times and places in the act mentioned; which said yearly rent should be in lieu and satisfaction of and full compensation for all the great and small tithes, &c. due or payable to the rector of the parish for the time being; that plaintiff, the rector of the parish, was assessed to the poor in the sum of 12*l.* in respect of the corn rent received by him in lieu of tithes, and because that sum remained unpaid, defendant, as overseer of the poor of the parish, distrained plaintiff's goods, &c. Demurrer to the avowry and joinder in demurrer.

Patteson, in support of the demurrer. The act of parliament directs that the corn rent payable to the rector in lieu of tithes shall be paid " free from all taxes and other deductions whatsoever, except the land tax." Those words are large enough to comprehend poor rates, therefore the corn rent is not liable to be assessed to the relief of the poor. The case of *Chatfield* v. *Ruston* (a) is directly in point, with this single difference only, that the act of parliament in that case contained the word " rates," which certainly is not to be found in the act of parliament in question. But that is immaterial, for the expression " all taxes and deductions whatsoever" necessarily includes " rates," the word " taxation" being used in the 43 *Eliz.* as descriptive of the assessments to be raised for the relief of the poor. In *Rex* v. *Toms* (b), an exemption from " parochial taxes" was held to operate as an exemption from poor rates. In *Lowndes* v. *Horne* (c) and *Rann* v. *Picking* (d), there were no words of exemption at all; therefore those cases do not apply. The same may be said of the more modern case of *Rex* v. *Boldero* (e).

(a) 5 D. & R. 675; 4 B. & C. 863.
(b) Dougl. 401.
(c) 2 W. Bla. 1252.
(d) Cald. 196.
(e) 6 D. & R. 557; 4 B. & C. 467.

Robinson, contrà. The argument on the other side assumes that the word "rates" is an unimportant word, having no definite meaning of its own, but being merely synonimous with the word "taxes." But that is a mistake. The two words have always been construed as descriptive of distinct species of charges. In *Chatfield* v. *Ruston* (a), the case relied on for the plaintiff, the word *rates* was treated in argument as applying to parochial burthens, and the word *taxes* as applying to parliamentary imposts; and all the judges, in delivering their opinions, seem to have relied upon the effect of the word *rates* in the exempting clause of that act of parliament. It is said that the words "other deductions," in the present act, necessarily include poor rates; but "other deductions," coupled with "taxes," must mean deductions *ejusdem generis,* which poor rates are not. Besides, a poor rate cannot, in any proper sense of the word, be called a deduction; for a deduction is something withheld by the payer, whereas the poor rate is not imposed until after the money has found its way into the pocket of the rector. It follows, therefore, that the rate in dispute in this case is neither a tax nor a deduction, and not within the exemption of the act of parliament.

ABBOTT, C. J.—Tithes, when received *quà* tithes, being liable to be assessed to the relief of the poor, there can be no doubt that a money payment substituted by an act of parliament for tithes, would be equally liable with the tithes themselves to be so assessed, in the absence of an express exemption of them in the act of parliament. But where a bargain is made, as in this and other inclosure acts, between the rector and his parishioners, the amount to be received by the rector must necessarily vary, according to the existence or non-existence of an agreement that he shall be exempted from taxes and other pecuniary burthens. The bargain in this instance was, that the corn rent substituted for the tithes should be paid " free from all taxes

(a) 5 D. & R. 675; 4 B. & C. 863.

and other deductions whatsoever, except the land tax." The question, therefore, turns upon the meaning of the words " all taxes and other deductions." The rector contends that upon the fair construction of those words his exemption includes payments to be made for the relief of the poor. His parishioners, on the other hand, insist that *taxes* and *deductions* are not *rates*, and therefore that the rector is liable to payment of the poor rates. Now it has been decided that " parochial tax" means, or at least comprehends, " poor rate." And I think most correctly. Is not the poor rate a tax? Would there be any thing absurd in speaking of a " poor *tax*" instead of a " poor *rate ?*" I consider the former expression equally appropriate with the latter ; each means merely that a certain aggregate sum is to be levied by division upon many ; and the very language of the statute of *Elizabeth* is, that " a fund shall be raised by *taxation*." Now money raised by taxation is a tax ; the poor rate is money raised by taxation : *ergo*, the poor rate is a tax. I am, therefore, of opinion, that the exempting clause in this act of parliament includes the poor rates, and that the plaintiff, upon this record, is entitled to judgment. If the words of this act of parliament did not exempt the rector from the poor rate, it would be difficult to fix upon any other burthen from which they would exempt him.

The other Judges concurred.

Judgment for the plaintiff.

COOKE v. LEONARD and another.

1827.

TRESPASS for an assault and false imprisonment. Plea, not guilty, and issue thereon. At the trial before *Burrough*, J., at the last summer assizes for the county of *Gloucester*, the case was this. One of the defendants, *Leonard*, was a constable of the parish of *Stroud;* the other was surveyor to certain commissioners appointed by a local act of 6 *Geo.* 4, *c.* 6(a), for improving, &c., the town of *Stroud.* On the 16th of *February*, 1826, two foreigners appeared in the streets of *Stroud*, exhibiting a dromedary and some monkies, beating a drum, and soliciting money from the bystanders. The high constable of *Stroud*, who was also one of the commissioners above-mentioned, apprehended one of the foreigners in the act of exhibiting the animals in the town and ordered the defendant *Leonard* to see that the animals were removed out of the town. The other foreigner had in the mean time withdrawn the animals out of the streets, and deposited them in a stable, where they were afterwards found by the defendants, who ordered the foreigner to remove the animals out of the town. The plaintiff, who happened to be present, thereupon interposed, advising the

Where a statute provides that "no plaintiff shall recover in any action commenced against any person for any thing done in execution or under the authority of the act, unless notice in writing shall be given to the person intended to be sued 28 days before such action shall be commenced;" no notice is necessary, where the defendant had not reasonable ground for supposing that he had acted in execution or under the authority of the act.

(a) By s. 68 of which, certain commissioners therein appointed are empowered to cause the streets of *Stroud* to be watched, and to appoint watchmen.

By s. 69, such watchmen may apprehend and secure, in some proper place, all rogues, vagabonds, vagrants, idle and disorderly persons, disturbers of the public peace, prostitutes, and all suspected persons who shall be found wandering or misbehaving themselves *during the hours of keeping watch* within the limits of the town.

By s. 70, such watchmen are to be sworn in as *constables*, and

are invested with the like powers and authorities, privileges and immunities, as any constables are invested with and enjoy by law.

And, by s. 111, "no plaintiff shall recover in any action commenced against any person for any thing done in execution of or under the authority of the act, unless notice in writing shall be previously given to the person intended to be sued twenty-eight days before such action shall be commenced." Upon the construction and operation of this latter section, the question in the cause entirely turned.

foreigner not to obey, and expressing his opinion that the defendant had no authority to issue such an order. The defendant *Leonard* then endeavoured to remove the animals by force, which the plaintiff assisted in preventing, and was thereupon taken into custody by the defendants. This was the assault and imprisonment complained of. No notice of action had been given to the defendants pursuant to the directions of the 111th section of the statute (*a*), and it was on that ground contended that the plaintiff must be nonsuited. The learned Judge being of opinion that the defendants had acted colourably under the authority of the statute, and were therefore entitled to notice, yielded to the objection, and nonsuited the plaintiff. In *Michaelmas* term last, a rule nisi having been obtained for setting aside the nonsuit, and for a new trial,

Ludlow now shewed cause. The nonsuit was right, for the defendants were clearly entitled to notice of action. In a case of this kind, all that is necessary in order to bring an officer within the protection of the statute, is to shew that he was acting in supposed pursuance of his authority, and with the *bonâ fide* intention of performing his duty. That was the rule acted upon with reference to another act of parliament, 53 *Geo.* 3, c. 127, in *Theobald* v. *Crichmore* (*b*), though the officer had clearly exceeded his authority; and Lord *Ellenborough* there said, that the protection afforded to public officers by that statute was evidently intended to be given where they had acted illegally, through ignorance or inadvertence, and with no other intention than that of executing their authority. [*Bayley*, J. In that case the defendant was acting under a magistrate's warrant: here there was no warrant.] Now in this case the foreigners were clearly " vagrants," or " idle and disorderly persons," within the terms of the 69th section of the statute (*a*), and were liable to be apprehended as such. They had created a nuisance in the streets of *Stroud* by publicly

(*a*) *Ante*, 339, (*a*).   (*b*) 1 B. & A. 227.

exhibiting their animals there. The defendants had been
called upon by the high constable to abate the nuisance.
If, in obedience to that call, they had merely apprehended
the foreigners themselves, or if, finding the animals in the
streets causing the nuisance, they had removed them from
thence, they would most clearly have been justified, either
at common law, or under the provisions of the statute.
Unfortunately they proceeded one step farther, and attempted to remove the animals from a stable, where they
were not immediately causing a nuisance. But even in
so doing it is plain that they acted *bonâ fide*, under the belief
that they were merely discharging their duty; and that
being the case, they are still entitled to the protection of
the statute.

C. Phillips, contrà, was stopped by the Court.

BAYLEY, J.—I entertain no doubt upon this case. The
general rule prevailing in all cases of this nature certainly
is, that where an act of parliament gives protection to persons acting in execution, or in pursuance of it, all persons
acting under its provisions are entitled to its protection,
although, in so doing, they exceed their authority. Such a
rule, however, ought to be restrained within its proper limits,
and there appear to me to be cases which warrant this distinction :—If an officer does an act, part of which is authorised by the statute, though part of it is not—or, if a
magistrate acts in a case where his general character empowers him to interfere—a mere excess of authority will
not deprive either the officer or the magistrate of that protection which the statute confers upon those who act in
execution of it; but where the party steps entirely out of
the provisions of the statute, and has no authority at all for
any part of that which he has done, there he is not entitled
to that protection. There are, I must admit, some very
strong cases in which magistrates acting beyond the limits
of their jurisdiction have been considered entitled to such
protection. Thus it has been held, that where a magistrate

acts upon a subject-matter of complaint brought before him, but which arose out of his jurisdiction, he is entitled to the notice required by the statute 24 *Geo.* 2, c. 44, before the party aggrieved can bring any action(*a*); but in that case he would have had authority to do the act he did, provided the subject-matter of complaint had arisen within his jurisdiction. In *Weller* v. *Toke* (*b*), *one* magistrate having committed the mother of a bastard child for not affiliating the child, was yet held entitled to the previous notice of action under the 24 *Geo.* 2, c. 44, though by the statute 18 *Eliz.* c. 3, s. 2, jurisdiction over the subject-matter is committed to *two* magistrates. In *Bird* v. *Gunston*(*c*) the magistrate was authorised by statute to commit the plaintiff, the driver of a waggon, for riding on the shafts in the highway. The magistrate, in fact, committed the driver for being on the shafts while the waggon was standing still; yet it was held, that though the commitment was illegal, the magistrate was entitled to notice of action. These cases all proceed upon the general principle applicable to this subject, namely, that where an act of parliament requires notice before action brought in respect of anything done in execution or in pursuance of its provisions, these latter words are not confined to acts done strictly in execution of the act of parliament, but extend to all acts done *bonâ fide* in pursuance of it. But where the act is done without any colour for supposing that it is authorised by the act of parliament, there the party is not entitled to notice of action. Thus, in *Lawton* v. *Miller*(*d*), a custom-house officer detained a man going abroad, whom he supposed to be an artificer. The man was not an artificer, nor, if he had been, would a custom-house officer have had any right to detain him. The plaintiff obtained a verdict and the defendant had liberty to move to enter a nonsuit, upon the ground that

---

(*a*) *Prestidge* v. *Woodman*, 2 D. & R. 43 ; 1 B. & C. 12.

(*b*) 9 East, 364. See *Ex-parte*

Martin, 9 D. & R. 65 ; 6 B. & C. 80.

(*c*) 2 Chit. Rep. 459.

(*d*) E. T. 1818. MS.

notice of action was necessary; and the motion was made, but the court refused the rule. In *Morgan* v. *Palmer(a)*, the mayor of an ancient borough, in which he was also a justice of the peace, took a fee of 4*s.* from a publican resident within the borough for renewing his annual license; and though it appeared that for fifty-seven years a similar fee had been uniformly received by the mayor for the time being from every publican within the borough applying to have his license, yet it was held that the fee was illegal; that it could not have been taken by the mayor by virtue or in execution of his office as a justice of the peace; and, therefore, that it might be recovered back in assumpsit for money had and received, without any notice of action. Let us then apply the principles deducible from these cases to the present. Had the defendants in this case any colour for acting as they did? Had they any reasonable ground for supposing, or could they have supposed that they were acting in execution or in pursuance of the statute? By different clauses of the statute, the commissioners are authorised to appoint watchmen, and the watchmen are authorised to apprehend all vagrants, all idle and disorderly persons, and all suspected persons found wandering or misbehaving themselves during the hours of keeping watch within the limits of the town. Two foreigners appeared in the town with a dromedary and monkey. How did the defendants act? They did not attempt to apprehend the owners of the animals, but they seized the animals themselves; and seized them, not while being exhibited in the public streets, where they might have been liable to be removed as a nuisance, but after they had been removed by their owners into a stable, where they had ceased to be a nuisance. They had not only no authority, but they had no colour or pretence for supposing that they had authority, under this act of parliament, to seize these animals while in the stable, for the purpose of removing them out of the town. Where an act of parliament provides, that in case

(*a*) 4 D. & R. 283; 2 B. & C. 729.

A A 2

of any action brought against any person, for any thing done in execution or in pursuance of the act, the defendant shall be entitled to certain privileges, the true meaning is, that the act done must be in its nature such, that the person doing it may reasonably suppose that he had authority from the act of parliament to do it. In this case I am clearly of opinion that the defendants had no reasonable grounds for supposing that either they, or the commissioners under whose instructions they acted, had any authority under this act of parliament to remove the animals from the place and under the circumstances they attempted to remove them; and, therefore, that no notice of action was necessary, that the nonsuit was wrong, and that the rule for a new trial ought to be made absolute.

Holroyd, J.—I am entirely of the same opinion. If the defendants had had authority under the act of parliament to do the thing complained of, and had inadvertently exceeded their authority in the course of doing it; or even if they had done the thing under colour of such authority, and with reasonable ground for believing that it existed; in either of those cases they would have been entitled to notice of action. But looking at the terms of this act of parliament, I think that it is quite clear that the defendants had no pretence or colour for believing that it gave them any authority for pursuing the line of conduct which they pursued. The 99th section of the act, which has not before been mentioned, inflicts a penalty of £5. upon persons committing certain acts in the streets of *Stroud*, and it subjects to that penalty, among other persons, " any person who shall, within any street of the town, exhibit or expose any stallion, or turn loose any horse, mule, ass, pig, or other beast." But even that section not only did not justify the defendants in their conduct, but did not furnish any colour or pretence for it. If they had interfered " during the hours of keeping watch," and while the dromedary and the monkies were being actually exhibited in the streets, so that they might be considered a nuisance, there would have been some colour and pretence for their interference, because, as constables of the town, they would have had authority, either by the common law, or under the act of parliament, to abate a nuisance. But they did not so interfere ; but, on the contrary, they waited till the animals had been removed from the streets to a stable, and had ceased to be a nuisance, before they attempted to seize them. In *Irving* v. *Wilson* (a), goods were seized as forfeited, which in fact were not so, by a revenue officer, who accepted money of the owner for releasing them. The owner brought an action to recover back the money, and it was held that no notice of action was necessary. And *Grose*, J. then laid it down as law, that if an officer seize goods as forfeited, he does it *colore officii;* but if he takes money for delivering up the goods, there is no pretence for saying that he does that *colore officii*. The case of *Morgan* v. *Palmer* (b), which has been cited by my brother *Bayley*, is an authority to the same effect. If the defendants in the present case had endeavoured to remove the animals while they were exhibiting in the streets, and forming an obstruction there, I should have thought that, though not strictly justified, they might still have been considered as acting *colore officii;* but when the animals were removed from the street into a stable and formed no nuisance or obstruction, the attempt to remove them was not an act done *colore officii*, because the defendants could not by possibility believe that they had any authority under the act of parliament to interfere in so summary and extraordinary a manner. For these reasons I agree in the opinion that there ought to be a new trial in this case.

LITTLEDALE, J.—I am of the same opinion. If the defendants could have reasonably believed that this act of parliament gave them any colour for their conduct, they would have been entitled to notice of action, although their

(a) 4 T. R. 435.   (b) 4 D. & R. 483; 2 B. & C. 729.

conduct would have been, strictly speaking, equally illegal. But they could not believe any such thing. The 69th section limits the period during which the persons therein described as " misbehaving themselves," may be apprehended, namely, " during the hours of keeping watch." Now it does not appear that the owners of these animals were " misbehaving themselves," or that the attempt to seize the animals was made, " during the hours of keeping watch." But even if that did appear, the clause in question empowers the watchmen to apprehend, not *animals*, but " persons," and persons " misbehaving themselves." I think it clear, therefore, that, under that clause, the defendants could have no ground for supposing that they had authority to remove the *animals* at the time when they attempted to do so. With respect to the 99th section, mentioned by my brother *Holroyd*, it is sufficient to observe that the animals were not in the streets at the time when the attempt was made to remove them; though I feel free to add, that I very much doubt whether the exhibition of such animals in the streets constituted a nuisance, within the fair meaning of that clause of the statute. At all events, I am clearly of opinion that neither the commissioners, nor, of course, the defendants who acted under them, had any authority to remove the animals after they had been placed in the stable. I think further, not only that they had no authority, but that they had no colour, or reasonable ground for believing that they had any such authority; and consequently that they were not entitled to notice of action, and that the rule for a new trial must be made absolute.

Rule absolute.

THOMPSON and another v. ATKINSON.

GURNEY on a former day obtained a rule nisi, calling on the plaintiffs to shew cause why the defendant should not have his costs pursuant to the 43 *Geo.* 3, c. 46, having been arrested for the sum of 179*l.* without any reasonable or probable cause. On shewing cause this day, the circumstances disclosed on affidavits were these :—Upon being arrested the defendant gave bail, and the cause went to issue. Before the case was called on, the parties agreed to a reference, and a verdict was taken by consent for the plaintiff, damages 500*l.*, subject to the award of an arbitrator, to whom the cause and all matters in difference between the parties were referred, and the costs of the cause were to abide the *event of the award*, and the costs of the reference were to be in the discretion of the arbitrator. The arbitrator published his award in the following terms :— " I find that at the time of the commencement of the said action, there was and is still due and owing from the defendant to the plaintiffs, upon a balance of accounts between them, the sum of 45*l.* 18*s.* And whereas it has upon the said reference been proved on the part of the defendant, that he, the defendant, was arrested in this action at the suit of the plaintiffs, on the 20th day of July, for the sum of 179*l.*, and he continued in custody under such arrest for the space of five weeks; and whereas I find that the plaintiffs had no reasonable or probable cause for arresting the defendant for so large a sum as 179*l.*, I do award, order, adjudge and declare, that the defendant, by reason *thereof*, is entitled to compensation or damages to the value and amount of 20*l.* And whereas no other matters were, upon the reference, alleged by either of the said parties to be in difference between them, I do order that the verdict in the said cause shall be vacated, annulled and set aside, and instead thereof, that a verdict shall be entered for the plaintiffs for the sum of 25*l.* 18*s.*, the same being the amount of the

A cause and all matters in difference were referred to an arbitrator, the costs of the cause to abide the event of the award. The arbitrator found for the plaintiff a certain sum to be due on balance of accounts, but as the defendant had been arrested without any reasonable or probable cause for a larger sum than was due, he awarded him a sum of money as a compensation for the unlawful arrest, to be deducted from the balance found to be really due to the plaintiff, and directed a verdict to be entered for the plaintiff for the difference :—Held, that the defendant was not entitled to costs under stat. 43 Geo. 3, c. 46, s. 3.

balance which I find due to the plaintiffs, after deducting
therefrom the amount of the damages I have awarded as
aforesaid to the said defendant." Under these circumstances, the question was whether the plaintiffs could be
deprived of their costs under the statute.

Denman and *Wightman* contended that as the costs of
the cause were to abide the event, and the finding of the
arbitrator was in favour of the plaintiffs, they were entitled
to their costs as a matter of course. It might be that the
defendant was originally arrested for the sum of 179*l*. without any reasonable or probable cause. For that he has had
a compensation allowed him by the arbitrator, still leaving
a verdict in favour of the plaintiffs, which concludes the
question of costs.

Gurney and *Comyn,* in support of the rule, urged that
notwithstanding the submission and the finding of the arbitrator ultimately for the plaintiffs, the defendant was by the
very terms of the statute entitled to costs. The statute
enacts " that the defendant shall be entitled to costs, if it
appear to the Court that the plaintiff had not any reasonable or probable cause for causing the defendant to be held
to bail for the sum for which he was arrested." Now here
the arbitrator has expressly found that the plaintiffs had no
reasonable or probable cause for arresting the defendant
for so large a sum as 179*l*. By this finding, the point is
determined.

Abbott, C. J.—Whether we consider the terms of the
reference, or the finding of the arbitrator, I think we cannot
make this rule absolute. By the terms of the reference,
the plaintiffs stipulate that they shall have the costs of the
cause if the verdict is entered in their favour. Subject to
that stipulation they give the arbitrator a further power of
taking into consideration whether the arrest was made for
too much money or not, but still stipulating as a term of

the reference that they shall have the costs of the cause if
the event of it be in their favour. The arbitrator determines that there was no probable ground for arresting the
defendant for so large a sum, and that, therefore, as a compensation for the imprisonment he has suffered, he gives
him the sum of 20*l.*, to be deducted from the sum of 45*l.*
18*s.*, which he finds to be due to the plaintiffs upon the
balance of accounts. It appears to me, therefore, that we
are bound by the terms of the reference and the finding of
the arbitrator, and, consequently, that this is not a case for
costs under the statute.

1827.

THOMPSON
v.
ATKINSON.

BAYLEY, J. and LITTLEDALE, J. concurred (*a*).

Rule discharged.

(*a*) *Holroyd.* J. was absent.

BRAZIER *v.* WILLIAM JONES, Esq.

THIS was an action against the Marshal of the Marshalsea
of this Court for an escape on mesne process. On a
former day a rule was obtained, calling on the defendant to
shew cause why the plaintiff should not be at liberty to
amend his bill by entitling it specially of a particular day in
term on payment of costs, under the following circumstances:—The bill was entitled generally of *Michaelmas*
term, 1828; the escape was alleged to have taken place on
the 15th *November*, 1828, and on that day the bill was filed.
To this bill there was a special demurrer, filed on the 22d
November, assigning for cause that the action had accrued
subsequently to the time when the bill must be supposed
to have been filed, inasmuch as by law it must have
relation to the first day of the term. It now appeared

Where a bill
was filed
against the
Marshal for an
escape, entitled
generally of the
term, and al-
leging the es-
cape to have
taken place on
the 15th day of
the same term,
to which there
was a special
demurrer, that
the cause
of action had
relation to
the first day of
the term, the
Court allowed
the plaintiff to

amend his bill by specially entitling it, upon payment of costs, although it appeared by
affidavit that the prisoner was recaptured before the motion was made for leave to
amend.

as a fact upon the affidavits that on the 21st *November* the prisoner had returned into the custody of the Marshal.

Campbell now shewed cause, and contended that as the defendant was clearly entitled to judgment on the special demurrer, the plaintiff was not at liberty to amend. If the plaintiff was allowed to amend, the defendant would be precluded from pleading to the present declaration the recaption of the prisoner, who appears now by affidavit to have returned into the custody of the Marshal on the 21st of *November*. The plaintiff must, therefore, be compelled to declare *de novo*, and then the defendant will be at liberty to plead the recaption; otherwise he will be prejudiced by the plaintiff's mistake.

Scarlett and *Comyn*, in support of the rule. It is too clearly settled to be now disputed, that so long as the proceedings are on paper and not of record, either party may have leave to amend on payment of costs. This is an ordinary application; *Deacon* v. *Vivian* (a), *Dickinson* v. *Plaisted* (b), *Coutaudre* v. *Le Reuz* (c), *Greenwood* v. *Richardson* (d), *Hodgson* v. *Mitchell* (e), *Smith* v. *Key* (f), *Wilkes* v. *The Earl of Halifax* (g), *Barnes* v. *Eyles* (h), *Duchess of Marlborough* v. *Widmore* (i), *Cross* v. *Kaye* (k), *Maddock* v. *Hammett* (l), *Petre* v. *Craft* (m). The Court cannot in this stage of the proceedings take notice of the fact that there has been a recaption. This appears only by affidavit; it is a matter dehors the record, which, if noticed in this way, may be productive of general inconvenience. But assuming that the Court can take notice of it, still it affords

(a) Barnes, 7.
(b) 7 T. R. 474.
(c) 1 East, 133.
(d) Barnes, 16.
(e) Ibid. 26.
(f) 1 Stra. 638.
(g) 2 Wils. 256.

(h) 2 J. B. Moore, 566; 6 Taunt. 19.
(i) 1 Wils. 149.
(k) 6 T. R. 543.
(l) 7 T. R. 55.
(m) 4 East, 433.

a stronger reason why the plaintiff should be at liberty to amend.

ABBOTT, C. J.—During the discussion of this case, I must own I was inclined to think that the better mode of disposing of the the rule was to order a stet processus to be entered; but upon consideration of the matter in conference with my learned brothers, I agree with them in thinking that the rule ought to be made absolute. There is no doubt that this was a mere slip or mistake, and according to the ordinary practice of the Court, the plaintiff would be allowed to amend upon payment of costs. If we were to allow the amendment by reason of the special circumstances laid before us by affidavit, we should not find it easy to avoid drawing this case into a precedent; and we should have the same sort of application made to us in a variety of cases in which, hitherto, such a course has not been countenanced. In my opinion we ought to be adverse to the discussion of any matters out of the record, and prevent the establishment of a precedent authorising parties to go into extraneous circumstances. We think justice will be better administered by making this rule absolute.

The other Judges concurred.

Rule absolute.

C. HINDLEY v. The MARQUIS of WESTMEATH.

THIS was an action of assumpsit for goods sold and delivered, to which the defendant pleaded the general issue, non assumpsit. At the trial before *Abbott*, C. J. at the

Where husband and wife agreed by deed to separate immediately and live apart, the former to allow the latter a maintenance, and they did not in fact separate immediately, but lived together for nine months afterwards, apparently as man and wife:—*Held*, that the deed was void.

If a wife lives apart from her husband against his wish, and he is willing to maintain her in his own house, he is not liable even for necessaries contracted for by her during the separation.

London sittings after *Michaelmas* term, 1823, a verdict was
entered for the plaintiff by consent, subject to the award of
a gentleman at the bar. The arbitrator made and published
his award as follows :—

" In pursuance of a certain order of reference made &c.,
I do award, order, and determine, that the verdict found for
the plaintiff by the jury be vacated, and that in lieu thereof
a verdict be entered for the defendant. I do also certify
by this, my award, that I do find and determine that the
plaintiff is entitled to recover against the defendant the
sum of 52*l.* 19*s.* in respect of a debt incurred by the defendant's wife, in case the defendant's wife, Lady *Westmeath,*
was living apart from the defendant under a deed of separation, valid at the time that debt was incurred. As to this
point, I do find the following facts, upon which my award
is founded. On the 17th day of *December,* in the year of
our Lord, 1817, a certain indenture, in three parts, was executed by the said defendant, then the Earl of *Westmeath,*
of the first part ; the Countess of *Westmeath* (his wife) of
the second part ; and *William Sheldon,* Esq. of the third
part."

The arbitrator then set out the deed, which recited that
disputes had arisen between the earl and his countess, and that
they had agreed to separate. From the terms of the deed,
however, it appeared that an immediate separation was not
contemplated, but provision was made for a future separation.

The arbitrator then went on to state the following facts :—

" After this deed was executed, the said Earl and
Countess of *Westmeath* were fully reconciled to each other,
and continued to live and cohabit together as man and wife.
In *August,* 1818, articles of separation, dated *May* 30th,
1818, were executed by all the parties thereto. These
articles were between the Earl and Countess of *Westmeath,*
of the one part, and Lord Viscount *Cranbourne* and *Henry
Widman Wood,* Esq. of the other part. And after reciting
that the Earl of *Westmeath* had, at the particular instance,

and at the sole desire of the said Countess of *Westmeath*, his wife, agreed to live separate and apart from her, and to allow to her and her assigns, during the joint lives of the said earl and the said countess, such separate maintenance and yearly provision for her and her child, or children, as was thereinafter mentioned, it was witnessed, that in consideration of and in pursuance of such agreement, he, the said Earl of *Westmeath*, granted unto Lord Viscount *Cranbourne* and *Henry Widman Wood*, their executors, &c., certain premises therein named, for the term of 99 years, if the said earl and countess should jointly so long live, upon trust, first to secure an annual sum of 1300*l.* for the first six years, for the sole use of the Countess of *Westmeath*, and payable to her, or such person as she might appoint, on certain specified days, with the usual powers to the trustees for that purpose, and then, in trust, to pay the surplus rents to Lord *Westmeath*. And it was thereby declared and agreed, that an additional yearly sum of 300*l.* was to be raised for the maintenance and education of Lady *Rosa Nugent*, the then only child of the said Earl and Countess of *Westmeath*, an infant of the age of five years or thereabouts, and of the child, whereof the said countess was then *enceinte*. But if either the said Lady *Rosa Nugent* or the said child, of which the said countess was then *enceinte*, should die before the expiration of six years from the date of that indenture, the yearly sum of 250*l.* only should be raised and paid, for the maintenance of such surviving child, in lieu of the sum of 300*l.*; and if both the said children should die before the expiration of the six years, then from and immediately after the death of such children, the said sum of 300*l.* or 250*l.*, as the case might be, should cease, and not be raised or paid. The deed also contained a proviso, that on the death of either the Earl or Countess of *Westmeath*, or other cessation of the said annuities, the term thereby granted should cease, in case all arrears had been then fully paid. The deed then contained covenants by the Earl of *Westmeath* with the trustees for

payment of the above annuities of 1300*l.* and 300*l.*, and
that he should not, after the execution of the deed, intermeddle or concern himself with any of the monies which
should be paid or come to the hands of the Countess of
Westmeath by reason of that indenture, or the trusts thereinbefore expressed, but that he would permit the trustees,
in trust for the Countess of *Westmeath*, and also the
Countess of *Westmeath*, to have and receive the said annual
sums or yearly rents, and every part thereof; and also that
it should be lawful for the Countess of *Westmeath*, notwithstanding her coverture, and as if she were sole and unmarried, by any deed or writing, or by her last will, at her pleasure, to dispose of the arrearages of the said several sums
or yearly rents, and also all her savings, and the proceeds
of the said sums, and all and singular sum and sums of
money, goods, chattels and effects, and personal estate
whatsoever, which she should at any time have, or which
should in anywise devolve or come to her during her life,
to such persons as she should think fit; and that he, the
Earl of *Westmeath*, should suffer such will to be proved
and acted on without obstruction, in the proper ecclesiastical court; and that upon receipt or disposal of all or any
sum or sums of money, she, the Countess of *Westmeath*,
should and might, notwithstanding her coverture, and as if
she were sole and unmarried, make and sign valid acquit-
tances; and, moreover, that the Countess of *Westmeath*
should and might, notwithstanding her coverture, live
separate and apart from the Earl of *Westmeath*, her husband, as if she were sole and unmarried; and that she, the
Countess of *Westmeath*, should from thenceforth be freed
and discharged from the power, command, restraint
control, authority and government of the said Earl of
Westmeath, and should and might live and reside in
such place and places, and in such manner as to her from
time to time should seem meet; and that he, the Earl of
Westmeath, should not molest or disturb the Countess of
Westmeath in her manner of living, nor should at any time
or times thereafter require, or by any means whatsoever,

either by ecclesiastical censures, or by taking out any process, or by commencing or intituting any suit whatsoever, compel her, the Countess of *Westmeath*, to cohabit or live with him the Earl of *Westmeath*, nor should or would for that purpose otherwise use any force, violence or restraint to the person of her, the Countess of *Westmeath*, or sue or molest or cause to be sued or molested, any person or persons whatsoever, for receiving, harbouring, lodging, protecting or entertaining her, the said Countess of *Westmeath;* and that she, the Countess of *Westmeath*, should and might in all things live as if she were sole and unmarried, without restraint or coercion of the Earl of *Westmeath*, or by any other person or persons by his means, privity, or procurement. The deed contained a covenant for further assurance, and other usual covenants for the protection of the trustees.

For a short time before, and at the time when these last articles were executed, Lord and Lady *Westmeath* had been and were living together in the same house apparently on friendly terms, and apparently also as man and wife. They continued so to live together after these last articles of agreement were executed. During this period, namely, in *November*, 1818, Lady *Westmeath* was delivered of a son and heir, and on that occasion Lord *Westmeath*, who was then residing in the same house with her, and attending her with great affection, communicated the intelligence to his and her friends and relations, and received their congratulations on the event. Subsequently to this period, at *Christmas*, 1818, Lord and Lady *Westmeath* visited Lady *Westmeath*'s father and mother, the Marquis and Marchioness of *Salisbury*, at *Hatfield*. During that visit they jointly occupied their usual suite of apartments there, and appeared to Lady *Salisbury* and the rest of the family as living together on friendly terms and in the usual manner as man and wife. They continued to live together in this way, and their mutual friends and acquaintance were not aware that they were not living together as man and wife. In fact, however, for a short time before and from the period of the execution of the last articles of agreement, Lord and Lady *Westmeath* had occupied different beds, and did not cohabit together, and this was known to the immediate personal attendant of Lady *Westmeath*, and on the part of Lady *Westmeath* there was, in fact, no real return of affection and kindness towards Lord *Westmeath*, after the execution of the last deed of separation. This continued till *May*, 1819, when it became apparent to their friends and relations that they were not living on good terms with each other. In *June*, 1819, Lady *Westmeath*, against the will and entreaties of Lord *Westmeath*, finally quitted his house, and ceased to reside with him. They have lived altogether separate ever since that period, but always against the wish and contrary to the entreaties of Lord *Westmeath*, who, during the whole period, was ready and willing to have received and provided for Lady *Westmeath* in his own house. Notwithstanding this, Lady *Westmeath* afterwards, in *November*, 1819, whilst so living apart from her husband, the defendant, against his will, and contrary to his entreaties that she would return to his house and reside with him, contracted a debt with the plaintiff for goods to the amount of 52*l*. 19*s*. This was the debt in question in the present case. I was of opinion, under the above circumstances, that the deed of separation, executed in *August*, 1818, was not intended to be accompanied by an immediate actual separation of the parties at the time it was executed. And that, not being accompanied nor intended to be accompanied by such actual separation, it was not valid from the beginning. And I also thought, that if valid at first, it had been avoided by what amounted to a subsequent reconciliation of the parties."

A motion having been made to set aside this award, the Court directed the matter to be argued as a special case; the question being whether the arbitrator should have directed the verdict for the plaintiff to be vacated, and a verdict entered for the defendant.

Erle, for the plaintiff. The question depends entirely

upon the validity of the deed of separation executed in August, 1818. It will be contended on the other side, that that deed is invalid on two grounds; first, that at the time it was executed it was not intended to be accompanied by an immediate actual separation; and, secondly, that at all events, as there was a subsequent reconciliation between the parties, the deed, by operation of law, became vacated. In support of the first point the case of *Durant* v. *Titley* (a) will be cited; but there is a marked distinction between that and the present case. There the parties, by the very terms of the deed, contemplated present cohabitation and future separation, and on that ground the deed was held invalid. But in the case now at bar, the deed in terms contemplates a present and continuing separation, for there are the terms " now and from henceforth." Nothing, indeed, can be more distinct than the expressions of this instrument to shew that the parties contemplated a state of separation, and consequently the case of *Durant* v. *Titley* does not apply. Then the difficulty, secondly, remains, whether these parties can be considered as having lived together in a state of matrimonial cohabitation after the execution of the deed, or whether the facts found by the arbitrator amount to a state of matrimonial cohabitation so as to avoid the deed. Now there is nothing found by the arbitrator to warrant the conclusion that the parties were so reconciled as man and wife as to vacate the instrument. All that he finds is, that for a short time before and at the time when the articles were executed, they had been and were living together in the same house *apparently* on friendly terms, and *apparently* as man and wife. He, however, goes on further and finds, that notwithstanding this apparent reconciliation, there was no real affection on the part of Lady *Westmeath* towards her lord, and that in effect, from the time of the execution of the deed until *June*, 1819, when she quitted his house altogether, she was exempt from his control as a husband, and that they did not, in fact, cohabit from the time the deed was

1827.

HINDLEY
v.
Marquis of
WESTMEATH.

(a) 7 Price, 577.

executed. They occupied different beds, and, in fact, did not live together as man and wife, and there was no real return of affection. It may be true that they lived in the same house, but unless there was an actual reconciliation, that has never been held sufficient to avoid a deed of separation. *Bateman* v. *Ross* (a), *Fletcher* v. *Fletcher* (b). This question must be determined by the same rules of strictness as where the forfeiture of valuable rights is sought. The wife has rights here which may be deeply involved, and therefore strict proof of a forfeiture is necessary. To vacate this deed there ought to be strict proof of mutual reconciliation and cohabitation. By the statute of *Westminster* 2, c. 34, a woman quitting her husband and living in adultery loses her dower. " *Nisi vir suus sponté et absque coercione ecclesiæ eam reconciliet et secum cohabitare permittat.*" Upon this Lord *Coke*, in 2 *Inst.* 436, makes a note which bears most pertinently upon the present case, " note, that cohabitation is not sufficient without reconciliation made by the husband, and, *sponte*, so as cohabitation only in the same house with the husband availeth her not." Cohabitation in this latter sense must be understood to mean co-residence. Here there may have been a co-residence, but no cohabitation, and clearly no reconciliation. The husband cannot avail himself of his offer and willingness to live and cohabit with the wife, so as to work a forfeiture of the wife's rights. This has been settled by *Seeling* v. *Crawley* (c), and *Guth* v. *Guth* (d).

Brodrick, contrà. Admitting that there is nothing on the face of this deed to render it void, still it is submitted that the facts found and the reasons stated by the arbitrator are sufficient for that purpose. The first material fact found by the arbitrator is, that at the time of the execution of the deed the parties were living together, that they did not intend to separate, and that no actual separation took place.

(a) 1 Dow, 235.   (c) 2 Vern. 386.
(b) 2 Cox, 99. 3 Bro. C. C. (d) 3 Bro. C. C. 614.
619, n.

It is clear from the case of *Durant* v. *Titley* (the authority
of which has not been disputed on the other side) that if it
had appeared on the face of the instrument itself that the
parties did not intend to live separate, the deed would have
been void. It is admitted that this does not appear on the
face of this deed, but the facts found by the arbitrator
supply the omission, and lead precisely to the same consequences as if it had been introduced into the instrument
itself. It cannot be contended that the facts found by the
arbitrator must not be admitted to control the effect of the
deed. The omission of any condition in a deed which
would vacate it, if truly set forth, will not preclude the control of the instrument by collateral evidence. This is constantly the case where there is usury or fraud. The finding
of the arbitrator here is equivalent to the finding of a jury.
Suppose a jury, upon an issue directed to try the validity of
this deed, had found that at the time it was executed the
parties lived together and did not intend to separate, and did
not in fact separate, is there any doubt that this would be
sufficient to vacate the deed? These facts are found by the
arbitrator, to whom the whole matter is referred, and the
same deference must be paid to his finding as to that of a
jury. This finding must have the same effect as if it were
incorporated into the deed, and therefore, on the authority
of *Durant* v. *Titley*, the deed is void. With respect to the
second point, namely, the effect of a reconciliation, the Defendant has no interest in disputing the authority of the
cases cited on the other side, or raising the general question
whether deeds of separation are lawful. It is sufficient for
him to rely upon those cases which determine that deeds of
separation, attended with circumstances similar to what appear to exist in this case, are void. As to the general question of what amounts to a reconciliation, the law is clearly
laid down by Lord Chancellor *Eldon*, in *Bateman* v. *Ross*,
in the following manner:—" In regard to the point of reconciliation, notwithstanding what might be found in some
of the reports, he held the general doctrine to be clear, that

a reconciliation after a separation entirely did away with the effects of it. This rested upon the ground of public policy, as it must not be permitted to parties to make agreements for themselves, to be held good whenever they chose to live separate. The question then was, whether in that case there was a reconciliation. It appeared to him there was not, unless their Lordships were prepared to say, that living under the same roof amounted to a reconciliation, *though in a state of the highest animosity.*" Lord *Redesdale* observed, that " the appellant was living at *Castle Gore,* the respondent went there not for the purpose of reconciliation, but to protect her property." In that case the case of *Fletcher* v. *Fletcher* was also adverted to. As a question of law therefore, the reconciliation in this case does not interfere with the effect of the deed of separation. To all outward appearance the parties were reconciled. It was unknown to any body that the fact was otherwise. Their mutual friends and acquaintance—nay, the lady's father and mother knew nothing to the contrary. It appears that the deed was executed at the sole desire of the lady—the wife compelled the husband to grant a deed of separation. Then the question comes to this: whether the wife having compelled the husband to grant a deed (admitted to be against the policy of the law and to be supported by prior decisions rather than by a sense of propriety,) can insist upon its operation, continuing, as she does to the world, to be living with her husband as before, because there is no return of his affection, and because, for some reason or other, she does not chuse to *cohabit* with her husband in that particular sense of the word—or sleep in the same bed with him. If the question of reconciliation in such cases is to be determined by such a test, it would lead to the most inconvenient and vague, not to say indelicate and improper inquiries. It may be that these parties did not sleep together, but it is quite clear that for all purposes as far as the world and the legal liabilities of the husband are concerned, they were reconciled. They were living in the same house apparently on friendly terms, occupying the same suite of apartments, and none but the lady's maid is acquainted with the fact that she does not sleep with her lord. It does not appear from the deed itself that there was to be an immediate separation, but even if that were stipulated, still the intention is negatived by the fact that they continued to live together. The cases of *Lord Rodney* v. *Chambers* (a) and *Chambers* v. *Caulfield* (b) went farther than this. There the parties were to separate, subject to the approbation of trustees; and that circumstance has always been relied upon in pointing out the distinction between those and subsequent cases, where no domestic tribunal was provided in order to determine whether the parties should or should not separate. Here no domestic tribunal is appointed—no reference to trustees provided for; but the question of separation or no separation is left to the mere caprice and will of the lady, after the husband has been compelled to execute the deed. The words of the Statute of Dower, and the note of Lord *Coke*, 2 *Inst.* do not apply to this case. The statute renders both reconciliation and cohabitation necessary to restore the wife's claim of dower. Cohabitation, however, there means nothing more than living in the same house with the husband. This deed also differs widely from other like cases in this, that here there is no covenant to indemnify the husband against debts contracted by the wife. This distinction was relied upon as shewing *consideration* in the cases of *Legard* v. *Johnson* (c) and *Lee* v. *Thurlow* (d). The last mentioned case has gone much farther than any others have gone. It is much to be regretted that these cases have been decided, and, probably, if the validity of such deeds were now res integra, the Courts would pause before they would recognize their validity.

Erle, in reply. It is now too late to question the lawfulness of deeds of separation. If this deed was valid at the time it was granted, the finding of the arbitrator cannot

(a) 2 East, 283.

(b) 6 East, 214.

(c) 3 Ves. 352.

(d) 4 D. & R. 11; 2 B. & C. 547.

control it. In terms it contemplates an immediate separation. The arbitrator merely gives it as his opinion that present separation was not intended. It is still open to the Court to consider that question. *Bateman* v. *Ross* was cited merely for the purpose of shewing, that living under the same roof does not amount to a reconciliation so as to avoid a deed of separation. Here the strong facts relied upon are the absence of cohabitation, and the want of the exercise of the marital privileges and control. Whether the husband would have been liable for necessaries supplied to the wife during the time she was under the same roof with him, is no test to determine this question. As to the third point made on the other side, that there is here no covenant to indemnify the husband against the debts contracted by the wife, that is no objection to the validity of such a deed, for the sealing and delivery of the deed imports consideration. The absence of such a covenant might render it invalid as against creditors, but in this case it is no objection. *Worrall* v. *Jacob* (a), *Nunn* v. *Wilsmore* (b), *Fitzer* v. *Fitzer* (c).

ABBOTT, C. J.—I am of opinion that in this case the award is good, and that the verdict should be entered for the defendant according to the directions of the arbitrator. This is an action brought by a person who has given credit for goods sold to Lady *Westmeath*. It is brought against her husband, Lord *Westmeath*. Now a person cannot by law sue a husband for goods furnished upon credit to a wife when that wife is living separate and apart from her husband, unless he can shew that she is so separate and living apart by his consent. The arbitrator in this case has found, as a fact, that at the time this debt was contracted by Lady *Westmeath*, she was living apart from her husband against his consent, and against his earnest will and desire, and that he was always willing to have received and provided for her in his own house. In order, therefore, to

(a) 3 Meriv. 268.   (b) 8 T. R. 521.   (c) 2 Atk. 511.

shew a consent on the husband's part, the creditor must
rely upon the existence of some deed valid in law, whereby
Lord *Westmeath* has bound himself irrevocably to permit
his wife to live separate and apart from him. The question
is, whether Lord *Westmeath* has executed such a deed. In
taking that question into consideration, I think it is important to look to the first deed, which it is not contended could
by any possibility be regarded as a valid deed. That is
made in *December*, 1817. In terms that deed was exactly
similar to the deed in *Durant* v. *Titley*, and was void on the
face of it; but it shews that there had at one time existed
differences between these parties—that there had been a
reconciliation contemplated—and that Lord *Westmeath* had
conveyed to his wife certain lands as a security for a separate maintenance in case future differences should arise
and she should herself be compelled to cease to live with
him—but not in case any mutual friend should think they
ought to live separate and cease to cohabit. That is the
effect of the first deed. After that deed was executed, the
parties unquestionably lived together, and what is called
matrimonial cohabitation took place between them, for this
deed is dated in the month of *December*, 1817, and in the
month of *November* following, Lady *Westmeath* is delivered
of a child, of which Lord *Westmeath* appears to be the
father. This deed having been executed, in the month of
August, 1818, another deed is executed; and upon the
perusal of that deed, it should seem, that the parties had
then actually separated, for in the language of the deed,
after reciting that they had agreed to live separate and apart,
and that he had agreed to allow to her during their joint
lives a separate maintenance and provision for her and her
children, he conveys to Lord *Cranbourne* certain hereditaments in trust, that she and the children shall receive a
certain income for six years, payable on certain days specified in the deed; and there are the several powers given to
trustees for that purpose; and then he covenants that Lady
Westmeath, notwithstanding her coverture, shall live as if

she were sole and unmarried, and shall from thenceforth be freed from his power, restraint, and control, and that he will not molest or disturb her. Reading this, it is an actual separation of the parties then immediately taking place. The actual separation, however, did not take place. On the contrary, Lady *Westmeath* continued to reside in his house till the month of *November*, when she was delivered of a son and heir. It further appears from the finding of the arbitrator, that after the birth of this child, they went to visit her ladyship's father and mother, the Marquis and Marchioness of *Salisbury*, at *Hatfield*, where they lived apparently as man and wife, and in the eyes of the world as if they were perfectly reconciled. It is found, however, that during the whole period, from a little before the execution of the deed in *August*, 1818, until their actual separation, what has been called a mutual cohabitation did not take place. The arbitrator then, upon these facts, has given his opinion, that under these circumstances, the deed executed in *August*, 1818, was not intended to be accompanied by an immediate actual separation of the parties. That is the conclusion of fact which he draws from the circumstances disclosed, and I think that conclusion is rightly drawn, for, although the deed imports actual present separation, yet, if the parties did not intend present actual separation, the deed does not speak the language of truth, and does not come within that class of cases by which validity to a certain extent is given to instruments of this kind. The arbitrator finds that the deed was not intended to be accompanied by actual separation immediately, and he finds that, in fact, they did not separate, but continued some months residing together as man and wife, namely, from *August*, 1818, until the month of *May* following. These facts being found, I think his conclusion is well warranted. It is to be observed, that the deed of *August*, 1818, provides for the payment of the annuity on certain days therein specified. For months after this period she was continuing to live with Lord *Westmeath*, and thereby rendered him liable on contracts for which husbands are ordinarily liable whilst their wives live with them; but if this is to be construed to the letter, he would be answerable to the trustees, and liable to pay them the annuity thereby agreed to be paid for her separate maintenance. Looking at the whole of this case, as it appears from the finding of the arbitrator that it was not intended by the deed that there was to be a present separation, but only to enable Lady *Westmeath* to separate from her lord when she pleased, I am of opinion, upon the authorities cited, that a deed of that description is void. I wish to confine my opinion to the point reserved for us by the learned arbitrator. At the same time I wish it not to be understood that I am by any means of opinion that the plaintiff could, merely on the ground of the existence of such a deed as this, even if it were a legal deed of separation, sue the husband for goods supplied to the wife living apart from the husband without his consent. On the contrary, I am disposed to think that he could not, but that the trustees would be bound to obtain the money from the husband and pay the wife's debts, and that the only remedy for the plaintiff would be to claim payment out of the fund provided by the deed of separation.

BAYLEY, J.—I take the general rule to be this:—Where the husband, without lawful excuse, turns away his wife, and will not maintain her, he gives her personal credit, and she has a right to maintenance upon his credit and in his name; but where a husband does not dismiss his wife, but is willing to maintain her in his own house, and she being in possession of his will upon the subject insists upon leaving his house, then the husband does not give her credit with the world, and a person who trusts her does so at his own peril. So if it turns out that there is a deed of separation subsisting between the husband and wife, and the wife being in possession of the fact that the husband is willing to maintain her in his own house, insists upon going away, it seems to me that a person who trusts the wife under such circumstances must not look to the husband, but to the means of maintenance provided by the husband under the deed of settlement; and then the wife, through the medium of her trustees, must endeavour to enforce payment out of the settlement money. In such case, however, the husband will not be liable to an unlimited extent for any debts the wife may have contracted; he will only be liable for such debts as are contracted for her necessary maintenance, and for such things as are suitable to her degree; but still his liability must be limited to the amount of money which he has covenanted to allow her by way of settlement. This was the mode of proceeding resorted to in the case of *Jee* v. *Thurlow*. The action was there brought, not by the creditor but by the trustee, to enforce the payment of money from the husband to enable the trustee to purchase those articles which were necessary for the wife's maintenance. I do not, however, think it necessary to decide this case upon that ground. My opinion is formed on the special finding of the arbitrator, which turns upon the validity of the deed of *August*, 1818. I am clearly of opinion that that is not a valid deed. There had been a previous deed executed in *December*, 1817, which, according to the authorities, could not be sustained, as being inconsistent with the policy of the law, the parties having contemplated a future and not a present separation. In *Jee* v. *Thurlow*, the Court decided that the parties being actually separated at the time the deed was executed, the case was not affected by the doctrine which had been previously established, and that they were bound to give effect to the deed; but they intimated their opinion that if it had appeared that the deed was executed with a view to a *future* separation, it would be invalid, and could not be upheld. Now I consider, from the circumstances found by the arbitrator to exist in this case, that this was a shift and contrivance to defeat and get rid of the decision in *Durant* v. *Titley*, and to make it appear upon the face of the deed that there was to be an immediate separation, whereas that was by no means within the contemplation of the parties. This conclusion one must come to, when it is found that from the month of *August*, 1818, down to the month of *May*, 1819, the parties are living not only in the same house and under the same roof, but living continually together in each other's company, apparently as man and wife. Surely under such circumstances they could not, during that time, be considered in legal contemplation as separated. They were living together during the whole of that period. It is said, however, that they were living together to *a certain extent only*. I think, however, that we should be violating principles if we were to take into consideration a living together *quoad hoc*. They were either separated altogether or they were not. The agreement was for an actual separation to all intents and purposes, whereas after it is executed they are found living together in each other's society, under the same roof, and apparently on friendly terms, as if nothing had happened. Their mutual friends and relations knew nothing to the contrary. *Res ipsa loquitur*. Their conduct shews that a separation was not contemplated. I am therefore of opinion, on that special ground, that the deed is invalid, and that the creditor, who could have no *locus standi in curiâ*, except upon the footing of the deed, (because the defendant had not turned his wife away, and had not refused to maintain her in his own house,) cannot rely upon the deed, and consequently that the award is perfectly right.

HOLROYD, J.—I also think that the award is right. It is found as a fact by the arbitrator that the wife was living apart from the husband without his consent. That being so, it is clear that the plaintiff could not maintain an action against the husband, unless the wife was entitled to live apart from him without his consent. Whether in the case of a valid deed of separation for such a purpose, a creditor could sue the husband for a debt contracted by the wife, would be a very different question from the present, but upon which I do not mean to give any opinion. It is quite clear that the deed of 1817 is not valid, because it provides for a future separation. Then is the second deed of 1818 valid? I think it is not, for although it imports upon the face of it that the parties intended to separate, yet it is found by the arbitrator to be otherwise, because the parties in fact lived together afterwards apparently on friendly and affectionate terms.

LITTLEDALE, J.—It seems to me that this action cannot be supported. If a married woman separates from her husband without his consent, and he is willing to maintain her in his house, he is not liable for her debts. But if they mutually agree to separate under a valid deed of separation, and there is no provision for the wife's maintenance, he is liable for her necessary support, because in that case she stands *quoad* the world in the same light as if she were living with him and he does not provide for her support. If, however, provision is made for her by a valid deed of separation, and it is regularly paid, then the husband cannot be liable for her debts. On the other hand, if the allowances be not regularly paid, then, according to the case of *Nurse* v. *Craig* (a), the husband is liable for the wife's debts, although *Mansfield*, C. J. differed in opinion from the other three judges. This case, however, turns upon the validity of the deed of 1818. Certainly that deed is valid upon the face of it, but the arbitrator having found as a fact that the parties at the time of executing it really did not intend to separate, but in fact lived together for many months afterwards, I think we are bound to consider it invalid, and consequently that the arbitrator has decided rightly.

Judgment for the defendant.

(a) 2 N. R. 148.

1827.

DAVIES v. PENTON.(a)

CASE to recover a compensation in damages for the breach of an agreement. The declaration set out articles of agreement bearing date the 23d day of *December*, 1823, made between the plaintiff of the first part, and the defendant of the second part, which recited, that the defendant for many years then past had carried on the practice and profession of a surgeon, apothecary, and accoucheur, and had established a considerable connection in such business; and that having determined to withdraw from the same, he had agreed with the plaintiff for the sale to him of all his then stock, and of the goodwill of his said business; and also to demise to him his house in *Great Surrey Street*, in which the business was then carried on, upon the following terms, that is to say, the sum of 800*l*. to be paid for the goodwill of the business of surgeon, apothecary, and accoucheur, and the influence and recommendation thereinafter agreed to be given by the defendant unto and in favour of the plaintiff, and the lease of the house in *Great Surrey Street*, for the term of nineteen years and one quarter, subject to the yearly rent of 80*l*. and the stock in trade to be taken and purchased by the plaintiff at a fair valuation; and that in part performance of the agreement the defendant had

A. agreed with *B.* to sell to him the stock and goodwill of his business as an apothecary, and to demise to him his house in which the business was carried on, for which *B.* was to pay 800*l*. and to take the furniture and fixtures at a fair valuation, which were afterwards valued at 170*l*. 4*s*. 400*l*. was paid in hand at the time of executing the agreement, and *B.* further agreed to accept and pay two bills of exchange, one for 400*l*. payable at twelve months after date, and the other for 170*l*. 4*s*. at two months after date; and *A.* agreed not to carry on the like business within five miles of the same house:

(a) It may be proper to state that this, and some succeeding cases, were decided before the full Court *in* Hilary term, and that others were decided before the three puisne Judges sitting *after* the term, under the statute frequently before mentioned in these Reports. The dates of the decisions are not given, but the mention or omission of the name of the Lord Chief Justice in the Report of the Judgment, will clearly shew when every case was decided, whether *in* term, or at the sittings *after* term.

and for the true performance of the agreement each party bound himself to the other in the *penal* sum of 500*l*. to be recoverable on breach of the agreement in a Court of law, as and by way of *liquidated damages* :—Held, that this was a *penalty*, and could not be pleaded by way of set-off as *liquidated damages* in an action by *B.* for a breach of the agreement in carrying on the business within five miles of the house. Held also, that although *B.* replied *bankruptcy* to part of *A.*'s plea, and demurred as to the rest, upon which there was a joinder in demurrer, *A.* could not avail himself of the bankruptcy to deprive *B.* of his judgment on demurrer.

accordingly demised to the plaintiff the said messuage or. tenement, with all and singular the appurtenances, for the term of nineteen years and one quarter of a year, wanting two days, from the 25th of *December*, 1823, at the yearly rent of 80*l.* The articles of agreement then stated, that the defendant, in further performance of the said agreement, and for and in consideration of 400*l.* to the defendant in hand paid by the plaintiff, at or before the signing of the articles of agreement, and for and in consideration of the further sum of 400*l.* (being the remainder of the said sum of 800*l.* consideration money therein-before mentioned,) secured to be paid to the defendant by a bill of exchange, bearing even date with the agreement, drawn by the defendant upon and accepted by the plaintiff for the said sum of 400*l.* and payable twelve months after date; and of the further sum of 170*l.* 4*s.* (being the ascertained value of the stock in trade, goods, fixtures, and effects used in and about the said business or profession, as agreed upon between the plaintiff and the defendant,) also secured to be paid to the defendant by a certain other bill of exchange, bearing even date with the said agreement, drawn by the defendant upon and accepted by the plaintiff, for the said sum of 170*l.* 4*s.* and payable two months after the date thereof, agreed to and with the plaintiff in manner following; that is to say, that he, the defendant, should permit the plaintiff to have, use, and exercise the said business, practice, and profession of a surgeon, apothecary, and accoucheur, from the 24th of *December*, 1823, and to carry on the same in and upon the same house and premises, and in the same way and manner as the defendant had been used and accustomed to do; and to have, receive, and take the whole of the profits and produce of such practice and profession to and for his own use and benefit; and that the defendant should use his best endeavours and influence with all his patients and friends to prevail upon them to employ the plaintiff in the way of his, said practice and business. And the plaintiff did thereby agree to and with the defendant, that he the plaintiff would

·well and truly pay and discharge the said two several bills
so drawn upon and accepted by him the plaintiff for the
sums of 400*l.* and 170*l.* 4*s.* as aforesaid, unto the defendant,
as and when the said bills of exchange respectively became
due and payable; and the defendant did by the said articles
of agreement, lastly, promise and agree to and with the
plaintiff, that he the defendant should not, nor would, at
any time thereafter use, exercise, or carry on the art, business, or profession of a surgeon, apothecary, or accoucheur,
within the distance of five miles from the said messuage,
being No. 12 in *Great Surrey Street* aforesaid, for his own
private benefit or emolument, in any manner howsoever;
*and for the true performance of all and singular the agree-
ments aforesaid, each of them, the defendant and the plaintiff,
did thereby bind and oblige himself unto the other of them
in the penal sum of 500l. to be recoverable for the breach of
the said agreement, in any court or courts of law, as and by
way of liquidated damages.* The declaration then set forth
mutual promises, and assigned for breach of the said agreement that the defendant did use, exercise, and carry on
the business or profession of a surgeon, apothecary, and
accoucheur, within the distance of five miles from the said
messuage. To this declaration the defendant pleaded, first,
the general issue; secondly, a plea of set-off as to all the
promises and undertakings in the said agreement mentioned,
because he says, that the plaintiff did not well and truly
pay and discharge the said two several bills of exchange,
according to the form and effect of the articles of agreement in that behalf, but wholly neglected and refused so to
do, and therein failed and made default; and thereupon and
according to the tenor and effect, true intent and meaning,
of the articles of agreement, the plaintiff forfeited and became liable to pay to the defendant the said sum of 500*l.*
in the articles of agreement mentioned, as and by way of
liquidated damages. The plea further alleged, that the
plaintiff at the commencement of the suit was indebted to
the defendant in the further sum of 500*l.* for work and

labour. To this plea the plaintiff replied, (except as to so much of the plea as related to the penal sum of 500*l.* first mentioned,) that the plaintiff before and on the 23d *December,* 1823, was a trader, &c. and that in *October,* 1824, he became bankrupt, and on the 27th *May,* 1825, obtained his certificate. Demurrer as to so much of the plea as related to the sum of 500*l.* first mentioned. Joinder in demurrer.

Tindal, S. G. in support of the demurrer. The question upon these proceedings is whether the sum of 500*l.*, which the defendant pleads by way of set-off under the agreement, is a penalty or liquidated damages. If it be a penalty, it cannot be pleaded by way of set-off; and if it be liquidated damages, it cannot be the sum justly and truly due according to the statute 8 *Geo.* 2, c. 24, s. 5. *Nedriffe* v. *Hogan*(a). Now it is clear, from the language of the agreement, that the parties themselves never intended that the 500*l.* should be paid by way of liquidated damages in the event of either of the bills being dishonoured and the other paid; nor, indeed, if both had been dishonoured when at maturity. Suppose both bills to be dishonoured, then the 500*l.* would be an incomplete measure of the damages, because the bills together amount to 570*l.* In that view of the case the parties never could have intended that the defendant was to lose the 70*l.*, which he must infallibly do if the 500*l.* is to be considered as liquidated damages. Again, suppose the bill for 170*l.* 4*s.* only to have been dishonoured, could it be contended that the defendant was entitled to the 500*l.*, at all events, as liquidated damages for that breach of the agreement? In the agreement the sum is called in one place a *penalty*, and in another *liquidated damages.* There are several cases applicable to this, where the words are left in doubt. In *Astley* v. *Weldon*(b) the plaintiff agreed to pay the defendant so much a week to perform at his theatre, and the defendant undertook to con-

(a) 2 Burr. 1024.   (b) 2 Bos. & Pul. 346.

form to certain regulations, and it was stipulated that "either
of them neglecting to perform that agreement should pay
to the other 200*l.*" In assumpsit upon this agreement,
stating several breaches and concluding to the plaintiff's
damage of 200*l.*, Lord *Eldon* held that the sum mentioned
in the agreement was in the nature of a penalty, and not of
liquidated damages. On the authority of that case the plea
of set-off is ill pleaded.

Chitty, contrà. The case of *Astley* v. *Weldon* is not at
all in point with this. That was an action against an actress,
because she refused to pay certain small fines for not attending to her stage duties, and it never could be contended
that for every such breach of duty she was to pay 200*l.* by
way of penalty. This is a very different case from that.
In the form in which this agreement is drawn up, the defendant has clearly evinced his understanding to be, that
the 500*l.* was to be the absolute measure of unliquidated
damages, if he did not pay his bills punctually when they
became due. In *Barton* v. *Glover* (a) the parties entered
into an agreement by which, in consideration of a sum to
be paid by the plaintiff, the defendant undertook to withdraw his stage coach from the road; and *Gibbs,* C. J. held,
that where the performance of an agreement for acts, not
consisting in the payment of money, is enforced by a stipulation for the payment of 500*l.*, to be considered as liquidated damages, or sum of money forfeited or due from the
party who shall neglect, &c., the jury are bound to give the
whole 500*l.* [*Holroyd,* J. It was determined by the House
of Lords in *Rann* v. *Hughes* (b), that in all agreements not
under seal the consideration must be co-extensive with the
promise. Now what consideration is there here to support
a promise to pay 500*l.* in case 170*l.* only should be due?
Would such a promise be valid unless by deed?] All that
the case of *Rann* v. *Hughes* decides is, that there must be

(a) Holt, N. P. C. 43.   See   (b) 7 T. R. 350, n.
Wibean v. *Ashton,* 1 Campb. 78.

a *quid pro quo;* but there is nothing to prevent a party from stipulating to pay 200*l.*, by way of liquidated damages, if he does not pay 100*l.* by a given time. The consideration for the promise here is the *jus disponendi* in the subject-matter of the agreement. [*Bayley,* J. But in construing the instrument are we not to collect the meaning of the words from the whole instrument taken together?] In *Reilly* v. *Jones* (a) the plaintiff and defendant entered into articles of agreement, by which the former, in consideration of 2,300*l.*, agreed to sell to the latter the lease of a public house, as he then held the same, for the expiration of his term therein, and also his goods, fixtures, and effects, at a valuation; and the defendant agreed to take an assignment of the lease, and pay the above sum for it, as also the amount of the goods, fixtures, and effects, and take possession of the premises on a given day, when the plaintiff agreed to give up possession of the said premises, goods, and effects, to assign licences, to repair or allow for all damaged outside windows, and to clear the rent and taxes to the day of quitting possession; and the expenses of the agreement were to be paid by the parties in equal moieties; and it was lastly agreed that on either party's not fulfilling all and every part of the agreement he should pay to the other 500*l.*, thereby settled and fixed as liquidated damages; and it was held that this latter sum was not a mere penalty to cover such damages as might be actually incurred by the non-performance thereof, but that, on a breach by the defendant for refusing to accept an assignment of the lease, or take possession, he was liable to pay the plaintiff the full amount of that sum. [*Abbott,* C. J. Here the party has paid the sum of 400*l.* Do you mean to contend that for the non-payment of the 170*l.* 4*s.* he is liable for the 500*l.* as liquidated damages?] That certainly is contended. [*Bayley,* J. Why then he may be still liable upon the bills, although he may have paid the 500*l.* *Littledale,* J. Do you really contend that after he shall have paid the penalty

(a) 8 J. B. Moore, 244; 1 Bing. 302.

of 500*l.* he is still liable for general damages ?] The party has entered into a specific agreement, and it is his business to take care and perform his contract strictly. [*Littledale*, J. You cannot recover both penalty and unliquidated damages.] But assuming this first point cannot be maintained, still, secondly, it is clear that the present plaintiff cannot maintain this action, because it appears upon the pleadings that he became bankrupt, and a commission issued against him after the agreement was entered into, consequently the right of action passes to the assignees.' [*Bayley*, J. But the bankruptcy comes in only by way of replication to part of the defendant's plea of set-off. Here is a plea of set-off applicable to the whole declaration. The plaintiff replies that, as to part of the set-off pleaded he is discharged by payment, and as to the residue he demurs. Can you upon demurrer avail yourself of facts which do not apply to one part of the plea, but do to another? I apprehend not.]

Tindal, S. G. in reply, was stopped by the Court.

ABBOTT, C. J.—I consider that this action is brought by the plaintiff to recover, not a sum certain by way of liquidated damages, but so much as he can get by way of damages. It is in fact an action upon the case to recover damages in proportion to the injury stated in the declaration. The proper form of action to recover a sum certain is debt. By the declaration it appears that the defendant agreed to sell the plaintiff the lease of his house, and the goodwill and business of a surgeon and apothecary, and his stock in trade, to be paid for in the manner therein set forth; and the defendant further agreed not to carry on the like business within the distance of five miles from the messuage aforesaid. The breach assigned by the plaintiff is, that the defendant did carry on the business of a surgeon, &c. within the distance of five miles from the said messuage. To this part of the declaration the defendant has pleaded that the plaintiff did not well and truly pay and discharge the said two several bills of exchange according to the form and effect of the articles of agreement in that behalf, but wholly neglected and refused so to do, and therein failed and made default; and thereupon, according to the tenor and effect, true intent and meaning, of the articles of agreement, the plaintiff forfeited and became liable to pay to the defendant the said sum of 500*l*. in the articles of agreement mentioned, as and by way of liquidated damages. Now the allegation as to the non-payment of the bills might be satisfied by proving that the bill for 400*l*. was paid on the day it fell due, but that the bill for 174*l*. was not paid until the day after it became due. As this would, strictly speaking, be a breach of the agreement, the defendant must contend that the plaintiff was liable to pay the whole sum of 500*l*. We are, therefore, to see whether in the language of this agreement there is any thing that can lead to such a strange and absurd conclusion. The declaration states, that " for the true performance of all and singular the agreements aforesaid, each of them, defendant and plaintiff, did thereby bind and oblige himself unto the other of them in the penal sum of 500*l*., to be recoverable for breach of the said agreement in any court or courts of law, as and by way of liquidated damages." Whoever framed this agreement seems to have had no very accurate notion of the distinction between a penalty and liquidated damages, for the sum of 500*l*. is described in the same sentence as a *penal sum* and as *liquidated damages*. Now both these expressions cannot be satisfied. The 500*l*. cannot be a penalty and also liquidated damages. We must, therefore, look to the whole of the agreement in order to give proper effect to this language; and it seems to me that we must say that this is liquidated damages and penalty only to secure such damages as the party by whom default is made ought to receive in justice, and not that this absolute sum of 500*l*. was payable at all events. It would be monstrous to hold, that if the bill of 174*l*. 4*s*. was not paid on the very day it was due, the plaintiff would be liable to pay the sum of 500*l.* The other ground taken by Mr. *Chitty* is, that inasmuch as it appears that the plaintiff had become bankrupt after the agreement was entered into, the plaintiff has no right of action, because it had then devolved upon the assignees, and consequently the defendant is entitled to judgment on this demurrer. It certainly is true that the plaintiff has himself set forth his own bankruptcy, but it is in a distinct part of the record from that upon which the present demurrer arises. Now although it is true that we are to look in general to the whole record, yet I apprehend that if a party demurs only to some specific part of a record, it is incompetent to him to go from that to another part to which there is no demurrer. Here the demurrer is only to so much of the plea as relates to the 500*l.*, and upon that demurrer I am of opinion that the plaintiff is entitled to judgment.

BAYLEY, J.—It depends upon the construction of this instrument, with reference to all its parts, whether the particular stipulation in question is to be construed by way of penalty or liquidated damages. I can well understand that parties might stipulate to pay each other a certain sum for the complete breach of the whole of an agreement, by way of liquidated damages; but where the payment is to depend, as in this instance, not upon the breach of the whole but upon *each and every part*, it appears to me that in some instances the amount fixed would be too little, and in others it would be abundantly too large. Where, therefore, there is any ambiguity as to the sense in which a stipulation of this kind is to be understood, I think the Court is bound to construe it as a stipulation, not for liquidated damages, but for a penalty, and a penalty only. Here the stipulation of the parties is, that for the true performance of *all and singular* the agreements, they bind themselves in the penal sum of 500*l.* as and by way of liquidated damages. It seems to me that when you have the words " penal sum" as well as "liquidated damages," and it is found that in the result in one case the sum to be paid would exceed and in another would be quite inadequate to the injury received, the Court is bound to hold that it never could have been intended that the sum was to be liquidated damages. Suppose the plaintiff wholly neglected to pay the two bills, amounting together to 574*l.*, and the 500*l.* was to be considered as a maximum of damages, why the defendant would lose 74*l.* On the other hand, if the 400*l.* bill had been paid, and the 174*l.* dishonoured, the 500*l.* would unjustly exceed the injury sustained by the breach of that part of the agreement. In the case of *Reilly* v. *Jones* (a) the sum there stipulated was a fixed maximum by way of liquidated damages. In this case the sum is not to be regarded as liquidated damages but as penalty, and consequently the set off is not valid. As to the second objection it seems to me that it would be confounding all principles of pleading if a party were at liberty to fly from one part of the record to another, and pray in aid a fact or statement which he has not brought under notice by way of demurrer. The demurrer here is confined specially to a particular point quite distinct from the plaintiff's alleged bankruptcy. There is nothing on the face of the declaration to shew that the right of action under the articles of agreement passed to the plaintiff's assignees. If the defendant meant to have relied on the plaintiff's bankruptcy, he might have pleaded it in bar, and then the plaintiff might have replied that his assignees had repudiated the agreement, and left him to sue for damages in his own right. On the whole, therefore, I am of opinion that the plaintiff is entitled to judgment upon this demurrer.

HOLROYD, J.—I am also of opinion that the sum of 500*l.*, which in the agreement is called a penal sum, is to be considered a penalty, notwithstanding it is stated that it is to be recovered as and by way of liquidated damages.

(a) 8 J. B. Moore.

We must look to the nature of the sum which is to be paid, and consider all the circumstances upon the face of the agreement itself, in order to ascertain whether it is absolute or not. The parties call it a penal sum. The sum which is to be paid, and the payment of which is to be secured by the penal sum, is 574*l.* Now 500*l.* cannot have been the amount of damages agreed upon for the nonpayment of 574*l.* If it be a penalty, the law will treat it as such, and the stipulation that it shall be recovered as liquidated damages will not prevent the party from insisting upon his being entitled to assess damages under the statute 8 and 9 *Wil.* 3, c. 11, s. 8. Then it is said that upon the face of the whole record the plaintiff has no right of action, because he appears to have become bankrupt since the agreement was executed. That point does not arise upon the demurrer, and if not, I think the defendant is not at liberty to resort to this circumstance, which comes in merely as collateral matter. Notwithstanding the general assignment of the plaintiff's effects to his assignees, they may have repudiated this agreement. It appears to me that on both grounds the plaintiff is entitled to judgment on this demurrer.

LITTLEDALE, J.—I am also of opinion that the plaintiff is entitled to judgment. Before the 8 and 9 *Wil.* 3, c. 11, the whole penalty might be recovered at law; and the party against whom it was recovered was driven to seek relief in a court of equity. That act only makes use of the word " penalty." Since then parties, in framing agreements, have got into the use of the words *liquidated damages;* but it seems to me that the change of the word will not change the nature of the thing. We are to look to the whole of the agreement together, and see whether from the nature of the subject-matter, although *liquidated damages* are mentioned, the parties contemplated any thing more than a penalty; for if they did, neither party ought to be deprived of the benefit of the statute allowing the assignment of breaches. A mere colour or shift in altering the word will not change the thing itself. Now it is quite clear from the whole of this agreement that the sum of 500l. was intended merely as a penalty to enforce the performance of the agreement. I perfectly agree with the reasons given by the Court upon this part of the case. Then as to the other objection, that the plaintiff cannot maintain this action, because upon the whole record he appears to be a bankrupt, I think it is without any weight. Now as to this sum of 500l., the plaintiff says, " You cannot set it off, because I became a bankrupt on such a day and obtained my certificate," and then he demurs to the other parts of the plea. Still, however, admitting that any thing would turn on the bankruptcy, we are bound by the rules of pleading to decide upon the plea and demurrer following one another; and cannot suffer the party to call in aid an allegation in one pleading to support another. We must treat the count, plea, and replication, and the count, plea, and demurrer, as distinct records, and give judgment upon each without reference to the other.

Judgment for plaintiff on demurrer.

DAVIS v. HARDY.

On the trial of an action for a malicious prosecution, the defendant produced a witness to prove the reasonableness and probability of the cause of prosecution, and there being nothing to contradict the evidence, or to shew that the statement was inconsistent with the truth:—Held, that the judge was warranted in acting upon the evidence at once and directing a nonsuit, without leaving the credit of the witness to the jury.

CASE for maliciously indicting the plaintiff for embezzlement, without any reasonable or probable cause. Plea, the general issue. At the trial before *Gaselee*, J. at the *Lent* Assizes for the county of *Somerset*, holden at *Bridgewater*, in 1826, the case was this:—The defendant had been keeper of *Ilchester* gaol, and the plaintiff was employed under him as a turnkey. A bankrupt debtor, confined in the gaol, had been ordered by commissioners of bankrupt to be brought from thence to *Taunton*, for the purpose of being examined touching his bankruptcy. The bankrupt was taken by the plaintiff to *Taunton* accordingly, and there the latter received from the assignees the expenses of the journey, including a fee of 2*l*. 2*s*. to the defendant, and also the sum of 1*l*. 10*s*. for the hire of a post-chaise to carry the bankrupt to *Taunton*. On his return to *Ilchester*, the plaintiff paid the defendant his fee, but said nothing of his having received the chaise hire from the assignees. This transaction took place in the month of *May*, 1823. In *April*, 1825, the defendant having made some complaints to the justices in quarter-sessions against the plaintiff, and amongst others, that he had not paid to him the chaise hire received from the assignees as above mentioned, the complaints were referred to a committee of magistrates for investigation. One of those magistrates was examined as a witness at the trial of the present action. He deposed that the plaintiff had admitted to him that he had received the chaise hire from the assignees, and had not paid it either to the defendant or the proprietor of the chaise; but he was not sure whether the plaintiff had admitted that he had desired the owner of the chaise not to tell the defendant that the chaise hire had not been paid. The owner of the chaise was examined before the committee of justices in support of this charge, and in consequence of the report made by the magistrates in *April*, 1825, the plaintiff was suspended from his office of turnkey. At the *July* sessions following, the defendant indicted the plaintiff for embezzling the amount of the chaise hire, but he was acquitted. The above mentioned facts being proved, the plaintiff's case was closed, whereupon the defendant's counsel contended that there ought to be a nonsuit, inasmuch as the facts proved established a probable cause for preferring the indictment. The learned judge, however, thought that there was sufficient proof of want of probable cause, and declined stopping the case. The defendant then went into his case, and called the owner of the post-chaise as a witness. He stated, that on the 25th of *May*, 1823, the plaintiff ordered the chaise in the defendant's name to go to *Taunton*. In about two months afterwards he asked him when he meant to pay the money he owed him. The plaintiff replied that he owed him some post-chaise hire of his own. The witness then said, " If you cannot pay me what you owe me yourself, pay me for the job to *Taunton*, or I will tell Mr. *Hardy*." The plaintiff then requested the witness not to tell Mr. *Hardy*, for it would do him a great deal of injury. The witness saw the plaintiff again in about a month, when the plaintiff promised to pay him. He went on to say that he did not tell the defendant that the chaise had been ordered in his name, till he heard that *Davis* had been suspended. Upon being cross-examined as to the time when the defendant had paid him the chaise hire, he said at first, it was a week or two after the examination by the magistrates, then a very short time before the indictment, and lastly, a day or two before the investigation. Upon this evidence, the learned judge was of opinion, that the circumstances proved on both sides, although not sufficient to sustain the indictment, yet established a sufficient probable cause for preferring it. The plaintiff's counsel then urged that it ought to be left to the jury to determine whether they believed the chaise-owner's evidence, after the manner in which he had conducted himself on cross-examination, for if he were not believed, the plaintiff was entitled to a verdict. The learned judge, however, said, that there was no contradictory evidence as to the fact of the plaintiff having desired the chaise-owner not to tell the defendant that the chaise hire had not been paid, and he refused to leave any question to the jury, and directed a nonsuit. In *Easter* term last the Court granted a rule nisi for setting aside the nonsuit, on the ground, that it ought to have been left to the jury to determine whether they believed the evidence of the chaise-owner.

Scarlet and *C. F. Williams* now shewed cause. There was nothing in this case to leave to the jury. If the chaise-owner's evidence had been adduced for the purpose of contradicting the evidence for the plaintiff, then the whole ought to have been left to the consideration of the jury. The fact, however, upon which the learned judge came to the conclusion that there was reasonable and probable cause for preferring the indictment, was an independent fact, which had not been mentioned before, and consequently the rule which requires that contradictory evidence shall be left to the jury does not apply. What took place on the cross-examination was not sufficient to invalidate the testimony of the witness upon the main fact to which he deposed, and therefore it was competent to the judge in the exercise of his discretion, in a case where the question was one compounded of law and fact, to act upon the evidence and direct a nonsuit.

Bompas and *Erle*, in support of the rule, contended, that there being evidence on both sides, the whole should have been left to the jury. The question of probable cause can only arise when the facts are ascertained, and it is the exclusive province of the jury to determine upon those facts. If it had appeared in the outset of this case that the defendant had a probable cause for preferring the charge against the plaintiff, then it was competent for the learned judge to have directed a nonsuit, because the onus of proving want of probable cause lay upon the plaintiff. In this case, however, the plaintiff had shewn in the outset that there was no probable cause for making the charge against him. Surely then when evidence was called on the part of the defendant to give a different account of the transaction, the whole case ought to have been left to the jury. In *Ravenga* v. *Macintosh* (a), and *Nicholson* v. *Coghill* (b), it was decided that reasonableness or probability of cause is a mixed question of law and fact for the jury to decide. In the present case the whole of the evidence ought to have been summed up for the jury with such di-

(a) *Ante*, vol. iv. 187; 2 B. & C. 693.
(b) *Ante*, vol. vi. 12; 4 B. & C. 21.

rections in point of law, as appeared to the judge to be proper, if the jury believed the evidence upon which the defendant relied. Here the whole case was withdrawn from the consideration of the jury, and the learned judge took upon himself to decide upon the only fact upon which the case hinged. The circumstance of the chaise-owner not being contradicted upon the main fact to which he deposed, was not a sufficient reason for shutting out the whole of his evidence and his demeanour in the witness box from the consideration of the jury, subject to such observations as the plaintiff's counsel might think it necessary to make upon his testimony. The plaintiff's counsel had a right, at all events, to observe upon the evidence produced by the defendant.

ABBOTT, C. J.—I am of opinion that the nonsuit in this case was properly directed, and that the rule nisi, obtained for setting it aside, ought to be discharged. The question for consideration is not whether the plaintiff was guilty of the charge preferred against him, nor whether the defendant chose to prefer it from an improper motive. The only question is whether there was reasonable or probable cause for preferring the charge, and upon the evidence adduced at the trial I think there was a probable cause. What were the facts? The plaintiff hired the chaise in the name of the defendant as his principal. At the end of the journey, he receives from the assignees of the bankrupt the amount of the chaise hire, which he ought to have paid over either to the defendant as his principal or to the person of whom the chaise was hired. He does neither the one or the other, but keeps the money in his own pocket for a long period of time; nor does he even mention to the defendant that he had received the money. After this some charges are preferred against him by the defendant, and among others there is a charge of having received this money without accounting for it or applying it to the proper use. His conduct is then investigated by the magistrates, and one of the magistrates was called as a witness on the part of the plaintiff, who proved that the plaintiff had admitted that most of the facts brought forward were true. Now upon this part of the case, left as it was by the plaintiff himself, I should have been inclined myself to say that there was probable cause for preferring the indictment, and that the plaintiff ought to be nonsuited on his own shewing; but the learned judge was of a different opinion, and allowed the case to proceed. Thereupon the owner of the chaise was examined as a witness on the part of the defendant, and he stated that the chaise was hired by the plaintiff of him in the name of the defendant, that the money was not paid, that he applied twice to him for the payment of it, and 'that upon his threatening that unless he was paid he would inform Mr. *Hardy* of it, the plaintiff requested him not to tell Mr. *Hardy* that it was not paid, as it would do him a great injury. Now it is quite clear that if that fact had been proved in the course of the plaintiff's case, it would at once have been a ground of nonsuit, as shewing a probable cause for preferring the charge. But it is said that because this fact came out upon the testimony of a witness called on the behalf of the defendant, the plaintiff's counsel had a right to address the jury as to the credit of that witness. But when a person comes into Court unimpeached in character and unimpeached in his testimony, and there is no want of probability in the story which he relates, I can see no reason for holding that the credit of such a witness ought to be left to the jury. Under such circumstances as these I think the judge is at liberty to consider the facts stated as being proved, and to act upon them accordingly without leaving them to the jury, especially when this was a matter upon which the minds of the jury might have been inflamed. It appears to me, therefore, that the judge was warranted in acting upon the evidence before him, and directing a nonsuit on the ground that there was probable cause for preferring the indictment.

BAYLEY, J.—I am of the same opinion. To support

an action of this kind, it is not sufficient to shew malice in the defendant, but also that there is a want of probable cause, for, his proceeding; for however strong the malice may be, yet if there is probable cause for preferring the charge, the plaintiff is not entitled to recover. Here there was clear evidence of probable cause, and such evidence as a jury ought to be directed to proceed upon. There is no doubt as to the general proposition that where there is contradictory testimony or evidence upon doubtful facts, the jury is the proper tribunal to exercise its judgment upon the weight and effect of the evidence; but I entirely agree with my Lord Chief Justice that if there is nothing in the demeanour of a witness, no improbability in the story he tells, nothing in his evidence at variance with any other parts of the case, it is not for the jury to determine upon the credit of the witness, nor need the testimony be left to their consideration. The chaise-owner told a consistent and a probable story, and he was uncontradicted in the material part of his evidence; and therefore it appears to me to be too much to say that his credit should be left to the jury. Suppose that the jury had been induced to find a verdict for the plaintiff on the ground that they disbelieved this man's evidence, I think we should have been bound to grant a new trial.

LITTLEDALE, J.(a)—I am of the same opinion.

Rule discharged.

(a) Holroyd, J. was in the Bail Court.

ADNAM *v.* WILKES, Gent. one, &c.

THIS was a rule calling on the plaintiff to shew cause why the names of the bail in error should not be struck out of the recognizance, or why an exoneretur should not be entered on the bail piece under the following circumstances.—In *Trinity* term, 1826, the plaintiff obtained a judgment for 220*l.* against the defendant. The defendant brought a writ of error, and on the 16th *June* he put in bail and gave notice thereof to the plaintiff's attorney, who on the same day excepted to the bail, and took out and served a rule for better bail. On the 20th *June* the defendant gave notice that the same bail would, on the first day of *Michaelmas* term, justify, or offer themselves for justification. The plaintiff gave a rule to transcribe the record, with which the defendant complied, after which no proceedings were had upon the writ of error, and the cause was still undetermined. Under these circumstances the question was, whether the bail in error were entitled to have their names struck out of the recognizance, or have an exoneretur entered on the bail piece.

Where plaintiff in error put in bail in vacation, and defendant in error excepted thereto, and gave a rule for better bail, and plaintiff gave notice for justifying the same bail on the first day of Michaelmas term, but they did not justify:—Held, that the bail in error were still liable upon the recognizance for the costs of the proceedings in error.

Hutchinson contended, that the bail in error were entitled to no relief, and he cited *Dickenson* v. *Heseltine* (a) as a case in point. There bail in error was put in in vacation and excepted to, and the plaintiff in error gave notice that they would justify on the first day of next term, and before that day non-prossed his own writ of error, and the bail did not justify; and under these circumstances it was held that the bail were not entitled to stay proceedings in an action against them upon the recognizance, nor to have an exoneretur entered on the bail piece, for, as Lord *Ellenborough* said, " this appears to be a trick to get all the effect of a writ of error without putting in bail. The pendency of a writ of error was a delay of the defendant in error in respect of his execution." So in the present case the bail by en-

(a) 2 M. & S. 210.

tering into the recognizance, and giving notice of justification, have prevented the defendant in error from having the benefit of his judgment and issuing execution from the 16th *June* until after the first day of *Michaelmas* term.

Chitty, in support of the rule, pressed upon the Court the distinction between this case and *Dickenson* v. *Heseltine*, inasmuch as in the latter the defendant had non-prossed his own writ of error; and he relied upon *Gould* v. *Holmström* (*a*), where bail in error, who were excepted to and did not justify, were relieved from proceedings against them, though no other bail had been put in, " for," said the Court, " the party who takes exceptions to the bail put in considers them as no bail unless they justify, and therefore not having justified they must be considered as no bail." In the present case the defendant in error having excepted to the bail, and taken out and served a rule for better bail, and no bail having afterwards justified, the case cited is an authority for relieving the bail in the present instance.

ABBOT, C. J.—I think we ought not in this case to relieve the bail in the manner desired. It is clear if we did so, we should allow them to become the instruments of working great injustice and doing mischief. They consent to become bail in error in the month of *June*. A rule is then taken out by the defendant in error for better bail. The form of that rule is, that unless the bail shall justify, the defendant in error shall be at liberty to sue out execution upon the judgment. The bail being put in in vacation, they could not justify until the first day of *Michaelmas* term. In the present instance, therefore, the effect of this proceeding was to delay the plaintiff below in his execution from *June* until *November*. It is stated on affidavit that in the meantime the goods of the defendant below had been sold off, and he himself being an attorney of the Court, and having therefore personal privilege, the execution could only,

(*a*) 7 East, 580.

have gone against his goods. Nobody, therefore, can doubt what the justice of this case is, namely, that those who have been the instruments of delaying the plaintiff ought not to be relieved from the effect of it. It appears to me that the case of *Dickinson* v. *Heseltine* will well warrant the Court in refusing relief to the bail. The distinction taken between that case and this is, that before *Michaelmas* term arrived the plaintiff in error in that case had non-prossed his own writ of error. Here the defendant below has not done so, but neither has he taken any step to prosecute his writ of error; and I am of opinion that we ought not to relieve the bail, but make them responsible so far as they may be made responsible.

BAYLEY, J.—I am of the same opinion. The form of the rule shews what the law is. Here the bail enter into a recognizance, by which they bind themselves that, if the defendant in error shall succeed, they will pay the debt and costs below, and the costs of the writ of error. Then the plaintiff says, " unless better bail is put in," (not that those bail already put in shall be a nullity, but unless better bail shall be put in,) " I shall issue a writ of execution, not for the whole for which they would be liable, but for the debt and costs recovered originally below." The plaintiff in error not having perfected his bail, the defendant in error is at liberty to sue out his execution to recover the debt and costs recovered below, but for no more. It seems to me, however, that there is no good reason why the bail in error should not continue liable to the residue of the responsibility which they had originally incurred, namely, the costs to which the defendant in error had been put. But it is said that as the defendant in error chose to except to the bail, they must be considered as no bail at all, and consequently that they are discharged from all responsibility, and the case of *Gould* v. *Holmstrom* was relied upon. I think, however, that that case proceeded entirely upon a mistake. All that the exception amounts to is this, " unless better bail is put in the plaintiff shall have execution for his original debt and costs." But it does not, therefore, follow that the bail shall be discharged altogether, but that they shall be relieved *pro tanto*, that is, they shall be no longer liable to the condemnation money, but that they shall remain liable for the residue, namely, the costs of the proceedings in error. The true principle of the case of *Gould* v. *Holmstrom* is this, that the plaintiff below, by non-prossing the writ of error on the ground of the bail not having justified, signified his consent that the bail in error should no longer stand liable upon their recognizance.

HOLROYD and LITTLEDALE, Js. concurred.

Rule discharged.

BARON *v.* MARTELL.

By the master's allocatur an attorney was ordered on the 12th *May* to pay over to his client a sum of 15*l* ; on the 20th *June* the attorney became bankrupt, and afterwards obtained his certificate:—Held, that it was then too late to move for an attachment for not paying the money pursuant to the master's allocatur.

ARCHBOLD had obtained a rule calling upon an attorney of this Court to shew cause why an attachment should not issue against him for not paying over a sum of 15*l*. pursuant to the master's allocatur. It being alleged that the attorney had retained more money in his hands for costs than he was entitled to, it was ordered by a rule of Court that his bill be referred to the master for taxation. The bill was taxed on the 12th of *May*, when the master awarded the sum of 15*l*. to be due to the client, and on the 20th of *June* the attorney became bankrupt, and had since obtained his certificate. It was now contended that the attorney was liable to an attachment for not paying over the money pursuant to the master's allocatur, notwithstanding his bankruptcy and certificate.

PER CURIAM.—The certificate is an answer to this demand. This is no more than a civil debt, and you cannot enforce payment of it by attachment.

Hutchinson was to have shewn cause.

Rule discharged.

CAMIDGE *v.* ALLENBY.

1827.

THIS was an action for goods sold and delivered, with the common money counts. Plea, the general issue.

At the trial before *Hullock*, B. at the last *Spring* Assizes for the county of *York*, a verdict was found for the plaintiff for £24, subject to the opinion of this Court on the following case :—This action was commenced to recover the sum of £24, alleged to be due from the defendant to the plaintiff for a quantity of corn sold and delivered by the plaintiff to the defendant at *York* on the morning of *Saturday, the* 10*th day of December,* 1825. On the same day, at three o'clock in the afternoon, the defendant delivered to the plaintiff at *York*, and the latter then and there received, as and for a payment of the price of the corn, four promissory notes for five pounds each, and four such notes for one pound each, of the bank of Messrs. *Dobson* and Sons, bankers at *Huddersfield*, in the county of *York*. The notes were in the following form, and the defendant's name was not written upon them :—

No.   *Huddersfield* Old Bank, £5.

I promise to pay the bearer on demand £5, value received. 1st day of *July*, 1823.

Entered, &c.   For *John Dobson* and Sons.

£5.   *W. Dobson.*

At eleven o'clock in the forenoon of the same 10th of *December, Dobson* and Sons stopped payment, having on the same morning and up to that hour paid all demands made upon them. They never afterwards renewed their payments, and shortly afterwards became bankrupts, and the plaintiff never received any part of the amount due on the notes. *Huddersfield* is distant from *York* about forty miles, and from *Laythorn*, the plaintiff's residence, fifty-two miles. At the time when the above notes were paid by the defendant to the plaintiff neither of them knew that *Dobson* and Sons had stopped payment or were insolvent.

Where goods were paid for by country bank notes in the afternoon of a day in the morning of which the bankers had stopped payment, without the knowledge of the vendor and vendee, and the latter, at the end of a week, offered to return the notes to the former, demanding payment of them: Held, that the vendee should have promptly presented the notes to the insolvent bankers, and given notice of nonpayment to the vendor according to the law-merchant, and that by his neglect to do so he had made the notes his own.

D D 2

The plaintiff never circulated the notes, nor did he ever present them to *Dobson* and Sons, the makers, for payment, but on *Saturday*, the 17th of the same month of *December*, the plaintiff required the defendant to receive back the notes and to pay him the amount of them, which the defendant then and ever since has refused to do. The question for the opinion of the Court is, whether the plaintiff is entitled to recover.

Dodd contended that the plaintiff was entitled to recover the price of the corn, unless the notes could be considered as payment, in consequence of laches in not presenting them for payment at the bank, or offering to return them earlier than he did. It will be urged on the other side that he was bound to do both or either. This argument will be found untenable. First, he was not bound to present the notes at the bank under the circumstances of the case; and secondly, the form of the notes rendered it unnecessary to offer to return them earlier than he did to the defendant. In the first place, it was not necessary to present the notes for payment, the defendant being no party to them, and consequently he could not be damnified by the neglect to present them. This case is distinguishable from those cases where the taking of the notes has been previous to the stoppage of the bankers, and in which presentment has been held necessary; but here there is the strong fact in the plaintiff's favour, that the notes were not taken by him until *after* the bank had stopped payment. Certainly, if they had been taken before *Dobson* and Sons had stopped, the plaintiff might have had more difficulty in his case, for want of proof of presentment. Here, however, presentment would have been of no use, because the bank had stopped payment, and therefore the defendant cannot have been prejudiced by the want of presentment. This case is distinguishable from *Howe* v. *Bowes* (a), because that was an action against the maker of the note, which was made pay-

(a) 5 Taunton, 30. 16 East, 112.

-able specially. But here the notes are made payable generally, and the defendant not being an indorser, presentment
was unnecessary. The cases establish this distinction, that
parties who merely pass bills or notes without becoming
parties to them, are not entitled to notice of presentment
and nonpayment; but where they are drawers and indorsers,
and their names are actually upon the instruments, it is
otherwise. It is also to be observed, that in this case the
action is not brought upon the notes, but merely for the
goods sold and delivered. The cases of *Warrington* v.
Furbor(a), *Swinyard* v. *Bowes* (b), and *Murray* v. *King* (c),
establish the principle, that a person who is not a party to
a bill cannot complain of laches in not giving him notice of
dishonour by the acceptor, unless he has sustained an actual
prejudice by the laches. It is true, that in *Phillips* v.
Astling (d), the want of presentment was held to be a good
defence to an action brought upon a guarantee given for the
price of goods to be paid for by a bill, but this was expressly on the ground that the acceptor was perfectly solvent at the time the bill became due. The case of *Hol-
brow* v. *Wilkins*(e) confirms the previous cases of *Warrington* v. *Furbor, Swinyard* v. *Bowes, Murray* v. *King,*
and *Phillips* v. *Astling,* and establishes the principle that the
want of presentment is no defence in this action, the defendant's name not being on the bill and he having sustained
no actual damage by the omission to present. The defendant by merely passing the notes to the plaintiff in
payment of a debt must be considered in the nature of a
surety for the solvency of the makers of the notes, and
rendering himself at all events liable in the event of their
failure. The statute 3 & 4 *Anne, c.* 9, does not apply to
this case, because that refers only to bills of exchange, and
does not comprehend bankers' notes payable to bearer.
But if even this were not so, the mere passing of these

(a) 8 East, 242.
(b) 5 M. & S. 62.
(c) 5 B. & A. 165.
(d) 2 Taunt. 206.
(e) *Ante,* vol. ii. 59; 1 B. & C.
10.

notes to the plaintiff by the defendant amounts to a guarantee for the solvency of the maker. Conceding that if
the bankers had not stopped payment before the time when
the notes ought in due course to be presented, the plaintiff
would have been guilty of laches in not having presented
them, still here there is no foundation for that argument,
because at the very time the notes were passed to the plaintiff the bankers had actually stopped payment. If presentment of bank notes under such circumstances were
necessary, it would be highly inconvenient in mercantile
transactions, and productive of no possible advantage, for it
would be a mere useless ceremony. On these grounds the
plaintiff was not bound to present these notes for payment.
Secondly. There was no obligation whatever on the plaintiff
to return the notes to the defendant, any further than as the
returning of them might amount to a notice of nonpayment.
He was not bound to give them up until he got his
money. [*Bayley*, J. If you had given him the notes up
promptly, and he had originally taken them from another
person under such circumstances as would have entitled
him to recover from such person, he might have taken immediate steps to enforce payment. By omitting, therefore,
to return them, may he not have sustained a damage?] A
party passing instruments of this kind is a guarantee for
their payment, and he must be taken to have knowledge of
the circumstances of the maker, and therefore bound himself to take notice of the maker's insolvency. He undertakes that the bankers shall pay, and if they do not, then
there is a breach of his implied guarantee. There is a
material distinction between the principle which applies to
the mere passer of a bank note, and the case of the drawer
or indorser of a bill of exchange. There is here no privity
between the plaintiff and the makers of the notes. He is
the mere holder of instruments which pass from hand to
hand as money, and consequently there is no duty imposed upon him to take those formal steps which are
required to be observed in the case of a bill of exchange

which has been dishonoured. There is no reasonable probability that, even if the defendant had had earlier notice
of the nonpayment of the notes, he could have enforced
payment of any body else. There was no attempt made at
the time of the trial to shew that the defendant had sustained any prejudice by want of earlier notice. If he had,
in fact, sustained any damage by reason of the want of
notice, that ought to have been proved in evidence and
relied upon in the defence. For instance, suppose he could
have shewn that between the time of passing the notes to
the plaintiff and the following Saturday he had gone to the
bankers for the purpose of paying a debt, and by reason of
the plaintiff's negligence he was prevented from setting off
these notes in payment of the debt, then there would have
been some ground for charging the plaintiff with laches.
But here there was no pretence for saying that the defendant could have derived any benefit from earlier notice,
because at the time the notes were passed the bankers had
stopped payment, and shortly afterwards they were declared
bankrupts.

C. Creswell, contrà, contended that this case came within
the operation of the statute 3 & 4 Anne, c. 9, s. 7, by which
it is enacted, " that if any person doth accept any bill of
exchange for and in satisfaction of any former debt, the
same shall be accounted a full and complete payment of
such debt, if such person accepting any such bill for his
debt doth not take his due course to obtain payment
thereof, by endeavouring to get the same accepted and paid."
Now here there was a former debt, the notes in question
were taken in payment of that debt, and upon all the cases
hitherto decided it will appear that the plaintiff has not
taken due course to obtain payment of them, and consequently they must be considered as a satisfaction of his
demand. But it is said on the other side, that this statute
does not apply to these notes, and is merely confined in its
operation to bills of exchange. It must also be contended,

that the law-merchant does not apply at all to promissory notes. Since that statute, however, it has been decided that promissory notes stand on the same footing as bills of exchange for all purposes whatsoever. Then if there be no distinction between a banker's note payable to bearer, and an ordinary promissory note made between private parties, it is clear that the plaintiff has not taken his due course to obtain payment of these notes, and cannot recover. Now according to the authorities of *Sanderson* v. *Bowes* (a) and *Dickinson* v. *Bowes* (b), bank notes are treated as promissory notes. Then what is the general principle in these cases? In *Bayley on Bills*, 187, it is laid down, that the receipt of a bill or note implies an undertaking from the receiver, to every party to the bill or note who would be entitled to bring an action on paying it, to present in proper time the one, where necessary for acceptance, and each for payment; to allow no extra time for payment, and to give notice without delay to such person of a failure in the attempt to procure a proper acceptance for payment. But it is said on the other side, that as the bankers were insolvent, there was no necessity for presenting these notes and giving notice to the defendant of their nonpayment. Now the cases of *Russell* v. *Langstaff* (c), *Howe* v. *Bowes* (d), and *Rohde* v. *Proctor* (e), shew that the insolvency of the drawer and acceptor of a bill of exchange does not cure the want of notice of dishonour; and it has even been held, that knowledge of the insolvency by the defendant does not dispense with the necessity of the demand for payment and notice to the defendant of the dishonour of the bill, *Esdaile* v. *Sowerby* (f); and in that case it was observed, that *notice* imports something *more than knowledge*, because it was competent to the holder to give credit to the maker. In point of law, and the authorities upon this subject, the mere

---

(a) 14 East, 500.
(b) 16 East, 110.
(c) Dougl. 514.
(d) 16 East, 112; 5 Taunt. 30.

(e) *Ante*, vol. vi. 610; 4 B. & C. 517.
(f) 11 East, 114.

keeping of these notes by the plaintiff for so long a time, was giving a new credit to the bankers, and upon that ground he has made them his own. It was upon this principle that the cases of *Moore* v. *Warren* (a) and *Home* v. *Barry* (b) were decided. The true test, in cases of this nature is, (as was laid down in *Cory* v. *Scott* (c),) whether, if the drawer pays the bill, he has any remedy against the other persons, if he has timely notice of the dishonour. Now would the defendant in this case have had a remedy over if he had had prompt notice of the nonpayment of these notes? Nobody doubts that he would have had his remedy against the bankers, not perhaps to the full extent of the amount of the notes, but he would have had a remedy *valeat quantum*. It is admitted on the other side, that if the defendant had been an indorser, he would have been entitled to prompt notice of the dishonour, but his name not being on the notes, he was to be deprived of that advantage. Why is an indorser entitled to notice? Because he may have his remedy over against the other parties to the bill. There is no sound distinction in principle, if a man has his remedy over, whether his name be on the bill or not. Suppose after the defendant had put his name upon the notes, he had struck his indorsement out, would that make any difference in his legal rights? The cases of *Warrington* v. *Furbor* and *Swinyard* v. *Bowes* do not touch the present case, because there the parties relying on the want of notice were wholly unconnected with the instruments, and would not, by paying them, have acquired any remedy over against other parties. Here these notes are taken as and for payment of a debt, and as the plaintiff has not taken due course to obtain payment of them, they are to be considered by the statute as a full and complete payment of the debt, inasmuch as by his laches he has deprived the defendant of his remedy over. The question

(a) Str. 415.
(b) Ibid.
(c) 3 B. & A. 619; Bayley on

Bills, 329; cited and commented on in *Firth* v. *Thrush*, 2 M. & R. 359.

then remaining is, whether the circumstance of *Dobson* and Sons having actually stopped payment at the time the plaintiff received the notes from the defendant makes any difference. According to the principle of the case of *Beeching* v. *Gower* (a), it makes no difference. In that case, a country bank note was given in payment while the bank continued open, but before the time allowed by the law-merchant had expired, the bank failed, and *Gibbs*, C. J. held that the holder was bound to present the note for payment in due time, and by neglecting to do so made it his own.

Here the Court stopped him.

Dodd was heard in reply.

BAYLEY, J.—I am of opinion that in this case we ought to give judgment for the defendant. One short observation will dispose of the cases of *Warrington* v. *Furbor* and *Swinyard* v. *Bowes*, the authorities cited to shew that it was not necessary in this case to prove presentment for payment. In those cases the persons insisting on the want of presentment were not parties to the bills. The defendant in this case was a party to the notes, for they were payable to the "bearer on demand," and he was the holder of them. Now I consider the holder of a bill as a party to it during the time he is holding it, and when he passes it away it passes by delivery from him. The party receiving traces his right to hold the bill from the person who had been the former holder, and consequently the former holder must be considered as a party to it. In the cases cited the persons relying upon the want of presentment never were parties to the bill, but were only parties to a collateral transaction, and on that ground the Court in each of those cases decided that the law-merchant did not apply. In this case it is perfectly clear, that if these notes had been given by the de-

(a) Holt, N. P. C. 313.

fendant to the plaintiff at the time when the corn was sold, he could have no remedy upon them in case of non-payment, because the defendant had not put his name upon the notes. ·The plaintiff might have insisted upon payment in money, but if he consented to take these notes as money, then he must be considered as taking them at his own peril, and as becoming the loser of the money in case of the insolvency of the bankers. If, indeed, he could have proved that at the time the defendant passed them to him he was guilty of a fraud, and that he knew that the notes were merely waste paper and of no value, then whether they were taken at the time of the sale or afterwards would be wholly immaterial. But in this case it appears that they were given at a later period than the date of the sale, and the question is, whether or not they are to be considered as payment and discharge of the debt due to the plaintiff in respect of the corn. I take the general rule applicable to all negotiable instruments of every description to be, that if they are taken in discharge of a pre-existing debt, they shall operate as a discharge of that debt, unless the holder who takes them does every thing which, according to the usage and custom of merchants applicable to such instruments, he ought to do in order to obtain payment of them. Then the question is, whether the plaintiff in this case has done all that he ought to do in order to obtain payment of these notes. They were intended for circulation, and it is contended by the defendant, that the plaintiff ought to have put them into circulation promptly, or else to have sent them immediately for payment at the bank. I certainly do not think that the plaintiff was bound to send them forth into circulation, or present them immediately at the bank, though he was not at liberty to lock them up in his desk for an unlimited time. Certainly he was bound to adopt one or other of two courses, either to put them into circulation within a reasonable time, or to take care that there was no neglect in presenting them for payment within a reasonable time. It is conceded on the part of the plaintiff, that if there had not been any insolvency of the bankers, the notes should have been circulated or presented on the *Monday*, unless there were some circumstances which would excuse his not sending them for payment on that day. I will assume that on the *Monday* he had ascertained that the bank had stopped, and that therefore it had become unnecessary to present them for payment; still he had another duty to perform. I apprehend that from the negotiable nature of these securities it was his duty to communicate to the party from whom he took them that the bank had stopped, and that he could not obtain payment, and that he, the plaintiff, would resort to the defendant for payment of the notes, and then it would be for the defendant to consider whether he could transfer the loss to any other person, for unless he had been guilty of some laches, he might perhaps have been able to resort to the person from whom he had received the notes originally. There is no doubt but that that person would be discharged if he had received no notice of non-payment, or of the insolvency of the bankers, till a week after he had paid them to the defendant. The neglect therefore on the part of the plaintiff to communicate to the defendant notice of the insolvency of the bankers, prejudiced, or had a tendency to prejudice the defendant. The law considers that the person upon whom the loss in cases of this kind is to fall, is entitled to have notice, in order that he may have time to exercise his own judgment whether he will or will not take legal steps against other persons who are parties to the bills or notes. Now if these notes had been returned to the defendant on the *Tuesday*, he might have taken steps against *Dobson* and Sons, and have endeavoured to enforce payment by pressure upon them, and he had a right to exercise his judgment whether he would do so or not, although they had stopped, or he might have had a remedy against the person from whom he received the notes. These steps he was precluded from taking by the plaintiff's neglect, and I think the loss ought to fall upon him. It may be very hard in a great variety of cases, that the entire loss should fall upon any one individual in consequence of his own neglect or laches. But it is a general rule applicable to cases of this description, not to be relaxed in particular instances, that the holder of such an instrument is to present promptly for payment, or to communicate without delay notice of non-payment, or of the insolvency of the acceptor of a bill or the maker of a note ; for a party is not only entitled to knowledge of insolvency, but to notice that in consequence of such insolvency he will be called upon to pay the amount of the bill or note. Suppose in this case, instead of having actually stopped payment, the bankers had been enabled to pay some of the notes, though not all, and that the plaintiff retained the rest in his hands without giving notice to the defendant until a considerable time afterwards, could it be contended that he would be liable on the dishonoured notes? If he could lawfully retain them a week, he might retain them six months, a year, or two years. I do not know where to draw the line, unless it is drawn where the law has drawn it in the manner I have pointed out. The case was very well argued by Mr. *Dodd*, and there appeared at first much difficulty and intricacy about it, but when we come to consider it deliberately, it appears to me to be free from any real difficulty consistently with all the rules applicable to bills of exchange and promissory notes. The case of *Beeching* v. *Gower* cuts down almost the whole of the argument for the plaintiff founded upon the fact that the notes were paid away after the bankers had stopped. But without any authority upon the subject, in my opinion, that circumstance made no difference in the case. I think the plaintiff must be considered as having been paid by these notes, and that he has by his neglect made them his own.

HOLROYD, J.—I think that under the circumstances stated in this case, notwithstanding the ingenious argument we have heard on the part of the plaintiff as well as on the part of the defendant, the plaintiff is not entitled to recover.

These notes, as a circulating medium, were paid by the defendant and received by the plaintiff as money, both parties being ignorant at the time of the important change which had taken place in the circumstances of the bankers. They are paid as money, and they are received and accepted as of the value they purported to be of; and if they are to be considered as money, they are, according to the case of *Miller* v. *Race*(a), to be considered in point of law as payment of the debt. But without determining whether the plaintiff was debarred in the first instance from electing to consider them either as negotiable instruments or as money, I think that under the circumstances of the case they operate as payment, for it appears to me that by not taking due steps to obtain payment, and delaying to give notice to the defendant, he treats them as money, and as his own property, and he cannot afterwards return them to the party from whom he took them after failing to do what the law imposed upon him. That is the short ground of my opinion. If bills of exchange or promissory notes are delivered over in payment and satisfaction of a debt, although they may not be considered as payment and satisfaction to all intents and purposes, but according to the result whether they should turn out to be available or not, still, if due means be not taken to obtain payment of them agreeably to the law and usages of merchants, they must be considered as payment and satisfaction of the debt, although they may not actually be available to the party. These bankers' notes are in point of law promissory notes, and therefore due diligence ought to have been used to obtain payment, and if payment had been refused, notice ought to have been given to the defendant of that refusal. It is found to be a fact that these notes were not presented for payment. True it is, that at the time when the plaintiff ought to have presented them for payment the bankers had become insolvent, but still that circumstance did not relieve the plaintiff from the obligation of giving notice at all events that the bankers

(a) 1 Burr. 452.

had become insolvent, and therefore required the defendant to pay the notes. Not having done so, I think he has made the notes his own, and that in point of law they are a satisfaction of his demand.

LITTLEDALE, J.—I think the plaintiff is not entitled to recover. If these notes were taken as negotiable instruments, as in the common case of a bill of exchange or promissory note, then they were taken subject to the condition that the holder should do all that was required to obtain payment. It was incumbent on the plaintiff to present them for payment within a reasonable time. It might not be required to present them the next day, but at all events he ought not to have gone beyond two days, and if they were not paid he ought to have given prompt notice to the defendant of the insolvency of the bankers. Waiting the time he did was much too long. If the notes were taken as money absolutely and without any condition at all, then the plaintiff took them for whatever they might turn out to be worth. It might be a different thing if the notes were actually forged, for then they would not be what they purported,- namely, genuine notes. Here, however, the notes were really the notes of *Dobson* and Sons, and it does not appear to me to make any difference whether the bankers had actually stopped payment at the time, or afterwards resumed their payments. I do not agree with the argument pressed upon us that there is any guarantee implied by law in the party passing a note, payable on demand to bearer, that the maker of the note is solvent at the time when it is so passed, and that consequently the defendant himself was bound to take notice of the bankers' insolvency.

Judgment for the defendant.

ELIZABTH BIDDELL, Widow, (she and one JOHN COXE, since deceased, being sued as executrix and executor of THOMAL BIDDELL, deceased,) v. MARY DOWSE.

(IN ERROR.)

1827.

An action at law cannot be maintained upon an order of a court of equity.

Where all matters in difference between parties to a suit in equity, some of whom were *infants*, represented by their next friends, were referred to arbitration by an order of the Vice-Chancellor, " with the consent of *the attornies* of the parties in the *said suit*," and an action was brought upon the award:—Held, (in error,) that the award was not binding on the infants.

ERROR from the Common Pleas, upon a judgment of that Court for breach, by the defendants below, of a promise to pay a sum of money awarded by an arbitrator. The first count of the declaration stated, that before the making of the promise and undertaking of the defendants as thereinafter mentioned certain differences had arisen, and a certain suit was then depending in the High Court of Chancery, in which the said plaintiff, *Mary Dowse*, widow, *J. Lightfoot Wilkinson* and *Mary* his wife, *Jane Dowse Wilkinson, G. Wilkinson, Mary Anne Wilkinson, J. T. Wilkinson, John Dowse Wilkinson, E. Wilkinson*, and *L. H. Wilkinson*, infants, by the said *J. L. Wilkinson*, their father and next friend, and *W. Jones* and *Elizabeth* his wife, *E. Jones, M. W. Jones, J. T. W. Jones, W. E. J. Jones*, and *J. D. Jones*, infants, by the said *W. Jones*, their father and next friend; *James May* and *Susannah* his wife, *J. May* the younger, *E. T. May*, and *M. May*, infants, by the said *J. May*, their father and next friend; and *T. May*, and *J. Boxer*, were plaintiffs; and *Peter King, Thomas Biddell*, since deceased, and *J. Keay*, were defendants; and that by an order of Sir *John Leach*, Vice-Chancellor, bearing date the 14th of *June*, 1823, it was amongst other things ordered, with the consent of the attornies of the parties in the said suit, that the several matters in question in the suit, and all disputes and differences then subsisting between the said plaintiff, *Mary Dowse, J. Lightfoot Wilkinson* and *Mary* his wife, *William Jones* and *Elizabeth* his wife, and *James May* and *Susannah* his wife, and *Peter King*, and *Thomas Biddell*, since deceased, should be referred to the award, arbitrament, and final determination of *W. C.*, who was to be at liberty to make one or more award or awards

of and concerning the matters thereby referred to him as he
should think fit, so as such award or awards should be
made in writing under the hand and seal of the said *W. C.*
ready to be delivered to the said parties, or such of them
as should require the same, on or before the 23d day of
June then next, or on or before such ulterior day or days
as the said *W. C.* should from from time to time appoint
in writing, by indorsement upon the said order. And in
case either of the said parties should happen to die before
the making of the final award under the said reference, the
reference was not to abate, but the executors and administrators of the parties so dying were to be considered and
taken as parties to the order in like manner as their testator
or intestate. The declaration then stated, that before the
making of the award thereinafter mentioned, to wit, on the
28th of *June*, 1824, the said *Thomas Biddell* died, to wit,
at &c., that the arbitrator enlarged the time for making his
award until the last day of *Trinity* term, 1824, and that he
during the enlarged time for making his award, to wit, on
the 7th *July*, 1824, at &c., made his award in writing between the parties aforesaid of and concerning the said differences, and did thereby then and there, amongst other
things, award that the defendants, as executor and executrix of *Thomas Biddell*, deceased, should, out of the assets
of *Thomas Biddell*, on the 27th day of *July* then next, between the hours of eleven and twelve in the forenoon, at
the chambers of Mr. *J. Boxer*, of *Furnival's Inn*, in the
county of *Middlesex*, pay to the plaintiff the sum of 225*l.* ;
of which award the defendant's executor and executrix as
aforesaid afterwards, to wit, on the said 7th day of *July*, in
the year last aforesaid, had notice, to wit, at &c., by reason of
which said premises, the defendants, as executor and executrix as aforesaid, became liable to pay to the plaintiff the
said sum of 225*l.*, according to the tenor of the award, to
wit, at &c.; and being so liable, they, the defendant's executor and executrix as aforesaid, afterwards, to wit, on &c.
at &c. in consideration thereof undertook and faithfully pro-

mised the plaintiff to pay her the said sum of 225*l.* at the time and in the manner as in the award was directed. The declaration went on to aver, that although the defendant's executor and executrix as aforesaid, to wit, on the 27th of *July,* in the year last aforesaid, were requested to pay the said sum of 225*l.* to the plaintiff according to the tenor and effect of the award, yet the defendant's executor and executrix as aforesaid, not regarding their promise and undertaking, did not nor would, when so requested, nor at any time before nor since, pay the said sum of 225*l.*, or any part thereof, to the plaintiff, but wholly neglected and refused so to do, to wit, at &c.

To this count there was a demurrer, upon which the Court of Common Pleas gave judgment for the plaintiff below.

Campbell, for the plaintiff in error, contended that the judgment ought to be reversed. First, the order of the Vice Chancellor could not be the foundation of an action at law, even in the lifetime of *Biddell.* It could only be enforced by attachment in the Court of equity, or by other process of that Court. No action will lie even upon a rule or order of this Court, but *à multo fortiori* it will not lie upon an order of the Court of Chancery. It has been determined that no action at law can be maintained upon the final decree or judgment of a Court of equity, unless it be for a debt which would be a debt at law, and the decree must shew it to be so. That was determined in *Carpenter* *v. Thornton* (a). If no legal debt would arise upon a final decree, much less would it arise upon an interlocutory order. In the present case there is no legal debt disclosed upon the face of the declaration. It merely recites that there was a suit in equity between parties, some of whom were married women and others infants. It does not appear that the object of the suit was to recover that which would be a debt at law. But, secondly, neither the infants nor the married women would be bound by this submis-

(a) 3 B. & A. 52.

sion, and, therefore, the award could not be enforced, there
being no reciprocity. It is a settled rule, that unless the
submission be mutual, the award is void(a). Therefore,
when it is found upon the face of the declaration itself, that
infants and married women are made parties to the submission, it could not be binding for want of mutuality; and
it cannot be said, that in such case the consent of the attornies can make it a binding agreement, especially upon
the infants, who may, when at majority, disclaim the authority and open the matter again. Suppose the award
had been, that a sum of money should be paid by the married women, it is clear that no action could be maintained
against them. It was said in the Court below, that this
Court would presume that the Court of equity would take
care of the interests of the married women and infants, but
a Court of law is not bound to take notice of that. It must
determine all actions at law upon the principles of law,
without reference to what a Court of equity would do.
But even in equity it is doubtful whether the Lord Chancellor would bind an infant under such circumstances. In
Cavendish v. ———— (b) an arbitrator awarded 450*l.* to an
infant, and that bond should be given by the guardian that
the infant, when he came of age, should convey the land in
question, but the Lord Chancellor *Nottingham* refused to
enforce the award, saying, that he would never decree an
award which would bind an infant. Supposing, however,
that an action could be maintained upon an award under
this order in the lifetime of the parties, no action would lie
against the representatives of one of the parties who died
before the award was made. The death of that party would
be a revocation of the arbitrator's authority. It must be
observed that this is an action upon the award, not upon a
promise of the testator that his executor would perform the
award. The award itself is considered the foundation of
the action. Such an award, made after the death of the
party, is not binding, for his submission is void, and whatever

(a) 2 Saund. 61, (n) 2.   (b) 1 Bro. Ch. Ca. 279.

E E 2

other remedies there may be, no action will lie upon the award made subsequently. There is no doubt that by the law of *England*, as well as of some other countries, the authority given to an arbitrator is revocable by the party giving it; *Vynior's* case (a), *Rolle's Abr. Authority* (D). So clear is this, that even where the submission is made a rule of Court, it may be revoked; *Milne* v. *Greatrix* (b). It is a settled rule, that the death of either of the parties to the submission is a revocation of the authority of an arbitrator, even where a verdict is taken for the plaintiff, and the submission is by order of nisi prius; *Potts* v. *Ward* (c), *Toussuint* v. *Hartop* (d), *Cooper* v. *Johnson* (e). The question then is, what is the effect of the clause in the submission by which the parties agreed that the reference should not abate by death, but that the personal representatives should be considered parties to the order. There may be many cases in which such a stipulation would be desirable if it could be acted on, but it cannot be by the rules of law. It is inconsistent with the very nature of a submission to arbitration, which is revocable, and by law revoked by the death of either of the parties to the submission, and consequently an executor cannot be bound by an award made after the death of his testator. A submission to an arbitrator is analogous to a power of attorney, which is revoked by the death of the party making it. In *Co. Litt.* s. 66, it is laid down, " If a man maketh a deed of feoffment to another, and a letter of attorney to one to deliver to him seisin by force of the same deed; yet if livery of seisin be not executed in the life of him who made the deed, this availeth nothing;" and in *Co. Litt.* 52 b, it is laid down that " a letter of attorney to deliver livery of seisin after the decease of the feoffor is void." The only authority the other way is *Roby* v. *Twelves* (f), where it was held that a custom for a copyholder to make a writing in the nature of

(a) 8 Rep. 162.
(b) 7 East, 608.
(c) 1 Marsh. 366.

(d) 7 Taunt. 571; 1 Moore, 287.
(e) 2 B. & A. 394.
(f) Styles, 423.

a letter of attorney to two copyholders of the manor to surrender his copyhold after his death was good ; but that being the *lex loci* makes all the difference. In *Rolle's Abr. Feoffment*, s. 1, it is said, " If a man makes a deed of feoffment, with a letter of attorney to *J. S.* to deliver seisin after his death, the attorney cannot deliver seisin during his life, and if he does he is a disseisor; nor can he deliver seisin after his death. But if mayor and commonalty or dean and chapter make a feoffment and letter of attorney to deliver seisin, this authority does not determine by the death of mayor or dean," *Bac. Abr.* tit. *Authority* (E). These passages shew that such an authority cannot be made irrevocable. In *Watson* v. *King* (a) it was held, that a power of attorney, though coupled with an interest, is instantly revoked by the death of the grantor ; and that an act afterwards *bonâ fide* done under it by the grantee, before notice of the death of the grantor, is a nullity. So in the case of *Murray* v. *The East India Company* (b), it was held that payment to an attorney after the death of the principal, without authority, was no discharge. This being so, an arbitrator, who, in law, represents the person of the party submitting to the reference, and who is in fact his attorney, ceases to have any authority upon the death of the person represented. This is not like the case of *Tyler* v. *Jones*(c), where a verdict was taken for a specific sum, subject to the award of an arbitrator, and a clause was inserted in the order of reference, at the suggestion of the Lord Chief Justice *Abbott*, to make the award binding on the personal representative, and in consequence of which the award was held good; but that was on the principle that the award of the arbitrator is the same as if the sum had been originally assessed by the jury. An award after verdict is considered the verdict and judgment of the jury, and the foundation of the award ; *Lee* v. *Lingard* (d), and *Borrowdale* v.

(a) 4 Campb. 272.   (c) 4 D. & R. 740; 3 B & C. 144.
(b) 5 B. & A. 204.   (d) 1 East, 401.

Hitchener (a). Now in this case there was no verdict, and unless the award be a binding instrument in itself, no action can be maintainable upon it. Let the case be considered in another point of view. It has been holden that the marriage of a woman is a revocation of a submission made by her when sole, and so of a power of attorney; *Anon* (b), *White* v. *Gifford* (c), *Charnley* v. *Winstanley* (d). Suppose a feme sole were to enter into a submission, expressly stipulating that her marriage afterwards should not avoid the reference, it is clear that an award made after marriage would not bind her husband; or if he were afterwards to die it would not bind the wife. They might be sued respectively for revoking the authority, but not for non-performance of the award. The case of *Powell* v. *Graham* (e) will be relied upon on the other side, but in that case the contract was irrevocable, and binding upon the personal representatives; but this being an action on an award after the death of one of the parties submitting to the reference, the action cannot be maintained. In addition to these objections arising on the other parts of the case, the form of the declaration itself is objectionable, for it alleges that the defendant undertook to pay without saying *as* executrix; it alleges a promise to pay in her own right, and this without any consideration stated. There is besides no allegation of assets. There may be a personal promise by an executor, but there must be a consideration to support it stated. Now in *Pearson* v. *Henry* (f) it was held, that a promise by an administratrix to pay the debt of the intestate, if there be no assets, is *nudum pactum*. [*Abbott*, C.J. The allegation here is, that the defendant promised to pay in the manner as in the award directed, and the direction of the award is to pay out of assets.] Which shews clearly that there ought to be an averment of assets. The omis-

---

(a) 3 B.&P. 244.

(b) Sir W. Jones, 388.

(c) Roll. Abr. Authority, (E.) pl. 4.

(d) 5 East, 266.

(e) 1 J. B. Moore, 305; 7 Taunt. 580.

(f) 5 T. R. 6.

sion of the word "as" deprives the defendant of the opportunity of pleading *plene administravit, Brigden* v. *Parkes* (a) and *Henshall* v. *Roberts* (b). But lastly, it is not even averred that *Thomas Biddell*, the testator, lived till the arbitrator entered upon the reference, or that the defendant ever had notice of the submission.

Holt, for the defendant in error. Three objections are made on the other side. First, that no action will lie upon an award made in pursuance of the order of the Vice Chancellor. Secondly, that the submission to arbitration was revoked by the death of *Thomas Biddell* before the award was made, and consequently the award is not binding. Thirdly, that the declaration is defective for want of averring assets. As to the first objection it may be conceded that no action would lie upon the Vice Chancellor's order, *per se*, nor would an action at law lie upon the final decree of a court of equity, unless there was a legal obligation to pay what was decreed. But in this case it will be observed that the Vice Chancellor's order is only a preliminary step; it is merely a suggestion, which the parties may adopt or reject; but having chosen to adopt the order and submit to it, their submission becomes the agreement, and that is the basis on which the award is made, and by which they must be bound. The only question then on this part of the case is whether there has been a binding consent to the submission. The consent is by their attornies. Now it has been holden that an attorney has authority to refer to arbitration a cause in which he is engaged, and his consent will bind his client. *Filmer* v. *Delber* (c). In *Curtis* v. *Barclay* (d), it was even held that a consignor of goods has authority to refer matters in difference between his principal and a third party relating to the goods consigned to him. If such an authority may

(a) 2 B. & P. 424.
(b) 5 East, 150.
(c) 3 Taunt. 486.

(d) *Ante*, vol. vii. 539; 5 B. & C. 141.

be exercised by an attorney at law, with greater reason may a solicitor in Chancery do so, considering the extensive nature of the jurisdiction of a Court of equity, which may bring all parties before it. It is clear that he may refer a suit on behalf of his client. His consent is only voidable as against infants on their attaining full age; it is not absolutely void. If, therefore, there be a sufficient consent to the submission, it is a good consideration for the award, and it stands on a legal valid basis, and there is no doubt that an action might have been maintained upon the award if made in the lifetime of *Thomas Biddell*. The question then, secondly, is whether the submission was revoked by the death of *Thomas Biddell*. The authorities cited on the other side upon this point are not disputed. It is conceded that either party to a submission may, by an act done by him, revoke the authority of the arbitrator, and that the death of either by law operates as a revocation; but it is clear that parties may agree not to revoke by their own act, or that the death of either of them shall not operate as a revocation of the authority of the arbitrator. Now here it was consented to by all parties " that in case either of the said parties should happen to die before the making of the final award under the said reference, the reference was not to abate, but the executors and administrators of the parties so dying were to be considered and taken as parties to the order, in like manner as their testator or intestate." Here then is a binding consent that the death of *Biddell* shall not operate as a revocation of the arbitrator's authority, and that consent will bind his executor. Lastly, the objection as to the want of an averment in the declaration of assets will not avail the plaintiff in error, because the knowledge of want of assets is peculiarly within the executor's knowledge, and it is upon him to shew as matter of defence that he had no assets. It is said that this executor is charged in his individual capacity, but the declaration shews clearly that he is sued in his representative character, and there is no doubt that execution would only go against the goods of the testator.

This case was argued in term time.

Cur. adv. vult.

ABBOTT, C. J. now delivered judgment.—This action against the plaintiff in error was brought in the Court below on an alleged promise to pay a sum of money awarded, the consideration for the promise being an assumed legal obligation to make such payment according to an award. Nothing appears to shew a legal obligation, arising after the award, to pay the money in pursuance of the award, unless there had existed previously, and before the award, a legal obligation to abide by and perform it when it should be made. Such a legal obligation, subjecting a party to an action for non-performance, must arise out of some valid and competent submission to the authority of the arbitrator. It therefore becomes necessary to consider, whether upon the facts set forth in the declaration there appears to have been such a valid and competent submission. The submission mentioned in the declaration is an order of the Vice Chancellor, made in a suit pending before him, by consent of the attornies of the parties in the suit. It is not alleged that the testator assented to the reference, or that he or his executors had any knowledge of it before the award was made. The order of the Vice Chancellor cannot be enforced by action. This was admitted. Then was the consent of the attornies of the parties to the suit, without more, a competent and valid submission? In order to answer this question it is proper to observe who were parties to the suit, and what were the matters submitted. Of the parties to the suit some of the plaintiffs therein appear to have been adults *sui juris*, others married women joined with their husbands, and others infants suing by their next friends. The defendants were all adults. The matters submitted are the several matters in question in the suit, and all disputes and differences between the adult plaintiffs, including the husbands and their wives, and the defendants in the suit. The matters in question in the suit must be taken to include the interest of the infant plaintiffs. Now if an action had been brought, and a declaration framed, not upon the award, as has been done, but upon the submission to the award, it would have been necessary to allege a promise to perform the award, and to have shewn also a consideration for that promise, which must have been a promise or some other binding matter on the other side. Admitting, for the sake of argument, but no further, that the consent of the attornies of such of the parties in the suit as were adult might be binding upon them, and equivalent to or evidence of a promise on their part to submit to and perform the award, and that this might have been a consideration sufficient to support the promise *of* the other parties to the suit, as far as regards the interest of the adult plaintiffs, still does it appear that any such consent was given or promise made by or on behalf of the infant plaintiffs? The only consent shewn in the declaration is the consent of the parties in the suit; but the infants cannot have had an attorney either in or out of the suit, and therefore no person representing them is alleged to have consented to the reference. And if by the attornies to the parties in the suit we are to understand the attornies of the next friends of the infants, can it be inferred merely from their character of attornies that they had authority to bind their principals, the next friends of the infants, to answer and become personally bound for the infants' acquiescence under and performance of the award, and to be responsible if they should refuse to do so when they came of age, and should chuse to open and re-agitate the matter? If we were to do this, we should impose upon the next friend of an infant an obligation far different from that which he takes upon himself when he consents to be named next friend for the purpose of a suit. We therefore think that the Court cannot do this by inference only, as by the frame of the present declaration the Court is required to do. If in fact the next friends of the infants did take this obligation on themselves, that matter ought to have been specially averred and shewn. Nothing of that kind is shewn, but the case is left to rest entirely on the consent of the attornies to the parties in the suit. There is a report of a case in the Court of Chancery very much resembling the present(*a*). It was shortly noticed at the bar; I shall quote it more at length. Matters in difference were referred by consent and order of the Court, and an award made; exceptions were taken to the award on one side, and the other side prayed it might be decreed; the Lord Chancellor *Nottingham* said, " When there is a reference by consent and order of the Court, if it will appear unequitable, this Court will not decree it; and accordingly in this cause set aside the award and bond of submission. The reason was because it concerned an infant, to whom 450*l.* was awarded, and that bond should be given by the guardian that the infant should at his full age convey the lands in question, which is not reasonable; for he may die, or if he live to full age, may refuse to convey. *It is not mutual.*" In like manner we think the submission in the case now before the Court was not mutual. It is true, that we cannot say whether in fact the interest of the infants is affected by this award; but if the submission fails as to one important part, we think it cannot stand as to the residue. A person may be willing to submit a suit in equity and all other matters to reference, and yet not willing to submit other matters, and leave the suit to proceed. And upon this ground, without adverting to the other objections that were taken in the argument at the bar, we think the plaintiff below has not shewn a good cause of action, and consequently that the judgment must be reversed.

Judgment reversed.

(*a*) Trinity Term, 28 Car. 2; 1 Cha. Ca. 279.

Doe on the demise of LLOYD v. PASSINGHAM.

By marriage settlement settlor limited his estate to *A.* and *B.* as trustees " to the only proper use and behoof of them their heirs and assigns for ever," in trust for settlor until his marriage, and from and after his marriage, in trust for husband and wife for life and the longest liver; then in trust for a term to other trustees to raise portions for younger children; then in trust for the first son and the heirs male of the body; then to the second son in like manner, and then to the daughters; and for default of such issue then over to the right heirs of the body of settlor:—Held, that the first set of trustees took the legal estate by common law, and not by the statute of uses, and that the second use could not be executed by the statute.

The purposes of the settlement, however, being at an end, in ejectment by the devisee of the person last seised, after the lapse of forty years, it was held that it might be left to the jury to presume a reconveyance of the legal estate from the trustees.

THIS was an ejectment to recover the possession of certain lands in the county of *Merioneth.* Plea, not guilty. At the trial before *Burrough,* J., at the last *Summer* Assizes for *Shropshire,* the case was this:—The lessor of the plaintiff claimed the land in question as devisee in tail under the will of *Catherine Lloyd,* who was co-heiress with her sister *Mary* of *Giwn Lloyd,* who died on the 26th *March,* 1774. On the 12th *May,* 1746, by indenture made and executed between himself, *Giwn Lloyd,* of the first part, *Sarah Hill* of the second part, Sir *Rowland Hill* and *John Wynne* of the third part, and Sir *Watkin Williams Wynne* and *Edward Lloyd* of the fourth part, in consideration of an intended marriage with the said *Sarah Hill,* and of a sum of 8000*l.,* being the marriage portion of the said *Sarah Hill,* paid or secured to be paid to him, *Giwn Lloyd,* he *Giwn Lloyd* did grant, release and confirm unto the said Sir *Watkin Williams Wynne* and *Edward Lloyd,* in their actual possession then being, by virtue of an indenture of bargain and sale, and to their heirs and assigns, certain premises therein particularly described, and amongst others the premises in question, " to have and to hold the said premises, with their appurtenances, unto the said Sir *Watkin Williams Wynne* and *Edward Lloyd,* their heirs and assigns for ever, upon trust, nevertheless, and subject to the several uses, interests and purposes thereinafter mentioned, that is to say, to the use of the said *Giwn Lloyd* and his heirs until the said intended marriage should take effect, and from and after the solemnization of the said intended marriage then to the use and behoof of *Giwn Lloyd* and *Sarah* his intended wife, and their assigns, for and during the term of their natural lives and the longer liver of them, as and for her jointure and in lieu and full satisfaction of dower; and from and after the decease of such survivor to the use of Sir *Rowland Hill* and *John Wynne*, their executors, administrators, and assigns, for the term of 1000 years, to and for the several intents and purposes thereinafter mentioned; and from and after the expiration or other sooner determination of that estate, to the use and behoof of the first son of the body of the said *Giwn Lloyd* on the body of the said *Sarah Hill*, his intended wife, lawfully to be begotten, and the heirs male of the body of such first son lawfully issuing; and for default of such issue, to the use and behoof of the second son in like manner; and then to the daughter; and for default of such issue to the use and behoof of the said *Giwn Lloyd*, his heirs and assigns for ever." And it was thereby declared and agreed by and between all and every the said parties to the said indenture that the term of 1000 years therein before limited to Sir *Rowland Hill* and *John Wynne* was upon trust, that they did and should, immediately after the decease of *Giwn Lloyd*, by sale or mortgage of the whole or any part thereof, raise the sum of 3000*l.*, to be paid and applied in manner thereinafter mentioned. And it was thereby further declared and agreed by and between the parties to the said indenture that a sum of 4000*l.*, part of the said sum of 8000*l.* should, immediately after the solemnization of the said intended marriage, be paid into the hands of them the said Sir *Rowland Hill* and *John Wynne*, upon trust that the same should be paid, laid out, and applied by them, with all convenient speed, in the purchase of freehold lands, tenements, or hereditaments, in fee simple, in the county of *Merioneth* aforesaid, or elsewhere in the principality of *Wales*, or in that part of *Great Britain* called *England*, with the approbation of them the said *Giwn Lloyd* and *Sarah Hill* his intended wife, or the survivor of them, testified by any deed or writing under the hands and seals of them the said *Giwn Lloyd* and *Sarah Hill*, and the survivor of them,

duly executed in the presence of two or more credible witnesses; and that the said lands, tenements, and hereditaments, when so purchased, and every part and parcel thereof, with their appurtenances, should be conveyed to them
the said Sir *Watkin Williams Wynne* and *Edward Lloyd*,
and their heirs, and to the survivor of them and his heirs,
to and for the use and behoof of the several persons and
for such estate and estates as the premises thereinbefore
mentioned, and thereby granted and released by the said
Giwn Lloyd, were conveyed, settled, limited and appointed.
And it was thereby also further declared and agreed that in
case there should be no issue of the said intended marriage,
and that the said *Sarah Hill* should be minded by her last
will and testament to give or devise any sum not exceeding
4000*l.*, or the estate thereby intended to be purchased
therewith, or any part thereof as aforesaid, to any person or
persons whatsoever, it should be lawful to and for her the
said *Sarah Hill*, notwithstanding her coverture, to give and
devise the same, or any part thereof, to such person or persons, and to and for such estate and estates, and such uses,
intents and purposes, as she should limit, direct and appoint; and in such case, they the said Sir *Watkin Williams
Wynne* and *Edward Lloyd* should stand seised of all and
every the lands, tenements and hereditaments so to be purchased as aforesaid, to them and their heirs, to and for such
uses, intents and purposes, as she the said *Sarah Hill*
should by such her last will limit, direct and appoint;
and then and from thenceforth all and every the uses and
limitations to the said *Giwn Lloyd* and his heirs, of and
concerning the said lands, tenements and hereditaments to
be purchased as aforesaid, should cease, determine and be
absolutely void to all intents and purposes whatsoever.

It appeared that *Giwn Lloyd* died in 1774 and *Sarah*
his wife in 1782 intestate, and without having had any issue.
The testatrix, *Catherine Lloyd*, continued in possession of
the estate from the death of *Sarah Lloyd* until the time of

her own death in 1787. Under these circumstances it was
contended that the legal estate was vested in Sir *Watkin
Williams Wynne* and *Edward Lloyd* by the deed of 1746,
and that consequently neither *Gwon Lloyd* nor the testatrix
had any legal estate in the lands in question, and therefore
the lessor of the plaintiff deriving no such estate from her
could not maintain ejectment. The learned judge thought
the legal estate was in the trustees, but reserved the point,
and the lessor of the plaintiff had a verdict, with liberty to
the defendant to move to enter a nonsuit. In *Michaelmas*
term last a rule nisi was granted accordingly; and now

1827.

Doe
v.
Passingham.

  W. E. Taunton, Campbell, and *R. V. Richards,* shewed
cause. Assuming that the learned judge, who tried the
cause, was correct in his opinion that the trustees under
this deed of settlement still have the legal estate, he ought
to have left it to the jury to presume after the lapse of so
long a time that there had been a reconveyance. On that
ground at all events there ought to be a new trial granted,
even if the Court itself will not presume a reconveyance.
But there are two grounds for contending that the legal
estate is out of the trustees. First, that looking to the
words of the limitation in the deed of 1746, the use was
not executed in Sir *W. W. Wynne* and *E. Lloyd,* but in all
the different persons in whose favour the limitation was
made; and secondly, that there cannot be a doubt that it
was the intention of the settlor that the use should be executed in the parties intended beneficially to take, and unless
that construction is given to the instrument, the manifest
intent of the settlor will be completely disappointed. As
to the first point, it is clear from the context of the settlement that the use was not executed in the trustees, but in
those persons to whose use the settlement is made. By
the first limitation the estate is conveyed to the trustees
" to have and hold the said premises with their appurtenances unto the said Sir *W. W. Wynne* and *E. Lloyd,*
their heirs and assigns." Now stopping there, they would

have had, not the use, but the seisin at common law, and out of that seisin the uses afterwards declared would be fed. The trustees are mere conduit pipes to supply the uses. In order that a use may arise there must be a seisin, but the use must be commensurate with the seisin. It may be very true that there cannot be a limitation of a use upon a use, but here the use is to shift according to circumstances. The effect of the statute of uses is to make the party to whom the first limitation is made seised of the estate, and then out of that seisin to feed and nourish the uses. The seisin is the fountain which supplies the uses. There is nothing in the language of the statute of uses which militates against this construction of the deed of settlement. The words of that statute are, " that where any person or persons stand or be seised of and in any honours, castles, &c. to the use, confidence, or trust of any *other* person or persons, &c. that in every such case such person and persons that have any such use shall hereafter be deemed and adjudged in lawful seisin, estate and possession of the same honours, &c." Here the subsequent limitations are not void, but are fed out of the seisin according to circumstances; for a use cannot be limited upon a use, a principle which was established soon after the passing of the statute of uses, and that for no other reason than that the uses are to be fed successively out of the seisin, and not to cross the common law. Lord *Bacon* in his reading on the statute of uses(a) observes upon the word " other," that the statute meant not to cross the common law, and that the word " other" was introduced, meaning the divided use, and not the conjoined use. As an instance of this he puts this case at p. 62, " If I enfeoff *A.* to the use of his right heirs, *A.* is in the fee simple, not by the statute, but by the common law." Again, in p. 63, he says, " The whole scope of the statute was to remit the common law, and never to intermeddle where the common law executed a use; therefore the statute ought to be expounded, that

(a) Law Tracts, p. 43.

where the party seised to the use and the *cestui que* use is
one person, he never taketh by the statute, except there be
a direct impossibility or impertinency for the use to take
effect by the common law." The cases of *Jenkins* v.
Young (a), reported also by the name of *Meredith* v.
Jones (b), and *Doe* v. *Prestwidge* (c), were decided upon
this doctrine. It appears from these cases that where the
limitation is to a person and his heirs, to the use of himself
and his heirs, they are consolidated together—the estate
passes by the seisin, and the use is absorbed or extinguished. Where therefore the limitation is to *A.* habendum
to him and his heirs, the use is merged, and the estate
unites in one and the same person, and the use thus becomes executed. This principle is broadly adopted in a
text book published by a gentleman who is entitled to considerable respect (d). Certainly no case is to be found
which decides, that where the estate is given to *A.* to the
use of *A.* with a second limitation to the use of *B.*, the
use is executed by the statute; but that is because *A.* is
in by the common law and not by the statute. *Tyrrel's*
case (e) is the first in which it was decided that a use cannot be engendered of a use; but that was the case of a
bargain and sale. Where a use is raised by way of contract of sale, there the use is executed by the statute, and
not by the common law. This is the principle upon which
there cannot be a use upon a use. Where there is a
bargain and sale to *A.* he has the use by means of the contract; the use is executed in him by the statute, and he has
the legal estate. It is probable that the case of *Hopkins* v.
Hopkins (f) will be urged against the plaintiff, where Lord
Hardwicke said, the statute of uses had no other effect
than to add at most three words to a conveyance; but that
learned judge only puts the common case which is found
in all the books, namely, where there is a limitation to *A.*

(a) Cro. Car. 230.   (d) 2 Preston's Conv. 483.
(b) Cro. Car. 244.   (e) Dyer, 155.
(c) 4 M. & S. 178.   (f) 1 Atk. 581.

and his heirs, to the use of *B.* and his heirs, in trust for *C.* The cases of Lady *Whetstone* v. *Bury*(a), and *The Attorney General* v. *Scott*(b), will also be relied upon on the other side.   In the first the terms of the settlement are not clearly stated, and there appears to have been no solemn judgment on the point; and in the second it is quite clear that it was the intention of the parties that *Barker,* to whom the estate was in the first instance conveyed, should take the legal estate.   Secondly, there can be no doubt that it was the intention of the settlor that the use should be executed in the parties beneficially interested, and the Court will not so construe the instrument as to defeat the manifest intent. According to all the authorities from the earliest times down to the present, beginning with the author of *Shepherd's Touchstone,* the Courts have always been anxious to found the interpretation of a deed upon the manifest intent of the parties, and for that purpose they have even taken great liberties with the language of the instrument, and even with the order in which the words are placed, so as to effectuate the intention.   Now in this case if the legal estate remained in the trustees, *Gwen Lloyd,* the settlor, could only have an equitable estate even though the intended marriage never took effect, and the wife would only have an equitable jointure in bar of dower, which clearly would not have that effect, although the object was expressly to bar dower.   Then the limitation to other trustees (Sir *R. Hill* and *J. Wynne*) for 1000 years, with power to sell or mortgage to raise portions for younger children, would be merely an equitable term, for without the legal estate they could not have power to sell or mortgage, which it was clearly the intention of the settlor that they should have.   Again, the clause respecting the lands to be purchased with the wife's fortune shews that the lands when purchased were to go to the same persons as the other property.   Now it is clear the trustees could not have the legal estate in the lands so purchased; so that if it is holden that the settlor had merely the equita-

(a) 2 P. Wms. 146.   (b) Cas. temp. Talb. 138.

ble estate in the lands in question, the express intention of the settlement will be defeated. Upon the subject of the construction of deeds so as to effectuate the intention, the case of *Packhurst* v. *Smith* (a) is an authority. Looking to the whole frame of this settlement, it is quite manifest that it was the intent of the testator merely to make the trustees conduit pipes for conveying the estate in succession to those parties in whose favour uses are declared. Granting, however, that the Court is constrained to decide against the lessor of the plaintiff upon the first and second points, still, thirdly, there is sufficient ground here for presuming, after so long a lapse of time, a reconveyance of the legal estate from the trustees, and for this *Warren* v. *Grenville* (b) is an authority.

Shadwell, *W. O. Russell*, and *E. V. Williams*, contrà. It cannot be denied that this instrument is most informal, and contains so many blunders throughout that it is impossible to collect the real intention of the settlor. In such a case therefore it is the duty of the Court, if there happen to be expressions so plain as to admit of no doubt as to their legal import, to give effect to those words in support of the analogies of the law, rather than speculate upon the intentions of the parties. The rule applicable to the construction of wills is different from that by which deeds are construed. As far however as the intention of the parties to this instrument can be collected, it is plain that the estate of inheritance was to be preserved. This could only be done by holding that the legal estate vests in the releasees for uses. If the legal estate did not so vest, the intent of the settlor would be defeated, because there being no trustees to preserve contingent remainders, it would have been in the power of the first tenant for life to defeat all the contingent remainders and destroy the estate of inheritance. So that admitting that intention is to be the key to this very obscure instrument, the trustees must have the legal

(a) Willes, 327.　　　　(b) 2 Stra. 1129.

estate. But taking the words of the settlement in their legal sense, as far as they are free from doubt, it is impossible to point out any substantial difference between this case and Lady *Whetstone* v. *Bury*(a), and *The Attorney General* v. *Scott* (b). In *Tipping* v. *Cousins*(c) a dictum of Lord *Hale* is cited, that whether feoffees take by the common law or by the statute, yet where the use is once disposed of to them and their heirs, whether the statute executes or not, there cannot be a use upon a use, nor a trust upon such use to be executed by the statute. To the same effect is the case of *Robinson* v. *Conyers*(d). The remaining question then is, whether it can be presumed that there was a reconveyance of the legal estate to the lessor of the plaintiff, or to the party from whom the title is not derived. This is not like the case of a surrender of a term. Here there is no probable ground for presuming a reconveyance. *Gwn Lloyd* died in 1774, his wife died in 1782, and the person under whom the lessor of the plaintiff claims had possession only for five years, namely, from 1782 to 1787. This point however was not made at the trial. Indeed it was not probable that it would, for it was inconsistent with the argument there maintained, that the legal estate never vested in the trustees. A strong *primâ facie* case should be made out even before it should be left to a jury to presume a reconveyance; *Doe* v. *Reed*(e). Here there was no circumstance to warrant a presumption of that kind, and therefore there was nothing to leave to the jury.

BAYLEY, J.—I am of opinion that we ought not to make the rule absolute for entering a nonsuit in this case, but that we ought to grant a new trial, because I think, considering the length of time that has elapsed since all the

(a) 2 P. Wms. 146.
(b) Cas. temp. Talbot. 138.
See Hargrave and Butler's Notes, 105, to Co. Litt. 206 a.
(c) Comb. 312.
(d) Cas. temp. Talb. 164.
(e) 5 B. & A. 232.

purposes of this deed were at an end, there was ground for
submitting to the consideration of the jury whether there
had not been a reconveyance of the legal estate to *Catherine*
and *Mary Lloyd*, or one of them.　The first question in
the case arises upon the construction to be put upon the
deed of settlement of the 12th of *May*, 1746, for if that
deed passes the legal estate, not to *Giwn Lloyd* and his
wife, or to the children, but vests the legal estate in Sir *W.
W. Wynne* and *E. Lloyd*, then the lessor of the plaintiff
had not at the time this ejectment was brought the legal
estate, unless it had been reconveyed to him by those trustees or by the heirs of the survivor of them.　That brings
us to the question, what is the legal construction of the
words of this deed.　The limitation is to Sir *W. W. Wynne*
and *E. Lloyd*, and their heirs and assigns, *habendum* to
them their heirs and assigns, to the only proper use and
behoof of them their heirs and assigns upon certain trusts.
I felt as the case was going on and Mr. *Taunton* was arguing it, that this was a very singular form of conveyance,
and I could not help thinking that the words " to the use
and behoof of them, their heirs and assigns," had by some
accident or other been introduced by mistake into this
part of the deed, but I now think they were introduced by
design, but through ignorance on the part of the person
who prepared it.　Unless effect is given to one particular
part of the deed, the whole will be inoperative.　The
limitation is to the trustees, their heirs and assigns, *habendum* to the use of them, their heirs and assigns, in trust for
Giwon Lloyd and his heirs until the marriage.　It certainly
strikes me as a singular thing that the moment the deed
was executed the settlor should dispossess himself entirely
of the legal estate, and become equitable owner of the fee
only; and that he and his wife should be equitable tenants
for life, with the legal estate for life in the trustees.　It is
also singular that the term created for raising portions should
be a mere equitable term, and that the lands to be purchased with the 4000*l*. should be limited in so confused a

manner as to leave it doubtful whether or not the *cestui que trust* would take the legal estate. That would not necessarily be the case, for the direction, that the estates purchased should be limited " for such estate and estates" as the other premises, might mean for equitable estates; and therefore this is not inconsistent with the idea that the trustees were to take the legal estate. The observation made by Mr. *Shadwell* is extremely cogent, namely, that unless the trustees had taken the legal estate the very moment the deed was executed, it would have been in the power of the husband and wife to defeat all the purposes of the settlement, and in the power of the husband alone, in the event of his surviving his wife, to have defeated the interests of the children. It seems to me, therefore, that so strong a purpose was to be answered by construing these words according to their legal operation, that I think we are not at liberty to put any other sense upon them than that in which they are generally understood in the law. During the many years I have been in the profession of the law, I have always understood that where there is a limitation of a use upon a use, the second use can never be executed, and that that is one of the distinctions between a trust and a use. Mr. *Taunton* concedes that that is the general principle, but he takes the distinction between this and the ordinary case, for here the trust use is limited to the same person who is the original settlor. He says, where you limit the estate to *A.* to the use of *A.* in trust for *B.* then *A.* is not in by the statute of uses, but by operation of the common law. To that I agree; but of what is he in? He is in of the estate clothed with the use, which is only absorbed in him but not extinguished. The case of *Jenkins* v. *Young* (a), cited in argument, was a case where the limitation was to husband and wife, *habendum* to the use of the husband and wife and their heirs. One of the questions was, whether they took under the statute of uses or at the common law, and it was decided

(a) Cro. Car. 230, 244.

that she took at common law; but what was the reason
given? The Court said, the use was not divided from the
estate, as where it is limited to a stranger, but that the use
and the estate went together. Therefore that case goes no
farther than to decide that, although the trustee in this
case might be in by the common law, yet they were in of
the estate and also of the use. In the course of the argument I asked Mr. *Taunton* if he knew of a case where the
limitation was to *A.* in trust for *B.*, in which it was decided
that the legal estate vested not in *A.* but *B.*, and he said there
was no such case to be found. Now there are two cases
in which the very point most directly arose, and the authority of which has never been since questioned in any Court
of law or equity. The first case I allude to is *Lady Whetstone* v. *Bury* (a), in which the words used were precisely
the same as those found in the deed in question. The
limitation there was to the trustees and their heirs, to the
use of them and their heirs, to the use of the husband for
life, remainder to the use of the trustees and their heirs,
and the Court held that the use of the estate was executed
in the trustees. So in the case of the *Attorney General* v.
Scott (b), which came before Lord *Talbot*, one of the
greatest real property lawyers that this kingdom ever knew,
the decision was to the same effect. These cases establish
that the legal estate vest in him to whom by the words of
the instrument the use is limited. On the authority of these
cases it is plain that we are under the necessity of holding
that the original estate in this case legally vested by means
of this deed in the persons named as trustees, Sir *W. W.
Wynne* and *E. Lloyd.* I think, however, that there ought
not to be a nonsuit, but a new trial granted. It is true that
all the purposes of this deed were at an end in 1782, and
we are therefore desired to presume that there had been a
reconveyance of the legal estate by the trustees. I think
we are not at liberty to form any such presumption. There
may be a case in which it would be the duty of the Court

(a) 2 P. Wms. 146.   (b) Cas. temp. Talb. 138.

to presume such an instrument, but I think if we were to do so here, we should be going much beyond what any Court has hitherto done, especially when this question has not yet been discussed before a jury. A jury is the proper tribunal to which such a question ought to be submitted, and therefore I think, considering the length of time that has elapsed since 1782, that the proper course will be to grant a new trial, and have the question of presumption left for the consideration of the jury.

HOLROYD, J.—For the reasons stated by my learned brother *Bayley*, I think there should be a new trial and not a nonsuit entered. When I first read this deed I had no doubt upon my own mind that the legal estate was in the trustees and not in the *cestui que trust*, having always understood it to be a well settled principle of law (without adverting to the statute of uses, or the distinction taken by Mr. *Taunton*) that a use cannot be limited upon a use. I was certainly very much struck with the argument used by Mr. *Taunton*, which went to shew that the first use was not executed by the statute, but by the common law, and that as the first use was of no effect, the second might be considered as executed by the statute as the only limitation to uses in the deed. But upon further consideration I am of opinion that this case cannot be decided on that principle, and that there are express authorities against it. It may be true that the trustees under the deed are seised by the common law and not by the statute, but still they are seised to the use of themselves, and to the use of another, in which case alone the use is executed by the statute. It appears to me, therefore, that the use is not executed in the *cestui que trust*, but in the trustees, and that they take the legal estate. As to the question of intention, I think we cannot reject the words " to the use and behoof of them their heirs and assigns," which if we did, that would render the deed inconsistent with other parts of it; but even if it should appear that the parties intended that the law should not

1827.

Dœ
v.
Passingham.

operate so as to execute the use in the trustees, yet if the settlor has given the estate to the use of the trustees, the intent of the parties cannot countervail the operation of law. I am, however, by no means satisfied that it was the intention of the parties that the deed should not take effect in the way which the words would by law operate. It is clear that the settlor meant to settle his property as an estate of inheritance. If he did not, then it was in the power of the husband and wife at any time to defeat all the provisions of the settlement. The absence also of trustees to preserve contingent remainders affords a strong reason for believing that the intention was that the legal estate should vest in the trustees. With respect to the estates to be purchased with the 4000*l*. I think there is nothing inconsistent in the terms of that part of the settlement with the former, so as to prevent us from giving effect to the words conveying the legal estate to the trustees.

LITTLEDALE, J.—I am of the same opinion. With respect to the intention that may be supposed to exist in the mind of the settlor, it is argued that that intention would be entirely defeated, if we were to hold that the legal estate is in the trustees. Certainly if we were not construing a deed, I should be disposed to give full latitude to words expressing a clear intent; but if the intention of parties is to be collected by collating various parts of a deed, and acted upon contrary to the plain words of the instrument, I am afraid we should open the door to great confusion in cases of this kind. I have never entertained a doubt that a use upon a use cannot be executed; and although there may be cases shewing that the trustees here took the estate by the common law, still it is equally clear that they took it coupled with a use. The cases cited on this point are decisive, and they are well collected by Serjeant *Williams*, in *Jefferson* v. *Morton* (a). I think, however, that although we are bound to hold that the trustees took the legal estate,

(a) 2 Saund. 11, n. 17 and 18.

1887.

Doe
v.
Passingham.

still there ought to be a new trial on the question, whether it ought not to be presumed that there was a reconveyance.

Rule absolute for a new trial.

BOYLE *v.* TAMLYN.

A. being possessed of two closes divided by a fence and gate, sold one to B., and afterwards the other to C. C. twice repaired the gate at his own expense, after notice from B. to do so, under a threat, in one instance, of impounding his cattle if he did not:—Held, that this was some evidence to go to the jury, from which they might presume a legal obligation on the part of B. to repair the gate. Such an obligation may be declared upon, as being "in respect of the defendant's occupation," though it is evidenced by a deed.

THIS was an action upon the case. The declaration stated that the plaintiff was possessed and in the occupation of a certain close of land in the parish of *East Down*, in the county of *Devon*, and that the defendant was possessed and in the occupation of a certain other close of land contiguous to and next adjoining to the close of the plaintiff, and divided therefrom by a certain fence, and in which fence there was, and of right ought to be, a certain gate and gateway between the close of the plaintiff and the close of the defendant; and the defendant, by reason of the possession of his close during all the time aforesaid, of right ought to have kept up and maintained, and still of right ought to keep up and maintain, the said gate between the close of the plaintiff and the close of the defendant, at all times of the year, in order that cattle lawfully feeding or being in the close of the plaintiff might not, for want of a sufficient gate between the plaintiff's close and the close of the defendant, escape from and out of the plaintiff's close into the close of the defendant, or into any other land or closes of any other person, over and through the close of the defendant, and do any damage there: yet the defendant unjustly unhung, took, and carried away the said gate between the plaintiff's close and the close of the defendant, and suffered and permitted the gateway to be and remain without a gate thereto for a long space of time, whereby the plaintiff's cattle escaped. The defendant pleaded not guilty. At the trial before *Littledale*, J., at the last summer assizes for the county of *Devon*, the case

was this:—The plaintiff was owner and occupier of some
land called the *Deans,* and the defendant was the owner
and occupier of a close called *Deadmoor,* adjoining to the
plaintiff's land. A fence in which was a gate, erected on
the defendant's land, separated the land of each party.
Both parcels of land formerly belonged to a person named
Coffin, who, about 30 years since, sold the *Deans* to the
plaintiff's father, and two years afterwards sold *Deadmoor*
to the defendant. The gate in the parting fence was repaired by the tenant of *Deadmoor* whilst the whole of the
lands belonged to *Coffin.* After the plaintiff's father had
bought *Deans,* but before the defendant bought *Deadmoor,*
the cattle belonging to one *Fry,* the then tenant of *Deadmoor,* having trespassed upon *Deans,* the plaintiff's father
gave notice to *Fry,* that unless he repaired the gate he
would impound his cattle. Upon this *Fry* repaired the
gate. After the defendant came into possession of *Deadmoor* the gate again got out of repair, upon which the
plaintiff's father called upon the defendant to repair the
gate, which he did accordingly. These were the facts
relied upon by the plaintiff to shew the defendant's liability
to repair the gate. On the part of the defendant it was
contended, that, in the absence of any express agreement
upon the subject, the mere fact of a gate having been
repaired twice, once by the former tenant of *Deadmoor,*
and the second time by the defendant himself, was no evidence to go to the jury to sustain an obligation to do an
act merely for the benefit of the plaintiff. The learned
Judge thought that there was evidence to go to the jury,
from which they might presume that there had been an
agreement between the plaintiff's father and the defendant
that the gate should be kept up by the latter for the benefit
of the plaintiff, telling them that, in point of law, the obligation to repair the gate, if any, could only be created by
specific agreement between the parties, regard being had to
the fact, that the land of each party had originally belonged
to *Coffin.* The jury found that the defendant was bound

by agreement to repair the gate. Liberty was, however, reserved by the learned Judge to move to enter a nonsuit, and in *Michaelmas* term last a rule nisi was granted accordingly for that purpose, against which

Merewether now shewed cause. The question is, whether the fact of the gate being repaired twice after notice to the tenant *Fry* and to the defendant respectively, does or does not raise the presumption of an agreement to repair, when accompanied with the fact that the plaintiff's father told *Fry*, " if you don't repair, I will impound your cattle." Now it must be admitted that this, if not conclusive, was cogent evidence of an agreement to repair, and at all events threw upon the defendant the burthen of shewing that the occupier of *Deadmoor* did not repair by virtue of a legal obligation. It cannot be denied that there was some evidence to go to the jury upon this point, and the case having been left to them by the learned Judge in that view, their finding ought not to be disturbed. The jury have presumed, upon the evidence, that an agreement had existed; but even upon much slighter evidence the Court would be slow in disturbing their verdict. In *Wilkinson* v. *Payne* (a) it was held, that the jury having found a verdict for the plaintiff upon a presumption contrary to evidence, the Court will not grant a new trial if the plaintiff be entitled to recover in conscience and equity. In giving judgment in that case, Lord *Kenyon* cited *Standen* v. *Standen* (b), where the jury presumed a legal marriage, though there was strong evidence to induce a suspicion that there had not been time enough for the bans to have been published three times. These cases shew, that where a presumption can be raised to support a verdict, the Court will not disturb the finding of the jury. Here there was evidence that the defendant and his predecessor in the occupation of the land had repaired the gate after notice, and that is evidence to shew that the reparation was in consequence of a legal obligation.

(a) 4 T. R. 468.   (b) Ibid. 469.

The general rule is, that where there is an existing fence between adjoining lands, the obligation of repairing is cast upon one or other of the occupants, and then the fact of its having been repaired by one is conclusive evidence of the obligation. [*Littledale*, J. Suppose this obligation to repair arose by deed or by a clause in the conveyance, or otherwise, would the declaration averring the defendant's liability to repair, " by reason of his possession," be sufficient? *Fentiman* v. *Smith* (a).] In that case the question was, whether as of *right* the party had the use of the watercourse. The obligation to repair may arise merely from possession. There are many cases which go to shew that it is sufficient to state in the declaration, that the defendant was bound to repair by reason of " his possession;" *The Queen* v. *Sir John Bucknall* (b), *Cheetham* v. *Handrom* (c), *Star* v. *Rookesby* (d), *Anonymous* (e), and *Rider* v. *Smith* (f). In the case last cited *Buller*, J. said, " the distinction is between cases where the plaintiff lays a charge upon the right of the defendant, and where the defendant himself prescribes in right of his own estate. In the former case the plaintiff is presumed to be ignorant of the defendant's estate, and cannot therefore plead it; but in the latter, the defendant knowing his own estate, in right of which he claims a privilege, must set it forth." [*Bayley*, J. But ought the fact of repair to be considered as presumptive evidence of an agreement to repair, when that fact has a double aspect or effect as to the right it determines? *Holroyd*, J. Inasmuch as a man is not bound to repair against himself, the obligation to repair between him and his neighbour may be extinguished by the unity of possession, but it may arise again by a subsequent liability; but can that liability be created without deed?] The question here is, whether the fact of repairing after notice, and even a threat of impounding cattle, is evidence of a legal obligation to

(a) 4 East, 107.
(b) 2 Ld. Raym. 804.
(c) 4 T. R. 318.
(d) 1 Salk. 335.
(e) 1 Taunt. 264.
(f) 3 T. R. 766.

repair as against a neighbour. [*Bayley*, J. Sometimes the necessity of a fence is taken into the consideration.] But the existence of the fence is evidence of the necessity of it, for one person has sacrificed part of his own land for the purpose of erecting it. Here there was a fence existing between *Deans* and *Deadmoor* at the time when the plaintiff's father purchased the land. He had a right, therefore, to expect that that fence which the owner or occupier of *Deadmoor* then maintained should be repaired by him in future. The case of *Churchill* v. *Evans* (a) is an authority to shew that if two persons have the concurrent possession of the same land, for the purpose that each might take profits of a special nature, distinct from but not inconsistent with the right of the other, the one is bound to guard against any casual damage which, during and by the fair enjoyment of his right, might happen to the other. In that case, however, the parties had distinct rights upon the same land; but here they had not any concurrent right on the land of each other. The original owner of the whole having always repaired the gate, and having sold part to the plaintiff's father, the latter had a right to expect either that the vendor or vendee of the other part would continue to repair it. The fact of continuing to repair it is evidence of an obligation to repair, and casts upon the defendant the burthen of rebutting the presumption arising from such evidence.

Manning, contrà. There was no evidence in this case to warrant the jury in presuming that there had been any agreement in fact entered into by the owner of *Deadmoor* to maintain, at his own expense, the gate in question, for the benefit of the owner or occupier of the plaintiff's land, and therefore the learned Judge ought to have directed a nonsuit. The doctrine of presumption as to the existence of a grant or an agreement does not apply to a case of this description. Where a grant is presumed, it is in conse-

(a) 1 Taunt. 529.

quence of long enjoyment by the supposed grantee, and acquiescence under a wrong by the supposed grantor. Now here there was no evidence of any such enjoyment or acquiescence. The foundation of the plaintiff's claim rests upon an incorporeal right affecting the land of the defendant, namely, a right to have fences maintained at the defendant's expense, for the plaintiff's sole benefit. To support this there ought to have been some evidence of a rightful imposition of the obligation upon the defendant, and his acquiescence under it. The act of repairing the gate did not appear to have been done in consequence of the assertion of any right on the part of the plaintiff, nor from any knowledge and consciousness on the part of the defendant that the obligation was rightful, and could not be resisted. Here, the enjoyment, as it is called, may be satisfactorily accounted for, and is consistent with the fact of there having been no grant or conveyance, and consequently there could have been no ground for presuming one. If it had appeared that the conveyance from *Coffin* to the plaintiff's father had contained the grant of an easement between one close and the other, that was capable of proof; but here there was no attempt to prove the existence of any grant or conveyance, and it was necessary that the jury should be satisfied that a conveyance of the right had in fact existed, before it could be presumed; *Doe* d. *Fenwick* v. *Reed* (a), *Livett* v. *Wilson* (b). There was, indeed, here nothing to leave to the jury. It does not necessarily follow that because the owner or occupier of *Deadmoor* repaired the gate, he did so in consequence of any legal obligation so to do. If it had appeared that the defendant had derived any exclusive advantage from repairing the gate, then there would have been some consideration to support the obligation; but if there were any advantage in maintaining the gate, it must have been mutual, in order to prevent mutual trespasses. If this case was one which ought to have been left to the jury, it ought not to have been withdrawn from

(a) 5 B. & A. 232.　　　_ (b) 3 Bing. 115.

their consideration that the gate was a convenience to both parties. The legitimate evidence was a deed to be produced on the part of the plaintiff, and, in the absence of such evidence, the Judge should have charged the jury to find for the defendant. Had such an agreement ever existed, it must have been made within 30 years, and have been in the possession of the plaintiff; and there is little doubt that if there were such an agreement, it would have been carefully preserved. None being produced, the plaintiff ought to have been nonsuited, or a verdict found for the defendant.

BAYLEY, J.—There is no doubt as to the general rule of law, that a man is only bound to take care that his cattle do not wander from his own land and trespass upon the lands of others. He is under no legal obligation to keep up fences between adjoining closes, of which he is owner; and even where adjoining lands which have once belonged to different persons, one of whom was bound to repair the fences between the two, afterwards become the property of the same person, the pre-existing obligation to repair the fences is destroyed by the unity of ownership. It follows also, that where the person who has so become the owner of the entirety afterwards parts with one of the two closes, the obligation to repair the fences will not revive, unless express words are introduced into the deed or conveyance for that purpose. We may, therefore, leave out of consideration all the acts of repair done by *Coffin* before *Boyle* became the purchaser of *Deans*, and also any acts done by his tenant of the land called *Deadmoor*, because it is quite clear that, during that period, there could be no legal obligation on the occupier of *Deadmoor* to repair; he must have repaired only for his own benefit. It appears, therefore, that within 30 years there was not any legal obligation on the owner or occupier of *Deadmoor* to maintain a fence for the benefit of the owner or occupier of the adjoining land. If any such obligation existed within that period, it must have arisen by deed or other obligatory writing. Then the question is, whether the fact of *Fry* and *Tamlyn* having repaired the gate, under the circumstances proved at the trial, ought to have induced the jury to presume that there had been some instrument binding the owner or occupier of *Deadmoor* to repair the same for the benefit of *Boyle.* That obligation must have been created either by the deed of conveyance from *Coffin* to *Boyle*, or by some subsequent grant or agreement between *Boyle* and the owner of *Deadmoor.* Now *Boyle* purchased *Deans* about 30 years since, and if *Coffin*, after that purchase, was under any legal obligation to repair the gate, that would appear by the deed of conveyance to *Boyle*, which must have been in his own possession, and which, if it were in existence, might have been proved at the trial. If by any clause in that deed *Coffin* became bound to repair the fence, it would be conclusive in favour of the plaintiff's right to recover; but no such deed of conveyance having been produced, I think the fair inference is, that *Coffin* did not bind himself by the deed of conveyance to *Boyle* to keep up the fence between the two closes. I agree that if there was proof of any such stipulation, it would support the allegation, that the defendant, "by reason of his possession," was bound to repair, *Compton* v. *Rulands* (a), for then the grant would be *evidence* only of the liability. Such a right to have fences repaired by the owner of adjoining lands is in the nature of a grant of a distinct easement, affecting the land of a grantor. The authorities referred to shew that it is usual in such cases to allege that the occupier of the land is, "by virtue of his possession," bound to repair. Assuming then that the deed of conveyance to *Boyle* was silent on the subject of repairing the fence, then the obligation to repair for the benefit of *Boyle* could only arise by some deed subsequently made between him and the owner of *Deadmoor*; by which the latter bound himself to repair the fence. If there ever was such a deed, it must have been

(a) 1 Price, 27.

in the possession of the plaintiff or his father, and it ought
to have been produced at the trial, or at least evidence
ought to have been given to shew that it was lost or destroyed; but no such deed having been produced, nor any
evidence given of its being lost or destroyed, I think that,
under the circumstances of this case, the fair inference is,
that no such deed in fact ever existed. The improbability
of such a deed ought at all events to have been presented
strongly to the consideration of the jury, and I think that
they ought to have found for the defendant. But then it
is insisted that there ought to have been a nonsuit. That,
however, could not be, if there was *any* evidence at all to
go to the jury to shew that the defendant was bound to
repair. Now the facts proved were these:—*Boyle*, the
plaintiff's father, purchased the *Deans* 30 years ago, and
the defendant purchased *Deadmoor* about two years afterwards. *Fry*, during those two years, having continued a
tenant of *Coffin*, repaired the gate. It appeared that applications were made by the plaintiff to the occupier of *Deadmoor* to repair. On the first occasion the plaintiff said,
" you must repair, or I shall impound your cattle." On
the second, the defendant was merely told that he must
repair, but he was not told that if he did not repair, and
the plaintiff sustained damage in consequence of his cattle
trespassing upon the lands of other persons, that he, the
plaintiff, should look for compensation from the occupier
of *Deadmoor*. The fact, therefore, of the gate being repaired on these two occasions did not distinctly shew that
the repairs were done by virtue of any legal obligation to
do so. Still it appears to me that there was some though
very slight evidence to go to the jury that the defendant
was bound to repair, for the fence might have been considered a mutual benefit to the plaintiff and defendant; and
if that were so, unless one of them were bound by law to
repair at his own expense, it might fairly be expected that
each would contribute to the repairs; but the proof being
that the gate was always repaired at the expense of the

occupier of *Deadmoor*, that fact afforded some evidence (I admit very slight) that he was bound to repair. Upon the whole, therefore, I am of opinion that the rule ought to be made absolute for a new trial; but as the weight of evidence appears to me to have been greatly in favour of the defendant, it ought to be without costs.

HOLROYD, J.—I have had very strong doubts whether there was any evidence to go to the jury, but I cannot say that there was none. The nonproduction of any deed, or of evidence to shew that a deed had ever existed, strongly negatives the liability charged upon the defendant. The probability is, that if this were intended to be an easement for the occupier of *Deans*, the right to it would have been expressed in the conveyance, as an appurtenant; and though such a stipulation should have been made, I think it is well declared upon in this case.

LITTLEDALE, J.—I am of the same opinion. There certainly was some evidence for the jury, and I did not think myself at liberty to withdraw it from their consideration, although I confess I was much surprised at their verdict. I told them, that when the whole of the land belonged to *Coffin*, he was under no legal obligation to keep up a fence between the different parts of his own land, and that when he sold one field to the plaintiff, it did not therefore follow that he sold him a privilege of having a gate or fence maintained by him, *Coffin*, on his remaining land, for the benefit of *Boyle*, for that was not necessary to the enjoyment of the land, although it might have been matter of specific agreement between the parties. I further told them, that when *Coffin* afterwards sold the land called *Deadmoor*, that would not necessarily throw upon the defendant the obligation to repair the gate for the benefit of the plaintiff; and if any such obligation existed, it must have arisen also in consequence of some express agreement between the plaintiff and the defendant. I pointed out the principle of the cases relating to rights of way and rights of common, and told them that that principle did not strictly apply to the present case, because in the case of every user of a way, or of a common, an act is done by one man upon the land of another, and unless it has been done with the acquiescence of the owner of the land, it must have been wrongful. I further told them, that the user of a way or a common for a long period, under circumstances which shew an acquiescence on the part of the owner of the land, raises an inference that the user has always been rightful, and affords evidence for a jury to presume in fact that there has been some grant or conveyance of the easement by the owner of the land to the person who has so used it. I pointed their attention to the fact, that in no instance had the defendant permitted the plaintiff to do any act upon his, the defendant's, land, and that he might fairly say that he repaired the gate for his own benefit, and to prevent his own cattle from trespassing upon the plaintiff's land. I told them, however, that if they thought the fact of the occupier of *Deadmoor* having always repaired the gate, and having in two instances repaired it after notice from the plaintiff to do so, amounted to an admission, on his part, that he was bound to repair the gate for the benefit of the plaintiff, they might presume that there had been an agreement between the parties to that effect. With these observations I left the case to the jury, and they found for the plaintiff; but as I am not satisfied with their verdict, I think there ought to be a new trial granted.

Rule absolute for a new trial.

Roe, on the demise of George Richley and Bridget, his wife, v. Burn.

THIS was an ejectment for an undivided fourth part of a dwelling-house and orchard, with the appurtenances, in the parish of *Corbridge*, in the county of *Northumberland*. The declaration contained two demises, first by *George Richley* and *Bridget* his wife, and secondly by *George Richley* alone. The demises were laid on the 2d of *April*, 1825. Plea, the general issue. At the trial before *Bayley*, J. at the summer assizes for the county of *Northumberland* in 1825, a verdict was found for the lessor of the plaintiff, subject to the opinion of the Court on the following case:—

William Burn, of *Corbridge*, in the county of *Northumberland*, being seised in fee of the premises, whereof one-fourth part is sought to be recovered in this action, on the 12th day of *March*, 1805, made the following will, which was duly executed and attested so as to pass real estates:—

"In the name of God, amen. I, *William Burn*, of *Corbridge*, gardener, in the parish of *Corbridge*, in the county of *Northumberland*, being in perfect understanding, but weak in health, praise be God, do make this my last will and testament, as followeth: that is to say, I give and bequeath unto my son *William*, which is now absent from home, 20*l.* of money of *Great Britain* extra, more than any other of my sons; and likewise unto *Ann Burn*, my wife, the whole of my effects during her life; also the freehold estate which I now enjoy, I bequeath as follows, *Ann Burn* my daughter, *James Burn* and *John Burn* my sons, likewise *Bridget Burn*, otherwise *Newbigun*, all the last-mentioned names, to be all equal sums, whatever it may amount to, except any of the aforementioned should die or be deceased, then their shares to be equally divided among the other that is surviving. In witness &c." The testator died within a few days after the making of this will, leaving all the persons therein named him surviving. *George*

Testator willed as follows: "I give and bequeath to my son W. 20*l.* extra more than any other of my sons; and likewise unto A. B. my wife, the whole of my effects during her life; also the freehold estate which I now enjoy, I bequeath as follows: A. B. my daughter, J. B. and I. B. my sons, likewise B. B. otherwise N., all the last mentioned names to be all equal sums, whatever it may amount to, except any of the aforementioned should die, then their shares to be equally divided among the other that is surviving:" —Held, that the freehold estate was devised to A. B., J. B., I. B. and that B. B. otherwise N. having been ousted by A.B. might maintain ejectment for one undivided fourth part.

Richley, one of the lessors of the plaintiff, after the testator's death, intermarried with the said *Bridget Burn*, otherwise *Newbigun*, the other lessor of the plaintiff. Upon the testator's death, his widow entered into possession of the house and orchard with the appurtenances at *Corbridge*, and continued to hold them until her death in *December*, 1824. Upon her death, the defendant, her daughter, and one of the devisees in the will, possessed herself of the whole of the said premises, and still retains the possession, having actually ousted the lessors of the plaintiff therefrom. The question for the opinion of the Court is, whether the lessors of the plaintiff are entitled to recover.

E. Alderson, for the lessors of the plaintiff. This, it must be admitted, is a very absurd will. The question is, whether, upon the construction of it, it is not a bequest for life to *Ann Burn*, the testator's widow, with remainder to the four children in fee, as tenants in common after her death. The rule in cases of this kind is, that if the intention of the testator can be collected, effect is to be given to it without a strict adherence to the mere words of the will. Now in this case it is quite clear that the testator meant to dispose of all his property; for after giving 20*l.* beyond what his other sons are to have, he goes on, " likewise unto *Ann Burn*, my wife, the whole of my effects during her life." The word " effects" will include landed property, if it can be collected that the intention was to pass the real estate; *Doe* d. *Andrew* v. *Lainchbury* (a). There the devise was of all the residue of the testator's " money, stock, property, and *effects*, of what kind or nature soever, to *A.* and *B.*" and it was held that these words would pass real as well as personal property, where from other parts of the will it appeared that the testator had applied the words *property* and *effects* to real estate. In *Hunter* v. *Brooman* (b) a devise of " all I am worth," which can mean no more than " all my property," was held to include realty. In

(a) 11 East, 290.   (b) 1 Bro. Ch. Ca. 437.

the present case, therefore, the devise is sufficient to pass
the realty to the wife for life by force of the word "effects."
This is the necessary conclusion if any operation is to be
given to the clause of the will which follows, bequeathing
the freehold estate to the four persons after named. The
bequest of 20*l.* to the son *William* cannot control this construction, because it clearly means no more than that he
shall have that sum extra his share of the personalty, if any
should be left. The devise to the wife will be inoperative,
if it be not held that she took for life with remainder to the
four persons afterwards named. [*Bayley,* J. Suppose the
estate does not go to the wife at all?] Then the freehold
is undisposed of. [*Bayley,* J. May he not have given all
his personal effects to his wife and his freehold estate to
his children? He says, " I give the whole of my effects to
my wife for life ; and the *freehold* estate which I now enjoy
I give to my children.] There was an adverse possession
in the wife until her death. The devise to the wife for
life shews that he intended to give the remainder in fee to
come into possession after her death, for otherwise the will
would be inconsistent.

C. *Cresswell,* contrà. It is not necessary in this case to
dispute whether the word "effects" is sufficient to pass
real estate. All that it is necessary to shew is that this will
is incapable of the construction contended for on the other
side. The true rule in construing wills apparently insensible, is well laid down by Lord *Kenyon* in *Lane v. Earl Stan-
hope* (*a*), where that learned judge says, " It is our duty in
construing a will to give effect to the devisor's intention as
far as we can consistently with the rules of law, not conjec-
turing but expounding his will from the words used." This
rule was afterwards mentioned with great approbation by Lord
Eldon in *Thompson* v. *Lady Lawley* (*b*). Now expounding
this will by that rule, it will be found that the construction
on the other side cannot be supported. At all events, if it

(*a*) 6 T. R. 352.   (*b*) 2 B. & P. 308.

can be shewn that the will is so insensible as to be capable of several different interpretations, then it will be void for uncertainty, and the heir at law will take, which will be a sufficient answer to this action. In the first place, the testator gives to his son *William* 20*l.* without pointing out the fund out of which that bequest is to come, nor does it appear that he had any personal property applicable to the payment of it. So that if the construction on the other side be correct, as the testator had only real property, *William*, who appears to be a peculiar object of the testator's bounty, would have less than his brothers and sisters. Whatever personal property was left, the whole of it was to go to the widow, and it could not be that the 20*l.* was to come out of that fund. He gives the whole of his *effects* to his wife during her life. This must be taken as a distinct and independent clause. He then goes on as with a new paragraph (for so it must be taken to be from the language of the bequest to the wife), " Also the *freehold estate* which I now enjoy I bequeath as follows." It is manifest the testator could not use the word *effects* as descriptive of his *real estate*, for immediately afterwards he uses the term " freehold estate." He could not use the words " effects" and " freehold estate" in the same line, as meaning the same thing. Certainly the principal point to be decided is whether the testator meant to make a full stop at the words " during her life." If the words " Also the freehold estate" &c. be taken as the beginning of a new sentence, then it is clear that the testator did not intend the persons named to take the estate itself, but that the estate should be sold and the proceeds divided amongst them in " equal sums." Then what becomes of the bequest of 20*l.* to the son *William*, who was to have more than any of his sons ? This also shews that the testator intended his freehold to be sold. No case precisely like this is to be found; but as far as one man's nonsense can be scanned by another's the case of *Thomas Hyde* v. *James Hyde*(a) is

(a) *Coram* the Vice Chancellor in 1819, but not reported.

something analogous to this. There the testator devised
an estate to his two sons, in trust for several grandchildren,
" share and share alike, and *to be paid* each of them their
shares, as they shall attain the age of twenty-one years;"
and it was held that this was a devise in trust to sell. It
being impossible, however, to give a safe and consistent
construction to the present will, it must be treated as void,
and the estate will descend to the heir at law. Such a construction will entitle the defendant to judgment on this
ejectment. Unless the Court decides that the estate was
devised to the wife for life, and then to the children in trust
to sell, and divide the proceeds amongst them, it is impossible to deal with the will on account of its uncertainty.

Alderson, in reply. The whole contents of the will shew
that the son *William* was to derive no benefit from the
devise of the real estate, because he is not named as one of
the four persons specified as takers. It is true that he is to
receive 20*l*. more than the *other sons;* but the devise of the
real estate is to four persons by name, two of whom are his
other sons, one a daughter, and the last a person who is
neither son or daughter of the testator. Assuming the
argument on the other side to be well founded, that the
estate was to be sold, still the four devisees would be entitled each to an equal share of the proceeds, and they are
the persons to sell. If a real estate is devised to be sold
for payment of debts, and the person to sell is not named,
as the proceeds are to pass through the hands of the executors, they are the persons to sell, *Bentham v. Wiltshire* (a),
Shepherd's Touchstone, p. 43. [*Bayley*, J. Out of what
fund is the son *William's* 20*l*. to come?] Out of the testator's personal estate, if any, for it is clear that the real estate
is to be divided in equal sums amongst the four persons
named in the devise.

Abbott, C. J.—It certainly is not very easy to say out

(a) 4 Maddox, 44.

of what fund the testator's son *William* was to have 20*l.*
more than his other sons. There is great difficulty in
making that out. Possibly there may have been personalty
sufficient to satisfy that bequest. It is suggested in argument, that he was probably to receive it out of the proceeds
of the real estate when sold; but I think we cannot connect
the clause giving 20*l.* to *William* with the clause giving the
freehold estate, not to *William* and other sons, but to two
sons named *James* and *John*, and to a daughter *Ann*, and
to a fourth person named *Bridget Burn*, otherwise *Newbigun*, which last was neither a son or a daughter of the
testator. It is, however, unnecessary to decide that point.
Neither is it necessary to decide whether the estate in land
was given to the wife for life, for no question turns upon
that, she having actually enjoyed the estate for her life. I
am of opinion that unless we disconnect the words " also
the freehold estate which I now enjoy," from the previous
words of the devise to the wife, there will be no subject-
matter on which the subsequent part of the will could
operate. It will then run thus, " also the freehold estate
which I now enjoy I bequeath as follows: *Ann Burn*, my
daughter, *James Burn* and *John Burn* my sons, likewise
Bridget Burn, otherwise *Newbigun*, all the last mentioned
names to be equal sums, whatever it may amount to, except
any of the aforesaid should die or be deceased, then their
shares to be equally divided among the other that is surviving." In order to give some sense to these words, to
supply some object, some matter of gift to the four persons
here named, it seems to me that we must connect with
them the words " also the freehold estate which I now
enjoy," and say that the testator has given his freehold
estate to these four persons for their equal advantage with
benefit of survivorship. That being so, I think we must
also say that those who were to have the benefit of the land
were the proper persons to sell it and make an equal
division of the proceeds, the will being silent as to the time
and mode of sale. It, therefore, follows that as the estate

has not in fact been sold, the lessors of the plaintiff are entitled to maintain ejectment for an undivided one-fourth.

BAYLEY, J.—I think that the gift to the son *James* of 20*l.*, when taken in connexion with the gift to the wife of the whole of the testator's effects, may fairly raise an inference that there was personal estate sufficient to give *William* 20*l.* more than any of the testator's other sons. He then goes on, " and likewise unto *Ann Burn*, my wife, the whole of my effects during her life." Stopping there, the gift of 20*l.* to *James* may be considered as a charge upon the personal estate only; for I cannot think the latter clause of the will, giving the freehold estate to four persons by name, would be subject to the charge of satisfying his legacy. It could only be a charge upon the personalty. Then, when the testator gives the whole of his effects to his wife during her life, it seems that the testator there came to a termination of the sentence. He says, " during life." That is a specification of the period of time during which she is to hold, and there, as it appears to me, the gift to the wife ceases, and that nothing more than effects were given to her. In all reasonable construction, when a testator concludes a gift in such words, the presumption is, that he there means to end the gift, and give no more to the object of his bounty thus mentioned. I think the word " also" may here be read as " item," which is the commencement of a new devise, according to the general rules. If so, then the freehold estate is by a new clause devised to the four persons afterwards named, as joint tenants or tenants in common ; whether one or the other is immaterial to the present case. I think the words " whatever *it* may amount to," shew clearly that these persons were to take the freehold estate, for to nothing else can those words refer.

HOLROYD, J.—I think that the devise to the son *William* of 20*l.* more than to the other sons was a charge upon the personal estate. I am also of opinion that the devise in the last clause was of the freehold to the four persons therein named; and that whether the estate itself was to be divided or whether it was to be sold and the proceeds divided, it was equally a devise to them. I, therefore, think the lessor of the plaintiff is entitled to the one-fourth part which she now claims (a).

Postea to the plaintiff.

(a) *Littledale*, J. was at the Old Bailey.

STEPHEN FORD v. HENRY WOODHAM TILEY.

A. agrees with B. to grant the latter a lease of a house as soon as he becomes possessed thereof, to bear date from the 21st of December, 1825, for fourteen or twenty-one years. At the date of the agreement the house was under a lease which would not expire till Midsummer, 1827; the legal estate being in trustees, first, to pay debts, and, secondly, to pay an annuity to T. and subject thereto to the use of A. if he attained twenty-four. In June,

THIS was an action of assumpsit for the breach of an agreement to grant a lease of a house and premises called the *King's Head*, situate in *Bartlett Street*, in the city of *Bath*. Plea, the general issue. At the trial before *Park*, J. at the last *Lent* assizes for the county of *Gloucester*, a verdict was found for the plaintiff, damages £300, the estimated value of the lease, with liberty to the defendant to move to enter a nonsuit, on the ground that the action was brought too soon, or to have a new trial on the ground that the damages were excessive. In *Easter* term last a rule nisi for that purpose was granted on the motion of *W. E. Taunton*. Cause was shewn in *Trinity* vacation at the sittings before *Bayley*, *Holroyd*, and *Littledale*, Justices, by *Campbell*. *Ludlow* was heard in support of the rule, and the Court having taken time to advise upon the case, judgment was now delivered by

1825, after A. had attained twenty-four, but before the out-standing lease had expired, he and the trustees joined in a fresh lease to C. for twenty-three years: Held, that A. was liable to an action before the expiration of the lease, which would not be out until Midsummer, 1827; but that the measure of damages would only be the value of a lease for so much of the term as upon a calculation of the probable period of the annuitant's death would be likely to be subsisting at the arrival of that period.

BAYLEY, J.—This case came before the Court upon a motion to enter a nonsuit. It was an action for breach of an agreement to grant the plaintiff a lease. The agreement, dated the 3d of *January*, 1824, was, that the defendant should, at the plaintiff's expense, with all possible speed after he should become possessed of or in possession of a certain public house, execute a lease thereof, and also of a furnace which stood upon the premises, from the 21st of *December*, 1825, for fourteen or twenty-one years, if required by the plaintiff, at the yearly rent of £105. It also bound the defendant to put the premises in good and tenantable repair, and to keep the roof in repair, and allow the water rents; and he was to have, as the consideration, £5 down, and £100 on the signing of the lease. The agreement also stipulated that if either party ran from the agreement, or did any thing to prevent the lease from being executed by all necessary parties, he should forfeit £200. The declaration contained three counts, the first and second generally upon the agreement, the third for the penalty. None of them stated that the defendant had been either possessed or in possession, but the first stated that the defendant might have been possessed, but that he fraudulently prevented himself from becoming possessed, and deceitfully refused to take possession. The second stated that he neglected to execute the lease, and ran from the agreement, and prevented the agreement from being executed by the necessary parties. The third was generally that he had run from the agreement, and no lease had been executed. It appeared in evidence on the trial, that at the time of the agreement the house was let upon a lease which would not expire till *Midsummer*, 1827, and that the legal estate was vested in trustees in trust, by lease or mortgage, to raise money to pay debts (which money was not wanted), and then in trust to receive and pay to *Betty Tyler* £25 per annum for her life, with powers to her of entry and distress, and subject thereto (and to the lease or mortgage, if any, to raise money to pay debts) to the use of the defendant, if he attained the age of twenty-four years. On the 24th of *June*, 1825, after the defendant had attained twenty-four, the defendant and the trustees joined in a new lease to

Messrs. Sims and Co. in whom the former lease was vested, for twenty-three years from the 29th of September, 1825, and it was for his concurrence in this lease that the action was brought. It was objected at the trial, and the question was saved, whether the action was not premature, on the ground that the lease, which was in *esse* at the time of the agreement, would not have expired until 1827, and was still, as to those parties, to be deemed as a subsisting lease; but though we are satisfied that that lease is, as between these parties, to be considered as subsisting, and that the defendant cannot hitherto have been taken to have been possessed, and has never had a right to have the possession, we are of opinion that the action is maintainable; because by the lease of *June*, 1825, the defendant has given up his right to have the possession, and has put it out of his power, so long as the lease of *June*, 1825, subsists, to grant the lease he stipulated to grant. It is very true the defendant may obtain a surrender of that lease before *Midsummer*, 1827, and then he will be in a condition to grant the lease he stipulated to grant; but the obtaining such a surrender is not to be expected, and the authorities are, that where a party has disabled himself from making an estate he has stipulated to make at a future day, by making an inconsistent conveyance of that estate, he is considered as guilty of a breach of his stipulation, and is liable to be sued before such day arrives. In 1 *Roll. Abr.* 248, pl. 1, (8 *Vin.* 225,) it is said, " If a day be limited to perform a condition, if the obligor once disables himself to perform it, though he be enabled again before the day, yet the condition is broken; as if the condition be to enfeoff another before *Michaelmas*; if, before the feast, he enfeoff another, though he after re-purchases, yet he cannot perform the condition;" and he cites 21 *Edw.* 4, 55, where *Choke*, who was then one of the Justices of C. B., so lays it down. The same may be collected from *Co. Litt.* 221 b., where, upon a feoffment on condition to re-enfeoff, on payment of a certain sum by the feoffor or his heirs before a certain day, a distinction is taken between a disability in the interim on the part of the feoffor or his heirs, and a disability on the part of the feoffee, a removal of the disability before the day from the feoffors or his heirs entitling them to require a re-enfeoffment, and the removal from the feoffee being no saving to him of the consequences of a breach; and Lord *Coke* adopts *Littleton's* reason, " maintenant, by disability of the feoffee, the condition is broken, and the feoffor may enter." Now if the feoffment of a stranger before the day be a breach of a condition to enfeoff *I. S.* at a given day, the granting of a lease to a stranger before the day will be the breach of a contract to grant a lease to *I. S.* at a given day, and, *a fortiori*, will it be a breach so long as the lease to such stranger remains in force. In this case, therefore, where the defendant has contracted to grant the plaintiff a lease as soon as he is possessed or in possession, and he will be entitled to the possession as soon after *Midsummer*, 1827, as *Betty Tyler*, the annuitant, shall die, and he has created a present disability in himself to grant such lease, if *Betty Tyler* shall die before the term to have been inserted in such lease would have expired, we are of opinion that the defendant's contract was broken by his joining in the lease of 1825, and, therefore, the rule for a nonsuit cannot be made absolute. It appears to us, however, that the damages, to the extent to which they have been given, cannot be supported; and we think (unless the parties can agree) that there ought to be a new trial, that the rule by which the damages should be regulated may be more distinctly laid down to the jury. The damages on the first count certainly cannot be supported; for that is founded upon the supposition that the defendant might have been possessed if he would; whereas, without the consent of the trustees, he had no right at law to possess himself until *Midsummer*, 1827, and the death of *Betty Tyler*. The second or third counts may be supported in respect of that part of them which charges that the defendant has run from his agreement, because we think his destroying his claim of the right of possession is running from his agreement; but then the measure of damages should be, not the value of a lease of fourteen or twenty-one years from *December*, 1825, but the value of a lease for so much of that term as, upon a calculation of the probability of the period of *Betty Tyler's* death, would be likely to be subsisting at the arrival of that period. The rule for a new trial must, therefore, be made absolute.

Rule absolute.

The Earl of FALMOUTH v. PENROSE.

Claim for
fish as toll for
the use of a
capstan and
windlass in
drawing fish-
ing-boats upon
the beach out
of the sea.
*Indebitatus as-
sumpsit* lies for
the fish so
claimed.

ASSUMPSIT to try the right of the plaintiff to have the second best fish out of the cargoes of all fishing-boats landing in a certain cove called *Senn Cove*, in the county of *Cornwall*, in respect of an alleged immemorial obligation to keep up a capstan and rope there for the purpose of hauling the fishing-boats out of the sea. The declaration contained twenty-eight counts. There were several special counts, in which it was alleged that the plaintiff was entitled to the second best fish of all sorts of fish. The declaration also contained several *indebitatus* counts for fish generally. The twenty-fourth count stated that the defendant was indebted to the plaintiff for divers other fish, to wit, one hundred fish of great value, to wit, of the value of £10, for divers other tolls or dues, due and of right payable from the defendant to the plaintiff, for and in respect of the defendant's having before then used and enjoyed, and having had the liberty and privilege of using and enjoying divers capstans, machines, windlasses, and ropes of the said plaintiff, to haul and assist in the hauling of divers boats of the defendant, and of divers other boats which the defendant had used, on to the beach, to wit, at, &c. in the county aforesaid ; and being so indebted, promised to pay, &c. upon request. The defendant pleaded the general issue. At the trial before *Gaselee*, J. at the last *Summer* assizes for the county of *Cornwall*, it appeared in evidence that it was usual for the

owner of every fishing-boat landing his cargo by the help
of the capstan, windlass, and rope provided by the plaintiff
in *Senn Cove*, to select a fish for himself, and for the plaintiff's agent then to select another fish, which fish, when so
selected, was rendered to the plaintiff. The evidence was
contradictory as to the point, whether the custom had been
to render the second best fish of all sorts, or only the
second best fish of all sorts, pilchards excepted. This
question went to the jury upon the evidence, and they
found the custom to have been to render the second best
fish of all sorts, with the exception of pilchards. In the
course of the trial the learned judge rejected the evidence
of a fisherman of *Senn Cove*, on the ground of his alleged
interest in the result of the cause. A verdict was ultimately found for the plaintiff on the *indebitatus* counts, but
the learned judge gave leave to move to enter a nonsuit, if
the Court should be of opinion that the evidence did not
support those counts. In *Michaelmas* term a rule nisi was
granted to enter a nonsuit, or have a new trial, on the
ground of the rejection of evidence.

R. Bayly and *Carter* now shewed cause. It will be
objected on the other side that *indebitatus assumpsit* will
not lie for tolls of fish, in respect of the use of the capstan
and rope. [*Bayley*, J. The word " indebted" may not of
necessity mean indebted for a money debt]. *Indebitatus
assumpsit* will no doubt lie for all sorts of personal chattels.
It would be an absurd refinement to draw any distinction
between money and goods for this purpose. There are
express authorities to shew that debt will lie for chattels,
and if so, it is equally clear that *indebitatus assumpsit* will
lie in respect of any parol contract upon which debt lies;
Fitzherb. N. B. 119 H.; *Com. Dig. Tit. Debt* (A. 5).
Debt lies though the lease be rendering corn or other collateral thing; 1 *Roll.* 591, l. 30; 4 *Leo.* 46; 3 *Leo.* 260;
and *Crawford* v. *Whittal*(a), and *The Mayor of Reading* v.

(*a*) Dougl. 4, (n.) 1.

Clark (a), are authorities to shew that *indebitatus assumpsit* will lie on a contract on which debt would lie. If there were any objection to the form of the declaration, the defendant should have demurred and not pleaded and gone to trial. Then, as to the motion for a new trial, on the ground that the learned judge rejected the evidence of one of the fishermen, it is quite clear that on the issue between these parties he was interested, as one of the body of fishermen frequenting *Senn Cove*, in defeating the right set up by the plaintiff; *Rhodes* v. *Ainsworth* (b), *Clanricard* v. *Denton* (c), *Company of Carpenters in Shrewsbury* v. *Hayward* (d).

C. F. Williams and *Halcomb*, contrà. Here the plaintiff claims fish generally, and not so many fish specifically, and therefore *indebitatus assumpsit* will not lie. Assuming that *indebitatus assumpsit* will lie generally for fish, upon a proper consideration to support the promise, still, in this case, the evidence did not support the counts upon which the verdict of the jury was founded. Those counts rest upon a claim of so many fish generally for tolls. The true ground of claim was for certain specific fish; for the evidence was, that when the owner of a fishing-boat landed his cargo at *Senn Cove*, the practice was for him to select a fish for himself, and then for the plaintiff or his agent to select another to be delivered to the plaintiff; so that if the plaintiff has any right of action he has mistaken his remedy. This being a fatal objection, there is no necessity for deciding the point as to the rejection of evidence.

At first the Court was inclined to think that the twenty-fourth count was free from objection and supported by the evidence, but next day, upon consideration,

BAYLEY, J. said:—We are of opinion that there must be a nonsuit entered. The substantial point for our determination is whether the plaintiff in this case can recover upon

(a) 4 B. & A. 268.   (c) 1 Gwill. 360; 1 Phill. Ev. 54.
(b) 1 B. & A. 87.   (d) Dougl. 373.

a general *indebitatus* count.   It appears to me that in form
the twenty-fourth count is free from objection, and that if
the evidence supported it, the plaintiff would have been entitled to recover.   That count states, that the defendant was
indebted to the plaintiff in divers, to wit, 100 fish, of the
value of £10, for divers tolls or dues, due and of right
payable from the defendant to the plaintiff, for and in respect of the defendant's having before then used and enjoyed, and having had the liberty and privilege of using and
enjoying, divers capstans, machines, windlasses, and ropes of
the plaintiff, to haul and assist in the hauling of divers boats
of the defendant, and of divers other boats which the defendant had used, on to the beach, to wit, &c. in the county
aforesaid, and being so indebted, the defendant, in consideration thereof, undertook and faithfully promised to pay him
the said plaintiff the said last-mentioned fish when he the
said defendant should be thereunto requested."   Now the
authorities cited in argument go to shew that debt will lie
for a chattel.   If so, we see no reason why *assumpsit* will
not also lie, but then the promise as well as the consideration must be proved.   Was there evidence in this case to
support the *indebitatus* counts?   According to the evidence,
it appears to have been the custom for the plaintiff or his
agent to select his fish, and that selection being made, the
same was rendered to him.   If, therefore, the defendant
had refused to render the fish so selected, or had refused to
let the plaintiff select one, he might have maintained a
special action on the case for damages; but there was no
legal liability on the part of the defendant to pay any given
fish to the plaintiff before selection, and, consequently, no
promise is implied by law on his part to do so.   The plaintiff, therefore, has failed to prove any promise or *assumpsit*
on the part of the defendant to render fish generally.   The
rule nisi for a nonsuit must therefore be made absolute.

HOLROYD, J. and LITTLEDALE, J. were of the same
opinion.

Rule absolute.

H. R. COLLING, Gent. one, &c. v. R. H. TREWEEK.

On the trial of an action for an attorney's bill it is not necessary to prove notice to produce the bill delivered before action brought; it is sufficient to give an examined copy in evidence.

ASSUMPSIT for an attorney's bill. Plea, the general issue. At the trial before *Littledale*, J. at the last *Summer* assizes for the county of *Devon*, the cause was undefended. In support of the plaintiff's case it was proved that in pursuance of the statute 2 *Geo.* 2, *c.* 23, *s.* 23, a copy of the bill, signed by the plaintiff, was duly delivered to the defendant one month before action brought. No notice, however, had been served on the defendant to produce the bill so delivered. The witness produced a paper purporting to be a copy of the bill so delivered, which he swore to be an exact copy in his own hand-writing, made at the time the original was made. This copy was not signed by the plaintiff, but his signature had been copied by the clerk. The plaintiff then offered to sign the copy in Court, but the learned judge was of opinion that this was not sufficient to dispense with the notice to produce the original bill delivered to the defendant, and that the copy produced was no evidence of a bill signed by the plaintiff having been delivered to the defendant in pursuance of the statute. Evidence was then given of the retainer and employment of the plaintiff by the defendant as an attorney, and that the business done, which was the subject of this action, was charged for at a reasonable amount. The learned judge, however, thought that the requisites of the statute had not been complied with, and directed a nonsuit, with leave to move to set the nonsuit aside, and enter a verdict for 10*l*. 0*s*. 1*d*., the amount proved. In *Michaelmas* term, *Wright* obtained a rule nisi for that purpose, on two grounds, first, that the bill delivered to the defendant was a notice to him of the amount of the plaintiff's demand, and of his intention to enforce payment by action, unless the defendant had the bill taxed; and, secondly, that assuming it not to be a notice, it was competent to the plaintiff at the trial to sign the copy then produced, and thereby to make it a duplicate original, and he cited *Ex parte Weston* (a), *Ex parte Titley* (b), *Ex parte Bury* (c), *Anderson* v. *May* (d), and *Kine* v. *Beaumont* (e).

Carter and *Tucker* now shewed cause. This case involves a simple point of practice as to the proof of the delivery of an attorney's bill. The plaintiff had given notice to the defendant to produce the bill delivered to him before action brought. That bill not being produced, the plaintiff's clerk produced a paper which he swore was a copy of the bill delivered, but not signed by the plaintiff himself. [*Bayley*, J. But it was a copy made at the time the original was made.] It is true that a duplicate original may be given in evidence without any notice to produce the counterpart, but that is where the duplicate is made at the same time with the corresponding instrument. Now here the copy of the bill could not be considered as a duplicate original, because the clerk only copied the plaintiff's name; it was not signed by the plaintiff himself at the time, which makes all the difference. Here the first paper is signed by the principal, the second by the agent, therefore they are not counterpart originals. In *Philipson* v. *Chace* (f), Lord *Ellenborough* said, "If there be two contemporary writings, the counterparts of each other, one of which is delivered to the opposite party, and the other preserved, as they may both be considered as originals, and they have equal claims to authenticity, the one which is preserved may be received in evidence without notice to produce the one which was delivered;" and he suggested that that must be the ground of the decision in *Anderson* v. *May* (g). In the present case, therefore, the copy of the bill could not be received without notice to produce the original, it not being a con-

(a) 1 Maddox, 75.

(b) 2 Rose, 83.

(c) Buck. B. C. 393.

(d) 2 B. & P. 237.

(e) 3 B. & B. 288.

(f) 2 Campb. 110.

(g) 2 B. & P. 237.

temporaneous duplicate written and signed by the plaintiff at the time the original was written and signed. Then could the fact of the plaintiff signing the copy at the time of the trial make it receivable without notice to produce the original? Clearly not, for still it was open to the objection that it was not a contemporaneous signature with the original. Having failed, therefore, to give the best legal evidence of his having delivered his bill one month before the action was brought, the nonsuit was right.

Wright, contrà. There are two points for consideration, first, whether the copy which was produced at the trial was that sort of instrument which ought to have been received, and if not, secondly, whether at the time the attorney offered to make it a duplicate, it was competent for him to do so. As to the first point, the case of *Philipson* v. *Chase* is not at all applicable, because there no copy of the bill was either proved to have been made or produced in evidence, but the proof attempted to have been given of the delivery of the bill was by reading the items of charge from the plaintiff's books, from which the bill was stated to have been copied. In the present case, a bill was made out and proved at the trial to have been signed by the plaintiff and delivered in time to the defendant, and a copy of that bill and of the plaintiff's signature to it was also produced in evidence. The ostensible object of the statute 2 *Geo.* 2, in requiring the bill to be delivered one month before action brought, is to give the party sought to be charged an opportunity of getting the bill taxed. It is, in effect, a notice of action containing the amount of the plaintiff's demand. On this ground alone the copy produced was legal evidence to dispense with notice to produce the original. In *Kine* v. *Beaumont* two of the learned judges are reported to have said that there was not any difference between a duplicate original and a copy made at the time and authenticated on oath. But the case of *Anderson*

v. *May* (a) is in all points decisive of this, where it was held that a duplicate copy of the bill is sufficient, without a notice to produce the original; and it does not appear in the report of that case that the copy produced had the signature of the plaintiff. Admitting, however, for the sake of argument, that the copy of the bill produced, as well as the original, ought to have been signed by the plaintiff, still it was competent to the plaintiff to sign it at the time of the trial, and to obviate the objection by making it an exact duplicate. The time when the signature is made is no way material, provided the instrument be in all other respects an exact copy. In *Ex parte Weston* (b) it was held, that a bankrupt petition, signed by the agent of the attorney who presented a bankrupt petition, was not a sufficient compliance with an order of the Court of Chancery relating to bankrupt petitions, which requires that the signature of each person signing a petition shall be attested by the petitioner actually presenting the petition; but the attorney and petitioner being in Court when the objection was made, they were permitted to sign the petition, and the objection was then cured. What difference in principle is there between this case and stamping instruments for the purpose of a cause by paying a penalty, or making a person interested a witness by giving him a release in open Court? The case of *Fory* v. *Orchard* (c) shews that it is not necessary to prove a notice to produce a notice of action where a copy is retained.

Curia advisare vult.

BAYLEY, J. delivered the judgment of the Court.—This was an action brought to recover the amount of an attorney's bill. There was a nonsuit, on the ground that a copy of the bill could not be received in evidence, because the plaintiff had not given the defendant notice to produce the original bill delivered to him. A rule nisi was obtained for

(a) 2 B. & P. 237; 3 Esp. 167. (c) 2 B. & P. 39.
(b) 1 Maddox, 75.

entering a verdict for the plaintiff on two grounds, first, that it was not necessary to give any notice to produce the bill delivered to the plaintiff, because that bill itself was a notice, and that it was not necessary in any case to give notice to produce a notice. Secondly, that the witness who proved the delivery of the bill to the defendant, having proved also that he made this copy of the bill and of the plaintiff's signature to it, which copy, if it had been signed by the plaintiff, would have been a duplicate original, and the plaintiff, at the trial, having offered to sign the copy, it was insisted that he ought to have been permitted to do so, and that if he had, it would then have been admissible evidence. Our opinion is not founded upon the latter point, but we think that notice to produce the bill delivered to the defendant was not necessary in this case, because the bill delivered to him was in the nature of a notice. There are three descriptions of cases in which notice to produce an instrument is not requisite. The first, where the instrument produced and that to be proved are duplicate originals; secondly, where the instrument to be proved is a notice; as a notice to quit, or a notice of the dishonour of a bill of exchange. In *Kine* v. *Beaumont* (a) the Court of Common Pleas, after consulting the judges of the other Courts, held, that the copy of an original letter giving notice of the dishonour of a bill was admissible without notice to produce the original letter, and *Dallas*, C. J. there said, that he could not see any very substantial difference between a duplicate original and a copy made at the time. It is not material for us to say whether there is or is not any difference. The third case is, where, from the nature of the suit, the opposite party must know that he is charged with possession of the instrument. Thus in an action of trover for any written instrument, or on an indictment for stealing a written instrument, you may prove the contents of it by parol evidence, without giving any notice to produce. Our opinion in this case is founded upon this, that

(a) 3 B. & B. 288.

1827.

COLLINS

v.

TREWEEK.

the bill delivered one month before action brought is substantially in the nature of a notice to the defendant of the amount of the plaintiff's demand, and that he will enforce that demand by action unless the defendant proceeds to tax his bill under the statute. The statute 2 Geo. 2, c. 23, enacts, that no attorney shall commence any action for the recovery of a bill for common law business done, until the expiration of one month or more after such attorney shall have delivered to the parties to be charged therewith a bill of fees, which bill shall be subscribed with the proper hand of such attorney; and it then enacts, " that the bill may be taxed upon application of the party chargeable by such bill, and upon his submission to pay the whole sum that upon taxation shall appear to be due." As no action, therefore, can be brought by an attorney to recover the amount of his bill, until the expiration of one month after he shall have delivered to the party to be charged a bill of fees, &c., the delivery of such a bill must, in effect, be a notice to the party sought to be charged, that unless he pays the amount or proceeds to tax the bill pursuant to the provisions of the statute, the attorney will bring an action to recover the amount, and when such a bill has been delivered, and an action is afterwards brought by the attorney, it is brought in pursuance of the notice. But this case may fairly be considered as falling within that class of cases where notice to produce has been held to be unnecessary, namely, on the ground that from the nature of the suit, the opposite party must know that he is charged with possession of the instrument. For here, from the very nature of the suit, the defendant must have known that the plaintiff sought to recover the amount of that bill which had been delivered to him, and which, in the ordinary course of things, must be in his possession. We do not proceed altogether without authority on this point. In *Anderson* v. *May* (a), a copy of an attorney's bill, the original of which had been delivered to the defendant, was held to be admissible in evi-

(a) 2 B. & P. 237.

dence without proof of notice to produce the original. From the report of that case in 3 *Espinasse*, 167, I think it is clear that the copy which was produced in evidence was not made contemporaneously with the original bill delivered, but had afterwards been made up from the same books from which the bill delivered had been made up. In *Philipson* v. *Chase* (a), Lord *Ellenborough* seems to have thought that the decision in *Anderson* v. *May* proceeded on the ground that they were duplicate originals, and made contemporaneously; but having ascertained satisfactorily that the instrument given in evidence in that case was not made contemporaneously with that which was delivered to the defendant, we think the decision in that case in point, and sustainable on the ground that the bill delivered was a notice to the defendant that unless the bill was paid within a month an action would be brought. Recollecting also that this is a mere technical objection, not deserving encouragement, we are of opinion that the copy of the bill delivered was admissible in evidence, without giving any notice to produce the bill delivered, and consequently the rule nisi for entering a verdict for the plaintiff for 10*l*. 0*s*. 1*d*. must be made absolute.

Rule absolute.

(a) 2 Campb. 110.

END OF HILARY TERM.

CASES

COURT OF KING'S BENCH

IN

EASTER TERM,

IN THE EIGHTH YEAR OF THE REIGN OF GEORGE IV.

MEMORANDA.

DURING *Hilary* vacation, *John,* Earl of *Eldon,* resigned the Great Seal, and was succeeded in the office of Lord High Chancellor of *Great Britain* by Sir *John Singleton Copley,* Knight, Master of the Rolls, who was created a Peer of the United Kingdom of *Great Britain* and *Ireland,* by the name, style and title of Baron *Lyndhurst,* of *Lyndhurst,* in the county of *Southampton.* His Lordship took his seat on the Bench of the Court of Chancery on the first day of this term.

Sir *Charles Abbott,* Knight, Lord Chief Justice of this Court, was raised to the Peerage by the name, style and title of Baron *Tenterden,* of *Hendon,* in the county of *Middlesex.*

Sir *Robert Graham,* Knight, one of the Barons of the Court of Exchequer, vacated his office, and was succeeded by *John Vaughan,* Esquire, one of His Majesty's Serjeants at law, who received the honor of Knighthood.

James Scarlett, Esquire, one of His Majesty's Counsel learned in the law, was appointed Attorney General, in the room of Sir *Charles Wetherell,* Knight, resigned, and was knighted.

ELIZABETH HOUSTON and CHARLOTTE GRIFFITH *v.*
HENRY ALWRIGHT HUGHES, C. DOWDING, ELIZA-
BETH CHARLOTTE STRONG, ANN STRONG, ELINOR
BERESFORD STRONG, SUSANNAH STRONG, CHAR-
LOTTE SARAH STRONG, NICHOLSON PEYTON, ELIZA
PEYTON, CHARLOTTE LEA PEYTON, REYNOLDS
PEYTON, THOMAS GRIFFITH PEYTON, HENRY PEY-
TON, and FRANCIS PEYTON.

Same Plaintiffs *v.* THOMAS LESINGHAM.

1827.

Same Plaintiffs *v.* WILLIAM PEYTON and ELIZABETH
PEYTON.

Tuesday,
1st May.

Same Plaintiffs *v.* ANNA MARIA SMITH.

Testator being
seised in fee of
freehold and
copyhold
lands, and
having also
leasehold for
lives and for
years, and
other personal
property, de-
vised and be-
queathed the
same to trus-
tees and their
heirs and as-
signs, haben-
dum in trust
for and during
all testator's
right, title and
estate therein,
upon trust,
first, to pay
debts and
funeral ex-

THE following case was sent by the Master of the Rolls
for the opinion of this Court :—

Henry *Lambert*, late of the *Bartons* in the parish of
Colwell and county of *Hereford*, Esq. duly made and
published his last will, bearing date the 26th of *September*,
1811, and executed and attested in the manner required by
law for devising freehold estates, in the words and figures
following (that is to say): " First, I will and direct, that all
my just debts, funeral and testamentary expenses, be fully
paid and satisfied.   I give, devise and bequeath unto *Abraham Robarts*, and unto *Henry Hughes*, and unto *John Platt*,
and to their heirs for ever, all my messuages or tenements,
farms, lands, hereditaments, estates and premises whatsoever
and wheresoever, freehold, copyhold or leasehold, (having
surrendered my copyhold estate to the use of my said will)
in possession, reversion, remainder or expectancy, or whereof

penses, and then to apply the annual income to the use of his two nieces for their
lives ; and after their decease there were devises to their grand-children, male and female,
in terms so ambiguous and contradictory, as to make it doubtful what equitable interest
the grand-children took :—Held, that the trustees took an estate in fee in the freehold
and copyhold lands, and an absolute interest in the leasehold for lives and years, and
that the devises over, though full of difficulties, did not make the will void for uncertainty.

This Court will not give any opinion upon a case sent from Chancery containing questions upon equitable estates merely.

I have a disposing power, with their several and respective
members, rights and appurtenances, to have and to hold
such of my said hereditaments and premises as are freehold
unto the said *A. Robarts, H. Hughes, J. Platt,* their heirs
and assigns, and to have and to hold my copyhold and all
such other of my estates as are less than freehold unto
A. R., H. H., J. P., for and during all my right, title and
estate, term therein or thereto respectively, according to
the nature and quantity of the said estate respectively. I
likewise give and bequeath to *A. R., H. H.* and *J. P.* all
my ready money, securities for money, household and other
goods, plate, china, linen, cattle, chattels, and all other my
personal estate of what nature or kind soever, as and for
and to the end that my trustees alone may have full power
and clear and absolute authority to release, convey, assign,
and assure all and every the estates and premises which, at
the time of making and of executing this my will and at my
death, may be vested in me as mortgagee in fee, or as a
trustee, without calling upon my heir-at-law to concur or
join in any release or transfer of any such premises, or have
any affirmation concerning what belongs to my real or personal estate whatsoever; and I do give and devise all my
estates, title, and interest in and to such premises as last
mentioned, together with all benefit and advantages thereof,
to *A. R., H. H., J. P.,* in trust and confidence that they
shall hold all my lands, tenements, real and personal estates,
for the uses hereinafter mentioned. I give *A. R., H. H.*
J. P., on condition that they undertake and execute the
office of trustees, also the several trusts therein this my will
contained, 200*l.* a piece to each, but only to such of them
as shall prove my said will; and that all the charges and
expenses of my trustees herein mentioned in this trust shall
be paid out of my personal estate; and that if any or either
of my trustees die or refuse to act in the trust, that then my
other trustee or my trustees shall have a power of chusing
a trustee in the place of such trustee or trustees so dying or
refusing to act, and so often as the same do happen, to the

intent of keeping a sufficient number of acting trustees, and that the trust may not descend to the heirs of the survivors; and my will is, that the said trustee or trustees so chosen shall have the same power and estate as given to the trustees herein named. I give to my niece Mrs. *S. Houghton*, formerly of *Grafton Street*, *Dublin*, and the eldest daughter of my sister, Mrs. *Ruth Leay*, 300*l.* a-piece each, upon the respective marriage of each of her grand-children, with the consent of their mother, or when they attain the age of 21 years; and if any die, their share to be equally divided between her male and female sons and daughters. And I give to Miss *Eliza Griffith*, the daughter of Mrs. *Charlotte Griffith*, late of *Grafton Street*, in the city of *Dublin*, in the kingdom of *Ireland*, five hundred pounds, on her respective marriage, with her mother's consent, or when she attains the age of twenty-one years. And I give to Miss *E. Kelly*, of the custom house, five hundred pounds. And I give to Miss *S. Kelly*, two hundred pounds. And I give to Mr. *Henry Hughes* of *Worcester*, three hundred pounds; and in trust and confidence that my trustees shall hold all my lands, tenements, real and personal property of what kind or nature soever, and all my estates and interest in the same, to be holden by my trustees in trust, and then apply the income and annual amount of such property to the use of my two nieces, *E. S. Houghton* and *C. Griffith*, for their lives and proper use and benefit, and after their decease to such child, or if more than one, to the use of such children in manner following: to wit, if male issue of my niece, Mrs. *S. Hough-ton*'s daughter, Mrs. *Strong*, then I give and devise to my trustees, *A. R.*, *H. H.*, *J. P.*, that they shall hold all my lands in trust and confidence, that they shall hold my will in whatsoever of my real estate or personal estate and interest therein come to my two nieces by virtue of this my will, be for their own sole and separate use, and not subject to the disposal of any husband; nor to sell, let or assign any part of the premises thereof; and that upon the payment of money that arises from my real or personal property of what nature soever, that *E. S. Houghton* or *C. Griffith*, their receipt only shall be a discharge for the money received; then from and after the decease of my two neices, *E. S. Houghton* and *C. Griffith*, and failure of their male issue, and satisfying my before mentioned gifts and bequeath, my trustees shall hold in trust for the use of *E. S. Houghton* and *C. Griffith*, my two nieces, their grand-daughters, when they attain the age of twenty-one years, or be married with the approbation and consent of their mother and my trustees, and not having such approbation and consent their share to be divided among the remainder, and as my two nieces by their will or deed in writing shall direct or appoint, then to the use of such child or children; and the profits arising from my real and personal estates, of what nature or kind soever, shall accumulate and be laid out and invest the same in stock or public funds, on real or government security, at interest, and the produce thereupon due or to become due, and securities in which the same shall be then invested, among all and every the child and children of my said two nieces, Mrs. *S. Houghton* and Mrs. *C. Griffith;* and my meaning is that if Miss *Eliza Griffith* marry and have issue, that *Eliza Griffith* and her children share in this my bequeathment equally with Mrs. *S. Houghton*, but not till after the decease of my two nieces, and if this happen, my trustees allowing what they shall judge proper for their maintenance and education of such child or children, till they arrive at the age before mentioned; and my will is, that every such child who shall take my surname, without the addition of any other surname, and shall inhabit the *Barton House*, and make it their residence and place of abode. Also I give and bequeath to my two nieces, *E. S. Houghton* and *C. Griffith*, all my plate, linen, china, household furniture, of what nature or kind soever as well in or about my dwelling-house at the *Barton* or elsewhere, upon trust during their natural lives, the use and enjoyment of all such, and after their decease, to the use of such son or sons and daughters. as my will directs as shall from time to time come into the possession of my estates and inhabit the *Barton House*, and also as often and from time to time renew the *Barton lease*, which is every seventh year, and also as often as the lives do fall in the lease of *Colwall Park*, that it be renewed, and three lives kept up to preserve it; and that all the building be kept in repair, and what is expended in needful repairs to be paid out of the rents and profits of the estate; and my will is, that whatsoever of my personal estate that comes to my two nieces, *E. S. Houghton* and *C. Griffith*, of my plate, linen, household goods and furniture, of any kind in my dwelling-house at the *Barton* shall remain, and after their decease to be for the use of such child, sons or daughters, that comes to the possession of my estate by virtue of this my will. But in case of failure of issue male, I devise to the female grand-daughters of *E. S. Houghton* and *C. Griffith*, grand-daughters. Then my will is that my trustees shall hold in trust all my lands, tenements, real and personal estates, after satisfying the before mentioned gifts and bequeaths in trust for the use of such grand-daughters of *E. S. Houghton* and *C. Griffith* as are then living, as tenants in common, and not as joint tenants; and if this happens, and any dispute to cause a difference of the bequeath of this my will, I direct that my said trustees do admit my bequeath, and determine absolute the same, and those that reject my bequeath be void, and then so avoidable and divided equally between such daughters as then living. And I do appoint my two nieces, *E. S. Houghton* and *C. Griffith*, executrix of this my last will and testament."

The testator was at the time of making his will, and thence up to and at the time of his death, seised of divers freehold lands and hereditaments for an estate of inheritance in fee simple in possession, and of divers copyhold lands and hereditaments, held of the manors of *Barton,* *Colwell, Coddington,* and *Bosbury Colwall,* in the county of *Hereford,* according to the custom of the said manors respectively, and of lands and hereditaments for the lives of certain persons named in the leases or grants thereof; and was also, at the time of his death, possessed of lands and hereditaments which had been demised to him for terms of years. All the testator's copyhold lands had been duly surrendered to the use of his will.

The testator died on the 25th *March*, 1814, without having altered or revoked his will, leaving *Dame Susannah Pritchard Tempest*, the wife of Sir *Henry Tempest*, baronet, his only child and heiress at law, customary heiress and sole next of kin. The plaintiff, *Elizabeth Houston*, who is the person designated in the will as Mrs. *Sheen Houghton*, and the plaintiff, *Charlotte Griffith*, who is the person designated in the will as *Charlotte Griffith*, were then and still are the only surviving children of the testator's sister, *Ruth Leay*, and they duly proved the testator's will.

At the date of the will, and at the time of the death of the testator, *Elizabeth Houston* had only one child *Elizabeth Strong*, then and now the wife of *Joseph Strong;* and *Charlotte Griffith* also had only one child, *Eliza Griffith*. Mrs. *Strong* had, at the testator's death, three children, viz. *Elizabeth Charlotte Strong*, *Elinor Beresford Strong*, and *Ann Strong*, and she has since had two children, viz. *Susannah Strong* and *Charlotte Sarah Strong*, all of whom are now living. *Eliza Griffith*, after the testator's death, intermarried with *Nicholson Peyton*, and has the following children: *Charlotte Leay Peyton*, *Reynolds Peyton*, *Thomas Griffith Peyton*, *Henry Peyton*, *Francis Peyton*, *William Peyton* and *Elizabeth Peyton*. No child of Mrs. *Strong* or of Mrs. *Peyton* has attained twenty-one or married.

Dame *Susannah Pritchard Tempest* survived her husband, and died on the 31st of *July*, 1821, without issue, and intestate as to her freehold estates, leaving the plaintiffs, *Elizabeth Houston* and *Charlotte Griffith*, her co-heiresses at law and sole next of kin.

On the 12th of *February*, 1825, letters of administration of the goods, chattels, rights and credits of the said Dame *Susannah Pritchard Tempest*, with her will annexed, were granted by and out of the Prerogative Court of the Archbishop of *Canterbury*, to *Thomas Lesingham*, and he is now the legal personal representative of the said Dame *Susannah Pritchard Tempest*.

On or about the 20th of *August*, 1822, the said plaintiffs filed their original bill in the High Court of Chancery against the defendants hereinbefore in that behalf named, and the said *John Platt* (since deceased), praying, amongst other things, that the will of the said testator might be established, and the rights of the several parties claiming thereunder declared, and that the plaintiffs might be declared under the will entitled to all and singular the messuages or tenements, farms, lands, hereditaments, and premises of which the testator died seised and possessed, or entitled to in fee, as tenants in common in tail male, and to all and singular the said copyhold and leasehold estates, and also to the whole of the personal estate and effects of the testator, subject only to the payment of his just debts and funeral and testamentary expenses and legacies, according to the several natures thereof, for their own use absolutely, in equal moieties; to which bill the defendants appeared and put in their answers. The said original bill was subsequently amended, and afterwards bills of supplement and revivor were filed to bring the necessary parties before the Court; and the original cause, and also the supplemental and revived causes being at issue, came on to be heard before the Master of the Rolls, on the 5th of *July*, 1826, when his Lordship directed the above case to be made for the opinion of the judges of this Court, and that the questions should be—

First. What estate and interest did the said *Abraham Robarts*, *Henry Hughes*, and *John Platt* take under the will of the testator in the freehold and copyhold lands and hereditaments in which the testator had at the time of his death an estate of inheritance to him and his heirs, and in the lands and tenements which were then held by him on leases for the lives of certain persons in the leases in that behalf named?

Secoudly. What estate and interest do the plaintiffs, *Elizabeth Houston* and *Charlotte Griffith*, respectively take under the will of the testator in the said freehold and copyhold lands and hereditaments, and in the said leaseholds for lives?

Thirdly. What estate and interest do the said *Reynolds Peyton, Thomas Griffith Peyton, Henry Peyton*, and *William Peyton*, the sons of the said *Eliza Peyton*, respectively take under the will of the testator in the freehold and copyhold lands and hereditaments, and in the leaseholds for lives respectively?

Fourthly. What estate and interest do the said *Elizabeth Charlotte Strong, Elinor Beresford Strong, Ann Strong, Susannah Strong*, and *Charlotte Sarah Strong*, the granddaughters of the said *Elizabeth Houston*, and *Eliza Peyton*, the daughter, and *Charlotte Leay Peyton* and *Elizabeth Peyton*, the grand-daughters of the said *Charlotte Griffith*, respectively take under the will of the testator in the said freehold and copyhold lands and hereditaments, and in the said leaseholds for lives respectively?

If the Court should be of opinion that by the will, as above stated, the whole legal estate in fee-simple in the aforesaid lands and hereditaments of inheritance, and the whole absolute interest in the leaseholds for lives, were vested in the said *Abraham Robarts, Henry Hughes*, and *James Platt;* then, in case they had been merely devisees to the uses, and the legal estate had not remained in them,

Fifthly, What estate and interest would the persons enumerated in the second, third, and fourth questions have respectively taken under the will of the said testator in the said freehold and copyhold lands and hereditaments, and in the said leaseholds for lives respectively?

This case was argued at the sittings in *Hilary* vacation, before *Bayley*, J. *Holroyd*, J. and *Littledale*, J. At the opening of the case, *Bayley*, J. asked the counsel whether the Court of Chancery expected this Court would certify what estates the plaintiffs would have taken if the legal estates had not remained in the trustees?

The Counsel replied, that in the case of *Murthwaite* v. *Jenkinson* (a) the Court had done so, and the questions in this case were framed in that manner, in order to obtain the opinion of this Court in the same way.

BAYLEY, J.—The old course used to be for the Court of Chancery to state the case upon assumption that all the estates were legal, and then to require this Court to give its opinion upon the case so stated as a mere question of law. I have, therefore, great difficulty in saying how a Court of law can give an opinion as to what will be the effect of a will if certain equitable devises had been legal devises.

Upon this suggestion it was agreed on both sides, that the only question to be argued was, whether the trustees took the legal fee in the freehold estates.

Denman, C. S. *Preston*, and E. H. *Alderson*, who severally and respectively represented the plaintiffs, their grand-daughters and their grandsons, contended that the legal fee in the freeholds vested in the trustees. It is a settled rule in construing instruments of this nature, that if any thing remains to be done by trustees after the life of the first taker, the trustees must take the continuing legal estate; *Doe* v. *Hicks* (b) and *Doe* v. *Willan* (c). Now here there were acts to be done by the trustees subsequently to the death of Mrs. E. S. *Houston* and Mrs. *Griffiths*, and, therefore, upon the authority of these cases the trustees clearly took the legal fee. There is no doubt that the trustees had the legal estate for some period in the whole of the testator's property. They must have had it to sustain the trust for the separate use of the married women, but there are various other purposes mentioned in the will which would require that they should have the fee. Amongst these are

(a) *Ante*, Vol. III. 765; 2 B.   (b) 7 T. R. 433.
& C. 357.   (c) 2 B. & A. 84.

the payment of legacies to grand-children and other persons, as well as the payment of his debts, funeral and testamentary expenses. If he left no personalty these would all have been charges upon the realty, and therefore for this purpose the trustees must have taken the legal fee. In short, every provision in the will shews that it was the intention of the testator to give the trustees the legal estate. In one clause he directs that the trustees shall have full power and authority to release, convey, assign and assure. That necessarily imports that he contemplated that they should possess the whole fee of those estates to which this clause is referable. Again, he directs that the trustees shall hold all his lands, tenements, real and personal property of what kind or nature soever, and that all his estate or interest in the same shall be holden by his trustees in trust. He then directs that, in a certain event, the rents and profits of the estate are to accumulate to be laid out by the trustees, and the buildings are to be kept in repair, and that what is expended in needful repairs shall be paid out of the rents and profits of the estate. In order to comply with these directions, it is essential that they should have the legal estate. Again, they are also to adjust the shares and ascertain the rights of the parties. The annual income of the property is to be paid to his two nieces, *E. Houston* and *C. Griffith*, and then from and after the decease of these nieces and failure of their male issue, he directs that the trustees shall hold in trust for the use of *E. Houston* and *C. Griffith*, his two neices, their grand-daughters, when they shall attain the age of twenty-one years or are married with the approbation and consent required. This latter provision shews that there must be an interval during which the trustees were to hold the real and personal estates. What is to be done by them during that interval? They are to accumulate the profits arising from the real and personal estates, and to invest the same in the public funds, and they are to apply what they think proper for the maintenance and education of the children till they respectively attain majority or become married. This is decisive to shew that these were acts to be done by the trustees after the death of Mrs. *Houston* and Mrs. *Griffith;* and, consequently, on the authority of the cases cited, it is clear that the trustees took the legal fee.

W. O. Russell, for the defendant *Thomas Lessingham,* contended that the trustees took only an estate for life during the lives of *Elizabeth Houston* and *Charlotte Griffith,* and that the devises over were void for uncertainty. He admitted that unless there was sufficient ground for contending that the devises over were void for uncertainty, the trustees must take the legal fee. It is quite clear that the subsequent parts of the will are perfectly insensible, and, consequently, the argument on the other side cannot be supported. It is sufficient for this purpose to call the attention of the Court to the nonsensical clause in the will following, " in trust and confidence that my trustees shall hold all my lands, &c. and all my estate and interest in the same, to be holden by my trustees in trust, and then apply the income and annual amount of such property to the use of my two nieces, *E. S. Houston* and *C. Griffith,* for their lives and proper use and benefit, and after their decease to such child, or if more than one to the use of such children, in manner following, to wit, if male issue of my niece, Mrs. *Houston's* daughter, Mrs. *Strong,* then I give and devise to my trustees that they shall hold all my lands in trust and confidence that they shall hold my will in whatsoever of my real estate or personal estate and interest therein, come to my two neices by virtue of this my will, be for their own sole and separate use, and not subject to the disposal of any husband, &c." Now this is perfectly unintelligible, and renders this part of the will absolutely void for uncertainty. No effect can be given to the will after the determination of the estates for life. [*Bayley,* J. There may be difficulties certainly as to the execution of the trusts over, but that is not the question we have to determine. If we hold that the trustees took the fee, a Court of equity will then have to determine whether all the purposes of the trust can be carried into execution. That Court may determine whether after the death of Mrs. *Houston* there are trusts so sufficiently expressed, that they can be carried into execution, because if they are not, then the Court of equity will take care of the interests of the heir at law or of the next of kin. The very existence of difficulty shews the necessity of holding that the trustees took the legal fee. It does not follow that because there are difficulties in carrying the will into effect that it is therefore void for uncertainty. There is, no doubt, difficulty in this will, but that is not a sufficient ground for holding it void for uncertainty.]

· *Campbell*, for the trustees, said it was their wish that the Court would so construe the will as to give them no more than an estate for life during the lives of Mrs. *Houston* and Mrs. *Griffith*. He submitted that if the other side had been heard adversely as to the different estates taken by the grandsons, by the grand-daughters, and the other claimants, there would have been found so much insurmountable difficulty in construing the will, that they would have felt it necessary to determine that the will, after the estates for life were determined, was absolutely void for uncertainty. [*Bayley*, J. Our determination upon the questions submitted to us will not prejudice the question as to the effect of the subsequent devises after the estate for life, but that will be for the after consideration of a Court of equity.]

Preston was heard in reply.

BAYLEY, J.—When a Court of equity sends a case for the consideration of a Court of law, it is not that the Court of law is to bind the Court of equity, but to assist it in the construction of the instrument. When a Court of equity sends a question for the opinion of this Court, that Court certainly pays respect to our opinion, but a Court of law

sits to give opinions upon legal questions and legal questions only. If a will is so framed as to present, like the
present, the consideration of questions upon equitable estates, it is peculiarly for a Court of equity to say in what
manner the will shall be moulded so as to present a legal
question for the consideration of a Court of law. If there
be difficulty in converting the equitable estates in the will
into legal estates, why that is peculiarly for the consideration of a Court of equity, which understands what is the
effect of an equitable devise, better than a Court of law.
Therefore it seems to me that if the Court of equity wishes
to have our opinion on those parts of this will which give
equitable interests, it is for that Court to mould the will into
such a shape as shall present a legal question for our consideration. If, therefore, we should be of opinion in this case
that the legal estate in fee is vested in the trustees, we shall
certify to the Court of equity in that respect, but forbear
answering any of the other questions stated. Upon the
question whether the trustees take the legal fee or not, I
think that according to the case of *Doe* v. *Willan*, where
you give an estate to trustees and their heirs indefinitely,
the trustees will take the fee if the purposes of the trust
require that they should have the absolute property in them,
or that they should take it for an indefinite period of time,
unless it can be seen on the face of the instrument that they
took a limited interest and not the fee. Now in this case
the freehold property being mixed with property in which
the trustees must have the whole interest, is a circumstance
which may assist the Court in determining whether the
trustees take the whole fee or less than the fee. In this
instance they must take an absolute interest both in the
copyholds and in the leaseholds for years, for if they did
not take an absolute interest in the freeholds of inheritance
and the freeholds for life, the consequence would be that
the one would be separated entirely from the other, which
would be directly contrary to the intention of the testator.
We shall, however, certify our opinion into Chancery.

The following certificate was afterwards sent to the
Master of the Rolls.

This case has been argued before us by counsel. We
have considered it, and we are of opinion that the said
Abraham Robarts, Henry Hughes, and *John Platt,* took
under the will of the testator an estate in fee simple in the
freehold and copyhold lands and hereditaments in which
the said testator had at the time of his death an estate of
inheritance to him and his heirs. And we are of opinion
that the said *Abraham Robarts, Henry Hughes,* and *John
Platt,* took the whole interest which the said testator, at
the time of his death, had in the lands and tenements which
were then held by him on leases for the lives of the persons
in the said leases in that behalf named. As we are of this
opinion, the interests of the other parties mentioned in the
questions are equitable interests only, and we have not given
any opinion as to them.

J. BAYLEY.
G. S. HOLROYD.
J. LITTLEDALE.

HOWELL v. HOWELL.

*Friday,
4th May.*

THIS was an action of assumpsit, tried before *Heywood,*
Serjeant, at the last Summer Great Sessions for the county
of *Caermarthen,* when the plaintiff was nonsuited, and at
that Great Sessions, namely, on the 26th of *August,* the
defendant had signed judgment. In *Michaelmas* term last
the plaintiff had obtained a rule nisi in this Court for setting
aside the nonsuit, and the transcript of the record had been
transmitted from the Court below into this Court, pursuant
to the Welsh Judicature Act, 5 *Geo.* 4, *c.* 106, *s.* 3, but no
recognizance conditioned to make and prosecute the application for the new trial, or setting aside the nonsuit and to
pay the costs, had been entered into pursuant to the 4th
section of the same statute, and

*A motion may
be made in
this Court for
a new trial
after judgment
and execution
in a cause tried
in the Courts
of Great Ses-
sions in Wales,
without enter-
ing into the re-
cognizance re-
quired by the
4th section of
stat. 5 Geo. 4,
c. 106.*

Sir *William Owen* now moved to have the cause struck out of the new trial peremptory paper, and to discharge the rule for setting aside the nonsuit, on the ground that it was not competent to a party to move for a new trial after judgment signed in a case tried before the Court of Great Session, unless the recognizance required by the 4th section of the Welsh Judicature Act was entered into. He contended that the recognizance required by that section must be entered into, as a condition precedent to a motion for a new trial. The reason for this was perfectly obvious, for after judgment signed and execution issued, the property taken in execution is bound and gets into other hands. The act enables parties to apply for new trials in the same manner as had been usually theretofore done in actions depending in the Courts of *Westminster Hall.* Now in those Courts a new trial cannot be moved for after a judgment and execution, for the reason that the property in the goods is changed by the execution. Unless, therefore, the Court holds that the recognizance shall be entered into before judgment and execution, one important provision in the Welsh Judicature Act will be defeated.

Lord TENTERDEN, C. J.—I am of opinion that we ought not to grant this application. By the second section of the 5 *Geo.* 4, *c.* 106, a party dissatisfied with any verdict in any action tried in any of the Courts of Great Sessions, may apply to any of the common law Courts of *Westminster* for a new trial, and it authorises those Courts to grant a rule for a new trial in the same manner as had been usually theretofore done in actions depending in the said Courts and tried at nisi prius before a judge of assize. So that the effect of this act is to place suitors in the Courts of Great Sessions precisely in the same situation as suitors in the common law Courts in *England.* In the Courts of *Westminster* the application for a new trial must be made within the first four days of term, before any judgment is signed, but by the practice of the Courts of Great Sessions the judgment is signed at the same sessions in which the cause is tried, and therefore it is impossible for a party dissatisfied with a verdict to apply to any of the common law Courts at *Westminster* before judgment is signed, and the consequence of that might·be that execution might issue upon the judgment before the party had an opportunity of making his application. In order, however, to remedy this inconvenience, the 4th section enacts, that nothing in the act shall be construed to extend to stay or delay the entering up judgment, which shall be given in any action in the Courts of Great Sessions and suing out execution thereon, unless the party intending to apply for a new trial thereof entered into the recognizance therein mentioned. The only effect of neglecting to enter into such a recognizance will be that execution may issue against him upon the judgment obtained in the Courts of Great Sessions, but the 4th section does not deprive him of the right given him by the 2d section to apply to the Courts of *Westminster* for a new trial. This makes the proceeding exactly analogous to a writ of error upon a judgment in the Courts of common law. In those Courts execution is not stayed unless bail in error be given, but the omission to put in bail does not prevent the party from going on with his writ of error, and if the judgment is afterwards reversed, he has his writ of restitution. So here if the party succeeds upon the second trial, and obtains a judgment, he will be in the like situation with a plaintiff in error in the common law Courts. In effect the object of the 4th section of the statute is to restrain parties from bringing frivolous writs of error.

BAYLEY, J., HOLROYD, J., and LITTLEDALE, J., were of the same opinion.

Rule refused.

CRIPPS v. BLANK.

Friday 4th May.

A person having title to land sued for use and occupation against A., who had received possession from a third person: —Held, that the declaration of A., " I don't consider the land as yours, but prove the right, and I'll pay you rent," would not support assumpsit for use and occupation.

ASSUMPSIT for the use and occupation of a certain piece of land. Plea, the general issue. At the trial at the last summer assizes for the county of *Bucks*, it appeared in evidence that a former occupier of the land in question had rented it of the landlord at five shillings per annum. After being in possession for fourteen years and paying rent, he quitted and another person took possession. After an interval of time, he gave up possession, and then the defendant came in. About two years before the trial the plaintiff became owner of the land, and he then applied to the defendant either to give up possession, or pay for it as the former occupiers had done. The defendant replied, " I do not consider the land as yours, but prove your right, and I'll pay you for it." The plaintiff then brought the present action, and after proving his title to the land, relied upon this conditional promise to sustain assumpsit for use and occupation. The learned judge was of opinion that under these circumstances the action would not lie in the absence of proof of unqualified attornement, and directed a nonsuit.

Robinson now moved for a rule nisi to set the nonsuit aside and obtain a new trial. The question is whether an action for use and occupation can be maintained upon evidence of title merely, without any proof of an unqualified recognition by the tenant of the landlord's right to sue. Now this case falls within the general principle, that in an action for use and occupation a tenant cannot call upon his landlord to shew title. *Cooke* v. *Loxley* (a). Here it is clear that the defendant is permitted to remain in the possession of the land by the plaintiff, and the defendant, after a notice that the plaintiff is the landlord, keeps possession. This is sufficient to entitle the plaintiff to maintain use and occupation without being driven to the necessity of bringing trespass or ejectment.

(a) 5 T. R. 4.

Lord TENTERDEN, C. J.—I think we are not called
upon in this case to decide the general abstract question,
whether it is competent for the owner of land to bring an
action for use and occupation, instead of trespass, against a
person who has entered upon the land without any communication with the owner of the land. It is sufficient for the
present case to say, that the evidence on this trial will not
sustain the action in the present form. It appeared in
evidence that a former occupier of the land in question consented to pay for it at the rate of five shillings a year, and
for some time he paid the money accordingly. Upon his
quitting, some other person came into the possession of the
land, and that person resigned the possession. After an
interval of time the defendant came in. Application is then
made to him by the plaintiff not to give up the land, but to
pay for it as former occupiers had done. The defendant
replies, " I don't consider the land as yours; prove your
right to it, and I'll pay you for it." This amounts to no
more than this, " When you have a title, I am contented to
be considered as occupying by your permission." The
learned judge thought that this could not be treated as an
unconditional promise to pay rent, or an acknowledgment
of the plaintiff's general right to recover for use and occupation, and I think his decision was correct.

BAYLEY, J.—I am of the same opinion. The general
rule certainly is, that if *A.* receives possession of land from
B. he cannot dispute the title of the latter in an action for
use and occupation, but where he receives possession from
another person, he may dispute the title of the party suing
as landlord. Here the defendant did not receive possession
from the plaintiff, and therefore the evidence produced
could not support use and occupation.

HOLROYD, J. and LITTLEDALE, J. concurred.

Rule refused.

1827.

Saturday,
5th May.

MOORE and others *v.* HAMMOND.

The deed of settlement of a joint stock company provided, that the directors should without summons meet together at their office once in every week on and at such day and hour as they should from time to time agree upon, and also at such other times as they should from time to time be convened in manner thereinafter mentioned or adjourned, and that three directors should be a board. Another clause authorised any three directors at any time to call a special board, by giving under their hands in writing three days notice to the other directors, which notices were to be countersigned by the secretary, and to be sent by him two days prior to the time appointed for such meeting: Held, that in order to constitute a good weekly meeting without summons the day and hour of meeting must have been previously agreed upon by the directors, and consequently that a meeting of three directors without previous agreement on their part to meet on any fixed day or hour was not a meeting duly convened within the meaning of the deed of settlement.

COVENANT. The declaration stated, that by indenture made between the several persons whose names were thereunto subscribed, and whose seals were thereunto affixed, except the said plaintiffs of the one part; and the said plaintiffs of the other part, after reciting as therein mentioned, it was witnessed, that for certain purposes in the indenture mentioned, each of the several parties to the indenture, except plaintiffs, did thereby for himself or herself, and his or her heirs, executors, administrators, and assigns, covenant with plaintiffs, their executors, administrators, and assigns, amongst other things, that the said several persons parties to the indenture, all of whom were thereafter distinguished by the title of proprietors, and the several other persons who should become proprietors as thereinafter was mentioned, should, while holding shares in the capital of a certain company thereinbefore proposed to be established, and until they should cease to be such proprietors in the manner thereinafter mentioned, be and continue for the term of fifty years from the date thereof, or until the same should be dissolved under the provisions thereinafter in that behalf contained, a company or partnership, society or association, by and under the name and firm of "The *Cornwall* and *Devonshire* Mining Company," and that the affairs and concerns of the said company or partnership society should be conducted and managed under and subject to the several rules, regulations, and conditions, restrictions, clauses, and agreements thereinafter contained, and amongst others the following, that is to say, that for the orderly and more effectual management of the affairs of the partnership society, there should during the continuance of it be kept up

a certain number of directors, and that the directors should
meet together at all times and according to the regulations
and conditions in the indenture in that behalf mentioned,
and that any such meeting of directors which should consist of three or more directors for the time being should be
and be styled a full board of directors, at their discretion,
from time to time to come to a resolution that the proprietors should be called upon to pay at any time within one
calendar month from the time of such resolution any further
instalment on each of their shares till the whole sum payable on each should have been paid, and that when the
board of directors should have come to a resolution to call
for any further settlement, they should call on all the proprietors to contribute the same rateably in proportion to
the number and amount in value of their several respective
shares, and that a circular letter should be delivered or sent
by the post to each proprietor, informing him or her of the
resolution, and of the day and place fixed by the board for
the payment of such further instalment, and that every proprietor should pay such instalment at the day and place so
fixed in that behalf as aforesaid.   The declaration then
went on to aver, that the defendant became and still was a
proprietor of divers, to wit, twenty shares of 50*l.* each in
the capital of the said company or partnership society, and
duly executed the indenture as such proprietor; that after
the making of the indenture, to wit, on the 14th *September*,
1826, at &c. at a meeting of the board of directors of the
company duly convened and held according to the regulations and conditions in the indenture in that behalf contained, the sum of 35*l.* then remaining due and payable on
each of the said shares; it was resolved, that the proprietors should thereby be called upon to pay on or before the
13th *October* then next, a further instalment of 5*l.* on each
of their shares, and that a board of directors should be held
on the last-mentioned day at eleven o'clock in the forenoon
precisely, at the offices of the company No. 26, *Lombard
Street*, for the purpose of receiving such further instalment;

that on the 14th *September*, 1826, a circular letter was sent by the post to the defendant, informing him of the resolution, and of the day and place fixed by the said board for the payment of such further instalment, whereby and by force of the indenture the defendant became liable to pay the sum of 100*l.* being the amount of the said instalment of 5*l.* on each of his twenty shares, at the time and place in that behalf mentioned as aforesaid, of which the defendant had notice. Breach, non-payment of the said sum of 100*l.* Pleas, first, *non est factum;* secondly, that there was no such meeting of a board of directors of the said company or partnership society, duly convened and held according to the regulations and conditions in the supposed indenture in that behalf contained. Issue thereon. At the trial before Lord *Tenterden*, C. J. at the *Middlesex* sittings after last term, it appeared in evidence that the plaintiffs were the trustees of a joint stock company, called the *Cornwall* and *Devonshire* Mining Company, and that the defendant was a partner or shareholder in that company. The deed of settlement establishing the company provided, that the directors should without notice or summons meet together at the house or office of the company, once in every week at the least, on and at such day and hour as they should from time to time agree upon, and also at such other times as they should from time to time be convened in manner thereinafter mentioned or assented to. Another clause provided, that any three directors might at any time call a special board or meeting of the directors of the company by leaving three days prior to the time appointed for such special board or meeting, with the secretary for the time being of the said company, notices in writing for the several other directors of the said company, which notices should be made under the respective hands of such directors convening such board or meeting, and should be countersigned by the secretary for the time being of the company, and should be sent by him by post or otherwise two days prior to the time appointed for such special board or meeting, which last-mentioned respective periods of three days and two days should be calculated exclusive of the days of sending or giving such notices, and exclusive of the day of holding such special meeting. In another clause it was provided, that every such meeting, whether weekly or otherwise, which should consist of three or more directors, should be and be styled a board of directors, and that no business should be transacted at any weekly or other meeting unless three directors at the least were present at the commencement of the business, and when a decision or determination should take place upon the whole or such part of the business as should be then under consideration, then the clause authorised the board of directors, at their discretion, from time to time, to come to a resolution that the proprietors should be called upon to pay at any time, within one calendar month from the time of such resolution, any further instalment of each of their shares, until the whole sum payable on each such share should have been paid. It appeared that a meeting of three of the directors, of which the chairman of the company was one, was held on the 14th of *September*, 1826, but the day of meeting had not been previously fixed or agreed upon by the directors, nor was it held in pursuance of an adjournment from a former meeting. The minutes of the proceedings made by the secretary at the meeting and signed by the chairman were produced, from which it appeared that a resolution was then come to, that a call should be made of 5*l*. on each share, to be paid on the 13th of *October*. On the part of the defendant it was contended, that the meeting of the directors at which this resolution was formed had not been convened in the manner prescribed by the deed of settlement, and therefore that the defendant was not liable for any breach of covenant in not paying the instalment pursuant to the call made by the directors. Of this opinion was the Lord Chief Justice, who directed a nonsuit.

Campbell now moved to set aside the nonsuit and obtain

a new trial, on the ground of misdirection, and contended that the provisions of the deed of settlement would authorise at all events, on a special emergency, a meeting of this description without any previous agreement amongst the directors as to the day on which the meeting should be held; and he urged that the Court ought not nicely to scan their proceedings, where there was no suggestion of fraud or misconduct.

Lord TENTERDEN, C. J.—I am of opinion that the nonsuit ought not to be disturbed. It is of the last importance to a joint stock company, consisting, as this does, of a large number of persons, who place the management and control of their affairs in a small number of individuals, that the regulations regarding the meetings of those intrusted with the management of their affairs should be held in pursuance of the directions of the deed. The deed in question provides for two classes of meetings of the directors; the one to be held without summons or notice, the other to be held upon summons. The class that may be held without summons or notice are weekly meetings; and they are to be held at such day and hour as the directors shall from time to time agree upon. Supposing, therefore, the directors at any meeting to have come to a resolution that there should be a meeting held on any one specified day in the week, a meeting on that day without notice or summons would be a good meeting within the provisions of this deed; but unless the directors have previously agreed upon the day on which the meeting shall be held, it appears to me that a meeting on any other day is not a good weekly meeting within the meaning of this clause. If it were held to be so, it would be in the power of any three of the directors, the chairman or deputy chairman being one, to hold a meeting to make an order for payment on shares, or to do any other act whatsoever regarding the affairs of the company, without any notice to the proprietors. I think that such was not the meaning of this clause, and that a meeting cannot be legally held unless by notice, or unless the directors have previously agreed to meet at a certain time and place, in order that every director may know the day on which such business will be transacted, and that he may have an opportunity of attending. I am therefore of opinion that this objection must prevail.

BAYLEY, J.—I am of opinion that this meeting was not duly held, there not having been any prior agreement of the directors to meet on the 14th of *September*.

HOLROYD, J. and LITTLEDALE, J. concurred.

Rule refused.

————◆————

BECKWITH *v.* PHILBY, WILKS, and SPICER.

TRESPASS for assaulting, beating, handcuffing, and imprisoning the plaintiff, and keeping and detaining him handcuffed and imprisoned, without any reasonable or probable cause, for forty-eight hours, on a false and pretended charge of felony. Plea, not guilty. At the trial before *Littledale*, J., at the last *Lent* assizes for the county of *Essex*, it appeared in evidence that about eight o'clock in the evening on the 31st of *January*, 1826, the plaintiff was seen by a farmer sitting on the battlements of *Loughton* Bridge, having with him a bridle and saddle. Shortly before this several horses had been stolen from the neighbourhood. The farmer immediately went to the defendant, *Philby*, who was high constable of *Ongar*, but resided at *Loughton*, and informed him of the circumstance and said he thought he ought to look after the man. The defendant, *Philby*, went out accordingly, and spoke to the plaintiff and asked him several questions. The plaintiff answered in a jeering and taunting manner and said he lived in *Titty-Ball Alley*. In consequence of these answers and seeing the bridle and saddle with him, *Philby* suspected that he had been steal-

*Monday,
7th May.*

A constable may arrest a person upon a reasonable suspicion of felony and take him before a magistrate, although no felony has in fact been committed.

K K 2

ing a horse or was about to do so. The plaintiff was then searched, and in his pockets were found some horsebeans and oats. *Philby* asked him where he had come from, and he told him that he had come from *Cheshunt*, that he had been to *Romford* market that day to sell a horse, that his name was *Beckwith*, and that he had got the horse of one *Bartlet*, who lived at *Cheshunt*. He then referred *Philby* to one *Noble*, who lived within a mile of *Loughton*, as a person who knew him. No inquiry, however, was made that night of *Noble* respecting the plaintiff. *Philby* then sent for the defendant *Wilks*, a constable of *Loughton*, to take the plaintiff to the watch-house, and on *Wilks's* arrival, ordered him to handcuff the plaintiff, which was done accordingly. At the plaintiff's own desire *Wilks* took him to a public house at *Loughton*, where he remained handcuffed all night. Next morning *Wilks* delivered him into the custody of the other defendant *Spicer*, who took him before a magistrate on that day. After taking examinations, the magistrate said he thought it his duty to detain the plaintiff, but told him if there was any body near who would be bound for his appearance, he might go home to his family. *Noble*, the person before mentioned, then came forward and became bound for the plaintiff's appearance when called upon, and he was then discharged. The defendant *Philby* was present at this examination. It appeared that the plaintiff was a blacksmith residing at *Waltham Cross*, in the county of *Hertford*, that he had bought a horse, as he had stated, of *Bartlet*, who resided at *Cheshunt*, and that on the day in question he had sold the animal at *Romford* market, and that he was a person of general good character. It was contended on the part of the defendant that there was reasonable and probable cause for suspecting the plaintiff of having committed a felony, and that the defendants were justified under the circumstances of the case in detaining him, although in fact it turned out that no felony had been committed. The learned judge told the jury that if upon the whole evidence they thought the defendants had reasonable cause for suspecting that the plaintiff had committed a felony, his arrest and detention were lawful. The jury found a verdict for the defendants, but leave was given to the plaintiff to move to enter a verdict for nominal damages if the Court should be opinion that the arrest and detention were unlawful.

Gurney now moved accordingly, and contended that as there was no charge of felony made, nor any felony committed, the defendant *Philby* was not justified in making the arrest in the first instance, and still less were he and the other defendants justified in detaining the plaintiff during the night, after he had referred to *Noble* as a person who could give an account of who he was. If, indeed, a charge of felony had been made against the plaintiff by a third person, or if it turned out that a felony in fact had been committed, then the defendants might have been justified in apprehending him and detaining him in custody. But here the defendant *Philby* thought proper to act upon his own suspicion, although furnished with the means afforded by the plaintiff at the time of ascertaining that his suspicions were without foundation. The defendants, therefore, stand on the same footing with private persons, who cannot be justified in arresting another, unless a felony has been actually committed.

Lord TENTERDEN, C. J.—I am of opinion that the verdict ought not to be disturbed. Whether there was reasonable cause to suspect that this man had committed a felony or was about to commit one, having·in his possession the implements proper and necessary for that purpose, was a question of fact for the jury. Whether he was detained also beyond a reasonable time was likewise a question of fact for the jury. They have determined both questions against the plaintiff, and I should say rightly. The only question of law in the case is whether a constable, having reasonable cause to suspect that a person has committed a felony, may detain such person until he can be brought be-fore a justice of the peace to have his conduct investigated, and I am of opinion that he may. There is this distinction between the case of a constable and a private individual. The private individual must not only shew a reasonable cause for suspicion, but he must prove that a felony has been actually committed, in order to justify the detention of the party; whereas a constable, who has reasonable ground to suspect that a felony has been committed, is au-thorised to detain the party suspected, until inquiry can be made by the proper authorities. Suppose a man goes about after nightfall with all the implements of housebreaking about him, would not a constable be justified in detaining him until he gave a proper account of himself before a magistrate? I apprehend that it would be a dangerous proposition for us to lay down that he would not. Here is a man having implements and every thing about him indi-cating an intention of stealing horses. After nightfall he is found with corn in his pockets to decoy, and a bridle and saddle to carry off the animal. I think under such circum-stances there was a reasonable ground of suspicion, which being found by the jury, the constable was justified in point of law. A constable may have a reasonable ground of suspicion to justify him in arresting a man without in-quiring into the truth of his statement, but it is for the jury to determine whether the ground of suspicion was reason-able. Here the jury have determined that question. The flippant conduct of the plaintiff in the first instance might very fairly have led the constable to suppose that the re-ference to *Noble*, who lived a mile off, might not be at-tended with any satisfactory result.

BAYLEY, J.—I am also of opinion that the verdict ought not to be disturbed. Having misled the constable in the first instance, the latter was not bound to make inquiry of the party to whom the plaintiff referred. If the plaintiff wished to remove the suspicion first cast upon him, he should himself have sent for *Noble,* and if he had done so and the inquiry turned out satisfactory, probably the result would have been different. It was the plaintiff's duty to have set the constable right after he had created a suspicion of his conduct in the first instance.

HOLROYD, J. concurred.

LITTLEDALE, J.—This being an action against constables, they would be justified in arresting and detaining a party if they had reasonable cause for suspecting him of felony, although it turned out that no felony had in fact been committed. This would not be so in the case of a private individual. In *Samuel* v. *Payne* (*a*) it was held that a constable might justify an arrest in the day time on a reasonable suspicion of felony, although a felony had not in fact been committed. So in *Lawrence* v. *Hedger* (*b*) it was held that watchmen and beadles have authority at common law to arrest and detain in prison for examination persons walking in the streets at night whom there is reasonable ground to suspect of felony, although there is no proof of a felony having been committed. Again, in *Hobbs* v. *Branscomb* (*c*) it was held that a peace officer may arrest a person charged with felony, no such offence having in fact been committed. It appears to me, therefore, that the jury having found that the defendant had reasonable cause for suspecting the plaintiff of felony, the verdict is right in point of law.

Rule refused (d).

(*a*) Doug. 358.
(*b*) 3 Taunt. 14.
(*c*) 3 Campb. 420.
(*d*) *Vide* Hawk. P. C. b. 2, c. 12, 13; *R.* v. *Tooley,* 2 Ld. Raym. 1301; *Theobald* v. *Chrichmore,* 1 B. & A. 227; *Cowles* v. *Dunbar,* 2 C. & P. 565.

1827.

Monday,
7th May.

If a negotiable instrument for the payment of money is framed in such equivocal terms as to render it ambiguous whether it be a bill of exchange or a promissory note, the holder has the option of treating it as either, as against the maker.

EDIS v. BURY

ASSUMPSIT for goods sold and delivered. Plea, the general issue. At the trial before Lord *Tenterden*, C. J. at the last sittings for *Middlesex*, the plaintiff proved that he had sold and delivered to the defendant two parcels of sheep to the value of £78 : 10s. and here closed his case. The defence to the action was, that the sheep had been paid for; and a bill of exchange for the sum of £35 : 2s. given by the defendant to the plaintiff, and honoured when at maturity in part payment of the sheep, was given in evidence under a notice to produce. The defendant gave the following instrument also in evidence, but which was not paid, although given for the remainder of the amount of the sheep, viz.

£44 : 11s. 5d.   *London, 5th August,* 1826.

Three months after date I promise to pay Mr. *John Bury*, or order, forty-four pounds, eleven shillings, and five-pence value received.

J. B. Gruthrot,	(Signed)	*John Bury.*
35, *Montague Place,*	(Indorsed)	*John Bury.*
Bedford Square.		

Mr. *Gruthrot's* name was written across the face of the instrument, but which was not paid when at maturity, and there was no proof of notice of the dishonour of it to the defendant. It was contended, on the part of the defendant, that the above instrument was a bill of exchange, and that the plaintiff being guilty of laches in not giving notice of the dishonour, it was a discharge from the defendant's liability for the remainder of the amount of the sheep. On the other hand it was contended, that the instrument was a promissory note, and that the defendant, as the maker, was at all events liable upon it as such. Of this opinion was the Lord Chief Justice, and the plaintiff had a verdict for the balance of his demand, with liberty, however, to the defendant to move to enter a nonsuit.

Campbell now moved accordingly, and contended that the instrument in question must be considered as a bill of exchange, and liable to all the rules applicable to such instruments by the custom of merchants; and he cited *Gray* v. *Milner* (a), *Allan* v. *Morson* (b), and *Shuttleworth* v. *Stevens* (c). In the first of those cases it was held not to be absolutely essential that the drawer's name should be mentioned on the bill by the drawer, if there be a place for payment fixed, and the drawee accept the bill in such form by writing his name thereon, which will be an adoption of the bill on his part. In the second case it was held, that an instrument in the common form of a bill, except that the word *at* was substituted for the word *to* before the name of the drawee, was a bill and not a note; but Lord *Ellenborough* intimated, that it might be treated as either by the holder; and the same doctrine was laid down in the third case, where the word *at* was written so as to be scarcely legible for the purpose of deceit. In the present case the instrument is addressed to *J. B. Gruthrot*, and his name is written across the face of it, which imports an acceptance, and therefore it has all the essential qualities of a bill of exchange.

Lord TENTERDEN, C. J.—I think the verdict ought not to be disturbed. It must be admitted that this is an instrument of, at least, very ambiguous character. In form it is a promissory note, for it begins with the words— " Three months after date I promise to pay." In the corner it is certainly addressed " *J. B. Gruthrot*," and that name is written across the instrument, so as in that respect to give it the form of a bill of exchange, although it does not in terms contain a request to *Gruthrot* to pay. It is therefore an instrument of an ambiguous nature, but whether the one or the other I shall not positively determine. The strong inclination of my opinion is, that it should be

(a) 3 J. B. Moore, 190; 8 Taunt.   (b) 4 Camp. 115.
739; 2 Stark. 336.   (c) 1 Camp. 407.

treated as a promissory note, but I think that where a party thinks proper to issue an instrument in so ambiguous a form, the law ought to allow the holder to treat it either as a promissory note or a bill of exchange at his option. On this ground, I think, the plaintiff was at liberty to deal with this instrument as a promissory note, and, consequently, that it was unnecessary to give the defendant notice of the dishonour.

BAYLEY, J.—I agree with my Lord Chief Justice in the opinion delivered by him in this case. I think this is a promissory note, and I regard the address at the corner, *J. B. Gruthrot*, and the name *J. B. Gruthrot* on the face of the instrument, as nothing more than an intimation on the part of *Bury*, the defendant, that the amount will be paid at *Gruthrot's* house, and a consent on the part of the latter that it may be paid there. But I agree also that if a person frames an instrument in this way, so that it may be taken to be either a promissory note or a bill of exchange, the holder is at liberty to treat it either as one or the other, and that he ought not to be defeated of his claim upon it by the party who framed it being allowed to say that the holder is guilty of laches in not treating it as a bill of exchange. If the maker puts the instrument into this ambiguous form, I think the holder has the option of treating it either as a bill of exchange or as a promissory note.

HOLROYD, J.—It is clear that this instrument was originally framed as a promissory note, for it contains the words " I promise to pay;" but adding the words in the corner, " *J. B. Gruthrot*," imports a design on the part of the drawer of the instrument that the holder might be at liberty to treat it either as a promissory note or a bill of exchange. Instruments of this nature, as well as others, ought to be construed most strongly against the party making them, especially if there is any supposition of fraud. In this case, even though the conduct of the party be *bonâ fide*, still if it be equivocal whether the instrument be a bill of exchange or a promissory note, it ought to be taken favourably for the plaintiff and against the defendant who made it. I think that the addition of *Gruthrot's* name on the face of the instrument afterwards does not prevent its operating as a promissory note.

LITTLEDALE, J.—I think this instrument is a promissory note. It begins originally with the words I promise, which is the usual form of a promissory note. But it is said that there is something written at the corner of the instrument and something on the face of it, and that these two writings convert it into a bill of exchange. I think not, for to make it a bill of exchange the words " I promise to pay" must be rejected. A bill of exchange is addressed to another person, and contains a request to the drawer to pay the same. A promissory note contains no such request, but is a personal undertaking to pay, and therefore there is an essential difference between the two sorts of instruments. Suppose the words " I promise" were rejected, could this instrument then have been declared upon as a bill of exchange before *Gruthrot* accepted it? If it could not, then it was not a bill of exchange at that time, and if it was once a promissory note, *Gruthrot*, by putting his name to it, could not make it a bill of exchange.

Rule refused.

COOKE v. JACKSON.

TRESPASS for breaking and entering the plaintiff's close, called *Broadmead.* Plea, *liberum tenementum;* and issue thereon. At the trial both parties proved that they were respectively possessed of parcels of land called *Broadmead,* both in the same parish. It was objected at the trial that of the same name will not prevent the plaintiff from recovering without a new assignment.

the plaintiff ought to have new assigned so as to make the defendant a trespasser in the *locus in quo*. The objection, however, was over-ruled by the learned judge, on the authority of *Cocker* v. *Crompton*(a), and the plaintiff had a verdict.

Ludlow now moved for a rule nisi to enter a nonsuit, and contended that this case was not governed by *Cocker* v. *Crompton*, but stood upon the old rule of pleading, by which the defendant was entitled to the benefit of the common bar, if he had a close corresponding in name with the close mentioned in the plaintiff's declaration, and he cited *Goodright* v. *Rich*(b), and *Hock* v. *Bacon*(c).

Lord TENTERDEN, C. J.—Two points have been settled in cases of this description; first, that if the plaintiff in a declaration of trespass names his close, and the defendant pleads *liberum tenementum* generally, he cannot by shewing that he himself is possessed of a close of the same name, and in the same vill, turn the plaintiff round and prevent his proving a trespass in his own close; and secondly, that where there is a general district of land known by one general name, and there are several occupiers in the same district, each person may call his own part of the district by the general name. Here the plaintiff has a part of the district called *Broadmead*, and he has a right to call his close by the name of *Broadmead*. The defendant also has a close called *Broadmead* in the same district, and he also has a right to call his close by that name; but that will not prevent the plaintiff without a new assignment from going into evidence to shew that the two closes are not connected one with another. It appears to me therefore that the verdict must stand.

(a) *Ante*, vol. ii. 719; 1 B. &   (b) 7 T. R. 335.
C. 489.   (c) 2 Taunt. 156.

BAYLEY, J.—I think this case falls within the principle of the decision in *Cocker* v. *Crompton.*

HOLROYD, J. and LITTLEDALE, J. concurred.

Rule refused(*a*).

(*a*) Vide *Stevens* v. *Whistler*, 11 East, 51, and *Pratt* v. *Groome*, 15 East, 235.

RICHARDS and another *v.* PORTER.

THIS was an action for goods sold and delivered, to which there was a plea of the general issue. At the trial before *Vaughan,* B. at the last assizes for the county of *Worcester,* it appeared in evidence that on the 22d of *January,* 1826, one of the plaintiffs being at *Derby,* where the defendant resided, made a verbal contract with the latter for the sale of five pockets of hops, which were to be forwarded from *Worcester* to the defendant by the common carrier. On the 25th of *January* the plaintiffs forwarded from *Worcester* by post a regular invoice of the hops, in which the plaintiffs were described as the sellers, and the defendant as the purchaser, and the plaintiffs by the letter inclosing the invoice informed the defendant that the hops would be forwarded the same day. Accordingly on the same day the plaintiffs delivered the five pockets of hops to the carrier to be conveyed from *Worcester* to *Derby.* The hops did not appear to have reached their destination. On the 28th of *February* the defendant wrote a letter to the plaintiffs in the following terms:—" The hops (five pockets) which I bought of Mr. *Richards* on the 23d of last month are not yet arrived, nor have I ever heard of them. I received the invoice; the last was much longer than they ought to have been on the road, however if they do not arrive in a few days I must get some elsewhere, and consequently cannot accept them."

Where the vendee of a quantity of hops acknowledged by letter to the vendor the receipt of the invoice, but said that the hops were not arrived, and added "if they do not arrive in a few days I must get some elsewhere:" Held, that the invoice and the letter taken together did not constitute a note in writing of the contract, to satisfy the statute of frauds.

This was the only evidence offered of any note or memorandum of a contract in writing to satisfy the statute of frauds, and the learned judge being of opinion that it was not sufficient to take the case out of that statute directed a nonsuit.

W. O. Russell now moved for a rule nisi to set aside the nonsuit, and enter a verdict for the plaintiff for the value of the hops, and contended that as the letter in question contained an acknowledgment that the invoice had come to the hands of the defendant, it was a sufficient memorandum of the contract to satisfy the statute. If the letter had falsified the contract, there are cases to shew that it would not have been sufficient, *Cooper* v. *Smith*(a); but here the defendant recognizes the contract as still subsisting, and although he complains that the hops are not yet arrived, yet it was no part of the contract that the hops were to be delivered within any specified time. The cases of *Saunderson* v. *Jackson*(b), *Schneider* v. *Norris*(c), and *Allen* v. *Bennett*(d), shew that a subsequent letter referring to or recognizing a contract may be connected with an invoice already delivered, so as to make a sufficient note in writing to satisfy the statute. Here the defendant acknowledges the receipt of the invoice, and that is a sufficient recognition of the contract to entitle the plaintiffs to recover.

Lord TENTERDEN, C. J.—I am of opinion that this is not a note or memorandum in writing of the contract sufficient to satisfy the statute of frauds. It appears to me that the letter is a very imperfect recognition of the contract, even connecting it with the invoice. If we were to hold this to be a sufficient note in writing to bind the party, we should in effect decide, that if a man were to write a letter saying, " I have bought of you goods, which I ought to have received, but which have never come to hand, and I

(a) 15 East, 103.

(b) 2 Bos.& Pul. 238; 3 Esp. 180.

(c) 2 M. & S. 286.

(d) 3 Taunt. 169.

give you notice that I will not be bound by the bargain," was nevertheless bound to pay for them, though he had never received them; which, if we were to do, I think we should be guilty of great violation of common sense and justice. I think the case of *Cooper* v. *Smith*(a) is not in substance distinguishable from this. In that case the contract was for a quantity of flour which was entered in a common order book by the plaintiff's rider, and in order to supply the defects in the memorandum contained in the book, a letter written afterwards by the defendant was produced, in which, though he recognized the order, yet he insisted that the flour had not been delivered in time, and the Court held that this was not a sufficient memorandum in writing within the statute to bind the defendant.

PER TOTAM CURIAM.

Rule refused.

(a) 15 East, 103.

HUTCHINS *v.* MORRIS and others.

CASE against excise officers to recover a compensation in damages for a loss incurred by the plaintiff in consequence of the improper conduct of the defendants in the treatment of certain quantities of wheat, malt, and utensils, seized under a warrant of distress for penalties incurred by the plaintiff under the Malt Act, 43 *Geo.* 3, c. 74, s. 13. The first count of the declaration stated, that the defendants having taken the goods in question as and for a distress for a certain penalty, whilst they were in their possession, and within six days of such seizure, the plaintiff paid to the defendants a certain sum of money in satisfaction and discharge of the said penalty, and then and there requested the defendants to re-deliver and restore the goods; that the

Where excise officers seized and carried away goods as a distress to satisfy a conviction for penalties under the Malt Acts, and immediately afterwards the owner released the goods by paying the penalty without demanding a return of the goods:—Held, that the officers were not

liable for injury done to the goods in carrying them back to the owner of their own accord.

defendants accepted and received the said sum in discharge
of said penalty, and ought to have then and there re-delivered and restored the goods upon such request; that the
defendants wholly neglected and refused so to do, and
wrongfully kept and detained them for a long space of time,
to wit, twenty days, and during all that time so negligently
kept the same, that by and through the mere negligence of
the defendants, divers quantities of malt and utensils became
wetted, damaged, and deteriorated, &c.   The second count
stated the seizing the goods as before for a distress for a
penalty, the payment of the money in satisfaction and discharge of such penalty, an allegation that the same sum
was sufficient to satisfy such penalty, and the acceptance and
receipt by the defendants in discharge of the same, and that
thereupon it became the duty of the defendants to restore
the said goods; that the defendants did not nor would re-
deliver or restore the same, but on the contrary thereof
wrongfully, &c. kept and detained, &c. and so negligently,
that, &c.   The third count stated the seizing, &c. as before,
the payment and receipt of a sum in discharge of the
penalty, and averred that thereupon it became and was the
duty of the defendants within a reasonable time to have
restored and re-delivered the goods, and to have kept the
same in a dry and clean state, concluding with charging as
a breach of their duty, that the defendants did not re-deliver
nor in the meantime keep in a dry and clean state, but on
the contrary thereof, &c. averring special damage, as in the
first and second counts.   Fourth count in trover for wrongfully converting the goods to their own use.   Plea, the
general issue, not guilty.   At the trial, before *Burrough, J.*
at the last assizes for the county of *Somerset*, it appeared in
evidence that the plaintiff was a maltster and the defendants were excise officers.   The plaintiff had been convicted
before two justices under the Malt Acts, 22 *Geo.* 2, c. 20,
and 48 *Geo*, 3, c. 74, s. 13, in a penalty of £200, which was
mitigated by the justices to £30.   A warrant was issued by
the justices, directing the defendants to levy the penalty

and to return the surplus to the plaintiff. The defendants accordingly seized a quantity of wheat, malt, and other goods belonging to the plaintiff, and removed them off his premises. Immediately afterwards the plaintiff paid the amount of the penalty, and expecting that the goods would be immediately returned to him, did not make any demand upon the defendants to re-deliver them. In about ten days afterwards, the defendants, of their own accord, brought the goods back in an open cart, and thereby becoming exposed to the rain, the wheat and malt were very much damaged, and some portion of the wheat was entirely lost. It was objected on the part of the defendants that the action was not maintainable; first, that they were not bound to restore the goods of their own accord to the plaintiff, but that the plaintiff himself was bound to come and demand and fetch them away; and secondly, that the defendants were entitled to retain the goods until the plaintiff paid or tendered the costs of the seizure. The learned judge directed a nonsuit on both these grounds.

Erskine now moved to set aside the nonsuit and obtain a new trial, and contended that it was the duty of the defendants to have brought back the goods in the same state in which they had seized them immediately on payment of the penalty by the plaintiff. The defendants, as seizing officers, were each entitled to a share of the penalty, and therefore it was their duty immediately to restore the goods in an undamaged state, without demand; and at all events, they were bound to take proper care of the goods during the period of time they were in the custody of the law. But assuming that the defendants were not bound to re-deliver the goods, yet as they had in fact done so, that dispensed with the demand and rendered them liable for the consequences of their negligence, whereby the goods were returned in a damaged state. Two acts of misconduct were attributed to them in the third count, first, for improperly detaining the goods, and secondly, for keeping them in an improper state. This was a divisible cause of action, and if the plaintiff proved either, he was entitled to recover a verdict.

Lord TENTERDEN, C. J.—I am of opinion that the nonsuit was right. The defendants are charged with a wrongful detention of the goods, but it appears to me, that in order to make them wrong-doers, there should have been a demand of the return of the goods as soon as the penalty was paid. The plaintiff cannot by forbearing to demand the goods cast upon the officers the burden and expense of carrying them back. It is true, they brought them back of their own accord, but in doing so they did more than they need have done, and the plaintiff complains of their doing something which they were not bound by law to do. Whilst the goods were in their possession, and before the penalty was paid, they were legally bound so to treat them that they should not be injured, but until demand made they were not liable for an unlawful detention. Their undertaking afterwards to return them without demand would not make them answerable for the injury done in the transit.

BAYLEY, J.—I am of the same opinion. It was the duty of the plaintiff, as soon as he had paid the penalty, to desire to have the goods back, but he cannot now take advantage of his own negligence, and cast the consequences of the injury to the goods upon the defendants.

HOLROYD, J.—The defendants were not bound to take care of the goods after the penalty was paid. The plaintiff does not complain of any improper treatment of the goods before the penalty was paid. As soon as it was paid, the plaintiff ought to have demanded the goods, and if the defendants had refused to deliver them on demand they would in that case have been responsible.

LITTLEDALE, J. concurred.

Rule refused.

MORRIS v. MELLIN.

THIS was a rule calling upon the plaintiff to shew cause why the warrant of attorney given by the defendant in this case should not be cancelled, and why the judgment signed thereon should not be set aside, under the following circumstances:—The warrant of attorney in question was executed on the 12th of *April*, 1824, and on the face of it purported to be given for the purpose of securing payment from the defendant to the plaintiff of 750*l*. In fact the warrant of attorney was executed upon the express condition that it was only to stand as a security for a sum to be awarded by an arbitrator named by the parties. It appeared that no award had been made, and the defendant *Mellin*, in *March*, 1825, took the benefit of the Insolvent Debtors' Act, and one *James Currie* was appointed assignee of his estate and effects. The warrant of attorney was filed and judgment entered up within twenty-one days from the date of its execution. The present rule was obtained at the instance of the assignee, on the ground that the warrant of attorney was void by the statute 3 *Geo.* 4, c. 39, s. 4, inasmuch as the defeazance was not written on the same paper or parchment before the time when it was filed. Cause was now shewn by

Thursday, 10th May.

A warrant of attorney subject to a defeazance not written on the same paper, is not void against the assignee of an insolvent debtor within 3 *Geo.* 4, c. 39, s. 4; *Holroyd*, J. dissentiente.

Bompas, who contended that the fourth section of the statute comprehended only such warrants of attorney as were mentioned in the preceding sections, which warrants of attorney are made void only as against assignees of a bankrupt. Now here there was no bankruptcy, and consequently this was not a warrant of attorney within the meaning of the fourth section.

W. O. Russell, contrà, contended, that as the object of the act was to prevent frauds upon creditors by the secret execution of warrants of attorney to confess judgment, the fourth section must be so construed as to effect this object

where a party was declared insolvent, although not a bankrupt within the meaning of the bankrupt laws. It would
be a strange proposition if secret warrants of attorney
would be void only against assignees of a bankrupt, and
not against the assignees of an insolvent debtor.

Lord TENTERDEN, C. J.—The question in this case is,
whether the words " such warrant of attorney or cognovit
actionem," contained in the 3 *Geo.* 4, c. 39, s. 4, extend to
every warrant of attorney, or such only as are described
particularly in the former sections, and are there declared
void in favour of the assignees of a bankrupt, unless they
are filed within twenty-one days, or unless judgment be
entered up on them within that time. It seems to me that
the question. does not depend on the actual filing of the
warrant of attorney. Now the act professes to be made
for the purpose of preventing frauds on creditors by secret
warrants of attorney to confess judgment. The preamble
recites, that injustice is frequently done to creditors by
secret warrants of attorney to confess judgment. The
recital as well as the title, therefore, shews that the object
of the act of parliament was to protect creditors; and one
might have expected that the enactment would be co-extensive with the mischief recited, and would in express terms
make all secret warrants of attorney void against creditors,
whether they were creditors under a commission of bankrupt or under a declaration of insolvency. The second
section, however, enacts, that unless the warrant of attorney
shall be filed or judgment entered up within twenty-one
days after the execution of it, such warrant of attorney shall
be fraudulent and void against the assignees of the bankrupt. So that the enactment.is thus far narrower than the
preamble. But if we were to give effect to the fourth
section in the way we are called upon to do, we should not
only extend the enactment to protect creditors, although
no commission of bankrupt had issued against the debtor
who gave the warrant of attorney, but also to render a.

warrant of attorney void in favour of the party himself.
Now it is a general rule of construction in the interpretation of acts of parliament, that an enactment, the effect of
which is to cut down, abridge, or restrain any written instrument, shall receive a limited and not any other construction. After the preamble to which I have already
alluded, the first section of this statute enacts, "that the
holder may, if he think fit, file the warrant of attorney and
defeazance within twenty-one days." The second section
then declares what shall be the consequence if it be not
filed within the twenty-one days, namely, that it shall be
null and void, not generally, but against the assignees of a
bankrupt. The third section contains a similar enactment
as to a cognovit actionem. Then comes the fourth section,
which enacts, that if such warrant of attorney or cognovit
actionem shall be given subject to any defeazance or condition, such defeazance or condition shall be written on the
same paper or parchment on which such warrant of attorney
or cognovit actionem shall be written, before the time when
the same shall be filed, otherwise such warrant of attorney
or cognovit actionem shall be void to all intents and purposes. Now, if we were to hold every warrant of attorney
not filed within the time mentioned in the second section to
be void to all intents and purposes, by reason of the defeazance not having been written on the same paper or
parchment, we should make the act not merely afford protection to creditors under a commission of bankrupt, but
to all creditors, and we should even enable a party who
gave the warrant of attorney to treat it as a nullity on that
ground. It appears to me, therefore, that the fourth section applies only to such warrants of attorney as would by
the former provisions of the act be fraudulent and void
against creditors under a commission of bankrupt, in consequence of their not having been filed within twenty-one
days after the execution thereof, or judgment not having
been entered up within that time, and consequently that
this rule ought to be discharged.

Bayley, J.—It appears to me that this is a case of very considerable difficulty; but I am inclined to think that all the clauses of the act are to be confined to the protection of creditors under a commission of bankrupt, and do not extend to protect all creditors or parties to the instrument, so as to enable them to treat it as a nullity. The general rule certainly is that which my Lord Chief Justice has just laid down, namely, that it must be clearly shewn that it was the intention of the legislature to cut down a written instrument, before that effect is given to the words of an act of parliament which admits of a doubtful construction. If the construction contended for in this case by Mr. *Russell* were to prevail, the party himself who executed the warrant of attorney might treat it as a nullity, on the ground that the defeazance was not written on the same paper or parchment as the warrant of attorney. Now the act does not purport to say what would be the effect upon the warrant of attorney under such circumstances as between parties. The title of the act professes to prevent fraud upon creditors by secret warrants of attorney to confess judgment. Creditors, therefore, were to be the objects of protection. The preamble also shews, that the only mischief contemplated was the injustice or fraud done to creditors. The first section then proceeds to enact, not that every warrant of attorney shall be filed, but that, if the holder shall think fit, it shall be filed. There is no obligation on the holder to file the warrant of attorney, but the second section provides that warrants of attorney not filed within the time therein mentioned, or on which judgment shall not be entered up within that time, shall be void, not against all creditors, but against the assignees under a commission of bankrupt. Such an instrument, notwithstanding this enactment, therefore, would be valid against the assignees of an insolvent debtor. The second section does not apply to cognovits, but the third section contains the same provision as to a cognovit; but that is not a general provision that every cognovit actionem shall be void against all creditors, but only against the assignees of a bankrupt. Therefore all the provisions of this act seem to give protection to assignees under a commission of bankrupt, and to no other class of persons. Then the fourth section enacts, that if such warrant of attorney shall be given subject to a defeasance, such defeazance or condition shall be written on the same paper before the time when the warrant of attorney shall be filed, otherwise such warrant of attorney shall be null and void to all intents and purposes. The question, as it seems to me, depends not only on the effect of the words " such warrant of attorney," but of the words " to all intents and purposes," whether the instrument is to be void to all intents and purposes, or void only to the intent and purpose of giving to creditors that protection contemplated by the former clauses of the act. Seeing that the provisions in the three preceding sections have in view the protection of creditors only, and there being no recital in this fourth section to shew a different intent, I incline to think that this clause does not entitle the assignee of an insolvent debtor to have a warrant of attorney vacated, on the ground of the defeazance not being written on the same paper or parchment as the warrant of attorney within the time prescribed. At the time this act of parliament passed there was a rule in this Court (a) applicable, not to cognovits certainly, but to warrants of attorney, which gave some protection to parties affected by such instruments. That rule required every attorney, who should prepare a warrant of attorney to confess judgment, which was to be subject to any defeazance, to cause such defeazance to be written on the same paper or parchment on which the warrant of attorney was written, or to cause a memorandum in writing to be made on such warrant of attorney, containing the substance and effect of such defeazance. Looking, however, to this act, and to the several provisions which have been pointed out, the inclination of my opinion is, that the fourth section makes null and void those instruments only

(a) Mic. T. 42 Geo. 3, 1801.

which should be void against the assignees of a bankrupt in case they were not filed in due time, and consequently that the rule for setting aside this warrant of attorney ought to be discharged.

HOLROYD, J.—I own that the inclination of my opinion is, that the fourth section extends to all warrants of attorney. I think that the effect of giving it a narrower construction might be to render successful those very frauds which it was the object of the legislature to prevent. I also think that the enactment ought not to be narrowed by reason either of the matter contained in the title or the preamble. The preamble recites, " that injustice is frequently done to creditors by secret warrants of attorney to confess judgments, whereby persons in a state of insolvency are enabled to keep up the appearance of being in good circumstances, and the persons holding such warrants of attorney have the power of taking the property of such insolvents at any time, to the exclusion of the rest of the creditors." In the preamble, therefore, the legislature contemplates the creditors of persons in a state of insolvency, and not merely the creditors of those who afterwards become bankrupt; and it appears to me that the words of the fourth section are sufficiently extensive to include all warrants of attorney which are within the mischief recited. If they are limited in their construction to such warrants of attorney only as would be void against the assignees of a bankrupt by the second section, the consequence would be, that the creditors of an insolvent debtor, whom it was equally the object of the legislature to protect, would be deprived of all benefit of the statute. There is no doubt it must be beneficial to the creditors of an insolvent, or even to the party giving or taking a warrant of attorney, that the defeazance should be written on the same paper or parchment as the warrant of attorney, in order that precise information of the nature of the instrument might be obtained at any subsequent time, and the legislature, therefore, may have

intended to require it in all cases. The words of the fourth
section are, that such warrant of attorney or cognovit actionem shall be void to *all intents and purposes.* Now if the
construction contended for were to prevail, the instrument
would be void only to the intent and purpose of protecting
the creditors of a bankrupt. It will not be void even in
favour of the creditors of an insolvent debtor; but as it is
clear that the legislature contemplated the injustice done to
the creditors of persons in a state of insolvency, I am
strongly inclined to think that a warrant of attorney, subject
to a defeazance or condition not written on the same paper
or parchment, is void against the assignee of an insolvent
debtor within the meaning of the fourth section of the
statute 3 *Geo.* 4, c. 39.

LITTLEDALE, J.—I think this rule ought to be discharged. The question arises upon the construction to
be put upon the words " such warrant of attorney," in the
fourth section. Now these words may refer to every warrant of attorney, or such warrants only as are mentioned
in the previous sections. The title and preamble of the
act shew that the object of the legislature was to prevent
frauds upon creditors. The second and third sections
make warrants of attorney in certain cases void against the
assignees of a bankrupt. The protection of creditors,
therefore, seems to be the object of the title, the preamble,
and those two sections. The fourth section enacts, " that
if such warrant of attorney or cognovit shall be given subject to a defeazance, such defeazance shall be written on
the same paper or parchment as the warrant of attorney or
cognovit, before the time when the same, or a copy thereof,
shall be filed, otherwise such warrant of attorney or cognovit shall be void to all intents and purposes." As this
section comes immediately after the preceding sections, we
must look to them to see what is the warrant of attorney or
cognovit actionem to which the word " such" in this section
refers. It is clear that the instruments mentioned in those

sections were warrants of attorney limited in their nature, and which were to be void against assignees of a bankrupt in case they were not filed or judgment entered up on them within twenty-one days. It has been urged that this section extends to all warrants of attorney where other creditors than those of a bankrupt are interested, or even where creditors have no interest whatever. There is, however, no provision made as to the consequences of not filing a warrant of attorney where the creditors of an insolvent debtor are concerned. The true reading of the fourth section, as it seems to me, is this, that those warrants of attorney which would be void within the preceding provisions of the act, by reason of their not having been filed within twenty-one days after execution, shall be null and void also within the fourth section, for want of having the defeazance written on the same paper or parchment as the warrant of attorney or cognovit actionem. I think that in this case some light may be thrown on the question by referring to the provisions of the statute 7 *Geo.* 4, c. 57, s. 35. That section recites that it is expedient to extend the provisions of the statute 3 *Geo.* 4, c. 39, and proceeds to enact, that that act shall extend to the assignee of every prisoner who shall, within the time therein mentioned, apply to the Insolvent Court for his discharge from his confinement, as if the said last-mentioned act had been expressly therein enacted; and it then declares, that all warrants of attorney which by the last-mentioned act were declared to be fraudulent against the assignees of a bankrupt, shall be deemed fraudulent and void against the assignees of an insolvent debtor. This I consider to be a legislative declaration, that the statute 3 *Geo.* 4, c. 39, did not make such instrument void against the assignees of an insolvent debtor. On these grounds I am of opinion that this rule ought to be discharged.

Rule discharged.

WEYMER *v.* KEMBLE and MASTERMAN.

THIS was an action of trover, for the wrongful conversion of certain bank notes, money, household furniture and stock in trade. Plea, not guilty. At the trial before Lord Tenterden, C. J. at the *Middlesex* sittings after last *Trinity* term, a verdict was found for the plaintiff, subject to the opinion of this Court on the following case :—

John Mileham, a grocer, being indebted to the plaintiff in the sum of 623*l.* 13*s.* for money lent, secured to the plaintiff by a warrant of attorney, dated 24th *February,* 1819, the plaintiff on the 10th *November,* 1825, entered up judgment by *non sum informatus* thereon, and a writ of *fieri facias* at the suit of the plaintiff, indorsed to levy 637*l.* 13*s.* was issued on the same day upon such judgment, by virtue of which writ the sheriff of *Middlesex* on the same 10th *November,* 1825, levied upon the stock in trade, goods and chattels of *John Mileham* within his bailiwick, and having caused them to be duly appraised, by bill of sale duly executed, bearing date the 5th *December,* 1825, in consideration of 402*l.* 17*s.* bargained and sold the said goods and chattels taken in execution at the suit of the said plaintiff, to have and to hold the same to the said plaintiff as his own goods and chattels, to his own use for ever, and on the same day formally delivered possession of the said goods and chattels, from which time subsequently, the plaintiff carried on the business of grocer on the same premises in his own name. On the 23d *December,* 1825, *John Mileham* declared himself insolvent, and on the 30th *December* a commission of bankrupt against him was sealed, and on the following day, the 31st of *December,* the messenger under the commission took possession of all the money, goods and chattels, upon the premises comprised in the said bill of sale, which messenger under such commission of bankrupt continued in possession until the 3d of *March,* 1826, when the defendants, who had before then

A person having the security of a warrant of attorney for his debt, entered up judgment by *non sum informatus,* and took out execution against the goods of his debtor, and by bill of sale from the sheriff took possession of the same. In a few days afterwards, the debtor became bankrupt, and the assignees retook the goods. In trover, held, that the plaintiff was not a creditor having security for his debt within the 6 *Geo.* 4, c. 16, s. 108, and was entitled to recover the goods back.

been chosen and were then assignees of the bankrupt, *John Mileham*, under such commission of bankrupt, sold by public auction the whole of the said goods and chattels on the premises, and received the proceeds thereof together with the money which the messenger possessed himself of, as aforesaid, and also such sums of money as had been realized by the sale of the goods on the premises during the possession of the messenger. The goods were demanded before the sale from the defendants who refused to deliver them up.

Parke, for the plaintiff, contended that the plaintiff was entitled to recover in this action, he having *bonâ fide* purchased the goods in question under an execution before the bankruptcy of *Mileham*. It will be contended on the other side, that the assignees of the bankrupt are entitled, notwithstanding the sale to the plaintiff, to retain possession of the goods by force either of the old bankrupt law or the new bankrupt law, 6 *Geo.* 4, c. 16. By section 108 of the last mentioned act, it is enacted, " That no creditor having security for his debt, or having made any attachment in *London* or any other place, by virtue of any custom there used, of the goods and chattels of the bankrupt, shall receive upon any such security or attachment more than a rateable part of such debt except in respect of any execution or extent served and levied by seizure upon, or any mortgage of or lien upon any part of the property of such bankrupt before the bankruptcy, provided that no creditor, though for a valuable consideration, who shall sue out execution upon any judgment obtained by default, confession, or *nil dicit*, shall avail himself of such execution to the prejudice of other fair creditors, but shall be paid rateable with such creditors." Now the question is, whether the property in these goods was bound by the sale to the plaintiff. According to the authorities before the passing of the late act, it appears that a bankruptcy subsequent to the seizure would not divest the execution creditor of the right of property in the goods. In *Smallcombe* v. *Cross* (a) it was held that goods were bound by a sale under a *fieri facias*, although they ought to have been seized under a prior writ, and *Holt*, C. J. said, " If a writ be delivered to the sheriff against *A.* and before it be executed *A.* becomes bankrupt, the execution is superseded." It was held also in *Coles* v. *Davies* (b) that a seizure of goods under a *fieri facias* was not affected by a subsequent bankruptcy. The question then in this case depends upon the construction of the 6th *Geo.* 4, c. 16, s. 108. By that section, the legislature recognises two descriptions of judgments; the first, a judgment after verdict, and secondly, a judgment by confession, or *nil dicit.* It is clear, therefore, that the enactment cannot comprehend both classes of judgments, for if it did, the assignees might rip up a transaction of this kind, taking place many years before the bankruptcy. This clause cannot reasonably be construed to affect a judgment after verdict, when the goods are actually seized before the bankruptcy. It may be otherwise in cases where the execution upon the judgment by *nil dicit* is not perfected by an actual sale. Here the execution was completely executed, and the sale and transfer of the property took place before the bankruptcy. The fruits, therefore, of the execution cannot be touched by operation of this clause. In the case of *Taylor* v. *Taylor* (c) the Court suggested that the construction of this clause now contended for was the true construction, and they refused an application by assignees of a bankrupt to set aside an execution issued before the bankruptcy, and intimated that it was a question for a Court of equity. That is an authority to shew that at all events the plaintiff is entitled to the judgment of this Court. If the seizure of the goods was the dividing point under the old bankrupt law, there seems to be no reason why the same rule should not be adopted in construing the modern act.

F. Pollock, contrà. The question certainly is, whether

(a) 1 Ld. Raym. 251. (b) Ib. 724. (c) *Ante*, vol. viii. 159; 5 B. & C. 392.

tion was intended to relate. He was not at the time of the
bankruptcy a *creditor* having security for his debt, because
he had ceased to have any security for his debt, having
actually availed himself of it by the sale of the bankrupt's
goods before the bankruptcy occurred. The words of the
section in question are, that " no *creditor* having security
for his debt, &c. shall receive upon any such security more
than a rateable part of such debt;" then follows an exception of certain cases, " except in respect of any execution
or extent served and levied by seizure upon or any mortgage
of or lien upon any part of the property of the bankrupt
before the bankruptcy." The plaintiff, therefore, comes
within the meaning of the description of a person having
security; for after seizure of the goods and before sale, he
may well be said to have a security for his debt by reason
of his right to have the goods sold. Then follows the proviso that " no creditor," though for a valuable consideration,
who shall sue out execution upon any judgment obtained
by default, confession, or *nil dicit*, shall avail himself of
such execution to the prejudice of other fair creditors, but
shall be paid rateably with such creditors." Now that
only limits the exception, and the exception applies only
to cases falling within the first part of the section, namely,
the cases of creditors having security. The present plaintiff
was not at the time of the bankruptcy a *creditor* having
security for his debt, because at that time his debt was
satisfied. It appears to me that this is the true construction
of the act of parliament, and that we ought to give judgment for the plaintiff.

Bayley, J.—I agree with my Lord Chief Justice in his
construction of this clause. I think the proviso ties down
the exception, and that the exception does not apply to any
persons who are not within the operation of the preceding
part of the section, namely, " creditors having security for
their debts." Here the plaintiff, at the time of the bankruptcy, had ceased to be a creditor, by the satisfaction of his

debt under the execution, and, therefore, he is not affected
by the statute. Unless we put this construction upon this
section it would lead to very serious consequences. It
would be in the power of the assignees of the bankrupt to
overreach every payment of a debt upon a judgment by
default, confession, or *nil dicit*, although the act of bankruptcy was committed ten years afterwards.

H𝙾𝙻𝚁𝙾𝚈𝙳, J.—I think the best construction that can be
given to this clause is that now put upon it by the Court.
At the time of the bankruptcy the plaintiff's judgment was
satisfied, and his debt actually paid, and, therefore, he was
no longer a *creditor*, and, consequently, not either within
the general words of the clause, or within the exception.
He stands entirely independent of the exception, whatever
may be the construction to be put upon it with respect to
other classes of persons.

L𝙸𝚃𝚃𝙻𝙴𝙳𝙰𝙻𝙴, J.—I am of the same opinion. The
clause is very obscurely worded, but I think upon the whole
the plaintiff is entitled to recover. Although the plaintiff
had a security before the act of bankruptcy, still that security
being at an end and satisfied before the act of bankruptcy,
the act of parliament does not apply to him. It seems to
me that this plaintiff is no more a creditor in respect of the
sum of 627*l.* 13*s.* than if the debt had been settled by the
bankrupt himself in ready money without the benefit of any
security. I, therefore, think that judgment ought to be
given for the plaintiff.

Postea to the plaintiff.

1847.

Wednesday,
16th May.

Where a surrender of a copyhold was made out of Court in 1790, and presented by the homage in 1792, but no entry of the surrender and presentment was made on the rolls of the manor, through the inadvertence of the steward, although the fee for that purpose was paid by the agent of the surrenderee, and the enrolment did not in fact take place until 1820:—Held, that the surrender and presentment might be proved by the draft of an entry produced from the muniments of the manor and the parol testimony of the foreman of the homage, who made such presentment. *Semble,* that a custom to present a surrender for enrolment within an indefinite time, is an unreasonable custom.

Doe on the Demise of J. PRIESTLEY and JANE his Wife, late JANE HUTTON, v. CALLOWAY.

THIS was an ejectment for certain premises, consisting of a messuage and lands, with the appurtenances, situate in *Weedon Beck,* in the county of *Northampton,* against the defendant as tenant in possession, but which ejectment was defended by the annuitants hereinafter mentioned. At the trial before *Holroyd, J.* at the *Summer* assizes for the county of *Northampton,* in 1823, a verdict was found for the lessors of the plaintiff, subject to the opinion of the Court on the following case :—

The premises, for the recovery of which the action was brought, are copyhold tenements of inheritance holden of the manor of *Weedon Beck,* under the provost and fellows of *Eton College,* who are the lords of the manor. *Thomas Bennett,* hereinafter mentioned, was seised in fee of the premises in 1790. The following written document, brought from among the muniments of the manor of *Weedon Beck,* was given in evidence on the part of the plaintiff :—" The manor of *Weedon Beck,* in the county of *Northampton.* The first day of *May,* in the year of our Lord, 1790. Be it remembered, that on the day and year above-written, *Thomas Bennett,* late of *Weedon Beck* aforesaid, but now of *Buckingham,* in the county of *Bucks,* grazier, a customary tenant of the manor aforesaid, and *Elizabeth* his wife, did, out of Court, surrender by the rod into the hands of the lords of the said manor, by the hands and acceptance of *Thomas Hearne,* Gent. (deputy-steward of the same manor, and for this turn and purpose only lawfully constituted and appointed), the said *Elizabeth* being solely examined apart from her said husband by the said deputy-steward and consenting, according to the custom thereof, all that messuage, &c. (setting out the premises for which the action was brought), to the use and behoof of *Jane Hutton,* of *Maids Morton,* in the county of *Bucks,* spinster, and of her

heirs and assigns for ever, according to the custom of the
said manor, by the rents and services therefore due and of
right accustomed: provided always, nevertheless, that if the
said *T. Bennett*, his heirs, executors, or administrators, or
any of them, do and shall well and truly pay or cause to be
paid unto the said *Jane Hutton*, her executors, administrators, or assigns, the full sum of 1000*l.* at the rate of
4*l.* 10*s.* for every 100*l.* by the year, upon the 1st day of
November, now next ensuing the day of the date of these
presents, then this present surrender shall be void and of
none effect, or else be and remain in full force.

Taken out of Court the day   *Thomas Bennett*,
   and year first above-   *Elizabeth Bennett.*"
   written, by me,
   Thomas Hearne, Deputy-Steward."

Under the signatures in the surrender was written a memorandum in the following words:—" Presented by *David
Atchison*, foreman of the jury, at a Court held the 10th day
of *December*, 1792." By the custom of the manor surrenders may be taken out of Court by a deputy-steward, and
surrenders so taken may be presented at any subsequent
Court. There is no limited time for presenting such surrenders; sometimes they are presented many years after
they are made, although there may have been Courts holden
in the mean time. A written document or paper (the first
two sheets whereof were missing), brought from among the
muniments of the manor of *Weedon Beck*, and relating to
the proceedings of the Court of the 10th of *December*,
1792, was given in evidence on the part of the plaintiff;
and that part which related to the premises in question
began thus:—" At this Court it is found by the homage,
that on the 1st day of *May*, in the year of our Lord, 1790,
Thomas Bennett, late of *Weedon Beck*, &c." (setting out a
surrender by the said *Thomas Bennett* similar in terms to
the one before-mentioned). The document lastly above set
out is indorsed with these words—" Draft of Court for

Weedon Beck, 92," in the handwriting of one Smith, a clerk of Mr. T. Barnard, the then steward of the manor. Barnard died in 1796. Smith died in 1818. The last-mentioned document was tendered in evidence on the part of the plaintiff, and objected to on the part of the defendant, but admitted by the learned judge, subject to the opinion of this Court both as to its admissibility and legal effect. David Atchison was foreman of the jury at a Court holden for the manor of Weedon Beck, on the 10th of December, 1792. The surrender of Thomas Bennett, in writing above set out, was brought to him at the said Court, as foreman of the jury, by John Harris, the then bailiff; he took it and presented it to Mr. Thomas Barnard, the steward, to be enrolled. The presentment was the act of the homage, and presented by Atchison as foreman of the jury, and he at the same time wrote the memorandum now appearing of the surrender and above set out. Mr. T. Barnard, the steward of the manor, received the presentment from Atchison, and demanded half-a-guinea for the enrolling of the said surrender, which was paid by John Harris, the then bailiff, on behalf of the mortgagee. The above-mentioned facts as to the holding of the Court on the 10th of December, 1792, and as to all the proceedings that took place at that Court, were proved by the said David Atchison from memory. This evidence was objected to on the part of the defendant, but received subject to the opinion of this Court as to its admissibility. Much other business was done at the same Court (some of which is referred to as done at a Court of that date by the rolls of subsequent Courts), but no other written document appeared to have been made at that Court, except the draft of the roll before-mentioned relating to the premises in question, and which relates also to other business of the manor done at the same Court; nor does there appear on the Court rolls any entry of a Court being holden in 1792, unless the Court should be of opinion that the draft above-mentioned can be considered as a court-roll; nor has there been any mutilation of, or erasure, in the

existing Court rolls. Interest was duly paid to the mortgagee for 1000*l.* up to the year 1818; but it did not appear
to have been so paid with the knowledge of the defendant
or of *Horlock* or *Yems*, or their trustees. On the 19th of
June, 1820, a Court was duly holden, the proceedings of
which, as far as relates to the premises in question, are contained in the following entry in the Court rolls :—" The
manor of *Weedon Beck*, in the county of *Northampton.*
The special Court-baron of the provost and college royal of
the blessed Mary of *Eton*, nigh *Windsor*, in the county of
Bucks, holden in and for the said manor, on Monday, the
19th day of *June*, in the year of our Lord, 1820, before
Edward Brown, Gent. the deputy of *Abraham Moore*, Esq.
the chief steward of the said manor. At this Court the
homage present, that at a Court holden in and for the said
manor, on the 10th day of *December*, 1792, a certain conditional surrender, bearing date the 1st day of *May*, 1790,
from *Thomas Bennett*, then late of *Weedon Beck* aforesaid,
but then of *Buckingham*, grazier, a customary tenant of the
said manor, and *Elizabeth* his wife, of all his copyhold or
customary messuages, lands, tenements, and hereditaments
whatsoever, lying within and holden of the manor aforesaid,
to the use of *Jane Hutton* of *Maids Morton*, in the county
of *Bucks*, spinster, and of her heirs and assigns for ever, for
securing the repayment of 1000*l.* and lawful interest, was
duly presented by the homage at that Court for enrolment,
but which, through inadvertence of the steward, was omitted
to be done, the homage therefore again at this Court present
the said additional surrender in the words and figures following." Then follows the surrender first above set out.
On the 15th of *May*, 1823, at a manor Court holden of the
manor of *Weedon Beck*, the lessors of the plaintiff were
duly admitted tenants to the said premises on the said surrender of *Thomas Bennett* and *Elizabeth* his wife, according
to the custom of the manor. On the part of the defendant
it was proved that *Thomas Bennett* died leaving a son,
John Bennett, his heir at law, who was admitted on the

22d day of *October*, 1807. *John Bennett* sold the premises to one *Thomas Smith*, who was admitted on the 27th of *October*, 1808, and who, on the 12th of *December*, 1814, granted an annuity to *Horlock* and *Yems* for 1998*l.* and duly surrendered the premises to trustees, (who previously to the completion of the purchase searched the Court rolls at *Eton* for incumbrances but found none), by surrender dated the 11th of *December*, 1814, and which surrender was duly presented and entered on the Court rolls at the next Court holden on the 3d of *May*, 1815, and the said trustees were admitted the 28th day of *February*, 1824 (*a*).

S. M. Phillips, for the plaintiffs, contended that there was a complete title proved in the lessors of the plaintiff to the premises in question. It appeared upon the case that *Thomas Bennett*, being seised in fee, had surrendered out of Court to one of the lessors of the plaintiff, *Jane Hutton*, by way of mortgage, and that she was admitted in *May*, 1823, the surrender being in 1790. The only question, therefore, in this case will be as to the effect of the presentment. It is admitted that by the old rule of copyhold law, the surrender must be presented in Court, and that the presentment must be made at the next Court, but by custom it may be at any subsequent Court, *Com. Dig. Copyhold, tit. Presentment*, *Moore* v. *Moore* (*b*). With respect, therefore, to the effect of the surrender, it is submitted that there was abundant proof to establish the fact of a presentment. In the first place the document in question is to be taken as an original of itself. It was delivered to the foreman of the jury, and by him to the steward of the Court for enrolment, the enrolment fee was paid to him by the agent of the surrenderee,

(*a*) In the statement of the case the point intended to be argued was omitted to be mentioned in the paper books, and the Court expressed strongly its disapprobation of this, which would lead to a very inconvenient practice, and

intimated that if, in future, gentlemen whose province it was to settle cases did not state the point intended to be raised, they would not hear the argument when the case was called on.

(*b*) 2 Ves. 601.

and the steward received it, and an entry was accordingly made of the document, and which was preserved amongst the muniments of the Court. The only question therefore is, whether this is to be considered as a complete and formal presentment, there being no case in the books which prescribes any particular form of presentment. Here is the fact of a surrender, and also the fact of a presentment. The document produced, to prove the latter must be treated as an original roll of Court. Admitting, however, that this is not to be taken as an original roll by itself, still it must be presumed that there was another roll of Court from which this was taken, that the original has been lost, and this document must be received and acted upon as secondary evidence. Even if it cannot be admitted as an original roll or as secondary evidence of a roll, still the parol evidence to shew that there was a presentment and surrender in fact, and the enrolment fee paid, and the steward being a public officer, it must be presumed that every thing was done properly by him. There is no case which holds that the presentment of a surrender cannot be proved without writing. Presentment is no part of the title so long as there is an actual surrender. It cannot, however, be disputed that there was a due presentment in *June*, 1820, and that, according to the custom of this manor, was a sufficient proof of a legal surrender.

Pennington, contrà. If the document in question can be considered as an original Court roll, then there is an end of the question. In order to support the lessors of the plaintiff's title, it was incumbent on them to produce either the original Court roll, or a copy of it, in order to establish a regular surrender. It is laid down in the books, that the usual and ordinary mode of proving a surrender and admittance is by producing the original Court rolls, or a copy thereof properly stamped. Indeed it is said that this is the only evidence of title to copyhold lands. In *Co. Litt.* section 75, it is laid down, that " copyhold tenants are called tenants by copy of Court roll, because they have no other evidence concerning their tenements but only the copies of Court rolls;" and in *Kite* and *Quintin's* case(a) the same rule is laid down. These authorities prove not only that the copies of the Court rolls are the usual evidence of alienation, but the only evidence of admittance. In *Calthorpe on Copyholds*, 47, there is this dictum, " if the lord in open Court doth grant a copyhold land, and the steward maketh no entry thereof in the Court rolls, this is not good, though it be never so publicly done, nor no collateral proof can make it good." He then goes on, " if the rolls be also lost, yet it seemeth that by proof he can make this good." This must mean that if the rolls having existed are proved to have been lost, then the party may go into secondary evidence, but here there was no proof of any roll having existed, but the defect was sought to be supplied by an instrument and by parol evidence to supply the place of a roll. The rolls, however, being perfectly silent as to any presentment having ever been made, the parol evidence, in the present instance, was inadmissible to prove the presentment and surrender. It is certainly laid down in several of the books that Court rolls are not records, and it is not insisted that Court rolls require the same degree of certainty as records, and it is admitted that there are several cases which have held that a party shall not be bound by the Court rolls. This doctrine is recognized in *Towers* v. *Moore* (b), where it was held that Court rolls not being records may be set right by parol evidence, if there be a mistake. In that case the Court said, that in case of a surrender made by the steward of a copyhold, if there be any mistake, that is only a matter of fact, and the Courts of law will admit an averment that there was a mistake either as to the lands or uses. [Lord *Tenterden*, C. J. If you can prove title to a copyhold by other means than the roll, then there is an end of the argument for which you are contending.] The second presentment of the surrender, made in

: (a) 4 Rep. 25.   (b) 2 Vern. 98.

1820, does not cure the objection to the proof of the plaintiff's title. That is bad for two reasons; first, it was too late; and secondly, it was informal. It is laid down in *Co. Litt.* s. 40, and in *Gilbert's Tenures*, 280, that a presentment by the general custom of manors is to be made at the next Court-baron immediately after the surrender, but by special custom in some places it will be good though made at the second or other subsequent Court. There is no authority to shew, however, that a custom to make a surrender at any indefinite time is good. That would be an unreasonable custom, and could not be supported. Admitting that the presentment in 1820 was not too late, still it was informal and insufficient, inasmuch as the jury do not present that the surrender was made out of Court according to the custom, which they ought to have done.

Phillips, in reply. It may be that the usual evidence of title to copyhold lands is the Court rolls themselves or copies, but it does not therefore follow that this is the only admissible evidence to prove title to such property. Indeed the authorities on the other side are conclusive upon this point.

This case was argued on *Tuesday*, the 15th *May*, during the absence of *Bayley*, J. The Court took time to consider of the case, and now on this day

Lord Tenterden, C. J. delivered judgment. This case was argued before us yesterday. The question was whether the surrender of a copyhold estate which had been made out of Court was sufficiently proved to have been presented to the Court so as to give a valid title under it. The surrender itself was made on the 1st of of *May*, 1790, and there is no doubt that if a surrender and presentment can be proved by any other evidence than an entry upon a fair roll of the Court, the surrender and presentment in this case was abundantly proved. There can be no doubt of that. There had been a presentment and enrolment of the surrender at a much later date than in 1790, namely, in 1820. It was contended that that presentment and enrolment was sufficient in point of law, but that could only be good upon a supposition that there was a custom in this manor, which is in fact found in this case, to present a surrender at an indefinite period of time from the time when the surrender actually took place. On the other hand it was contended that though such a custom does exist in this manor, still it is unreasonable and therefore cannot be supported. It is not necessary for the Court to give any opinion in the present case on that point. I can only say that I should hesitate long before I determined that such a custom was good in point of law. The surrender made in 1790 was, as it appears by the evidence, not presented at the next Court, but at the Court holden in *December*, 1792. The surrender was made out of Court to the deputy-steward of the manor, and it was presented in Court by the homage on the 10th of *December*, 1792. That was proved by the actual production of a surrender from the muniments of the lord, with an indorsement in the handwriting of the steward, purporting that it was presented by *Atchison* at a Court holden on the 10th of *December*, 1792, and *Atchison*, the person named as having made the presentment, being still living at the time of the trial, was examined as a witness and proved that fact. There was this further proof, namely, a paper indorsed on the back " Draft of Court for *Weedon Beck*, 92," in the handwriting of the then steward of the manor. That paper was imperfect, some part of it having been torn, but the entry of this surrender and of its presentment was perfect. But the question is whether independently of such an entry in the Court rolls, properly so called, the evidence I have stated is not abundantly sufficient to shew that the surrender was made and presented in proper time so as to give a title under it. It was contended that the title to a copyhold tenement cannot be proved by anything but the Court roll, or a copy of it, and *Co. Litt.* s. 75, was cited in support of that position. But the general expressions there used must be understood with this qualification, that the proper proof of copyhold title is by the rolls of the manor Court, in contradistinction to other species of evidence as to matters in pais or matters of record, such as a feoffment, a charter, or a fine and recovery. Now if it be held that the title to a copyhold tenement could be proved by nothing but the production of the Court rolls, or a copy thereof, great inconvenience might ensue. Suppose the rolls of the manor to be all destroyed by an accidental fire, and copies either not to have been delivered out through the delay of the steward, (which too often occurs,) or actually to have been delivered to the tenant and lost, as writings of that description which are contained in a small compass may easily be, could it be said that all the copyholders, if they had not copies to produce, would lose their titles to their estates? It appears to me to be impossible to maintain such a proposition. Then if it cannot be said that the production of a roll itself, or of a copy taken from it, is the only evidence, it seems to me that in the case before the Court there was abundant evidence to satisfy all that was by law requisite. There are cases which have been decided in Courts of law, which shew that the entry upon the roll is not conclusive upon the parties, but that if there be a mistake in the entry, that mistake may be shewn by averment in pleading, or by proof of the fact before a jury, and not merely that it may be corrected by a decree of a Court of equity to set the roll right and make all appear correct. That has been decided in two instances, in one of which there was a mistake in the date of the Court roll. By the Court roll it appeared that the Court was held on a particular day, that day did not answer the party producing the roll, and it was held that he might, notwithstanding the entry therein mentioned, shew that the Court was not held on the day there specified, but on another. That point was settled in the case of *Burgess* v. *Forster*(a). I need

(a) 1 Leon. 289.

only read that part of the report which relates to this point. The surrender was entered on a roll of the Court dated the 2d of *May*, and the letter of deputation to the steward before whom it was taken was dated the 3d of *June*, in the same year, and the Court were clearly of opinion " that this entry of the date of the Court should not prejudice the party, for that entry was not matter of record, but was but an escrow, and if the parties had been at issue upon the time of the surrender made, or of the Court holden, the same should not be tried by the rolls of the manor, but by the country, and the party might give in evidence the truth of the matter, and should not be bound by the roll, and according to this resolution of the Court judgment was given." The next case was *Biend* v. *Biend*(a). There a father being seised of freehold and copyhold lands settled the same upon his second son and his male issue upon the death of his eldest son without male issue, and covenanted to surrender his copyholds to those uses, but instead thereof the surrender was entered on the roll to the use of the heirs general; this surrender was vacated by a decree, and a new surrender made according to the settlement. This was a decision of a Court of equity. In another case an additional surrender was added to the roll in order to pass other lands(b). That is a still stronger case. This is reported on the authority of *Dyer*. These lands were held of the manor of *A*. The surrender in the roll was by the name of " all the lands, tenements, and hereditaments," and the question was whether more land passed than was specified in the surrender, which, says the reporter, was matter of doubt for twenty-one years, and according to the report of the opinion of *Dyer*, no more lands would pass than were expressed in the surrender, but the Lord Chief Justice and many others were of a different opinion. In *Co. Copyholder*, s. 40, it is laid down, " that if a conditional surrender be presented, and the steward in entering it omitteth the condition, yet upon sufficient proof made in Court, the surren-

(a) Cas. temp. Finch, 254.　　　(b) See *Jerningham's* case.

der shall not be avoided, but the roll amended, and this shall be no conclusion to the party to plead or give in evidence the truth of the matter;" and *Kite* and *Quintin's* case is to the same effect. There is one other case which I am inclined to mention, namely, a decision of Lord *Holt* at *nisi prius,* reported anonymously in Ld. *Raym.* 735. The dispute was between the lord and the devisee of the copyholder, and Lord *Holt,* C. J. was of opinion as against the lord, that the rough draft of the surrender and admittance made by the steward of the manor was admissible evidence. It certainly does not appear in that case whether a fair roll had been engrossed and lost by the lord, but I cannot think that that is material, for the draft is not properly speaking a copy, but is the original from which the fair roll is afterwards made out. The draft itself is more in the nature of an original than the fair copy, though the latter is more convenient for reference, and therefore is the document which is generally resorted to. For these reasons, we who have heard the case argued are of opinion that there was sufficient proof to entitle the lessors of the plaintiff to recover.

1827.

DOE
v.
CALLOWAY.

Postea to the plaintiff.

SAUNDERS *v.* MUSGRAVE, Bart.

Wednesday,
16th May.

An agreement for the sale and assignment of a term in certain premises contained a stipulation that the vendee should

THIS was an action for money had and received. Plea, *non assumpsit.* At the trial before Lord *Tenterden,* C. J., at the sittings in *London* after last *Michaelmas* term, the case was this:—In *December,* 1824, B. F. *Tucker* entered into a contract with one J. *Moon* for the sale of a term of years in a house and premises situate at *Clifton,* and in con- " in the meantime and until the assignment was made, pay and allow to the vendor at the rate of 100*l.* per annum, from the time of taking possession of the premises until the completion of the purchase:"—Held, that this constituted the relation of landlord and tenant, and that a half-yearly payment having become due before the completion of the purchase, the landlord was entitled to be first satisfied out of the proceeds of the tenant's effects sold under a *fieri facias.*

sideration of 1260l. to be paid by Moon, he agreed that he would on payment of that sum at the request of Moon execute to him an effectual assignment of the premises for the residue of a certain term of years then unexpired, and would on or before the 25th of March then next erect an additional room and make certain other alterations, and put up certain fixtures, and in consideration thereof Moon agreed to pay the 1260l. on or before the 21st of December, 1825. It was farther agreed that in the meantime and until the assignment was made, Moon should pay and allow to Tucker at the rate of 100l. per annum, from the time of taking possession of the premises until the completion of the purchase; in equal half-yearly payments; and Tucker agreed to furnish an abstract within three months. In the month of January, 1825, Moon took possession of the premises and continued in possession until the month of November in the same year, when a writ of fi. fa. issued against him at the suit of the present plaintiff for 150l., and was delivered to the defendant, being then sheriff of Gloucestershire, to execute. Upon this Tucker gave notice to the defendant that 75l. for three quarters of a year's rent was due to him, and the defendant paid over to him out of the proceeds of the levy 50l. for half a year's rent. The remainder of the goods produced only 80l., and the present action was commenced against the sheriff to recover the sum of 50l. so paid over to Tucker, on the ground that the relation of landlord and tenant subsisted between him and Moon. It appeared that after Moon took possession of the premises, Tucker agreed to allow him 12l. in lieu of some fixtures which were to have been put into the house, and in February, 1825, Moon, after he had been in possession, paid Tucker in advance a sum of 10l. It farther appeared that Tucker had never completed the repairs and alterations stipulated for in the agreement. On the part of the defendant it was contended that the 100l. per annum, which Moon had agreed to pay until the completion of the purchase, was a rent, that one half-year's rent was due at the time of the execution, and that consequently the sheriff was justified in paying over the 50l. On the part of the plaintiff it was insisted that the 100l. was not a rent, and that at all events the plaintiff was entitled to a verdict for the two sums of 12l. and 10l. The noble and learned judge was of opinion that the 100l. was a rent, and directed the jury to find a verdict for the plaintiff for 50l., with liberty however to the defendant to move to enter a nonsuit. In Hilary term Campbell obtained a rule nisi for entering a nonsuit or reducing the verdict to the sum of 22l.

Marryat and *F. Kelly* now shewed cause. The question in this case turns upon the construction of the agreement entered into between *Tucker* and *Moon*. That agreement does not constitute the relation of landlord and tenant. It is merely a contract for the sale of the remainder of a term of years in the premises. It contains no words of demise, no reservation of rent; no letting, in short nothing that imports a tenancy, or which would give to the supposed landlord a power of distress under the statute. In the case of *Dunk* v. *Hunter* (a) it was held that a landlord cannot distrain unless there be an actual demise at a specific rent. There a tenant was in possession under a memorandum of agreement, whereby the defendant as lessor agreed to let a house on lease for twenty-one years, at the net clear rent of 68l. per annum; the tenant to enter at any time on or before a particular day on paying the sum of 50l. on entry, and there was a purchasing clause in the lease. Under these circumstances the Court held that this only amounted to an agreement for a future lease, and that no lease having been executed, and no rent subsequently paid; the landlord was not entitled to distrain. Now that case is perfectly analogous to the present. Here there was no demise, nor was there any reservation of rent. It is merely a contract of purchase, with the stipulation that in order that the vendor may not be prejudiced, the vendee shall pay 100l.

(a) 5 B. & A. 322.

per annum until the former shall be enabled to complete the contract, and until the latter shall pay the purchase money. It cannot be contended that *Moon* was to pay at all events 100*l.* per annum if *Tucker* did not perform his agreement to repair and improve the premises, or if he failed to furnish an abstract and to do any thing towards the completion of the contract. Another objection, shewing that the relation of landlord and tenant did not subsist betwixt these parties, is, that the payment until the completion of the purchase was to be *at the rate* of 100*l.* per annum. Now according to the case of *Parker* v. *Harris*(a), a reservation of rent *at the rate* of 18*l.* per annum is bad. [*Bayley*, J. But here the stipulation was that 100*l.* per annum should be paid from the time of taking possession of the premises until the completion of the purchase, " in equal half-yearly payments."] At all events the plaintiff is entitled to a verdict for the 10*l.* actually paid and the 12*l.* which *Tucker* had agreed to allow *Moon.*

Campbell, in support of the rule. The claim for the two sums of 10*l.* and 12*l.* was quite a surprise upon the defendant at nisi prius, because there had been admissions entered into between the parties in order to raise the next question whether the landlord was entitled to be paid any thing before the goods were removed from the premises. The plaintiff alleged that the payment of 50*l.* to the landlord was illegal, and that was the only point in dispute. It did not, however, appear that the sum of 10*l.* was paid as part of the rent, nor that the sum of 12*l.* was to be considered as such a payment *quâ* rent. The question then is what was the relation subsisting between *Moon* and *Tucker*? There is no doubt *Moon* was to pay something. Then what was that something? It was a hundred pounds per annum for the time he was in possession of the premises, payable *in equal half-yearly payments.* The rent was to run from the time of taking possession, the sum was fixed,

(a) 1 Salk. 262; 4 Mod. 77.

and the time of payment agreed upon. Here, therefore, there was every essential requisite of a demise and reservation of rent. This case is distinguishable from *Dunk* v. *Hunter,* because there was no fixed yearly rent there. There is here. The agreement to repair is not a condition precedent to the payment of the rent, for whether the repairs were done or not, still *Moon* was liable to pay a fixed rent of 100*l.* per annum. The breach of the agreement to repair might give *Moon* a right of cross action, but that would not relieve him from the stipulation to pay rent.

Lord TENTERDEN, C. J.—I am of opinion that the relation of landlord and tenant, at a fixed rent of 100*l.* per annum, payable half-yearly, to commence from the time of taking possession of the premises, was created between *Moon* and *Tucker.* I think *Tucker* had a right of distress if the rent was not paid every half-year. Then as to the right to an abatement on account of the neglect to repair, I think that the breach of the agreement in that respect does not give *Moon* any right to an abatement from the rent, but merely to maintain a cross action. I am, however, of opinion that when *Tucker* agreed to allow 12*l.*, that meant that it should be allowed out of the first payment that became due, and I think it must also be considered that the 10*l.* was part payment of the half-year's rent. The plaintiff will therefore be entitled to have a verdict entered at all events for those two sums.

BAYLEY, HOLROYD and LITTLEDALE, Js. concurred.

Rule absolute for reducing the verdict to 22*l.*

1827.

*Wednesday,
16th May.*

The Court, without a judge's certificate, will not enter a suggestion on the roll to deprive the plaintiff of his costs under 5 *Geo.* 4, c. 106, in an action where the defendant resided in *Wales* at the time of serving process, although the sum recovered was under 50*l.*

MORTIMER *v.* HARRIS

W. E. TAUNTON moved for a rule to shew cause why a suggestion should not be entered on the judgment roll, that the plaintiff had not recovered more than 50*l.* so as to entitle the defendant to judgment of nonsuit and costs thereon. It was an action of assault and battery tried in an *English* county, the cause of action having arisen within the principality of *Wales.* By stat. 5 *Geo.* 4, c. 106, it is enacted, " that in case the plaintiff in any action on the case for words, or of debt, trespass on the case, assault and battery, or other personal action, where the cause of such action shall arise within the dominion of *Wales,* and which shall be tried at the assizes at the *English* county nearest to that of *Wales* in which the cause of action is laid to arise, shall not recover by verdict a debt or damages to the amount of 50*l.*; then, if the judge who tried the cause, on evidence appearing before him, shall certify on the back of the nisi prius record that the defendant was resident in *Wales* at the service of the mesne process on him in such action, (or on such fact being suggested on the record or judgment roll,) a judgment of nonsuit shall be entered, and the defendant shall have like judgment and remedy thereon to recover costs against the plaintiff as if a verdict had been given for him by the jury." In the present case the learned judge who tried the cause, in consequence of a doubt entertained by him whether it was sufficiently proved at the trial that the cause of action arose, and that the defendant was resident in *Wales* at the time of service of mesne process upon him, refused to grant a certificate, although the plaintiff only recovered 20*l.* damages. Now beyond all doubt (as he was prepared by affidavit to shew) the defendant resided in *Wales* at the time of the service of process, and continued so to reside down to the time of trial. There were no means of bringing the propriety of the learned judge's decision under consideration, except in the present mode, and he submitted that this application ought to be granted.

BAYLEY, J. (a)—I am of opinion that we have no authority to order a suggestion to be entered. The statute 5 *Geo.* 4, c. 106, which repeals the 13 *Geo.* 3, c. 51, prohibits, by the 21st section, certain actions under 50*l.* being brought out of the Courts in *Wales*(b), and provides that in any action of assault and battery where the cause of action shall arise in *Wales* and shall be tried in *England,* and the plaintiff shall not recover damages to the amount of 50*l.*, then if the judge who tried the cause, on evidence appearing before him, shall certify on the back of the nisi prius record that the defendant was resident in *Wales* at the service of process, a judgment of nonsuit shall be entered and so forth. Now the act of parliament makes it a condition, to entitle the defendant to enter a suggestion, that the judge who tried the cause shall have certified on the back of the nisi prius record that the defendant was resident in *Wales* at the service of the process. Here the learned judge has refused so to certify, and we cannot order a suggestion to be entered without his certificate.

HOLROYD and LITTLEDALE, Js. concurred.

Rule refused.

(a) Lord *Tenterden,* C. J. was absent.   (b) See 1 C. & P. 468.

N N 2

1827.

*Saturday,
20th May.*

A lease contained a proviso, " that if the rent should be in arrear for twenty-one days after demand, or if any of the covenants should be broken, the term granted, or so much thereof as should be then unexpired, should be void; and that it should be lawful for the landlord to re-enter:"—Held, that the lease was only voidable by breach of the covenant, and that the landlord was bound to make an actual re-entry in order to take advantage of the forfeiture, of which a subsequent receipt of rent was a waiver.

ARNSBY *v.* WOODWARD.

THIS was an action of assumpsit. The declaration stated, that on the 31st of *May*, 1824, it was agreed between the plaintiff and the defendant, that the former should purchase for £400 a lease of certain premises theretofore granted by one *William Yems* to one *John Ellis*, and should accept the said lease or an underlease from persons named *Farr* and *Newman*, to whom *Ellis* had agreed to underlet; that the plaintiff deposited £90, which was to be forfeited, if the purchase was not completed on or before the 24th of *June* then next, and that the plaintiff was to have the lease with the same covenants that were contained in the lease granted to *Ellis*; that in pursuance of the agreement the plaintiff took possession of the premises, and was willing to perform the agreement in all things. The declaration went on to aver as breach, that before the making of the said agreement, *Ellis* had wholly vacated, annulled, and forfeited the said lease so granted to him by the said *W. Yems*, and that the said term therein mentioned, together with the term for which *Ellis* had demised or agreed to demise to *Farr* and *Newman*, had before that time thereby become and then was wholly ended and terminated, whereby the plaintiff could not at any time after the making of the said agreement have nor hath he had the said lease so granted by the said *Yems* to *Ellis*, or an underlease from the said *Farr* and *Newman*, or any lease with the same covenants as in the lease granted by *Yems* to *Ellis* as he ought to have been enabled by the defendant to have had; by means whereof the plaintiff lost the £90 which he had deposited, and had to pay *Yems* the costs of an action of ejectment brought by him to recover possession of the premises, and sustained other special damage stated in the declaration. The defendant pleaded non assumpsit. At the trial before Lord *Tenterden*, C. J. at the *Middlesex* sittings after last *Michaelmas* term, the case was this:—In the year 1818, *Yems* granted a lease to *Ellis* of the premises in question, containing among other

covenants one not to assign without the license in writing
of the lessor. The lease also contained a proviso in these
terms, " that if the rent should be in arrear twenty-one days
after demand made, or if any of the covenants should be
broken, then the term thereby granted, or so much thereof
as should be then to come and unexpired, should cease, determine, and be utterly void, and it should be lawful to and
for *Yems*, and to and for the superior landlord of the said premises for the time being, into or upon the demised premises
wholly to re-enter, and the same to hold to his own use, and
to expel and remove *Ellis*." An agreement to underlet the
premises to *Farr* and *Newman* was entered into by *Ellis* in the
year 1820, and the defendant, as agent for *Farr* and *Newman*,
entered into with the plaintiff the agreement, for the breach
of which this action was brought. In the month of *June*,
1824, the plaintiff took possession of the premises, and in
the month of *July* following *Yems* was willing to give *Ellis*
a license to assign to him, but the plaintiff insisted upon
seeing *Yems's* title, which he refused to comply with. At
Christmas, 1824, *Yems* received rent from the plaintiff. At
Lady-day, 1825, the plaintiff not having paid the rent then
due, *Yems* brought an action of ejectment for the following
breaches of covenant, namely, nonpayment of rent due at
Lady-day, 1825, not repairing and keeping the premises in
repair at any period after the commencement of the term, not
insuring from fire, not painting, assigning without license, and
keeping swine on the premises. Upon the ejectment being
brought, the plaintiff gave notice of it to the defendant, but
he refused to interfere, upon which the plaintiff gave a
cognovit, and judgment was signed thereon, and he was
turned out of possession. It was objected on the part of
the defendant, that this action was not maintainable, inasmuch as upon receiving rent at *Christmas*, 1824, *Yems* had
waived all the breaches of covenant alleged to have been
committed before that time, and that for any subsequent
breaches the defendant was not responsible. It was further
contended, that as *Yems* was at one time willing to allow

Ellis's term to be assigned to the plaintiff, which he refused to accept, he could not maintain this action. The Lord Chief Justice was of opinion that the acceptance of rent by *Yems* at *Christmas*, 1824, was a waiver of the breaches of covenant committed before that time, and directed a nonsuit. In *Hilary* term, *Scarlett*, A. G. obtained a rule nisi for setting the nonsuit aside and granting a new trial.

Gurney and *E. Lawes* now shewed cause. In order to support this action the plaintiff must make out, not only that the lease to *Ellis* was voidable, but that it was absolutely void, by breach of the covenants therein contained; and that it could not be revived by any subsequent act of the landlord. Now it is clear and settled law, that a forfeiture for breach of covenant for nonpayment of rent may be cured by subsequent acceptance of rent by the landlord. The cases of *Doe* v. *Banks* (a) and *Read* v. *Farr* (b) establish that point. Admitting that there was a forfeiture by breach of any of the covenants, still that could only be perfected by an actual re-entry of the landlord. The lease here was only voidable, but the breaches were cured by the subsequent acceptances of the rent. The proviso here is, not that the lease shall be void upon the breach of covenant, without a re-entry, but that if the rent shall be in arrear by the space of twenty-one days after demand made, it shall and may be lawful to and for *Yems*, &c. into or upon the demised premises wholly to re-enter and the same to hold to his own use, and to expel and remove *Ellis*. There is therefore only a permission to the landlord to re-enter if he chuses,—he may do so, but if instead of making his election, he accepts rent after forfeiture committed, he sets up the lease again. This case is not so strong as the cases cited, because in those the lease was to become absolutely void in certain events, but here it was only voidable, and consequently the defendant in this case is not liable.

(a) 4 B. & A. 401.   (b) 6 M. & S. 121.

Scarlett, A. G. contrà. The proviso in this case in terms declares, that if the rent should be in arrears twenty-one days after demand made, or if any of the covenants should be broken, then the term thereby granted should cease, determine, and be utterly void. Nothing can be stronger than this language. A re-entry therefore was not necessary to determine the lease. There is a provision that it should be lawful not only for *Yems* but for the superior landlord to re-enter. Now there is nothing to shew, at all events, that the superior landlord has waived the forfeiture, for the argument on the other side must go to that extent. The principle of the cases cited on the other side applies to the immediate relation of landlord and tenant, but not to a case of this description. Until the case of *Read* v. *Farr* was determined, it had always been considered that where a proviso made a lease void in certain events, re-entry by the landlord was not necessary in order to enforce the forfeiture. In that case, however, as well as in *Doe* d. *Bryant* v. *Banks* a distinction was taken in favour of the landlord, and it was held, that although the proviso declared that for certain breaches of covenant the lease should be void, yet the tenant should not be allowed to insist upon the forfeiture, because that would be permitting him to take advantage of his own wrong. This rule, however, does not apply to the case of a landlord, because he is entitled to insist upon the terms of the proviso, without actual re-entry, whereas in this case, upon breach of covenant, the lease is declared to be utterly void.

Lord TENTERDEN, C. J.—I am of opinion that in this case the nonsuit was right. The ground on which the plaintiff contended that he was entitled to maintain this action was, that the lease which the defendant had bargained to sell had been made void by the conduct of *Ellis*. From the evidence, it appeared, that an action of ejectment had been brought against the plaintiff by the person granting the lease to *Ellis*, and that notice of that ejectment was given to the defendant, who refused to interfere. The plaintiff afterwards thought fit to give a cognovit and suffer judgment in ejectment to be signed against him, and he was thereupon turned out of possession, had to pay costs, and lost the benefit of some expenditure which he had made on the premises. I admit that if *Yems*, the lessor of the plaintiff in that action, was not entitled to recover in the ejectment, the present plaintiff could not now turn round upon the present defendant and make him liable for what was done under a mistake. But it is said further, that whether *Yems* could have recovered or not, still the lease was void as against the superior landlord, and that the superior landlord might have succeeded in that action. That, however, is not the ground of complaint alleged in the declaration; but even if it were, I cannot collect from the evidence that the superior landlord had attempted to recover, or could have recovered, or even thought of proceeding for a forfeiture, for so far as he was concerned, all the covenants with him had been performed and he had no right of action. At the trial of this cause there was not a tittle of evidence to prove, nor was there any reason to suppose, that the superior landlord had any right to recover. We must therefore, as it appears to me, hold, that this case is to turn upon the question whether *Yems* was entitled to recover as against *Ellis*, or in other words, whether the lease to *Ellis* had become void. Now the proviso in this case is by no means expressed in the same language as in the two cases cited, for here, after a statement that in certain events the term should cease and be utterly void, it is added, " and it shall be lawful to and for *Yems* and to and for the superior landlord of the said premises for the time being, into or upon the demised premises wholly to re-enter, and the same to hold to his own use and to expel and remove *Ellis*." If we read these two clauses of the proviso together, as I think we ought to do, it seems to me that the sound and reasonable construction of the lease is that *Yems* the landlord may enter if he will, and if he chuses so to do the lease shall be void, but not otherwise. Unless we put this construction upon this proviso, the latter words of it, namely, those which give the power of re-entry to *Yems*, are utterly useless. We can give no effect to those words at all, unless we take them in connection with the preceding words, and give the same sense to them as if the two members of the sentence were transposed. That being so, then the two cases which have been cited are authorities in point, and we must put the same construction upon this lease. There can be no doubt, therefore, that *Yems* having received rent after a forfeiture had accrued, he by that receipt of rent waived the forfeiture, and established the lease as a good lease, up to the time when he actually received rent. If he had received rent in part up to the time *Ellis* had anything to do with the premises, and for a portion of the time after the plaintiff himself had become possessed, it seems to me that the ejectment brought by *Yems* might have been well defended by *Arnsby*, except for any breach of covenant committed in his own time, for which he certainly could not call upon the defendant to reimburse him. Assuming, however, that the proviso in this case had been expressed in the very terms found in the two cases cited, I should still be of opinion that it follows as a consequence from those decisions, that if upon a lease so worded the landlord waives his right of entry for a forfeiture by receiving rent afterwards, he thereby acknowledges in either case that the title continues in the tenant up to the time of receiving rent, and that he cannot at a subsequent period revert to a bygone act of forfeiture, and say that the lease was forfeited. If we were to hold otherwise, the effect of such a decision would be this, that a tenant can never say when the lease is to be considered void by his landlord; and that the landlord may at any distant period of time, after giving the lessee reason to believe by the receipt of rent that he has done away with the forfeiture, after going on for a considerable time treating the lease as valid, and peradventure inducing the tenant upon the faith that the lease is still subsisting, to incur considerable expense in the improvement of the premises, re-enter upon the premises and claim a forfeiture after he has been so slumbering on his own rights. As such a decision would be productive of great injustice, I think that the rule for a new trial must be discharged.

BAYLEY, J.—I agree with my Lord Chief Justice in the opinion delivered by his lordship. I think the receipt for rent up to *Christmas*, 1824, deprived *Yems*, the landlord, of the right of insisting upon a forfeiture for any breach of covenant committed prior to that time. If the plaintiff *Arnsby* has sustained any damage it was through his own neglect. He came into possession in *June*, 1824. The ejectment was not brought until after *March*, 1825. In the meantime, from *Christmas*, 1824, he was in the occupation of the premises. During that time there were continuing breaches of the covenants, which would entitle the landlord, *de die in diem*, to enter for a forfeiture; for instance, non-repair, neglecting to insure against fire, and keeping a piggery on the premises. The receipt for rent at *Christmas*, 1824, would not cure these subsequent breaches of covenant, and as they arose from the plaintiff's own neglect, the defendant could not be answerable for the consequences of the ejectment.

HOLROYD, J.—I am of the same opinion. I see nothing in this case to take it out of the old rule by which it is settled that a landlord receiving rent after a forfeiture thereby waives the forfeiture, provided the forfeiture is known to him at the time he receives the rent. In the case of *Doe* d. *Gregson* v. *Harrison* (a) there was a similar provision to that contained in the present case, and the Court held, that the receiving of rent after forfeiture incurred was a waiver, the landlord being acquainted with the forfeiture at the time.

(a) 2 T. R. 425.

LITLLEDALE, J.—I am of the same opinion. I think
this lease was not absolutely void by the breach of covenant, but only voidable. It gave the landlord a power of
re-entering if he chuse to exercise it, but it was absolutely
necessary for him to make an actual entry, in order to take
advantage of the forfeiture, as in the case of a freehold
estate.

1827.

ARNSBY
v.
WOODWARD.

Rule discharged.

TOMKINS *v.* ASHBY.

Saturday,
20th May.

THIS was an action for money had and received. Plea,
the general issue. At the trial before Lord *Tenterden*, C. J.
at the *London* sittings after last *Michaelmas* term, the
plaintiff, in support of his claim, tendered in evidence a
paper writing in the following terms: " *September* 15th, 1824,
Mr. *Tomkins* has left in my hands 200*l.*" It was contended
on the part of the defendant that this paper required a
receipt stamp to render it admissible in evidence, but the
Lord Chief Justice received it, and the plaintiff had a verdict, with liberty to the defendant to move to enter a nonsuit. A rule nisi to enter a nonsuit was granted in *Hilary*
term, against which

A memoran-
dum in these
terms,—" Mr.
T. has left in
my hands
200*l.*," may be
given in evi-
dence in sup-
port of an ac-
tion for money
had and re-
ceived,without
a stamp.

Marryat now shewed cause. By the Stamp Act, 55
Geo. 3, c. 184, the duty is imposed, in terms, upon receipts
or discharges given for or upon the payment of money.
There is, therefore, no pretence for contending that this
piece of paper requires a receipt stamp. It does not import proof that the debt has been satisfied nor even a promise to pay. It is nothing more than an acknowledgment
that so much money belonging to the plaintiff is in the
hands of the defendant. In *Israel* v. *Israel* (a) it was held,
that a written paper containing a bare acknowledgment of a
debt is good evidence under the money counts without a

(a) 1 Camp. 499.

stamp. The same point was ruled in *Fisher* v. *Leslie* (a).
In *Childers* v. *Bouhois*(b) it was held, that two unstamped
slips of paper with I. O. U. 400*l*. and I. O. U. 250*l*. written
thereon, were not receipts, and might therefore be received
in evidence in assumpsit for money lent, without being
stamped. So in *Wellard* v. *Moss*(c) it was held, that a
written acknowledgment at the foot of an account, stating
that such account was correct, might be given in evidence
without a receipt stamp.

Scarlett, A. G. in support of the rule. There is no
doubt that this paper was offered in evidence as and for a
receipt of money, and the Stamp Act comprehends any sort
of receipt or acknowledgment for the payment of money.
If, therefore, this was given in evidence as a receipt it requires a stamp. The mere form of the instrument cannot
affect the question, for the stamp laws cannot be evaded by
mere form. The only exemptions from receipt duty contained in the act are receipts given for money deposited in
the Bank of *England,* or Royal Bank of *Scotland,* or of the
Bank of *British Linen Company* in *Scotland,* or in the
hands of any banker or bankers, to be accounted for on demand. This defendant not being a banker and not being
within the exception, the acknowledgment in question required a receipt stamp.

Lord TENTERDEN, C. J.—I am of opinion that this instrument did not require a stamp. I take it to be a settled
principle that Acts of Parliament imposing duties are to be
so construed as not to make any instruments liable to them,
unless it is manifestly the intention of the legislature that
such was the object. The description of instruments, commonly called receipts or stamps, mentioned in the 55 *Geo.* 3,
c. 184, as liable to a stamp duty, are " every receipt or discharge given for or upon the payment of money."" Then, in

(a) 1 Esp. 426.   (c) 7 J. B. Moore, 503. 1 Bing.
(b) 1 D. & R. N. P. C. 8,   134.

order to prevent evasions, follows this declaration, "that any note or memorandum given to any person upon payment of money, whereby any sum of money, debt or demand, or any part of any debt or demand therein specified, and amounting to 2*l.* and upwards, shall be acknowledged to have been paid, settled, balanced, or otherwise discharged, shall be deemed a receipt." All these words import that something formerly due has been discharged or settled. It appears to me therefore that the paper in question is not within the act, and does not require a stamp. Then comes the clause of exemption, " receipts given for money deposited in the Bank of *England,* &c." Certainly, according to the construction which we are now putting on the act, a receipt or an acknowledgment for money, to be accounted for on demand, would not be within the operation of the act. Probably, for the sake of avoiding difficulties and captious objections, the Bank of *England* and the bankers in general stipulated to have a specific legislative declaration that their receipts should not be included in the general clause, provided they should not be expressed to be receipts or discharges for money previously due. The distinction between a receipt for money repayable upon demand and a discharge of a debt previously due is broad and manifest. Without therefore any very critical construction, but attending to the plain words used by the legislature, " receipt or discharge given for or upon the payment of money," I think we are bound to hold that those words apply only to a receipt or discharge for an antecedent debt, and not to an acknowledgment of a sum of money to be accounted for on demand. I am therefore of opinion that the rule ought to be discharged.

BAYLEY, J. and HOLROYD, J. were of the same opinion.

LITTLEDALE, J.—The exemption in the act, as it appears to me, will apply to all acknowledgments for money to be accounted for on demand, but when the receipt or acknowledgment is to operate as a discharge of a debt, the stamp duty is incurred.

Rule discharged.

Saturday,
20th May.

Trover is not a cause of action within the operation of the *Bath* Court of Requests act, 45 *G.* 3, c. 67.

WEARE *v.* CALDER.

THIS was an action of trover, to which the defendant pleaded not guilty. At the last assizes for the county of *Somerset*, the plaintiff recovered a verdict for a sum under 10*l.* On a former day a rule *nisi* was obtained for entering a suggestion on the roll to deprive the plaintiff of his costs, under the *Bath* Court of Requests Act, 45 *Geo.* 3, c. 67, s. 47. It appeared that both parties resided in the city of *Bath*, within the jurisdiction of the Commissioners of the Court of Requests. The 16th section of the act gives the Commissioners therein named jurisdiction to decide and determine all disputes and differences between party and party for any sum not exceeding 10*l.* in all actions or causes of debt for rent, upon leases, articles, or securities, and in all causes of assumpsit. By the 17th section the Commissioners are prohibited from determining the right or title to any lands, tenements, or hereditaments, or real estates whatsoever, or to decide on any debt where the title of a freehold or lease for years of any lands, tenements or hereditaments, or of any chattels real, shall be brought into question. By section 12, power is given to any person, whether resident or not within the jurisdiction of the Court, having any debt or debts, on the balance of accounts or otherwise howsoever, not exceeding the value of 10*l.* due or owing to him by or from any person or persons whatsoever, residing or being within the said city, or the liberty or precincts thereof, or keeping or using any house, warehouse, wharf, quay, lodging, shop, shed, stall or stand, or using or frequenting the markets there, or seeking a livelihood, or in any way trading or dealing within the same, to apply for a summons against such debtor, &c.; and by section 47, if any action or suit for any debt recoverable by virtue of the act in the Court of Requests shall be commenced in any other Court whatever, or elsewhere than in the said Court, the plaintiff in such action shall not, by reason of a verdict for him or otherwise, be entitled to any costs whatsover, &c. The question was, whether an action of trover was an action within the meaning of this statute.

.. *Merewether* was heard for the defendant and *Coleridge* for the plaintiff.

Lord TENTERDEN, C. J.—I am of opinion that trover is not a cause of action within the operation of the statute. It would certainly be difficult to find an Act of Parliament giving jurisdiction to a Court of Requests in terms more extensive than are contained in this, to prevent a party from suing in any other Court; but I cannot say, upon looking through the whole of this act, that an action of trover is contemplated. The evident object of the framer of the act was to prevent suits for small debts and on money contracts from being brought into the superior Courts, but I think we cannot extend the operation of the act, however beneficial it may be, to an action of this nature. This is a motion to enter a suggestion to deprive the plaintiff of his costs, and as I think he is unnecessarily brought here, it is reasonable that those who are desirous of raising the question should pay the costs of the experiment.

BAYLEY, HOLROYD, and LITTLEDALE, Js., concurred.

Rule discharged with costs.

1827.

Wednesday,
23d May.

A *general*
notice of the
defendant's in-
tention to dis-
pute *the bank-*
ruptcy in an
action by as-
signees of a
bankrupt, is
not sufficient
under 6 *G.* 4,
c. 16, s. 90.

TRIMLEY and others, Assignees of THOMAS DORNFORD,
a Bankrupt, *v.* UWINS.

THIS was an action for money had and received, to which
the defendant pleaded the general issue. At the trial before
Bayley, J. at the sittings in *London* after last *Michaelmas*
term, it appeared that a commission of bankruptcy against
Dornford was issued on the 2d of *February,* 1826. The
defendant had given a general notice of his intention to dispute " the bankruptcy," and the plaintiffs having failed in
proving an act of bankruptcy, the learned judge directed a
nonsuit. In *Hilary* term a rule *nisi* for a new trial was
granted, on the ground that the notice of the defendant's
intention to dispute the bankruptcy was too general, and
therefore that the plaintiffs were not bound to give the
evidence required to support their title to sue as assignees.

Marryatt shewed cause against the rule, and *Scarlett,*
A. G. was heard in support of it.

Lord TENTERDEN, C. J.—I am of opinion that the
notice of disputing the bankruptcy given in this case was
too general. By the statute 6 *Geo.* 4, c. 16, s. 90, it is
enacted, " that in any action by or against any assignee, &c.
no proof shall be required at the trial of the petitioning
creditor's debt or debts, or of the trading or act or acts of
bankruptcy respectively, unless the other party in such
action shall, if defendant at or before pleading, and if the
plaintiff before issue joined, give notice in writing to such
assignee, &c. that he intends to dispute *some and which of*
such matters." Now bankruptcy comprises three distinct
matters, namely, the trading, the petitioning creditor's debt,
and the act of bankruptcy. These three things are necessary to constitute a bankrupt, and the statute requires no
proof of the bankruptcy to be given unless the party intending to dispute it gives a notice that he intends to dis-

pute some and which of such matters. So that it is quite
manifest this notice is too general. The rule for a new trial
must therefore be made absolute, but it is reasonable that
the defendant should be at liberty to plead *de novo*, and
have an opportunity of delivering a fresh notice.

BAYLEY, J.—The notice should specify what part of the
proceedings in bankruptcy the defendant intends to dispute.
In this case, if the defendant had given notice of his intention to dispute the act of bankruptcy, it would have been
sufficient, that being the point intended to be raised.

HOLROYD and LITTLEDALE, Js. concurred.

Rule absolute for a new trial, with liberty to the defendant to plead *de novo*, and give fresh notice (*a*).

(*a*) Vide Archbold's B. L. 12, 15, 57, 261, 267.

1827.

TRIMLEY
v.
UWINS.

TANNER *v.* SMART.

*Saturday, 26th
May.*

THIS was an action of assumpsit on a promissory note,
dated the 19th *January*, 1816, payable on the 30th of *November* then next. The declaration was of *Hilary* term,
1826. The defendant pleaded *actio non accrevit infra sex
annos;* and issue thereon. At the trial before Lord *Tenterden,* C. J. at the sittings in *London* after last *Michaelmas*
term, it appeared in evidence, that in 1818 the note was
presented to the defendant, and in reply to a demand of
payment, he said, " I cannot pay the debt at present, but I
will pay it as soon as I can." No evidence was offered
that the defendant had ever since been possessed of means
of paying the note. The Lord Chief Justice was of
opinion that the promise proved, being only conditional, it
was incumbent on the plaintiff to prove that the defendant
the case out of the statute of limitations, without proof on the part of
the defendant's ability to pay.

On issue taken
upon the plea
of *actio non
accrevit infra
sex annos,* in an
action of as-
sumpsit, it was
proved that the
defendant said
within six
years, on being
applied to for
payment, " I
cannot pay the
debt at present,
but I will pay
it as soon as I
can:"—Held,
that this was
not a sufficient
acknowledg-
ment to take

was of ability to pay since the promise; but entertaining doubt upon the point, he allowed the plaintiff to take a verdict, with liberty to the defendant to move for a new trial for the purpose of raising the question, whether the acknowledgment proved was sufficient to take the case out of the statute of limitations, without proof of the defendant's ability to pay. In *Hilary* term last a rule nisi was granted accordingly, and

Scarlett, A. G. and *D. F. Jones*, now shewed cause, and contended that according to decided cases, the acknowledgment proved at the trial, amounting as it did to an admission that the debt was due and unsatisfied, was sufficient to take the case out of the statute. They relied mainly upon *Leaper* v. *Tatton* (a), which was an action of assumpsit against the defendant, as acceptor of a bill of exchange, and upon an account stated. It was proved that the defendant acknowledged his acceptance, and that he had been liable, but said ·that he was not liable then, because the bill was out of date, and that he could not pay it, as it was not in his power. This was held sufficient to take the case out of the statute.

F. Pollock, contrà, contended that the acknowledgment only amounted to a conditional promise, which, according to modern decisions, would not take the case out of the statute without proof on the part of the plaintiff that the defendant was of ability to pay since the acknowledgment. This proof did not lie upon the defendant, because he could not be called upon to prove a negative. ·

Lord TENTERDEN, C. J.—This is a question of considerable importance. As at present advised, we all think that some proof ought to have been given by the plaintiff of the defendant's ability to pay, but we shall take time to consider of our judgment.

(a) 16 East, 420.

The case was argued on *Wednesday*, the 23d instant.

Cur adv. vult.

The judgment of the Court was now delivered by

Lord TENTERDEN, C. J.—The question in this case was, whether an acknowledgment, which implied that the debt for which the action was brought had not been paid, was an answer to the statute of limitations. The action was in assumpsit. Issue was joined upon the statute, and the acknowledgment proved was " I cannot pay the debt at present, but I will pay it as soon as I can." The point, therefore, is, whether this is such an acknowledgment as, without proof of any ability on the part of the defendant, takes the case out of the statute. There are, undoubtedly, authorities that the statute is founded on the presumption of payment, but that whatever repels that presumption is an answer to the statute, and that any acknowledgment which repels that presumption is, in legal effect, a promise to pay the debt, and that though such an acknowledgment is accompanied with only a conditional promise, or even a refusal to pay, the law considers the condition or refusal void, and treats the acknowledgment of itself as an unconditional answer to the statute ; and if these authorities be unquestionable, the verdict which has been given for the plaintiff ought to stand, and the rule for a new trial ought to be discharged. I refer to the cases of *Yea* v. *Fouraker* (a), *Lloyd* v. *Maund* (b), *Bryan* v. *Horseman* (c), *Leaper* v. *Tatton* (d), *Dowthwaite* v. *Tibbut* (e), *Frost* v. *Bengough* (f), *Rowcroft* v. *Lomas* (g), *Swan* v. *Sewell* (h), and *Mountstephen* v. *Brooke* (i). But if there are conflicting authorities

(a) 2 Burr. 1099.
(b) 2 T. R. 706.
(c) 5 Esp. 81; 4 East, 599; 1 Smith, 125.
(d) 16 East, 420.
(e) 5 M. & S. 75.

(f) 8 J. B. Moore, 180; 1 Bing. 266.
(g) 4 M. & S. 457.
(h) 2 B. & A. 759.
(i) 3 B. & A. 141.

upon the point, if the principles upon which the authorities I have mentioned are founded appear to be doubtful, and the opposite authorities more consonant to legal rules, we ought at least to grant a new trial, that the opportunity may be afforded of having the decision of a Court of error upon the point, and that for the future we may have a correct standard by which to act. The statute of limitations directs that all actions of trespass *quare clausum fregit*, all actions of trespass, detinue, trover, or replevin for goods, all actions of account and on the case, other than actions concerning trade between merchants, and all actions of debt grounded on any lending or contract, without specialty, shall be commenced and sued (with an exception of actions for slander) within six years next after the cause of action or suit, and not afterwards. Though this statute puts all these actions upon the same footing, it is only in actions of assumpsit that an acknowledgment has been held an answer; and when, in the case of *Hurst* v. *Parker* (a), it was decided to be inapplicable to actions of trespass, Lord *Ellenborough* gave what appears to be the true reason, that in assumpsit " an acknowledgment of the debt is evidence of a fresh promise," and that promise is considered as one of the promises laid in the declaration, and one of the causes of action which the declaration states. If an acknowledgment have the effect which the cases in the plaintiff's favour attribute to it, one should have expected that the replication to a plea of the statute would have pleaded the acknowledgment in terms, and relied upon it as a bar to the statute, whereas the constant replication ever since the statute to let in evidence of an acknowledgment is, that the causes of action accrued (or that the defendant made the promise in the declaration) within six years, and the only principle upon which it can be held to be an answer to the statute is this, that an acknowledgment is evidence of a new promise, and as such constitutes a new cause of action, and supports and establishes the promises which the declaration states.

(a) 1 B. & A. 92; 2 Chit. Rep. 249.

Upon this principle, whenever the acknowledgment supports any of the promises in the declaration, the plaintiff succeeds. When it does not support them, (though it may shew clearly that the debt never has been paid, but is still a subsisting debt,) the plaintiff fails.   In one of the earliest and leading cases upon the statute, *Heylin* v. *Husting* (a), in assumpsit by an executor for goods sold by his testator, the defendant pleaded the statute, and the plaintiff proved that within six years the defendant had said, " If you can prove your debt I will pay it." The debt had been contracted about six years when this occurred, and whether this evidence would prove the issue for the plaintiff, *Holt*, C. J. doubted.   On motion in Court it was agreed by the whole bench, that if six years elapse after a debt is contracted, and then the debtor acknowledges the debt and promises to pay, evidence of such a promise and acknowledgment is good to maintain an action ; but they doubted whether such evidence would support an action upon the first contract, and whether the plaintiff should not have declared specially upon the conditional promise ; and *Rokeby*, J. thought that an acknowledgment in such case without a promise would not bind ; but *Holt*, C. J. thought it would, and said it had been often so held, though the contrary had also been held.   Afterwards *Holt*, C. J. talked the point over with ten judges at *Serjeants' Inn*, including the *King's Bench* judges, and they agreed upon consideration, that this promise, after six years elapsed, was sufficient evidence to maintain the declaration, for the defendant expressly promises payment on proof of the debt, which proof may be made in the said action.   They all agreed also, that if a man acknowledged a debt after six years, it was good evidence of an assumpsit, upon *non assumpsit infra sex annos* pleaded, for the jury to find a verdict for the plaintiff, but it is not a matter npon which, if found specially, the Court could give judgment for the plaintiff, and the reason for this is, because the jury must draw the conclusion from

(a) Com. 54 ; Ld. Raym. 389, 421 ; Salk. 29 ; 5 Mod. 425 ; 6 Mod. 309.

evidence, not the Court. Lord *Raymond* and *Salkeld*, in their reports of the same case, both state that the judges thought that a general *indebitatus assumpsit* might be well maintained, because the defendant had waived the benefit of the statute; but as the pleadings do not appear to have been calculated to raise the question of waiver, and as neither of the reports in the 5th and 6th of Modern Reports notice this point, we have cited the case from *Comyn's* Reports, because that report appeared to accord best with legal principles. In *Green* v. *Crane* (a), in assumpsit by an executor, upon promises to his testator, and *non assumpsit infra sex annos* pleaded, the plaintiff proved that within six years the defendant owned the debt, and promised payment, but the acknowledgment and promise were made, not in the testator's lifetime, but after his death, and whether that evidence could maintain the issue was the question; and after the case had been stirred twice, and the Court had taken further time to advise, *Holt*, C. J. delivered the resolution of the Court, that they were all of opinion that the action could not be maintained, the promise being made to the executor, and so out of the issue. In *Sarrell* v. *Wine* (b) the facts were exactly similar to those in *Green* v. *Crane*, and the Court acted upon that decision. In *Ward* v. *Hunter* (c) there was a similar determination. In *Manton* v. *Sculthorpe* (d) the same point occurred again in the King's Bench, and they decided accordingly, that the acknowledgment to the executor was not evidence upon promises to the testator, and a nonsuit was entered. In *Pittam* v. *Forster* (e), in an action against *Forster* and *Norris* and wife, upon promises made by *Forster* and the wife *dum sola*, the defendants pleaded the statute, that the cause of action did not accrue within six years. Issue was taken thereupon, and the plaintiff proved an acknowledgment by

(*a*) 2 Ld. Raym. 1101; 6 Mod.
309; Salk. 28; 11 Mod. 37.
  (*b*) 3 East, 409.
  (*c*) 6 Taunt. 210.

(*d*) Trinity, 1818.
  (*e*) *Ante*, vol. ii. 363; 1 B. &
C. 248.

Forster after the marriage of *Norris* and wife; and whether that supported the issue and entitled the plaintiff to a verdict was the question; and upon argument, the Court was clear it did not, for the issue was whether there was any such promise within six years as the declaration stated, namely, a promise whilst the wife was sole; and a promise after the wife was married was not within that issue. All these cases proceed upon the principle that, under the ordinary issue on the statute of limitations, an acknowledgment is only evidence of a promise to pay, and unless it is conformable to and maintains the promises in the declaration, though it may shew to demonstration that the debt has never been paid and is still subsisting, it has no effect. The question then comes to this, is there any promise in this case which will support the promises in the declaration? The promises in the declaration are absolute and unconditional to pay, when thereunto afterwards requested. The promise proved here was, " I will pay as soon as I can," and there was no evidence of ability to pay, so as to raise that which in its terms was a qualified promise into one that was absolute and unconditional. Had it been in terms what it is in substance, " prove that I am able to pay, and then I will pay," it would have been what the promise was taken to be in *Haylin* v. *Hasting,* a conditional promise, and when the proof of ability should have been given, but not before, an absolute one. Upon a general acknowledgment, where nothing is said to prevent it, a general promise to pay may and ought to be implied, but where the party guards his acknowledgment and accompanies it with an express declaration to prevent any such implication, why shall not the rule " *expressum facit cessare tacitum,*" apply? In *Bicknell* v. *Keppell* (a), where the question was, whether the case was taken out of the statute by a letter, in which the defendant referred the plaintiff to his solicitors and said, " they are in possession of my determination and ability," *Mansfield,* C. J. seemed to think the defendant's

(a) 1 N. R. 20; see *M'Culloch* v. *Dawes, ante,* 40.

ability would come in issue upon the trial, and that the solicitors might be examined as to the defendant's ability as
well as to the determination he had communicated to them;
and in the late case of *A'Court* v. *Cross* (a), where the defendant said, " I know I do owe the money, but the bill I
gave is upon a three-penny stamp, and I will never pay it,"
Gaselee, J. thought this acknowledgment did not amount
to a promise to pay, or take the case out of the statute, and·
the Court upon argument on both sides were of opinion
that he was right, and that where the defendant distinctly
and expressly declared that he would not pay, a promise
could not be raised by implication that he would. Upon
legal principles, therefore, it appears to us that this decision
was right, and that in this case the rule for a new trial
ought to be made absolute.

Rule absolute for a new trial.

(a) 3 Bing. 329.

Where an
award was
sought to be
set aside on the
ground that
the arbitrator
had not deter-
mined all mat-
ters in dif-
ference :—
Held, that if
the affidavit
coupled with a
rule nisi dis-
closes the ob-
jections to the
award, it is a
sufficient com-
pliance with
the rule E. T.
2 G. 4.

RAWSTHORN *v.* ARNOLD.

BY an order of nisi prius this cause and all matters in difference were referred to an arbitrator, who made his award
on the 28th of *December* last, and directed a verdict to be
entered for the defendant, the order of nisi prius having
previously been made a rule of Court. On a former day
in this term a rule nisi was obtained for setting aside the
award on the ground that the arbitrator had not determined
all matters in difference. The rule did not specify particularly those matters pursuant to the general rule of Court of
Easter term, 2 *Geo.* 4 (b), but the affidavit in support of
the motion set forth certain alleged causes of difference be-

(b) 2 B. & A. 539.

A motion to set aside an award made under an order of nisi prius, must be made within
the time allowed for moving for a new trial, unless a sufficient reason is shewn for the delay.

tween the parties, which were not mentioned in the award.

Cross, Serjt. now shewed cause, and contended, first, that the rule for setting aside the award should have set forth those matters in difference which it was alleged that the arbitrator had omitted to determine, and, secondly, that the motion to set aside the award came too late, the award having been made in *December,* and the judgment having been entered up early in *January,* so that the application should have been made in *Hilary* term.

Scarlett, A. G. contrà. First, the affidavit annexed to the rule nisi, stating the grounds of objection to the award, is a sufficient compliance with the general rule of *Easter* term, 2 *Geo.* 4. Secondly, as this was not a reference under the statute 9 and 10 *Wil.* 3, c. 15, the plaintiff was not bound to move the Court to set aside the award before the end of the term next after the award was made and published; but *non constat* that the plaintiff had notice of the award time enough to apply to set it aside in *Hilary* term, which the defendant was bound to shew by affidavit.

Lord TENTERDEN, C. J.—With respect to the preliminary objection, I am of opinion that the rule, coupled with the affidavit, sufficiently explains the grounds of objection made to the award. But as to the objection that the application is made too late, I think it was not necessary for the defendant to shew the time when the plaintiff had notice of the award. When a party makes an application to the Court after the time generally allowed for that purpose, it is incumbent on him to shew a sufficient excuse for the delay. It appears to me, therefore, that it lay on the plaintiff to shew that he had not timely notice of the award so as to enable him to move in *Hilary* term. There is no doubt that the reference in this case, being by a rule of Court made in a cause, is not within the statute of *William;* but then the party seeking to disturb the award should have made his application within the period allowed by the practice of the Court on moving for a new trial, although the Court might not insist rigidly upon a compliance with that rule, if any sufficient grounds were stated for asking indulgence.

BAYLEY, HOLROYD and LITTLEDALE, Js. concurred.

Rule discharged with costs.

Tuesday,
22d May.

BERRY *v.* ADAMSON, Gent. one, &c,

In an action for maliciously arresting and imprisoning the plaintiff until he gave bail, it was proved that in consequence of a verbal message sent, the plaintiff voluntarily went to the bailiff's house, and gave a bail-bond :—Held, that this was not an arrest and imprisonment to sustain an action on the case against the original plaintiff, although the latter had no cause of action.

THIS was an action on the case for maliciously and without probable cause arresting the plaintiff and causing him to be kept in prison until he gave bail. The defendant pleaded not guilty. At the trial before Lord *Tenterden*, C. J., at the *Middlesex* sittings after last *Michaelmas* term, it appeared in evidence that on the 29th *October*, 1825, the defendant sued out an attachment of privilege against the plaintiff, indorsed for bail to the amount of 90*l.* and upwards. Instead of actually arresting the plaintiff the sheriff's officer sent his assistant without the warrant, with a verbal message to the plaintiff that he had a writ against him, and requested that he would fix a time for attending at the lock-up house and giving a bail-bond. The plaintiff accordingly fixed a time, attended at the house of the sheriff's officer with two bondsmen, and executed a bail-bond. The original cause of action was referred to arbitration, and an award was made in favour of the present plaintiff. On the part of the defendant it was contended that there was no arrest here proved to sustain the allegation in the declaration of an actual arrest, and *Arrowsmith* v. *Le Mesurier* (a) was relied upon as an authority in point. The Lord Chief

(a) 2 New Rep. 211; 2 Saund. 59 a.

Justice was of opinion that no arrest had been made out to
sustain this action and directed a nonsuit. *Brougham* in
Hilary term had obtained a rule nisi for setting the nonsuit
aside, and

1827.

BERRY
v.
ADAMSON.

Scarlett, A. G. and *D. F. Jones* now shewed cause.
The declaration complains that the defendant had maliciously arrested and held the plaintiff to bail. Now merely
proving that the plaintiff was held to bail, is not sufficient
to sustain this allegation. It was necessary to prove an
actual arrest as well as a holding to bail. All the evidence
went to negative the fact of an arrest. The defendant not
wishing to have the plaintiff arrested, delivered the warrant to
the officer on a *Saturday* night, and expressly told him not
to arrest the plaintiff, because it would be inconvenient for
him to lie in prison until the *Monday* following. The
officer accordingly sends the plaintiff word that he has got
a writ against him and requests that he will come on *Monday* and give bail. The plaintiff, without even seeing the
warrant, voluntarily comes on the *Monday* and puts in bail.
Now this cannot be considered as an arrest, there having
been no restraint whatever upon the plaintiff's person.
Suppose the plaintiff, instead of coming on the *Monday*
and putting in bail, had absconded or concealed himself,
could it be contended that the sheriff would be liable to an
action for an escape? If not, then there was no arrest.
It may be true that a man may be virtually arrested, although the officer does not lay hands upon him, as where
the officer desires the man not to leave the room, or locks
a door upon him, but there must be either a corporal touch
or a capacity in the officer to arrest, and a submission by
the party to restraint upon his liberty. The cases of *Homer*
v. *Battyn* (a), and *Arrowsmith* v. *Le Mesurier,* are authorities in point. At the utmost this was a metaphysical
arrest.

(a) Bull. N. P. 62.

Brougham and *Chitty*, in support of the rule. The plaintiff having submitted to the process of the law and given a bail-bond, that is in law an arrest. Suppose when the plaintiff went to the lock-up house, in consequence of the message sent to him, he had refused to execute a bail-bond, it is clear that then he was in the custody of the law, and the sheriff would have been liable to an action for an escape, if he had been allowed to depart. His voluntarily going to the lock-up house, in consequence of the message from the sheriff's officer, was a submission to process, and would therefore be an arrest in point of law. In *Homer* v. *Battyn* it was said, that if a bailiff, having process against one, says to him when he is on horseback or in a coach, " you are my prisoner, I have a writ against you," upon which he submits, turns back, or goes with him, though the bailiff never touched him, yet it is an arrest, because he submitted to the process. So here the plaintiff, by giving the bail-bond, submitted to the process, and that is an arrest. Having given bail, the sheriff would be bound to return *cepi corpus,* and if he afterwards allowed him to escape, not only the sheriff, but the party who caused the process to be sued out, would be estopped from saying that the plaintiff had not been arrested. By giving bail the plaintiff was virtually in custody. *Norton* v. *Moseley* (a). The case of *Arrowsmith* v. *Le Mesurier* is not at all in point, for that was only the case of a summons to go before a magistrate. The sheriff here is the obligee to the bail-bond, which necessarily supposes an arrest.

Lord TENTERDEN, C. J.—This was an action for arresting and keeping the plaintiff in prison. Now has he actually or constructively been arrested and kept in prison? The case of *Arrowsmith* v. *Le Mesurier* is a decisive authority to shew that he has not, and that case was much more favourable to the argument in support of a constructive arrest than this. There a constable went with a war-

(a) *Ante,* 107; 6 B. & C. 106.

rant, which had been granted by a magistrate for apprehending the plaintiff upon a charge of conspiracy, and
shewed the warrant to the plaintiff. After conversing some
time with the constable, the plaintiff desired to have a copy
of the warrant, which the constable permitted him to take,
after which the plaintiff attended the constable to the magistrate, and after being examined upon the subject of the
charge, he was dismissed, and Sir *James Mansfield*, C. J.
said " I can suppose that an arrest may take place without
an actual touch, as if a man be locked up in a room, but
here the plaintiff went voluntarily before a magistrate.
The warrant was made no other use of than as a summons.
The constable brought a warrant, but did not arrest the
plaintiff. How can a man's walking freely to a magistrate
prove him to be arrested?" Here the bailiff's follower did
not even take the warrant with him, but merely went to the
plaintiff, told him that there was a writ in the sheriff's
office against him, and desired him to appoint a day to
come and put in bail. He does appoint a day and comes
accordingly. I cannot, however, consider that as an arrest
and imprisonment according to the authority of the case
cited. It is not necessary to decide whether an action
could be maintained against the sheriff, if after the officer
had told the plaintiff to come and put in bail he had refused
to come. As between these parties it is sufficient to decide
that there was no arrest and imprisonment.

BAYLEY, HOLROYD and LITTLEDALE, Js. were of the
same opinion.

Rule discharged (a).

(a) Vide *Williams* v. *Jones*, Cas. temp. Hard. 301; and *Garner* v.
Sparks, 1 Salk. 79.

ROPER *v.* COOMBES.

By an agree-
ment between
A. and *B.* on
the 31st of
March, the
former agreed
to grant a
lease to the
latter of a
public-house
for the term of
21 years, to
run from the
29th of *Septem-*
ber then next,
in considera-
tion of £1000,
of which £10
was immedi-
ately paid
down, £90
was to be paid
on the 13th of
April, and the
residue on
having posses-
sion of the
premises. *B.*
being re-
quired to pay
the £90 called
upon *A.* to
prove his title,
which being
refused, he
gave notice
that he would
rescind the
contract, and
brought an ac-
tion to recover
the £10 which
he had paid:
—Held, that
he had a right
so to do, and
that he was
not bound to
wait until the
29th of *Sep-*
tember, from
which time
the lease was
to run.

THIS was an action of assumpsit for money had and received, with the common counts. Plea, the general issue.
At the trial before Lord *Tenterden,* C. J. at the *Middlesex*
sittings after last *Michaelmas* term, the case was this:—On
the 31st of *March,* 1826, the defendant entered into an agreement to grant to the plaintiff a lease of a public-house for a
term of twenty-one years, to commence from the 29th of
September then next ensuing, at the annual rent of £60, in
consideration of £1,000, of which £10 was paid down by
the plaintiff. The sum of £90 was to be paid on the 13th of
April 1826, and the residue of the money when the plaintiff obtained possession of the premises. The sum of £90
was not paid on the 13th of *April,* and on the 20th of the
same month the plaintiff called upon the defendant to shew
title to the premises. Instead of this the defendant insisted
upon being paid the £90, and notified to the plaintiff that
he was not bound to grant the lease or shew a title until the
29th of *September.* Upon this the plaintiff gave notice to the
defendant that he would rescind the contract, and called for
the repayment of the £10 he had deposited, which being
refused, he brought the present action in *Trinity* term,
1826. It was proved that at that time the defendant was
not in a condition to grant a lease according to his contract.
On the part of the defendant it was objected, that this
action could not have been commenced until after the 29th
of *September,* 1826, because up to that time he might have
been in a condition to execute such a lease as he had
agreed to grant to the plaintiff, and that it was not necessary for him to have a good title to the premises at the time
the contract was entered into, it being sufficient if he had a
good title when the lease was to take effect. The Lord
Chief Justice, however, was of opinion, on the authority of
Bartlett v. *Tuchin and another* (a), that the plaintiff was at

(a) 1 Marsh. 583; 6 Taunt. 259.

liberty to rescind the contract before the 29th of *September*, and was entitled to recover back his deposit of £10; and the plaintiff had a verdict accordingly, with liberty however to the defendant to move for a nonsuit. In *Hilary* term, *Gurney* obtained a rule nisi accordingly, against which

Scarlett, A. G. and *Dodd* now shewed cause. The case of *Bartlett* v. *Tuchin* is an authority in favour of the plaintiff. In that case the plaintiff purchased by auction certain premises belonging to the estate of a bankrupt. The plaintiff, after having paid a deposit, gave notice to the assignees that he would abandon the purchase for a supposed defect in the title, and it was held, that as the assignees at the time when they received notice from the purchaser had not a good title to the estate, they could not enforce the contract, nor consequently retain the deposit. In the present case, although the agreement is silent as to the time when the lease was to be granted, yet it must have a reasonable construction. The plaintiff had bound himself to pay £90 on the 13th of *April*, as part of the premium, but he was not bound to pay that money until the defendant satisfied him that he could make a good title to the premises. The defendant having failed to complete his part of the contract upon request, the plaintiff was clearly entitled to rescind the contract and sue for his deposit. If the defendant could have shewn that on the 20th of *April* he had a good title to the premises, the case might have been different. It may be true that the lease was only to run from the 29th of *September*, but it is quite consistent with the agreement that it should be executed before that time, inasmuch as part of the premium was to be paid on the 13th of *April* previously.

Gurney and *F. Kelly* in support of the rule. At the time the plaintiff commenced this action he had no right to rescind the contract. The sum of £90 was to be paid within a fortnight after the date of the agreement. It was not in the contemplation of the parties at the time the deposit was paid that the plaintiff should be at liberty to call upon the defendant immediately to execute the lease. At all events he was entitled to a reasonable time, but here the plaintiff, within a week after he refuses to pay the £90, requires the defendant to exhibit his title. Now that is an unreasonable condition, which was not warranted by the agreement. So long as the defendant could shew title at the time the lease was to commence, that would be a sufficient compliance with his part of the contract. For this *Thompson* v. *Miles*(a) is an authority. In that case it was held by Lord *Kenyon*, that where a party sells an estate or any interest therein, and at the time has no title or not such as he sells, if he nevertheless obtains such estate or interest before he is called upon to complete the purchase, it is sufficient. So here, if the defendant was able to make a good title on the 29th of *September*, that would prevent the plaintiff from rescinding the contract, and therefore the action is brought too soon. The case of *Bartlett* v. *Tuchin* is not in point, because that was a case of vendor and vendee. [Lord *Tenterden*, C. J. This is also the *sale* of a lease for a term of years at the price of £1000.]

Lord Tenterden, C. J.—The question in this case properly is, whether the plaintiff had a right, under the circumstances proved at the trial, to rescind the contract. Now unless he had a right to rescind the contract, it is clear that the defendant would be entitled to maintain an action for the sum of £90, which was agreed to be paid on the 13th of *April*. The contract was properly for the sale of a lease, to be granted at some future day, though the day for granting it was not particularly specified. The plaintiff having agreed to pay £90 on the 13th of *April*, I think it but reasonable that he should not be called upon to pay so large a sum of money without knowing that the defendant had the power of completing his part of the contract. The defendant gave the plaintiff no notice of any right he had to grant the lease; he had many days allowed him for

(a) 1 Esp. 184.

that purpose, and even at the trial it was proved on the part of the plaintiff himself, that the defendant could not be in a condition to grant a lease for a term of twenty-one years, because the title was vested in some other person, to whom an application had been made to grant a lease. The onus of proof that he had title lay properly on the defendant; but negative proof came from the other side that he had no title. Under such circumstances it would be unjust to say that the defendant had a right to insist upon the payment of the £90 before he was called upon to prove title, because the plaintiff was not to take his chance whether at some future time the defendant would be enabled to grant a lease. It appears to me that the defendant having refused to shew title when called upon, the plaintiff had a right to rescind the contract and bring his action for the £10 which had been paid.

BAYLEY, J. was absent.

HOLROYD, J.—I think that under the circumstances proved, the plaintiff had a right to rescind the contract, and that he was not bound to pay the £90 before the defendant exhibited his title. He ought not to be called upon to pay so large a sum of money upon an uncertainty. There was a case lately before this Court, which decided that where a party has disabled himself from fulfilling a contract, although before the expiration of the time allowed for that purpose he may be in a condition to do so, still, in the mean time, the other party has a right to rescind the contract.

LITTLEDALE, J. was of the same opinion.

Rule discharged.

1827.

Saturday,
26th May.

The KING *v.* RUSSELL and others.

Where certain machines called staiths were erected in the river *Tyne* for the purpose of loading vessels with coals:— Held, by two justices, on the trial of the owners of the staiths for a public nuisance to the navigation of the river, that the defendants might be acquitted if the jury were of opinion upon the evidence that the abridgment of the right of passage occasioned by the staiths was for a public purpose, produced a public benefit, were erected in a reasonable situation, and left a reasonable space for the passage of vessels on the river; and that they might take into consideration that by means of the staiths coals were supplied to the public at a cheaper rate, and in better condition than they otherwise could be.

The want of a previous writ of *ad quod damnum* in such a case is not conclusive against the defendants.

THIS was an indictment for a nuisance in the river *Tyne.* The first count of the indictment stated, that the river *Tyne* was, and from time immemorial had been, an ancient river, and the king's ancient common public highway for all the liege subjects of the king and his predecessors, with their ships, keels, lighters, cobles, boats, wherries, and other vessels, to navigate, sail, row, put, set, pass, and repass without obstruction, and that the defendants on, &c. and from thence until the taking of that inquisition, did unlawfully keep and continue certain geers, spouts, piles, posts, waggon-ways, railways, platforms, and erections, that is to say, ten geers, &c. which before then had been unlawfully, &c. erected, placed, fixed, put, and set in, upon, and over the said river and king's ancient common and public highway, near to a certain place called *Wallsend*, and which had been and were erected, &c. upon and over the said river to a great extent, to wit, to the extent of 300 feet towards the middle of the stream, by means whereof the navigation, course, stream, and passage of, in, through, along, and upon the said river, and the king's ancient and common public highway thereon, &c. and from thence continually up to that time had been, and still were greatly straightened, narrowed, lessened, obstructed, and blocked up, and thereby divers large quantities of coals, stones, gravel, sand, soil, silt, mud, and other substances became and were collected near to the said place where the said geers, &c. were placed, and in other parts of the river and king's ancient common and public highway there, and divers dangerous sandbanks, quicksands, banks, and shoals were formed therein, to wit, at, &c. so that the liege subjects of the king navigating, &c. with their ships, &c. in, through, and along

the said river and king's ancient common public highway
there, could not navigate, &c. in so free, safe, and uninter-
rupted a manner as of right they ought, and before had
been used and accustomed to do, to the great damage and
common nuisance, &c. The second count charged the
defendants with a nuisance in making certain additions to
geers before erected. The third, with erecting geers, &c.
The fourth, with keeping and continuing certain chains and
anchors fixed to certain buoys in the navigable part of the
river. The fifth, with placing buoys with chains and anchors fixed to them in the river. The sixth, with unlawfully and without lawful excuse causing and permitting
divers vessels to stay and remain in the river near a certain
staith belonging to the defendants, for a long space of time,
to wit, &c. to the obstruction of the navigation. The seventh, with straightening, narrowing, and obstructing the
navigation generally. The eighth, with casting a great
quantity of coals, stones, and other substances into the
river, and thereby obstructing the navigation. The defendants pleaded not guilty. At the trial before *Bayley*, J. at
the *summer* assizes for the county of *York* in 1824, it appeared in evidence that the defendants were the owners of
a coal mine on the north side of the river *Tyne*, at a place
called *Wallsend*. In order to ship the produce of the
mines with convenience, they had erected two stages or
staiths projecting into the river, supported on piles, there
called geers, driven into the bed of the river. On the top
of these were erected railways, over which waggons laden
with coals from the mine passed, and the coals were deposited
into vessels moored at the extremity of the staiths by means
of a machine called a drop. One of these staiths extended
nearly 150 feet, and the other 130 feet from high-water
mark, and both extended a few feet beyond low-water mark.
The drops, when let down, extended 40 feet farther, and
vessels taking in their cargoes were obliged to lie at that
distance from the staiths; but when drawn up, the drops
did not occasion any obstruction to the navigation. It ap-

peared that when vessels are not laden by means of staiths the coals are conveyed from the shore on board small craft called keels, and cast by hand from the keels into the ships. When vessels are laden in this manner they generally have a keel lying on each side, and thus occupy a greater space in the river than when laden by means of the staiths and drops, and their cargoes cannot be put on board in less than double the time. The expense also of shipping coals in this manner is much greater, and the coals are in worse condition than when loaded by means of staiths. The staiths in question at particular periods of the tide occasion considerable obstruction to small craft navigating against the stream, and for some time both before and after high water occupy a considerable space, which would otherwise be navigable with large vessels. It was proved, however, that if there were no staiths used in loading vessels the number of keels used on the *Tyne* would be greatly increased, and the river much crowded with them. On the south side of the river, opposite to one of the staiths indicted, there was a sandbank, which had increased after the staiths were erected, in consequence of the change thereby produced in the current of the stream. The defendants had obtained permission to erect the staiths from the Corporation of *Newcastle*, who are conservators of the river · *Tyne* and port of *Newcastle*. No writ of *ad quod damnum* was ever executed. The learned judge, in summing up the case for the jury, told them that in his opinion the use of a large navigable river was not for passage only, but for other important advantages, which might supersede the right of passage. It appeared to him that where a great public benefit accrued from that which occasioned the abridgement of the right of passage, that abridgement was not a nuisance, but proper and beneficial, and he directed the jury to acquit the defendants if they thought that the abridgment of the right of passage in this case was for a public purpose and produced a public benefit, and if it was in a reasonable situation, and a reasonable space was left for the passage

of vessels navigating the river *Tyne;* but otherwise to find
a verdict of guilty. His lordship called the attention of the
jury to that part of the evidence which went to shew that
the staiths were not merely a private but a public benefit,
for by means of them the coals were brought to market at a
smaller expense and in a better condition, in both which
particulars the public were benefited. He then left the
following questions for the decision of the jury:—1. Were
the staiths erected in a reasonable place? 2. Was there a
reasonable space left for the public in navigating the river
Tyne? 3. Were the staiths a public benefit? 4. Did the
public benefit countervail the prejudice done to individuals?
The jury found the defendants not guilty, stating that they
did so in consequence of the learned judge's direction.
Before the learned judge had begun to sum up it was
agreed on both sides, that if the jury acquitted the defendants the prosecutor's counsel might move to enter a verdict
for the crown, or for a new trial, if they should be dissatisfied with his lordship's directions in point of law. Accordingly in *Michaelmas* term, 1824, *Brougham* moved for
and obtained a rule nisi, for entering a verdict for the crown
or for granting a new trial.

In *Hilary* term, 1826, the case was argued.

Scarlett, A. G. J. *Williams,* *Coltman,* and *Ingham,* shewed
cause, and contended, on the part of the defendants, that
the direction of the learned judge to the jury was correct in
point of law, and that the finding of the jury was supported
by the evidence.

Brougham, Tindal, E. Alderson, and *Parke,* were heard
contrà.

The arguments and authorities bearing upon the question
being noticed by the judges in their decision, it is unnecessary here to enter into detail.

There being a difference of opinion upon the bench, the

case stood over by adjournment until this term, and now the judges who heard the case delivered their opinion seriatim. *Littledale*, J. who had been of counsel in the cause when at the bar gave no opinion.

HOLROYD, J. delivered his opinion to the following effect:—This was an indictment for wrongfully continuing two geers or staiths with spouts in the *Tyne*, a public navigable river, to the public nuisance of the navigation. There was a verdict for the defendants. A motion was made to set it aside, and instead thereof to enter a verdict for the crown. It was agreed at the trial that if the judge's direction was wrong, a verdict should be entered for the crown, if the Court should be of opinion that the jury ought so to have found; or that a special verdict should be entered if the Court should think it right. I am of opinion that there is not sufficient ground to set aside the verdict on account of any misdirection of the judge, or on any other account of which I am aware. The facts proved were as follows:—Two geers had been erected by the defendants for loading ships therefrom with coals, each extending below the low-water mark a foot or two, with spouts therefrom, one of which extended thirty-six feet; the other parts of the geers were between high and low-water mark. One of these geers was in existence in 1800. The other was not erected till afterwards. It appeared that they were substituted for loading the ships instead of loading them by keels. Subsequently statutes (a) passed, giving to the public rights of loading in turn at these spouts so long as they continue, which thereby have become clothed as long as they continue with public rights, in addition to the private rights of the proprietors. These statutes therefore consider that the spouts are not to be taken *per se*, and at all events nuisances or illegal. But independently of these statutes there are public and private rights with regard to the port for traffic and commerce in coals and also other merchan-

(a) 57 *Geo.* 3, c. 30, in operation at the time of this indictment.

dize. There is a public right of navigation on the river for that and other purposes. There are also public or private rights of fishing, public or private rights on the shore. For traffic there are rights, not only of navigation *eundo et redeundo*, but *morando* (so far as necessary or reasonable) for loading and unloading, or for a wind, &c. The enjoyment of each of those rights by some is frequently and necessarily an obstruction to the free and complete enjoyment either of the same right or of some of the above rights by others; for example, ships at anchor in the channel of the river are an obstruction to ships sailing, &c., boats and wherries plying, keels lying in the river, are also an obstruction. But such obstruction is not necessarily or as a matter of law a public or a private nuisance. Each of the rights thus mentioned must at times occasionally yield and become subordinate as may be necessary or reasonable, at least in part, to some of the others. The public, that is, each individual, has not an absolute right to navigate or sail over every part of the river, but only where there is not otherwise a legal pre-occupation (as in some cases there may be) by others. Ships, in order to load, must lie, if not at the staiths, in the channel of the river, with their loading keels. So in other trades, the ships lie at the wharfs or elsewhere in the river or port to load or unload, and their obstruction to others is or is not, as well as the erection of the wharf itself, a nuisance to the navigation, in like manner as the staith or geers themselves in the coal trade are or are not a nuisance according to circumstances. Whether they are so or not is dependent upon circumstances, and is, therefore, according to Lord *Hale*, in his treatise *De Portibus Maris*, 85, a question of fact for the jury. After specifying as a nuisance " the straightening of the port by building too far into the water, where ships or vessels might have formerly ridden," he adds, " it is to be observed that nuisance or not nuisance in such a case is a question of fact. It is not, therefore, every building below the high-water mark, nor every building below the low-water mark, that is *ipso facto* in law a nuisance." The only objection to the geers on the indictment is that they are unlawful, as being a public nuisance to the navigation. The defendants' right to have them there, and to continue and use them, is not impugned on any other ground. The defendants getting their coals by a proper access to and upon the river would have a right to load ships lying and continuing in the river for that purpose by the means of keels, although the doing so might be a temporary, and by doing it successively to different ships might be a continued though not a total obstruction or inconvenience to the navigation. And there would be a right to keep the ships and keels in the river for that purpose in convenient and proper places, at times not confined to the times of their being in actual use. And the evidence on the part of the defendants went to shew that the mode of loading the ships by the geers in question was less an obstruction to the navigation, and was more beneficial to the public, in fact, that it was a benefit instead of a nuisance, and therefore not subject to the present indictment. And the jury, upon the evidence, were of that opinion, and upon the learned judge's directions with regard to the law of the case, they found a verdict for the defendants. Now are the staiths to be deemed a nuisance, if they be such as the conservators of the river and port and the jury would *pro bono publico* be desirous should be made, or as a jury would deem upon the evidence a beneficial instead of an injurious change, or a general use of the port and river? Loading by the spouts is not necessarily a nuisance, because it is recognized by statutes, (the public local acts of 57 *Geo.* 3, c. 30, s. 17, and 5 *Geo.* 4, c. 72, s. 9, 10, 17,) and so long as the geers and spouts continue, the public have a right to have their ships loaded in turn at them with coals, supposing them not to be illegal. But it is objected that they are at all events illegal for want of a writ of *ad quod damnum*, and a favourable return of the inquisition thereof, and also that the jury have been or may have been misled by the direction of the learned judge, that his direction is incorrect in point of law, and further, that the jury ought to have found a verdict for the crown. First, as to the want of a writ of *ad quod damnum*: this is not like the case of shutting up a public highway and setting out another in lieu; that cannot be done so as to do away the former public right and to create a new public right without a writ of *ad quod damnum*. The former can only be abrogated by the writ of *ad quod damnum*, and the proceedings, and the king's license thereon; but that is not, as I conceive, requisite here, where the question is whether the mode of enjoyment in question of some of the public rights of the port, river and navigation, is or constitutes in fact a public nuisance. If that mode of enjoyment be not in fact such a nuisance, it does not as I conceive become so for the want of a writ of *ad quod damnum*, though without such a writ and a favourable inquisition thereon, they who erect such works act at their peril; and though the want of such a writ may be a good ground for the Lord Chancellor's interfering for the security of the public, and by injunction restraining any person from erecting works or buildings that interfere with the exercise of a public right, till it be ascertained by the writ of *ad quod damnum* that they are so doing, it is not a public nuisance or injurious to the king or his subjects. I now come to the consideration of the learned judge's direction to the jury, which forms the second ground of objection. The following observations were made by him as to the question of law arising upon the evidence which had been given:—" If wherever there is a power of passage over the water of a navigable river, there is a public right of way for all the king's subjects, not only in the channel but in all the places where vessels can go at the height of the tide; if that is a right of way which is to yield to nothing, but which the public is at all times entitled to insist on for the purpose of passage; then the prosecutor's counsel shall be at liberty to apply to the Court to enter a verdict for the crown, because these staiths interfere, where at high water the river was navigable

before they were erected. But my opinion is that the use
of a public water is not for passage only, but for many other
purposes, and that many of those purposes are entitled to
supersede the right of passage, and to narrow the right of
passage to those parts which may not be requisite for
greater and more beneficial purposes. Where there is a
space of water of very considerable extent, some part may
be most usefully applied for the purposes of commerce,
and that which is so applied may be over and above that
which is sufficient for navigation; and where a great public
benefit results from the abridgement of the exercise of the
right of passage, the great public benefit makes that abridgement no nuisance, but a useful, beneficial, and a proper
purpose. Therefore if in this case you shall say that that
which has been taken from the opportunity of passage has been
taken for public purposes, and for the public benefit, and
that it is placed in a reasonable situation, and that enough
is left for the ordinary and reasonable purposes of passage,
I shall recommend it to you certainly to find this not a nuisance." That which was taken from the opportunity of
passage was taken for public purposes and for the public
benefit, that is to say, for the exercise of public rights,
deemed by the statutes which I before referred to to be
beneficial, and to be vested in and exercised by the public.
Then the learned judge proceeded to make certain qualifi-
cations of that which had fallen from him;—" If you shall
be of opinion that this is in a place which, for public benefit,
it ought not to be in; that reasonable space is not left for
the purposes of passage; if you shall think that no public
benefit (and this was properly a question for the jury) results from this erection; I should recommend it to you to
find a verdict for the crown. And if you shall find that
this in any part of it goes further than for public purposes
it ought to go, then, as to that part, you pointing out in
your verdict what part it is, I should recommend it to you
certainly to give a verdict for the crown." Then the
learned judge proceeded: " It was suggested, while the

case was going on, that this was a staith for the private purposes of the individuals, and not for the public benefit. I beg to suggest for your consideration, because my opinion is different in that respect, that notwithstanding the individual is the proprietor of it, notwithstanding it gives him the opportunity of bringing his commodity to the market, yet it is beneficial to the public that that thing should be brought to the market, and brought to the market in that way, therefore the thing is, as it seems to me, useful to the public, who come to that staith for the purpose of having their vessels loaded, and to the people who want to carry coals to the *London* market. Both the man who receives the coals at the staith, and the man who buys his coals at *London*, coming from that staith, are benefited, if they are either got by those means cheaper, or if they are got by those means better than they otherwise would be; thus it is of public benefit that the thing should be there." These are observations merely in answer to the assertion that the staiths were for private benefit only, to shew that public benefit also may result from them, and are observations well founded in fact, and true, as it appears to me. But then it is said they are inapplicable to the question the jury were to try, and ought not to be taken into consideration by them. But it seems to me that so far as and for the purpose for which they were urged, namely, as an answer to the allegation that those staiths were for private purposes and not for public benefit, and to do away with the effect of such an assertion, they might be taken into consideration by the jury, and were warrantably used. They were a mere answer to an unfounded suggestion of the prosecutor, and not part of the direction to the jury; but if they had been so, yet qualified as they were by what followed, which were the points left to the attention and consideration of the jury, I think no fault is to be found. The learned judge proceeds: " Therefore the points to which I wish your attention to be directed will be, was this staith in a reasonable place, and is it applied to purposes of public benefit? Was reasonable space left for the purposes of navigation? And do the purposes of public benefit resulting from the staith countervail the prejudice which individuals may sustain by having the exercise of their right of passage narrowed?" At the conclusion he says, " Thus, gentlemen, I apprehend I have pointed out to you the true ground on which your verdict is to be founded. If you think this is placed not in a reasonable part of the river, that it does an unnecessary damage to the navigation, or that this is not of any public benefit, or that the public benefit resulting from it is not equal to the public inconvenience which arises from it, then you will find your verdict for the crown; if on these points you are of a different opinion, then for the defendants." Upon this the jury found a verdict for the defendants. The whole of this direction, taken together, is in substance correct, qualified in the different parts as it is; and I see no sufficient reason to enable me to say the jury have drawn such a conclusion from the evidence as to warrant the Court in setting aside the verdict.

BAYLEY, J.—I agree with my brother *Holroyd* in this case that there ought not to be a new trial; and though I regret extremely that there should be a difference of opinion on the part of my lord, I am happy to think the difference between us is limited to a single point, and that too one which would hardly be likely to lead to a different result upon a new trial. I have, indeed, considered the subject with every degree of attention on my part, and should willingly act on his judgment in preference to my own, but I feel so strong a conviction in my own mind, that I think I cannot in justice to the defendants give up my own opinion. I believe we are all agreed that a writ of *ad quod damnum* was not requisite in this case, and that if these staiths are not upon the facts and merits a nuisance, the neglect to make them the subjects of an *ad quod damnum* will not make them so. The points submitted to the jury were, whether these staiths were erected in a part of the river where it was reasonable ships should load, whether a reasonable space was left for navigation, whether the loading of vessels by means of them was a public benefit, whether they extended into the river further than the public benefit required, and whether the public benefit they produced was greater than the public injury they occasioned. Upon each of these points the verdict shews that the jury were in favour of the defendants. The only point on which our difference rests is, I believe, the point of public benefit, not the point upon the preponderance of public benefit, but the question what might be taken into consideration as matter of public benefit. I certainly suffered the jury to take into their consideration, as part of the public benefit, the possible reduction of price at the staith, the possible reduction of price in the *London* market, and the improved condition in which the coals would arrive there, and if I was wrong in suffering them to take any of these points into their consideration, the verdict may have proceeded upon a wrong principle, and there ought to be a new trial. Mr. *Brougham* had strongly pressed on the consideration of the jury, that these staiths were beneficial only to the individuals to whom they belonged, and that they conferred no benefit on the public; and in answer to this point I submitted to the consideration of the jury, that if by means of these staiths an article of great public use found its way to the public at a lower price and in a better state than it otherwise would, I thought these were circumstances of public benefit, and points they might take into their consideration upon that head; and upon the best attention I have been able to give the subject, I am bound to say I continue of that opinion. The right of the public upon the waters of a port or a navigable river is not confined to the purposes of passage; trade and commerce are the chief objects, and the right of passage is chiefly subservient to those ends. Unless there are facilities of loading and unloading, of shipping and landing, much of the public benefit of a port is lost.

In the infancy of a port, when it is first applied to the purposes of trade and commerce, unless the water by the shore be deep, the articles must be shipped in shallow water from the shore and landed in shallow water on the shore. Boats or vessels of small draught must be employed to fetch and carry from and to the shore, and the commodity must pass from boat to ship, or from ship to boat. Breakage, and pilferage, and waste, besides the expense of boating, are some of the probable concomitants of such a mode. As trade advances the inconvenience and mischief of this mode are superseded by the erection of wharfs and quays, and what is, perhaps, an improved species of loading wharf, a staith. The loading or unloading is then immediate from the wharf or staith into the ship, or from the ship upon the wharf. But upon what principle can the erection of a wharf or staith be supported? It narrows the right of passage; it occupies a space where boats before had navigated, it turns part of the water-way into solid ground; but it advances some of the other purposes, the main purposes of a port, its trade and commerce. Is there any other legal principle upon which they can be allowed? Make any erection for pleasure, for whim, for caprice, and if it interfere in the least degree with the public right of passage, it is a nuisance. Erect it for the purposes of trade and commerce, and keep it applied to the purposes of trade and commerce, and subject to the guards with which this case was presented to the jury, the interests of trade and commerce give it a protection, and it is a justifiable erection, not a nuisance. What says Lord *Hale, De Portibus Maris,* c. 7, p. 85? "In the case of building into the water where ships or vessels might formerly have ridden, whether it be nuisance or not nuisance is a question of fact. It is not every building below high or low-water mark that is *ipso facto* in law a nuisance, for this would destroy all quays, which are all built below high-water mark, otherwise vessels could not come at them to unload, and some are built below low-water mark." In what does the

1827.

The King
v.
Russell.

trade and commerce of any port consist? In its exports and its imports. And to whom do the public benefits of a port result? To the port and its neighbourhood, and to the places with which it trades. The exports may, and in many instances do, consist of the produce of the neighbourhood of the port, and the individuals to whom they belong are induced to send them, not from patriotic views of encouraging the shipping interest, of promoting a nursery for seamen, or of benefiting the place to which such produce is sent, but from the mere selfish principle of individual advantage; but if public benefit results, is it a right view of the question to look at the motive instead of considering the effect? If the conduct of many individuals, though proceeding wholly and exclusively from private motives of private profit, produce results of great public benefit, and the question is proposed, whether public benefit be or be not produced, am I to answer the question in the negative, because public benefit was never in the contemplation of the individuals by whom it is produced? If then the exportation of the produce of a neighbourhood will increase the trade and commerce of a port, and that trade and commerce will benefit every place to which that produce is sent, how is that exportation to be advanced? By giving facilities to exportation, by reducing the expense to the owner of that produce, by enabling him to export upon terms which will insure him a profit and a market. What is the great export trade of *Newcastle?* The produce of its neighbourhood, coals. Who are the first movers in that trade? The owners of the neighbouring mines. Why do they send the coals to market? For the sake of profit only, their motive is selfish only. But are the owners of these mines the only persons interested in the export of coals? Exclusively of the shipping interest, and the persons who are concerned in the carrying trade, when the owners are tempted by the hope of private profit to join in the exportation, what is to be said of the great body of purchasers at the market to which the coals are carried? Have they no interest in having coals, and having them cheap and good? Stop the *Newcastle* coal trade, and where is the inconvenience felt? In *Newcastle* and its neighbourhood, to a certain extent undoubtedly. But in *Newcastle* and its neighbourhood only? Certainly not. To a much greater extent in *London* and in the other markets to which *Newcastle* coals are sent. Throw any impediment upon the trade, deteriorate the coals, or increase the price, and where does the pressure fall? Undoubtedly upon the market to which this coal is sent. Encourage the trade, make the article cheap, and improve its quality, and who reaps the benefit? The market to which the article is sent. Facility in loading is one of the chief means to give the trade encouragement. It brings to market produce, which otherwise would not pay for bringing. It increases the number of sellers, and has a tendency to produce such a competition as will keep the price low. The staiths in question save the ship one fourth of her loading time, prevent pilfering, breakage and waste, and send to market a better commodity by 6d. a chaldron than would otherwise arrive there. And is this nothing to the *London* purchaser? He has from these two staiths 600 cargoes, above 100,000 chaldrons of prime coals, coals in an unbroken state, instead of the same quantity of coal in an inferior condition, keel coals. And if from the benefit which the owner of the mine has from the staith, and the purchaser at the staith has from expedition and otherwise, the coals are sold in the *London* market at a lower price, I cannot help thinking that a public benefit results to the *London* buyers, and that the jury were entitled to take that into their consideration. I did not assume that the article would be cheaper, that was for the consideration of the jury; but if it were, I thought it an ingredient to be considered upon the question of public benefit. Is the place in which the public benefit accrues material? Does it signify whether it accrues in the port of *Newcastle* or in any other part of the kingdom? The king is equally the guardian of the public rights of all his subjects; all his subjects are equally under his care; and if public benefit results, it is immaterial whether it is to his subjects in *London* or to his subjects in *Newcastle*. Nor can it be a question whether the benefit results from a public or a private staith; from the staith confined to the goods of a single individual, or from a public one, which any one may use. In estimating the amount of public benefit which a staith produces, the extent to which it is used may be material; but if a private individual, with his own coals, keeps it in full employ, I think it equally entitled to protection, on account of the benefit it confers upon the distant market, the market to which the coals are carried, whether it be public or private. I have hitherto considered the case with reference to these two staiths only, and to the public benefit which they confer upon the distant market; but when the question is considered with reference to the state of the port of *Newcastle*, the necessity of taking into consideration the effect upon the distant market appears to me more prominent. There are twenty-eight similar staiths, many, if not all, for the private purposes of particular coal owners. Exclude the question of public benefit to the *London* market from the staiths in question, and must it not be excluded from each and every one of those staiths, and what will be the state of the *London* market when the purchaser can meet with nothing but keel coal? But will he be able, even to get keel coals? There must be staiths, as was in evidence upon the trial, for loading keels. And if a ship staith is to be proscribed because it is erected and used for the private benefit of the proprietor of a particular coal mine, and, because the public benefit to the market cannot be taken into consideration, must not keel staiths, when erected and used for the private benefit of a like proprietor, be excluded also? It will interfere, though in a less degree, with the freedom of passage, and though a nuisance of less magnitude, will still be a nuisance. For these reasons, I am of opinion, that upon the question of public benefit, the probable effect upon the price and meliorated condition of the coal, were

proper for the consideration of the former jury ; that if the
case were to go to another jury, they would still be proper
ingredients for their consideration, and that the direction
given in that respect is free from objection.

Lord TENTERDEN, C. J.—I am sorry that I cannot
concur in the opinion of my two learned brothers on the
present occasion. I am not prepared to say that I think
the verdict ought to be entered for the crown, but with all
deference to them, I am compelled to own that my mind
would be better satisfied if the cause were again sent to
trial by another jury. I do not think the want of a previous
writ of *ad quod damnum* conclusive against the defendants.
Such a writ is highly proper where the crown is applied to
for a grant of any liberty or franchise; and so far at least
necessary, that probably no person would think himself
justified in advising the King to make any such grant where
possible injury to an existing right could be surmised without the sanction of a previous inquiry under the writ. It
may also be, and I think it is, a prudent and proper measure
before a subject takes upon him to act for himself and on
his own judgment. The want of it furnishes an argument
against the propriety of his act, because it shews that he is
apprehensive of the consequence of a previous inquiry, and
fears that its result may be unfavourable to his views. And
when the object of any proceeding is to prevent the accom-
plishment of an act intended or begun, as an application for
an injunction, the want of this previous proceeding may
properly form a very material ingredient in the consideration
of the question. It is also deserving of consideration and
attention on the trial of an indictment. But the finding
under this writ, when favourable to those at whose instance
it has issued, is traversable, it is not conclusive in their
favour, it is not a bar to an indictment for a nuisance.
The jury, by whom such an indictment is to be tried, have
a right to exercise their own judgment upon the matter, and
may find that to be a perfect nuisance which, under this

writ, has been found not to be to the prejudice of his Majesty's subjects. And as the finding is not conclusive on one side, I cannot think the absence of any finding conclusive on the other. In my opinion, speaking with great deference to the high authority that is reported to have spoken of the want of such a proceeding as conclusive, the jury who are to try an indictment, for a nuisance have a right to exercise their own judgment on the question, as well in the absence of such a proceeding, as where such a previous inquiry has taken place. I come now to mention my reasons for saying that my mind would be better satisfied if the cause were sent to another trial. The erections in question are said to be in the port of *Newcastle*, by which I understand to be meant, that they are within the limits of the jurisdiction of that port. They are certainly at a considerable distance below the public quays and places of general resort of vessels trading to that port, and must be passed by vessels resorting to and from such places. And I take it to be clear that the passage of such vessels is, in certain seasons at least of wind and tide, rendered less free and commodious; that the water way is in some degree narrowed at present, and may possibly and not improbably be further narrowed in process of time by the gradual accumulation of sand and silt carried to the opposite side of the river. The erections were made and maintained for the private convenience of the owners of particular collieries; all who think proper to purchase their coals from these collieries have a right, under a particular act of parliament, to be supplied in turn, by application at some office at *Newcastle*. The owners of the collieries cannot chuse to whom they will vend, but they may chuse at what seasons they will vend, and whether they will vend at all, and seasons may occur when they have no commodity to vend. It was proved that coals put into vessels from these staiths are less broken and come to market in distant places in a somewhat better state than those which are brought to the vessel's side in keels or barges, and so undergo a double shipment or removal. But I think it may well be doubted whether they come to market at any cheaper rate, or at a rate so much cheaper as to be worth consideration. When all arrive at a market, I should apprehend those which are found in the best state will fetch the best price, and so the advantage, as far as price is concerned, will be to the owners of the staiths and collieries, and not to the public. Admitting, however, that there is some public benefit both from the price and condition of the coals, still I must own that I do not think those points could properly be taken into consideration in the question raised by this indictment. That question I take properly to have been, whether the navigation and passage of vessels on this public navigable river was injured by these erections. Upon this question there was evidence on both sides, regard being had to that obstruction which must necessarily take place by the transfer of coals from keels or other vessels confined to the navigation of the river into ships of a different kind passing to sea. And if the question had been left entirely in this form, and a verdict found for the defendants, I do not, as at present advised, see that any objection could have been properly made to it. In some parts of my learned brother's direction to the jury, and especially towards the close, the case appears to have been left mainly on this ground. But in other parts remarks were made on the public benefit, of the nature I have alluded to, which might probably, in my judgment, have an effect upon the minds of the jury, coming as they did from so high and from so respectable an authority, that I think ought not to have been produced. I am far from thinking that where the direction of a judge is, in the main and taken altogether, right and consonant to law, a verdict is to be set aside on account of occasional or casual expressions, that, upon more mature consideration, may be thought incorrect. And I desire that no such inference may be drawn from my present judgment. It would be a very ill compliment to juries to suppose that they are likely to be misled by such accidental expressions. But in the present case, I am bound to say that I think the matter went further, and that my mind is by no means satisfied that the verdict was not materially influenced by considerations that I think ought not to have affected it. For these reasons I should have been better satisfied with a new trial; but as those of my learned brothers who have felt themselves at liberty to take any part in the consideration of this question, think the verdict ought to stand, the rule for setting it aside and entering a verdict for the crown must be discharged.

Rule discharged.

Bastock v. Ridgway.

FEIGNED ISSUE, to try whether the hamlet of Single-borough, in the parish of *Great Horwood*, in the county of *Buckingham*, was legally separated and divided from the township of *Great Horwood*, in the same parish, for the relief and maintenance of the poor. At the trial before *Alexander*, C. B., at the *Buckinghamshire* summer assizes, 1825, a verdict was found for the plaintiff, subject to the opinion of this Court upon the following case:—

A parish cannot be legally separated into districts for the relief and maintenance of the poor, unless it cannot otherwise reap the full benefit of the statute 43 Eliz. c. 2.

The parish of *Great Horwood* consists of the township of *Great Horwood* and of the hamlet of *Singleborough*, which hamlet is a distinct and immemorial vill. The township of *Horwood* contains about 3000 acres, consisting almost entirely of open fields and waste or common lands. The hamlet of *Singleborough* contains about 900 acres. It was inclosed upwards of 20 years ago under an act of parliament, and the lands are of much greater value in proportion to their extent than those of the township of *Horwood*.

The case then went on to state, with a verbose particularity which it would be inconvenient and does not appear necessary to imitate, a vast variety of facts relating to the extent, population, and circumstances of the parish; and to set out a great number of certificates and bastardy bonds, varying in date from 1679 to 1753, some directed " to the overseers of the poor of *Great Horwood cum Singleborough*," others " to the overseers of *Great Horwood*," and others " to the overseers of *Singleborough*." It then proceeded as follows :—

On the 8th of *October*, 1690, an agreement was made under the hands and seals of *Hugh Barker* and 32 other persons, including the rector of the parish, therein described as of *Great Horwood* and *Singleborough*, whereby they agreed to have a house built at *Singleborough* for the use of *W. Gayton*, at the costs and charges of *Horwood* and *Singleborough*, and so to continue for the use of the poor of *Singleborough*, each hamlet paying their usual proportionable allowance for their relief; and that the poor of *Singleborough* and *Horwood* be kept in their respective hamlets.

On the 24th of *April*, 1753, the following agreement was made by and between the churchwardens and overseers of the poor of the township of *Great Horwood* and certain inhabitants of the said township, and the churchwardens and overseers of the poor of the hamlet of *Singleborough* and certain inhabitants thereof :—" Articles of agreement indented, made, concluded and agreed upon, this 24th day of *April*, 1753, between *J. H.* and *J. J.*, churchwardens, and *W. K.* and *H. C.*, overseers, and *W. K.*, *R. W.*, *R. B.*, *W. C.*, *N. W.*, *H. H.*, *T. E.*, and *T. V.*, and others, whose hands and seals are hereunto set and subscribed, occupiers of lands and tenements within the town, precincts, or division of *Great Horwood*, in the county of *Bucks*, for and on behalf of themselves, and, as far as by law they can, on behalf of the future churchwardens and overseers and occupiers of lands and tenements within the said town, precincts, or division, of the one part, and *T. B.*, churchwarden, and *T. B.*, senior, overseer, and *T. B.* the elder, and *T. B.* the younger, and *J. H.*, and others, whose hands and seals are hereunto set and subscribed, occupiers of lands and tenements within the hamlet, liberty, or division of *Singleborough*, in the parish of *Great Horwood* aforesaid, on behalf of themselves, and, as far as by law they can, on behalf of all and every future and succeeding churchwardens and overseers and occupiers of lands and tenements within the said hamlet, of the other part, as follows:—Whereas frequent disputes do arise between the occupiers of lands in the said town and the said hamlet, concerning the reception of poor persons sent by orders or otherwise to each of the said places, and concerning the proportion of the poor rates to be raised in each place, occasioned in some measure by considerable private donations given for the maintenance and relief of the poor of one place, independent and exclusive of the other, by which great expenses frequently are incurred, disorder and confusion do ensue, and the poor by such means become more burthensome than they otherwise would be: Now for the prevention of such inconveniences for the future," &c. The deed then contained an agreement that for the future each district should separately maintain its own poor, and that the township and hamlet should, in all matters concerning the poor, be considered as two distinct and different parishes; it provided for the division of certain private donations and of certain almshouses between the two districts: and it contained a covenant to support and keep the articles of agreement, and to admit the same as evidence in any controversy which might arise touching the poor of either of the said places. Ever since the date of this agreement the township and hamlet respectively have maintained their poor separately, and paupers have been removed, by orders of justices, from foreign parishes to the township and hamlet respectively, and from the hamlet to the township.

Since the year 1753 there have been separate poor rates for the township and hamlet, and also separate appointments of overseers of the poor, with the exceptions hereinafter mentioned: that is to say, that in each of the years 1815, 1816, and 1817, a joint appointment of overseers of

the poor of the whole parish was made by two justices of
the peace, on the application of the inhabitants of the
township of *Great Horwood*, without the consent and against
the will of the inhabitants of the hamlet of *Singleborough;*
but notwithstanding such joint appointments of overseers,
the poor of the hamlet of *Singleborough* continued to be
maintained and employed by the inhabitants thereof separately as theretofore, and without any interference on the
part of the overseers or inhabitants of the township of
Horwood, and separate rates were likewise made by the
township and hamlet respectively for the relief of their
respective poor.

If the Court shall be of opinion that the legal presumption to be formed from the facts stated is, that the hamlet
of *Singleborough* was legally separated from the township
of *Great Horwood*, for the relief and maintenance of the
poor, the verdict is to stand; otherwise, a verdict is to be
entered for the defendant.

B. *Monro*, for the plaintiff.   The Court must come to a
decision in the affirmative of this issue, that the hamlet of
Singleborough has been legally separated from the township
of *Great Horwood*, for the purpose of relieving and maintaining its own poor.   There is no doubt that it may have
been legally separated for that purpose, if at the time when
the statute 13 & 14 *Car.* 2, c. 12, passed, the parish could
not receive the benefit of the statute 43 *Eliz.* c. 2.   For
this position *Rex* v. *Leigh* (a), and *Rex* v. *Walsall* (b), are
express authorities; and in the former of those cases
Buller, J. declared the meaning of that phrase to be, not
that there must be an absolute *impossibility* for the inhabitants of a parish to maintain their own poor, *as a parish*,
for that would not be the case even if the parish were a
hundred miles in circumference, but that it must be *inconvenient* for them to do so (c).   The question, therefore, is,

(a) 3 T. R. 746.   (c) " The statute does not mean
(b) 2 B. & A. 157.   that it is absolutely impossible for

whether this parish has been able conveniently to receive
the benefit of the statute 43 *Eliz.* c. 2. Now it is found
by the case, that during the last seventy-two years it has
not in fact received that benefit, for there have been re-
movals, not only from foreign parishes to the hamlet of
Singleborough and to the township of *Great Horwood*, but
from the hamlet to the township; and the not receiving the
benefit during such a period is, according to the opinion of
Bayley, J., in *Rex* v. *Walsall*, strong evidence to lead to
the conclusion that it was not capable of doing so. [*Bayley*, J. In that case the agreement to separate had been
acted upon ever since the time of passing the statute 13 &
14 *Car.* 2.] It appears here that even prior to the last
seventy-two years, the parish had not the full and ordinary
benefit of the statute 43 *Eliz.*, for in 1690, not quite thirty
years after the passing of the statute 13 & 14 *Car.* 2, an
agreement was made for keeping the poor of *Singleborough*
and of *Great Horwood* separately in their respective hamlets.
[*Bayley*, J. It does not appear by that agreement that it
was, in the language of the twenty-first section of that
statute, " by reason of the largeness of the parish" that it
could not receive that benefit.] The words of the enactment are general, and it has never been decided that they
must be restrained by the recital to those cases only where
the largeness of the parish is the only reason why it cannot

them to maintain their own poor
as a parish, but that it is inconvenient so to do. I even go further,
for though it should appear that a
parish had enjoyed the benefit of
the statute of *Elizabeth*, yet if they
could not now conveniently maintain their own poor jointly, we
would permit them to divide themselves, provided there be such legal
divisions as are capable of maintaining their own poor separately."
Per *Buller*, J., in *Rex* v. *Leigh*, 3

T.R. 746. And in *Rex* v. *Horton*,
1 T. R. 374, the same learned Judge
said, " we must consider what is
meant by the *benefit* of the statute.
It is that the parish may maintain
their poor *as a parish*, for unless
they can do it *as such*, they cannot
have the benefit of the statute.
Now it is stated that two of the
townships maintain their own poor,
but unless they all join, they cannot have the benefit of the statute."

receive the benefit of the statute of *Elizabeth* (a). In *Rex*
v. *Leigh* (b) the parish was not very large, five miles long
and four miles broad; and here there are 4000 acres in the
parish, of which *Singleborough* contains only one fourth.
In 1714 a certificate was given, directed to the churchwardens and overseers of the poor of the hamlet of *Singleborough* and parish of *Great Horwood*. It is true that the
agreement of 1753 shews that the private donations were
in some degree the cause of disputes between the hamlet
and the township; but it does not shew that they were the
only cause of those disputes; and it does shew clearly
that at that time there existed a necessity for a separation.
If a joint appointment of overseers should now be held
proper, what security is there that the same disputes and
expense which were obviated by the agreement will not be
again occasioned? In an anonymous case (c), recognised
by Lord *Kenyon* in *Rex* v. *Newell* (d), where different districts of a parish situated in two counties had distinct
officers, made distinct rates, and had used, time out of
mind, to make distinct accounts to the justices of each
county, the Court held that they were entitled to maintain
their own poor separately. In *Rex* v. *Leigh* (b), where a
township had for 60 or 70 years past, (and before, for any
thing that appeared to the contrary,) had separate overseers,
and maintained its own poor separately from the parish at
large, it was held that it was still entitled to the same
privilege.

Bligh, contrà, was stopped by the Court.

Lord TENTERDEN, C. J.—The question reserved for our

(a) " To enable the townships
of a parish to separate from each
other, where it appears that the
parish has had the benefit of the
43 *Elizabeth*, it must be shewn
that, *from an increase of population,*
or *some other cause*, it is impossible that they can continue to reap
the benefit of that statute." Per
Ashhurst, J., in *Rex* v. *Leigh*, 3
T. R. 746; 1 Nolan, 46, 3d edit.
  (b) 3 T. R. 746.
  (c) Sir Tho. Ray. 476.
  (d) 4 T. R. 266.

opinion upon this special case is, whether the legal presumption to be formed from the facts stated in that case is, that the hamlet of *Singleborough* has been legally separated from the township of *Great Horwood*, for the relief and maintenance of the poor. Now, looking to the statute 13 & 14 *Car.* 2, c. 12, s. 21, upon which alone such a separation can be founded, it is apparent that the largeness of the parishes is expressly assigned as the reason why particular parishes are unable to enjoy the benefit of the previous statute, 43 *Eliz.* c. 2. I must not be understood as meaning to say, that because the largeness of the parishes is so mentioned, that must be considered as the only reason why the benefit of the statute of *Elizabeth* cannot be enjoyed; because that benefit might be lost by means of an increasing and superabundant population in a district not itself very large. But I do mean to say, that there must be some evidence to shew that the parish has not received, and could not have received, the benefit of the statute of *Elizabeth*. Looking at the present state of things in this parish, I see nothing to justify me in coming to such a conclusion; and looking at the former state of things there, I see nothing shewing that this parish might not have had the *full* benefit of that statute. What are the facts here? These. In 1758 the hamlet and the township thought fit to separate. The instrument by which they separated was clearly invalid, unless it was founded on that necessity which the statute of *Charles* points out. The instrument recites, that frequent disputes had arisen between the occupiers of lands in the town, precinct, or division of the township of *Great Horwood* and the hamlet of *Singleborough*, concerning the reception of poor persons sent by orders of removal to each of those places, and concerning the proportion of poor rates to be raised in each of those places, occasioned in some degree by considerable private donations given for the relief and maintenance of the poor of one place, independently and exclusively of the other, by which great expenses were incurred, and disorder and confusion ensued, and the poor became more burthensome than they would otherwise have been. All that I can infer from such an agreement is, that there had been disputes originating in a want of proper attention to the subject; not that there was any real inability on the part of the parish to maintain all its poor collectively, but merely that the hamlet and the township thought proper to fall into disputes upon the mode of doing it. Those disputes are said to have been occasioned in some degree by the private donations, but that does not prove that they were unable to receive the benefit of the statute of *Elizabeth;* indeed the donations, if properly applied, could not have caused any difficulty in that respect; for if the poor rates of the whole parish were applicable to the relief of all the poor, the private donations would not be so, but would, properly, be applicable to those only who did not receive any assistance from the poor rates, but who, having some assistance from another source, were thus enabled to maintain themselves. In the present case the agreement for the separation was of so recent a date as 1753. In *Rex* v. *Walsall* (a) the separation took place very shortly after the passing of the statute of *Charles.* Now in the interval between the statute of *Elizabeth* and that of *Charles,* there could not be any legal valid separation. Then if we find that as soon as an act of parliament makes a separation legal, a parish which could not have the full benefit of the statute of *Elizabeth* actually effects such a separation, that is, in my opinion, satisfactory evidence, that at and before that time it had been thought that the parish could not have the benefit of the statute of *Elizabeth.* But the same inference does not arise in a case where the separation has been effected so recently as 1753. Upon the whole, therefore, I am of opinion that the facts of this case do not warrant us in presuming that the hamlet of *Singleborough* has been legally separated from the township

(a) 2 B. & A. 157.

of *Great Horwood* for the relief and maintenance of the
poor.

. The other Judges concurred.

Judgment for the defendant.

———◆———

COATES and another *v.* RAILTON and another.

TROVER for 500 pieces of printed calico. Plea, not
guilty; and issue thereon.   At the trial before Lord *Tenterden*, C. J. at the last *London* sittings, the case was this:—
The plaintiffs were calico printers at *Manchester;* the defendants were commission agents at the same place, acting
also as packers in respect of such goods as they sent abroad.
James, *Richard*, and *Robert Butler* were merchants, carrying on business in *London* under the firm of *Butler*, Brothers, and in *Lisbon* in partnership with one *Krus*, under
the firm of *Butler*, *Krus* & Co.   The course of dealing
between the parties was this:—When *Butler*, *Krus* & Co.
wanted goods to be purchased for them at *Manchester*, they
sent a letter addressed to the defendants under cover to
Butler, Brothers, in *London*.   That letter *Butler*, Brothers,
forwarded to the defendants, who purchased the goods in
the name of *Butler*, Brothers, and forwarded them, *viâ
Liverpool*, to *Butler*, *Krus* & Co. at *Lisbon;* and the seller
then drew on *Butler*, Brothers, at three months for the
amount.   On the 7th of *January*, 1826, the defendants
received a letter from *Butler*, Brothers, inclosing one from
Butler, *Krus* & Co., of the 19th of *December*, desiring the
defendants to purchase on their account 500 pieces of
printed calico, and on the following day the defendants did
purchase the same of the plaintiffs in the name of *Butler*,
Brothers, informing the plaintiffs that they were to be sent
to *Lisbon* as on former occasions.   On the 28th of *January*
the goods were delivered to the defendants at their ware-

*Goods pur-
chased by an
agent at Man-
chester, for
the avowed
purpose of
being sent to
his principal at
Lisbon, are in
transitu until
they arrive at
Lisbon, and,
on the insol-
vency of the
principal, may
be stopped by
the seller in
the warehouse
of the agent at
Manchester.*

house in *Manchester*, with an invoice, in which *Butler*, Brothers, were made debtors. The defendants sent the goods to their calenderer, who calendered them, made them up, and returned them to the defendants on the 31st of *January*. The defendants were to forward the goods to *Liverpool*, to be shipped to *Butler*, *Krus* & Co. at *Lisbon*. Neither *Butler*, Brothers, nor *Butler*, *Krus* & Co., had any warehouse at *Manchester*. On the 1st of *February* the plaintiffs drew upon *Butler*, Brothers, a bill for the price of the goods at three months' date, and transmitted it to *London*, but it was dishonoured. *Butler*, Brothers, stopped payment on the 6th of *February*, and a commission afterwards issued against them, under which they were declared bankrupts. The goods remained in the defendants' warehouse at the time when intelligence reached *Manchester* that *Butler*, Brothers, had stopped payment, and the plaintiffs then claimed them, but the defendants refused to deliver them. The Lord Chief Justice was of opinion that *Lisbon* being the place of ultimate destination of the goods, they continued to be *in transitu* while they remained in the defendants' warehouse, and therefore that the plaintiffs had a right to stop them. The plaintiffs therefore had a verdict.

Denman, C. S. now moved to enter a nonsuit. Neither *Butler*, Brothers, nor *Butler*, *Krus* & Co. had any warehouse in *Manchester*, but the defendants acted in the transaction in the double capacity of factors and warehousemen; therefore the delivery of the goods to them was a delivery to the buyers, and put an end to the *transitus*. There are several cases directly in point. In *Dixon* v. *Baldwin* (a), *A.* and *B.*, traders, living in *London*, were in the habit of ordering goods of the defendants, cotton manufacturers at *Manchester*, to be sent to *M.* & Co. at *Hull*, for the purpose of being afterwards sent to the correspondents of *A.* and *B.* at *Hamburgh*. On the 31st of *March*, *A.* and *B.* sent orders to the defendants for certain goods to be sent to

(a) 5 East, 175.

M. & Co. at *Hull*, to be shipped for *Hamburgh*, as usual. It was held that, as between buyer and seller, the right of the defendants to stop *in transitu* was at an end when the goods came to the possession of *M.* & Co. at *Hull*; for they were for this purpose the appointed agents of the vendees, and received orders from them as to the ulterior destination of the goods; and the goods, after their arrival at *Hull*, were to receive a new direction from the vendees. In *Leeds* v. *Wright* (a), *A.*, the general agent of *B.* & Co., a house in *Paris*, with power to export for them to such markets as he should think fit, purchased goods in the name of *B.* & Co. of *C.* at *Manchester*, and directed them to be sent to *D.*, a packer in *London*. After their arrival *A.* had some of the goods unpacked and sent away, and the remainder repacked. News then arrived of the failure of *B.* & Co. It was held that the goods in *D.*'s hands were no longer *in transitu*, and that *C.*, therefore, had no right to stop them. In *Rowe* v. *Pickford* (b), a trader in *London* was in the habit of purchasing goods at *Manchester*, and exporting them to the *Continent* shortly after their arrival in *London*. The goods consigned to him remained in the waggon office of the defendants, who were carriers, until they were removed by his agent for the purpose of being shipped. It was held that such trader having become bankrupt, his assignees were entitled to recover goods deposited with the defendants before the bankruptcy, and that the consignor had no right to stop them *in transitu*, as the trader had no warehouse of his own; and that the *transitus* of the goods was at an end on their arrival at the waggon office.

Lord TENTERDEN, C. J.—I think we ought not to grant the rule prayed for in this case. The goods were purchased of the plaintiffs by the defendants as agents, in the name of *Butler*, Brothers, but in reality for *Butler*, *Krus* & Co., to whom they were to be sent at *Lisbon*. The defendants

(a) 3 B. & P. 320; 4 Esp. 243.   (b) 8 Taunt. 83; 1 Moore, 526.

were packers and warehousemen, as well as the general agents of the purchasers. If they had been only warehousemen, it is perfectly clear that as the goods were purchased for the avowed purpose of being sent to *Lisbon*, the vendors would have been entitled to stop them at any moment while they were in a course of conveyance to *Lisbon.* I was of opinion at the trial, that the fact of the defendants in this case having been the general agents of the purchasers as well as warehousemen made no difference; and that the goods having been delivered to them by the vendors for the purpose of being forwarded to *Lisbon*, the *transitus* was not at an end, and the plaintiffs had a right to stop the goods. I am of the same opinion now.

BAYLEY, J.—I think my Lord Chief Justice was right in the view which he took of this case at Nisi Prius. The general rule is, that where goods are sold for the purpose of being sent to a particular place of destination named by the purchaser, the right of the vendor to stop them continues until they arrive at that place of destination. In the several cases cited, the goods were sent to the place where the purchaser directed them to be sent, and the principle deducible from those cases is, that the *transitus* is not at an end until the goods have reached the place named by the purchaser to the vendor as the place of their destination. Here the place of destination named by the purchasers to the vendors was *Lisbon*, and not the defendant's warehouse, and therefore I think the goods were *in transitu* while they continued in the possession of the defendants, and the vendors had a right to stop them.

HOLROYD, J., and LITTLEDALE, J., concurred.

Rule refused.

1827.

VAVASOUR *v.* ORMROD.

DEBT for rent. The declaration stated that by a certain indenture made between plaintiff and one *J. S.* (profert of which was made,) plaintiff demised, &c. to *J. S.*, his executors, &c., certain premises, *habendum*, &c., " yielding and paying therefore the yearly yent of 160*l.*, by two even and equal portions, in each and every year during the said term, that is to say, on, &c.," as by the said indenture, reference being thereunto had, would more fully and at large appear. It then averred the entry of *J. S.*, his assignment to the defendant, the entry of the latter, and that rent had since accrued due. Plea, *nil debet;* and issue thereon. At the trial before *Hullock*, B., at the last *Lent* assizes for the county of *Lancaster*, the reservation of rent in the indenture produced was in these words:—" yielding and paying during the said term, *except as hereinafter mentioned;*" and then proceeding in the terms set forth in the declaration. It appeared also that the lease contained a covenant by the lessor to expend 600*l.* in erecting a steam engine, and a proviso that in case the lessee should within three years pay to the lessor 300*l.* in part discharge of the 600*l.* to be so expended by the lessor, the rent should be reduced from 160*l.* to 130*l.*, and that if the remaining 300*l.* should be paid within six years, the rent should be further reduced to 100*l.* There was no proof of payment of any part of the 600*l.* It was contended on the part of the defendant that there was a fatal variance between the lease and the declaration; that on a plea of *non est factum* to a declaration in covenant on a lease, the omission of an exception in a reservation or a covenant created a variance, although a distinct proviso, if not insisted upon, might be omitted; (for this 1 *Saund.* 234, note (2) c. 5th ed. was cited;) that although the proviso in this case was a distinct one, the ex-

Marginal note: If the reservation of rent in a lease refers to a subsequent proviso, by which the rent is to be reduced if a certain event happens, the plaintiff in an action of debt for the rent must set out the reservation with the proviso in his declaration, although the event has not happened.

ception referring to it was in the body of the reservation,
and the reservation, therefore, must be read as if it had
contained the proviso itself in the form of an exception;
that this, therefore, would have been a fatal variance on a
plea of *non est factum*, and was equally so on a plea of *nil
debet*, which put in issue the execution of the indenture set
out in the declaration as much as a plea of *non est factum*.
It was admitted on the part of the plaintiff that the reservation must be read as if it had contained the proviso itself in
the form of an exception, but it was contended that the
distinction between a proviso and an exception did not consist in mere form of expression; that this was strictly in its
nature a proviso and not an exception, because it depended
upon a contingency which might or might not happen, and
which in fact had not happened; that the supposed exception was to be a nullity in case of the not happening of the
contingency, and, as the contingency had not happened,
had become a nullity, and was properly omitted in the reservation stated in the declaration; and that in declaring
upon written instruments in general, that part only need be
set out upon which the plaintiff intends to rely. The
learned judge was of opinion that this was properly speaking
an exception and not a proviso; that as by the terms of the
reservation the whole rent was to be payable only under particular circumstances, such a limitation should have been
noticed, although a proviso for a distinct purpose, as for re-
entry on nonpayment of rent, would stand upon a different
footing. His lordship, therefore, directed a nonsuit.

F. Pollock now moved to set aside the nonsuit and for a
new trial. The question is whether the conditional clause
in the subsequent part of the lease referred to in the red-
dendum was an exception or a proviso. If it was an exception, the plaintiff undoubtedly was bound to notice it;
if it was a proviso, he was not, but the defendant, if he intended to rely upon it, should have set it out in his plea.
Now this is not an exception, but a proviso. The distinc-

tion between the two is this:—an exception defeats, absolutely, the operation of the covenant; a proviso limits its operation, conditionally. [*Bayley*, J. There may be words which amount to neither the one nor the other, but to a qualification only.] At any rate this is not an exception, and it is submitted that it is a proviso, its effect being to limit the plaintiff's right to rent, conditionally, under certain contingent circumstances. It was sufficient, therefore, for the plaintiff to set out the reservation, and it was for the defendant to shew the proviso which was to limit the operation of the covenant. He cited *Elliott* v. *Blake* (a) and *Hotham* v. *The East India Company* (b).

Lord TENTERDEN, C. J.—The established rule of pleading in such cases is this:—if an act of parliament, or a private instrument, contains, first a general clause, and afterwards a separate and distinct clause, which has the effect of taking out of the general clause something which would otherwise be included in it, the party relying upon the general clause in pleading may set out that clause only, without noticing the separate and distinct clause which operates as an exception. But if the exception itself is incorporated in the general clause, the party relying upon it must in pleading state it with the exception; and if he states it as containing an absolute unconditional stipulation, without noticing the exception, it will be a fatal variance. In this case the exception is not in express terms introduced into the reservation, but by reference only to some subsequent part of the lease; for the words are, " except as hereinafter mentioned." The maxim of law, " *verba relata inesse videntur*," applies to such a case. The clause *thereinafter mentioned* must be considered as an exception in the general clause, by which the rent is reserved; and then, according to the rule I have adverted to, the plaintiff ought to have set out both the reservation and the excep-

(a) 1 Levinz. 88.   (b) 1 T. R. 638, 645.

R R 2

1827.

Vavasour
v.
Ormrod.

tion in his declaration. Not having done so, I am of opinion that the variance is fatal, and that there is no ground for setting aside the nonsuit.

The other Judges concurred.

Rule refused.

AUSTIN v. DENNIFORD.

Where assignees under a second commission of bankrupt have refused to interfere, and the bankrupt has not paid 15s. in the pound, but has effects whereon to levy, a creditor may take out execution upon a judgment recovered before the second commission.

THIS was a rule calling upon the plaintiff to shew cause why the execution in this case should not be set aside, on the ground that the defendant, who had been once a bankrupt and obtained his certificate, had had a second commission of bankruptcy sued out against him, under which he had not paid fifteen shillings in the pound, and it was objected that, as the assignees had declined interfering in the present case, the plaintiff was not at liberty to take out execution upon a judgment recovered between the first and second commissions.

Follett was for the plaintiff, and *Barry* for the defendant.

Lord TENTERDEN, C.J.—If the assignees do not chuse to interfere, I do not see what is to prevent a creditor from taking out execution upon his judgment. The rule must therefore be discharged.

The other Judges concurred.

Rule discharged.

FREE, D.D. *v.* BURGOYNE.

1827.

THERE had been a demurrer to a declaration in prohibition in this case, upon which the Court gave judgment that the prohibition should stand so far as regarded the proceeding against Dr. *Free,* upon a charge of incontinence, *pro salute animæ vel reformatione morum,* but that, as regarded the proceeding upon that charge for the purpose of suspension or deprivation, a consultation should be awarded (*a*). The judgment was completed, and a consultation issued. A writ of error was brought (*b*), and was still pending, the clerk of the errors having declined to make the transcript, because the judgment so completed had no award of costs. The plaintiff's attorney then took out an appointment to tax costs, and the master, in spite of the remonstrance and protest of the defendant's attorney, allowed the plaintiff full costs. A rule nisi having been obtained for rescinding and erasing from the record the allowance of costs,

A plaintiff in prohibition obtaining judgment after demurrer, is not entitled to costs, except his case is within 8 & 9 W. 3, c. 11, s. 3; and if the judgment he obtains is for a partial prohibition, and a partial consultation, his case is not within that statute.

Denman, C.S. now shewed cause. This is a case within the statute 8 & 9 *W.* 3, c. 11, s. 3. By that section it is enacted, " that in all actions of debt upon the statute for not setting out tithe, &c., and in all suits upon any writ of *scire facias,* and suits upon prohibition, the plaintiff obtaining judgment, or any award of execution after plea pleaded or demurrer joined therein, shall likewise recover his costs of suit; and if the plaintiff shall become nonsuit, or suffer a discontinuance, or a verdict shall pass against him, the defendant shall recover his costs," &c. Here the plaintiff in prohibition has obtained judgment after demurrer, he is consequently entitled to costs within the very words of the statute. The case of *Middleton* v. *Croft* (*c*) is decisive of the present. There the plaintiff in prohibition obtained judgment upon one point, and upon the other

(*a*) 8 D. & R. 179; 5 B. & C. 400.   (*c*) 2 Stra. 1056.
(*b*) 8 D. & R. 587; 6 B. & C. 27.

points a consultation was awarded. The plaintiff applied for costs, and the Court said that the words of the act which gave costs to a plaintiff under such circumstances were too strong to be got over. It was there further said, that the same question was considered by the House of Lords in Dr. *Bentley*'s case, where the prohibition was allowed to stand upon some points, and a consultation was awarded upon others.

Marryat, contrà. This was not a "judgment obtained in a suit upon prohibition" within the meaning of the statute. The statute means a judgment complete and absolute upon all the points raised in the suit; here the plaintiff obtained only a qualified judgment upon one point raised in the suit. In this case there has been no judgment obtained by the plaintiff in prohibition, such as bars the defendant from proceeding in the Spiritual Court, for he is at this moment entitled to proceed in that Court upon every article contained in the libel, in a qualified mode. A judgment similar to that pronounced in the present case was pronounced in the case of *Townsend* v. *Thorpe* (a). The roll in that case has been found, but no judgment is indorsed upon it. The present is an instance, among many others, of a *casus omissus* in an act of parliament; the statute does not provide for the case of a judgment in part for a prohibition and in part for a consultation. There is another instance of the same sort in the same act of parliament, for it does not provide that a defendant in prohibition obtaining judgment after demurrer shall be entitled to costs.

Lord TENTERDEN, C. J., after conferring with the other Judges.—There is a writ of error pending in this case, therefore our decision upon this point, if deemed unsatisfactory, may be assigned as a ground of error. As at present advised we are of opinion that this is not a case within the statute. At common law no costs could be allowed in

(a) Ld. Raym. 1507.

prohibition; therefore, if the case is not within the statute, we, of course, cannot award costs. Considering, at present, that the case is not within the statute, we shall make this rule for rescinding the allowance of costs absolute; but we shall permit the plaintiff to amend his judgment by entering upon the record a prayer for costs, and a refusal of them by the Court, and also to assign that refusal of costs as a ground of error.

Rule absolute accordingly.

POWNAL, Gent., one, &c. *v.* FERRAND.

ASSUMPSIT for money paid by the plaintiff to the use of the defendant. Plea, non assumpsit; and issue thereon. At the trial before Lord *Tenterden*, C.J., at the last *Middlesex* sittings, the case was this:—The defendant was the acceptor of a bill of exchange for 350*l.*, payable three months after date, drawn on the 11th of *March*, 1825, by one *Ford*, and indorsed by *Ford* to the plaintiff, by the plaintiff to one *Hayes*, and by *Hayes* to one *Field*. The bill was dishonoured, whereupon *Field*, the holder, brought actions and recovered judgments against all the parties to the bill, and the present plaintiff in consequence paid *Field* 40*l.* on account of the bill. The present defendant refusing to pay the costs of the actions against the other parties, *Field*, who had recovered against him as acceptor 350*l.* and 30*l.* costs, levied upon his goods 340*l.*, giving credit for the 40*l.* he had received from the present plaintiff; and this action was brought to recover the 40*l.* which the plaintiff had been compelled to pay *Field* on account of the bill. It was contended on the part of the defendant, that the plaintiff could not recover that money in this form of action, because there was no privity between them; that the money was not paid in exoneration of the defendant, but of the plaintiff himself, who was a party to the bill, and

If the indorser of a bill is compelled by the holder to pay him part of the amount, he may recover it back from the acceptor in an action for money paid to his use.

liable upon it; and that it would be a great hardship upon the acceptor of a bill if several indorsers could, by making partial payments, acquire a right of action against him. Lord *Tenterden* was of opinion that as the defendant was liable in point of law to the whole amount of the bill, and had been exonerated to the extent of 40*l.* by the plaintiff's paying that sum, that sum must be considered as money paid to his use; his lordship, therefore, directed the jury to find a verdict for the plaintiff, which they did.

Starkie now moved for a new trial. This action cannot be supported. In order to entitle the plaintiff to recover, it must appear either that he had some legal interest in the bill, or that he was a party to some contract collateral to the bill. Now, first, he had no legal interest in the bill at the time when he paid the 40*l.* He had parted with his interest in the bill by indorsing it; and his part payment of the bill did not restore him to his original interest in it, though a full payment would have done so. Even if he had paid the bill in full, and thereby recovered his original right upon it, still his only remedy would have been an action upon the bill. For this the case of *Death* v. *Serwontes* (a) is a clear authority. Secondly, the plaintiff was not a party to any contract collateral to the bill. There was no privity between him and the acceptor, and unless there is some privity between a party paying a bill and the acceptor, the mere act of paying the bill creates no new contract between them. An indorser, by paying the bill, is simply restored to his original right, and upon that principle it has been held, that where an indorser pays a bill after the bankruptcy of the acceptor, the certificate of the acceptor is a bar to an action by the indorser; *Cowley* v. *Dunlop* (b), and *Houle* v. *Baxter* (c). The indorser of a bill does not, as such, stand in the situation of a surety for the acceptor, so as to make a payment to an indorsee a payment to the use of the acceptor; that appears clearly

(a) 1 Lutw. 886.   (b) 7 T. R. 565.   (c) 3 East, 177.

from the two cases last cited. There is no liability on the part of the indorser, except that which arises from the law and custom of merchants; and for all that appears in this case the payment made by the plaintiff was voluntary: there was no evidence to shew that he received notice of the dishonour of the bill, or that he was liable upon it. [Lord *Tenterden*, C.J. We cannot assume that he made the payment without being liable.] *Exall* v. *Partridge* (a) may at first sight appear to be an authority against the defendant in this case, but it is not so in reality. There *A.*, *B.*, and *C.* were lessees of premises by deed from *D.*, to whom they covenanted to pay the rent. *B.* and *C.* assigned their interest to *A.*, subsequent to which assignment, and with knowledge whereof, the plaintiff placed his goods on the premises under the care of *A.*, where they were distrained by *D.* for rent, and the plaintiff, in order to redeem them, was obliged to pay the rent. It was held that the plaintiff might maintain an action for money paid against *A.*, *B.*, and *C.*, on the ground that the three defendants were liable to the landlord for the rent in the first instance, and as, by the payment made by the plaintiff, all the three were released from the demand of the rent, and as such payment was not voluntary, but compulsory, the law would imply a promise by the three defendants to repay the plaintiff. In that case there was clearly an implied assumpsit on the part of *Partridge*, under whose care the goods were placed, that they should not be distrained for rent due by his default. There was consequently a privity between the plaintiff and *Partridge*, who was, jointly with the other two defendants, bound to pay the rent; and the only question was, whether the plaintiff's right of action was against *Partridge* alone, or extended to all. The whole case turned upon privity of contract. There, if the plaintiff could not have recovered, he would have had no remedy at all; here the plaintiff has a legitimate and proximate remedy, for there is an instrument in writing, the construction of which ought alone to regulate the rights and liabilities of the parties.

(a) 8 T. R. 308.

Lord TENTERDEN, C. J.—Considering the very peculiar nature of the facts in this case, I think we may decide that the plaintiff is entitled to recover, without thereby giving rise to any mischievous consequences. The defendant, as acceptor, was originally liable to the plaintiff on the bill. The defendant was the first defaulter, and he having made default, *Field*, the holder of the bill, sued the plaintiff and obtained a verdict against him, upon which the plaintiff paid *Field* 40*l.* on account of the bill. *Field* also sued the defendant as acceptor of the bill, and obtained a verdict against him for 350*l.*, and judgment was signed for that sum and 30*l.* costs, and an execution issued against the defendant, under which 340*l.* was levied. The present action was brought to recover from the defendant the sum of 40*l.*, which he had been compelled to pay as indorser of the bill. *Cowley* v. *Dunlop* (a), and *Houle* v. *Baxter* (b), were very different cases from the present. There the acceptors had become bankrupts and obtained their certificates before the indorsers made any payment on account of the bills; so that the acceptors had ceased to be liable upon the bills at the time when the payments by the indorsers were made. Here, the money paid by the plaintiff was money which the defendant was liable to pay, and in my opinion justice requires that the plaintiff should be allowed to recover it back. It has been urged that he cannot recover in this particular form of action, and that he ought to have sued upon the bill. But the bill was not in his possession; and even if it had been, he would have had great difficulty in suing upon it, because the defendant might have pleaded a former recovery of the full amount of the bill. That difficulty the plaintiff avoids by resorting to this action for money paid to the use of the defendant. I am of opinion that the plaintiff is entitled to recover, upon the general principle, that one man who is compelled to pay money which another man is bound by law to pay, is entitled to be reimbursed by the latter; and I think that

(a) 7 T. R. 565.   (b) 3 East, 177.

money paid under such circumstances may properly ·be considered as money paid to the use of the person who·is so bound to pay it. I see no ground, therefore, for disturbing the verdict in this case.

'Bayley, J.—I am of the same opinion with my lord. The defendant, as acceptor of the bill, was bound to pay it when due. He has no right to complain of any hardship resulting to him by reason of his non-payment of the bill, for it arises from his own breach of duty. If he pays the bill when due, no party can call upon him. But the holder of a bill has a right to demand payment from all the parties to it, though the acceptor is the only person who ought to expect to be called upon to pay it. The other parties, if called upon, may each pay a portion, and in that case the acceptor will be responsible to those parties to the extent of the sums which they have respectively paid. Here the plaintiff, as one of the indorsers, was called upon by the holder to pay the bill. If the defendant had done his duty as acceptor, the plaintiff would not have been so called upon. The plaintiff has paid 40l. to the holder on account of the bill, and the question is whether he is to lose that sum, or can recover it back from the defendant, by whose default he was compelled to pay it. It is undoubted law that one man by voluntarily paying the debt of another acquires no right of action against that other; but if he pays that debt because he is compelled to do so, he does acquire a right of action, for the law implies a promise on the part of the person whose debt he so pays to reimburse him. That principle was fully established in the case of *Exall* v. *Partridge* (a). In this case the plaintiff paid part of the debt owing by the defendant because he was compelled to do so, therefore he is entitled to recover it back from the defendant; and I think it makes no difference that he paid part only, and not the whole amount of the bill, because the defendant has equally been benefited to that extent.

(a) 8 T. R. 308.

HOLROYD, J.—I am of opinion that this action is maintainable for the reasons already given by my Lord Chief Justice and my brother *Bayley*. With respect to the argument that the plaintiff by making the payment was only restored to his original right in respect of the bill, and should, therefore, have sued upon the bill, I am of opinion that he is entitled to recover in this form of action upon the same principle upon which a surety is entitled to recover money from his principal. I think that a party is not bound to resort to the original engagement unless it be by deed, but that he may at his election found his action upon the original engagement, or bring *indebitatus assumpsit* for money paid.

LITTLEDALE, J.—The authorities to which we have been referred induced me for some time to doubt whether the plaintiff, as indorser, could recover in this form of action; but upon further consideration, I am satisfied that although the plaintiff by making the payment may be restored to his original right upon the bill, he may, nevertheless, maintain an action for money paid to the defendant's use. It is a general rule that a man who is compelled by legal process to pay money which another is by law liable to pay, may recover it back in an action of *indebitatus assumpsit* for money paid to the use of that other. The present case is within the principle laid down in *Exall* v. *Partridge* (a), and that is a sound and just principle. It is true that in a case like the present the acceptor may become liable to several actions; but of that he has no right to complain, because he has brought it upon himself by not paying the bill when it became due, as he ought to have done. The same inconvenience might occur in a case like *Exall* v. *Partridge*, for if the goods of several persons were distrained, and they severally contributed sums towards payment of the rent, the lessees would be liable to several actions.

Rule refused.

(*a*) 8 T. R. 308.

BRANDLING v. BARRINGTON.

CASE, against the sheriff of the county palatine of *Durham*, for wrongfully removing the goods of a tenant from premises rented by him of the plaintiff, without paying the plaintiff one half year's rent then due, contrary to the statute 8 *Ann*, c. 14. Plea, not guilty; and issue thereon. At the trial before *Hullock*. B., at the *Summer* assizes for *Durham*, in 1824, a verdict was taken for the plaintiff, damages 125*l.*, subject to the opinion of the Court upon the following case:—

John *Hudson* was tenant to the plaintiff of certain lands and premises in the parish of *Chester-le-Street*, in the county of *Durham*, from the 12th of *May*, 1822, to the 12th of *May*, 1823, and on the 22d of *November*, 1822, the sum of 125*l.* was due from him to the plaintiff for one half-year's rent of the same premises, and continued to be due until and at the time of the defendant's entry as hereinafter mentioned. On the 17th of *January*, 1823, the defendant, as sheriff of the county, entered upon the premises and seized certain goods of *Hudson's* then being on the premises, and to a greater amount than the rent due, by virtue of a writ of *pone per vadios*, tested the 10th of *January*, and issued on the 15th out of the Court of Chancery of the said county palatine, at the suit of one *William Thompson*, and returnable in the Court of Pleas at *Durham* on the 25th of the same month. *Hudson* did not appear at the return of the writ, and thereupon on the same day was issued out of the said Court of Pleas a process called an extract, directed to the defendant as sheriff, on receipt of which he made his warrant to the bailiff, who had seized and had continued in possession of *Hudson's* goods under the writ of *pone per vadios*, requesting him thereby to deliver over to the plaintiff in the action the goods which had been attached, in satisfaction of his damages. The bailiff, on receipt of the warrant, proceeded to a sale of the goods by auction on the

A tenant's goods were seized under a writ of *pone per vadios* issued out of the Court of Pleas at *Durham*. He made default, and his goods were forfeited to the bishop, by whose order the sheriff sold them and paid the proceeds to the plaintiff:—

Held, that the writ of *pone per vadios* was not an *execution* within 8 *Ann*, c. 14, s. 1, and that the landlord could not claim from the sheriff half a year's rent due to him before he removed the goods.

12th of *February,* he being an auctioneer, and acting as such at the sale. On the 26th of *January* the sheriff had notice that the sum of 125*l.* was due from *Hudson* to the plaintiff for rent of the said premises; but the bailiff, without paying over any part of such rent, delivered the goods to the purchasers at the sale, who removed them off the premises, the rent being then and still unsatisfied. The bailiff paid over the proceeds of the sale to the attorney of *Thompson,* the plaintiff in the action, and received from him thereout the amount of his charge for keeping possession, from the attachment of the goods under the writ of *pone per vadios,* up to and with the day of sale, and the expenses of the sale. The bailiff returned the auction sheet to the defendant, who certified thereon that the goods had been attached by virtue of a writ of *pone per vadios,* and afterwards sold by virtue of a writ of extract, in satisfaction of *Thompson's* damages and costs; and upon this certificate the auction duty was remitted under the 19th *Geo.* 3, c. 56, s. 15.

The practice of the Courts of the county palatine of *Durham,* as respects this question, is as follows:—When the plaintiff sues the writ of *pone per vadios* out of the Court of Chancery, he makes an affidavit of the amount of the debt due to him, which is filed in that Court, and which amount being indorsed on the writ is a guide to the officer who executes the writ, as to the value of the goods by which he attaches the debtor. If the writ is executed more than four days before the return, the debtor has till twelve o'clock of the morrow of the return day to appear; if within four days of the return, he has, by a modern rule of Court, four days after the return to appear, and on appearance he may cast an essoign to the next Court-day. If he does not appear at the regular time, a minute of his default is marked upon the writ by the prothonotary of the Court of Pleas. The plaint of the writ is afterwards entered in a book, called the Remembrancer's Book, and immediately after the entry in the book, the word " default" is added, and at the instance of the plaintiff an extract is issued, directed to the sheriff, and the sheriff makes his warrant to the bailiff in the forms respectively used in this case. No judgment is signed, nor other proceedings taken in Court, save as above stated. On the receipt of the warrant, the bailiff to whom it is directed, and who is always the same officer who has made the attachment under the writ of *pone per vadios*, proceeds to sell the goods. If he is himself an auctioneer, he acts as such at the sale, if not, the auctioneer is engaged by him or by the plaintiff's attorney; and the expenses of the sale, together with those of keeping possession of the goods under the writ of *pone per vadios*, up to and with the day of sale, are in all cases paid by the plaintiff's attorney, or otherwise delivered to the bailiff from the proceeds of the sale. The plaintiff is then satisfied his demand, according to the amount sworn to by him in his affidavit of debt, and the surplus, if any, is refunded to the debtor. In case the debtor's goods have been attached at the several suits of two creditors, and extracts have issued in both suits, the demands of the several creditors are satisfied in the order in which the respective writs of *pone per vadios* have been executed by the seizure and attachment of the defendant's goods under them respectively. The sheriff does not receive any poundage on these sales, but in the present case, and in every case since the passing of the 19 *Geo.* 3, c. 56, the sheriff has made a certificate to the excise under the fifteenth section. These proceedings are final; and after his default has been recorded by the prothonotary, as stated above, the defendant is not permitted to come in subsequently and contest the debt upon any terms whatsoever.

The following are copies of the writs of *pone per vadios* and extract:—" *George* the Fourth, by the grace of God, &c., To the Sheriff of *Durham* greeting: If *William Thompson* make you secure of prosecuting his claim, then put by gages and safe pledges *John Hudson*, late of the city of *Durham*, in your county, yeoman, that he be before our justices at *Durham*, on the 25th day of *January* instant, to shew for that," &c.   Here followed counts in assumpsit for goods sold, and the money counts, concluding to the plaintiff's damage of 500*l.*   The sheriff returned that he had attached *John Hudson* by certain goods mentioned in a schedule annexed.   The writ of extract was as follows:—

" an extract of the fines, amerciaments, and forfeitures lost, charged, and coming forth at the Sessions or Court of Pleas, held at *Durham* the 25th day of *January*, in the third year of the reign, &c., before *James Baker*, M. A., Spiritual Chancellor of the Diocese of *Durham*, *Alexander Engum* Esq., and others, their fellow justices of our Sovereign Lord the King, in the county palatine of *Durham* and *Sadberge*.

" The Honourable *William Kepple Barrington*, Sheriff of *Durham*, 1954, upon him charged for the value of divers goods and chattels specified in a certain schedule hereunto annexed, late of *John Hudson*, late of the city of *Durham*, in his county, yeoman, *which were attached by the said sheriff, and forfeited to the Bishop of Durham*, at the same Sessions or Court of Pleas, because the said *John Hudson* did not appear on that day to answer *William Thompson* of a plea of trespass on the case, to the damage of the said *William Thompson* of 500*l.*, as he was attached by the said plaintiff.

" Mr. Sheriff,

The goods and chattels above named were forfeited to the Lord Bishop of *Durham*; his lordship is pleased that they be assigned over to the said plaintiff in satisfaction of so much of his damages above specified as the value thereof doth amount unto, which is to be allowed you in your account by the said bishop, and which his lordship hath empowered us to signify unto you.

J. G.
H. D. } Commissioners."

Ingham, for the plaintiff.   The claim of the plaintiff of his half-year's rent depends upon the construction which the Court shall give to the statute 8 *Ann*, c. 14, s. 1(*a*). That is a remedial statute, and is to be construed liberally. This case is within the mischief intended to be remedied, therefore it ought to be held within the remedy, even though it may not be within the very words. Com. Dig. Parliament (R. 15.) The statute is entitled, " An act for the better security of rents, and to prevent frauds committed by tenants," and the object of the first section seems to be, to protect the landlord whenever he is by legal process deprived of his remedy by distress. That is a fair provision as regards the landlord, because the stock must have been fed and the crop produced upon his soil; and it is beneficial to the tenant also, because it enables the landlord to grant him indulgence without risk of loss. It was decided in *Henchett* v. *Kimpson* (*b*) that the act extends to an execution at the suit of a *defendant* for costs, notwithstanding the direction at the end of the section that the sheriff shall pay the *plaintiff* as well the rent as the execution money. It was there objected that the act applied only to executions at the suit of plaintiffs; but the Court said it was to

(*a*) Which, " for the more easy and effectual recovery of rents reserved on leases for life or lives, term of years, at will, or otherwise," enacts, " that no goods or chattels whatsoever, lying or being in or upon any messuage, lands or tenements which are or shall be leased for life or lives, term of years, at will, or otherwise, shall be liable to be taken by virtue of any execution on any pretence whatsoever, unless the party at whose suit the said execution is sued out shall, before the removal of such goods from off the said premises by virtue of such execution or extent, pay to the landlord of the said premises or his bailiff, all such sum or sums of money as are or shall be due for rent for the said premises at the time of the taking such goods or chattels by virtue of such execution: provided the said arrears of rent do not amount to more than one year's rent; and in case the said arrears shall exceed one year's rent, then the said party, at whose suit such execution is sued out, paying the said landlord or his bailiff one year's rent, may proceed to execute his judgment, as he might have done before the making of this act; and the sheriff or other officer is hereby empowered and required to levy and pay to the plaintiff as well the money so paid for rent as the execution money."

(*b*) 2 Wilson, 140.

be construed liberally, and overruled the objection. The like liberal construction was put upon the act in the case of *Dixon* v. *Smith* (a), where the landlord was allowed his rent as against a sequestration; the Court, upon the equity of the statute, considering a sequestration as a species of execution. In *Greaves* v. *D'Acastro* (b), the tenant's goods were seized and sold under process of outlawry, and the Court of Exchequer ordered the landlord to be paid one year's rent in arrear out of the money in the sheriff's hands; and that decision was cited with approbation by *Lawrence*, J. in *St. John's College* v. *Murcott* (c). That decision is strongly in point here, for outlawry is a forfeiture to the crown, *Hartwicke* v. *Porter* (d), and the forfeiture to the crown there is equivalent to the forfeiture to the bishop here. Perhaps it will be said that the *capias utlegatum* is a complete execution, and that there is no complete execution here, because there is no judgment. The answer is, that there is a judgment here, namely, of forfeiture to the bishop for nonappearance. In *Gilbert on Distresses*, 16, 4th ed., it is said respecting process of attachment, " Where this process issues out of a Court of record, there is no doubt

(a) 1 Swanst. 457.

(b) Bunbury, 194.

(c) 7 T. R. 264. But in *Rex* v. *Southerby, Bunbury,* 5, it is said, " *Southerby* was outlawed, and an extent issued, and an inquisition was taken thereupon, and his house and goods seized by virtue thereof: *Etchins*, the landlord, moved upon the stat. 8 *Ann*, to have the goods delivered to him, suggesting that they had been distrained by him for rent three days before the extent. *Per curiam*, Not the party, but the King only is concerned in the outlawry, and we cannot relieve the landlord upon this motion." And in a note to that case it is said, " the same motion was made in *Michaelmas*

term, 1717, between *The King* and *Burgess*, but the defendant was not relieved." And in *Rex* v. *Pritchard, Bunbury,* 269, it is said, " Upon the 19th of *Feb.* 1728, an extent issued against *Pritchard*, tenant of *Sambrook*; the 27d of *April,* 1729, *Sambrook* distrains for rent; 30th of *April,* 1729, the inquisition finds the goods then in the possession of *Pritchard*. Note, the extent was not executed till the 23d of *April*, the day after the distress. Mr. *Foley* moved that *Sambrook* might have the benefit of the statute, 8 *Ann*, for his rent, notwithstanding the extent; but it was denied *per curiam*.

(d) Cited in *Lawrence* v. *Nethersell, Dyer*, 199.

but if the defendant makes default, the goods he was attached by are forfeited, because in such case *there is a*
judgment of the King's Court of record condemning the
goods, which alters the property." If it should be said
that *capias utlegatum* is necessary to execute the judgment
of outlawry, and that, therefore, the case of outlawry differs
from the present; the answer is, that although the goods
here were forfeited to the bishop without the writ of extract, still that writ was necessary to perfect the title of the
party, and the statute speaks of executions *at the suit of*
the party. These authorities concur in shewing that the
statute is to be construed liberally, and so as to extend the
remedy to every case within the mischief. Now the mischief is the loss sustained by a landlord when he is deprived
of the opportunity for distraining for rent, which is the case
whenever the goods of the tenant are taken into the custody
of the law. In *Gilbert on Distresses*, 50, it is said, " Goods
in the custody of the law are not distrainable, for it is *ex vi*
termini repugnant that it should be lawful to take goods
out of the custody of the law; and that cannot be a pledge
to me which I cannot bring into my actual possession."
The intention of the legislature in all such cases seems to
have been that the landlord should be satisfied to the extent
of one year's rent before the goods of the tenant could be
applied to the payment of a private creditor. The present
is even a stronger case than one of outlawry; for there the
judgment may be reversed, the goods may be restored to
the tenant, and the right of distress to the landlord; but
here the case finds expressly that the proceedings are absolutely final.

F. Pollock, contrà. The present case is not within
either the words or the policy of the act of parliament.
This is a declaration charging the sheriff with *wrongfully*
removing the goods of a tenant from off the premises without paying the landlord one half-year's rent then due to
him. Now when the defendant in the action made default,

the goods became forfeited to the bishop, and he, pleading that they should be assigned over to the plaintiff, made an order to that effect, in obedience to which order the sheriff sold the goods and paid over the proceeds to the plaintiff. Therefore it is impossible to say that the sheriff, when acting in obedience to that process, was a wrong-doer, nor can any case be found to warrant such a proposition. Even the equity of the act could not extend its operation to a case like this; besides, that cannot be taken into consideration in a Court of law: therefore, *Dixon* v. *Smith* (a), where the application was to the Court of Chancery, and *Greaves* v. *D'Acastro* (b), where the application was to the equity side of the Court of Exchequer, are no authorities for the present case. The writ of *pone per vadios* in this case cannot be regarded in a Court of law as an execution within the meaning of the statute. The statute was never intended to apply to a case like the present. It speaks of the party *executing his judgment*, which proves beyond a doubt that the word *execution* in the enactment means execution upon a judgment; and that was the opinion of Lord *Ellenborough* in *Lee* v. *Lopes* (c): here there was not an execution upon a judgment, for there was no judgment signed.

Ingham, in reply. The case last cited is an authority rather in favour of the plaintiff than against him, for the ground of the decision there was, that the sheriff had taken in execution goods which belonged to the assignees of the tenant, and the landlord had a right to distrain for the rent in arrear, notwithstanding the bankruptcy, the commission not being an execution within the meaning of the statute. There the landlord, not being deprived of his right of distress, could have no claim to the benefit of the statute; here the landlord was deprived of his right of distress.

Lord TENTERDEN, C. J.—I am of opinion that the

(a) 1 Swanst. 457.   (b) Bunb. 194.   (c) 15 East, 230.

plaintiff is not entitled to recover. This is an action charging the defendant, as sheriff of the county palatine of *Durham*, with wrongfully removing the goods of a tenant from premises occupied by him without paying the landlord one half-year's rent then due, contrary to the statute 8 *Ann.* c. 14, s. 1. That statute speaks only of goods taken by virtue of any " execution," but it adverts to the party " executing his judgment," and I think it perfectly clear that its operation was intended to be confined to executions on judgments. In this case, the process by virtue of which the sheriff seized and sold the goods was not process of execution on a judgment, it was not, therefore, an " execution" within the words of the statute. But it was said that it was within the equity of the statute. I cannot help observing, individually, that it appears to me an extremely dangerous course to give effect to what is called the equity of a statute, and that I think it much safer and better to abide by and decide upon the plain words, even though there may be ground for believing that the legislature would probably have provided for other cases, if their attention had been directed to them. Then a case was cited from *Bunbury's* Reports, as to the allowance of rent in the case of outlawry on civil process; but there the proceeding was not, as here, by action against the sheriff, but by application to the equity side of the Court of Exchequer: and in other cases, mentioned by the same Reporter, where the outlawry was at the suit of the crown, similar applications were refused(*a*). So in *Dixon v. Smith* (*b*) the application was to the Court of Chancery, into which the proceeds of a sequestration had been paid, and there was no complaint made against the sequestrator. In *St. John's College* v. *Murcott* (*c*) an outlawry had taken place, after which a distress was made for the rent, and the outlawry was reversed; so that the case became the same as if the outlawry had never taken place, and the distress remained available. None of these cases govern the present. The plaintiff seems to me to have mistaken his course of proceeding. Instead of suing the sheriff, I think

(*a*) *Vide ante*, 614, n.(*c*).   (*b*) 1 Swanst. 457.   (*c*) 7 T. R. 264.

he should have applied by way of petition to the Bishop's Court. I cannot, of course, undertake to say what would have been the effect of such a petition, but upon the authority of the cases which have been referred to, it probably would not have been rejected without much consideration. If the party appears in obedience to the writ of *pone per vadios,* his goods are released; if not, they become forfeited to the bishop, *jure regali,* and are at his disposal. An application to him under such circumstances would be very similar to the application to the Court of Exchequer in the case of outlawry on civil process, and it would be equally in his power, and doubtless in his inclination, to grant relief to the landlord. But the landlord clearly cannot treat the sheriff as a wrong-doer, and therefore our judgment in this case must, as it seems to me, be for the defendant.

BAYLEY, J.—I certainly feel that the present case comes within the mischief intended to be remedied by the statute 8 Ann. c. 14, s. 1, and it would have given me satisfaction if it could, by fair construction, have been brought within the words of that enactment. Unfortunately, I am convinced that the operation of the statute cannot be extended to a case like the present, without resorting to a mode of construction wholly unwarrantable. The policy of the enactment doubtless was, to secure to the landlord the payment of one year's rent in preference to any other creditor, the effect of which was equally beneficial to the tenant, because it secured to him the forbearance of his landlord, whom, but for the statute, he would expect to distrain upon him as soon as his rent became in arrear. Still I think we should be attributing too comprehensive a meaning to the words of the statute, if we were to hold that they entitled the present plaintiff to payment of the rent due to him. The goods of the tenant in this case cannot properly be said to have been taken in execution, though that which was done may have had the effect of an execution. The writ of *pone per vadios* cannot be called an execution; it resembles the writ of *distringas*, which issues out of this Court for the purpose of compelling an appearance, under which the sheriff may, by order of the Court, sell the goods he has seized, and deliver over the proceeds to the plaintiff without paying a year's rent to the landlord. The writ of *pone per vadios* issues for the purpose of compelling an appearance; if the party attached does appear, his goods are released; if he makes default they become forfeited to the bishop, who may dispose of them as he thinks fit. The bishop's order to assign over the proceeds of the goods to the plaintiff is made entirely *ex gratiâ*, and the sheriff, who acts merely in obedience to that order, is clearly entitled to protection in so acting. The distinction taken by my Lord Chief Justice is conclusive to shew that the cases of outlawry are not authorities in favour of the plaintiff's right of action in the present case. For these reasons I am of opinion, not without regret, that this action cannot be maintained, and that a nonsuit must be entered.

HOLROYD, J.—I entirely concur in the view that has been taken of this question. I think that a case like the present was not within the contemplation of the legislature, though it may, perhaps, be within the mischief which they intended to remedy by means of the statute of *Anne*. The assignment of the goods to the plaintiff in the original action was a purely voluntary act on the part of the bishop, to whom they had become forfeited, and who had power to dispose of them as he should think fit. The proper course for the present plaintiff would have been to apply to the bishop by way of petition, who might, and I make no doubt would, have granted him relief; but I think it quite clear that he has no remedy as against the sheriff, who has merely performed his duty.

LITTLEDALE, J.—I am also of opinion that this case does not come within the statute. The writ of *pone per* cannot is clearly not an execution, though in some cases it may have the effect of an execution. Besides, as applied to this case, it is evident that the directions of the statute could not be complied with. It provides that the party at whose suit the execution issues shall pay to the landlord the rent in arrear, provided that does not exceed one year's rent; and that he may then proceed to execute his judgment as he might have done before the passing of the act; and it then requires the sheriff to levy the money paid over for rent as well as the execution money. But here the authority of the sheriff as to seizure was at an end as soon as the party's goods had been taken under the writ of *pone per vadios*; and when he was afterwards ordered by the bishop to sell those goods, and to pay over the proceeds to the plaintiff, the statute did not give him authority to levy in addition any sum that was due for rent.

Judgment for the defendant.

WILMOT v. WILKINSON.

By writing not under seal, *A.* agrees, in consideration of 7000*l.*, to present the nominee of *B.* to the next turn of a rectory, and to furnish an abstract of title to, and execute a conveyance of, the next presentation, to *B.* :

ASSUMPSIT on a special agreement, with the common money counts, to recover 500*l.* and interest. Plea, non assumpsit; and issue thereon. At the trial before Lord *Tenterden*, C. J., at the *Middlesex* sittings after *Michaelmas* term, 1825, a verdict was found for the plaintiff, subject to the opinion of the Court upon the following case.

On the 22d of *March*, 1824, an agreement in writing was made between Messrs. *Goodacre* and *Buzzard* and the plaintiff, as follows :—

"Agreement between the undersigned *M. Buzzard*, on

such a writing is only an agreement, not a conveyance, and does not require an *ad valorem* stamp. Afterwards *A.*, by consent of *B.*, agrees to sell the next presentation to *C.* for £7,500, on having such title as *A.* had received, *C.* paying to *B.*, absolutely, on a day certain, the odd £500. *A.* furnishes an abstract of such title as he had received, which *C.* refuses to accept, and no conveyance is tendered to him. *B.* sues *C.* for the £500. There is a good consideration to support the action, and *A.* having done all that his contract required, it is no answer to the action that no conveyance was tendered to *C.*

behalf of himself and his partner, J. Goodacre, and their
respective heirs, executors and administrators, of the one
part; and the undersigned E. C. Wilmot, on behalf of himself and his heirs, executors and administrators, of the other
part; as follows: In consideration of the sum of 7000l. of
lawful money of Great Britain, to be paid in manner hereinafter mentioned, he the said M. Buzzard doth hereby, for
himself and his said partner J. Goodacre, agree to present
such person to the rectory of Presteign, in the county of
Radnor, vacant by or immediately upon the death, resignation, or sooner determination of the incumbency of the
present incumbent, with all the great and small tithes,
oblations, &c., as he the said E. C. Wilmot, his executors,
&c., shall nominate or appoint; and further, that M. Buzzard
shall forthwith furnish an abstract of title to the same presentation, and deduce, at the costs and charges of himself
and his said partner, or one of them, a good, valid, and
marketable title to the same; and also execute a proper
conveyance of the same to him the said E. C. Wilmot, his
executors, &c.; such conveyance to be prepared at the
expense, costs, and charges of the said E. C. Wilmot, his
executors," &c.

On the 12th of July, 1824, another agreement was entered into between the said Messrs. Goodacre and Buzzard
and the defendant, as follows:—

"Memorandum, July 12th, 1824. Messrs. Goodacre
and Buzzard, with the consent of E. C. Wilmot, agree to
sell to T. Wilkinson the next presentation to the living of
Presteign, Radnorshire, which they have purchased of Lord
Oxford, for the sum of 7,500l., to be paid for at Michaelmas
next, on having such title as they have received from Lord
Oxford and Lord Harley and their trustee, Mr. Moore,
with their covenant for the return of the money in the event
of their being unable to procure the nominee of Mr. Wilkinson induction and quiet possession of the living for six
months after the next vacancy of the same. Mr. Wilkinson
to have the option of paying the 7000l., part of the 7,500l.,

absolutely to Messrs. G. and B., or to have the same invested in their names and that of Mr. *Wilkinson's* trustee, he, Mr. *W.*, paying interest at 5l. per cent. on the 7000l., and receiving the dividends or interest resulting from the same, Mr. *Wilkinson* paying at *Michaelmas* the remaining 500l. absolutely to Mr. *Wilmot*, with G. and B.'s consent."

At the foot of this agreement was written and signed by the plaintiff, as follows: " I hereby ratify, on my part, the above agreement."

The above-mentioned agreement of the 22d of *March*, 1824, was stamped with a 1l. stamp. An abstract of the title to the said next presentation was delivered to the defendant's attorney on or about the 20th day of *June*, 1824, and two original deeds of the 18th day of *July*, 1823, whereby Lord *Oxford*, Lord *Harley*, and Mr. *Moore*, conveyed to *Goodacre* and *Buzzard*, were in due time shewn to and examined by the defendant's attorney, and were well executed, and corresponded with the said abstract. No other of the deeds or muniments set forth in the said abstract were at any time produced to the defendant or his attorney. The defendant, after *July*, 1824, offered the benefit of his interest under the said agreement for sale, such as it was, if the purchaser chose to take his chance. After the death of *Buzzard*, and before the 29th of *September*, 1824, *Goodacre's* attorney required the defendant to pay the 7000l., and offered to enter into a covenant pursuant to the said agreement. The defendant required *Goodacre* and *Buzzard's* attorney to give him an inspection of the other deeds mentioned in the abstract, which he did not do, declaring it was not in his power. The plaintiff, on the 29th of *September*, 1824, demanded the 500l., but never tendered any draft of a conveyance to the defendant. *Buzzard* died on the 22d of *September*, 1824. *Goodacre* did not consent, but objected to the payment over of the 500l. to the plaintiff. No evidence was given on the part of the plaintiff of any consent by the devisees or representatives of *Buz-*

zard, or by *Moore*. No money was ever paid by the plaintiff to *Goodacre* and *Buzzard*, or either of them.

Chitty, for the plaintiff. Two objections were taken on the part of the defendant at the trial; first, that the agreement required an *ad valorem* stamp, as being a conveyance; and secondly, that the plaintiff should have tendered a conveyance to the defendant. There is no weight in either of these objections. First, the deed was adequately stamped, for it had the usual agreement stamp of 1*l*., which was sufficient, for the deed was not itself a conveyance. Secondly, it was not necessary that a conveyance should be tendered to the defendant, for as the agreement was silent respecting the expenses, they would, as a matter of course, fall upon the purchaser, and he was the person whose duty it was, after the abstract was delivered, to have a conveyance prepared. If any point is now made as to the non-production of the other deeds, the answer is, that the vendors did all that could be required of them towards the completion of the purchase; they undertook to sell the interest which they derived from Lord *Oxford*, and they produced the deeds by which that interest was conveyed to them; that was all they were bound to do or could do. Then with respect to the question of consent, no evidence of the consent of *Goodacre* and the other parties to the payment of the 500*l*. was necessary, because the agreement is to pay the plaintiff 500*l*. on a particular day, " absolutely," that is, *at all events*.

D. F. Jones, contrà. First, the instrument of *March*, 1824, should have had an *ad valorem* stamp, as a conveyance. From the very nature of the property which was the subject-matter of sale, that instrument would have the effect of a conveyance. If the church had become vacant before any formal conveyance was executed, a Court of equity would, upon that instrument, have decreed the next presentation to the purchaser, and if so, it clearly required an ad valorem stamp upon the amount of the purchase-money. [*Bayley*, J. A Court of equity might have compelled the execution of a conveyance; but the Stamp Act imposes the ad valorem duty upon the actual " conveyance" of the property, not upon the right to call for such a conveyance. *Littledale*, J. The question is whether the stamp was or was not sufficient at the time when the instrument was executed.] Secondly, the plaintiff is not in a situation to sue, because the contract between *Goodacre* and *Buzzard* and the defendant was never completed, and there was no evidence of the vendors' consenting to the payment of the £500 to the plaintiff. The word " absolutely" has been relied on by the other side as shewing that the plaintiff is entitled to the £500 *at all events*, and independently of the other circumstances in the case; but that word is evidently not used in the sense of " at all events," but means absolutely only in contradistinction to the option reserved to the defendant with respect to the £7000. Thirdly, the vendors ought to have produced all the deeds mentioned in the abstract, without which they did not make out a complete and satisfactory title. The fair meaning of the agreement is that they will convey Lord *Oxford's* title, and if so, it was incumbent upon them to shew that he had a good title according to the stipulation in the first agreement. Fourthly, the plaintiff might and ought to have tendered a draft of a conveyance. In *Jones* v. *Barkley* (a) it was held that before such an action as this can be maintained, the plaintiff must have done all in his power, and in that case a draft of a conveyance was tendered.

Lord TENTERDEN, C. J.—I am of opinion that the plaintiff is entitled to recover the £500 demanded by this action. The objection to the stamp has been already sufficiently answered, therefore I say nothing upon that subject. Then as to the instrument: it is no conveyance, either in its effect, or in the intention of the parties. What-

(a) 2 Dougl. 684.

ever might have been its language, it could not possibly operate as a grant of the next presentation, because it was not under seal; and I think it was not intended so to operate. The case then stands thus: the plaintiff having made one bargain with *Goodacre* and *Buzzard* for the next presentation, another bargain was afterwards made, with the plaintiff's consent, between *Goodacre* and *Buzzard* and the defendant, by which they agreed, not to make a good title, but to sell the next presentation for £7,500, to be paid on a particular day, on having such title as the vendors had received; with a covenant for a return of the money in a certain event, and an option to be exercised by the defendant as to the £7000 for his further security, but from which the £500 was expressly exempted. That agreement the plaintiff ratified, having previously acquired an interest in the subject-matter of it, so that, without his consent, *Goodacre* and *Buzzard* could have made no agreement with the defendant; there was, consequently, a good consideration for the promise to pay the £500 to the plaintiff. Then come the objections that the vendors did not shew a good title, and did not tender any conveyance. If they did all that their contract required, and more was demanded, that released them from the obligation of taking any further steps in the transaction. I am at a loss to conceive what language a man is to use who intends to sell such a title as he has received, and nothing more, if the language of this agreement is not sufficient so to limit his undertaking. If a purchaser will bargain thus rashly to pay for such a title as the seller has, it is his own fault if his money is placed in hazard by the insufficiency of that title; though here no hardship could be sustained, because the principal money was secured. Then, as there was a good consideration for the defendant's promise, and as the vendors have done all that their contract required, the only remaining question is, whether the stipulation for the consent of *Goodacre* and *Buzzard* means a consent to be given at the time when the money was to be paid, or at the time when the contract was entered into. I

1827.

WILMOT
v.
WILKINSON.

think it means the latter; that such consent was a part of the consideration for the plaintiff giving up his bargain; that it was incorporated in the agreement, and could not afterwards be recalled. I am, therefore, of opinion that the plaintiff is entitled to judgment.

The other judges concurred.

Postea to the plaintiff.

GLANVILLE *v.* STACEY.

The rakings of corn are tithable, where, from the course of husbandry used, their quantity is necessarily considerable, though no fraud is practised or intended.

DEBT on the statute 2 & 3 *Edw.* 6, c. 13, for not duly setting out tithes of barley and oats. Plea, the general issue. At the trial before *Gaselee*, J. at the *summer* assizes for the county of *Cornwall*, 1825, a verdict was found for the plaintiff for three shillings, subject to the opinion of this Court on the following case:—

In the year 1823 the plaintiff was farmer of the tithes of corn and grain in the parish of *St. Germains*, in the county of *Cornwall*, and the defendant was then the occupier thereof twenty-three acres of land tilled to barley, and of one acre of land tilled to oats. No composition for tithes existed between the parties. The usual mode of harvesting and tithing of barley and oats in the parish was as follows. The crop is first cut by the scythe into swathes, which women and children then collect into sheaves by means of rakes; the sheaves are next bound and put into shocks, consisting of eight, ten, or twelve each, and then the tithing immediately takes place. The portion of the crop which remains on the ground after this process is then collected into rows with large rakes, and with small ones into bundles, which are called wads, and these are bound and placed together in heaps, and afterwards carried by the farmer to the mow. After the carrying, there is generally some scattered corn left in the places of the heaps, and the whole field is then raked a second time as before. Both the first and second rakings are carried by the farmer to the mow and treated as the rest of the crop. After the two rakings have taken place, and not before, the gleaners are admitted, and cattle, sheep, geese, &c. turned into the field. The average crop per acre through the parish, including both the tithe and what was collected by raking, was thirty bushels, and the average quantity of that which was left after the tithing took place was about three bushels, but the state of the weather, the length of the stalk, and the degree of skill and care exercised by the labourers, both in carrying the corn on the scythe, in mowing clean to the swathe, and in raking clean for the binding of the sheaves, will make a considerable difference in the quantity left on the ground. In the year 1823 the defendant followed the mode of harvesting above described, the tithe was set out before the rakings had been made into wads; but the tithe collector, who came with the plaintiff's waggons to take away the tithe, saw the quantity of the corn lying on the ground, and stated in evidence, that, in his opinion, the quantity left would produce about three bushels per acre. The defendant was guilty of no fraud, and great care was taken by his directions in the mowing clean as aforesaid, and in raking clean for the binding of the sheaves, and as little rakings were left as possible in that mode of harvesting.

Coleridge, for the plaintiff. The right of the tithe owner is to one tenth of the entire crop, as accurately as it can be ascertained, without, of course, expecting mathematical precision. The only principle upon which the rakings can be exempt from the tithe, is that they come within the maxim *de minimis non curat lex;* therefore, when they are considerable in quantity, and are reduced, or reducible, to a tithable shape, as in this case, they are clearly tithable. It must be admitted that the cases upon the subject are somewhat contradictory and difficult to reconcile; but the balance of them is in favour of the plaintiff; and some of those which are against him are capable of explanation. In ancient times, as appears by the old cases, it was considered, as a matter of course, that the rakings were by the common law subject to tithe, and whenever an exemption was claimed, it was in respect of a custom or prescription; *Anonymous*(a), *Bird* v. *Adams*(b), *Jesop* v. *Paine*(c), *Grysman* v. *Lewis* (d) citing Sir *C. Morrison's case*, *Ledger* v. *Langley*(e): and it was not unfrequently held that such custom or prescription was void, and tithe of the rakings payable. In a somewhat later case of *Fosse* v. *Parker* (f), where an action was brought for tithes of neck wool, *Houghton*, J. said, " There may be much deceit in this, as in the case of rakings; if purposely they will scatter corn, the parson shall have tithe of this, unless it be *minus voluntarié.*" So, in *Andrews* v. *Lane* (g), *Richardson*, C. J. said, " As to rakings, I hold that where rakings are of great value, *or* if they are left on the land covinously, tithes shall be paid of them; but if they are left there in a small quantity *and* involuntarily, it is otherwise; and therefore the words of the suggestion in such case are *minus voluntarié.*" Here the rakings must be considered to have been left voluntarily, because it was impossible in the mode of harvesting adopted to avoid leaving them. In *Staughton* v. *Hide*(h) it was alleged to be the custom of the parish with respect to grass, " that the parishioners are not to rake together the grass round the cocks." The Court, however, " declared that the custom insisted upon by the defendants not to rake up their grass into cocks in order to the setting out the full tithes thereof, is a void custom." In *Howard* v. *Bovingdon*(i) a similar custom was set up with respect to the aftermath of hay, and the rakings of barley and oats; and " the Court declared the plaintiff entitled to the second crop of grass mowed for hay; to have the barley set out for tithing in cocks or heaps; to have the corn, scattered

(a) 2 Leon. 70.
(b) Anderson, 199; Moor, 278; Saville, 100.
(c) Cro. Eliz. 363.
(d) Cro. Eliz. 446.

(e) 1 Sid. 283; 2 Keb. 85.
(f) 3 Bulstr. 242.
(g) 2 Gwillim, 473.
(h) 1 Wood, 394.
(i) 4 Wood, 546.

around such cocks or heaps, raked up to the same before it is tithed; and to take away the said tithes with the rakings thereto belonging." In a modern case, *Filewood* v. *Kemp* (a), Lord *Stowell* said, " As to barley rakings, I have no hesitation in saying that I conceive the law to be that the clergyman being entitled to one tenth, is entitled also to the rakings of every tenth cock, as composing part of the proportion belonging to him." All these cases bear clearly and directly for the plaintiff, and present a body of authorities upon which the Court would be justified in acting. The rakings are in all of them treated as titheable; and even where custom is alleged to the contrary, it is not allowed to prevail against the right: and custom is the strongest ground the defendant has to rest upon in this case. There certainly are cases of a different bearing to be found, some of which admit of explanation; but it must be conceded that others of them cannot be so disposed of. *Perry* v. *Soam* (b) is equivocal, and the reports of it do not agree. In *Leonard's* report of it it is said, " There was a case lately in this Court betwixt the Lord *Howard* and *Nichols*, where the suit in the Spiritual Court was for the tithes of rakings, and the surmise for a prohibition was, that the inhabitants had used to till and sow their lands, &c. and they had used to be discharged of their tithes and rakings after that the shocks had been carried away; and *Coke*, who was of counsel for the parson, durst not demur upon it, but traversed the prescription." In *Johnson* v. *Aubrey* (c) it is said, apparently with reference to the same case, " *Coke* cited one *Nichols'* case to be adjudged in this Court, that tithes shall not be paid for rakings of corn, unless it can be averred that they are foul rakings, and covinous to defraud the parson." In *Sherrington* v. *Fleetwood* (d) there is a *dictum*, but only a *dictum*, of *Popham*, C. J. to the same effect, where he is reported to have said, " it hath been here adjudged that tithes shall not be paid for rakings, unless

(a) 1 Haggard, 487.   (c) Cro. Eliz. 660.
(b) 2 Leon. 27; Cro. Eliz. 139.   (d) Cro. Eliz. 475.

1827.

GRENVILLE
v.
STACEY.

they be *foul* rakings." The same case is reported in
Moor (a), where nothing is said about "rakings." In
Green v. *Hun* (b) it was held, that a prescription generally
to pay the tenth cock of barley in satisfaction of the tithes
of the barley and rakings was good; and that if they were left
voluntarié, that must be shewn by the other side: but there
the exemption was claimed by prescription. In *Pitt* v.
Harris (c) a prohibition had been granted in a suit for
tithes of rakings, without any special ground for it appearing. But, afterwards, Serjeant *Finch* told the Court
that the farmer made great gain of the rakings, and carried
them to his barn; and *Coke* said, " the prohibition has been
granted, but you may plead this if you wish to have a consultation." None of these *dicta* or decisions can be held
strictly applicable to a case like the present; where the quantity of rakings is admitted to be, of necessity, large and out
of proportion to that which would result from a different
course of husbandry. The cases which bear more directly
against the plaintiff, and which are less open to explanation,
are, *Parry* v. *Chauncey* (d), *Anonymous* (e), *The case of
Modus Decimandi* (f), and *Cecil* v. *Scott* (g); but even these
cases, strong as they are in themselves against the plaintiff,
are consistent with and, as it is submitted, subordinate to
the principle already alluded to, namely, that where the
farmer chuses to adopt a mode of husbandry by which the
quantity of rakings left is unavoidably large, the tithe-owner
is not to be deprived of his right to the tithe of those
rakings.

Carter, contrà. The case expressly finds that the defendant was guilty of no fraud; that great care was taken by
his directions in the mowing clean and in raking clean for
the binding of the sheaves; that as little rakings were left as

(a) Moor, 909.
(b) Cro. Eliz. 702.
(c) 1 Roll. Rep. 379.
(d) Noy, 15.

(e) 1 Freeman, 334; 12 Mod.
235.
(f) 13 Co. Rep. 12.
(g) Litt. Rep. 31.

possible in the mode of harvesting adopted; and that the mode of harvesting adopted was that which prevailed by custom in that country. It cannot therefore be said that the rakings in this case were left covinously or *voluntarié;* and if so, the only question is whether involuntary rakings are titheable; and it is quite clear that they are not. Lord Chief Baron *Comyns,* speaking of corn tithes, says (*a*) " The manner of payment shall be such as the usage or custom of the country allows; as when it has been usually paid in the sheaf or bundle, it shall be a good manner of setting out of tithes. *But no tithe ought to be paid for the rakings of corn, where it is not dispersed by fraud."* For the latter position he cites as authorities *Pitt* v. *Harris* (*b*), 1 Roll. Abr. *Dismes* (Z), pl. 11, and 2 Inst. 652. Now the last-mentioned authority is Lord *Coke's* commentary on the 2 *Edw.* 6, c. 13, in which, after enumerating the articles not titheable by the common law, he says, " tithes shall not be paid of rakings left without *covin,* nor of after-pasture." [*Bayley,* J. But a reason is assigned in *Rolle's* Abridgement, namely, that rakings are exempt from tithes by the Levitical law. Now that was because they were left for the gleaners, from whence we must infer that the word " rakings" is properly applicable to that which is usually left for the gleaners, and not to that of which the farmer makes a profit.] The meaning of the word is not so re-strained in any of the cases. As to the cases where the exemption was claimed by prescription, the exemption must have been allowed at common law and not on the ground of prescription; because a prescription to pay tithe of part of the corn in satisfaction of tithe of the whole would be clearly bad; it was so held in *Grysman* v. *Lewis* (*c*), and *Watson,* in his *Clergyman's Law* (*d*), states the result of all the cases to be the same. In *Erskine* v. *Ruffle* (*e*), *Parker,* C. B. after alluding to the case of *Green*

(*a*) Com. Dig. *Dismes,* (H.) 1. (*d*) Page 550.
(*b*) 1 Roll. Rep. 379. (*e*) 3 Gwill. 961.
(*c*) Cro. Eliz. 446.

v. *Hun* as reported by *Croke* (a), says, " but the true reason of the judgment was, that no tithes were payable for involuntary rakings." So the anonymous case in *Freeman* (b)
decided, that no tithe was payable for rakings of corn if they
were involuntary, but if, *by fraud*, more was left than necessary, *secus*. *Parry* v. *Chauncey* (c) and *Cecil* v. *Scott* (d)
are also express authorities to the same effect in favour of
the present defendant. All these cases proceed upon the
same, and that a very equitable principle, namely, that the
farmer shall pay tithe upon the crop cut and gathered, fairly
and without fraud, in the customary course of husbandry,
but that for any trifling surplus which may result from extraordinary care and diligence on his part, he shall not pay
tithe. *Howard* v. *Bovingdon* (e) does not militate against
this principle, for there the corn was put up into cocks with
a fork, and the scattered corn was raked up before the cocks
were carried, but the farmer insisted upon a right to set out
the tithe before the raking took place. In *Filewood* v.
Kemp (f) the mode of husbandry is not mentioned, but it
would appear from the judgment to have been the same as
in *Howard* v. *Bovingdon*.

The case was argued on a former day in this term, when
the Court took time for deliberation. Judgment was now
delivered by

Lord TENTERDEN, C. J.—This case was lately argued
before us, and the several authorities bearing upon the
question were quoted and commented upon at the bar. It
is not necessary to go through them again. They are very
numerous and not very consistent. The principle that may
be extracted from them appears to us to be, that for small
quantities involuntarily left in the process of raking, tithe
shall not be payable; otherwise, if there be any particular

(a) Cro. Eliz. 702.
(b) 1 Freeman, 334; 12 Mod.
285.
(c) Noy, 15.
(d) Litt. Rep. 31.
(e) 4 Wood, 546.
(f) 1 Haggard, 487.

fraud or intention to deprive the parson of his full right. His right is to a tenth of the corn, to be taken generally when it comes to such a state or stage as that the parson may see he has his fair tenth. In the case now before the Court particular fraud or deceit is negatived. The defendant is found to have followed the practice usual in the parish. But it is further found that about thirty bushels of barley were collected by the first raking, and three bushels left on the ground, so that the tithe of the thirty being set out, the parson would have an eleventh part only and not a tenth, and this although great care was taken in mowing and raking clean for the binding of the sheaves. And we are of opinion that a course of harvesting, by which so large a portion is not subjected to the tithing even when great care is taken, and by which, consequently, a much larger portion may be withdrawn if the process be less carefully conducted, operates in itself as a deceit, and cannot be sustained at law, and, consequently, that the plaintiff was certainly entitled to the tithe of what was left after the first raking. The quantity left at the second raking was probably too small to be worth attention.

The verdict, therefore, is to stand, and the postea to be delivered to the plaintiff.

Postea to the plaintiff.

1827.

GLANVILLE
v.
STACEY.

DOE on the demise of the Rev. THOMAS MORGAN, Clerk, v. JOHN MORGAN.

EJECTMENT, for lands situate in the parish of *Llywell*, in the county of *Brecon*. Demise, 13th of *January*, 1826. At the trial before *Garrow*, B., at the *Herefordshire* summer assizes, 1826, a verdict was found for the defendant, subject to the opinion of the Court upon the following case :—

Thomas Morgan, the lessor of the plaintiff, was the eldest to my brother; but my mother is at liberty to give 1000*l*. of my property where she pleases:"—Held, that testator's real estate passed to his brother.

Testator, after giving some pecuniary legacies, proceeded thus: " All my property and effects of all claims I shall have, I give

brother and heir at law of *David Morgan*, deceased. *David Morgan*, being seised in fee of the premises in question, made his last will and testament in writing, bearing date the 3d day of *January*, 1822, duly executed and attested to pass real estates *(verbatim et literatim)* as follows:—

    " Jany 3rd 11822 In the name of God Amen I give
          as in the bond
to W^m 500 as intrest of 500*l*. during his life to *Howell Jones* apprentice if he will wake a sobor life with the securiety of porson of the parish where he lives the sum of 5*l*. p^r yeer and all my property and effects of all claimes I shall have I give to my brother *John Morgan* of *Tull Glase* in *Cray* but my mother is at liberty to give 1000*l*. of my property where she please of
    This is my last will by me   *David Morgan*."

 David Morgan, the testator, died before the 13th of *January*, 1826, without altering such will, being so seised, and also possessed of personal property to the amount of 6000*l*. *John Morgan* the defendant, and *John Morgan* mentioned in the will, are one and the same person.

Campbell, for the plaintiff. It might almost be contended that this will is altogether void, for being wholly unintelligible; but without going that length, it may safely be contended that the will is not sufficient to pass real estate. The lessor of the plaintiff is the heir at law of the testator, and it is an established principle, that the heir at law cannot be disinherited except by express words or necessary implication. The language of this will, so far as it is at all intelligible, is confined entirely to the mention of personalty. It contains no introductory words indicating that the testator had any intention to dispose of his real estate. There is no mention of lands, or of the heir at law. It is true that the will contains the word " property," and that it has been held that real estate will pass under the word " property," and even under the words " *personal* property," if it is apparent from other parts of the will that such was the intention of the testator; *Doe* v. *Tofield* (a). But in that case such an intention was apparent; here there is nothing in the will to shew it: indeed the effect of the will is the other way, for as it never mentions the heir at law, the natural inference is, that the testator meant the law to take its course, and intended his real estate to go by course of law to his heir. In *Markant* v. *Twisden* (b) it was held, that real estate would not pass under the words " the residue of my estate, chattels, real and personal," because the latter words explained the former, and shewed that the whole sentence pointed to personalty; and here, the word " property," which is less comprehensive in its meaning than the word " estate," is followed and explained by the word " effects," which *ex vi termini* relates to personalty. In *Timewell* v. *Perkins* (c), the testator, after devising particular freehold lands, gave all the residue of his estate, consisting in ready money, plate, &c., or in any other thing whatsoever or wheresoever; and it was held that the latter words would not pass real estate. There are many other decisions proceeding upon the same principle. It has been held that real estate will not pass under a devise of " all the rest of my estate and effects, of what nature soever," *Doe* v. *Buckner* (d); nor, after a disposition of the real estate for life, under a devise of " the residue of my effects wheresoever and whatsoever," *Camfield* v. *Gilbert* (e); nor, after a bequest of personalties, under a devise of " all the remainder of my *property* whatsoever and wheresoever," *Roe* v. *Yeud* (f); nor, after language clearly descriptive of personal property, under a devise of " all other my *property*," *Doe* v. *Rout* (g); nor under a devise of the residue of the estate to trustees upon trust to sell, *Doe* v. *Hurrell* (h); nor under a bequest of " all and singular my effects," unless, indeed, a contrary intention is apparent in other parts of

---

(a) 11 East, 246.
(b) 1 Eq. Ca. Abr. 211.
(c) 2 Atk. 102.
(d) 6 T. R. 610.

(e) 3 East, 516.
(f) 2 N. R. 214.
(g) 7 Taunt. 79.
(h) 5 B. & A. 18.

the will, Doe v. Dring (n). It was, indeed, decided in Doe v. Tofield (b), that real property may pass under the description of " personal estates" in a will; but under these peculiar circumstances, that it was manifest from the whole of the will, as by terms of direct reference to that description of property in ulterior dispositions of the same real property, that such was the intention of the testator. In Doe v. Chapman (c), a devise of " all the rest and residue of my estate, of what nature or kind soever," was held to include real as well as personal property, though accompanied with limitations peculiarly applicable, and usually applied; to personal property alone; but there the testatrix had surrendered her copyholds to the use of her will, thereby clearly manifesting her intention not to die intestate as to any part of her property. In Doe v. Lainchbury (d), a devise of all the residue of the testator's " money, stock, property, and effects, of what kind or nature soever," to A. and B., " to be divided equally between them, share and share alike," was held to pass real as well as personal estate, because it appeared from other parts of the will that the testator had applied the words " property and effects" to real estate. Doe v. Langlands (e) is the strongest case against the present plaintiff. There, a testator, possessed of real and personal property, after several pecuniary legacies, " gave and bequeathed all and every the residue of his property, goods, and chattels, to be divided equally between A. and B., share and share alike, after all his debts paid." It was held that the word " property," though followed by the words " goods and chattels," was sufficient of itself to carry the realty. But nothing else appeared there to restrain the meaning of the word " property," and the personalty was not in fact sufficient to pay all the debts and legacies. The result of all these authorities is, that although the word " property" may in some cases suffice

(a) 2 M. & S. 448.   (d) 11 East, 290.
(b) 11 East, 246.   (e) 14 East, 370.
(c) 1 H. Bla. 223.

to pass real estate, it is not always and necessarily sufficient for that purpose; and that the whole will must be looked at in order to see whether the testator used that word to denote real as well as personal estate. Now looking at the whole will in this case, there is nothing to shew that the testator intended to devise his real estate. He begins by giving two pecuniary legacies, one of 500l., and the other of an annuity to his apprentice; and immediately afterwards he gives " all his property and effects of all claims he shall have" to his brother. The word " property," therefore, coupled as it is with the word " effects," is evidently meant to denote personal property only. But supposing that this latter clause, standing by itself, would have passed the real estate by virtue of the word " property," it is followed by another which shews most clearly that the testator did not consider his real estate to have passed by the former clause, because he adds, " but my mother is at liberty to give 1000l. of my *property* where she pleases." In that clause he most unquestionably uses the word " property" to denote " personal estate," which fairly raises the inference that he used it in the same sense in the preceding clause. If the personal estate, at the time of the testator's death, had been insufficient to discharge his debts, his mother could have obtained her 1000l. only out of the real estate; and yet it must be insisted on the other side that the testator has already passed the real estate by the previous gift to his brother. At all events, therefore, the gift to the mother renders it extremely doubtful whether the testator intended to include his real estate in the gift to the brother; and then the rule of law applies that the heir at law is not to be disinherited but by express words or necessary implication.

W. E. Taunton, contrà, was stopped by the Court.

Lord TENTERDEN, C. J.—I am of opinion that the verdict which has been found for the defendant in this case is right, and ought not to be disturbed. This is undoubtedly the will of a very unlettered man, and I believe it is not unusual for such men to use the word " property" as denoting all they are worth in the world, real as well as personal estate; though our decision cannot, of course, be governed by that consideration. It has, however, been decided in many cases, and is established as a principle, that the word " property" in a will is of itself sufficient to pass real estate, unless there is something in other parts of the will which shews clearly that that word was used in a more confined and limited sense. Now the only part of this will which it is contended can have such an effect, is that by which the testator declares that his mother is at liberty to give 1000l. of his property where she pleases. But that, at the very utmost, renders it doubtful whether he intended that sum to come out of his real or his personal property; and the want of certainty in that latter clause cannot take away from the preceding clause the certainty which belongs to it. Then as the word " property," *per se,* has been held to include real as well as personal estate, and as there is nothing in this will to shew that it is there used in a more limited sense, I am of opinion that the real estate did pass under it, and that the defendant, consequently, is entitled to the judgment of the Court.

BAYLEY, J.—Where a testator uses words calculated to pass the real estate, the real estate will pass, unless it is shewn clearly by other expressions in the will that those words were used in a different sense. It was decided in *Doe* v. *Langlands* (a), that the word " property," when used in a will, would pass the real as well as the personal estate; and if there are other expressions in the will calculated to raise a judicial doubt only whether the testator intended to apply the word " property" to his personal estate alone, I think those expressions cannot be allowed to control the effect of the word " property," that having

(a) 14 East, 370.

been held, *per se,* to include real as well as personal estate. Here, after some pecuniary legacies, the testator gives " all his property and effects of all claims he shall have" to his brother; meaning clearly that all his property and the produce of all his claims shall go to his brother. It seems to me much the same thing as if he had said " all I have, and all I, die worth;" and there can be no doubt that the real estate would have passed under those words. The testator afterwards empowers his mother "to give 1000*l*. of his property where she pleases;" which may raise a judicial doubt whether he intended that sum to come out of his real or his personal estate; but I think a mere doubtful expression such as that should not be allowed to control the prior clause, by which the testator gave all his property to his brother. The bequest to the mother may be satisfied out of the personal effects, or, if there were no personal effects, would enable her, in a Court of Equity, to charge the real estate, though devised to another.

HOLROYD, J., and LITTLEDALE, J., concurred.

Judgment for the defendant.

———◆———

FAYLE *v.* BIRD.

ASSUMPSIT by the drawer against the acceptor of a bill of exchange. The bill was dated 31st *January*, 1826, and requested the defendant to pay, two months after the date thereof, to the plaintiff's order in *London,* 59*l*. 12*s*. 6*d*. for value delivered to the defendant in potter's clay; and was accepted by the defendant, *payable at W. Metcalf, Esq., Coal Exchange, London.* The declaration averred presentment for payment *at W. Metcalf, Esq., Coal Ex-*

change, *London*. Plea, non assumpsit; and issue thereon. At the trial before Lord *Tenterden*, C. J., at the *London* sittings after *Trinity* term, 1826, the plaintiff, being unable to prove a presentment at *Metcalf's*, was nonsuited, but had leave to move to enter a verdict in his favour. A rule nisi having afterwards been granted accordingly,

F. Pollock now shewed cause. The nonsuit was right, for the plaintiff was bound to prove a presentment of the bill at *Metcalf's* in *London*. If a bill of exchange is " accepted, payable at the house of *P.* and Co.," it is a qualified acceptance, restricting the place of payment, and the holder is bound to present the bill at that house for payment, in order to charge the acceptor of the bill. If he brings an action upon the bill against the acceptor, he must aver in his declaration, and prove at the trial, that he made such presentment; and for want of such averment, a declaration is bad on demurrer. This was the solemn decision, after much argument, in the late case of *Rowe* v. *Young*, in error (a), and to remedy the inconvenience arising from that decision, the statute 1 and 2 *Geo.* 4, c. 78, was passed. That statute is entitled, " An Act to regulate *Acceptances* of Bills of Exchange." It recites that, " Whereas according to law as hath been adjudged, when a bill is *accepted* payable at a banker's, the acceptance thereof is not a general but a qualified acceptance; and whereas a practice hath very generally prevailed among merchants and traders so to *accept* bills, and the same have among such persons been very generally considered as bills generally accepted, and accepted without qualification; and whereas many persons have been and may be much prejudiced and misled by such practice and understanding, and persons *accepting* bills may relieve themselves from all inconvenience by giving such notice as hereinafter mentioned, of their intention to make only a qualified acceptance thereof:" and then enacts, " that if any person shall *accept* a bill of ex-

(a) 2 Bligh, 391; 2 Bro. & Bing. 165.

change, payable at the house of a banker, or other place, without further expression in his acceptance, such acceptance shall be deemed and taken to be to all intents and purposes a general acceptance of such bill; but if the acceptor shall in his acceptance express that he *accepts the bill, payable at a banker's house, or other place, only, and not otherwise or elsewhere,* such acceptance shall be deemed and taken to be to all intents and purposes a qualified acceptance of such bill, and the acceptor shall not be liable to pay the said bill, except in default of payment when such payment shall have been first duly demanded at such banker's house, or other place." Looking at the whole tenor of that statute, it is clear that it applies only to cases when the bill is *drawn* payable *generally,* but is *accepted* payable *at a particular place.* The present case, therefore, is not within the statute, because here the bill is *drawn* payable in *London.* Here the drawer himself points to a particular place of payment; he desires the acceptor to pay to his order " in *London;*" and the acceptor, adopting the direction of the drawer, accepts the bill payable " at *W. Metcalf, Esq., Coal Exchange, London.*" The qualification here is no act of the acceptor's, it is part of the compact between the parties; therefore the case is governed by the decision in *Rowe* v. *Young* (a), and is left untouched by the statute. Then the plaintiff, not having proved a presentment in *London,* cannot recover; because before the statute, presentment to the acceptor in *London* would clearly have been a condition precedent to the holder's having any claim against him. *Saunderson* v. *Bowes* (b), *Dickinson* v. *Bowes* (c), and *Howe* v. *Bowes* (d).

Hutchinson, contrà. The plaintiff is entitled to recover. The statute was clearly intended to apply to all bills made

(a) 2 Bligh, 391; 2 Bro. & Bing. 165.

(b) 14 East, 500; Bayley on Bills, 175.

(c) 16 East, 110.

(d) 16 East, 112; *S. C.* in error, 5 Taunt. 30.

payable at a particular place, whether so made payable by the drawer or the acceptor. The bill here being *drawn* payable in *London* makes no difference, because the acceptor has *accepted* it payable in *London*, within the very words of the statute. The point has recently been decided in the Court of Common Pleas in the case of *Selby* v. *Eden* (a), and this Court will, if possible, assimilate the practice of the two Courts. There the bill was drawn payable to the order of the drawer in *London*, and was accepted by the defendant payable in *London*, *according to the usage and custom of merchants.* It was contended that it was not a case within the statute, and that presentment in *London* ought to have been proved. But it was held, after argument and deliberation, that it was within the statute, and that proof of presentment for payment in *London* was not necessary. That case must decide the present.

Lord TENTERDEN, C. J.—But for the authority cited on the part of the plaintiff, I should certainly have doubted whether this case fell within the statute 1 and 2 *Geo.* 4, c. 78. It appears, however, that the Court of Common Pleas have decided in the case of *Selby* v. *Eden* (a), that the statute embraces every bill payable at a banker's or other place; and that it makes no difference whether the bill is rendered so payable by the language of the drawer, or by the language of the acceptor. It is of the highest importance to the public that there should be uniformity in the decisions of the several Courts of *Westminster Hall* upon all questions, but especially upon questions affecting negotiable instruments of this description. Upon the authority of that case, therefore, I am of opinion that this case is within the statute, and that the rule for entering a verdict for the plaintiff must be made absolute.

The other Judges concurred.

Rule absolute.

(a) 3 Bing. 611.

STONE and another v. W. MARSH, J. H. STRACEY, and
G. E. GRAHAM.

1827.

Monday,
28th May.

THIS was an issue directed by the Lord Chancellor to try
whether the defendants and one *Henry Fauntleroy* were, at
the date and issuing forth of certain commissions of bankrupt against the defendants and *H. Fauntleroy*, indebted
to the plaintiffs and *H. Fauntleroy* in any and what sum
of money, his lordship having ordered that on the trial of
that issue no objection should be taken to the proceeding
to the final determination of the said issue, on the ground
that *Fauntleroy* was interested as a trustee jointly with the
plaintiffs, and also a partner with the defendants. At the
trial before Lord *Tenterden,* C. J., at the *London* sittings
after *Hilary* term in 1826, a verdict was found for the
plaintiffs, subject to the opinion of this Court on the following case:—

On the 26th day of *May,* 1819, there was standing in
the books of the Governor and Company of the Bank of
England, in the name of the plaintiffs jointly with *H.
Fauntleroy,* deceased, the sum of 17,061*l.* 12*s.* 4*d.* in the
capital stock of navy 5 per cent. annuities, which were
held by the plaintiffs and *Fauntleroy* as trustees under the
will of Sir *Thomas Bemers Plaistow,* deceased. The defendants and *Fauntleroy,* and Sir *James Sibbald,* Bart.,
until the death of Sir *J. Sibbald,* and the defendants and
Fauntleroy, since the death of Sir *J. Sibbald,* carried on
the business of bankers in *Berner's Street,* under the firm
of *Marsh* and Co. On the 25th of *May,* 1819, instructions were given by the house of *Marsh* and Co. to their
broker, *J. H. Spurling,* to sell as much of the said stock
as would produce 16,000*l.* sterling; previously to which
time there had been lodged at the Bank of *England*
a letter of attorney, purporting to be executed by the
plaintiffs and *Fauntleroy* to sell, assign, and transfer all
or any part of 16,000*l.* part of the said annuities, which
letter of attorney was executed by *Fauntleroy;* but the

*Fauntleroy,
being one of
three co-trus-
tees, pro-
prietors of
stock, and also
one of three
co-partners in a
banking-house,
forged the
names of his
co-trustees to
a power of at-
torney, under
which he sold
the stock, and
paid the mo-
ney into his
banking-house.
Neither his co-
trustees, nor
his co-partners,
were privy to
the transac-
tion. Faunt-
leroy was exe-
cuted for ano-
ther forgery.
The surviving
trustees sued
the surviving
partners for
the money.
On an issue
from Chan-
cery, directing
that no objec-
tion should be
taken that
Fauntleroy
had been in-
terested both
as a trustee
and a partner
in the bank-
ing-house:—
Held, that the
money consti-
tuted a debt
due from the
bankers to the
trustees.*

execution thereof by the plaintiffs was forged by *Fauntleroy*. Pursuant to such instructions, *Spurling* entered into contracts with various stock-jobbers for the sale to them of 15,811*l.* 13*s.* of the said navy five per cent. annuities, at prices which upon the whole yielded 16,019*l.* 15*s.* 4*d.* the 19*l.* 15*s.* 4*d.* being the amount of the brokerage. On the 26th of *May,* 1819, *J. H. Spurling* caused transfers to be prepared in the books of the Governor and Company of the Bank of *England,* of part of the said annuities to the amount of 7000*l.* to the purchasers thereof or their nominees; and on that day the defendant, *J. H. Stracey,* attended at the Bank and signed the demand to act, indorsed on the said power of attorney, and then executed two several instruments of transfer so prepared in the books kept at the Bank of *England,* of two sums, part of the annuities, viz. 6895*l.* 10*s.* 5*d.* to the Rev. *W. Yates* and *T. Norris,* Esq. and 104*l.* 9*s.* 6*d.* to one *Henry Neil;* and the annuities were thereupon carried by the Governor and Company to the credit of the said transferees in the books kept at the Bank of *England* for transfer thereof, and the plaintiffs and *Fauntleroy* ceased to have credit for the same in the said books kept at the Bank. On the 28th day of *May,* 1819, the residue of the annuities was in like manner transferred to the purchasers, the instruments of transfer having been executed by *Graham;* and the annuities were thereupon carried by the said Governor and Company to the credit of the transferees in the books kept at the Bank of *England* for transfer thereof, and the plaintiffs and *Fauntleroy* ceased to have credit for the same in the said books kept at the Bank. The defendants' house had an account with Messrs. *Martin, Stone* and Co. bankers in the city, in the usual way of a banker's account, and a pass-book went from one house to the other from time to time, according to the usual practice between bankers and their customers; and to this account *Spurling,* the broker, usually paid the money received by him for stock sold by order of the defendants' house. The consideration-money of the annuities was re-raised by *Spurling*, and was paid by him to *Martin, Stone* and Co. to the credit of the house of *Marsh* and Co. according to the usual practice, together with the sum of 9*l.* 17*s.* 8*d.* one moiety of the broker's commission, which was allowed by him to the house of *Marsh* and Co., according to the usual practice on sales effected by him on their account; since which payment the account of *Marsh* and Co. with *Martin* and Co. had been frequently balanced, before the bankruptcy. *Fauntleroy* was permitted by the partners to conduct the greater part of the business of the house without their interference, and drew upon the account of *Martin, Stone* and Co.'s in the partnership firm, (as he thought fit), without the knowledge and in fraud of his partners, more than the amount of the said sums so paid in. Upon the apprehension of *Fauntleroy*, shortly before the bankruptcy, a paper was found in his private desk, whereof he kept the key, in the handwriting of the defendant *Graham*, in pencil, of which the following is a copy :—

"26th *May*, 1819.   £15,000 odd, navy fives.

"7105*l.* paid into *Martin's* on the 26th, and on the 28th, 8900*l.* odd, to make up the account to raise 16,000*l.* money, of *H. F. Gahagan* and *Stone.*"

There was no account with the defendants' house in the names of the plaintiffs and *Fauntleroy*, but there was an account in the names of the executors of Sir *Thomas Plaistow.* The executors were, in fact, the plaintiff, *Gahagan*, Messrs. *Plaistow* and *Fauntleroy.* The defendant, *Stracy*, knew that the plaintiff, *Stone*, was in *India* in the year 1819. The money raised by the transfers was not carried to the executors' account. A broker's note of the sale was transmitted by the said *J. H. Spurling* to the house of *Marsh* and Co. in the usual course.

Bosanquet, Serjt. for the plaintiffs. The question in this case is, whether there was a debt due from the bankers to the trustees of the property referred to, at the period of the bankruptcy of the former. For the plaintiffs it is contended that there was; that the money produced by the sale of the stock and received by the bankers, constituted a debt due from them to the plaintiffs. The case must be considered in two points of view: first, independently of the forgery, and, secondly, as connected with it. First, looking at the case independently of the forgery, this was money had and received by the bankers to the use of the trustees. The stock belonged to the plaintiffs; the contract for the sale of it was made by the defendants through their broker; it was sold to an innocent party; the price was received by the broker, and paid into the house of *Stone* and Co. together with half the brokerage, to the credit of the defendants, and afterwards drawn out by checks drawn in the name of their firm. The money so received by the bankers, not having been paid over to the trustees, constitutes a debt due to them. It is true the stock was sold and the money paid to the defendants, without the authority of the trustees; but as the purchaser takes no objection to the sale, and makes no claim to have his money back, the defendants can have no colour of right to retain it from the plaintiffs. *Marsh* and Co. assumed to have authority to sell the stock; under that assumed authority they did sell it, and received the money; the former owners of the stock then are entitled to adopt their act and claim the money, and the defendants cannot be allowed to say, in answer to that claim, that they had not authority. A principal, under such circumstances, has a right to adopt and to claim the benefit of the acts of a person assuming to have the authority of an agent; at least as against the agent himself; *Routh* v. *Thompson* (a), *Lucena* v. *Crawfurd* (b), *Hagedorn* v. *Oliverson* (c). The fraud of *Fauntleroy*, in giving authority to sell without the knowledge or consent of his co-trustees, is no part of their title; they do not claim through the forgery: their title is equally valid

(a) 13 East, 285.   (b) 2 N. R. 323.   (c) 2 M. & S. 485.

whether the authority to sell was good or bad. Suppose there had been no apparent authority at all, but the bankers had assumed it, could they claim to retain the money? Surely not. A fraud has been committed, but that cannot affect the trustees, because it was not committed for the benefit of the trustees, but for the benefit of the bankers. The object of the fraud was to raise money on the stock belonging to the trustees, and thereby to increase the funds of the banking-house, upon which *Fauntleroy* was authorised to draw in the name of the firm. The defendants, as the partners of *Fauntleroy*, may have been defrauded, but that has happened through their own fault, and the improper confidence which they thought fit to repose in him with a view to their own advantage. Such a fraud cannot affect the right of the trustees to insist upon their debt. Besides, no man can take advantage of the fraud of another to his own benefit; independently, therefore, of the forgery, there is nothing to prevent the plaintiffs from recovering. Secondly, considering the case as connected with the forgery, the fact of the power of attorney which authorised the sale having been forged by one of the partners in the banking-house, cannot affect the right of the plaintiffs to recover. They do not claim through the forgery; their title does not originate in the power of attorney or the sale, but in the receipt of the money by the banking-house. If it were otherwise it would be immaterial, because the transfer of the stock was not a felony nor any indictable offence, any more than the payment of the money by the purchaser or the receipt of it by the defendants. The rightful owner of property is not deprived of his civil remedy because his property has been taken from him by means of a felonious act. Where goods are feloniously stolen out of the possession of a bailee, as an innkeeper or a carrier, the owner may recover their value, and that even against a purchaser, unless the sale were in market-overt. So if a bank-note be stolen, the owner may recover it from the holder, if the latter has not exercised due caution in receiving it (*a*). *Willett* v. *Chambers* (*b*) is a strong authority in favour of the present plaintiffs. There *Dadley*, in 1771, obtained from *Bindley*, 350*l.* by forging a mortgage to him from *Hughes.* In 1776 *Dadley* and *Chambers* became partners. Then, *Bindley* wishing to call in his money, *Dadley* agreed with *Willett* to procure him a mortgage for 500*l.*, being 150*l.* in addition to the 350*l.* An assignment of the pretended mortgage was made to *Willett*, who paid 180*l.* to *Chambers* and 300*l.* to *Dadley*. *Dadley* died. *Chambers* was not privy to the forgeries, and no procuration money was paid. Yet, although *Willett's* money was obtained by forgery, he recovered against *Chambers* the whole 480*l.* It will be said here that the debt is merged in the felony, but it is an incorrect expression to say that a debt or a trespass is merged in a felony. The felon cannot be sued for the debt or the trespass for a time, but the right of action is not gone for ever. The rule that a person injured by a felonious act cannot sue the felon is founded on principles of public policy, to secure the punishment of the offender; but if the offender is dead, or has been brought to trial, the case is not within the principles on which the rule is founded, and, *cessante ratione, cessat et ipsa lex.* The civil remedy against the felon is only suspended until he has been tried for the felony; when that has taken place and he has been either convicted or acquitted, an action for the civil injury resulting from his wrongful act is maintainable. It is said in *Brooke's Abridgement* (*c*) to have been agreed, that if a man be indicted, arraigned, and *acquitted* of the robbery of *J. S.*, he shall not have an action of trespass, for the trespass is *extinct* in the felony, *et omne majus trahit ad se minus;* but a *quære* is added, and 31 H. 6, 15, is cited: and indeed this cannot be law to the extent of the terms in

(*a*) *Egan* v. *Thredfall*, 5 D. & R. 326, n; and see *Gill* v. *Cubitt*, 5 D. & R. 324; and *Downe* v. *Halling*, 6 D. & R. 455, and the cases there cited.

(*b*) Cowper, 814. See *Gow on Partnership*, 55, 147, 3d edit.

(*c*) Tit. *Trespass*, pl. 415.

which it is stated, because the acquittal may have proceeded upon the ground that the offence charged did not
amount to felony.   Moreover, it appears, upon referring to
the Year Book, 31 H. 6, 15, that the question arose upon
a writ of conspiracy for indicting the plaintiff for an assault
and battery, and stealing from his person feloniously four
shillings.   The objection to the writ was that it comprehended assault and battery as well as robbery, for which
former the writ of conspiracy did not lie; and the Court
seem to have thought that they made part of the felony, and
that being acquitted of the felony, he was also acquitted of
the trespass.   In *Higgins* v. *Butcher*(a) it was held, that
trespass would not lie by the husband for an assault upon
his wife, whereof she lingered and died, " because the private wrong was drowned in the offence to the Crown;" but
the rule was well applied in that case, because the defendant, the offender, was still alive, and had not been prosecuted.   In *Markham* v. *Cobb* (b), *Jones*, J. held that the
action of trespass was barred by production of a record
hat the taking was felonious; but *Doddridge* and *Whitlock*,
Js., in the same case, held that where the party robbed has
not been a party to the prosecution, he may maintain an
action of trespass; and the rather, because he would otherwise be without remedy.   The like point was ruled in
Dawkes v. *Coveneigh*(c), where *Roll*, C. J. said that the
action would not lie *before* prosecution, for the danger that
the felon might not be tried.   After trial, the party is clearly
at liberty to pursue his remedy for the private wrong.   Lord
Hale lays this down as a principle; because the offender
having been prosecuted, there can be no mischief to the
commonwealth (d).   In *Master* v. *Miller* (e), *Buller*, J. said,
" The law, proceeding upon principles of public policy, has
wisely said, that where a case amounts to felony you shall

(a) Yelv. 89.   (d) 1 Hale, P. C. 546.
(b) Noy, 82; Latch. 144.   (e) 4 T. R. 332.
(c) Styles, 346; 2 Rol. Abr.
557.

not recover against the felon in a civil action; but that rule does not appear to have been extended beyond actions of trespass or tort, in which, it is said, the trespass is merged in the felony." That learned judge, at the same time, expressed doubts whether the rule extended to any case "after the offender is brought to justice." All these authorities were reviewed in *Crosby* v. *Leng*(a), where Lord *Ellenborough* laid down the broad principle thus: "The policy of the law requires, that before the party injured by any felonious act can seek civil redress for it, the matter should be heard and disposed of before the proper criminal tribunal, in order that the justice of the country may be first satisfied in respect of the public offence; and after a verdict, either of acquittal or conviction, the judgment is so far conclusive in any collateral proceeding *quoad* the particular matter, that the objection is thereby removed of bringing that *sub judice* in a civil action, which was the proper subject-matter of a criminal prosecution." The rule, therefore, is satisfied by the conviction or acquittal, without collusion, of the offender, and the authorities cited fully establish that it is a mistake to lay it down as a rule that the right of civil action is *merged* in the felony. The civil right is only *suspended;* and was only suspended here: for there is no pretence for saying that there was any collusion on the part of the present plaintiffs. It was impossible to prosecute *Fauntleroy* for this forgery, for it is even now not known in what county he forged the power of attorney, nor by whom it was left at the Bank of *England.* The

(a) 5 T. R. 601. "But the liability of the firm in such cases depends on the knowledge the other members have of its being trust-money; and therefore, if one partner, being a trustee, bring trust-money into the trade without the knowledge or privity of his co-partner, it cannot be proved against the joint estate as a joint debt; for although the partner abuses his trust, and advances the money to the partnership, it will not raise a contract between the partnership and the *cestui que trust,* nor convert the innocent partners into implied trustees. *Ex parte Apsey,* 3 Bro. C. C. 265." *Gow on Partnership,* 285.

plaintiffs, therefore, could not have prosecuted him with effect either for the forgery or the uttering, and therefore cannot be charged with fraud or collusion for neglecting to do so.

F. Pollock, contrà. There is no debt due from the banking-house to the trustees; at any rate no *legal* debt, to support this action: their claim, if any, is a purely *equitable* one. The case may be regarded in three points of view: first, considering *Fauntleroy* as a trustee and not a partner in the banking-house; secondly, considering him as a partner and not a trustee; thirdly, considering him as both a trustee and a partner. First, considering *Fauntleroy* as a trustee only and not a partner in the banking-house, he must be taken to have employed the bankers, to have sold the stock through their agency, to have paid the money to them on his own account, and to have received it back again from them. That is, really, the substance of the transaction. He has, in some form or other, paid the money in, and he has drawn it out again. The defendants, indeed, may have known that it was not his own money; but still, if he paid it in to his private account, and drew it out again himself, they cannot be liable for it to his co-trustees. In the first view of the case, therefore, there is no debt due from the defendants to the trustees. The circumstance of the half brokerage having been paid to the credit of the banking-house, has been relied upon as shewing that the defendants interfered in the sale, and are, therefore, liable; but bankers take half the brokerage in every case where they employ a broker on behalf of a customer: therefore no conclusion adverse to the defendants can be drawn from that circumstance. Secondly, suppose *Fauntleroy* to have been a partner in the banking-house and not a trustee, and that he brought the power of attorney, and put the money to his own account, and afterwards drew it out again; then, his co-partners would not be liable. In *Smith*

v. *Jameson* (a), where one of two partners applied trust-money in the trade, *with the privity of the other partner*, and they having afterwards separated, the partnership effects were assigned to the former partner, who undertook to discharge the joint debts; it was held, that this private arrangement did not operate to discharge the retiring partner, but that both were liable to reimburse the trust-money. But that case is distinguishable from the present in this most important particular, that there the misapplication of the trust-money by the one partner took place *with the privity of the other partner*. Besides, there the plaintiff had a *legal* title *ab initio;* here the plaintiffs have, at most, a merely *equitable* claim. Suppose *Fauntleroy* had defrauded his partners, and repurchased the stock with their money; his partners would not have been entitled to recover that money from the trustees; and that shews that the partners, in this view of the case, are not liable to the trustees. Thirdly, considering *Fauntleroy* both as a trustee and a partner, the blending of the two characters cannot make the partners liable, if they would not be so, taking *Fauntleroy* as acting in either character separately. The money did, undoubtedly, get into the partnership funds; but the hand that paid it in was the hand to draw it out: so that there can be no claim against the other partners, who were not privy either to the paying of the money, or to the drawing it out (b).

Then, as to the effect of the felony, it must be conceded, according to the authorities cited, that after the conviction of the felon, an action may be maintained against him. But this concession will not assist the present plaintiffs, because here the transaction is wholly void. The plaintiffs cannot adopt a felony, without doing which they cannot maintain this action. Their remedy is against the purchaser of the stock, or against the Bank of *England*. The statute 24 *Geo.* 3, c. 99, s. 14, requires transfers to be entered and registered,

(a) 5 T. R. 601.   (b) *Vide ante*, 650, (a).

and signed by the party or attorney lawfully authorised. The transfer in this case was not so made. In *Davis* v. *The Bank of England*(a), the Court of Common Pleas decided that property in stock is not transferred from the owner by being placed, under a forged power of attorney, to the name of another person in the books of the Bank of *England*. The plaintiffs, therefore, may recover against the Bank of *England*, and need not resort to the present defendants. A man cannot adopt a felony. An assent to a battery formerly done, or to a tort punishable by statute, as an assent to a riot, or to a forcible entry, after it be done, shall not make a man punishable; *Vin. Abr. tit. Ratihabitio; Bishop* v. Lady *Montague*(b). Lord *Coke* lays it down that confirmation cannot work upon an estate that is void in law (c). Here the transfer is void in law, therefore the plaintiffs cannot confirm or adopt it.

Cur. adv. vult.

Lord TENTERDEN, C. J. now delivered the judgment of the Court, and after stating the facts of the case, proceeded as follows:—The defendants in this case are by the order of the Lord Chancellor prevented from taking any objection on account of the particular situation of *H. Fauntleroy*, as being both a proprietor of the stock sold and a partner in the banking-house; and the case is, therefore, to be considered as a case between the plaintiffs, proprietors of navy five per cent. annuities, on the one part, and the defendants, as a banking-house, on the other part. And it appears by the case, that the defendants' house, by means of sales of the annuities made under the orders of the house, and transfers signed, part by one of the defendants and part by another, received the price and proceeds of the annuities; that the money was paid by the broker, who effected the sales, into the defendants' house by a payment to their agents in the city; that it was so paid generally, and was

(a) 2 Bingh. 393.   (b) Cro. Eliz. 824.   (c) Co. Litt. 295 b.

never appropriated by the house to any particular account, not to the account of *H. Fauntleroy*, as was assumed in one part of the argument for the defendants, not to the account of the trustees, who had not in fact any account with the house, nor to the account of the executors of the person, of whose estate these annuities had formed a part, and who had an account with the house; and therefore being so paid in, and not placed to any particular account, cannot have been drawn out, but must be taken to have remained in the hands of the house at the time of the bankruptcy. Upon this state of facts it cannot be doubted that it was the duty of the house to place the money to the credit of the trustees, and retain it for their use, and subject to their order; and that no ignorance on the part of any of them, even supposing all but one to have been ignorant of the facts, (which, however, cannot have been,) nor any neglect on the part of the house, arising from a misplaced confidence reposed by them in one of themselves, or otherwise, to which the plaintiffs were no parties, can deprive the plaintiffs of their right to their money. And these facts were all that was incumbent on the plaintiffs to prove in order to shew their right to the money. It was not necessary for them to shew that the sale of the annuities was made with their authority; for even if made without their authority, and by an act wrongful towards them, they might by law waive the wrong, and demand the money, as is done in many other cases. The other facts stated in the case, of which one alone is of any importance, are brought forward on the part of the defendants; and it remains to be considered whether that fact defeats the plaintiffs' claim. That fact is, that the transfers were made under a forged power of attorney, forged by *H. Fauntleroy*, a member of the defendants' house. The authority was forged *by* and not *to* him; the *instrument* does not profess to give him any authority to sell the annuities; the authority is expressed to be given to the other members of the house jointly and severally, and could only be executed by some of them, as in fact it was. They

ought to have satisfied themselves of the validity of the
authority before they acted upon it. This forgery was a
capital felony, and it is therefore urged on the behalf of the
defendants that there has been no valid transfer of the annuities; that the Bank of *England* is answerable to the
plaintiffs for having permitted the transfers to have been
made without their authority; and that the buyers are also
answerable as having taken by purchase from persons who
had no authority to sell. It is not necessary to say whether
the plaintiffs had or had not these remedies, or either of
them, because, generally speaking, where an injured party
has different remedies against different persons, he may
elect which he will pursue. So that the question is, whether the plaintiffs have the remedy they now seek. The
transfers were made and the money received in pursuance
of a felony committed by a member of the defendants'
house. Can the house set up this felony as an answer to
the plaintiffs' claim? In general a man cannot defend himself against a demand by shewing on his part that it arose
out of his own misconduct, according to the maxim, " *Nemo
allegans suam turpitudinem est audiendus.*" There is, indeed, another rule of the law of *England*, viz. that a man
shall not be allowed to make a felony the foundation of a
civil action: not that he shall not maintain a civil action to
recover from a third and innocent person that which has
been feloniously taken from him, for this he may do if there
has not been a sale in market-overt, but that he shall not
sue the felon; and it may be admitted that he shall not sue
others, together with the felon, in a proceeding to which
the felon is a necessary party, and wherein his claim appears by his own shewing to be founded on the felony of
the defendant, *Gibson* v. *Minet* (a). This is the whole extent of the rule. The rule is founded on a principle of
public policy, and where the public policy ceases to operate
the rule shall cease also. This point was very ably shewn
in the argument on the behalf of the plaintiffs. The autho-

(a) 1 H. Bla. 612.

rities were quoted, and need not be repeated; and it was shewn that the familiar phrase, " the action is merged in the felony," is not at all times and literally true. Now public policy requires that offenders against the law shall be brought to justice, and for that reason a man is not permitted to abstain from prosecuting an offender by receiving back stolen property, or any equivalent or composition for a felony, without suit, and of course cannot be allowed to maintain a suit for such a purpose. But it is not contended that any such policy or rule is applicable to the present case; the offender has suffered the extreme sentence of the law for another offence of the same kind. It does not appear that the plaintiffs had any knowledge of the particular forgery mentioned in this case at such a time as might have enabled them to bring the offender to justice sooner; or even if they had been acquainted with the fact of the forgery, that they could, in ignorance of the place of the forgery, and of the means by which the forged instrument was placed in the Bank of *England,* have instituted a prosecution with success. And it was very properly admitted by the learned counsel for the defendants, that he could not contend that an action might not be maintained after conviction of the felon. But it was contended that the maxim of ratifying a precedent unauthorised act, and taking the benefit of it, cannot apply to a void or to a felonious act; and that here the plaintiffs were seeking to ratify the felonious act of *H. F.* and were making that act the ground of their demand. In this latter assertion lies the fallacy of the defendants' argument. The assertion is incorrect in fact; the plaintiffs do not seek to ratify the felonious act; they do not make that act the ground of their demand. The ground of their demand is the actual receipt of the money produced by the sale and transfer of their annuities. The sale was not a felonious act, neither was the transfer, nor the receipt of the money. The felonious act was antecedent to all these, and was complete without them, and was only the inducement to the Bank of *England* to allow the transfer to be

made. If public policy had required that the felonious inducement should prevent a claim to the money afterwards
received, as it would do if an action were brought against
the felon for the money received by a transfer obtained by
his felony, in lieu of a prosecution for the felony, a defence
of another kind would be given. But that is not the present case, and not being so, we think the plaintiffs may
entirely pass by the felony, and rely on the transfer and receipt of the money, and that the defendants cannot protect
themselves against the demand for the money which they
have received, by shewing this felony on the part of one of
the members of their house. The postea, therefore, is to
be delivered to the plaintiffs.

Postea to the plaintiffs.

Monday,
28th May.

GARNETT *v.* FERRAND and another.

TRESPASS, for assaulting plaintiff, and turning him out
of a room. Pleas, first, not guilty. Second, that before
and at the time when, &c. defendant *Ferrand* was one of
the coroners for the county palatine of *Lancaster*, and being
such coroner, was just before the time when, &c. in the
room in the declaration mentioned, within the county, and
within his jurisdiction as such coroner, for the purpose of
taking an inquisition upon view of the body of *B. C.*, then
and there lying dead, within the jurisdiction of defendant
Ferrand, as such coroner, touching the death of the said
B. C., and that afterwards and just before the said time
when, &c. and while defendant *Ferrand* was in the said
room as such coroner, and for the purpose aforesaid, plaintiff not having been summoned as a witness or juror touching the said inquisition, nor coming before defendant *Ferrand*, as such coroner, to testify any knowledge concerning
the same, with force and arms, &c., wrongfully broke and
entered into the said room, and intruded himself upon de-

Trespass will
not lie against
a coroner for
turning a per-
son out of a
room in which
he is about to
hold an in-
quest.

fendant *Ferrand*, so being therein as such coroner, and for the purpose aforesaid; and thereupon defendant *Ferrand* requested plaintiff to go and depart from and out of the said room, which he wholly refused to do, and continued in the same room in contempt of defendant *Ferrand* as such coroner, and to the disturbance and violation of due order and decency in the administration of justice, and to the great hinderance thereof; and thereupon defendant *Ferrand*, and the other defendant as his servant and by his command, gently laid their hands on plaintiff and turned him out, &c. Third, as before, that defendant *Ferrand* was about to hold an inquest, and that plaintiff wrongfully broke and entered the room, for the purpose of wrongfully and illegally taking notes of and publishing the proceedings of the said inquisition; and plaintiff was then and there wrongfully and illegally about to take notes of and publish the said proceedings, and would then and there wrongfully and illegally have taken notes of and published the same, if he had been permitted to remain in the said room during the said proceedings, to the great hinderance of public justice; and thereupon defendant *Ferrand*, in order to prevent plaintiff from so wrongfully and illegally taking notes of and publishing the said proceedings before the termination of the same, then and there requested plaintiff to depart, &c. concluding as before. Fourth, that defendant *Ferrand* was in the said room, the same being a private room hired by him for certain business therein, and plaintiff wrongfully broke and entered the said room; whereupon defendant *Ferrand* requested him to depart, &c. concluding as before. Replication to the second plea, that true it is defendant *Ferrand* was a coroner, and was in the room for the purpose in the plea mentioned, and that plaintiff entered, not being summoned, &c. and refused to depart; and plaintiff further saith that afterwards, and while defendant *Ferrand* was in the room for the purpose in the second plea mentioned, and after all the jurors had been duly sworn to inquire touching the death of the said *B. C.*, plaintiff, then and still being a

liege subject of the realm, peaceably and quietly entered
into the said room, the door thereof being then and there
open, to witness and be present at the said inquisition so
then about to be taken, the said room being then and there
sufficiently capacious to admit the presence of plaintiff at
the said inquisition, without any obstruction or hinderance
to the taking thereof, and then and there continued, &c.;
without this that defendants committed the trespasses in the
second plea mentioned, with the residue of the cause in that
plea alleged. Replication to the third plea, making the
same admissions, alleging the same facts, and traversing the
residue of the cause in the third plea stated. Replication
to the fourth plea, that defendant *Ferrand* was coroner, and
about to hold an inquest on *B. C.* in the said room, and
that plaintiff, being a liege subject, peaceably entered the
said room, the door being open, and the room having been
hired for the purpose of taking the inquisition, to witness
and be present at the said inquisition so about to be taken,
the said room being sufficiently capacious to admit the presence of plaintiff at the inquisition without obstruction to
the taking thereof, and continued in the said room, con-
ducting himself peaceably and quietly, and in an orderly and
proper manner, for the purpose of witnessing and being
present at the said inquisition, until defendants turned him
out, &c. Special demurrers to the replications to the
second and third pleas, for that they did not tender any
single or material issue, and were argumentative; and also
for that plaintiff had not in the inducement to the special
traverse expressly alleged any new matter, nor admitted nor
expressly denied the allegation in the pleas; and also for
that the special traverse in each concluded with a verification, without any sufficient allegation of new matter. General demurrer to the replication to the fourth plea. Joinder
in demurrer.

Follett, in support of the demurrer. The main question
in this case arises upon the replication to the fourth plea.

That plea states matter which constitutes a good defence to the action, therefore the question is, whether the replication is a good answer to the plea. It must be considered as admitted that the plaintiff was not in any way connected with the proceedings; that he was not summoned, nor accused, nor suspected; that he was not a relative of the deceased; and that he was not even an inhabitant of the mill in which the body was found. The ultimate question then will be, whether every person, under such circumstances, has a right to be present at a coroner's inquest, or whether the coroner, the presiding officer, has not a right, in the exercise of his discretion, to order the removal of any individual so circumstanced, whose presence he may deem prejudicial to the ends of justice, without rendering himself liable to an action at the suit of that individual. It is submitted that the coroner has this right. His is not an open court, for the inquest is only a preliminary investigation; but if it is an open court, still the judge has the power to exclude any person not connected with the proceedings, whom he may think fit to exclude. That the inquiry before a coroner, when it relates to the death of a person supposed to have been feloniously killed, is preliminary only, is clear from the language of the statute 4 *Edw.* 1, st. 2, *De Officio Coronatoris* (a). Before the statute of *Magna Charta*, c. 17, coroners held pleas of the crown; but by that statute, which enacts that "*nullus vicecomes, constabularius, coronator, vel alii ballivi nostri, teneant placita coronæ,*" their power in proceeding to trial and judgment is taken away (b). Lord *Coke,* in his commentary upon this, says (c): "And what authority had the coroner? The same authority he now hath, in case when any man come to violent or untimely death, *super visum corporis*, &c.; abjurations and outlawries, &c; appeals of death by bill, &c." This authority of the coroner, viz., the coroner solely to

---

(a) See the statute set out and commented on in *Jervis on Coroners,* 21, et seq.

(b) *Jervis on Coroners,* 21.

(c) 2 Inst. 32.

take an indictment *super visum corporis*, and to take an appeal, and to enter the appeal; and the Court remaineth to this day. But he can proceed no further, either upon the indictment or appeal, but to deliver them over to the justices; and this is saved to them by stat. Westm. 1, c. 10."
But it may be said that as to some matters arising out of this inquiry, the inquest of the coroner is final, as, that the deceased was *felo de se*; that a certain thing was deodand; that a certain person was guilty and *fugam fecit*. It appears by the best authorities that the inquests of the coroner are in no case conclusive, and that one affected by them, either collaterally or otherwise, may deny their authority and put them in issue. The only inquiries upon which any doubt has been entertained are those of flight and *felo de se* (a), *Rex* v. *Alderman* (b), *Ripley's case* (c), *Rex* v. *Parker* (d), *Holland* v. *Ellis* (e), *Anonymous* (f); *Vin. Abr.* Coroner, (F.); 2 *Haw. P. C.* c. 9, s. 55; *Com. Dig.* Officer, (G. 12); 1 *Hale, P. C.* 416. In the last mentioned authority the law upon this subject is thus stated:—" But although an inquisition taken before the coroner *super visum corporis*, in the point of *felo de se*, is of great authority, and a sufficient record, whereupon process may be made against those that detain the goods found in the inquisition, yet it seems to me that it is traversable in the very point so found, for it is but an inquest of office, and whereupon the party grieved thereby can have no attaint; but otherwise it is of a presentment of a *fugam fecit* before the coroner." That the finding of a deodand is traversable, is clear from 1 *Hale, P. C.* 421; and in the late case of *Rex* v. *Evett* (g), where a *venire* issued to bring in the defendant to answer for a deodand, and he appeared, and demurred to the inquisition, the Court, after argument, quashed the inquisition. By the current of authorities, it seems to be taken for

(a) *Jarvis on Coroners*, 282.

(b) 3 Keb. 564, 604; 2 Lev. 182.

(c) Sir T. Jones, 198.

(d) 3 Keb. 489.

(e) 1 Ventr. 278.

(f) 1 Ventr. 239.

(g) *Ante*, 237; 6 B. & C. 247.

granted that the presentment of a *fugam fecit* is not traversable. This opinion rests upon a *dictum* in 8 *Ed.* 4, quoted by Lord *Hale* and *Staunford;* but there appears to be no instance in which the Court has acted upon it. Indeed Lord *Hale* does not express his assent to this *dictum*, but after arguing that a finding of *felo de se* is traversable, cites it as an authority, and adds, " but indeed it holds that a *fugam fecit*, presented before the coroner, is not traversable, *quia ancient ley de Corone*," and in the same page (a), he says, " the doubt of Mr. *Staunford* is only upon a *fugam fecit*." Indeed, upon principle, there is no reason why a *fugam fecit* found by the coroner is not equally traversable as any other inquisition, and the doubt in this respect rests upon no better foundation than the *dictum* before alluded to (b).

But assuming that the proceedings are not traversable, and that persons interested in them have a right to be present, that will not assist the present plaintiff, because he admits upon the record that he was not interested in the proceedings. In *Rex* v. *Fleet* (c) it was held illegal to publish in a newspaper a statement of the evidence given before a coroner's jury, even though the statement was correct, and the party publishing was not actuated by any malicious motive. So the publication of *ex parte* proceedings before magistrates has been held to be illegal, *Rex* v. *Fisher* (d), and it has been decided by this Court that a Court of general gaol delivery has power to make an order prohibiting the publication of the proceedings pending a trial, and to punish disobedience to such order by fine; *Rex* v. *Clement* (e). In all cases of preliminary inquiry care is taken that the evidence given shall not be published. Grand jurors are sworn to secrecy; and there is no sub-

(a) 1 Hale, P. C. 417.

(b) 1 Saund. 363; 1 East, P. C. 391.

(c) 1 B. & A. 379.

(d) 2 Campb. 563; and see *Duncan* v. *Thwaites*, 5 D. & R.

447; 3 B. & C. 556; *Cox* v. *Coleridge*, 2 D. & R. 86; 1 B. & C. 37; *Paley on Convictions*, 3d ed. by *Dowling*, 67, n. (1).

(e) 4 B. & A. 218; 11 Price, 82.

stantial difference in their nature between proceedings before a grand jury and proceedings before a coroner. But then it will be contended that the coroner's Court is an open Court, and *Rex* v. *Killinghall*(a), and *Rex* v. *Eriswell*(b), will be cited as authorities for that argument. In the former, a grand jury had found that a horse was deodand, and upon motion to quash the inquisition it was argued that " this is an office of entitling, and ought to be publicly and openly found," to which Lord Mansfield said, that was so " by express statutes;" and added, " inquisitions before the coroner are traversable." In the other case, Lord *Kenyon* said, the examination before the coroner is an inquest of office: it is a transaction of notoriety, to which every person has a right of access; and writs of *ad quod damnum* have been frequently set aside for want of this notoriety in the execution of them by the sheriff." Now no such statutes as those alluded to by Lord *Mansfield* can be found. He probably alluded to the statutes of escheators, 34 *Ed.* 3, c. 13; 36 *Ed.* 3, c. 13; 36 *Hen.* 6, c. 16; and 1 *Hen.* 8, c. 8; but they were made to protect the public from the oppressive conduct of those officers, and with that view required that their inquests should in future be taken openly; and they do not in the slightest degree refer or apply to inquests before coroners. The *dictum* of Lord *Kenyon* may also be referred to the same source, namely, the confounding the statutory provisions relating to these inquests of office with coroners' inquests. The statute of *Marlbridge* (c), indeed, declares that at inquests for the death of a man, all persons being twelve years of age ought to appear, unless they have reasonable cause of absence; but that relates only to such persons as are summoned by the coroner, as is evident both from the language of the statute and that of Lord *Coke* in his commentary upon it(d).

(a) 1 Burr. 17.   (c) 52 *Hen.* 3, c. 25.
(b) 3 T. R. 707.   (d) 2 Inst. 147.

But, assuming secondly, that the coroner's Court, is an open Court, still it is a Court of record, of which he is the judge, and as such he possesses, in common with every judge of a Court of record, power to exclude any person not connected with the proceedings, whose presence he deems likely to obstruct the administration of justice, without thereby rendering himself liable to an action. It is not meant to say that the law authorises the judges of the superior Courts to act arbitrarily, and to make the Courts, in effect, close; but the right to have them open is the right of the public and not of any individual, therefore no individual can maintain an action against a judge of record for excluding him. If such a judge acts corruptly in excluding any individual, he is liable to punishment by proceedings of a different kind; but no action can be maintained against him. This power of exclusion is constantly exercised by the judges of various Courts which are confessedly open Courts. The Lord Chancellor hears causes in his private room; can it be contended that an action of trespass would lie against the Lord Chancellor for directing the expulsion of a reporter, or any other individual, who intruded upon him there? Surely not. The judges of assize, when decency requires it, are in the constant habit of ordering all females, and males of tender age, to be excluded from the Courts, Witnesses also, who have been subpœnaed to give evidence, and whose duty it is to be in Court, are frequently ordered out of Court until their testimony is required, when it is suggested that such a course is necessary for the due administration of justice. If every person for whom there is sufficient space has a right to be in Court, he may also have a right to chuse his own station there, and he may chuse to occupy the bench, by the side of the judge, if there is sufficient space for him there. The inconvenience which might result from the exercise of such a right, is a strong argument against its existence. Should a judge act corruptly, either in excluding any individual from his Court, or in

closing his Court from the public, or in giving an improper judgment, or in doing any other wrongful act in his judicial capacity, he is liable to punishment by proceedings of a different kind; if a judge of one of the superior Courts, he may be proceeded against by impeachment; if of one of the inferior Courts, by criminal information or indictment. But it is settled law, that no action at the suit of an individual can be maintained against any judge of a Court of record for any act done by him in the exercise of his judicial functions: the present plaintiff, therefore, has mistaken his remedy, even if he was improperly excluded from the room.

Parke, contrà. The real and highly important public question to be decided in the present case is this: What is the nature of the proceedings before the coroner? Is the inquisition an inquiry of a public nature, for the purpose of publicly ascertaining the fact, and such as takes place in ordinary Courts of justice, or on an inquest of office; or is it an *ex parte* and secret inquiry, such as takes place before grand juries and magistrates, for the purpose of accusing a particular individual? It is confidently submitted that it is the former, and upon three distinct grounds. First, ancient statutes and authorities defining the duties of the coroner and the obligations of the public towards him. Secondly, authorities establishing that individuals have certain rights in respect of inquests, which they cannot exercise unless they are present, and therefore that they have a right to be present. And thirdly, the express *dicta* of judges in modern times. First, the office of coroner is very ancient. "They," said *Doddridge*, J., in *Grange v. Denny*(a), speaking of coroners, "are of so great antiquity, that their commencement is not known." His Court is a Court of record, *Britton*, cap. 3, fol. 3; his functions are various, for besides taking inquests of death, he is to inquire of treasure trove, of wrecks of the sea, and of deodands; 4 *Edw.* 1, st. 2, *De*

(a) 3 Bulst. 176.

Officio Coronatoris, 4 Inst. 271. [*Bayley*, J. By the common law the coroner had authority to hear and determine felonies; while that was the case his Court was analogous to the ordinary Courts of law; but he was deprived of that authority by *Magna Charta*, c. 17.] He has still authority to inquire of the death of man; that inquiry does not necessarily lead to the accusation of any individual, but is often conclusive, as that the deceased was *felo de se*, or died by the visitation of God, &c.; and the possibility that it may lead to such an accusation is not sufficient ground for making such an inquiry, which from its very nature ought to be public. The trial of an action for slander, where words imputing felony are justified, may lead to the accusation of the plaintiff, for he may be tried for the felony on the finding of the jury; yet no lawyer can contend that the trial of the action should therefore be secret. The statute of *Marlbridge* (a) in express words declares, that at inquests for the death of man, all persons being twelve years of age ought to appear; nor can it be maintained with reason, as has been contended on the other side, that this which imposes the obligation of attending inquests, does not also confer the right to attend them. The former part of that chapter remedied the grievance which had been previously felt of amercements imposed upon townships, because all persons of the age of twelve years did not attend the coroner's inquest on all occasions, and provided that there should be no amercement if a sufficient number attended to take the inquest; but it excepts out of that provision inquests for the death of man, and there is nothing, either in the statute or the commentary, indicating that it was intended to apply to such persons only as should be summoned by the coroner. That statute has never been repealed. In *Sir Thomas Smith's History of the Commonwealth* it is said (b), "The impannelling of this (the coroner's) inquest, and the view of the body, is commonly in the street, in an open place, and *in coroná populi;*" and in an anonymous

(a) 52 Hen. 3, c. 25.   (b) Page 96.

case reported by *Freeman*(a), where the Court held that an inquisition of *felo de se* was traversable, Lord *Hale* distinguished it from a *fugam fecit*, observing, that " all the parties that were present at the death of the party are *bound to attend* the coroner's inquest, and their not appearing there is a flying in law, and cannot be contradicted." Secondly, the public have many rights connected with coroners' inquests, which must be defeated if they are not allowed to be present. Lord *Hale*, after stating the argument on both sides, says(b), " The coroner's inquest ought in all cases to hear the evidence upon oath, as well that which maketh for as that which maketh against the prisoner, and the whole evidence ought to be returned with the inquisition;" and *Barclee's case*(c) and *Rex* v. *Scarey*(d), are authorities to the same effect. Now if a person has not a right to be present, he cannot know whether evidence tending to criminate him has been given or not, and cannot, in case it has, be prepared to adduce evidence in answer. It was admitted in the argument of *Cox* v. *Coleridge*(e), that a party has a right to attend by counsel before the coroner's inquest; *à fortiori*, therefore, he has a right to attend in his own person. A party has a right to move to set aside an inquisition for irregularity, *Rex* v. *Hethersall*(f), where the Court said, that " upon affidavit that the jury did not go according to the evidence, or of any indirect proceedings of the coroner, they would grant a *melius inquirendum;*" but if the party is not present he cannot know whether any irregularity has occurred or not. It is said that the proceedings are preliminary, and that therefore they should be private. It must be admitted that to a certain extent they are preliminary and *ex parte*, and that to a certain extent the finding is traversable; but it does not necessarily follow that the inquiry should be private. It partakes of the nature of an

(a) Freeman, 419.

(b) 2 Hale, P. C. 62.

(c) 2 Sid. 90; 2 Hale, P, C. 60.

(d) 1 Leach, C. C. 43, 4th ed.

(e) 2 D. & R. 86; 1 B. & C. 37.

(f) 3 Mod. 80.

inquest of office, at which all the public have a right to be present. That right was secured by the statutes of escheators, which were declaratory of the common law. In *Rex* v. *Bickley* (a), it was held, that the witnesses might be cross-examined, and adverse testimony adduced, by the party interested in the property which was the subject of inquiry, although the finding was traversable; and in *Rex* v. *Killinghall* (b), Lord *Mansfield* assimilated coroners' inquests to other inquests of entitling. The proceedings before a coroner are very different from the proceedings before a grand jury. There, a particular individual is in the first instance accused of a crime; here, no individual is accused in the first instance; that is a proceeding for accusation; this is a proceeding for information only. The oath taken by the jurors is very different: those of the grand jury are sworn to keep their counsel secret; at the coroner's inquest the Court is opened by proclamation, and the oath does not require secrecy. Before the grand jury the party accused cannot produce witnesses; the coroner is bound to hear all the evidence on both sides. The depositions made before the grand jury are not evidence against the prisoner in case of the death of the witnesses; those made before the coroner are, upon the very ground that the party affected by them has a right to be present and cross-examine the witnesses. Thirdly, there are express *dicta* of judges in modern times, that the coroner's inquest is a proceeding to which all persons have a right of access. In *Scott* v. *Shearman* (c), *Blackstone*, J. speaking of a presentment of *fugam fecit* by the coroner's jury, says, " the reason given in some books why this inquest is not traversable, like other inquests of office, is, because of the notoriety of the coroner's inquest *super visum corporis*, at which the inhabitants of all the neighbouring villages are bound to attend, and so the finding of the flight is but in effect recording the absence of the party." In *Rex* v. *Killinghall* (d), Lord *Mansfield*

(a) 3 Price, 454.   (c) 2 H. Bla. 981.
(b) 1 Burr. 17.   (d) 1 Burr. 17.

likens the coroner's inquest to other inquests of office,
which are open by express statutes. And in *Rex* v. *Eriswell*(a), Lord *Kenyon* expressly says, that " the examination
before the coroner is a transaction of notoriety, to which
every one has a right of access." It has been said that the
plaintiff had no right to be present, because if he had that
right, he would also have a right to publish the proceedings, and *Rex* v. *Fisher*(b) and *Rex* v. *Fleet*(c) were cited.
But those cases only shew that a person cannot justify a
publication on the ground of its being a statement of the
proceedings before a coroner, provided it would be otherwise illegal, as where the matter published is of a libellous
or indecent nature. Other cases to the same effect might
be cited, as *Rex* v. *Lee*(d) and *Rex* v. *Carlisle*(e), but none
of them touch the present case; they merely shew that it is
not lawful to publish even a correct account of the proceedings of any Court of justice, if such account contains
matter of a libellous, blasphemous, or indecent nature.
Besides, in arguing the general question here, it cannot be
assumed that the plaintiff was present at the inquest for
the purpose or with the intention of publishing the proceedings. Lastly, it is said that the coroner, as judge of
his Court, has a right to exclude all persons whose presence he may deem likely to interfere with the due administration of justice. It is not necessary to inquire whether
the coroner possesses such a discretionary power or not, because the pleadings do not raise that question; the defendant
has not averred that any such occasion existed for excluding
the plaintiff: he claims by his pleas, not a discretionary
power of excluding persons whom it would be inconvenient
should remain, but an arbitrary, absolute, uncontrollable
right to exclude any person at his own will and pleasure,
and that right, at least, the law does not give him.

Cur. adv. vult.

(a) 3 T. R. 707.   (d) 5 Esp. 123.
(b) 2 Camp. 563.   (e) 3 B. & A. 167.
(c) 1 B. & A. 379.

Lord TENTERDEN now delivered judgment, and after stating the substance of the pleadings, proceeded thus:— Upon this state of the record, it does not appear that the plaintiff had any interest in the matter of the inquest which the coroner was about to take, or any information to offer which might further the objects of the inquiry. If any thing of this kind existed it ought to have been shewn on the part of the plaintiff, and not being shewn, it must be taken not to have existed. I would not, however, be understood to intimate, that if any such matter had appeared our judgment would have been different. But the general question arising upon this record, is only whether a person, in the absence of such matters, can maintain an action of trespass against the coroner for causing him to be put out of the room after his refusal to depart. We are all of opinion that he cannot; and this being our opinion on the general question, it is not necessary to notice the particular points that were suggested in the argument at the bar. The Court of the coroner is a Court of record, of which the coroner is the judge; and it is a general rule, of very great antiquity, that no action will lie against a judge of record for any matter done by him in the exercise of his judicial functions; *Floyd* v. *Barker* (a), *Poole* v. *Gwynne* (b), *Dr. Groenveldt* v. *Dr. Burwell* and others (c), *Hammond* v. *Howell* (d). I shall mention the particulars of the case last cited only. *Hammond* and other jurymen had been fined and imprisoned by the Court at the Old Bailey, for acquitting certain persons of a riot, whom the evidence shewed to be guilty. This was certainly a very strong exercise of authority, calculated to excite, and in fact exciting, great public interest. It was determined by the Court of *Common Pleas*, on a writ of *habeas corpus*, that the fine and imprisonment were contrary to law, and the parties were discharged out of custody. After this, *Hammond* brought an action of trespass against the Recorder of

---

(a) 12 Co. 24.   (c) 1 Ld. Raym. 454.
(b) Lutw. 935, 1560.   (d) 1 Mod. 184; 2 Mod. 218.

London, one of the judges in the commission, for this imprisonment. The defendant, by his plea, shewed the proceedings before the commissioners, and averred that the jury had pronounced an acquittal against plain evidence, and the direction of the Court in matter of law. The plaintiff traversed the finding against evidence, and upon these pleadings it was held, that the action did not lie, because the defendant was a judge of record. This freedom from action and question at the suit of an individual is given by the law to the judges, not so much for their own sake as for the sake of the public and for the advancement of justice, that being free from actions they may be free in thought and independent in judgment, as all who are to administer justice ought to be. And it is not to be supposed beforehand, that those who are selected for the administration of justice will make an ill use of the authority vested in them. Even inferior justices, and those not of record, cannot be called in question for an error of judgment, so long as they act within the bounds of their jurisdiction. In the imperfection of human nature, it is better even that an individual should occasionally suffer a wrong, than that the general course of justice should be impeded and fettered by constant and perpetual restraints and apprehensions on the part of those who are to administer it. Corruption is quite another matter; so also are neglect of duty and misconduct in it. For these, I trust, there is and always will be some due course of punishment by public prosecution. To come, however, to the particular case now before the Court. It is argued, on the part of the plaintiff, that the Court of the coroner is a public Court, that it is and ought to be open to the entrance of all his Majesty's subjects, or at least of so many as the place will contain; and it is averred, and not denied on the record, that on the occasion in question there was room for the presence of the plaintiff. The Court was assembled for an inquest on the view of the body of a person then lying dead. Now it is obvious that such an inquiry ought, for the purposes of justice, in some cases to be conducted in secrecy; it is a preliminary inquiry, which may or may not end in the accusation of a particular individual; it may be requisite that a suspected person should not, in so early a stage, be informed of the suspicion that may be entertained against him, and of the evidence on which it is founded, lest he should elude justice by flight, tampering with witnesses, or otherwise. Another matter, as that of deodand, may be consequential to the inquiry; but nothing that is done will be conclusive upon the person to be affected by it. All is traversable. It was admitted in the argument, that secrecy and exclusion may be proper and necessary when charge and accusation begin. It is obvious that this may begin as soon as the evidence begins. Cases also may occur in which privacy may be requisite for the sake of decency; others in which it may be due to the family of the deceased. Many things must be disclosed to those who are to decide, the publication whereof to the world at large may be productive of mischief without any possibility of good. Who then is to decide whether privacy be necessary or proper? We answer, the coroner, and the coroner alone, and that the propriety of his decision cannot be questioned in an action. In the case of *Hammond* v. *Howell*, before mentioned, the plaintiff, by his traverse, attempted to put in issue for trial before a jury, the question whether the verdict was or was not against evidence, but he was not allowed to do so. And if the reason which may lead the coroner or judge to think privacy necessary cannot be tried, it need not be alleged or shewn in pleading, for nothing need be alleged that is not traversable. Further, it was properly asked in the argument for the defendant, if every man has a right to be present at such an inquest for whose presence there is room in the place where it is holden, why has he not a right to be present at every part of that place? And if every man has a right to chuse his station, and to decide for himself whether there be space to contain his person, it is easy to see that much disorder and confusion may often arise.

1827.

GARNETT
v.
FERRAND,

Even in cases where absolute privacy may not be required, the exclusion of particular persons may be necessary or proper. Who then is to decide upon this? We again answer, the coroner, and the coroner alone, and that the reason of his decision cannot be tried in an action. It will be, in many cases, impossible that a proceeding should be conducted with due order and solemnity, and with the effect that justice demands, if the presiding officer, whether he be judge, coroner, justice or sheriff, have not the control of the proceeding, and the power of admission or exclusion, according to his own discretion. It is not to be expected that any person will act at the peril of being harassed by a multiplicity of actions, and of having his reasons and motives weighed and tried by juries at the suit of individuals who may be dissatisfied with his conduct. There are very few who will not prefer rather to admit disorder and confusion, and all the evil consequences that may follow from the indiscriminate admission of those who may chuse to intrude, than to place themselves in a situation of so great jeopardy. The power of exclusion is necessary to the due administration of justice. There is nothing to shew that it has been abused in the present instance, nor are we aware that it has been abused in any other. For these reasons we are of opinion that the judgment should be entered for the defendant.

Judgment for the defendant.

BENNETT v. APPERLEY, Clerk.

Monday,
28th May.

A writ of sequestration need not be published before the return-day of the writ of levari facias, on which it is founded, nor need a copy of it be affixed on the church door.

THIS was a rule calling upon the Bishop of Hereford to shew cause why he should not make a return, stating what he had levied under a writ of levari facias in this cause, and why he should not give precedence to the sequestration issued upon that writ before the sequestration issued by him in a cause of Devereux v. Apperley.

The affidavits disclosed the following facts:—On the 15th of *August*, 1826, the defendant gave the plaintiff a warrant of attorney to confess judgment for 1400*l.* and upwards. On the 17th of *August* judgment was entered up and a writ of *fieri facias* was issued, directed to the sheriff of *Hereford*, returnable on *Monday* next after the morrow of *All Souls*. The sheriff returned *nulla bona*, but certified that the defendant was a beneficed clerk, rector of the rectory of *Stoke Lacy*, and vicar of the vicarage of *Ocle Pritchard*, both in his bailiwick, and within the diocese of the Bishop of *Hereford*. On the 7th of *November*, 1826, the plaintiff sued out a writ of *levari facias de bonis ecclesiasticis*, directed to the Bishop of *Hereford*, returnable on *Monday* next after eight days of the *Purification*. This writ was delivered at the registry office of the bishop on the 8th of *November*, for the purpose of having sequestrations issued immediately, but none were in fact issued until the 26th of *December*, when they were issued, directed to the plaintiff's attorney, who, on the 7th of *January*, 1827, caused them to be read in the parish churches of the rectory and vicarage before mentioned, and at the church doors; and on the same day caused copies to be fixed on the church doors. On the 3d of *October*, 1826, the defendant gave a warrant of attorney to *Devereux* for 1400*l.* upon which judgment was entered up on the 26th of the same month, and a writ of *fieri facias* was issued, directed to the sheriff of *Hereford*, returnable on the 6th of *November*. That writ was delivered to the sheriff on the 5th of *November*, who, on that day, returned *nulla bona*, and certified that the defendant was a beneficed clerk, &c. On the 6th of *November* a writ of *levari facias* issued at the suit of *Devereux*, returnable on *Wednesday* next after the morrow of *Saint Martin*, and was delivered at the registry office of the Bishop of *Hereford* on the 7th of *November*. At the latter end of *November* writs of sequestration issued at the instance of *Devereux*, directed to one *Evans*, who, on the 3d of *December*, caused the same to be read in the parish churches of *Stoke Lacy* and *Ocle Pritchard*, and at the church doors; but no copies were fixed on the church doors. *Evans*, under these sequestrations, obtained possession of the profits of the livings. It was not usual in the diocese of *Hereford* to publish sequestrations in any other way than by reading them in the church and at the door. The warrant of attorney given to *Devereux* was not stamped when this rule was obtained, but before cause was shewn a proper stamp had been put upon it.

Campbell and *Holroyd* shewed cause. The warrant of attorney being now properly stamped, the rule cannot be sustained upon the objection originally made on that ground, for the Court will not inquire when the stamp was affixed. *Devereux's* writs of sequestration, therefore, founded upon the judgment entered up on that warrant of attorney, are entitled to precedence, inasmuch as the publication of them in the mode usual in the diocese of *Hereford* took place before the issuing of the writs granted to the plaintiff. The fact of that publication having been made after the return day of the writ of *levari facias*, presents no material difficulty; because that writ is a continuing execution, and the bishop has authority to act under it until it has been actually returned, or the debt has been satisfied. *Marsh* v. *Fawcett* (a), *Legassicke* v. *The Bishop of Exeter* (b).

Follett, contrà. The bishop, to whom the writ of *levari facias* is directed, stands precisely in the same situation as the sheriff, when he is called upon to execute the ordinary writ of *fieri facias*. Each derives his authority solely from the writ which he is to execute, and the bishop by his writ of sequestration empowers the sequestrator to seize and take the profits of the benfice, just as the sheriff by his warrant empowers his officer to levy under a *fieri facias*. The mode of executing the process is, in the case of the

(a) 2 H. Bla. 582.   (b) Cited ibid.

sheriff, by seizure, and in the case of the bishop, by publication. But both seizure and publication must be made before the return day of the writ. In *Doe* v. *Bluck* (a) it was held, that a sequestration did not take effect until it was published; and the cases cited on the other side support the same position. Those cases, indeed, only establish, that if the sequestration is published before the writ is returnable, the execution is continuing until the authority of the bishop is terminated by an actual return made. The usual mode of publication in the diocese of *Hereford* cannot control the law which regulates every publication; and the law requires that a copy of the writ shall be fixed on the church door. *Burn's Eccl. Law, tit. Sequestration; Tidd's Practice,* 1060, 6th ed.

Lord TENTERDEN, C. J.—I think this rule ought to be discharged. I am not convinced by any of the cases cited that publication is necessary before the day upon which the *levari facias* is returnable. *Doe* v. *Bluck* (a), as it appears to me, only decided that, until publication, the right of the rector to hold possession and to take the profits of the benefice was not determined, and, therefore, that he might maintain an action of ejectment upon a demise laid of a date prior to publication. But the learned judge who tried that cause expressly said, that after publication, the lessor of the plaintiff could not sue out a writ of possession. I am also of opinion that the mode of publication adopted in this case was sufficient; and that there is no absolute necessity, though it may be convenient, to fix a copy of the writ on the church door.

BAYLEY, J.—I am of the same opinion. The property is bound from the time when the sequestrator is appointed. The only object of publication is to determine, in case of

(a) 3 Campb. 447; 1 Cromp. Prac. 359.

dispute, to whom the right of priority belongs. The justice of the case is palpably against the present plaintiff.

HOLROYD, J. and LITTLEDALE, J. concurred.

Rule discharged.

GENERAL RULE OF COURT.

Easter Term, 8 Geo. 4, 1827.

WHEREAS some doubts have arisen in practice as to the number of defendants' names to be inserted in mesne process in actions by bill:—It is hereby ordered, that from and after the last day of this present term, in all actions by bill, the mesne process shall contain the name of the defendant, (or, if more than one, of all the defendants,) in that action, and shall not contain the name or names of the defendant or defendants in any other action.

BY THE COURT.

The KING *v.* The Inhabitants of RIDGEWELL (*a*).

A paper writing in the form of an agreement between father and son, purporting to be a conveyance of land, with a stipulation for quiet enjoyment of the premises absolutely and for ever, not being under seal, was holden to operate as an agreement, and not to require a deed stamp.

BY an order of two justices *George Aylen* and his wife were removed from *Ridgewell* to *Ashen*, both in the county of *Essex.* On appeal the sessions quashed the order, subject to the opinion of this Court on the following case:—

At the trial of the appeal the respondents proposed to establish a derivative settlement for the pauper *George Aylen,* from his father *Joseph Aylen* the younger, by proving that the father was settled by estate in the appellant parish of *Ashen,* and for that purpose offered in evidence an instrument which had been originally written on unstamped paper, but which, for the purposes of the appeal, had been stamped with a 20*s.* agreement stamp, and a fine of 5*l.* paid at the stamp-office on procuring such 20*s.* stamp to be impressed thereon. The instrument was in the following words:—" An agreement made the 20th day of *February,* 1805, between *Joseph Aylen,* of *Ridgewell,* in the county of *Essex,* blacksmith, of the one part, and *Joseph Aylen* the younger, of the same, blacksmith, of the other part, as follows:—The said *Joseph Aylen* the elder, in consideration of the natural love and affection which he has and bears to his son *Joseph Aylen,* and for the further consideration of the sum of 19*l.* 19*s.* of lawful money of *Great Britain,* does fully, clearly, and absolutely remise, release, and for ever quit claim unto his son *Joseph Aylen* the full and peaceable possession of, in, or to all that moiety or two thirds of a tenement or cottage situate in *Ashen,* otherwise *Esse,* together with the yards and premises and appurtenances thereunto belonging, to hold all the said moiety or two thirds of the aforesaid messuage or tenement, with the hereditaments and appurtenances to the same belonging, to my said son *Joseph Aylen,* and to his heirs and assigns, absolutely and for ever: and I the said *Joseph Aylen* the elder, nor my heirs, nor any other person or persons for me or them, or

(*a*) This and the following cases were decided after the term, by the three puisne Judges sitting in *Banc,* as on former occasions.

Y

in my or their names, or in the right or stead of any of
them, shall or will, by any ways or means, hereafter have,
claim, challenge, or demand any estate, right, title, or interest, be it by last will or testament or otherwise, of, in, or
to the said premises, or any part or parcel thereof, but
from all and every action, right, estate, title, interest, or
demand, of, in, or to the said premises, or any part thereof,
they and every of them shall be utterly excluded and barred
for ever." The execution of the instrument was duly
proved, but the appellants' counsel objected to its admissibility in evidence, on the ground that it had not a proper
stamp; whereupon the Court of Quarter Sessions decided
that it could not be received in evidence, and on that ground
quashed the order of removal, subject to the opinion of
this Court, whether it was admissible in evidence for the
purpose of proving a derivative settlement for the pauper in
the parish of *Ashen*.

Knox and *Mirehouse*, in support of the order of sessions,
contended that the instrument in question was an instrument of conveyance, and therefore required a stamp of 30s.
by statute 44 *Geo*. 3, c. 98, the stamp act then in operation.
Whatever might be the form of the instrument, it is quite
clear that it was intended by the parties that it should
operate as an absolute conveyance, and not as an executory
agreement. It was offered in evidence at the trial of the
appeal as an absolute conveyance, to support a settlement
by estate.

Jessopp and *Dowling*, contrà, contended that this paper
writing was not an instrument of conveyance, it not being
under seal. The intention of the parties had nothing to do
with the question. The paper was offered in evidence, not
to prove title by conveyance, but to explain under what
circumstances the pauper's father had been in possession
of the premises in *Ashen*. All that was contended for on
the part of the respondents was, that it ought to have been

received in evidence, whatever its legal effect might be in determining the settlement.

BAYLEY, J.—The objection made to the production of this instrument in evidence was, that it had only an agreement stamp. Now whether an agreement stamp was sufficient or not, must depend upon the legal effect of the instrument. It is said, that if it had borne a deed stamp, or a 30s. stamp, impressed upon it, that would have been the right stamp, under statute 44 *Geo.* 3, c. 98, which requires that every deed or other instrument of conveyance, surrender, lease, release, grant, appointment, confirmation, assignment, transfer, covenant, or any obligatory instrument, (not otherwise charged in the schedule,) which may be enrolled, shall have a 30s. stamp. Now this is not a deed, because it is not under seal. It is not a conveyance, because it conveys nothing in such a form as to make it operate as a conveyance of land. There cannot be a conveyance of property of this description without a deed. It is not, therefore, a release, grant, &c. Then the only question is, whether it falls under the other words, " any obligatory instrument not otherwise charged in the schedule"? Is this an obligatory instrument? It does not divest the father of his interest in any portion of the land which it purports to convey. At the utmost it is only an executory instrument, and operating as an agreement only. It is an agreement made between father and son, whereby, in consideration of natural love and affection, &c., the father does fully, clearly, and absolutely remise, release, and for ever quit claim, unto his son, the full and peaceable possession of the premises. Does the instrument operate in that way? Clearly it does not, because, not being under seal, it cannot operate as a remise, release, or quitting claim. It can only operate as an agreement on the part of the father that he will forbear to disturb the son in the enjoyment of the premises. Then the instrument goes on, " to hold to the son and his heirs and assigns absolutely and for ever, and the father nor his heirs, nor any other person, &c., shall or will, by any ways or means, thereafter have, claim, challenge, or demand any estate, right, title, or interest, be it by last will or testament or otherwise, to the premises, but from all and every action, right, estate, title, interest, or demand, of, in, or to the premises, they and every of them shall be utterly excluded and barred for ever." Now this is only binding to the extent of an agreement on the part of the father, but it does not transfer any right of property to the son. Operating, therefore, by way of an agreement only, and having an agreement stamp upon it, I think it should have been received in evidence *valead quantum.* Very likely, however, it would not advance the case of the respondents materially, if it be only an agreement and not a conveyance. The case must, however, go back to the sessions to be reheard.

HOLROYD, J.—I am of the same opinion. Assuming that this instrument could operate in point of law as a release, independently of other circumstances, as it would if it were by deed, still it would require a release stamp; but when it depends on other circumstances whether it could operate as a release or not, it does not require a release stamp. Supposing that this could be considered as a lease in writing not under seal, still if it operates as a lease it ought to have been impressed with a lease stamp. Probably the parties themselves thought this instrument would operate as a conveyance, but we cannot look to their intent, if it cannot be carried into operation by force of the instrument itself. This instrument could not operate as a release of any interest in land without being under seal. At the utmost it is only an agreement, being founded on valuable consideration that the father would not molest the son in the enjoyment of the premises. The instrument conveyed no legal estate or interest in land, and as it operates only as an agreement, and, as it has an agreement stamp, I think it ought to have been received in evidence. What effect it will have on the settlement is another matter.

LITTLEDALE, J.—We must look to the legal effect of the instrument, and not to the intention of the parties executing it. This instrument does not convey an interest in land. It professes to be merely an agreement not to disturb the party in possession. In that point of view, probably, the instrument would not require any stamp at all, even as an agreement. At all events, as it has an agreement stamp, and not being a conveyance, it was admissible in evidence. There might be grounds for going into a Court of Equity, for that Court to consider whether the agreement was not sufficient to decree a conveyance. As an agreement it certainly was admissible on the trial of this appeal, whatever effect it might have on the question of settlement or no settlement. Whether the party being let into possession and enjoying the estate, pursuant to the agreement, would gain him a settlement, we are not called upon to determine.

BAYLEY, J.—Although this instrument conveys nothing, yet with actual occupation I am inclined to think a settlement would be thereby gained.

Order of Sessions quashed, and the appeal directed to be reheard (a).

(a) At the rehearing of the appeal at the following sessions the settlement was determined on another ground.

The KING v. The Inhabitants of GREAT YARMOUTH.

Where an order of removal was made by two justices, one of whom appeared by the order to be one of the churchwardens making the complaint:—Held ill.

BY an order of two justices, R. Lenny, his wife and three children, were removed from the parish of Woodbridge, in the county of Suffolk, to the parish of Great Yarmouth, in the county of Norfolk. On appeal, the sessions confirmed the order of removal, subject to the opinion of this Court, whether the order of removal was or was not bad, on the ground that George Thomas, Esq. one of the justices who signed the order, was, at the time when the order was made, one of the churchwardens of the parish of *Woodbridge*.

B. Andrews and *Prendergast*, in support of the order of sessions, admitted that Mr. *Thomas*, the magistrate, was a rated inhabitant as well as a churchwarden of *Woodbridge*, but contended that the order of removal was not bad on that account. Certainly if this point had been argued before the passing of the statute 16 *Geo.* 2, c. 18, the case of *Great Chart* v. *Kennington* (a) would be an authority against the validity of the order; but the statute alluded to was passed for the express purpose of remedying the inconvenience resulting from that decision. By that statute justices for any county, city, borough, or town corporate, within their jurisdiction, are enabled to do all acts appertaining to their office as justices, so far as the same relates to the laws for the relief, maintenance, and settlement of poor persons, and notwithstanding such justices are rated to or chargeable with the taxes, levies, or rates within the parish, township, or place affected by such acts. Where, indeed, the justice is called upon to exercise an appellant jurisdiction, he is disqualified from acting: and by the same act it is enacted, " that no justice shall act in the determination of any appeal to the quarter sessions from any order relating to such parish, township, or place where such justice is charged, taxed, or chargeable." Now it must be contended on the other side, that a justice, who happens to have the whole property in the parish, can make no order to relieve himself from improper burthens, because he is a churchwarden. The only ground upon which this magistrate could be disqualified would be on the ground of interest; but a churchwarden can have no interest in the removal of a pauper, except as a rated inhabitant; and the statute expressly removes all objection to him on that ground, if he happens to be a removing justice. This is not like the case of a justice sitting to investigate his own

(a) Burr. S. C. 194.

accounts as churchwarden. A churchwarden has nothing to do in the removal of a pauper, but to lay an information and complaint before the magistrates; the complaint and information are not taken on oath, and the order of removal is not conclusive, but may be appealed against on the merits. But it does not necessarily follow that Mr. *Thomas* in this case heard the complaint, although he may have subsequently signed the order; for one set of justices may have heard the complaint and another may have signed the order, which would not be irregular, *Rex* v. *Westwood* (a), *Rex* v. *Stanstead* (b). Churchwardens are disinterested public officers, and they are bound to take care of the interests of the inhabitants; and as they are in no way personally interested in the result of a removal, there is no ground for contending that the justice is disqualified from signing the order, although he happens to be a churchwarden.

T. Andrews and *Blunt*, contrà. On the face of it the order of removal involves an absurdity quite inconsistent with law, for the complaint purports to be made by one of the churchwardens *to himself.* Now it never could be in the contemplation of the statute referred to that an order of removal should be made by the person acting as churchwarden. The characters of justice and of churchwarden are quite incompatible. But it is said, on the other side, that the churchwardens had no interest in the event; but that is not so, for, in the event of an appeal, they may be liable to costs. Again, they may be liable personally for removing a pauper maliciously or even improvidently; and it is doubtful whether they could call upon the parish to reimburse them for the consequences of such a proceeding. In *Rex* v. *Gudderidge* (c) it was held, that a justice of the peace, who is a rated inhabitant of a parish, cannot vote at the sessions, either upon the determination of an appeal

(a) 1 Stra. 73.   (c) *Ante*, vol. viii. 217; 5 B. & C. 459.
(b) 2 Salk. 488.

against the accounts of the overseers of his parish, or upon the propriety of granting a case for the opinion of the King's Bench; and the Court there said, that they thought it the safer course to hold that magistrates should not interfere in cases where they were at all interested. The most remote interest ought to be a ground of objection in cases of this nature, even for the sake of appearances. If the objection now made be not upheld, it will involve this absurdity, that the removing justices may be both churchwardens, and then a pauper may be removed against his will from a parish, at the pleasure of two individuals. The removing justices are judges, their act is judicial, and may be appealed against. So that here is a person, a judge in his own suit, determining a complaint made by himself to himself, which is contrary to the principles of natural justice. By law a pauper is only to be removed by justices upon the complaint of parish officers. The concurrence of two distinct classes of persons is essential to the removal of the pauper. The removal of a poor person interferes with his personal liberty, and therefore the protection of that liberty ought not to be narrowed, by allowing the office of magistrate and churchwarden to be exercised by the same person.

BAYLEY, J.—If this case turned upon the question of interest only, and there were no other objection, I think that the fact of this magistrate being a churchwarden would not be a fatal objection to the order of removal. By the statute 16 *Geo.* 2, a person may act in the character of justice although he is a rated inhabitant of the parish; and I do not see that, upon the question of interest, it is possible to predicate of a churchwarden or overseer that he has any interest in the removal of a pauper except in his character of rated inhabitant. He may, indeed, be liable to the payment of costs, if he does the act improperly; but that shews that it is against his interest as churchwarden to do an act which may bring a burthen upon himself, for by so doing he subjects himself to a responsibility which could not otherwise attach to him. In the case of *Rex* v. *Bermondsey* (a) it was decided that the governors of the poor were excluded from being witnesses, although there was a clause in the act of parliament by which rated inhabitants might be witnesses; but in that case the Court thought, that as the governors were made liable to the costs of an appeal in the first · instance, and being parties to the appeal were in that respect to be considered as interested, though in truth only trustees, and entitled to be reimbursed out of the parochial fund, they did not come within the general exception, which rendered rated inhabitants eligible as witnesses. I think, however, that in this case the supposed interest of the magistrate forms no objection, because he has no interest beyond the fact of his being a rated inhabitant. I take the true objection to be this, that as this gentleman is one of the individuals complaining, he is not a competent person to hear and determine his own complaint. I cannot consider him as divested of the character of churchwarden, when he acts as a magistrate. The magisterial act is to be done upon the complaint of the churchwardens and overseers.. The order of removal imports on the face of it, that it is made upon the complaint of the churchwardens and overseers. By the statute 43 *Eliz.* c. 2, the management of the poor is committed to the churchwardens and overseers. Why then, from the nature. of the thing, the complaint must be made by the churchwardens and overseers to the justices. Here there is a. complaint made by churchwardens and overseers, one of whom is Mr. *Thomas*, and he is one of the persons to whom the complaint is made. It appears to me, therefore, that he has been acting in two incompatible characters, and that this order of removal cannot be supported.

HOLROYD, J.—I think likewise, upon the ground intimated by my brother *Bayley*, that, as this order was made by a gentleman acting both as overseer and magistrate, it

(a) 3 East, 5.

1827.

The King
v.
GREAT
YARMOUTH.

cannot be supported. Previous to the passing of the statute 16 *Geo.* 2, c. 18, magistrates, by reason of being rateable to the relief of the poor, were not competent to act in the making of an order of removal, because they were virtually parties to the complaint of chargeability, but by that act this objection has been removed. In this case, however, it appears to me that the churchwardens are not only virtual but actual parties to the complaint. It is quite incompatible and inconsistent that a party should sustain the two characters of complainant and the person to whom the complaint is made, he being a party to the cause, whether otherwise interested or not. The justices are entitled to examine the party making the complaint, and determine upon that examination. Now how could this gentleman hear and determine his own complaint? It appears to me to be quite inconsistent that a man should be a complainant and judge of his own complaint, although he may not have any personal interest in the matter.

LITTLEDALE, J.—I am of the same opinion. Although the act of parliament which has been cited enables justices having an interest in the removal of a pauper, by reason of their being rateable in the parish, to act in the removal, still that does not contemplate cases where there are one set of persons to complain and another to adjudicate, that is to say, churchwardens and overseers contradistinguished from justices who are to hear and determine a complaint. It never contemplated the case of a justice being an overseer, and hearing and determining his own complaint.

Order of Sessions quashed.

The KING v. The Inhabitants of RAMSGATE.

Under 6 *Geo.*
4, c. 57, no set-
tlement can be
acquired by
renting a tene-
ment, unless
the entire rent
for the term of
one whole year
at the least,
whatever its
amount, is
actually paid.

BY an order of two justices, *George Sweetman, Sarah* his
wife, and their two children, were removed from the parish
of *Ramsgate,* in the *Isle of Thanet,* in the county of *Kent,* to
the parish of *St. Lawrence,* in the *Isle of Thanet,* in the
same county. On appeal, the sessions quashed the order,
subject to the opinion of this Court upon the following
case :—

In the month of *April,* 1825, *Sarah Sweetman,* the wife
of the pauper, (the pauper himself being of unsound mind,)
hired of *Robert Croft,* Esq. a house in the parish of *St.
Lawrence,* for one year, at a rent of 15*l. per annum,* payable
quarterly.

The pauper and his family occupied the house for the
year, and the pauper's wife paid the sum of 6*l.* 15*s.* towards
the rent. Soon after the expiration of the year, the landlord distrained upon the pauper's goods for the rent remaining due, and received under such distress, after payment
of the expenses thereof, the sum of 4*l.* 17*s.* 6*d.,* making the
total rent received amount to 11*l.* 12*s.* 6*d.*

Bolland, in support of the order of sessions. The pauper
did not acquire a settlement by renting a tenement in the
parish of *St. Lawrence,* because the whole year's rent was
not paid. Before the 59 *Geo.* 3, c. 50, the coming to settle
and residing forty days on a tenement of the annual value
of 10*l.* conferred a settlement, whether the rent was paid or
not. That statute required, amongst other things, that the
rent should be paid for the term of one whole year. But
that statute applied only to settlements by *renting* tenements, and did not abrogate the old law, under which a settlement might be acquired by paying parochial rates and
taxes in respect of a tenement of the annual value of 10*l.*;
so that it continued necessary to prove the value of the
tenement, which gave rise to expensive litigation. To

remedy this evil, the 6 *Geo.* 4, c. 57, which took effect from the 22d of *June*, 1825, was passed, and the second section of that statute enacts, " that no person shall acquire a settlement in any parish, &c. by reason of settling upon, renting, or paying parochial rates for any tenement, unless such tenement shall consist of a separate and distinct dwelling-house or building, or of land, or of both, *bonâ fide* rented by such person in such parish, &c., at and for the sum of 10*l.* a year at the least, for the term of one whole year; nor unless such house or building, or land, shall be occupied under such yearly hiring, and the rent for the same, *to the amount of* 10*l.* actually paid, for the term of one whole year at the least." Now, the concluding words, " for the term of one whole year at the least," must be construed as applying to both branches of the sentence, and as regulating, therefore, the payment of the rent, as well as the occupation of the tenement. The words " to the amount of 10*l.*" may admit of an argument the other way; but their true import seems to be only, that the yearly rent must be 10*l.* at the least, and so construed they leave the section a positive enactment, that the rent for the term of one whole year, whatever its amount may be, shall be paid, in order to entitle the occupier to a settlement.

. *F. Pollock*, contrà. The construction contended for on the other side would make a dead letter of the most important proviso in the present statute, 6 *Geo.* 4, c. 57. The former statute, 59 *Geo.* 3, c. 50, *did* require payment of one year's entire rent, whatever its amount might be. From thence followed this equally absurd and unjust consequence, that one person renting premises at 1000*l.* a year, and paying 999*l.* of his rent, could not acquire a settlement, while another renting a tenement at only 10*l.* a year, and paying that 10*l.* rent, did acquire a settlement. One of the objects in passing the present act of parliament was to remedy this evil. It is well known that such was the intention of the legislature; the only question is whether they

have adopted words clearly expressive of their intention.
Now the present statute repeals the former, and there is a
marked and important difference in the language of the
two as regards the payment of rent. The 59 Geo. 3, c. 50,
required that *the rent* should be actually paid. The 6 Geo.
4, c. 57, requires that the rent, *to the amount of* 10l. shall
be actually paid. Those are words of limitation; they are
here introduced for the first time; those who so introduced
them must have had a meaning under them; and what
meaning could they have, except that the payment of rent
to the amount of 10l., in respect of one year's occupation,
should be sufficient, although the amount of the rent reserved might exceed 10l.? The only mode of giving a reasonable construction to this enactment seems to be, to read
the words " and the rent for the same to the amount of
10l. actually paid," as if they were in a parenthesis, and
then the construction will be, that in order to acquire a settlement, although the tenement must be occupied for a
year, the payment of rent to the amount of 10l. will be sufficient; which will be the more reasonable, because then
the acquiring of a settlement will depend, as it ought, upon
the ability of the party to pay a certain limited sum.

BAYLEY, J.—It is very desirable in all cases to adhere
to the words of an act of parliament, giving to them that
meaning which they naturally bear in the order in which
they are placed. The statute 59 *Geo.* 3, c. 50, enacts,
" that no person shall acquire a settlement in any parish,
&c. by reason of his dwelling for forty days in any tenement
rented by such person, unless such tenement shall consist
of a house or building within such parish, &c. being a separate and distinct dwelling-house or building, or of land
within such parish, &c., or of both, *bonâ fide* hired by such
person, at and for the sum of 10l. a year at the least, for the
term of one whole year; nor unless such house or building
shall be held, and such land occupied, *and the rent for the
same actually paid,* for the term of one whole year at the

least, by the person hiring the same." That statute, therefore, required that the rent (whatever its amount might be)
should be paid for the term of one whole year. But as
that statute applied only to settlements which might be
gained by reason of the *renting* of a tenement, a settlement
might still be gained by paying parochial rates in respect of
a tenement of the annual value of 10*l.* without complying
with the requisites of that statute ; and that was the cause
of much litigation. The statute 6 *Geo.* 4, c. 57, was passed
to remedy that inconvenience ; and it recites, that the settlement of the poor had in some instances been made to
depend upon the annual value of tenements which they
might have rented, or upon the annual value of tenements
in virtue of which they had paid parochial rates ; and that
the ascertaining such value in such respective cases had
given rise to very expensive litigation ; and that doubts had
been entertained whether the act of 59 *Geo.* 3, c. 50, had
been effectual for the purpose of altering the law in respect
of the necessity of proving the annual value of tenements
so rented ; and that it was expedient that further provision
should be made relating thereto." It then repeals the
former statute, and enacts, " that no person shall acquire a
settlement in any parish, &c., by reason of settling upon,
renting, or paying parochial rates for any tenement, not
being his own property, unless such tenement shall consist
of a separate and distinct dwelling-house or building, or
of land, or of both, *bonâ fide* rented by such person, in such
parish, &c., at and for the sum of 10*l.* a year at the least,
for the term of one whole year ; nor unless such house or
building, or land, shall be occupied under such yearly hiring,
and the rent for the same, to the amount of 10*l.* actually
paid, for the term of one whole year at the least." It is
very material to observe the situation of the words " for
the term of one whole year at the least." They are the
concluding words of a sentence, and must be read according
to the true rule of grammatical construction, as applying to
both branches of the sentence. It is contended that they

apply to the first branch of the sentence only, the occupation of the tenement, and that the words " and the rent for
the same to the amount of 10*l.* actually paid" should be read
as if they were in a parenthesis; but I can find nothing,
either in the recital, or in any of the previous provisions of
the act, that warrants me in so reading them. I think they
must be read in the plain sense attributable to them in the
order in which they are placed in the act. If the legislature
had intended that payment of rent to the amount of 10*l.*
should be sufficient for acquiring a settlement, they should,
and I cannot help thinking they would, have introduced the
words, " for the term of one whole year at the least," immediately after the words relating to the occupation. I
admit that the words " to the amount of 10*l.*" create some
difficulty, but I think that difficulty is not such as to justify
us in construing them as if they were placed in an order
different from that in which we find them. Taking them in
that order, their application cannot be confined to the first
branch of the sentence. The effect of this construction
will certainly be, that a person renting premises at however
high a rent, and not paying a year's entire rent, will not
acquire a settlement. But the other construction would
have this effect, that a person who rented premises at 15*l.*
a year, and held them three years, would acquire a settlement by paying 10*l.* on account of one year's rent; and I
cannot think that was intended. Upon the whole, I think
we are bound to read the words of this statute in the sense
naturally belonging to them in the order in which they are
placed, and so reading them I am of opinion that the words
" for the term of one whole year at the least," cannot be
confined to the first branch of the sentence, and, consequently, that the whole rent reserved, whatever its amount,
must be paid for the term of one whole year at the least.
That not having been done in this case, I am of opinion
that the pauper gained no settlement in the parish of *St.
Lawrence*, and, therefore, that the order of sessions must
be quashed.

HOLROYD, J.—I am of the same opinion. The question is not without difficulty, but I think, upon the whole, that the words " for the term of one whole year at the least" must be construed according to their nature and import in the order in which they stand in the act of parliament, and so construing them, it seems to me that the entire rent, which must amount to 10l. a year, but which may exceed that sum, must be paid for the term of one whole year at least, whether it exceed 10l. or not.

LITTLEDALE, J. concurred.

Order of sessions quashed (a).

(a) The decision in this case was afterwards confirmed, by the whole Court, in the case of Rex v. Ashby-de-la-Hay, 2 M. & R. 21; 8 B. & C. 27; 1 M. & R. Mag. Cas. 273. The legislature have, however, since proved that these decisions were contrary to their intention, in passing the statute 6 Geo. 4, c. 57, for by a later statute, 1 Will. 4, c. 18, it is expressly enacted that a payment of rent to the amount of 10l. shall be sufficient to confer a settlement.— ED. June, 1831.

There was another point argued in this case, namely, that part of the rent having been paid by means of a distress, that was not a payment to satisfy the statute 6 Geo. 4, c. 57; but as the judgment of the Court did not proceed on that ground, it was deemed unnecessary to state the arguments. It may be observed, however, that the point does not appear to have been ever expressly decided. In Rex v. Carshalton, ante, 132; 6 B. & C. 93; 4 D. & R. Mag. Cas. 249, where part of the rent was paid by means of a distress, the point was raised, but not settled. There the pauper occupied more than a year, but the rent was not paid until after his death, and it was held that a payment after his death by the means of distress and sale of his goods, did not satisfy the statute. But it was admitted in argument, that if the distress had been made before the pauper's death, the statute would have been substantially complied with. And see Rex v. Ampthill, 4 D. & R. 447; 2 B. & C. 847; 2 D. & R. Mag. Cas. 297.

The KING v. KENYON.

A return to a *certiorari* signed by justices, without their descriptions as such, and without their seals, is bad; but the Court will send it back to them for amendment.

An order for stopping up an unnecessary *footway* under 55 *Geo.* 3, c. 68, s. 2, must state distinctly the parish in which the footway lies, must describe its length and breadth, and, *Semble,* must order it to be sold as well as stopped up.

TWO magistrates for the county of *Lancaster*, by an order made in petty sessions, certified as follows:—

"We have viewed a certain public footway over and across the lands of *W. R.* in the parish of *Flixton*, beginning at, &c. and ending at, &c. and two public footways, being branches of the said first-mentioned footway, one of which runs from the east side of the said first-mentioned footway, across *the said lands* of the said *R. W.* from, &c. to, &c. and the other runs from the west side of the said first mentioned footway, across *the lands* of the said *W. R.* from, &c. to, &c.; and also one other public footway, beginning at, &c. and running over and across *the lands* of the said *R. W.* to, &c.; and we do certify, that the said several public footways did, and each of them did appear to us to be unnecessary. We therefore, pursuant to the statute in that case made and provided, do hereby, at the said special sessions, order the said footways to be severally stopped up."

This order was confirmed by the sessions on appeal, but was afterwards duly removed into this Court by *certiorari*, directed to the justices of *Lancashire*, and a rule obtained for quashing it. In *Michaelmas* term, 1826,

Courtenay, in support of the order, took a preliminary objection, that the return to the *certiorari* was bad, it being signed by four persons, who did not describe themselves as justices of *Lancashire*, and had not put their seals to the return.

The Court then suggested that he should take a rule to shew cause why the return to the *certiorari* should not be quashed, and that the other side should take a cross rule for leave to amend. In *Hilary* term, 1827,

Courtenay, Armstrong, and *Aglionby,* shewed cause against the latter rule. The return is clearly bad, and must be quashed, unless · the Court shall allow an amendment, *Ashley's case* (*a*); which they will not do in the present case. Indeed, it seems very doubtful whether they have authority to do so. Such amendments are never allowed, except where they are authorised by some express act of parliament. Thus the 21 *Jac.* 1, c. 13, expressly provides, that, after verdict, judgment shall not be stayed for want of the signature of the sheriff or other proper officer to the return of the *venire facias.* The subsequent statutes of 16 and 17 *Car.* 2, c. 8, 9 *Ann.* c. 20, and 5 *Geo.* 1, c. 13, give the power of making amendments in certain other instances, the inference from which is, that such an authority is not inherent in the Court, but must be conferred upon them by legislative enactment (*b*). But supposing the Court have the power, they will not have the inclination to allow this amendment. The object of this amendment is to reverse the judgment of the Court of quarter sessions, and Lord *Holt,* C. J. said, in *Walker* v. *Slackoe* (*c*), that the statutes only authorised amendments in support of judgments. In *Rex* v. *The Mayor of Grampound* (*d*), Lord *Kenyon,* C. J. said, " I wish that could be attained which Lord *Hardwicke* in the case before him (*e*) lamented could not be done, namely, ' that these amendments were reducible to some certain rules ;' but there being no such rule, each particular case must be left to the sound discretion of the Court. And the best principle seems to be that on which Lord *Hard-*

1827.

The KING
v.
KENYON.

(*a*) 2 Salk. 479. That case only decided that a return to a *certiorari* made, not by two justices, but by the clerk of the peace, who was not the person to whom the *certiorari* was directed, was bad; and in· *Rex* v. *Pickersgill,* Cald. 297, it is said that a return to a *certiorari* need not be under seal.

(*b*) In *Rex* v. *The Mayor of Grampound,* 7 T. R. 699, which

was a motion to amend a return to a *mandamus* made by a corporation, Lord *Kenyon,* C. J. said, " Amendments of this kind are not made under the, statutes of *jeofails,* but under the general authority of the Court."

(*c*) 5 Mod. 69.

(*d*) 7 T. R. 699.

(*e*) *Rex* v. *Ellames,* Rep. temp. Hardwicke, 42.

z z 2

wicke relied in the same case, that an amendment shall or shall not be permitted to be made, as it will best tend to the furtherance of justice:" a principle which is not shewn to apply to the present case. In *Rex* v. *Newton*(a), where the objection to the return to a *certiorari* was that it was not made by the proper persons, no hint of an amendment was thrown out, but the party moved to quash their own *certiorari*, which was done. *Rex* v. *Atkinson*(b) will be relied on by the other side. There the caption of an indictment, which had been removed into this Court by *certiorari*, was allowed to be amended; but that was upon the ground that a copy only of the caption had been returned, and that the amendment would make the copy correspond with the original. In this case the return is not a copy, and there is really nothing to amend by. At all events, the return cannot be taken off the file and sent back to the justices: they must be brought into Court to make the amendment, *Rex* v. *Franklin*(c), *Rex* v. *Serjeant*(d).

Scarlett and *Coltman*, contrà, were stopped by *Abbott*, C. J. and

PER CURIAM.—We think we ought not only to permit the justices to perfect the return, by putting their own proper descriptions and their seals to it, but that we ought to compel them to do so, because otherwise we should enable them, either wilfully or by negligence, to defeat the process of this Court.

Rule absolute.

The return was amended accordingly, and the sufficiency of the order was now discussed.

Courtenay, Armstrong, and *Aglionby,* in support of the order. Three objections are taken to this order. First,

(a) Burr. S. C. 157.

(b) E. 24 *Geo.* 3, 1 Saund. 249, n. (1).

(c) 11 Mod. 413.

(d) 1 Saund. 250, e.

that the lands over which the footways pass are not stated to be in the parish of *Flixton*. Secondly, that the length and breadth of the footways are not stated. And, thirdly, that there ought to have been a separate order for each footway. First, the footway first mentioned in the order is expressly stated to run " over and across the lands of *R. W.* in the parish of *Flixton*;" and that next mentioned is stated to run " across *the said* lands of *the said R. W.*;" so far, therefore, the order is clearly unobjectionable. It is true that 'the' other lands are described as running " across the lands, (omitting the word *said*,) of *the said R. W.*;" but no other lands of *R. W.* are mentioned in the order besides those which are expressly alleged to be in the parish of *Flixton*, therefore the Court will intend that all the lands and all the footways are in that parish; *Rex* v. *Normanton* (d). Where an order of justices is doubtful, the Court will intend that they have done right; *Rex* v. *Mayfield* (b). At all events the order is good for the two footways expressly alleged to be in the parish. [*Bayley*, J. There are cases in which an order may be good in part and bad in part; but I think this is not one of them: here the validity or invalidity of the order as to one part may be most essential as to the residue.] Secondly, it is quite unnecessary to set out the length and breadth of the footways. It can be of no advantage to the public to know the dimensions of a road that is stopped up. Whatever its dimensions are, it is equally stopped up, and the public have nothing more to do with it. Where a new road is set out the case is different; there it may be necessary to state the dimensions, in order that the public may know what they have a right to use; *Davison* v. *Gill* (c). [*Bayley*, J. The eighteenth form in the schedule to the 13 *Geo.* 3, c. 78, states both the length and breadth of the road stopped up.] But that applies only to cases where the soil of the old road is to be sold; and the soil of an old footway cannot be sold either under the provisions of that statute or of the

(a) Burr. S. C. 213.   (b) Burr. S. C. 453.   (c) 1 East. 64.

55 *Geo.* 3, c. 68. The second section of the latter statute will be relied upon as bearing against the order on this point; but the argument will prove fallacious. That clause commences, after enumerating highways, bridleways, and footways, by empowering justices at petty sessions to divert, turn, and stop up *footways;* and to divert, turn, stop up and inclose, *sell and dispose of,* highways, and bridleways, *omitting footways;* and then proceeds to enact, that if it shall appear to the justices upon view that any highway, bridleway, *or footway,* is unnecessary, they may make an order to stop up, *and sell and dispose of,* such unnecessary highway, bridleway, *or footway.* Now there can be no doubt that in the latter part of that clause the word " footway" has been inserted by mistake; for there can be no reason for empowering the justices to sell an old footway when it is only stopped up, and withholding the same power from them when it is diverted and stopped up. At any rate, for the purpose of this objection, it ought to appear upon the face of the order, which it does not, that the public had a right to the soil of the footway, so that there would be a subject-matter of sale. Thirdly, it was not requisite to have a separate order for each footway. It is true that in the margin to the eighteenth form in the schedule to the statute 13 *Geo.* 3, c. 78, it is said, " if there are more highways than one to be stopped up, there should be a separate order for each." It must also be admitted that the same note is to be found in the margin of the Parliament Roll. But still it cannot be considered as an authority upon the point, because it is not supported by anything in the body of the statute. There is no such legislative provision to be found either in the 13 *Geo.* 3, c. 78, or in the 55 *Geo.* 3, c. 68; nor does reason or expediency appear to make it necessary. Besides, the note itself is confined to *highways;* it does not mention *footways:* and still further, all the footways in this case in reality constitute but one footway.

Coltman, contrà, was stopped by the Court.

BAYLEY, J.—There are two grounds upon which I am of opinion that this order cannot be supported. In the first place, I think it does not sufficiently describe the parish in which some of the footways ordered to be stopped up lie. Secondly, it does not in any degree describe the length or breadth of those footways, or order them to be sold. Now, upon the first point, the order is notice to the inhabitants of the parish that the footway is about to be stopped up; that is a measure in which they are all more or less interested. Therefore the order ought clearly and explicitly to describe the local situation of the footway, so that every inhabitant may have the opportunity of appealing against it, if he is so minded. The first of these footways is described as running across lands of *R. W.* in the parish of *Flixton*; the second as running across the *said* lands of the said *R. W.*; and, though the parish is there omitted, I think the word " said" sufficiently fixes the situation of the lands, and, consequently, of the footway. But in the description of the third and fourth footways, both the name of the parish itself, and the word " said," as a reference to it, are dropped, and they are merely stated to run across *the lands* of *R. W.*, and we cannot assume that *the lands* are *the said lands;* and then the order is bad, because there is nothing to shew that those footways are in the parish of *Flixton*. As to the other objection, I agree that under the 13 *Geo.* 3, c. 78, no power is given to stop up any highway, bridleway, or footway, except where another is substituted for it. But the 55 *Geo.* 3, c. 68, s. 2, provides, first, for the case of substituting a new way for an old one; and then follows the provision upon which this question turns—" and also when it shall appear upon the view of any two or more of the said justices of the peace, that any public highway, bridleway, or footway, is unnecessary, it shall and may be lawful, by order of such justices, or any two of them, to stop up and to sell and dispose of such unnecessary highway, bridleway, or footway." By the words of this enactment it is clear that an order to stop up a footway must also be an order to sell; but it is said that the word "footway" has been inserted there by mistake, and that the legislature did not intend this power of sale to include old footways. Now, referring to the former statute, 13 *Geo. 3,* c. 78, it seems clear to me that such was their intention. It is true that by that statute no power was given to stop up an old footway without making a new one; but wherever that was done, the old footway was to be disposed of by some mode or other, though not by sale; and the subsequent statute having given power to stop up unnecessary footways, it was reasonable that the legislature should make a provision for converting them into money for the use of the public. Then if the justices are to make an order for stopping up *and* selling, it cannot be good unless it applies to both. The provision for each of those acts must be made at the same time, and even if that were not so, still the order must state the length and breadth of the footway stopped up, in order that it may be known what is afterwards to be sold. For these reasons I am of opinion that this order is bad, and must be quashed.

HOLROYD, J. and LITTLEDALE, J. concurred.

Order quashed.

W. R. BROWNE *v.* LEE.

"Grant of annuity" is a sufficient description in the memorial of an annuity deed containing special covenants.

A surety may sue a co-surety for payments made by the former, on account of an annuity, notwithstanding the bankruptcy and certificate of the latter; a surety not being a creditor within the 49 *Geo.* 3, c. 121, s. 17.

Where the grantor of an annuity assigned it, together with all the securities, for a valuable consideration, to *A.,* part of which belonged to *B.,* one of the co-sureties for payment of the annuity, and it was agreed by deed between *A.* and *B.* that the former should retain out of the annual payments sufficient to pay him the principal sum advanced, together with interest, and that when he should have been paid principal and interest the annuity should be for the benefit of *B.*: Held, that the annuity did not thereby become extinguished, and that the co-sureties still remained liable to contribution to *A.* although *B.* had assigned stock for further securing the payment of the annuity.

THIS was an action of assumpsit for the sum of 454*l.* 8*s.* money paid by the plaintiff to the defendant's use. Pleas, 1st. non-assumpsit, and, secondly, the defendant's bank-

ruptcy and certificate. At the trial before Lord *Tenterden*,
C. J. at the sittings in *London* before *Michaelmas* term,
1825, a verdict was found for the plaintiff, subject to the
opinion of the Court on the following case:—

By indenture, made the 24th of *November*, 1818, between
J. H. *Browne*, of the first part, the plaintiff of the second
part, the defendant and H. H. *Browne* of the third part,
B. *Hey* of the fourth part, and T. *Horton* of the fifth part;
J. H. *Browne*, in consideration of 2000*l.* paid in manner
in the indenture mentioned, covenanted with B. *Hey* to pay
for his use one annuity of 230*l.* 10*s.* during the life of him
J. H. *Browne;* and the plaintiff, the defendant, and H. H.
Browne jointly and severally covenanted and agreed with
the said B. *Hey*, his executors, &c. that they would effec-
tually guarantee the payment of the annuity to B. *Hey*, and
would well and truly pay to him, B. *Hey*, on demand, all
or such part of the annuity as should be in arrear, together
with all costs, &c. which should or might have been incurred by him, B. *Hey*, in consequence of the non-payment
of the same or any part thereof. The plaintiff also by the
same deed, at the request of J. H. *Browne*, granted, sold,
assigned, transferred, set over and confirmed unto the said
T. *Horton*, his executors, &c. all that the balance or residue
or so much as should remain of the sum of 5000*l.* four per
cent. annuities therein mentioned, (after setting apart and
deducting the principal sum of 2000*l.* as therein-before was
mentioned,) to which the plaintiff, his executors, &c. should
or might become, or, if the said indenture had not been
made, would have become entitled, upon the decease of one,
Johnson, therein mentioned, under the will of H. H. *Browne*,
deceased. The annuity was payable by quarterly payments
on the 24th of *February*, 24th of *May*, 24th of *August*,
and 24th of *November*, in each year. This indenture was
duly executed by all the parties. A memorial, pursuant to
the 53 *Geo.* 3, was inrolled on the 4th of *December*, 1818,
and in the column headed, "nature of the instrument,"
were the words "grant of annuity." About the beginning

of 1821, *J. H. Browne*, the grantor, and *H. H. Browne*, one of the sureties, became insolvent, and on the 30th of *June*, 1821, a commission of bankrupt was issued against the defendant, under which he was found bankrupt, and duly obtained his certificate on the 11th of *September* following. At the time such commission issued, there were two quarterly payments of the annuity due and unpaid. After the defendant's bankruptcy the plaintiff, his co-surety, made the following payments in respect of the arrears of the annuity, viz. 110*l.* on the 21st of *January*, 1822, and 100*l.* on the 5th of *November*, 1822; the plaintiff received from the defendant, on the 17th of the same month of *November*, 1822, 70*l.* as being in satisfaction of one-third of the said sums of 110*l.* and 100*l.* together with costs, upon a settlement between them of two actions then pending in respect of such payments. Subsequent to this transaction, viz. on the 8th of *October*, 1823, the plaintiff paid to Mr. *Hey* 75*l.*, and on the 17th of *November*, 1823, the defendant paid the plaintiff, under threat of arrest, the further sum of 67*l.* 10*s.* for contribution, and the plaintiff's attorney thereupon gave the following receipt, without any specification as to time: —" Received, 17th *November*, 1823, of Mr. *Lee*, 67*l.* 10*s.* in respect of Mr. *W. R. Browne*'s claim on him for contribution for Mr. *Hey*'s annuity." On the 1st of *May*, 1824, there being at that time arrears of the annuity due, *Hey*, by indorsement on the indenture, in consideration of 1995*l.* granted, sold and assigned this annuity to *Wilkinson*, his executors, &c. and the full benefit and advantage of all covenants, powers, and remedies thereby given for securing and enforcing payment of the annuity, and all the estate, title and interest of him (*Hey*) therein and thereto; *habendum* to *Wilkinson* thenceforth during the natural life of *J. H. Browne*, subject to the proviso for re-purchase therein contained; and further, all arrears of the quarterly or other payments of the annuity then due and unpaid, and all costs and expenses on account thereof, or of the non-payment thereof, and also the judgment entered up by virtue of the warrant of attorney therein mentioned against *J. H. Browne* the defendant, the plaintiff, and *H. H. Browne*, at the suit of *Hey*, in the Court of *King's Bench*, for 1000*l.*, and all sums of money thereafter to become payable for the redemption or re-purchase of the annuity or otherwise in relation thereto. *Habendum* the same to *Wilkinson*, his executors, &c. as his and their own proper goods and chattels and effects absolutely. By another indenture of the same date, viz. 1st of *May*, 1824, made between *Wilkinson* of the one part, and the plaintiff of the other part, after reciting among other things that the sum of 995*l.*, part of the said sum of 1995*l.*, the consideration money before mentioned for the purchase of the annuity and the arrears thereof, and the costs, charges and expenses aforesaid, was the money of the plaintiff *W. R. Browne*, and not the money of *Wilkinson*, but that 1000*l.*, the residue thereof, was the money of *Wilkinson*, and that upon the treaty for the purchase of the annuity by *Wilkinson* from *Hey*, it had been agreed between *Wilkinson* and the plaintiff that the annuity, with the arrears thereof and the securities for the same, should be so purchased by or in the name of *Wilkinson*, to secure to him the re-payment of the said sum of 1000*l.* and interest; and then for the benefit of the plaintiff *W. R. Browne*, it was witnessed, that in pursuance of the agreement and for better securing the payment of the 1000*l.*, part of the 1995*l.*, *Wilkinson* should stand and be possessed of the annuity, and the arrears and the other securities for the same, upon trust that he, *Wilkinson*, should receive and enforce payment of the same when and as the same should from time to time become due, and should take and prosecute all actions, &c. and out of the monies to be received to retain and repay himself the 1000*l.* advanced by him, and interest at the rate of 5*l.* per cent. from the date thereof, and subject thereto for the absolute benefit of the plaintiff; and the plaintiff covenanted that he would, on demand, pay or cause to be paid to *Wilkinson* the 1000*l.* and would in the meantime pay to him, *Wilkinson*, 5*l.* per cent. interest for the same, such interest to be payable half-yearly from the date of the said indenture. In making the above arrangement with the grantee, *Hey*, by which he assigned the annuity to *Wilkinson* for 1995*l.*, the parties made up the account, taking it as a mortgage at 5*l.* per cent. from the beginning, and giving credit for the difference between 5*l.* per cent. upon 2000*l.* and the annuity. The grantee was entitled to more. After the assignment to *Wilkinson*, he received from the plaintiff, by credit on transactions of business, sums equal to the amount of the annuity, up to *December*, 1824, and gave a receipt as for the annuity, but he considered the money as interest and partial payment of his principal.

F. Pollock, for the plaintiff. The defendant is at all events liable to contribution to the extent of one third of the amount which the plaintiff has been compelled to pay on account of the annuity. On the other side it will doubtless be contended that the annuity deed was void for want of a proper memorial pursuant to the statute. That objection, however, cannot prevail. The description of the instrument in the memorial is a " grant of annuity." Now this is a sufficient description of the nature of the instrument as required by the annuity act, 53 *Geo.* 3, c. 141. In *Horwood* v. *Underhill* (a) it was held, that if the grantor of an annuity secures it by a bond, whereby he binds himself, his heirs, &c., it is not necessary that the memorial of the bond should describe it as binding his heirs. That case depended upon the annuity act, 17 *Geo.* 3, c. 26; but the present annuity act is framed in like manner with that, as to what the memorial shall contain. A covenant to pay an annuity may well be called a grant of it. The substance of the deed is a grant. But the late case of *Crowther* v. *Wentworth* (b) is an authority expressly in point. There an annuity was granted by an indenture which also contained a release of a former annuity, and it was held that it was

(a) 4 Taunt. 346.   (b) *Ante*, 286; 6 B. & C. 366.

sufficient to describe the annuity deed in the memorial as a grant of an annuity. This objection therefore being thus disposed of, and it being manifest that the plaintiff has been compelled, as one of the sureties, to pay money on account of the annuity, it is clear that the plaintiff has at least a right to call upon the defendant, his co-surety, to contribute that portion of the sum paid which he ought in justice to have paid himself. It is clear that the defendant would be liable in equity, but it is no less clear that he would be also liable in a Court of law, because the claim is founded upon a fixed principle of justice. There is no doubt that a creditor has a right to resort to any one of several sureties for the whole of his debt, or to each for a proportion, but if he thinks proper to sue one only for the whole, that one may in his turn resort to his co-sureties for their respective contributions, so as to prevent his being damnified beyond the amount to which, in natural justice, he was individually liable. This point seems scarcely disputable. It certainly would not be in equity, *Peter* v. *Rich* (a), *Craythorne* v. *Swinburne* (b); and there is no reason why the like principle should not be acted upon in a Court of law. Then, thirdly, the defendant's bankruptcy and certificate is no bar to this action, because at the time of the bankruptcy the plaintiff was not in a condition to prove the present claim as a debt. At that time it was uncertain whether he would ever have any claim against the defendant as his co-surety, for until the default of the principal, the plaintiff himself could not have become liable, and the statute, 49 *Geo.* 3, c. 121, s. 8, applies only to those cases where the surety is in a condition to prove. But in *Flanagan* v. *Watkins* (c) it was held, that a surety under an annuity deed is not entitled, under the statute above-mentioned, to prove the value of the annuity as a debt under the commission, and therefore where such a surety had redeemed the annuity subsequently to the bankruptcy, the Court decided that he was entitled to maintain an action for the value against the

(a) 1 Bro. C. C. 34.   (b) 14 Ves. 164.   (c) 3 B. & A. 186.

bankrupt, who had obtained his certificate, and that, although the grantee had proved under the 17th section of the statute. Then the last question is, whether the annuity was extinguished by the deed of the 1st of *May*, 1824. It will be contended, on the other side, that that in substance was a re-purchase of the annuity by the plaintiff. In terms that is not quite so. [*Bayley*, J. At law *Wilkinson* is the holder of the annuity.] That certainly would be the most favourable manner in which the transaction could be viewed. The annuity was assigned by the grantee to *Wilkinson* for 1995*l*. Part of that money belonged to the plaintiff and part to *Wilkinson*, and the latter was to have the annuity as a security for the re-payment of his 1000*l*., but as soon as that was repaid, together with interest, the annuity was to belong to the plaintiff; but still this arrangement would not deprive the plaintiff of his remedy against the defendant as his co-surety for the payment of the annuity. As between the plaintiff and the defendant it continued a subsisting annuity, and as the transaction continued perfect in point of form, the legal liability of the several parties remain undisturbed. On these grounds the plaintiff is entitled to recover against the defendant at least one third of the amount which he has been compelled to pay in respect of the annuity.

E. Alderson, contrà. The defendant is entitled to the judgment of the Court. The first objection arising on the case is, that the memorial of the annuity deed is defective, for not stating the assignment of stock as a farther security to the grantee. It may not be necessary to set out in the memorial all the parts of the deed, and all the covenants, as was held in *Crowther* v. *Wentworth*, but as the assignment of stock was to be an additional security to the grantee, it was most material to record that part of the transaction in the memorial, for that was something more than the mere grant of an annuity. The statute requires that the nature of the whole instrument shall be described in the memorial. Now here the instrument is described only in part. This is a much stronger case than *Butler* v. *Capel* (a). In that case the memorial described the instrument by which the annuity was secured as an assignment of certain hereditaments, and it appeared that the instrument was in fact an underlease; but the Court held that in popular language such an instrument was sufficiently described in compliance with the terms of the statute. Secondly, the question is to what amount the defendant is liable for contribution, assuming he is liable at all. This being an action for money paid to the use of the defendant, the principle on which such actions are founded is stated in *Deering* v. *Earl Winchelsea* (b), and *Cowell* v. *Edwards* (c), namely, that sureties are, as between themselves, in *æquali jure*, and shall contribute only in their respective proportions. So that according to the authority of these cases the defendant is at law only liable to pay his proportionate share, namely, one third. Thirdly, however, even as to this proportion, the defendant is discharged by his bankruptcy and certificate. The statute 49 *Geo.* 3, c. 121, s. 17, makes no distinction between a principal and a surety. By that statute it is competent for any annuity creditor of the bankrupt to prove under the commission as a creditor for the value of his annuity, and the certificate is made a bar against all demands in respect of such annuity, the arrears and future payments thereof, in the same manner as it would be' with respect to any other debt which might be proved under the commission. Therefore as the value of the annuity is considered a debt, the grantee might have proved the amount as a debt under the commission. It follows then that as the grantee of the annuity was a creditor of the defendant, the certificate is not only a bar to the grantee, but to the claim of the plaintiff as surety. In the case of *Baxter* v. *Nichols* (d) it was held that the bankruptcy and

(a) *Ante*, vol. iii. 485; 2 B. & C. 251.

(b) 2 Bos. & Pul. 270.

(c) *Ib.* 268.

(d) 4 Taunt. 90.

certificate of one of several joint grantors of an annuity and covenantors for payment discharges the bankrupt, but not his co-defendants; but there the Court recognized no distinction between a principal and surety. [*Bayley*, J. In that case the surety was considered as a grantor. The surety may not be liable until the default of his principal.] Then lastly, the question is whether this annuity has not been extinguished by the deed of the 1st of *May*, 1824. The effect of that deed is, in law, to relieve the defendant as a surety from all subsequent liability to the payment of the annuity. Before the payments, in respect of which the defendant is sought to be made liable, the plaintiff had purchased the grantee's interest in the annuity. If a principal redeems an annuity he cannot call upon his sureties. So if one of several sureties redeems an annuity, he cannot call upon his co-sureties. Here the plaintiff, by becoming substantially the assignee of the annuity, has made himself the party to receive and to pay it. He therefore stands in the situation of a principal who has redeemed an annuity. *Darwin* v. *Lincoln* (a). [*Bayley*, J. All that the Court there decided was, that a surety, who charges his estate in fee simple, of which he was seised in possession at the time of granting an annuity, with the payment of it, and which estate is of greater annual value than the annuity, is a grantor within the meaning of the statute, and therefore no memorial is requisite.] But the effect of this arrangement betwixt *Wilkinson* and the plaintiff is materially to alter the sitituation of the defendant, and renders him liable to a greater responsibility than he otherwise would be subjected to. The plaintiff had originally conveyed property to the grantee for better securing the payment of the annuity, but by this arrangement that property as well as the annuity having become again vested in the plaintiff, the defendant would lose the benefit of that additional security for the arrears which might become due.

(a) 5 B. & A. 441.

BAYLEY, J.—It seems to me that in this case the plaintiff is entitled to recover. I think, however, that he can only recover at law one third of the money which he has paid on account of this annuity. There are indeed cases in equity in which a different doctrine has been held, but they proceeded on equitable principles. In one case (a) one of three sureties having paid a sum of money, it was holden that he was entitled to recover one moiety from another of the co-sureties, the third having become insolvent, but I think that at law co-sureties are only liable to the extent to which they would be originally liable, and that the insolvency of one does not cast any additional obligation on other persons who are under suretyship. The second objection which has been argued is, that the nature of this annuity deed has not been properly described in the memorial in compliance with the annuity act. It has been described as merely " a grant of annuity." By the second section of the statute 53 Geo. 3, c. 141, it is required that within thirty days after the execution of every deed, &c. there shall be a memorial enrolled in the High Court of Chancery, of what?—of the date of the instrument, the names of all the parties and of all the witnesses thereto, of the persons for whose lives the annuity is granted, of the persons by whom the same is to be beneficially received, the pecuniary consideration for granting the same, the annual sum or sums to be paid, in the form and to the effect following, with such alterations therein as the circumstances or nature of any particular case may require. Now there is nothing in the enacting part of this clause which requires the nature of the instrument to be described. We are left to collect from the schedule which follows and the columns therein, what is meant by " the nature of the instrument." One of those columns is headed " nature of the instrument," and under that head there are given instances of the description of the nature of the instrument which the statute requires, namely, " lease and release;" " Warrant of at-

(a) Peters v. Rich, 1 Bro. C. C. 34.

torney to confess judgment;" " Bond and penalty." There is no obligation here on the party to describe the property on which the annuity is secured. Now this part of the statute has received a judicial decision in the case of *Butler* v. *Capell*, referred to in the course of the argument. There, under the head of " nature of the instrument," the memorial described it as an assignment of " certain hereditaments." It appeared in fact that the instrument was an under-lease and not an assignment. The parties had mistaken the nature of the instrument as to its strict legal effect, but that was held to be a sufficient description of the nature of the instrument within the statute, and the Court said that it was not necessary in the column of the schedule to observe a strict adherence to the form of the instrument, and to describe it according to its legal operation. It seems to me that the words " grant of annuity" are as good a description of the nature of an instrument by which an annuity is secured as the words " lease and release." This memorial contains as much, and as true a description of the instrument as, I apprehend, the legislature intended. It is clearly not necessary to set out the covenants contained in the instrument. The next objection is, that the bankruptcy and certificate of the defendant exonerate him from all obligation to reimburse the plaintiff any portion of the sum of money he may have paid on account of the annuity since the bankruptcy, and it is contended that if the defendant was exonerated from all obligation to pay *Hey*, the grantee, he is exonerated also from all obligation to pay the plaintiff. Now I do not agree in that argument. This must depend upon the effect of the statute 49 *Geo*. 3, c. 121, s. 17, by which it is enacted, " that it shall be competent to any annuity creditor of any person, against whom a commission of bankrupt shall issue, to prove under the commission for the value of such annuity, which value the commissioners are to ascertain, and the certificate of every bankrupt under whose commission such proof shall be or might be or might have been made

shall be a discharge of such bankrupt." It is quite clear
that that clause applies only to annuity creditors. The
plaintiff and defendant were only co-sureties for the grantor
of the annuity. Was the plaintiff then an annuity creditor
of the defendant? Clearly he was not. Was *Hey*, the grantee of the annuity, an annuity creditor of the defendant?
Certainly not, because he could only be made liable in the
event of the grantor's default. The grantee was the annuity creditor of the grantor. The object of the act was
to put annuity creditors of a bankrupt upon the same footing with other creditors, as to annuity debts, and power is
given to the commissioners to set a value upon the annuity.
But in the case of a surety, who may never be liable if the
principal does his duty, and who never can be ultimately
responsible to any material extent, provided the principal
continues solvent, it cannot be predicated that this statute
applies. Besides how could a value be put on the plaintiff's
interest in this annuity? That value is not to be estimated
soley with reference to the duration of the life of the *cestui*
qui vie; but the present responsibility of the grantor of the
annuity and of the different co-sureties must be taken into
consideration. This would be the value of the interest of
the grantee, but how would the value of the interest of a
surety be estimated? It seems to me that the 17th section
of the 49 *Geo.* 3, c. 121, does not apply to the case of the
present plaintiff, and that he could not have proved under
the defendant's commission. The case of *Baxter* v.
Nichols(a) is clearly distinguishable from this, because
there the question arose betwixt grantor and grantee. The
defendant in that case was a grantor, and as between him
and the other persons, they were annuity debtors to the
grantee. That case came within the very words of the act
of parliament. The fourth objection is, that the plaintiff,
by the bargain entered into between himself and *Wilkinson*,
had redeemed the annuity, that this was no longer a subsisting annuity, and consequently that the money paid by

(a) 4 Taunt. 90.

the plaintiff to *Wilkinson* was not a payment made on account of the annuity, and that the defendant is under no
obligation to contribute towards that payment. Now that
argument is put on two grounds: first, it is contended that
at all events, without considering the fact that the present
plaintiff had pledged a certain portion of his property to
the grantee of the annuity in order to supply a fund in aid
of any deficiency in the original securities, but considering
the plaintiff and the defendant as in *æquali jure*, the bargain
of the first of *May*, 1824, entirely put an end to and extinguished the grant of the annuity; and secondly, that as the
relative condition of the defendant as a surety was altered
by that transaction, he is completely discharged. Now it
seems to me, upon the first ground of argument, that the
mode by which this arrangement has been effected between
the plaintiff and *Wilkinson* does not discontinue the annuity
or determine the obligation subsisting between the plaintiff
and the defendant. I think great injustice would be done
to the plaintiff, if we were not to consider this as a continuing annuity, and that we are not at liberty so to treat it,
(unless the defendant had thought fit to repudiate the bargain,) and to take away from the plaintiff the power of
binding himself by the arrangement alluded to, so far as it
contributes to bind him. By the bargain of 1st *May*, 1824,
Hey ceases to be grantee of the annuity, and *Wilkinson* is
put in his place, and became entitled to receive the annual
payments. The money paid to *Hey* is 1995*l*. It is true,
that as between *Wilkinson* and the plaintiff the former was
to receive 1000*l*. and interest, and that after payment of
that sum and interest, the plaintiff was to receive the annual payments; but at the time when the plaintiff made
the payments in respect of which he seeks to recover contribution, *Wilkinson* was entitled both at law and in equity
to receive them. I therefore think that the mode which
these parties have adopted is not inconsistent with the justice of the case, and that as between the plaintiff and the
defendant we are bound to consider this as a subsisting an-

nuity, until the defendant shall have made his election to repudiate the bargain entered into between these parties. The remaining question is, whether, in consequence of the provision introduced into the deed of the 1st *May*, 1824, by which the plaintiff pledges part of his property as a further security for the payment of the annuity, that property must be exhausted before the plaintiff can call for any contribution from the defendant. Now looking at the nature of this deed, it seems to me that the provision by which the plaintiff pledges part of his property has not the effect of relieving the sureties. What are the nature and terms of the instrument by which the sureties originally became bound for the grantor? Three persons guarantee the payment of the annuity to *Hey*, and covenant that they will well and truly pay 230*l*. 10*s*. This is a stipulation on the part of those three guarantees. What is the legal operation of that guarantee? Why, that if one of those persons shall be called upon to pay the annuity, he shall be entitled to recover contribution from the rest. But there is another clause in a subsequent part of the deed, by which one of the sureties pledges certain property as a further security for the payment of the annuity. If that clause was intended for the benefit of the sureties, then any arrangement which would have the effect of depriving them of that benefit would relieve them from liability. But that clause purports to have been inserted at the request of the grantor of the annuity, and was introduced for the purpose of giving a better security to the grantee, and not for the purpose of releasing the sureties from the responsibility which they had incurred by a prior clause guaranteeing the payment of the annuity. I am therefore of opinion, upon the whole of this case, that the plaintiff is entitled to recover one third of the amount of payments made by the plaintiff since the 17th *November*, 1823, down to *December*, 1824.

Hᴏʟʀᴏʏᴅ, J.—I am of the same opinion. I think the plaintiff is entitled to recover at law one third part of the payments in question, and that he is not entitled to recover any more. I likewise think that the words "grant of annuity" are a sufficient description of the nature of the instrument within the meaning of the annuity act. It seems to me also to be perfectly clear that the 17th section of the 49 *Geo.* 3, c. 121, does not relate to sureties for the payment of an annuity, but to annuity creditors only, whose interest may be ascertained by the commissioners by putting a value upon the annuity itself. The next question is, whether the annuity is to be considered as at an end by the transaction of the 1st of *May*, 1824. I think it cannot, and that the annuity as between these parties must be treated as a subsisting annuity, and that the defendant still continued liable to pay his contribution by reason of his suretyship. The remaining question is, whether the assignment by the plaintiff of certain stock, as a further security for the payment of the annuity, makes any difference as to the liability of the sureties. I think it does not. The assignment of stock was intended not for the benefit of the sureties, but of the grantee. Even if the payment had been made out of that fund, it seems to me that the co-sureties would have been entitled to recover.

LITTLEDALE, J.—I am of the same opinion. I think the objection stated as to the insufficiency of the memorial is not tenable, and that the instrument was properly described as far as it goes, and that it was unnecessary to specify the assignment of stock for better securing the payment of the annuity. If it were necessary to set out this, it would on the same principle be necessary to set out the obligations of the three sureties. With regard to the bankruptcy it appears to me that the defendant's certificate is no bar to this action, and that the 17th section of the act referred to does not apply to this case. That section applies only to the case of an annuity creditor, but the plaintiff was not an annuity creditor, although he may be a creditor in respect of a transaction arising out of an annuity. I also think that this is a subsisting annuity notwithstanding what has taken place between the plaintiff and *Wilkinson*, and I do not think that the plaintiff, by having pledged some of his own property as a further security, has precluded himself from recovering against the defendant for contribution.

Postea to the plaintiff.

HUGHES v. HUMPHREYS and another.

COVENANT. The declaration stated, that by a certain indenture of apprenticeship made between plaintiff of the first part, *Owen Hughes* of the second part, and defendants of the third part, defendants did covenant &c., to and with plaintiff, his executors, &c., that they, defendants, would use their best endeavours to teach and instruct *Owen Hughes* in the business and profession of surgery and pharmacy, and all other the branches of the same; and also find and provide for *Owen Hughes* good, sufficient, and suitable meat, drink, and lodging, during the term of five years next ensuing from the day of the date of the indenture. Breach, first, that defendants did not nor would, after the making of the indenture, use their best endeavours to teach and instruct *Owen Hughes* in the business and profession of surgery and·pharmacy, during the said term; but, on the contrary thereof, they, defendants, afterwards, and after the making of the indenture, and before the expiration of the term, to wit, on 5th *October*, 1825, at &c., wholly refused then, or at any other time, to teach and instruct *Owen Hughes* in the said business and profession, contrary to the tenor and effect, true intent and meaning of the indenture, and of the covenant of defendants. Secondly, that defendants did not nor would, after the making of the indenture,

Covenant, by the father of an apprentice against the master, for not teaching the apprentice. Plea, that defendant did teach, until the apprentice ran away and never returned. Replication, that on a certain day defendant refused, then or ever, to take back the apprentice, and thereby discharged him. Rejoinder, that the apprentice had previously enlisted as a soldier, and that plaintiff never requested defendant to take back the apprentice when he was able to return. Surrejoinder,

that soon after the apprentice had enlisted, defendant refused, then or ever, to take him back, and wholly discharged him. Demurrer. Held, that the surrejoinder was bad, and no answer to the rejoinder; and that the plea was good, and an answer to the action.

find and provide for *Owen Hughes* good, sufficient, and suitable meat, drink, and lodging, during the said term; but, on the contrary thereof, afterwards, to wit, on &c., at &c., discharged *Owen Hughes* from their employ, and neglected and then and there wholly refused, then or at any other time, to receive him into their employ, or to find and provide for him good, sufficient, and suitable meat, drink, and lodging, contrary to the covenant of defendants. Plea, that *Owen Hughes*, after the making of the indenture, and before the expiration of the term, to wit, on &c., at &c., without the license or consent of defendants, or either of them, wrongfully deserted from and left the service and employ of defendants, his masters, and did not at any time afterwards return into such service and employ, but hath thence continually hitherto continued absent therefrom; and defendants further say, that they did continually, from and after the making of the indenture, until *Owen Hughes* so deserted and left the service and employ of defendants as aforesaid, use their best endeavours to teach and instruct *Owen Hughes* in the business and profession of surgery and pharmacy, and all other the branches of the same; and did also, during all that time, find and provide for *Owen Hughes* good, sufficient, and suitable meat, drink, and lodging, according to the form and effect of the indenture, and of the covenant of defendants in that behalf. Replication, to so much of the plea as relates to the time upon and subsequent to 5th *October*, 1825, that after *Owen Hughes* so left the service and employ of defendants as aforesaid, and during the term, and before the exhibiting of the bill of plaintiff in this behalf, to wit, on 5th *October*, 1825, at &c., defendants wholly refused then, or at any other time, to receive back *Owen Hughes* into their service or employ as such apprentice, or to use their best endeavours to teach and instruct *Owen Hughes* in the business and profession of surgery and pharmacy, and all other the branches of the same, or to find and provide for *Owen Hughes* good, sufficient, and suitable meat, drink, and lodging, according to the covenant of defendants, and thereby then and there discharged *Owen Hughes* from their service and employ. Rejoinder, that before the time of the supposed refusal in the replication to part of the plea of defendants mentioned, and before the exhibiting of the bill of plaintiff in this behalf, to wit, on 5th *October*, 1825, *Owen Hughes* enlisted and entered into the service of his Majesty as a common soldier, and remained and continued in the service of his Majesty as such common soldier for a long space of time, to wit, hitherto, and was thereby during all that time wholly incapacitated from serving defendants as such apprentice: and defendants further say, that plaintiff did not at any time after *Owen Hughes* so quitted and left the service and employ of defendants as such apprentice, and before *Owen Hughes* so enlisted as such soldier, or at any other time, request defendants to receive back *Owen Hughes* into their service as such apprentice, when *Owen Hughes* was ready and willing and capable of returning into such service; nor did *Owen Hughes* tender himself to defendants, or offer during that time to return into the service and employ of defendants as such apprentice. Surrejoinder, that a little time after *Owen Hughes* so enlisted and entered into the service of his Majesty as a common soldier, as in the rejoinder of defendants is in that behalf alleged, to wit, on 5th *October*, 1825, to wit, at &c., defendants refused, then or ever, to receive back *Owen Hughes* into their service and employ as such apprentice, and then and there wholly discharged *Owen Hughes* from their service and employ as such apprentice, and discharged *Owen Hughes* from returning or offering to return, then or ever, into the service of defendants as such apprentice. Demurrer and joinder.

W. O. Russell, in support of the demurrer. First, the plea is good, and is a bar to the action. It states a sufficient excuse for the neglect to maintain and teach the apprentice, which is charged in the declaration as a breach of covenant on the part of the defendants. The plaintiff alleges that the defendants refused to instruct or to provide meat, drink, &c., for the apprentice during the term. The defendants answer, that they did instruct and provide for the apprentice up to a certain time, and that then the apprentice left the service without their consent, and never returned to it. Their covenant must be considered as an undertaking to instruct an apprentice who remains in the service, and thus renders his instruction practicable. It is impracticable to instruct or provide for an apprentice who runs away from the service, therefore his absence is a good excuse for the non-performance of the covenant. Secondly, the surrejoinder is bad. It does not traverse or avoid any of the facts alleged in the rejoinder, and those facts are an answer to the replication. The replication states, that the defendants, on the 5th of *October*, 1825, refused to receive back the apprentice into their employ, and *thereby* discharged him. The rejoinder shews, that before that time the apprentice had enlisted, and had become incapacitated from serving the defendants; and that he in fact never returned, or offered to return, into the service. That, according to the *dictum* of *Bayley*, J., in *Winstone* v. *Linn*(a), is a sufficient excuse for not giving instruction, &c., during the term for which the apprentice was bound; and *Cuff* v. *Browne* (b) is also an authority to the same effect. That being so, the surrejoinder is bad for not traversing or avoiding the facts stated in the rejoinder.

Rumball, contrà. First, the surrejoinder answers the rejoinder. It states, that on a certain day the defendants wholly discharged the apprentice from returning, or offering to return, into their service. That operates as a continuing refusal to take back the apprentice, extending over the whole of the residue of the term mentioned in the indenture, and the fact of the apprentice being afterwards incapacitated from returning was quite immaterial. If his dis-

(a) 2 D. & R. 474; 1 B. & C. 467;   (b) 5 Price, 297.
1 D. & R. Mag. Cas. 337.

ability had been removed the very next day, he would still have continued discharged from the service of the defendants. If the surrejoinder had alleged only a refusal to take back the apprentice, it might have been necessary to aver a willingness and offer to return, *Co. Litt.* 207, *Rawsthorne* v. *Johnson* (a); but the allegation that the defendants wholly discharged the apprentice from their service, renders an offer to return unnecessary, and a disability of returning immaterial; 1 *Roll. Abr.* 458, N. pl. 5, *Jones* v. *Barkley* (b). [*Bayley*, J. It is laid down in *Co. Litt.* 221, that if there be a feoffment upon condition to be performed before a certain day, and the feoffee incur a disability, the condition is broken, and the feoffor may re-enter, although the disability may be removed before the day.] Secondly, the plea is clearly bad; it contains no sufficient answer to the declaration. There are two breaches of covenant assigned, the neglecting to instruct the apprentice, and the neglecting to provide necessaries for him; and neither of these is traversed. The absence of the apprentice is not, in point of law, an excuse for the non-performance of the covenant, because the law implies a covenant on the part of the master that the apprentice shall remain with him and receive instruction; and where a party covenants that something shall be done or accepted by a third person, he is liable to an action for the refusal of such third person to do or accept the act; *Com. Dig. Covenant,* (L. 14); *Bro. Abr. Condition,* pl. 4; *Lamb's case* (c); *Doughty* v. *Neal* (d); *Hesketh* v. *Gray* (e); *Worsley* v. *Wood* (f). It is true that in those cases the act was to be done to or accepted by a stranger, and therefore they might be distinguishable from the present case, if there was any thing here to shew that the apprentice was a party to the indenture. But there is nothing to shew that he was either party or privy to the indenture; no such averment appears upon any part of the record; and in the

(a) 1 East, 202.

(b) 2 Dougl. 684.

(c) 5 Co. Rep. 24.

(d) 1 Saund. 216.

(e) Sayer, 185.

(f) 6 T. R. 710.

absence of such an averment, the fact cannot be presumed: *Hollingworth* v. *Ascue* (a), *Moor* v. *Jones* (b), *Ashmore* v. *Ripley* (c). In *Branch* v. *Ewington* (d), and *Cuming* v. *Hill* (e), the latter of which comes very near the present case, it was held, that a father, who had covenanted that his son should serve as an apprentice, was not exonerated by the refusal of the son, although the latter was a party to the indenture. Here the justice of the case is clearly and strongly with the plaintiff; for he, as the father of the apprentice, and a party to the indenture, can neither release himself from his covenants, nor compel the apprentice to return to his service: whereas the defendants, as the masters, have ample powers given to them by the law, under which they may either compel the apprentice to return to his duty, or procure the indenture to be cancelled.

BAYLEY, J.—I fully concur in the principle, that where a covenant is made that a stranger shall do or accept particular acts, that covenant must be performed at the peril and risk of the covenantor. But the first question in this case is, have the defendants covenanted for the performance of those acts on the part of the apprentice, the non-performance of which is assigned as a breach of covenant? That question can only be answered by looking at the nature of the instrument, the relation of the parties, and the language which they have adopted in the transaction. The declaration describes the instrument as an indenture of apprenticeship, made between the plaintiff of the first part, the apprentice of the second, and the defendants of the third; but the only covenant it sets out is one upon the part of the defendants, to instruct and provide for the apprentice. Now it is usual, in indentures of apprenticeship, to find some third party who receives covenants for the benefit of the apprentice, and makes covenants for him.

(a) Cro. Eliz. 355.
(b) 2 Ld. Raym. 1541.
(c) Cro. Jac. 420.
(d) Dougl. 518.
(e) 3 B. & A. 59.

The case of *Branch* v. *Ewington* (a) shews what the character and situation of such third party are; that he is not a stranger to the apprentice, but in a great degree identified with him. There, the parties to the indenture were the master, the apprentice, and his father. They all entered into covenants—the master to teach, the apprentice to serve, and the father to find clothing—and each party bound himself to the other for the performance of all the covenants in the indenture. The apprentice having broken his covenant, the father was sued and held liable. Why? Might it not have been said in answer to that action, as it is said in support of this, that the master had impliedly covenanted to compel the apprentice to stay and serve, if that were the true meaning of the indenture? The argument would equally apply to both cases; but no such argument was urged there. The plea in this case is in substance this:—" I did perform my covenants so long as the apprentice gave me the opportunity of doing so." It therefore answers the alleged breaches of covenant up to the time of the apprentice quitting the service, and excuses them after that time. Then the question is, who covenanted to compel the apprentice to remain and serve? If the masters so covenanted, the statement in their plea is no excuse; if they did not, it is. Upon this case, as disclosed upon the pleadings, I am of opinion that the masters did not so covenant, and that consequently they are not liable for the alleged non-performance of their covenants to instruct and provide for the apprentice. Then if the plea is good, as I think it is, it follows that the subsequent pleadings are bad. The replication states a refusal by the defendants to take back the apprentice, and avers that they *thereby* wholly discharged him from their service. The defendants rejoin, that the apprentice had contracted another relation, which disabled him from returning to their service. In answer to that, and in order to render the defendants liable for not taking the apprentice back, at all events an offer to return

(a) Dougl. 518.

should have been alleged; but the surrejoinder contains no such allegation. For these reasons I am of opinion that the defendants are entitled to judgment.

HOLROYD, J.—It seems to me that the plea in this case is good, and that the subsequent pleadings to avoid it are bad. If so, the defendants are entitled to judgment. I assent to the principle laid down in the cases which have been cited, as regards the performance of covenants to or by strangers; but they do not apply here, for the apprentice in this case was not a stranger. It is not, indeed, averred that the plaintiff and the apprentice executed the indenture, but they are stated to be parties to it. In an indenture of apprenticeship the master and the apprentice stand in different and opposite situations, and there is generally a third party who covenants on behalf of the apprentice. The master does not covenant that the apprentice shall remain in his service, or receive his instructions; the fair effect of the indenture is, that the master shall use his best endeavours to give instruction, and the apprentice covenants, either by himself or by a third person, to receive that instruction.

LITTLEDALE, J.—I am of the same opinion. The contract made by the defendants was, that they would use their best endeavours to instruct the apprentice; and when the apprentice absented himself, he made it impossible for them to perform that contract. It is argued that the absence of the apprentice is no excuse, because he is a stranger to the contract. It is true there is no averment that he executed the indenture, and in some respects, therefore, he may be considered as a stranger, but not as regards the present question; and I think he is so far identified with the plaintiff, that his default is the default of the plaintiff, and furnishes, therefore, an answer to the action.

Judgment for the defendants.

Cook and others, Assignees of Griffin, a Bankrupt, *v.*   1827.
                    Pallmer.

ASSUMPSIT, for money had and received. Plea, non *A bailiff had taken in execution goods of a trader more than sufficient to satisfy the levy. The trader became bankrupt, and his assignees authorised the bailiff to sell all the goods by private contract for a certain sum, which he did, and received the money. The bailiff then satisfied the execution creditor, but never paid over the surplus to the assignees. The assignees sued the sheriff for the surplus:—Held, that they could not recover, because the bailiff in selling goods beyond the amount of the levy was the agent of the assignees and not of the sheriff.* assumpsit; issue thereon. At the trial before Lord *Tenterden*, C. J. at the *London* sittings after *Trinity* term 1825, a verdict was found for the plaintiffs, damages 603*l.*, subject to the opinion of the Court upon the following case:—

The plaintiffs are the assignees of *D. Griffin*, a bankrupt. The defendant was sheriff of *Surrey* at the time when the transactions hereinafter mentioned occurred. On the 12th of *April*, 1822, *J. Theobald* entered up judgment against *Griffin* on two several warrants of attorney, and issued writs of *fieri facias*, returnable on *Wednesday* next after fifteen days of *Easter*, directed to the defendant, as sheriff of *Surrey*, indorsed to levy the two sums of 509*l.* 13*s.* 4*d.* and 1019*l.* 10*s.* 1*d.* The defendant issued his warrants directed to *Jarvis*, his bailiff, who, on the same 12th of *April*, seized the stock in trade of the bankrupt, to answer those two sums. *Jarvis* remained in possession until *June*, when a commission of bankrupt issued against *Griffin*, on an act of bankruptcy committed on the 1st of *May*, 1822. During the time that *Jarvis* was in possession, he suffered part of the bankrupt's stock to be sold, and received the proceeds, amounting to 400*l.* After the commission issued, *Jarvis* directed the sheriff's brokers to remove from the premises goods sufficient to satisfy the two writs; which they did. In *June*, the defendant being ruled to return the writs, as to one returned that he had levied part, and had goods to satisfy the residue, which remained in his hands for want of buyers, and as to the whole sum to be levied under the other writ, he made the same return, that he had levied goods which remained in his hands for want of buyers. On the 18th of *June*, a commission of bankrupt issued against *Griffin*, under which the plaintiffs were chosen assignees; and on the 7th of *August* following they gave the defendant notice

in writing of the commission. While the goods remained
in the hands of the sheriff's brokers, one *Martin*, having
inspected them, offered to buy the whole for 1803*l*, 18*s*.,
and a memorandum was drawn up and signed by *Theobald*
and the plaintiffs, as assignees, which, after reciting that
the goods were in the custody of the sheriff of *Surrey*, and
that it was for the interest of all parties that they should
be sold to *Martin* for 1803*l*. 18*s*., stated that the parties
" did thereby consent and agree, that the sheriff should be
at liberty to deliver the goods to *Martin*, and to receive
that sum as the full value of the goods." *Martin*, accompanied by *Theobald's* attorney, then went to *Jarvis*, and
paid him the purchase-money, whereupon *Jarvis* gave him
an order to the sheriff's brokers to deliver the goods.
Jarvis afterwards went with him to the brokers, and saw
the goods delivered. The remainder of *Theobald's* claim
was satisfied out of the money paid by *Martin* to *Jarvis*;
but the latter never paid over to the plaintiffs, or any other
person, the balance due to them, and he afterwards, and
before the commencement of this action, became bankrupt.
The action was defended by his sureties.

Hutchinson, for the plaintiffs. At the trial two points
were made for the defendant. First, that *Jarvis*, by seizing
goods exceeding in value the sums indorsed upon the writs,
had exceeded his authority, and that, consequently, the
sheriff was not responsible for his act. Secondly, that the
agreement afterwards made between the execution creditor
and the plaintiffs, was such an interference by them in the
transaction as deprived them of the right to sue the sheriff;
that it was an adoption by them of the act of *Jarvis*, without
the knowledge of the defendant; and that it made *Jarvis*
their agent, and thereby released the defendant, as sheriff,
from all responsibility. Now there can be no doubt that
the sheriff was originally liable for the amount of the goods
seized by his officer; and the subsequent agreement could

.1827.

Cook
v.
Pallmer.

not discharge him from a liability which had attached at the moment the goods were seized. *Theobald* might have sued the sheriff, if his executions had not been satisfied; and this action is brought by third persons, who were not connected with the executions, and whose rights had not arisen at the time when the seizure was made.

F. Pollock, contrà. The sheriff is generally liable for the wrongful acts of his officer; but they must be acts done by the officer in the course of his employment, and in the exercise of his authority. Thus, if a bailiff being directed to arrest *A.*, arrests *B.*, the sheriff is responsible; but if he arrests *B. and C.*, the sheriff is not responsible. Where a bailiff seizes goods exceeding in value the amount indorsed on the writ, the sheriff is liable for the whole, but the usual and proper course is for the bailiff to sell by auction sufficient to satisfy the levy, and then to stop the sale. Suppose there had been a sale by auction in this case, and the plaintiffs had been present, and when sufficient had been sold to satisfy *Theobald's* executions, they had requested *Jarvis* to proceed and sell the remainder of the goods, and he had done so and received the money, would the sheriff have been responsible for the surplus money so raised? Clearly not, because *Jarvis* would then have been, for that portion of the sale, the agent of the plaintiffs and not of the sheriff; and yet that is, in substance, the present case. The plaintiffs authorised *Jarvis* to sell the whole of the goods to *Martin*, and to receive the whole of the purchase-money. By so doing they made *Jarvis* their own agent, and exonerated the sheriff. They knew their own interests and were bound to protect them, which they might easily have done, by taking care that *Jarvis* received no more of the purchase-money than was sufficient to satisfy *Theobald's* executions.

Bayley, J.—I am of opinion that the plaintiffs cannot recover. The defendant was no party to the agreement under which all the goods were sold, and all the purchase-money paid to the sheriff's officer; that was an arrangement made between *Theobald*, the execution-creditor, and the plaintiffs. *Theobald* had issued two executions. Part of the money had been raised, and was in the possession of the officer, together with goods more than sufficient to satisfy the residue. The duty of the officer was to raise the residue by the sale of those goods, and when that was done, to stop the sale; but *Theobald* and the plaintiffs authorised the officer to sell all the goods for a certain sum. Upon that sale the officer was the agent of the sheriff to the extent of the sum to be levied, but no further, for his authority to sell to a greater extent was not derived from the sheriff, but from *Theobald* and the plaintiffs, who by giving him that authority made him their agent as to that part of the transaction. The sheriff never had any right to call upon the officer to pay over the surplus to him, nor was it the duty of the officer to do so; and as the sureties are only responsible for the due performance of the officer's duty to the sheriff, the plaintiffs cannot be entitled to recover, even considering the sureties as the real defendants in this action. I am, therefore, of opinion that a nonsuit must be entered.

Holroyd, J. and Littledale, J. concurred.

Judgment of nonsuit.

———◆———

Davis, Executrix of Griffith, *v.* Bryan, Gent. one &c.,

A. purchased and paid for an annuity for his life, which was regularly paid up to the time of his death. No memorial was inrolled: —Held, that his executrix could not recover back any part of the consideration money.

DECLARATION in *indebitatus assumpsit*, containing counts for money had and received by the defendant to the use of the testator, for interest due from the defendant to the testator upon an account stated with the testator, for money had and received by the defendant to the use of the plaintiff as executrix, and, lastly, a count upon an account stated between the defendant and the plaintiff, as executrix, of monies due to her in that character. The defendant pleaded the general issue, the statute of limitations, and a set-off for money lent and advanced, and paid, laid out and

expended by the defendant for the use of the testator. On
these pleas issues were joined. At the trial before Lord
Tenterden, C. J. at the *Middlesex* sittings after *Easter* term,
1826, a verdict was found for the plaintiff on the second
issue, and also on the first and third issues with the damages
laid in the declaration, subject to the opinion of the Court
upon the following case :—

The testator in 1814, and from thence until his death,
resided in or near *Ross* in *Herefordshire*. The defendant,
an attorney, resided during the same period at *Monmouth*,
and acted as the attorney and agent of the testator. On the
25th *November*, 1814, the testator agreed to purchase of
the defendant an annuity of 24*l.* for his (testator's) life, for
the price of 300*l.* which was then paid by him to the defendant; and the defendant, to secure the annuity, signed
the following instrument, which instrument was found
among the testator's papers after his death, and was produced by the plaintiff at the trial:—

" Received this 25th *November*, 1814, of Mr. *William
Griffith*, the sum of 300*l.* being the purchase-money for an
annuity of 24*l.* to be paid by me, my heirs, executors, or
administrators, to the said *William Griffith*, during the term
of his natural life, by two equal half-yearly payments, on
Midsummer-day and *Christmas-day* in every year; the said
annuity to commence from the 25th *December* next, and
the first half-yearly payment to be made on the 24th *June*
next; and the payment of the said annuity to be secured at
any time after the expiration of two years, from the 25th
December next, on freehold lands, messuages, or tenements,
of equal or greater annual value, if so required by the said
William Griffith, on his giving three months' previous
notice in writing for that purpose."

No memorial of this instrument was inrolled, nor was
any other security for the annuity given by the defendant,
or applied for by the testator. The defendant was able to
have given the freehold security, if it had been required.
The testator died in *December*, 1823, and from the time of

the contract for the annuity to the time of his death, the annuity was regularly paid to him half-yearly by the defendant, and frequently in advance. The defendant and the testator were on terms of great intimacy, and the defendant often lent him money, the balance of which was paid to the defendant by the plaintiff, after the testator's death.

. The question for the consideration of the Court is, whether the plaintiff is entitled to recover from the defendant any and what sum in respect of the sum of 300*l.* so paid by the testator to the defendant, and whether the same is subject to any and what deduction in respect of the annuity so paid as aforesaid.

R. V. Richards, for the plaintiff. The plaintiff is entitled to recover the balance of the 300*l.* after deducting the payments made by the defendant. The testator, if he had brought the action, might have recovered the whole 300*l.*, because no memorial of the grant of the annuity having been inrolled, the grant was " null and void to all intents and purposes," within the very words of the statute 53 *Geo.* 3, c. 141, s. 2. The provision in that act is precisely the same as that in the former act, 17 *Geo.* 3, c. 26, s. 1, with respect to which it has been repeatedly decided that where the grant of an annuity is void for non-compliance with the requisites of the law, the consideration given for it may be recovered back; *Shove* v. *Webb* (a), *Scurfield* v. *Gowland* (b). [*Bayley,* J. In those cases the annuity was set aside for informality in the memorial.] True, but that makes no difference; there the memorial was held bad, and it was set aside; here no memorial has ever been inrolled; the parties, therefore, are in the same situation. It will be contended that the executrix cannot maintain the action, although the testator might have done so ; but it is difficult to say upon what principles such an argument can be rested. [*Bayley,* J. In this case the grantee has received

(a) 1 T. R. 732.   (b) 6 East, 241.

the whole consideration for which he paid the 300*l.*, for the
annuity was regularly paid to him during his life; so that
your argument must go this length, that even if the testator
had received the annuity for thirty years together, his executrix might still recover back the consideration money.]   It is
not proposed to push the argument to that extreme length;
nor is it necessary to do so, because the defendant would
be entitled to set off the payments made on account of the
annuity, *Hicks* v. *Hicks* (a): and the present plaintiff only
seeks to recover the balance of the 300*l.* after deducting such
payments.   In the case last cited Lord *Ellenborough* said,
that if the consideration money was money had and received, it must be money had and received with all its consequences; and one of those consequences is that the executrix may recover it.

G. R. Cross, contrà.   The present case is distinguishable
from all those in which the consideration money given for
an annuity has been recovered back after the grant of the
annuity had been set aside.   In all those cases the grant
was set aside upon the application of the grantor, and the
action to recover the consideration money was brought in
the lifetime of the grantee.   The action for money had and
received is an equitable action, and all the equity in this
case is in favour of the defendant, because the testator has
received the full benefit of his contract.   From the moment
of his death the contract ceased to be executory, and there
is an important distinction between contracts executed and
executory; the former cannot be rescinded, the latter may,
Lowry v. *Bourdieu* (b), *Tappenden* v. *Randall* (c), *Aubert*
v. *Walsh* (d).   Here the contract has expired, and cannot,
therefore, be rescinded; besides, the testator has had the
full benefit of it.

BAYLEY, J.—This is a plain case as regards both law

(a) 3 East, 16.   (c) 2 B. & P. 467.
(b) 2 Dougl. 468.   (d) 3 Taunt. 277.

and justicé. The action for money had and received is an equitable action, and cannot be maintained when it is against good conscience that the money should be recovered. Here it is clearly against good conscience that the plaintiff should recover. Look at the facts. A bargain is made, and the testator pays 300*l*. upon condition that he shall receive 24*l*. a year during his life. He did receive 24*l*. a year during his life, therefore he has received all that he bargained for, and now his executrix claims a return of the money which he paid for the annuity which he bargained for and has enjoyed, upon the ground that the bargain was void from the beginning. Is there any thing like good conscience in such a claim? Decidedly not. Or is it warranted by law, that is, is the grant of the annuity void? I think not. The statute, indeed, says, that unless a memorial of the deed is inrolled, the deed shall be void; but there are many cases in which those words have been held to make the instrument voidable only at the pleasure of the party, and I think we are at liberty to give them that construction in the present case. It is said that the statute, as explained by the case of *Hicks* v. *Hicks*, shews the contract to have been absolutely void; but that was a very different case from the present. There the grantor of the annuity insisted that the contract was void, therefore the grantee had a right to do the same; and the only point decided was, that the grantor was entitled to set off the payments which he had made on account of the annuity in an action brought by the grantee to recover back the consideration money. Besides, here the contract is no longer *in fieri;* it has been executed, and cannot now be rescinded.

HOLROYD, J., and LITTLEDALE, J., concurred.

　　　　　　　　　　　　Judgment for the defendant.

MILNES *v.* DUNCAN, Gent., one, &c.

1827.

ASSUMPSIT for money had and received. Plea, *non assumpsit;* and issue thereon. At the trial before Lord *Tenterden,* C. J., at the *Middlesex* sittings after *Trinity* term, 1826, the plaintiff had a verdict for 150*l.*, subject to the opinion of the Court upon the following case:—

Money paid in ignorance of a fact, and without full means of obtaining knowledge of that fact, may be recovered back, by the party paying it, in an action for money had and received.

The plaintiff, an attorney at *Matlock,* in *Derbyshire,* was employed by the defendant, an attorney in *London,* to receive the rents of an estate near *Matlock* belonging to the defendant. On the 11th of *February,* 1826, the plaintiff, having previously received rents exceeding 150*l.*, inclosed, in a letter of that date, to the defendant, the following *Irish* bill of exchange for 150*l.*, in part liquidation thereof:—

". £150.   *Glen Anne Mills, Nov.* 24, 1825.

Three months after date pay to our order 150*l.* sterling, in *London,* value received.

                    Atkinson, Chomney, & *Atkinson.*

To Mr. *Gerald Atkinson, Liverpool.*

    Accepted, payable at *Williams* & Co. bankers,

                              G. *Atkinson.*"

The bill had several indorsements, but there was nothing in them to shew that it had been drawn or indorsed in *Ireland.* On the 13th of *February* the defendant acknowledged the receipt of the bill. On the 27th of *February* the bill became due, but was not then presented for payment. On the 20th of *March* the defendant wrote to the plaintiff as follows:—" I am sorry to acquaint you that the bill for 150*l.* you sent me for the rent has not been honoured. The bill is drawn by or in the name of *Atkinson* and two other names from some mills, but the writing is so bad that I cannot make the name or the place out: what am I to do in this?" The plaintiff received this letter the next day, and applied to his immediate indorsers, *Arkwright* & Co., bankers at *Wirksworth,* to take up the bill, which they refused to do, because it had been so long overheld. These facts the plaintiff communicated to the defendant, by letter, on the same day. On the 25th of *March* the defendant wrote to the plaintiff, and said, " it is unnecessary for me to enter upon the subject of supposed delay, for the bill is an absolute nullity, by being drawn on a stamp of inferior value: I must request you will, with as little delay as possible, remit me the amount of the rents, and I will return you the void bill." On the 27th of *March* the plaintiff answered that he had again applied to *Ark-wright* & Co., and they had refused to have any thing to do with the bill, because it had been so long overheld, and that he had directed his agent, *Forbes*, to call upon the defendant, and to confer with him on the subject, and he requested him to shew *Forbes* the bill. On the 29th of *March* a clerk of *Forbes* called upon the defendant, and after inspecting the bill, said it was drawn on a 4*s.* stamp. On the 30th of *March*, the defendant wrote to the plaintiff that he declined presenting the illegal bill to any person for payment, because he might thereby subject himself to a penalty, as the other parties on the bill had; and that if the plaintiff's bankers obstinately refused to have any thing to do with the illegal bill he should resort to other means; and that as his determination was formed, it would be better to act on it immediately, and that he therefore requested the plaintiff to inform him in the course of a post or two if the plaintiff would instruct *Forbes* to appear for him. On the 3d of *April*, a clerk of *Forbes*, by the plaintiff's direction, called again upon the defendant, and informed him that he had written to the plaintiff, and expected to receive the amount of the bill in a post or two, till which time he requested no proceedings might be taken; and on the 7th of *April*, the same clerk, by the direction of *Forbes*, paid the amount of the bill, and at the same time again inspected the bill, which the defendant delivered up to him, and gave the following receipt :—" 7th *April*, 1826. Received of *J. Milnes*, Esq. by the payment of Mr. *Forbes*, his agent, two bank post bills, value 150*l.* for a void bill of exchange sent to me by Mr. *Milnes* for rent." Up to this period the bill in question

had been considered and treated by both parties as an
English bill, but it afterwards proved to be an *Irish* bill,
and impressed with a proper stamp suitable to such bill.
Upon the discovery of which, on the 12th of *April*, the
plaintiff presented the bill at *Williams* and Co.'s for payment, which was refused by them. But if it had been presented when it became due, there were at that time assets
in their hands, and it would have been paid. The acceptor
became bankrupt on the 20th *June*, 1826, which was after
the present action had been commenced.

Coleridge, for the plaintiff. The plaintiff is entitled to
recover, because he paid the money, not under a mistake of
the law, but under a mistake of the facts. That mistake
was orignally occasioned by the defendant himself, and that,
at a time when he, by his own negligence, had made the bill
his own. The plaintiff received no consideration for paying
the money, and never intended to pay it without consideration. He has been guilty of no delay in making his claim,
and has done nothing to alter the defendant's situation in
relation to the other parties on the bill. The money, therefore, is recoverable upon general principles as money had
and received. It is a well established principle that money
paid under a mistake of the law cannot be recovered back;
but it is also a principle equally well established, that where
it is against conscience that the party who has received the
money should retain it, or where the money is paid in
ignorance of the facts, and there is no illegality in the transaction, it may be recovered back, *Moses* v. *Macfarlane* (a).
This principle was also recognised in *Bize* v. *Dickason* (b),
and by *Mansfield*, C. J. and *Chambre*, J. in *Brisbane* v.
Dacres (c). The facts of this case clearly bring it within the
operation of this principle. The defendant received a good
bill which, from mere negligence, he omitted to present for
payment when due. By that negligence he rendered the
bill, as against all prior indorsers, a nullity. He was in-

(a) 2 Burr. 1005.　　(b) 1 T. R. 285.　　(c) 5 Taunt. 143.

formed of this, and that the indorsers would not hold themselves liable. He then declared the bill to be void for want of a proper stamp, and finally threatened to sue the plaintiff, and thereby induced him to pay the money. Under such circumstances the defendant had no right in conscience to receive the money, therefore it is against conscience that he should retain it. He either did or did not know that the bill was drawn in *Ireland,* and, therefore, properly stamped. If he did know it, he obtained the money by fraud; if he did not, he cannot profit by a mistake into which he first fell himself and afterwards led the plaintiff. It will be said that the plaintiff had the means of knowledge respecting that fact, and therefore cannot recover, and *Bilbie* v. *Lumley* (a) will be relied on. The marginal note of that case certainly does state that money paid with full means of knowledge of the facts cannot be recovered back, but the decision in the case does not warrant that statement. The real decision in that case was that money paid with knowledge of the facts could not be recovered back on the ground of ignorance of the law; it was cited by *Lawrence,* J. as an authority to that extent only in *Lothian* v. *Henderson* (b), and was treated in the same light both by the bench and the bar in *Brisbane* v. *Dacres* (c). *Chatfield* v. *Paxton* (d) is in favour of the present plaintiff, for there Lord *Kenyon* laid down the rule as being, " that where a man, knowing all the facts explicitly, and being under no misapprehension with regard to any of them, nor of the law acting upon them, chuses to pay a sum of money, *volenti non fit injuria,* he shall not recover it back again." The defendant here had all the means of knowledge that the plaintiff had; if he had knowledge, he obtained the money by fraud; to avoid the imputation of fraud, he must say that he had not knowledge or the full means of knowledge, and if so, he must also admit that the plaintiff had neither knowledge nor the full means of knowledge of the facts.

(a) 2 East, 469.
(b) 3 B. & P. 520.
(c) 5 Taunt. 143.

(d) 2 East, 471, n.; Chitty on Bills, 304, n. 3.

Comyn, contrà. The plaintiff in this case paid the money at a time when he had the full means of knowledge of the facts; therefore he cannot recover it back. *Bilbie* v. *Lumley*. In that case Lord *Ellenborough* referred to the decision in *Chatfield* v. *Paxton* as one that could not be relied on. When the plaintiff was informed that the bill was void for want of a proper stamp, it became his duty to use every means in his power to ascertain whether that information was correct or not. He had ample means in his power for that purpose, for he might not only have inquired of the persons from whom he received the bill, where the bill was drawn, but he might have traced it through the different indorsers up to the drawer, and have made the same inquiry there; and if he had done so, he would have ascertained that the bill was drawn in *Ireland*, and was therefore properly stamped.

Bayley, J.—I think the plaintiff is entitled to recover. The rule of law applicable to this case is clear. When money is paid under a mistake of the law, it cannot be recovered back. When it is paid under a mistake of the real facts, there being no neglect to employ the existing means of knowledge, it may be recovered back. Then the question is, whether the present plaintiff, when he paid the money, was ignorant of the real facts respecting the bill, and whether he was guilty of any negligence in not employing the means of knowledge which he possessed. The bill was remitted to the defendant before it was due. He neglected to present it for payment when it became due, and held it a month; and in consequence of that neglect it was not paid. Supposing the bill to be a valid bill, this negligence of the defendant destroyed the plaintiff's right to recover against the prior indorsers, and varied, therefore, materially, the situation of the parties. Some time after the bill had become due the defendant communicated to the plaintiff that it had not been paid, but without then mentioning or appearing to know of any infirmity in the bill. The plaintiff applied to his indorsers, who refused to pay, because the bill had been held over so long. The defendant then, for the first time, declared that the bill was void for want of a proper stamp, and refused to present for payment what he termed " the illegal bill." It is clear that at that time the defendant believed that the bill was not drawn upon the proper stamp. The fact of his being led into that error goes far to shew that the bill itself could not furnish either him or the plaintiff with adequate means of knowing whether it was properly stamped or not. The plaintiff, also believing the bill to be void, paid the amount. That appears from the receipt, which speaks of a void bill of exchange. The defendant received the money, still believing the bill to be void. Afterwards it turned out that the bill was drawn in *Ireland*, that it bore the proper stamp, and that it was a valid bill. The money, therefore, was paid and received, under a mistake as to a particular fact, namely, the place where the bill was drawn. Then is there any negligence imputable to the plaintiff? I think not. The bill did not appear upon the face of it to be an *Irish* bill; all the circumstances connected with it were as much calculated to give knowledge to the defendant as to the plaintiff: and as they did not inform the defendant that the bill was drawn in *Ireland*, it may reasonably be inferred that they were not adequate to inform the plaintiff, or any other person, of that fact. I think the plaintiff, when he paid the money, had no adequate means of knowing that the bill was not a void bill; and that being so, it is clear that he paid the money under a mistake of fact, without any negligence on his part, and therefore that he is entitled to recover it back.

HOLROYD, J. and LITTLEDALE, J. concurred.

Judgment for the plaintiff.

END OF EASTER TERM.

CASES.

ARGUED AND DETERMINED

IN THE

COURT OF KING'S BENCH

IN

TRINITY TERM,

IN THE EIGHTH YEAR OF THE REIGN OF GEORGE IV.

MEMORANDA.

IN the course of last term, Mr. Serjeant *Bosanquet* took his seat within the bar as King's Serjeant; and on the first day of this term, the following gentlemen took their seats within the bar:—

Serjeants *Taddy*, *Cross* and *Wilde*, as King's Serjeants.

Henry Brougham, of *Lincoln's Inn*, Esq., to whom a patent of precedence had been granted to rank immediately after *Charles Pepys*, Esq., the latter having taken his seat within the bar as King's Counsel on the first day of last *Michaelmas* term.

As King's Counsel, *Thomas Crosby Treslove*, of *Lincoln's Inn*, Esq.; *George Rose*, of the *Inner Temple*, Esq.; *Henry Bickersteth*, of the *Inner Temple*, Esq.; *John Williams*, of the *Inner Temple*, Esq.; *John Campbell*, of *Lincoln's Inn*, Esq.; *Frederick Pollock*, of the *Inner Temple*, Esq.; and *Horace Twiss*, of the *Inner Temple*, Esq.

1827.

In the course of this term, the following gentlemen were called to the degree of the coif, viz. *Thomas Andrews, Henry Storks, Edward Lawes, Edward Ludlow, Henry Alworth Merewether, William Oldnall Russell, David Francis Jones, John Scriven, Henry John Stephen,* and *Charles Carpenter Bompas,* Esqrs. The first seven gentlemen gave rings with the following motto, " *More majorum,*" and the remaining three, with the motto " *Lex ratione probatur.*"

M'INTOSH *v.* R. SLADE, J. SLADE and C. VOY.

The master of a vessel laden with wine and fruit, which latter, being stowed above the former, was, by the bill of lading, to be delivered at *Coxe's Quay,* which is higher up the river *Thames* than the *London Docks,* where the wine was to be delivered, conveyed her first to the *London Docks,* where he discharged the pilot, but the vessel did not break bulk. The consignees of the fruit refused to let it be landed in the *London Docks,* whereupon the master took on

CASE, to recover damages for the injury sustained by the plaintiff, in consequence of his barge, called the *Smelt,* being run foul of and sunk in the river *Thames* by the brig *Stanley,* of which the defendants *R. Slade* and *J. Slade* were owners, and the defendant *Voy* was pilot, at the time of the accident. At the trial before Lord *Tenterden,* C. J. at the *London* sittings after last *Michaelmas* term, a verdict was found against all the defendants, subject, as to the liability of the defendants *R. Slade* and *J. Slade,* to the opinion of this Court on the following case :—

The brig *Stanley,* belonging to the port of *Poole,* of which the two defendants *R. Slade* and *J. Slade* were owners, sailed from *Lisbon* in *February,* 1826, with a cargo of fruit and wine for *London,* and by the bills of lading the fruit was to be delivered at *Fresh Wharf* or *Coxe's Quay,* both in *Thames Street,* and the wine was to be delivered in the *London Docks.* The brig was navigated from *Gravesend* to the *London Docks* by and under the charge of *J. Pashley,* a duly licensed pilot, and arrived in the *London Docks* on the 21st *February,* 1826, where *Pashley* was

board another pilot to convey the vessel to *Coxe's Quay.* In the passage, the vessel ran foul of a barge and sunk it:—Held, that the pilot who had charge of the vessel was alone answerable for the loss under 6 *Geo.* 4, c. 125.

discharged, and the brig remained in the *London Docks* until the 25th of the same month. During the time the brig was so lying in the docks, application was made to the consignees of the fruit, to allow the same to be discharged in the docks, which was refused, and no part of the brig's cargo was discharged in the docks, nor did she break bulk there. On the 25th *February* the brig proceeded from the *London Docks* towards *Coxe's Quay* in *Thames Street* for the purpose of discharging the fruit, which constituted the upper part of her cargo, and there delivered the same according to the bill of lading. The defendant *Voy*, a pilot duly appointed and licensed to conduct ships and vessels from *London Bridge* to *Gravesend*, and from *Gravesend* to *London Bridge*, was employed by the other defendants, as such pilot, to conduct and navigate the brig from the *London Docks* to *Coxe's Quay*; and whilst she was proceeding from the *London Docks* to *Coxe's Quay* with *Voy* on board, and under his charge and management, the accident in question happened. *Coxe's Quay* is situate between *London Bridge* and the *London Docks*, and is about a mile from the *London Docks*. The port of *London* extends from *London Bridge* to below *Gravesend*. The question for the opinion of the Court is, whether, under the above circumstances, the defendants *R. Slade* and *J. Slade* were or were not entitled to be acquitted under the provisions of the pilot act, 6 *Geo.* 4, c. 125, the vessel being *sect. 55.* under the care of a duly licensed pilot at the time of the accident.

Wightman, for the plaintiff. This case must be governed by the determination of the question whether the master of the vessel was bound to have a pilot on board to navigate her from the *London Docks* to *Coxe's Quay*. If he was so bound, then the owners are not liable for the accident, but if not so bound they are responsible. The 55th section of the pilot act enacts, " that no owner or master of any ship shall be answerable for any loss or damage which shall happen to any person from or by reason or means of any neglect, default, or incapacity of any licensed pilot acting in the charge of any ship, under or in pursuance of any of the provisions of that act." Now as the master was not bound to take a pilot on board from the *London Docks* to *Coxe's Quay*, it cannot be said that the pilot was acting in pursuance of any of the provisions of the pilot act at the time the accident happened. By the bill of lading, the voyage was at an end at the time the vessel arrived in the *London Docks*. The employment, therefore, of the pilot to take the vessel from the *London Docks* to *Coxe's Quay* was a mere voluntary act of the owners. In this point of view he was merely their servant, and they are liable for his negligence. For this *Carruthers* v. *Sydebotham* (a), *Attorney General* v. *Case* (b), and *Abbott on Shipping*, 160, 5th ed. are authorities. It is true, that by the second section of the act " all vessels sailing, navigating, and passing up or down or upon the rivers *Thames* or *Medway*, and the several channels, creeks and docks thereof, or therein, between *Orfordness*, the *Downs*, or *Isle of Wight*, and *London Bridge*, shall be conducted and piloted (except as hereinafter provided) within those limits by licensed pilots, and by no other pilots or persons whomsoever;" but that enactment does not apply to vessels which have once arrived at their place of destination ; and cannot be extended to vessels removing afterwards to another place, though within the same port. *Rex* v. *Lambe* (c), *Rex* v. *Neale* (d). Without referring to the 63d section, which clearly exempts this vessel from the liability to take a pilot on board, the circumstances of this case would, upon principle, shew that the master was not bound to take a pilot on board ; but that section is decisive upon the subject, because it expressly exempts ships brought into any port in *England* by any pilot duly licensed, afterwards removing in such port or ports for the purpose of entering

(a) 4 M. & S. 77.   (c) 5 T. R. 76.
(b) 3 Price, 302.   (d) 8 T. R. 241.

into or going out of any dock, or for changing the moorings of such ship or vessel. Here the vessel had been piloted to the *London Docks*, and the pilot was discharged. Circumstances rendered it necessary for her to change her moorings and go to some other place in the same port. Surely, under such circumstances, the master was not bound to take another pilot on board for that purpose. This was a mere voluntary act, and the owners are liable. The schedule to the act contains the rates of charge to be made by pilots upon ships to the *London Docks*, or to moorings, as well as from moorings into the *London Docks;* but there is no rate from the *London Docks* to a place nearer the bridge, nor from moorings to moorings. The removal of the vessel in this case from the *London Docks* to *Coxe's Quay* was no more than a change of moorings. The case of *Thornton* v. *Bolland*(a) will be cited on the other side; but that differs very materially from the present. There, the master of a vessel from the westward had been piloted into *Standgate Creek* by a Cinque Port pilot, and discharged him there, and sailed *a mile* towards *London*, with a signal flying for a *Trinity House* pilot, who came on board at *Sheerness;* and it was held that the master was liable to a penalty under the statute, and did not fall within the exception of removing a vessel for the purpose of entering into or going out of dock, or changing her moorings; " for," said the Lord Chief Justice, " the defendant proceeded *on the voyage* for the distance of one mile without a pilot on board."

Campbell, contrà. The defendants, Messrs. *Slade*, are exempted from liability by force of the pilot act, 6 *Geo.* 4, c. 125. First, under the circumstances of the case the owners were compellable to take a pilot on board to navigate the vessel from the *London Docks* to *Coxe's Quay*, and secondly, even if not compellable, still as there was in fact on board the ship, at the time the accident happened, a

(a) 9 J. B. Moore, 403; 2 Bing. 219.

pilot regularly licensed, according to the provisions of the act, and the ship was within the limits pointed out by the statute, and under the pilot's management, the owners are not liable. First, as to the necessity of taking a pilot on board, it is material to draw the attention of the Court to the facts of the case. By the bill of lading, a material part of the cargo was to be delivered at *Coxe's Quay;* and being fruit, and placed at the top, it required to be first delivered before the wine could be got at. The voyage, therefore, was not at an end until the vessel got to *Coxe's Quay.* The case also states, that the port of *London* extends from *Gravesend* to *London Bridge,* so that *Coxe's Quay* was within the port. It may be true that the vessel was duly piloted into the *London Docks* at first, but not having broken bulk there, she cannot be said to have arrived at her destination. Suppose she had broken bulk at *Gravesend,* could it have been contended that she might afterwards have gone into the docks without a pilot? Certainly not. If not, then what difference is there between such a state of circumstances and the circumstances found in this case? Again, suppose the vessel had not stopped at the *London Docks* in the first instance, and the accident had happened in the passage between the *London Docks* and *Coxe's Quay,* is there any doubt that she must have had a pilot on board? What difference then does it make that she has unnecessarily stopped at the *London Docks* for a nugatory purpose? The case, therefore, falls within the meaning and spirit of the second section, this being a vessel sailing, navigating and passing upon the river *Thames* within the limits therein set out, and, therefore, requiring to have a licensed pilot on board. The cases of *Rex* v. *Lambe* and *Rex* v. *Neale* are different from this. The decisions in those cases were founded on the statute 5 *Geo.* 2, c. 20, which is materially different in its provisions from the modern pilot act. Taking it that *primâ facie* this is a case within the second section, is there any thing in the circumstances of the case, which will bring it within the exception contained in the 63d section? It is said that this vessel was only removing from moorings to moorings after she had come into port. Now that is not so; for at the time the accident happened the vessel was actually sailing to her destination. The fact of her having stopped in her way at the *London Docks* without breaking bulk does not alter the case. That was an useless and unnecessary stoppage, no way contributing to the performance of her voyage. In going to *Coxe's Quay*, she was going for the necessary purpose of discharging her cargo according to the bill of lading. Changing moorings must be understood to apply to the case of a vessel which has once broken bulk, and discharged her cargo in port, and getting out of the way for the convenience of other vessels or for her own. It does not apply to a case like the present, where the vessel was passing from one part of the port to another for the purpose of discharging her cargo. The case of *Thornton* v. *Bolland* is directly in point. That was the case of a vessel proceeding from one part of the same port to another without a pilot. Here the circumstances are alike; and in both cases the words of the act of parliament are precisely similar. Secondly, conceding that the owners were not under any legal obligation to take a pilot on board during this part of the voyage, still having in fact a licensed pilot on board when the accident happened they are exempt from responsibility. The 55th section is very general in its terms. It exempts owners from responsibility for any damage accruing by default of any licensed pilot acting in the charge of any vessel, in pursuance of the provisions of that act, so long as such pilot shall be duly qualified to have the charge of the vessel. There is no doubt that in this case *Voy* the pilot was duly qualified to have charge of this vessel in her passage from the *London Docks* to *Coxe's Quay*, therefore the owners are exempt from all liability.

Cur. adv. vult.

BAYLEY, J.—This was an action against the owners and pilot of a brig for an injury done by the brig whilst moving from the *London Docks* to *Coxe's Quay*, and the question was, whether, under the late pilot act, 6 *Geo.* 4, c. 125, the owners were entitled to an acquital. There was no question but that the injury was occasioned by the neglect or default of the pilot, so that the owners were clearly entitled to an acquittal under the fifty-fifth section of that act, if, under the circumstances, it was necessary that the brig should have a pilot on board at the time; but it was insisted that the protection under section 55 extended to no case where the ship was under no obligation to have a pilot on board, and it was contended that at the time this injury was done this brig was under no such obligation. It is upon this latter point our opinion is founded, and we have had the benefit of conferring with Lord *Tenterden* upon the subject. By this act, all ships and vessels navigating and passing up or down or upon the rivers *Thames* or *Medway*, and the several channels, creeks and docks thereof or therein, between *Orfordness*, the *Downs*, or *Isle of Wight*, and *London Bridge*, are to be conducted and piloted within those limits (except as thereinafter is provided) by licensed pilots and no other pilots or persons, and the only exception applicable to this case was section 63, which gave an exemption from penalties for removing a ship in port for the purpose of entering into or going out of any dock or for changing its moorings, and it was urged in this case, that at the time in question this brig was merely changing her moorings. The brig was loaded with fruit and wine, the former deliverable at *Fresh Wharf* or *Coxe's Quay*, both in *Thames Street*, and considerably above the *London Docks:* the latter deliverable in the *London Docks*. The fruit constituted the upper part of the cargo and the wine could not be delivered until the fruit was out, so that unless the owners could come to some new arrangement with the persons who were to have the fruit, *Fresh Wharf* or *Coxe's Quay* was the place to which the ship should in the first

1827.

M'INTOSH
v.
SLADE.

instance have proceeded, and they had no right to stop her short of one or the other of those places. It was thought fit, however, to put into the *London Docks* and stop short there, under the chance that they might be able to come to some arrangement with the consignees of the fruit to procure their consent for discharging the fruit there, and upon being disappointed in that respect, they got a fresh pilot, left the docks, and were proceeding to *Coxe's Quay*, when the injury, for which the action was brought, was committed, and under these circumstances we are of opinion that this brig was not to be considered as merely changing her moorings. It is not necessary for us to decide whether, where a ship's cargo is deliverable at different parts of the port of *London*, and a removal becomes necessary after she has reached the place where she is first to begin her delivery, such removal shall be deemed a change of moorings; but our opinion is this, that if a ship stops short before she reaches the place at which she ought to stop, a removal thence to the place to which she ought to have gone in the first instance is not a mere change of moorings, and is not within the exemption in question. This brig had no right to stop at the *London Docks*, she ought to have proceeded in the first instance to *Fresh Wharf* or *Coxe's Quay*, and when she was proceeding thither from the docks she was going to what was properly her original destination, she was sailing to reach what was the end of her voyage, and not merely changing her moorings. For these reasons we are of opinion, that the master was bound at that time to have a pilot on board, and, consequently, that the owners are exempt from liability. The verdict, therefore, must be entered for *Robert* and *John Slade*, and against *Voy.*

E. BRYDGES *v.* H. PLUMPTRE.

Where, after the lapse of six years, a defendant, being asked for the payment of a debt, said, " I owed the money, but I have a receipt in full of all demands, I shall search for it, and let you know in the event of my not being able to find it :"— Held, that this was not sufficient to take the case out of the statute of limitations.

THIS was an action of debt to recover a sum of six guineas, claimed to be due from the defendant to the plaintiff for the balance of wages. The defendant pleaded, first, the general issue, and, secondly, the statute of limitations. At the trial before *Graham*, B. at the last *Summer* assizes for the county of *Kent*, it appeared that the plaintiff had quitted the defendant's service in 1816, at which time there was due to him the sum of six guineas. In order to take the case out of the statute of limitations, it appeared that, shortly before action brought, the defendant was applied to for payment of the money, and he said, " *Brydges* quitted my service in 1816. I owed him six guineas, but I have his receipt in full of all demands ; I shall search for it, and I shall let you know in the event of my not being able to find it." It was contended that this was an admission of the debt, and that the defendant was bound to pay it, and that he was liable for the amount in failure of proof of the receipt in full of all demands. The learned Judge was inclined to think, that as the defendant had relied then upon a receipt in full of all demands, and did not produce it, his statement must be considered as an admission that he was bound to pay, and the plaintiff had a verdict. In *Easter* term a rule nisi was granted for entering a nonsuit, against which

Adolphus and *Platt* now shewed cause. The question is, whether the expressions used by the defendant are sufficient to take the case out of the statute of limitations. Now it has been ruled in many cases, that where a defendant acknowledges the existence of the debt, and puts his reason for not paying it upon the ground of some document in his possession, and he fails to produce such document, he cannot avail himself of the statute. *Hellings* v. *Shaw*(a). Here there was abundant evidence of the ac-

(a) 1 J. B. Moore, 340; 7 Taunt. 608.

knowledgment of the debt, and of an admission that the
defendant was bound to pay, and having failed to produce
the receipt in full of all demands, the statute of limitations
is no defence.

1827.

E. BRYDGES
v.
H. PLUMPTRE.

Marryat, contrà, was stopped by the Court.

Lord TENTERDEN, C. J.—I am of opinion that the
rule must be made absolute for entering a nonsuit. In the
case of *Tanner* v. *Smart* (a), it was decided by us last term,
that in order to take a case out of the statute of limitations,
the evidence must be such as fairly shews a promise to pay
the debt supposed to be due. In that case there was a
positive promise to pay the debt in these terms, " I cannot pay the debt at present, but I will pay it as soon as I
can." We held that as there was no proof that he could
pay the money, or was of ability to pay, even that promise
was not sufficient to take the case out of the statute. According to our decision in that case, which was very much
considered, I am clearly of opinion that this rule must be
made absolute. Taking the whole of what the defendant
said, it is quite manifest that he did not intend to pay the
debt, and I cannot infer a promise to pay, if a man does
not intend to pay a debt which he has all along resisted,
even though the ground of his resistance cannot be afterwards sustained in evidence.

HOLROYD, J.(b).—I am of the same opinion. It is said
that the learned Judge considered this as an admission on
the part of the defendant that he was bound to pay. I do
not think that it is by any means such an admission. When
applied to for payment, he says he has a receipt in full of
all demands, but he cannot find it, and that he considered
all the claims between him and the plaintiff at an end.

(a) *Ante*, 519 ; 6 B. & C.
603.

(b) *Bayley*, J. had left the
Court.

LITTLEDALE, J.—The statute of limitations enacts, that the action shall be brought within six years and not after; but a great many decisions have taken place since the statute, which have gone to say that it may be brought after the original cause of action upon a fresh cause of action arising upon a new promise; but in such cases there must be something said by the party which is tantamount to a new promise to pay. Now so far from this being a promise to pay, it is a denial of the debt, and although the defendant says he has a receipt in full of all demands, still he is not bound to produce the instrument. I cannot say that his saying, whether true or false, that he has a receipt in full of all demands is to be construed into an admission of his liability.

Rule absolute.

HARE v. TRAVIS.

ASSUMPSIT on a policy of insurance on pearl ashes, on board the ship *Smyrna*, at and from *Liverpool* to *London*. The plaintiff sought to recover an average loss. The policy contained the usual clause that all goods were to be free from average under 3 per cent., unless general or the ship was stranded. Plea, the general issue. At the trial before Lord *Tenterden*, C. J., at the sittings in *London* after last term, the facts proved in evidence were these:— the pearl ashes in question were loaded at *Liverpool*, with other goods, which last were destined for the port of *Southampton*. The pearl ashes were stowed in the lower tier. The vessel sailed from *Liverpool* on the 23d of *September*. She was compelled by stress of weather to put into *Holyhead* twice, and the captain having called a survey there, it appeared that she had made a good deal of water.

She left *Holyhead* on the 30th of *October*, and from that time she was never free from water. In the *Bristol* channel she was pumped, and the water brought up was so charged with a solution of the pearl ashes, that it took the colour out of the captain's clothes. The vessel arrived at *Southampton*, and there the goods shipped for that port were delivered, but no examination of the pearl ashes took place. On the 4th of *November* she left *Southampton* for *London*, and arrived there on the 10th of that month. During the voyage from *Southampton* to *London* there were no heavy seas, the weather was tolerably fair, but the ship made water, though not so much as she had done previously. In four or five days after the vessel arrived in *London*, the pearl ashes were unloaded, and were found damaged to such a degree as to be sold only for one-third of what they would have originally fetched, had they been delivered in a sound state. It was proved by persons acquainted with the article, that the damage sustained could not have happened from coming in contact with salt water in less than three or four weeks, but certainly not in three or four days. Upon these facts it was contended on the part of the defendant, that the plaintiff ought to be nonsuited on two grounds, first, because the vessel did not sail on the voyage insured, which was from *Liverpool* to *London*, which was the first port of her destination, but on a voyage to *Southampton*, for which port the master must have cleared, he having taken in goods for that place; and, secondly, assuming that the putting in to *Southampton* was a mere deviation, there was no evidence upon which the jury could come to any reasonable determination that the loss had happened, for which the underwriters were liable, before the deviation took place. The Lord Chief Justice was of opinion, that the vessel did sail on the voyage insured, the captain having an intention to deviate, which intention was afterwards carried into effect by his actually going into *Southampton*, and that the underwriters were therefore not liable for any damage which had occurred after that time; but he left it as a question of fact to the jury on the evidence, whether, before the vessel put into *Southampton*, the pearl ashes had been damaged to the amount of 3 per cent. by a peril of the sea. The jury found that the damage exceeded 3 per cent. before the deviation to *Southampton*.

Campbell now moved for a rule nisi to enter a nonsuit on both points made at the trial. First, the captain having been clearly guilty of a deviation from the voyage insured, the underwriters are not liable unless it appeared clearly that the loss happened before the deviation; and there is no case to be found in which the underwriters have been held liable for a loss arising after deviation. From the first there was an intention to deviate, by taking goods in for *Southampton*, and that intention being executed, the underwriters are discharged. Secondly, there was no proof of any sea damage before the deviation, and it is quite clear that they would not be answerable for a loss arising afterwards. No examination of the pearl ashes took place at *Southampton*, and therefore the presumption is that the injury arose afterwards. The pearl ashes were warranted free from average if under 3 per cent., and the plaintiff was bound to shew a damage to that extent by a peril of the sea whilst the goods were under the protection of the policy. *Parkin* v. *Tunno* (a). Here there was no evidence of that kind. Between the 1st and the 10th of *November*, whilst the vessel was on her voyage to *Southampton*, she was frequently pumped, and for any thing that appeared to the contrary the damage may have arisen in that interval.

Lord TENTERDEN, C. J.—I am of opinion that we ought not to grant a rule. The voyage insured was at and from *Liverpool* to *London*. The captain having taken goods on board at *Liverpool* for *Southampton*, intending to leave them at *Southampton* on his way to *London*, it seems to me that the ship must be understood to have sailed on a

(a) 2 Campb. 53.

voyage to both places, and that so long as the vessel continued in that course which was common to a voyage either to *Southampton* or *London*, she was sailing on the voyage insured. Inasmuch, however, as the policy did not contain any clause giving liberty to the vessel to put into *Southampton*, I think the putting into that port was a deviation, and that the plaintiff was not entitled to recover for any damage arising subsequently. The question is then whether there was any evidence of a loss to the extent of 3 per cent. before the deviation at *Southampton*. It appeared that in the course of her voyage to *Southampton* the vessel met with a great deal of bad weather, and had suffered so greatly that she was obliged to put in at *Holyhead* twice, and upon her survey there it appeared that she had made much water. In the *Bristol* channel she was pumped, and that then the pearl ashes were in a state of solution, and that the water brought up discharged the colour from the captain's clothes. It appeared further, that between *Southampton* and *London* she encountered better weather, though it was still necessary to keep the pump going, but not so frequently as before she put into *Southampton*. Under these circumstances I left it to the jury to say whether in their judgment a loss exceeding 3 per cent. had accrued by a peril of the sea before the ship arrived at *Southampton*, it having been agreed before hand that the precise amount should be settled out of Court. The jury found in the affirmative, and I see no reason for disturbing their verdict.

BAYLEY, J.—If a voyage is insured to a given place, and when the ship sails the captain does not mean to go to that place at all, he never sails on the voyage insured, and the policy does not attach. But if at the time of sailing the captain means to go ultimately to the place originally intended, but by a circuitous route, the voyage is to be considered as the same until the vessel comes to the dividing point, and the policy still attaches upon the subject of in-

surance; the departure from the course of the voyage insured then becomes a deviation; but before the arrival at the
dividing point, there is no more than an intention to deviate,
which, if not carried into effect, will not vitiate the policy.
This principle was established in the case of *Kewley* v.
Ryan (a). The policy there was at and from *Granada* to
Liverpool. The vessel sailed for *Liverpool*, but before the
commencement of the voyage the captain had formed the
design of touching at *Cork* on her way. Before, however,
she had arrived at the dividing point, she was totally lost;
but the termini of the intended voyage being really the
same as those described in the policy, the Court held
that it must be considered as the same voyage, and that
a design to deviate not effected would not vitiate the
policy; and they observed, that the ship was bound for
Liverpool, although she had also clearances for *Cork*.
Here also this vessel must be considered as sailing on her
voyage to *London* until the deviation to *Southampton* took
place. It appears to me, upon the second point, that
there was evidence to go to the jury that a loss by a peril of
the sea to the amount of 3 per cent. had arisen before the
deviation, and therefore I am of opinion that there ought
to be no rule.

HOLROYD, J. and LITTLEDALE, J. concurred.

                                        Rule refused.

            (a) 2 H. Black. 248.

The KING v. The Inhabitants of THORNHAM.

Where a shep-
herd hired him-
self under an
agreement for 12s. per week, and to have " twenty-one ewes *going* :" —Held, that as it
was no part of the contract that the sheep should be pasture fed, no settlement was
gained, although the feed was worth more than 10l. a year, and might have been in fact
pasture feeding.

BY an order of two justices *Richard Hammond*, labourer,
Sarah his wife, and their four children, were removed from

Sedgeford to *Thornham,* both in the county of *Norfolk.*
The sessions, on appeal, confirmed the order, subject to
the opinion of this Court on the following case :—

The pauper, being a married man, went on the *Midsummer-day,* 1812, to live with Mr. *Barsham,* a farmer, residing in the appellant parish of *Thornham,* as his shepherd,
under a written agreement, which was in the following
words :—" *April* 28th, 1812. Hired *Richard Hammond,*
shepherd, at 12*s.* per week, 6*d.* per head a lamb at clip-day,
three weeks' board in lambing, meat of victuals, and pluck
when he kills a pig, and to have *twenty-one ewes going,* to
come to his place at old *Midsummer-day* next. (Signed)
James Barsham." The pauper came to live with Mr. *Barsham* under this agreement, with the ewes and lambs and
his furniture. For the first quarter of a year he resided
in Mr. *Barsham's* farm-house, and for the remainder of
the two years he lived in a cottage of his master's near the
farm-house, with his wife and family, rent free. The going
of the twenty-one ewes was worth more than 10*l.* a year.
During a fortnight or three weeks of the first year the
ewes were fed off Mr. *Barsham's* farm on the turnips of
a neighbouring farmer, and during part of the second
winter they were fed on straw.

Nolan and *Maltby* in support of the order of sessions.
The first question in this case is, whether an agreement for
the " going" of twenty-one ewes is not an agreement under
which the sheep were at all events to be fed on the growing produce of the master's farm ; and, secondly, whether,
supposing the growing produce might be, and in point of
fact *was* taken, that is not substantially a contract that the
sheep should be fed on the farm. With respect to the first
point, there are authorities to shew, that the term " going"
means that the sheep should " go on the farm," and is to
be understood as equivalent to grazing, in contra-distinc-
tion to dry feeding or foddering in the yard. The term
has the same meaning as a " gate," and it has been held

that a " cattle gate" in a stinted pasture is a tenement sufficient to confer a settlement. *Rex* v. *Whixley* (a), *Rex* v. *Tolpuddle* (b). The case of *Rex* v. *Dersingham* (c) is still stronger, for there it was held that a right of common in gross was a tenement within the statute. That was a " going of cattle on the common," and in that sense the word " going" *ex vi termini* means a certain portion of the growing produce. In this case, it was not even optional with the master to have the sheep fed anywhere else but upon his own land. [*Bayley*, J. Might he not have foddered them with hay not grown upon his own land ?] The term " going" has a definite meaning in the law, and means going upon the farm and to be fed upon the pasture. [*Littledale*, J. The sessions have not found that by " going" it was meant that the sheep were to be fed on pasture.] In *Rex* v. *Benniworth* (d) the cow was to be fed on the master's land, but that did not necessarily shew that the animal was to be pasture fed, or fed upon the growing produce of the master's land, but yet the Court drew that conclusion from all the circumstances of the case. So in *Rex* v. *Cherry Willingham* (e) the same construction was put upon the contract. The case of *Rex* v. *Bardwell* (f) was decided upon the ground expressly that the sheep should be pasture fed, and, therefore, the meaning of the term " going" was not brought under consideration. Secondly, assuming that the contract between these parties did not give an absolute interest in the growing produce of the master's land, yet if, under the contract, there might be a right to take growing produce, and if this was in fact enjoyed for more than forty days, it is sufficient to confer a settlement. Under this agreement it was clearly competent to the master to feed the sheep forty days on the pasture ; and, therefore, it may be considered as an optional

---

(a) 1 T. R. 137.

(b) 4 T. R. 671.

(c) 7 T. R. 671

(d) *Ante*, vol. iv. 355; 2 B. & C. 775.

(e) *Ante*, vol. iii. 13; 1 B. & C. 696.

(f) *Ante*, vol. iii. 369; 4 B. & C. 161.

agreement, the giving an alternative either for the going on
the land itself or for the feeding in the farm-yard. There
is no doubt that if the agreement had been in terms drawn
up in the alternative, and the master had fed the sheep on
growing produce for forty days, it would have been suf-
cient to have conferred a settlement, and so it would
have been sufficient, if, at the master's option, they were
fed all the time, except for forty days, in the farm-yard.
The cases of *Rex* v. *Fillongley* (a), and *Rex* v. *Minster* (b)
are authorities to shew that such an optional agreement, if
acted upon, would be sufficient to confer a settlement.

Marryat and *Wightman*, contrà, were stopped by the
Court.

BAYLEY, J.—This appears to me to be a very plain
case. If the sessions had intended that the word "going"
had the meaning which has been ascribed to it to-day,
we should probably have pronounced a different opinion
from that which we are now called upon to deliver. They
should have told us what was the meaning of the parties
at the time the contract was entered into, or what was the
understanding or interpretation of the word "going" in
that part of the country. I think the fair meaning of the
word "going" is, that the pauper's twenty-one ewes were
to be with, and to go with his master's flock, and were to
be fed from time to time upon growing produce, or upon
hay, or upon turnips, as his master's flock was. Without
any explanation given to us, as to the meaning of the word
"going," as understood in the part of the country where
the agreement was entered into, we must understand it in
that sense in which it is usually understood. It appears to
me, therefore, that the word "going" does not necessarily
mean feeding upon the growing produce of the land, and
consequently that the pauper has not gained a settlement
by a tenement of 10l. a year. In order to make out a settlement of this kind, it must be part of the bargain itself,

(a) 1 T. R. 458.   (b) 3 M. & S. 276.

3 E 2

that the sheep shall be fed to the extent of 10*l.* a year, out of the growing produce of the land, and if it does not stipulate that they shall be so fed, the mere circumstance of their being in fact so fed out of the growing produce of the land to the extent of 10*l.* a year will not confer a settlement. The authorities go to shew that this must be part of the original bargain. I find this laid down in a text book, in very extensive use, published by a gentleman who has favoured the world with a valuable work upon the poor laws (a), and he cites as authorities to this effect, *Rex* v. *Bardwell* (b), *Rex* v. *Tisbury* (c), and *Rex* v. *Darley Abbey* (d). In this last case it was solemnly determined that it must be part of the contract that the cattle should be pasture fed. So also the case of *Rex* v. *Oswald Twissle* (e) it was determined that the contract must be to feed the cattle with the growing produce of the land. In that case, the pauper rented the milk of a cow by the year. The keep of the animal might be, and was in fact, by pasture feeding, but it was held that inasmuch as it did not appear to be made matter of bargain that she should be pasture fed, hiring her milk was not necessarily taking a tenement of 10*l.* a year, and, consequently, did not confer a settlement. In the case of *Rex* v. *Sutton St. Edmunds* (f) the terms of the bargain were, that the master was either to find the pauper two cows, or the pauper was at liberty to provide himself with two, and feed them on his master's farm during the year, and in that case, *Abbott*, C. J. said, " In the case of *Rex* v. *Oswald Twissle* the contract was for the feed of a cow, without saying on the farm, and inasmuch as it did not appear that the cow was to be pasture fed, the Court held that no settlement was gained, and quashed the order. In the case then at bar, he observed the contract was not

(a) Mr. *Nolan's* Treatise upon the Poor Laws, vol. ii. pp. 19, 20.

(b) *Ante,* vol. iii. 369; 2 B. & C. 161.

(c) Mic. 43 *Geo.* 3, cited in *Rex* v. *Darley Abbey,* 14 East, 280.

(d) 14 East, 280.

(e) Cited in *Rex* v. *Sutton St. Edmunds, ante,* vol. ii. 800; 1 B. & C. 536.

(f) *Ante,* vol. ii. 800; 1 B. & C. 586.

for the growing produce, and he added that in *Rex* v. *Oswald Twissle* the attention of the Court had been called to the distinction between taking the growing crop and the severed crop, and it being found in *Rex* v. *Sutton St. Edmunds* that the growing crop was less than the value of 10*l.*, he thought that no settlement was gained. Of this opinion were the other judges, and the Court determined that the contract must be to feed the cattle with the growing produce of the land in order to confer a settlement. In the cases cited and relied upon by Mr. *Nolan*, the contracts were, that the feeding was to be upon the growing produce of a particular piece of land. Such was the case of the " cattle gate," which imports, in the north of *England*, the going of cattle upon a particular piece of land, there to be fed on the growing produce of that land. In the case of *Rex* v. *Dersingham*, the agreement was for the going of three heads of cattle on the common. That necessarily meant going and feeding on the growing produce of the common. That gave a clear right that the cattle should be pasture fed; and, consequently, if the pasture was worth 10*l.* a year, it would confer a settlement. In the present case, looking at the terms of the contract between the master and servant, and believing that neither of them had any very accurate idea of the meaning of the word " going," they must be taken to have used that word in its ordinary sense, namely, that the twenty-one ewes, should go with the master's flock, wherever it went, and should be fed from time to time, as his flock was, either on pasture or on dry food, and there being no specific agreement that they should be pasture fed to the extent of 10*l.* a year, it falls within the principles laid down and acted upon in the several cases to which I have adverted. For these reasons, it appears to me that the pauper gained no settlement in the parish of *Thornham.*

HOLROYD, J.—I am of opinion that no settlement was gained under this contract. I think the word " going" has no technical meaning, and that unless it can be made out on the face of the case itself that it imports that the sheep were to be going on the pasture, there to be fed, it must be taken in its ordinary sense, and the doctrine of the cases referred to by my brother *Bayley* must govern our decision. I think the word " going" here does not mean any thing more than was expressed in *Rex* v. *Bardwell*, namely, that the servant's should go with the master's cattle, that is, to be fed upon pasture or dry food, as the case might be. It appears to me, therefore, that as the word " going" does not necessarily import feeding on pasture, no settlement was gained.

LITTLEDALE, J.—I am of the same opinion. The case turns entirely upon the meaning of the word " going." If that word had a well-known meaning in the part of the country in which this question arose, it ought to have been expressly found by the case, or if it was to be understood by these parties themselves that it was meant that the sheep were to be pasture fed, it ought to have been so stated. I am not aware that the word " going" has any such signification. It does not necessarily mean pasture feeding, but if that be the meaning, the quarter sessions should have so found it in the case. Not having so found it, it appears to me that we must understand it in its common and ordinary sense, namely, that the pauper was to have the going of his sheep with his master's flock, whether it were fed on pasture or dry food. The case of *Rex* v. *Bardwell* gives an interpretation of the word " going," which ought to bind our judgment.

Order of Sessions quashed.

The KING v. GOSSE.

THIS was an appeal against a rate made for the relief of the poor of the parish of *St. James*, in *Poole*, in the county of *Dorset*. The sessions confirmed the rate, subject to the opinion of this Court upon a case. The case stated that the defendant *Gosse*, and two other persons, carried on business in co-partnership, in the parish of *St. James*, in *Poole*. The defendant was the only partner resident within the parish, and he was rated in respect of the whole of the partnership property in which he and his copartners were jointly interested, and not in respect of his third share only.

Where one only of several partners was resident in a parish, and a poor rate was made upon him in respect of all the partnership property, and not upon his individual share:—Held, that the rate could not be supported.

Tindal, S. G., *Brougham*, and *W. D. Bayley*, contended that the rate was properly made, inasmuch as it was impossible for the overseers to make a rate in respect of the interest which each partner may have in a firm. They must look to the person who is in the visible possession of the property. The defendant, *Gosse*, had an undivided interest in the whole partnership property, and therefore he was primarily rateable for the whole, as the resident partner. This was not like either of the cases of *Rex* v. *North Currey* (a) and *Rex* v. *Fryer* (b), in the first of which not any of the partners was resident in the parish; and in the second all the partners were rated, although one only resided in the parish.

Scarlett, A. G. and *Parke*, contrà, were stopped by the Court.

Lord TENTERDEN, C. J.—We are of opinion that this rate must be amended. By the statute 43 *Eliz.* c. 2, it is " inhabitants" that are to be rated according to their ability. Now if this rate were to stand, the defendant, *Gosse*, would be rated, not according to his own ability, but the ability of

(a) *Ante*, vol. vii. 424; 4 B. & C. 953. (b) *Ante*, vol. vii. 426, n.; 4 B. & C. 961, n.

himself and others.　It is suggested that there will be difficulty in ascertaining the quantity of interest which each of the several partners has in the concern.　That difficulty may be easily obviated by imposing the rate in respect of the whole property, and the party overrated may come and discharge himself by proving the extent of his interest.

The other Judges concurred.

Rate to be amended.

The KING *v.* The Company of Proprietors of the
REGENT'S CANAL.

The *Regent's* Canal Company are rateable to the poor only in respect of the annual value of the land occupied by their canal *quâ* land, and not in respect of the value of the rates and tolls arising therefrom, which being made personal property is not rateable.

A slip of land in a natural state, used as a landing-place for goods on the edge of a basin belonging to the company, is not a wharf within the meaning of the statute 52 *Geo.* 3, c. 195,

UPON an appeal by the defendants against a rate for the relief of the poor of the parish of *St. Ann, Limehouse*, the sessions confirmed the rate, subject to the opinion of this Court on the following case:—

In the rate or assessment the appellants stood rated thus:—

		£.
No. 1.	Company of Proprietors of *Regent's Canal*, for wharfs and banks adjoining the basin leading to the *Regent's Canal* . . . . themselves,	130
No. 2.	Ditto, for land covered with water, comprising the part of the basin within the respondents' parish . ditto,	150
No. 3.	Ditto, for land covered with water, comprising that part of the *Regent's Canal* and the towing-path and banks within the respondents' parish . . . . . ditto,	150
No. 4.	Ditto, for one double lock in *Limehouse Fields*, and for one other double lock leading from the basin to the canal in the respondents' parish, . . . themselves, for each lock, ...	25

The rate was duly allowed and published, and was in all respects correct in point of form.　By the 52 *Geo.* 3, c. 195, s. 101, it was provided, " that lands, whether covered with water or not, and also all dwelling-houses, wharfs, ware-

nor rateable as such to the poor.

houses, lock-houses, and other houses, of and belonging to the company, should be rateable and chargeable to the maintenance of the poor, and to all other parochial rates and taxes in the several parishes and places where they were respectively situated, the lands according to their quantity and quality, and the dwelling-houses, wharfs, warehouses, lock-houses, and other houses, according to the nature and respective uses, dimensions, and descriptions thereof, and should be charged and assessed in like manner as lands of a like quality, and dwelling-houses, wharfs, warehouses, lock-houses, and other houses of a like and similar size, nature, dimension, or description, in the respective parishes where the same should be situate, were or should be assessed or charged; and that the rates, duties, and other personal property of the company liable to be rated to the poor or other parochial taxes, in any such parishes or places, should be rated and assessed in like manner and in the same proportion as other personal property rateable in the said parishes and places respectively should be rated and assessed, and according to the length of line of the said navigation in such respective parishes and places, and not otherwise or in any other manner; provided that, before such personal property should be rated, fourteen days' notice should be given in writing to or left at the dwelling-house of the treasurer or clerk, or any other officer of the company residing in the parish or place where such rate should be intended to be made, by the respective overseers of the poor, of the intention so to do."

As to No. 1, the facts were as follow:—The land rated was the margin of a large basin or dock belonging to the appellants. This basin communicates on the one hand with the *Thames*, by means of a lock capable of admitting ships of a large burthen; and on the other hand with the *Regent's Canal*, by means of a double lock of only sufficient size to admit the barges used in the internal navigation. On the east, and on part of the south and north sides of this basin is a narrow slip of land, the property of the appellants, and containing altogether one acre, two roods, and fourteen perches, situated in the respondents' parish. Over this land, on the south and east sides, there was originally made a towing-path for barges proceeding between the canal and the *Thames*. This is still occasionally used in times of frost, but at all other times the barges cross the basin diagonally, and have no occasion for it. At the end next the double lock it is terminated by a fence and gate, which is kept locked by the defendants, and is only opened by their servants, who keep the key of the gate, for persons having navigation business, who are always freely admitted, and use the towing-path as a foot-path on those occasions. Next adjoining the slip of land on the east side of the basin are situate the bonding yard for timber of Messrs. *Richardson* and of Messrs. *Watkins* and *Fry*. The vessels bringing cargoes from foreign parts and other places to these yards take their births along the east side of the basin, and unload their timber and other goods by means of stages belonging to such ships, on the slip of land of the defendants, rated as a wharf, the upper edge of the slip of land next the basin consisting of the natural ground, and not being faced with brick, stone, or timber, and the ground below the water gradually sloping down to the bottom of the basin. The timber is measured and marked on this slip of land by the officers of the revenue, and is after that, with the other goods, conveyed either into the bonding yard, or, on payment of the duties, into the private premises of the above persons. For this privilege of landing their goods neither Messrs. *Richardson* nor Messrs. *Watkins* and *Fry* pay any acknowledgment or rent to the defendants; they only pay, as all other persons do, the rates and duties imposed in respect of the tonnage of the ships entering the basin, but the number of the ships coming into the basin of the defendants is greatly increased by reason of the establishment of Messrs. *Richardson's* premises as a bonding yard, and the access thereto from the basin; and there has been, in consequence thereof, a considerable increase in the tonnage rates and duties paid on such ships to the company since the bonding yard has been established. No other persons are allowed to land their goods there, nor is there any crane or convenience for landing goods. In another part of the basin, situate in *Ratcliffe* hamlet, there are cranes and wharfs regularly built, where the defendants, in addition to the tonnage rates, charge both for the cranage and wharfage of all goods there landed. Neither the south nor the north side of the basin within the respondents' parish was used for landing goods. If the land on the east side of the basin be to be considered as a wharf, of which the defendants were the occupiers, its annual value, together with the value of the land on the north and south sides of the basin, was 130*l.*, as stated in the rate. The annual value of the land within the respondents' parish on the east, south, and north sides, if assessed as land of a like quality, was only 8*l.* As to Nos. 2, 3, and 4, the facts were as follow:—The basin, canal, towing-path, and locks, if liable to be assessed in respect of the profits arising to the defendants from the rates and duties received by them, were of the value stated in the rate; and they were also of the value stated in the rate, if the defendants were liable to be rated for the rent at which the basin, canal, towing-path, and locks, would let to any other company similarly situated as the appellants; but their value, if liable to be rated as land of a like quality within the parish, was only the sum of 34*l.* No personal property was rated in the parish at all, nor were there any rates due specially for passing either of the two double locks rated, but only for passing for certain distances along the canal. There were no other profits derived to the defendants from those premises, except the rates and duties imposed by the *Regent's Canal* act. The questions for the opinion of this Court were, first, as to that part of the rate or assessment marked No. 1, whether, under the circumstances stated relating thereto, the land

on the east side of the basin ought to be rated as a wharf.
And if it ought not to be so rated, then the sessions were
of opinion that the rate ought to be amended, by reducing
the sum of 130*l.* to the sum of 8*l.*: and, second, as to that
part of the rate or assessment marked Nos. 2, 3, and 4,
whether, under the 101st clause of the act of the 52 *Geo.* 3,
c. 195, the basin, canal, towing-paths, and locks, are liable
to be rated merely as land of a like quality within the parish.
And if so, the sessions were of opinion that the rate ought
further to be amended, by substituting the sum of 34*l.* for
the sum of 350*l.*

Andrews and *Adolphus*, in support of the order of sessions. The first question is, whether the defendants are
rateable to the poor for the slip of land adjoining the basin
on the east side, as a wharf. If it be a wharf, there is no
doubt they are rateable. The use to which the slip of land
is applied must determine that question. The case states
that it is used for the purpose of a wharf; that ships
approach it for the purpose of landing goods, and conveying them to the premises of Messrs. *Richardson* and
Messrs. *Watkins* and *Fry*. It is used to all intents and
purposes as a landing-place, which is generally the sole
use of a wharf. A wharf does not necessarily mean something erected or constructed. If the land, though in its
natural state, be used as an unloading place, that is suf
ficient. It may be true, that no wharfage dues are payable
in respect of the privilege of landing goods on this piece of
land, but if the defendants derive an increased tonnage in
consequence of ships entering their basin for the purpose
of landing their goods there, that will make it rateable as a
wharf. The circumstance of their paying no wharfage dues
may be matter of mere agreement or arrangement between
the parties, and the liability of the wharf cannot be evaded
by such an arrangement. The defendants derive all the
benefit which can be derived from this slip of land as a
wharf, and therefore they are properly rateable for it within

the meaning of the act of parliament. The slip of land is
used also as a wharf for the purpose of collecting the
public revenue. The case finds that foreign timber is
marked on this slip of land, and is then conveyed into the
bonding warehouses. By the 43 *Geo.* 3, c. 132, s. 12, it
is enacted, " that before any goods shall be lodged in the
bonded warehouses, the same shall be duly entered with
the proper officers of the customs, and regularly landed."
Therefore if this be a place used for the purpose of landing goods in the manner required by the public service, it
must be treated as a wharf, and rated accordingly. The
company indirectly derive a revenue from it, by reason of
the increased tonnage dues payable by ships entering the
basin for the purpose of landing goods there. The second
question is, whether the canal and basin are rateable as so
much land covered with water. By the act of parliament
the land upon which the canal and basin are constructed,
is to be assessed to the poor as other land of the like quality
in the parish. That must mean land covered with water
and used by the company for the purpose of a canal or basin,
and the land having acquired an increased value by this
mode of application, it must be assessed rateably according
to its annual value. Here the land covered with water has
acquired an improved value by means of the purposes to
which it is applied, and it is rateable in respect of that
improved value.

Brodrick and *Ellis*, (with whom was *F. Pollock*,) contrà.
It must be conceded that the land mentioned in the assessment Nos. 2, 3, and 4, is rateable for that value which
it has acquired from the circumstance of its having been
used for the purpose of a canal, unless there be some
clause in the act of parliament expressly exempting it from
such charge. But there is a distinction broadly taken in
this act of parliament between land and profits arising from
rates and tolls. The rates and tolls are by the act considered as personal property, and are not rateable *per se*,

and consequently cannot be considered as giving an improved value to the land itself. The act exempts rates and tolls, unless other personal property in the parish is rateable. Now the case finds that personal property is not rateable in the parish of *St. Ann, Limehouse*. By the act the land is to be rated according to quantity and quality, and dwelling-houses, &c. according to their uses, dimensions, &c. As land, therefore, the land on which the canal and basin are constructed is not rateable according to the uses to which it is applied. Here the use is for the purpose of levying rates and tolls, but by the act these rates and tolls are treated as personal property, and are not rateable to the poor unless other personal property is rateable in the parish, which is expressly found not to be so in this case. If the land thus occupied by the company is rateable in respect of the tolls, as giving it an improved annual value, the company might be rateable twice over for the same subject-matter, first, for the profit as land, and second, in the event of other personal property being rated, in respect of the rates and duties, as giving an improved value arising from an incorporeal hereditament. But the cases of *Rex* v. *The Grand Junction Canal Company* (a), and *Rex* v. *St. Peter the Great* (b), are authorities to shew that the company in this case are rateable for the lands at the same value as other adjacent lands, and not for the land used for the purposes of the canal according to its improved value. Then, secondly, the question is, whether the slip of land mentioned in the assessment No. 1, is rateable as a wharf. Now it is clear that no profit arises from this slip of land except in respect of the rates and dues payable by vessels entering the basin for the purpose of landing goods there, and therefore the same argument is applicable in this instance as in the others; for if this slip of land is rateable as a wharf, it might be rateable twice over, first, as land, and secondly, in respect of the increased value of the rates and tolls. But in point of fact this is not a wharf, and in

(a) 1 B. & A. 289.　　(b) *Ante*, vol. viii. 391; 5 B. & C. 478.

no respect comes up to that definition. Lord *Hale*, in his Treatise " de Portibus Maris," c. 2, p. 46, says, " that a port consists of something that is natural, viz. an access of the sea, whereby ships may conveniently come, &c., and something that is artificial, as quays and wharfs, and cranes and warehouses," &c. It is clear from this, that a wharf means something artificial—something constructed by the art of man. It is so treated by the act of parliament in question, in the sections 86, 107, 125, and 126. By the 86th section it is enacted, " that if the owners of any lands through which the canal passes, shall not make, build, and construct proper and sufficient wharfs, warehouses, and other conveniences for the use of the navigation, as the company shall think necessary, then the company shall have full power to do it." By the 126th section, any individual through whose land the canal passes, is enabled to make or erect any wharf, quay, landing-place, crane, weigh-beam, or warehouse, for his own private and exclusive use. So by the public act, 46 *Geo.* 3, c. 153, for the preservation of the public harbours of the united kingdom, it is enacted, " that it shall not be lawful for any person to make, construct, or erect any pier, quay, wharf, &c., in any public harbour, without giving a month's notice to the Admiralty." The slip of land, therefore, in question cannot be considered as a wharf; and although it may for some purposes be used in fact as such, still it is only rateable as land in like manner with other lands in the same parish.

Bayley, J.—I am of opinion that the assessment in this case must be reduced. It seems to me that the property comprised in the assessment No. 1, is rateable not as a wharf, but simply as so much land, and that the property comprised in Nos. 2, 3, and 4, is rateable as land, but not for the value it has acquired from being used for the purposes of a canal. The statute 52 *Geo.* 3, c. 195, recites, that the making of the *Regent's* canal will be of great public utility. Now that gives us a clue to the construction of the act of parliament. If the canal had not been made, and the land had remained in its original state, it would have been rateable in the same proportion as other land in the parish. On the other hand, if there had been no express provision in the act of parliament regulating the mode in which the land taken for the purpose of the canal was to be rated, the general principle in such cases would have applied, namely, that the company would be rateable in respect of the improved value of the land by its application to the purposes of a canal. But the making of the canal being a work of great public utility, and attended with great expense, it is but just to relieve the undertakers of it from a burthen which will attach to them only by reason of the improvements they make at a very heavy expense in the property used by them for their canal. It is not unusual, therefore, to insert in canal acts clauses to exonerate the undertakers from contributing a larger sum to the maintenance of the poor, in respect of the land used by them for the purposes of their canal, than would have been contributed in respect of that same land, if it had not been so used. Accordingly we find in the *Regent's* canal act a clause to that effect, namely, section 101. One of the objects of that clause is to exonerate the company from rates and taxes to a greater amount than the land would be liable to before it was converted to the purposes of a canal. The clause enacts, " that lands, whether covered with water or not, shall be rateable to the maintenance of the poor, according to their quantity and quality." We shall see what is meant by the word lands by what follows : " and the dwelling-houses, wharfs, warehouses, lock-houses, and other houses, according to the nature and respective uses, dimensions, and descriptions thereof, and shall be charged and assessed in like manner as lands of a like quality, and dwelling-houses, wharfs, warehouses, lock-houses, and other houses of a like and similar size, nature, dimension, or description, are assessed or charged." The act having provided in the first instance for the rating of

land, whether covered with water or not, and for buildings, &c., then introduces an additional subject of rateability, but not absolutely and at all events, but only on condition that other property of the like description is rateable
in the parish. It enacts, " that the rates, duties, and other
personal property of the company liable to be rated to the
poor in any such parishes or places, shall be rated and
assessed in the like manner and in the same proportion,
as other personal property rateable in the said parishes
and places respectively shall be rated and assessed." The
introduction of the word " other," clearly shews that the
rates and duties were contemplated by the legislature as
a species of personal property, for there is this proviso
contained in the clause, " that before such personal property should be rated, fourteen days' notice should be given
in writing to, or left at the dwelling-house of the treasurer
or clerk, or any other officer of the company residing in
the parish or place where such rate should be intended to
be made, by the respective overseers of the poor of the
intention so to do." There are, therefore, three distinct
subjects of rate; first, lands whether covered with water
or not, secondly, dwelling-houses, warehouses, and other
buildings, and, thirdly, rates and duties. The two former
are rateable at all events, and the latter only on condition
that personal property also is rated in the parish. Now
the property described in the assessments Nos. 2, 3 and 4,
seems to me to be nothing but land partly covered with
water, and, consequently, is only to be rated in the same
manner as other land of the same quality in the parish
would have been, if it had not been converted into a basin
or applied to the other purposes of the canal. If it had
been intended by the legislature that the land should be
rated according to its improved value by the construction
of docks, basins, and the canal, I apprehend this would
have been distinctly expressed. It is clear that but for
the exemption I have pointed out, there would have been
no occasion, as far as the land is concerned, to have intro-.

duced such a provision, because the land would have been rateable according to its improved quality, by the construction of docks, canals and basins. What I have now said, is an answer to the objection to the assessments Nos. 2, 3, and 4. The remaining question is, whether the property which is the subject of the assessment No. 1, can properly be rated as a wharf. If it be a wharf, it must be so within the meaning of the act of parliament. Now the word wharf is classed in the act with all those things which are artificial and requiring expense in their erection. The words are " dwelling-houses, wharfs, lock-houses and other houses.". Clearly this piece of land is not that description of wharf upon which any expense has been incurred. It is merely made use of as land in its character of land, applicable certainly to the purposes of landing customable goods and for other public purposes. The term "wharf" in its ordinary signification imports a place built or constructed for the purpose of loading or unloading goods. The act of parliament itself contains some clauses referable to wharfs in this sense, and it appears to me from the language of those different clauses, that the legislature contemplated something made and erected according to the general meaning of the word wharf. These clauses have been pointed out and dwelt upon by Mr. Brodnick in his argument. Looking to the language of the act of parliament, and considering those different clauses together, it appears to me, that this is not to be considered as a wharf, but at the utmost as a landing-place. For these reasons, it appears to me, that the whole of the property comprised in the four assessments can only be rated as land, and that the assessments must be reduced accordingly.

Holroyd, J.—For the reasons so fully stated by my brother *Bayley*, I am also of opinion that the assessments must be reduced. The exempting clause in favour of the company would be wholly inoperative if the land occupied by their canal, docks and basins, were rateable in respect of the beneficial improvement of the land by the creation of the works in question. It appears to me, that the property comprised in the several assessments can only be rated as land. I also think that the slip of land comprised in assessment No. 1, is not a wharf in common intendment, nor a wharf within the meaning of the act of parliament.

LITTLEDALE, J.—I am of the same opinion. It appears to me that the slip of land in question is not a wharf. It is not an artificial construction so as to make it in common parlance a wharf. But it is said, that inasmuch as it is used as a landing-place, it must be treated as a wharf. It is, however, not used properly as a wharf, for the goods are landed by means of stages. Goods may be, and frequently are, landed on the sea-beach, but it does not, therefore, follow that the sea-beach is a wharf. If this were a wharf, it might reasonably be expected that the company would charge wharfage dues, but no remuneration whatever is paid to the company for the use of the piece of land specifically, though they do receive wharfage dues for the use of other premises. It is clear, from the act of parliament, that by the wharfs thereby contemplated are meant artificial buildings, constructed by the hand of man, and not pieces of land which may be used for the purpose of landing goods. Then as to the property comprised in the assessments Nos. 2, 3 and 4, I think it ought to be rated merely as land. The *Regent's* Canal Company take up a great quantity of land for the purposes of their canal, and they incur great expense in the making of it. The act of parliament, however, makes a marked distinction between lands and houses and the rates and duties, as the subjects of assessment to the poor. Lands and houses are rateable as lands and houses of the same description in the parish, but the canal rates and duties, which are the profits arising from the particular use of the land, are to be rated in the parish. Now if the land is to be rated as land, according to the value which it has acquired in consequence of the

1827.

The KING
v.
REGENT'S
CANAL
COMPANY.

1827.

The KING
v.
REGENT'S
CANAL
COMPANY.

purpose to which it has been applied by the company, and which value arises from the canal duties, then if other personal property in the parish happens to be rated also, it might happen that the company would be liable to be rated twice over for the same property, once for the land in respect of its improved value, and a second time for canal rates and duties, but that, I apprehend, never could have been intended by the legislature. The rate must, therefore, be amended by reducing it.

Rate amended by reducing it according to the directions of the Court.

The KING v. The Justices of the Borough of LEICESTER.

54 *G. 3, c. 84,*
which enacts
that the *Mi-
chaelmas* quar-
ter sessions
shall be holden
in the week
next after the
11th of *Octo-
ber,* is merely
directory, and
those sessions
may be legally
holden at
another time.

A high con-
stable, by the
direction of
justices, em-
ployed and
paid special
and ordinary
constables to
suppress riots
at an election:
—Held, that
the sums so
paid were ex-
traordinary
expenses in-
curred by the
high constable within 41 *Geo.* 3, c. 78, s. 2, which the justices might make an order upon the treasurer to reimburse him.

BY an order of two justices of the borough of *Leicester,* made 10th *October,* 1826, after reciting that *A. B.,* high constable of the borough, had applied to them for certain extraordinary expenses incurred by him as high constable in several cases of riot and felony occurring within the borough, before and during an election for members of parliament recently had therein, and that they had examined into and considered the same, the justices thereby adjudged and allowed to *A. B.* 1343*l.* 17*s.* as the reasonable and necessary allowance to be made to him for his extraordinary expenses so incurred, and thereby, in pursuance of the statute, &c., ordered and directed the treasurer of the borough to pay to *A. B.* 1343*l.* 17*s.* By an order of the Court of Quarter Sessions, held 12th *October,* 1826, the order of the two justices was confirmed. In *Hilary* term, 1827, a rule nisi for a *certiorari* to remove both orders was obtained, upon affidavits suggesting that the expenses of the high constable had not been incurred *bonâ fide;* and also upon the following objections appearing on the face of the orders, namely, first, that they did not describe the nature and date of the riots, nor what allowances had been made; secondly, that the order of confirmation was not made at the sessions held next after the time when the riots were supposed to have occurred; and thirdly, that it was made at a sessions not duly held according to the statute 54 *Geo.* 3, c. 84, which requires the *Michaelmas* quarter sessions to be held in the first week after the 11th *October*, whereas the sessions in question were held in the same week in which the 11th *October* fell. The affidavits impugning the *bona fides* of the expenditure were answered by others, shewing that, during the election in *June*, 1826, there were several serious riots in *Leicester;* that the high constable, by order of the magistrates, had a large body of special constables sworn in, who, with the ordinary constables and head-boroughs, were actively employed throughout the election in endeavouring to preserve the peace; and that the entire sum allowed to the high constable had been *bonâ fide* paid by him to the ordinary and special constables. Upon these affidavits a fourth objection was founded, namely, that the money allowed was not for the *personal expenses* of the high constable, but for payments made by him to others, namely, the ordinary and special constables.

Scarlett, A. G., and *Parke*, now shewed cause, confining themselves, by direction of the Court, to the third and fourth objections, the Court being clearly of opinion that the affidavits impugning the expenditure of the money had been satisfactorily answered; that the orders sufficiently described the nature and date of the riots; and that the first order was confirmed at the sessions next after the time when it was made. The ancient statutes which regulated the holding of the Courts of Quarter Sessions were always considered as directory only, and Courts held at other times than those specified in the statutes were always held good: 2 Haw. P. C. b. ii. c. 8. The 54 *Geo.* 3, c. 84, which merely alters the time of holding the *Michaelmas* quarter

1827.

The King
v.
Justices of
Leicester.

sessions from the week after *Michaelmas* to the week after the 11th of *October*, must receive the same construction as the earlier statutes; and if so, it is directory only, and there is an end of that objection. The other objection is, that the 41 *Geo.* 3, c. 78, s. 2, which empowers justices to order reasonable allowances to be made to high constables for extraordinary expenses incurred by them in cases of riot, applies only to *personal expenses.* Now the language of that clause would not warrant such a construction, even if the meaning of the term " personal expenses" were clearly defined; and the fair sense of the thing seems to be, that whatever the high constable finds it necessary to expend, in the execution of his duty for the preservation of the peace, is a personal expense, for which he should be reimbursed.

Campbell, contrà. First, the regulation in 54 *Geo.* 3, c. 84, s. 1, must be considered as imperative; because otherwise the exception in s. 2, in favour of *London* and *Middlesex*, becomes wholly nugatory: and indeed if the justices may still hold the sessions when they please, it is difficult to discover any utility in the first section. The former statutes may have been directory only, but this clearly is not so, for it appoints a new time for holding the sessions *instead* of the old one, and thereby absolutely deprives the justices of their previous discretionary power. Secondly, the 41 *Geo.* 3, c. 78, s. 2, does not apply to such expenses as those incurred in the present case. That statute applies exclusively to the *personal* expenses of the high constable *himself*, and the payments in question do not come within that description. The proper mode of remunerating the other constables is pointed out in another statute, 1 *Geo.* 4, c. 37, s. 3, which might and ought to have been adopted in the present instance.

Lord Tenterden, C. J.—I think this rule ought to be discharged. The matter has been very fully discussed, but.

as the only effect of granting a *certiorari* to remove the order would be to impose upon us the duty of sending them back to the justices, instead of quashing them, I think we ought not to do that unnecessary act. The first and general point made by way of objection to the order itself is, that the quarter sessions at which it was made, being holden on the 12th of *October*, were not legally holden, because they were not a general quarter sessions within the meaning of the act of parliament, so as to give the justices jurisdiction. Looking at the older statutes upon this subject, we find that by 12 *Ric.* 2, c. 10, the justices are required to hold their sessions in every quarter of a year, at least, but no particular days are mentioned on which they are to be holden. By the 2 *Hen.* 5, st. 1, c. 4, it was enacted, " that they shall make their sessions four times in the year, viz. in the first week after *Michaelmas, Epiphany, Easter,* and the translation of *St. Thomas the Martyr,* and oftener if need be." The question now raised would be precisely the same if it had been brought under consideration before the passing of the late act of parliament, 54 *Geo.* 3, c. 84, which merely substitutes the week after the 11th of *October* for the week after *Michaelmas,* so that the question must therefore receive the same consideration as if that statute had never been passed. Now we find it mentioned so long ago as the time of Sir *Matthew Hale,* that the earlier statutes to which I have referred were directory only. After pointing out what, according to a strict construction, would be required by those statutes, that learned person says (a), " Yet it is very plain that the quarter sessions are variously held in several counties, some at one day some at another, yet it hath been ruled that these are each of them good quarter sessions, within the several acts that relate to quarter sessions, for these acts, especially that of 2 *Hen.* 5, is only directive and in the affirmative, and therefore though the sessions are held at another day, according to the general direction of the statute 12 *Ric.* 2,

(a) 2 Hale's P. C. 50.

yet they are quarter sessions." It is now contended that
the statute 54 *Geo.* 3, c. 84, is imperative, and that the
sessions shall be holden at the time therein mentioned, and
that it is impossible for any thing to be more positive.
Now if there had been negative words declaring that the
sessions should be holden at no other time but that specified, we might give that effect to the statute; but the
words used being only affirmative, I think the authority of
Lord *Hale* is sufficient to warrant us in saying that the
statute is merely directory, and that we cannot hold that the
proceedings at the sessions in question were all *coram non
judice.* This brings me to the objection made as to the
remuneration given to the high constable for the extraordinary expense incurred by him in the case of a riot and
disturbance. It is contended that the statute 41 *Geo.* 3,
c. 78, s. 2, merely authorises the justices to make an allowance for his personal expenses; but that would be a very
narrow construction of a statute authorising them to reimburse him the expenses incurred in suppressing a riot.
One can hardly suppose that, if he is to act at all on such
an occasion, he is not to be reimbursed such expenses as
he may reasonably incur. The question is, whether special
constables, who are sworn in and act under his directions,
shall in the first instance be remunerated by him, and he
may afterwards receive from the justices an allowance in
respect of that expense. Now I think he may, without
the special authority given under the act 1 *Geo.* 4, c. 37,
which gives power to remunerate special constables; and
that both acts are perfectly consistent with each other.
If the high constable, whether called upon by others or
upon his own view, thinks it necessary, for the preservation of the public peace, to call in the assistance of special
constables or other persons to assist him, it is proper that
his should be the hand to pay for their services; but if
special constables are sworn in by the justices without the
intervention of the high constable, they should likewise
pay them according to the directions of the statute. These

are the observations which I think it necessary to make respecting the special constables. With respect to the regular or ordinary constables, it appears to me that they are also entitled to remuneration for their extraordinary exertions. It is urged that they are not entitled, without some express act of parliament, to any extraordinary remuneration. But as far as any general principle can be collected from the statute 41 *Geo.* 3, c. 78, or the 18 *Geo.* 3, c. 19, it is in favour of the payment to them for their extraordinary exertions, and I think the justices were well warranted in considering such payment as an extraordinary expense incurred by the high constable, for which they might make him an allowance. For these reasons it appears to me that the order of sessions, confirming the order of the two justices, is well founded, and that this rule ought to be discharged.

BAYLEY, J., HOLROYD, J., and LITTLEDALE, J.; concurred.

Rule discharged (*a*).

(*a*) As to the periods now fixed for holding the quarter sessions, see the statute 1 *Wm.* 4, c. 70, s. 35, which, however, does not alter the period for holding the *Michaelmas* sessions.

The KING *v.* The Justices of BUCKINGHAMSHIRE.

BY the 54 *Geo.* 3, c. 103, a local act, the justices of *Buckinghamshire* were empowered to make an equal county rate, and for that purpose to order certain returns, after obtaining which they were required to assess and tax every parish, &c. rateably and in due proportions. By s. 10, if the churchwardens, &c. of any such parish, &c. or any other persons, should think themselves aggrieved by any thing done in pursuance of the act, they might appeal to the general quarter sessions for the county, holden next after

Where a county rate is made under a local act giving a limited right of appeal, parties aggrieved have still the unlimited right of appeal given by the general act, 55 *G.* 3, c. 51, s. 14.

the cause of complaint should arise, upon giving a specified
notice. The returns were made, and the proportion of the
rate for each parish was fixed. At the *Epiphany* sessions,
1827, a rate was made, and a certain sum assessed upon the
parish of *Iver*: and at an adjourned sessions in *February*,
1827, another rate was made and another sum assessed upon
that parish. At the next *Easter* sessions the parish officers
of *Iver* appealed against both rates, upon the ground that
their parish was assessed higher than the parish of *Langley*.
Fourteen days' notice of appeal and the grounds of it had
been given to the parish officers of *Langley*, to the clerk of
the peace for the county, and to the high constable of the
hundred in which both parishes were situate. The sessions
refused to hear the appeal, and a rule nisi for a mandamus
having been obtained, ...

Tindal, S. G. and *Maltby* shewed cause. The sessions
were right. The appeal was clearly too late with reference
to the local act, and *Iver* had no right of appeal under the
general act, 55 *Geo.* 3, c. 51, s. 14. The words of that
clause are undoubtedly large, for they empower parish officers to appeal against the county rate if they have *at any
time* reason to think their parish aggrieved by it, whether
on account of the proportions assessed upon the parishes
being unequal, or on account of their parish being rated at
a higher proportion than some other parish. But s. 21
empowers the justices of a county for which a local act has
passed, to act either under that, or under the general act, at
their option; and as the rate in question was made under
the local act, the appeal should have been made under that
also.

Munro, contrà. The general act, 55 *Geo.* 3, c. 51, s. 21,
gives the justices the option alluded to only in cases where
the provisions of that statute are not inconsistent with those
of the local act. But if this parish had a right of appeal
under the general act, which did not exist under the local

1827.

The King
v.
Justices of.
Buckingham-
shire.

act, the two statutes are in that respect inconsistent, and the justices were wrong in acting under the local act. Now, the general act gives the parish aggrieved a right of appealing at any time when the grievance is felt. The proportions of the rate in this case may have been perfectly fair at the time when they were fixed, and may have become very unequal afterwards; and whenever that happened, a right of appeal accrued: *Rex* v. *The Justices of the City of York(a).*

Lord TENTERDEN, C. J.—Considering this as an appeal under the general act, 55 *Geo.* 3, c. 51, s. 14, it seems to me to have been made in due time. The rate was made under the local act; but the appeal clause of the general act refers to acts and rates of a prior date. It gives a right of appeal to the churchwardens and overseers of any parish who " shall at any time have reason to think that such parish is aggrieved by any rate *now existing*, or hereafter to be made, either in pursuance of this act or of *any act or acts now in force.*" Those are general words, clearly applicable to all prior statutes, whether local or general. As to the twenty-first section, that relates only to the authority of the justices in assessing and levying the county rate. All the powers given to them for those purposes may be well exercised under the local act, without depriving parishes of the right of appeal given by the general act; and I think we ought not to give the appeal clause of the general act a more limited construction, because it is very convenient that the right of appeal should be the same in every county. Parties aggrieved may have a difficulty in ascertaining whether the rate is made under the general or the local act, and may, consequently, upon a more limited construction, lose their opportunity of appealing, without any default of their own.

The other Judges concurred.

Rule absolute.

(a) 2 B. & C. 771.

1827.

The KING v. The Inhabitants of LIVERPOOL.

An act of parliament vested a dock and the dues arising therefrom in trustees, and provided that those dues should be applied to paying off the debt incurred in making the dock, and to keeping it in repair, and then that the dues should be lowered. Held, that the trustees were not rateable to the poor, either for the dock dues, or for the premises purchased or rented for the purposes of the dock, there being no beneficial occupation of either by any person.

BY a rate for the relief of the poor of the parish of Liverpool, made 21st July, 1825, and duly published and allowed, the trustees of the docks and harbour of Liverpool were assessed in the sum of 50,952l., in respect of the annual value and profits of the dock estates within that parish, vested in them as trustees of the docks and harbour, according to the following schedule:—

On the dock duties £50,000

On three cranes at the New Wall and the
　　Parade Slip 40

Engine House, *Bridge Street* 17

Office, *Salthouse Dock* 8

Ditto, *King's Dock* 26

On office, *Queen's Dock* 26

Ditto, *Bridge Street* 54

Ditto, *Old Dock* 270

Ditto, *Goree* 11

Ditto, Yard, &c. *Trektham Street* . . . 185

Ditto　　　　　Ditto 315

Against this assessment the trustees appealed to the Court of Quarter Sessions of the borough of *Liverpool*, on the ground that the dock estates within the parish were not rateable to the poor. That Court, being of opinion that the trustees were not rateable, amended the rate, by striking out the foregoing assessment, subject to the opinion of this Court upon the following case:—

The dock estates within the parish of *Liverpool* are vested in the mayor, aldermen, bailiffs, and common councilmen of *Liverpool*, as trustees of the docks and harbour of *Liverpool*, by virtue of several acts of parliament, (namely, 8 *Ann.* c. 12, 3 *Geo.* 1, 11 *Geo.* 2, c. 32, 2 *Geo.* 3, c. 86, 25 *Geo.* 3, c. 15, 39 *Geo.* 3, c. 59, and 51 *Geo.* 3, c. 143, all of which, excepting the second, are public acts,) and consist of a large quantity of land, to the extent of

100 acres. Part of those estates was granted voluntarily by the corporation of *Liverpool*, part was sold by that body to the trustees for a pecuniary consideration, and other parts have been purchased by the trustees from private individuals, according to the powers given to them by the said acts. Before the construction of the present works, part of the land was waste, both above and below high water mark, but other parts consisted of lands and buildings in the occupation of individuals rated to the relief of the poor of the parish.

The dock estates at present consist of several wet docks, in which vessels may be constantly afloat, dry basins, that is to say, dry at low water, wharfs, piers, slips, cranes, weighing machines, offices, and yards for storing goods, and other conveniences requisite to form a complete dock; and the trustees are authorised to receive large sums, under the name of dock rates and duties, for accommodating vessels in the docks, by virtue of the acts of parliament.

The trustees manage the dock estates by their servants and agents, who receive and account to them for the dues and profits so arising, and no part of the estates and premises above assessed is let off to other persons.

With regard to the application of the monies received as dock duties, it is enacted by 8 *Ann.* c. 12, s. 9, under which the first dock was built, " that all and every sum and sums of money that shall be raised and received by the duties aforesaid, after payment of the expenses of collection, shall be, by the trustees for the time being, applied and disposed of in the building and repairing the said new dock or basin, and other works, and in the securing, preserving, and maintaining the said dock or basin and harbour of *Liverpool, and to no other use or purpose whatsoever.*" By the same section the collector is required to keep accurate accounts of all his receipts and disbursements.

By s. 15 of the same act, nine commissioners are appointed for the inspection of the accounts, who " shall and may order and appoint all monies which shall rest due upon such account to be laid out and expended to and for the uses and purposes in the act mentioned, and to, and for no other use whatsoever."

By 11 Geo. 2, c. 32, s. 4, passed for building another dock, "there shall be twelve commissioners to inspect, audit, and adjust the accounts of all the collectors' receipts and disbursements of all the monies collected and levied by virtue of the former act, who shall be invested with such and the same powers and authorities in all respects, and to all intents, constructions, and purposes, as were given to and vested in the commissioners appointed in pursuance of the former acts, or either of them."

By 51 Geo. 3, c. 143, s. 125, the mode of appointing the commissioners is altered, but the electors are authorised to appoint them as commissioners, for the purposes in this and the former acts mentioned.

By 11 Geo. 2, c. 32, s. 8, all the collectors of dock duties are required to keep regular accounts of their receipts and disbursements, and to produce the same to the commissioners when ordered; and by s. 9, the treasurer of the dock duties is required to print his account yearly, the expense of such printing to be deducted out of the dock duties, and to deliver a copy to any person paying dock duties who may require the same.

All the dock rates payable by the former acts were repealed by 51 Geo. 3, cap. 143, which imposed the present duties. Sect. 27 of that act, which relates to the application of the present dock duties, is as follows:—" And be it further enacted, that all monies which shall be collected, received, levied, borrowed and raised by and under this act, shall be applied in paying and defraying the charges and expenses attending the obtaining and passing this present act, and to the paying the expenses and charges attending the levying and collecting the said rates and duties; and after the paying and appropriating one-third part of the said monies to and for the purpose of making and completing the southernmost of the north docks, as hereinafter is mentioned, then to the paying off and discharging the present bond debt of £114,705. 19s. 4d., and the debt of £67,406. 18s. 7d. owing by the trustees to the corporation of Liverpool, for the purchase of land and strand intended for the site of the southermost of the two northern docks, and any future bond debt, and the interest on the same, and to the paying and discharging the interest on all other monies which may be hereafter borrowed and taken up at interest under the provisions of this act, upon the credit of the dock rates and duties, and to the carrying into execution the purposes of this act and the said recited acts, in the making, erecting, building, finishing, and maintaining such docks, basins, piers, and other works and buildings in the port of Liverpool, under the said acts and this act, and to the paying, defraying, and satisfying all other charges and expenses already incurred, or hereafter to be incurred in the carrying into execution, or under or in consequence of any of the former acts or this present act; and the residue or surplus of all monies arising from such rates or duties, which shall remain after such application thereof as aforesaid, shall from time to time be applied in or towards the repayment of the principal monies which shall have been borrowed under this act, until all such principal monies shall be repaid, and all assignments of or mortgages upon such rates and duties are paid off, satisfied, discharged, and redeemed; and when, by the means last mentioned, all the principal monies which shall have been borrowed shall be repaid, and all assignments and mortgages upon the said rates are satisfied and redeemed, then and in such case it shall be lawful for the trustees, and they are hereby required to lower and reduce the rates and duties hereby granted and made payable, as far as the same can be done in the then state of the docks, basins, buildings, and other works and buildings of the said port, and leaving sufficient for all charges of management and collection of rates and other concerns of the said docks, basins, piers, works, and other buildings, and improving, repairing, and maintaining the same, and for carrying into execution the provisions of the former acts and this act." The present duties have been invariably applied by the trustees according to the direction of the last-mentioned section, and they derive no private advantage or emolument whatsoever from the execution of the trusts of the dock estates.

The three cranes mentioned in the schedule were erected by the trustees out of the dock funds, in pursuance of the power given them by 51 *Geo.* 3, c. 143, s. 78. For the use of these cranes in landing and discharging cargoes the trustees charge a certain sum, which goes to the general dock estate, in the same way as the dock duties, and is applied as the general dock funds are and must be applied, by the various acts of parliament, and the trustees derive no individual benefit from them.

The engine house is used for the purpose of keeping a fire engine, which the trustees have provided out of the public funds, for the security of the shipping, as empowered by the same section, and no rent is charged to or paid by any one for the same.

Of the different offices enumerated in the schedule, some are for the accommodation of the dock-masters and gate-men at the various docks, as places of shelter, and merely for the dispatch of public business; others are occupied by the collector of the dock rates, the harbour-master, and other public officers of the trustees, solely for the purposes of the dock business. No rent is charged to them for the use of these offices, and no part of them is occupied as a residence by any one.

The two yards mentioned in the schedule are hired by the trustees at an annual rent, as a place necessary for the deposit of the various articles used in the erection and maintenance of the docks, and from the occupation of which they derive no personal benefit.

Tindal, S. G. and *Gregson,* in support of the order of sessions. The case finds that all the dock funds are by the

1827.

The King
v.
Liverpool.

different acts of parliament expressly and entirely appropriated to public purposes; therefore, there is no beneficial occupation by any persons of the property in respect of which the trustees are rated: and that being so, the rate cannot be supported. Upon this point *Rex* v. *Agar*(a) is no authority against the appellants in this case, while *Rex* v. *The Commissioners of Salters-load-sluice*(b) is a direct authority in their favour. So in *Rex* v. *Terrott*(c), Lord *Ellenborough* said, " The principle to be collected from all the cases on the subject is, that if the party rated have the use of the building, or other subject of the rate, as a mere servant of the crown, or of any public body, or in any other respect, for the mere exercise of public duty therein, and have no beneficial occupation of or emolument resulting from it in any personal and private respect, then he is not rateable:" and his lordship afterwards assigned this reason for the rule, that " the occupation is throughout that of the public, and of that public occupation the individuals are only the means and instruments." The decision in *Lord Amherst* v. *Lord Somers*(d) proceeded upon the same principle. Even in *Rex* v. *The Hull Dock Company*(e), where the company were held to be rateable, *Holroyd*, J. had the same principle in view, for he said, " If under the section requiring the company to repair the dock and other works, the specific rates had been, so far as they were required, appropriated to that purpose only, I should have entertained considerable doubt whether any property vested in the trustees which could properly be made the subject of rate, beyond the surplus which might happen to remain in their hands after satisfying the expenses attending the maintenance and repair of the works." In this case there can never legally be a surplus in the hands of the trustees, because as soon as certain objects specified in the acts are accomplished, they are bound to reduce the rates.

(a) 14 East, 256.			(d) 2 T. R. 372.
(b) 4 T. R. 730.			(e) 5 M. & S. 402.
(c) 3 East, 513.

Scarlett, A. G. and *J. Williams*, contrà. This property is rateable in its nature; it is therefore liable to be rated whether producing any profit or not: *Rex* v. *Parrott(a)*. The rates being received by trustees makes no difference, for the trustees of a Methodist chapel have been held rateable. *Rex* v. *Agar(b)*. [Lord *Tenterden*, C. J. Because, if there had been no trustees, and the minister had received the pew rents in the first instance, he would have been rateable in respect of them, and as he ultimately received the surplus, after payment of the expenses of the chapel, the rate was substantially upon him, through the medium of the trustees.] The trustees here may derive no benefit from the docks individually, but as the Corporation of *Liverpool* they do, for they possess large property in the neighbourhood, which must of necessity be increased in value by the docks and by the expenditure of the rates upon them. No doubt the public do derive a benefit, but that does not exempt the property from rateability, where there is also a private benefit. At all events the last two items of the rate are good, for they are in respect of premises rented by the trustees. If they had rented a farm for the purpose of paying their labourers in corn and other produce, that would clearly have been rateable, and the rate upon the premises in question may be supported upon the same principle.

Lord TENTERDEN, C. J.—I am of opinion that the order of sessions made in this case ought to be confirmed. It appears to me that there is no solid ground for the distinction which has been taken with respect to those parts of the property rated which are rented by the dock company, because if there is no beneficial occupation it must be wholly immaterial whether the occupier is the owner or not. Then upon the main question, I consider the case of *Rex* v. *The Commissioners of Salters-load-sluice(c)* as decisive of the present. There the tolls received were by act of parliament directed to be applied to the purposes of the

(a) 5 T. R. 593.   (b) 14 East, 256.   (c) 4 T. R. 730.

act, and to and for no other use or purpose whatsoever. It is true that in this case the act of parliament under which the present dock rates are levied does not expressly declare that they shall be applied to the purposes therein specified, and no other; but it directs that certain debts shall be discharged out of them, and then provides for the application of the surplus, by directing that the dock rates shall be lowered: so that any application of the dock rates to any purpose not specified, would clearly be a violation of the act of parliament. Nothing of that sort is suggested, and therefore there is not in reality any difference between this case and the former. The principle of not rating property of which no person is the beneficial occupier is not confined to docks and canals, or to property of that nature. Thus it has been held, that the trustees of a Quakers' meeting-house, of which *no* profit is made by letting the pews, or otherwise, are not rateable; *Rex* v. *Woodward*(a); and the same rule would apply to a chapel with the rites of the Church of *England*, or to a dissenting meeting-house. On the other hand it has been held, that where the pews of such a meeting-house are let, and a profit thereby made, the trustees are rateable, although they receive the rents, not for their own benefit, but for that of the minister: *Rex* v. *Agar*(b). In this case the trustees are not occupiers in the ordinary sense of the word, and no profit is received for the benefit of any person. If private property belonging to the trustees in their character of the Corporation of *Liverpool* is improved by means of the docks, that property may be rateable for the improved value.

The other Judges concurred.

Order of Sessions confirmed (c).

(a) 5 T. R. 79.
(b) 14 East, 256. And see *Robson* v. *Hyde*, Cald. 310.
(c) See the next case.

The KING *v.* The Trustees of the River WEAVER.

1827.

Trustees are not rateable to the poor in respect of the tolls of a navigation received by them, the surplus of which is by statute made applicable to the repair of public bridges and highways.

ON appeal against a rate for the relief of the poor made by the overseers of the poor of the township of *Moulton,* in the county of *Chester,* upon the trustees of the river *Weaver,* the sessions confirmed the rate, subject to the opinion of this Court upon the following case :—

By 7 *Geo.* 1, entitled " An Act for making the river *Weaver* navigable from *Frodsham Bridge* to *Winsford Bridge* in the county of *Chester,"* it was enacted, " that from and after the said work shall be finished, and all the charges thereof, &c. fully paid, that then the clear produce of the rates and duties shall, from time to time, be employed for and towards amending and repairing the public bridges within the county of *Chester,* and such other public charges upon the county, and in such manner as the justices at the *Michaelmas* quarter sessions shall yearly order, direct and appoint." And, after reciting that the roads leading to the river would be much injured by the increased traffic upon them, it was provided, that so much of the rates as the justices might think fit should be expended in repairing those roads, and that if any surplus remained, it should be expended in repairing such other highways in the county as the justices in sessions should appoint.

By 33 *Geo.* 2, further provisions as to the navigation were made, but it directed that the surplus duties, after payment of the expenses of the navigation, should be applied to such public purposes as before mentioned.

The tonnage rates and duties upon the *Weaver* are not charged by the mile, but 1*s.* per ton is charged upon the whole line of river; and a vessel navigating the whole or any part of the length of the navigation is subject to the same charge. This tonnage is paid quarterly at the River *Weaver* Navigation Office in *Northwich,* which is a distinct township from *Moulton.* The annual accounts up to the 5th of *April* in each year are regularly audited by the clerk of the

peace, and filed at the *Michaelmas* quarter sessions, when
the balance arising from the rates and duties in the hands
of the treasurer, over and above the necessary charges and
expenses for the maintenance and support of the navigation, is directed by the magistrates there assembled to be
paid, and the same is invariably paid to the county treasurer, to be applied for the general purposes of the county,
according to the acts of parliament, and to none others.
The township of *Moulton* rated the trustees as follows:—

Occupiers.	Property rated.	Rental.	Sum assessed.
The Trustees of the River *Weaver* Navigation.	Lands used for the River *Weaver*, with the tolls, dues and duties arising therefrom, or in respect thereof, within the township of *Moulton*.	£. s. d. 234 13 4	£. s. d. 35 4 0

The amount at which the trustees are assessed in the said
rate, provided they are rateable at all, is correct.

Alderson, Brown and *Trafford,* in support of the order of
sessions. The question is, whether these trustees are beneficial occupiers. It is submitted that they are. *They*
need not enjoy the benefit: if benefit accrues to any
person, *that* makes the property rateable. In such a case
the trustee and the cestui que trust are one. In *Rex* v.
Agar(a) the trustees of a Methodist chapel were held to
be rateable for the pew rents, though the surplus, after
payment of the current expenses, was paid over to the
minister. It cannot be said that the surplus profits here
are to be applied to the purposes of the public, and that
therefore the trustees are not rateable. They are to be
applied to the purposes of the county, not of the public;
and being so applied, they relieve the county rate *pro tanto,*
and confer a benefit upon every landholder in the county.

(a) 14 East, 256.

That is a private benefit, and the principle of exemption does not apply except in cases of public benefit, that is, a benefit conferred upon the public at large. *Rex* v. *The Commissioners of Salters-load-sluice* (a) and *Rex* v. *Sculcoates* (b) are both distinguishable from the present case. In the first, all the money received was to be applied in the drainage of the lands adjoining the navigation. Those lands would become rateable for the improved value so conferred upon them; so that if the money had been rateable in the hands of the commissioners, it would, in effect, have been rateable twice over. In the second case, no person derived any benefit within the parish from the lands used for the purposes of the drainage.

Nolan and *Cottingham*, contrà. The trustees must derive some private and personal profit from their occupation, in order to render them rateable: *Rex* v. *Terrott* (c). They derive none such. They have no interest in the soil; it is not vested in them by the acts of parliament. The tolls are payable for the right of passage, not for the use of the soil; therefore they are not rateable: *Rex* v. *Nicholson* (d), *Williams* v. *Jones* (e), *Rex* v. *Bell* (f), *Rex* v. *Tynemouth* (g), *Rex* v. *Coke* (h), *Rex* v. *Fowke* (i). Besides, these tolls are applicable entirely to public purposes, and upon that ground they are not rateable. *Rex* v. *The Commissioners of Salters-load-sluice* (k) and *Rex* v. *Sculcoates* (l) are express authorities upon this point, and cannot be distinguished from the present case.

This case was argued at a former sittings in Banc, when

BAYLEY, J. delivered himself to this effect:—There is

(a) 4 T. R. 730.
(b) 12 East, 40.
(c) 3 East, 506.
(d) 12 East, 330.
(e) 12 East, 346.
(f) 5 M. & S. 221.

(g) 12 East, 46.
(h) 3 D. & R. 666; 5 B. & C. 797.
(i) *Ante*, 120; 5 B. & C. 814.
(k) 4 T. R. 730.
(l) 12 East, 40.

not any clause in the acts of parliament set out in the case which vests the soil of the river *Weaver* in the trustees; they cannot, therefore, be rateable to the relief of the poor in respect of the tolls. Upon this point we are all agreed: upon the other point we prefer postponing our judgment until the case of *The King* v. *The Inhabitants of Liverpool* (a) has been argued.

Cur. adv. vult.

That case having been since argued and determined,

BAYLEY, J. now said—We think the principle of the decision in *Rex* v. *Liverpool* is applicable to the present case. The surplus tolls are made applicable to the repairing and maintaining the county bridges and highways. Those are public purposes; and as no part of the money received can be applied to private purposes, that money is not rateable in the hands of the trustees. Upon both points, therefore, we are of opinion that the order of sessions confirming the rate must be quashed.

Order of sessions quashed.

(a) *Ante,* 780.

GOODE v. LANGLEY, BAYLEY, RANGER, and WEDDELL.

THIS was an action of trover to recover the value of a gig wrongfully converted by the defendants to their own use. Plea, the general issue. At the trial before *Parke,* J. at the last *Yorkshire* summer assizes, the case was this:— In 1826 the defendant *Langley* was high sheriff of the county of *York,* and *Bayley* was one of his officers. The defendant *Weddell* carried on the business of a coachmaker

Where, under a fi. fa., a judgment creditor was left in possession by the sheriff's officer of a chattel taken in execution, and with the consent of the debtor and

creditor, it was delivered to *A.,* and the officer retook it to pay poundage:—Held, that *A.,* who had *bonâ fide* paid the price of the chattel, might maintain trover for it against the sheriff.

at *Knaresborough*, and the defendant *Ranger*, who was his step-father, resided with him at the period in question. In *April*, 1826, the plaintiff employed *Weddell* to make him a gig; the price agreed upon was 37*l.*, against which was to be set off an old debt of 20*l.* 12*s.* 6*d.* due from *Weddell* to the plaintiff. The plaintiff had selected at *Weddell's* shop an unfinished gig, which was to be completed and delivered in a few days. Before the gig was finished, the plaintiff paid to *Weddell* a sum of money sufficient to make up the difference between the old debt of 20*l.* 12*s.* 6*d.* and the sum of 37*l.*, which was to be the price of the gig. On *Thursday* the 11th of *May*, the plaintiff went to *Weddell's* premises for the gig. The defendant, *Ranger*, who was present, assisted *Weddell* in drawing it out of the yard and putting the horse to. The plaintiff then drove away the gig. At this time there had been an execution put into *Weddell's* premises, at the suit of *Ranger*, for the sum of 459*l.*, for a debt due upon a judgment recovered, and on the 6th of *May*, *Bayley*, the sheriff's officer, took possession of *Weddell's* goods, at which time the gig in question was upon the premises in an unfinished state. After the seizure *Weddell* had been permitted to complete the gig, which was delivered to the plaintiff on the 11th of *May*, as above mentioned. On the 13th of *May*, *Bayley*, the sheriff's officer, finding that the gig had been taken away from *Weddell's* house, went to the plaintiff's premises and took it back again; whereupon the plaintiff brought the present action, after a demand and refusal, to recover the value of the gig. Evidence was offered on the part of the plaintiff to shew that there was a juggle between *Ranger* and *Weddell*, and that the judgment and execution were collusive. Upon this point the case went to the jury, and they found their verdict for the plaintiff, damages 37*l.* In *Michaelmas* term last *Parke* moved for and obtained a rule to shew cause why there should not be a new trial granted, on the ground that the property in the gig not having vested in the plaintiff at the time the sheriff took possession under the fieri facias, trover was not maintainable.

Scarlett, A. G., and *E. H. Alderson*, now shewed cause. It being found by the jury that the judgment and execution at the suit of *Ranger* were collusive, there is no doubt that at all events the plaintiff is entitled to recover, even though the gig was not finished at the time the execution was put into *Weddell's* premises. Independently, however, of this point, the gig having been delivered to the plaintiff in a complete state on the 11th of *May*, with the assent and even the personal assistance of *Ranger*, the judgment creditor, that delivery completely vested the property in the plaintiff. One mode of trying this question would be, whether *Ranger* could have maintained trover against the sheriff for the gig. It is clear that he could not, because he had concurred in the delivery of it to the plaintiff after the execution issued. If this be so, then it follows that the sheriff himself could not have maintained trover against the present plaintiff. Why is it that, in general, a sheriff may maintain trover for goods which he has seized in execution? Because he is answerable to the judgment creditor for the value of the goods so seized. But if the plaintiff in the execution assents to the property being delivered up, the sheriff's liability is discharged. Under such circumstances the sheriff could not retake the goods for his poundage. He has a lien upon them for the poundage so long as they are in his possession, but if he is so imprudent as to part with possession, his lien is gone.

Parke, in support of the rule. The seizure having been made on the 6th of *May*, at which time the gig was not completed, the property in it was bound by the execution, and consequently this action is not maintainable. There is no doubt that until the gig was actually finished and delivered to the plaintiff he acquired no property in it, although be might have paid the price agreed upon. In *Mucklow* v. *Mangles* (a) it was held, that if a person contracts with another for a chattel which is not in existence at the time of the contract, though he pays him the whole value in advance, and the other proceeds to execute the order, the buyer acquires no property in the chattel till it is finished and delivered to him. The same principle was recognised in *Woods* v. *Russell* (b), which was the case of a ship to be built, and paid for by instalments of so much when the vessel had arrived at certain stages of completion; but in that case there was an express stipulation upon the subject. If there be no such stipulation, and the article is destroyed by fire before it is finished and delivered, the part or the whole of the purchase-money paid must be refunded to the purchaser, and the vendor must sustain the loss; but this is upon the principle, that until actual delivery the property does not vest in the vendee. It may be true, that in this case the execution creditor assented to the delivery of the gig to the plaintiff on the 11th of *May*, but still that would not vest the property in the plaintiff. At that time the gig was in the custody of the law, and the assent of *Ranger* alone could not bind the sheriff, who had a lien upon the gig for his poundage. Neither could fraud and collusion between *Weddell* and *Ranger* affect the sheriff, for under the writ of fieri facias he was bound to obey the exigency of it, whatever defect there might be in the judgment; and a fraudulent judgment ought not to place him in a worse situation.

Lord TENTERDEN, C. J.—I think this rule ought to be discharged. Upon the evidence produced at the trial it must be taken that the whole sum of 37*l.*, as the price of the gig, was paid by the plaintiff. Without entering into the question how far the property in the gig had passed to the plaintiff before it was seized by the sheriff on the 6th

(a) 1 Taunt. 380.   (b) 5 B. & A. 942; 1 D. & R. 587.

of *May*, it seems to me that there was sufficient evidence to sustain the present verdict. The sheriff's officer entered the premises of *Weddell* by virtue of a writ of fieri facias issued on the 5th of *May*, at the suit of *Ranger*, and seized the property. The officer, instead of taking upon himself to protect the property thus seized in execution, leaves the judgment creditor and his step-son, the debtor, to mind the concerns of the business. *Ranger*, the judgment creditor, remains on the premises, and takes upon himself the management of the business, pays the workmen, and so forth. The judgment creditor being so left in possession, he and the debtor concurred in delivering the gig to the plaintiff. As against them, therefore, the plaintiff is clearly entitled to retain it. After the delivery has taken place, the sheriff's officer returns and retakes the property. I think he had no right so to do. It is said that he had the right, in order to receive his poundage, but I am of opinion that it was his duty not to permit it to go out of his possession, and by doing so his lien for poundage was gone. It appears to me, that by leaving the gig in the care of the judgment creditor he was bound by the act of the latter in delivering it to the plaintiff. The poundage being the sheriff's own debt, I think he had not such an interest in the goods as to entitle him to resume possession after the judgment creditor had consented to part with them to the plaintiff.

BAYLEY, J., and LITTLEDALE, J., concurred (*a*).

Rule discharged.

(*a*) *Holroyd*, J., had left the Court.

———◆———

SANDIMAN *v.* BREACH.

THIS was an action of assumpsit, to recover the expense of hiring a post-chaise to carry the plaintiff from *Clapton* to *London.* Plea, the general issue. At the trial before Lord *Tenterden,* C. J. at the sittings in *London* after last *Michaelmas* term, it appeared in evidence, that the plaintiff had gone to spend the day on a *Sunday* at *Clapton,* and had booked himself a place in the defendant's stage-coach to return by it in the evening to *London,* and paid half the fare at the booking office, the defendant being the proprietor of the stage-coach duly licensed to travel from *Clapton* to *London.* In the evening the defendant refused to go to *London,* finding that he had no other passenger willing to go but the plaintiff. Upon which the plaintiff immediately hired a post-chaise in the neighbourhood to convey him to town, which put him to the expense of 13s., for which sum the present action was brought, in consequence of the defendant's breach of contract. On the part of the defendant it was insisted that the contract was illegal, it being made on the *Lord's day,* in violation of the statutes 3 *Car.* 1, c. 1, and 29 *Car.* 2, c. 7, and, consequently, that the defendant was not bound to perform it. Lord *Tenterden* saved the point, and the plaintiff had a verdict for 13s. with liberty to the defendant to move for a nonsuit. A rule nisi having been granted accordingly in *Hilary* term last, cause was now shewn against it by

Dodd. The ground upon which it is sought to disturb the verdict in this case is, that the contract in question is void, it having been entered into on a *Sunday.* Upon an examination, however, of the words of the statutes relied upon at the trial, it will be found that there is nothing in either of them that will render the travelling of stage-coaches on a *Sunday* illegal. The statute 3 *Car.* 1, c. 1, begins by reciting, that the *Lord's day* " is much broken and profaned by carriers, waggoners, carters, wainmen, butchers, and drovers of cattle," and then it enacts, " that no carrier with any horse or horses, nor waggonman with any waggon, nor carman with any cart, nor wainman with any wain, nor drovers with any cattle, shall by themselves or any other travel upon the said day, upon pain that every person so offending shall forfeit 20s. for every such offence." Now it is quite clear that the only word contained in that act which is at all applicable to the driver of a stage-coach is the word " carrier," but that evidently means the carrier of goods and not passengers. In the case of *Rex* v. *Middleton* (a) the Court held that the driver of a stage-van, travelling to and from *London* to *York*, was a common carrier within the meaning of the statute, but they studiously avoided giving any opinion as to whether the driver of a stage-coach was liable to the penalties of that statute, for *Abbot*, C. J. there said, " We are not called upon to give any opinion whether the drivers of mail and stage-coaches are carriers within the purview of this statute." Then does the 29 *Car.* 2, c. 7, apply to the defendant? By the first section of that statute it is enacted " that no tradesman, artificer, workman, labourer or other person whatsoever, shall do or exercise any worldly labour, business, or work of their ordinary callings upon the *Lord's day*, or any part thereof, works of necessity and charity only excepted, and that every person being of the age of 14 or upwards offending in the premises, shall for every such offence forfeit the sum of 5s." It cannot be said on the other side that the defendant falls within the description of persons here mentioned, unless he comes under the words " or other person whatsoever;" but by the general rule of construction in such cases, those words must be understood to apply to other persons of the like kind previously mentioned. It is true that the second section prohibits certain persons from travelling on a *Sunday*, but as those persons are specially mentioned, the Court will limit so penal a statute to such persons only, and not extend

(a) *Ante*, vol. iv. 825.

its provisions to others. The second section enacts that "no drover, horse-courser, waggoner, butcher, higgler, their or any of their servants, shall travel or come into his or their inn or lodging upon the *Lord's day*, upon pain that every such offender shall forfeit 20s. for every such offence, and that no person shall use, employ or travel upon the *Lord's day* with any boat, wherry, lighter, or barge, unless it be on some extraordinary occasions, to be allowed by some justice of peace." Conceding, for the sake of argument, that the defendant comes within the operation of the first section of the act, still his employment might come within the words of the exception, " works of charity and necessity." There are many acts done on *Sundays* which are essentially necessary, not only to the comfort, but convenience of life, which would be protected by the statute. For instance, medical men are often called upon to travel on a *Sunday*, and witnesses on their way to the assizes, and so forth. The exception in the statute has always been liberally construed. For instance, in *Rex* v. *Cox* (a), and *Rex* v. *Younger* (b), it was decided that baking pies and puddings, and such things for dinner on *Sunday*, is not an offence within the statute. If the statute were construed so strictly as will be contended for on the other side, in the present state of society it would lead to great public inconvenience. It would stop all communication between different parts of the country, and all transactions must be put an end to on the *Sabbath day*; nay, all correspondence through the medium of the royal mails must terminate, because it is notorious that mail-coaches must travel on the *Sunday*. Then secondly, assuming that any offence was committed against the statute, the offence was committed by the defendant, and not by the plaintiff, and he cannot take advantage of his own wrong. [*Bayley*, J. But do you not employ him to break the law?] The mere knowledge on the part of the plaintiff that the defendant is going to break the law, will not affect the plaintiff's right to recover; it is the

(a) 2 Bur. 785.   (b) 5 T. R. 449.

person who exercises his ordinary calling on the *Sabbath*, who is alone guilty of the offence against the statute. *Hodgson* v. *Temple* (a), *Bloxsome* v. *Williams* (b). Thirdly, however, the defendant is in possession of a license under the 29 *Geo.* 3, c. 51, s. 4, which in express terms authorises him to carry on *Sundays* 12 outside, and six inside passengers. In the face of this license, therefore, it does not lie in the mouth of the defendant to say that the contract was illegal.

Gurney, contrà. The argument pressed on the other side would with more propriety be addressed to the legislature for a revision of the law than to this Court; for it is quite clear, that by the law, as it at present stands, the defendant comes within the spirit and the words of the statute. The only question is, whether the driver of a stage-coach, having " an ordinary calling" and exercising that calling on the *Sabbath day*, is liable to the penalties of the statute 29 *Car.* 2, c. 7, for if he be, then it follows as a consequence, that the defendant having made a contract with the plaintiff in violation of the law, no action will lie against him for refusing to perform that contract. Now the words " or other person whatsoever," in the first section of the statute, are comprehensive enough to include all classes of persons exercising their ordinary callings on the *Lord's day*. [Lord *Tenterden*, C. J. If that be so, why should drovers and waggoners be specially mentioned in the second section?] That circumstance will not destroy the effect of the sweeping words contained in the first part of the act. It is clear that the fifth section considers all persons travelling on *Sunday* as offenders, inasmuch as it deprives them of all remedy against the hundred in case of robbery. The fact of the defendant having a license under the Hackney-coach act, to carry passengers on a *Sunday*, can avail the plaintiff nothing, if the license be in contravention of the general

(a) 5 Taunt. 181.   (b) *Ante*, vol. v. 82; 3 B. & C. 232.

law of the land. The case of Fennel v. Ridler (a) decides that the statute 29 *Car.* 2, c. 7, applies to private as well as public conduct, and it was determined that a horse dealer cannot maintain an action upon a private contract for the sale and warranty of a horse, if made on a *Sunday.* In *Rex* v. *Cox* the only point decided was, that a criminal information would not lie against a baker for baking pies on a *Sunday,* and this was on the ground that he came within the exemption in favour of cook-shops, contained in the third section.

This case was argued on a former day in the term. The Court took time to consider of the case, and judgment was now delivered by

Lord TENTERDEN, C. J.—We are of opinion that the rule nisi granted in this case must be discharged. It was objected that the plaintiff could not recover, because the contract for the breach of which the action was brought was to have been performed on the *Sabbath day,* and that it could not be legally performed on that day. But upon looking into the statutes 3 *Car.* 1, c. 1, and 29 *Car.* 2, c. 7, upon which the objection was founded, we are of opinion that this case does not come within them. There have been subsequent statutes containing regulations as to hackney-coaches, but they are too ambiguous to be taken as legislative expositions of the former acts. By the first of these, the 3 *Car.* 1, c. 1, it was enacted, " that no carrier with any horse, nor waggonman with any waggon, nor carman with any cart, nor wainman with any wain, nor drover with any cattle, shall by themselves or any other travel on the *Lord's day;*" and by the 29 *Car.* 2, c. 7, it is enacted, " that no tradesman, artificer, workman, labourer, or other person or persons, shall do or exercise any worldly labour, business or work of their ordinary callings upon the *Lord's day.*" It was contended that under the words " other person or persons," the drivers of stage-coaches are included. But where general words follow particular ones, the rule is to

(a) *Ante,* vol. viii. 204; 5 B. & C. 406.

construe them as applicable to persons *ejusdem generis.*
Considering then that in the 3 *Car.* 1, c. 1, carriers of a
certain description are mentioned, and that in the 29 *Car.*
2, c. 7, drovers, horse-coursers, waggoners, and travellers
of certain descriptions are specifically mentioned, we think
that the words " other person or persons" cannot have
been used in a sense large enough to include the owner and
driver of a stage-coach. On these grounds we think that
the rule for entering a nonsuit must be discharged.

1827.

Sandiman
v.
Breach.

Rule discharged.

Browning and another *v.* Aylwin and another.

THIS was a rule calling upon the defendants, who were
sworn brokers of the city of *London,* to shew cause why
the plaintiffs should not be at liberty to inspect their books
and take a copy of a contract therein entered by them for
the purchase of 39 casks of fine Olive oil, on their behalf
and for their account, the property of one *B. Valle.* It
appeared from the affidavits, that in *November,* 1826, the
plaintiffs employed the defendants to purchase on their
account the oil in question. The defendants accordingly
purchased the oil, and delivered to the plaintiffs a bought-
note, purporting that they had bought the oil for the plaintiffs' account. The owner of the oil, however, refused to
deliver it, on the ground that he was not bound by any contract so to do. It appeared that the sold-note, delivered
by the defendants to *Valle,* varied from the bought-note
received by the plaintiffs. The plaintiffs, therefore, being
unable to enforce the contract against *Valle,* brought the
present action against the defendants to recover damages
for the loss which they had thereby sustained. The defendants, as sworn brokers of the city of *London,* had given
the usual bond to the corporation, one of the conditions of

A sworn bro-
ker of the city
of *London* is in
the nature of
a public agent,
and, therefore,
in an action a-
gainst him for
negligence in
making a con-
tract, the Court
will, on motion,
compel him to
produce his
books for the
purpose of
enabling the
plaintiff to in-
spect them and
take a copy of
the contract.

1827.

BROWNING
v.
AYLWIN.

which was, that they should enter in a book to be kept for that purpose all contracts made by them, and that either of the parties to such contracts, whether buyer or seller, should be at liberty to inspect the original entries of such contracts. The plaintiffs had demanded of the defendants an inspection of their books, which being refused the present application was made.

F. Pollock shewed cause against the rule, and contended, that this being an action against the defendants for negligence, the plaintiffs had no right to compel the defendants to produce evidence against themselves, which was the effect of this application. No authority was to be found which had gone that length.

Parke, contrà. This, in principle, is an application of very ordinary occurrence. It is a general rule, that if there be an instrument in the hands of the opposite party, which is essential to the plaintiff's case, the Court will compel him to produce it, but *à multo fortiori* this rule applies in the case of a public officer, such as a sworn broker of the city of *London*. By the bond entered into by the defendants to the corporation of the city, it is a condition imposed upon them, that they shall enter all contracts in their books, and shall allow the parties interested to inspect them. In the case of *King* v. *King* (a), the Court compelled a defendant in covenant, on a deed which he held, to produce it to the plaintiff for the purposes of the cause. So in *Morrow* v. *Saunders* (b) it was held, that if one part of a deed be executed by the plaintiff alone, but remains in the possession of the defendant's attorney, the Court will order the latter to give an inspection and copy of it to the plaintiff. Unless this application be granted the plaintiffs will have no remedy, for the contract entered in the bidder's book and signed by him is the best evidence of the transaction. This is not like the case of *Geam* v. *Aflalo* (c),

(a) 4 Taunt. 666.
(b) 3 J. B. Moore, 671; 1 B. & B. 318.
(c) *Ante*, 148; 6 B. & C. 117.

because there there was no entry in the book of the contract signed by the broker, and therefore the bought and sold notes were the best evidence.

This matter was argued on *Wednesday* the 27th of *June,* when the Court took time to look into it, and now the judgment of the Court was delivered by

BAYLEY, J.—We think that a sworn broker is in the nature of a public agent, having a public duty to perform, and consequently that the parties for whom he acts are entitled upon principle to inspect the documents by which they are to be bound.

Rule absolute (a).

(a) *Vide* 1 Chitty, 98, and the cases there collected.

SMITH and others *v.* FERRAND.

THIS was an action of assumpsit for goods sold and delivered; to which the defendant pleaded the general issue. At the trial before *Park,* J., at the last summer assizes for the county of *York,* it appeared in evidence that the plaintiffs carried on business at *Gomersal,* near *Leeds,* under the firm of *The Gomersal Mill Company,* and were in the habit of employing a person named *John Kaye* to sell goods and receive money on their account. The defendant resided at *Almondbury,* near *Huddersfield,* and in the month of *September,* 1825, *Kaye* sold him, on the plaintiffs' account, some worsted yarn, which was afterwards delivered, to the amount of 195*l.* According to the evidence of *Kaye,* who was examined as a witness in support of the case, it appeared that the yarn was sold to be paid for on delivery by a bill at two months, which was to be considered as a money payment. On the 11th of *October* the defendant which was dishonoured:—Held, that the vendor could not sue the vendee for the price of the goods.

An agent for the vendor of goods received from the vendee an order upon his banker for the price to be paid out of funds specifically deposited for that purpose with the banker. The latter offered to pay in cash, deducting discount, or by a bill upon a third person. The agent, without the knowledge of the vendee, took the bill, gave *Kaye* an order, without any signature, address, or date, upon Messrs. *Dobson* & Co. bankers at *Huddersfield*, in the following terms:—" Please to pay *The Gomersal Mill Company* 193*l.*, equal to six months." When *Kaye* presented this order he received from Messrs. *Dobson* & Co. a bill at three months for 100*l.* drawn on a house in *London*, and their own bank notes to the amount of 89*l.* 11*s.* The sum of 3*l.* 9*s.* was deducted from the total amount of the order, as discount upon the 100*l.* bill, and for six months on the 89*l.* 11*s.* The cashier told him at the time that he might have the whole amount in cash, minus the discount. Immediately after receiving the 100*l.* bill and the money, *Kaye* called upon the defendant, and wrote on the invoice of the goods the word " settled," but at the same time said he would not give credit for more than he had actually received. The 100*l.* bill was duly presented in *London* when at maturity, on the 13th of *January*, but was dishonoured by the drawees. Messrs. *Dobson* & Co. had stopped payment in the previous month of *December*. It appeared in evidence on the part of the defendant, that it was the usual course of trade at *Huddersfield* to sell goods of the description in question to be paid for by a bill at six months, and that *Kaye*, on the day he received the order from the defendant, admitted that he had agreed to allow six months' discount. It further appeared that the defendant had paid in to Messrs. *Dobson* & Co. a bill for 2000*l.*, which was duly paid when at maturity, and delivered to them a list of different persons to whom he wished payments to be made, and amongst these was " *John Kaye*, *Gomersal*, 193*l.*" When *Kaye* presented the order above mentioned, he was asked at the banker's how he wished to be paid, and he replied that he would take a bill for 100*l.* at three months, and the remainder in bank notes. When the discount was deducted he made no objection. Under these circumstances *Park*, J., was of opinion, that inasmuch as *Kaye* might have received cash for the order, as he was told by the bankers, but chose to take a bill which turned out to be worth nothing, the defendant was discharged. With respect to the deduction for discount, the right of the plaintiffs to recover that depended upon whether in fact *Kaye* had agreed to allow six months' discount. That question he left to the jury, and they being of opinion that *Kaye* had so agreed, found their verdict for the defendant. In *Michaelmas* term last a rule nisi for a new trial was obtained, on the ground that the order given by the defendant to *Kaye* upon *Dobson* & Co. was not a check, and as the latter must be considered as agents for the defendant, it was in effect a payment by the defendant; and the 100*l.* bill having turned out waste paper, it was not *pro tanto* a discharge of the plaintiffs' original demand.

Scarlett, A. G. and *Campbell*, now shewed cause, and contended, that after the finding of the jury upon the facts disclosed on the trial, the conduct of *Kaye*, who must be taken to have acted within the scope of his authority as an agent, bound the plaintiffs as his principals. *Kaye* might have received bank notes or money upon the defendant's order, instead of which he chose to take a bill upon *London*, which had three months to run, at his own risk. By this election he was bound, and although it turned out that the parties to it had failed before the bill became due, it operated as a discharge of the defendant, the original debtor.

Parke, (with whom was *Cross*, Serjt.) in support of the rule, contended, that as the order given by the defendant to *Kaye* was neither directed to Messrs. *Dobson* & Co. nor signed by the defendant, it could not be considered as a check, which made all the difference. At the utmost it was a mere memorandum to denote *Kaye* as one of the persons mentioned by the defendant in the list sent by him to the bankers who were to receive payment out of the proceeds of the 2000*l.* bill. In this respect *Dobson* & Co. were merely the agents of the defendant, and they having given *Kaye* a bill which turned out to be unproductive, the defendant continued liable upon the original demand. Suppose the defendant himself had given this bill to *Kaye*, it clearly would have been no discharge of the debt. Then what difference in principle does it make that it was given by his agents, *Dobson* & Co., by whose act he must be bound? In the case of *Ex parte Blackburn* (a) Lord *Eldon* was of opinion, that where there is an antecedent debt, and a bill is given for it without any indorsement by the debtor, the law implies a contract that the bill shall be paid when at maturity, and if it is not, the original debt remains. If, therefore, *Dobson* & Co. are to be considered as the defendant's agents, this case falls directly within the principle of that doctrine. But the case of *Everett v. Collins* (b) is precisely in point with the present, even assuming that the order in question might be considered as a check. In that case the plaintiff had employed the defendant to sell cattle for him, and, on demanding the money produced by the sale, the defendant took the plaintiff's son to *Mingay, Nott* & Co., his agents, and they offered to pay him in bank notes, but he preferred a check on their bankers. He took the check, but it was not paid; and it was held that this did not discharge the defendant, although *Mingay* & Co. failed with a balance of his in their hands. That decision was founded on the principle that *Mingay* & Co. were the defendant's agents, and that their offer to pay by notes or their check was equivalent to an offer by the defendant himself to pay by notes or his check. There is no doubt that in the present case the order in question gave *Kaye* the option of taking a bill at six months, or at any less time, or money, allowing discount; and therefore as he was warranted by the order in taking the bill in question, which turned out to be of no value, it does not operate as a discharge of the debt *pro tanto*. This principle is to be collected from *Ex parte Dixon* (c). This is not like the case of *Bolton* v. *Richards* (d), where the party received

(a) 10 Ves. 206.   (c) MS. cited in argument 6 T. R. 142.
(b) 2 Campb. 515.   (d) 6 T. R. 139.

payment in a mode not warranted by the order. In that
case, A. sold goods to B., for which the latter was to pay
by a bill at three months; B. gave A. a check on his bankers, (who were also the bankers of A.) requiring them to
pay A. on demand in a bill at three months. A. paid the
check into the bankers and took no bill from them, but the
amount was transferred in the bankers' books from B.'s
account to A.'s, with the knowledge of both. The bankers
failed before the check became due, and it was held that A.
could not recover the value of the goods against B. In
the present case, however, Kaye had an option given him
by the order either to take money or bills. It is true that
he has made his election, by taking part of the amount in
cash and part in a bill, but as he was authorised so to do
by the order itself, and, as the bill was dishonoured, the
original debt *pro tanto* remains unsatisfied, and the defendant is still liable.

Lord TENTERDEN, C. J.—I am of opinion that this rule
ought to be discharged. The facts of the case appear to
be these:—The defendant had sent a bill for 2000*l.* (which
was afterwards paid) to his bankers, Messrs. *Dobson & Co.*,
for the purpose of meeting payments on his account. He
gave to *Kaye*, the plaintiff's agent, a note in these terms:
" Please to pay *The Gomersal Mill Company* 193*l.*, equal
to six months." Previously to this the defendant had sent
to *Dobson* & Co. a general list, containing the names of
persons to whom he wished them to make payments, and
amongst others *John Kaye*. I am clearly of opinion, that
by the terms of the instrument given by the defendant to
Kaye, when the latter went to *Dobson* & Co., he had a right
to insist on payment in ready money, on allowing six months'
discount, and if they refused to give him that, he or his
principals might have taken his or their remedy against the
defendant. Whether the order upon *Dobson* & Co. assumed
the form of a regular check or not, does not appear to me
to make any difference. When *Kaye* presented the order

to, *Dobson* & *Co.,* it appears that he might have had cash if he would, but he chose to take a bill for 100*l.* which had nearly three months to run; so that he took a security very different from that which was taken from *Mingay* and *Co.* in *Everett v. Collins.* There the party took nothing but a check or order on a banker to pay the money immediately; but here the plaintiff's agent takes a bill of exchange having other names upon it, and having a certain time to run; not an instrument importing immediate payment, like a check. I think, therefore, that this case is clearly distinguishable from that cited. It is also to be observed, that *Dobson* & Co. are not merely agents in the common understanding of that term, but agents entrusted with funds for the special purpose of paying this demand amongst others. It appears to me, that as the plaintiffs or their agent *Kaye* thought proper to waive the right to immediate payment, and to take the security of a bill of exchange which has turned out to be fruitless, it is fit that they should sustain the loss which has happened through their own fault.

BAYLEY, J.—I consider *Dobson* & Co. in this case as debtors to the plaintiffs for the amount of this bill. I take it to be clear, that if a creditor refers a third person to his debtor for payment, entitling him to demand payment in ready money, and instead of taking ready money, such third person receives payment in any other way, he does so at his own peril. In the case of *Embleton v. Cremer*(a), tried before Lord *Kenyon* on the 26th of *February,* 1796, it was decided, that if a debtor refers his creditor to a third person for payment in ready money, and the creditor gives to the third person indulgence without the knowledge and consent of the debtor, and the third person becomes insolvent, the loss must fall on the creditor, because, as between himself and the debtor, the giving indulgence without notice operates as an agreement on his part to look to the third person, and discharges the debtor. Now in this case

(a) Cited by the learned Judge from his own MS. notes.

Kaye received an order for 193*l.* upon *Dobson* & Co., who
stood in the situation of debtors to *Ferrand* for that amount.
It follows that *Kaye* had a right to demand payment in cash,
and it appears from the evidence that he might have had
cash, if he thought fit, but he chose to take a bill at three
months. The defendant was no party to the arrangement,
he never authorised *Kaye* to take the bill. The taking of
the bill was an act of *Kaye's*, and an act of indulgence
given to *Dobson* & Co.; and being an act of indulgence,
the loss arising from the failure of *Dobson* & Co. must fall
upon *Kaye* or the plaintiffs, his principals, with whom he
is identified. I think that the fact of *Kaye's* taking the bill
without having made any communication upon the subject
to the defendant *Ferrand*, is conclusive to shew that the
plaintiffs are not entitled to recover the amount against the
defendant. The case of *Everett* v. *Collins* (a) is very different from this, because in that case the check taken was
an order for immediate payment, equivalent to payment in
cash; for when a party is offered the option of having either
a check on a banker or bank notes, it is in effect an offer
to pay in one species of cash or another. This is a very
different thing from giving indulgence or forbearance to
postpone payment. I think, therefore, that the verdict
found for the defendant ought not to be disturbed.

LITTLEDALE, J.—I am of the same opinion (b).

Rule discharged (c).

(a) 2 Campb. 515.
(b) *Holroyd*, J., was in the Bail
Court.

(c) See *Robinson* v. *Read*, 4 M.
& R. 349, and the authorities there
cited.

1827.

F. H. RENNELL, administratrix of THOMAS RENNELL,
clerk, v. The Bishop of LINCOLN, T. H. MIREHOUSE,
and W. S. MIREHOUSE.

A prebendary, who had the advowson of a rectory in right of his prebend, died while the church was vacant:—Held, that his administratrix had the right of presentation for that turn: Lord Tenterden, C. J. dissentiente.

QUARE impedit. The declaration stated that whereas one *William Dodwell*, clerk, doctor in divinity, late prebendary of the prebend or canonry of *South Grantham*, founded in the cathedral church of *Salisbury*, heretofore to wit on &c., at &c., was seised of and in the said prebend or canonry, with its appurtenances, to which said prebend or canonry the advowson of the rectory of the parish church of *Welby* with its appurtenances then belonged and still belongs, in his demesne as of fee in right of the said prebend or canonry. And so being such prebendary as aforesaid, and so being seised of and in the said prebend or canonry with its appurtenances, to which &c., afterwards to wit on &c., at &c., presented to the said church of *Welby*, being then vacant, one *William Dodwell*, master of arts, his clerk, who, on the said presentation of the said *W. D.*, doctor in divinity, was admitted, instituted and inducted into the same in the time of peace &c. That the said *W. D.*, being so seised of the prebend or canonry with its appurtenances, to which &c., in his demesne as of fee in right of the said prebend or canonry, afterwards to wit on &c., at &c., died so seised; after whose death to wit on &c., at &c., one *Robert Price*, clerk, was lawfully admitted &c., and afterwards died; after whose death to wit on &c., at &c., *Thomas Rennell*, the intestate, was lawfully admitted &c., whereby the said *Thomas Rennell* then and there became and was seised of and in the said prebend or canonry with its appurtenances, to which &c., in his demesne as of fee in right of the said prebend or canonry. And the said *Thomas Rennell* being so seised, the said church afterwards to wit on &c., at &c., became vacant by the death of the said Rev. *William Dodwell*, clerk, the late parson and incumbent thereof, and still is vacant, whereby it then and there belonged to the said *Thomas Rennell* to present a fit person to the said rectory of the said parish church so vacant as aforesaid.   Averment, that afterwards and while the said church was so vacant as aforesaid, to wit on &c. at &c., the said *Thomas Rennell* died intestate, so seised of and in the said prebend or canonry with its appurtenances, to which &c., in his demesne as of fee in right of the said prebend or canonry, without having presented any person to the said rectory of the said parish church; after whose death, and while the said church was so vacant as aforesaid, to wit on &c., at &c., administration was granted to the plaintiff, whereupon and whereby it then and there belonged, and now belongs to the plaintiff, as administratrix as aforesaid, to present a fit person to the said rectory of the said parish church, so being vacant as aforesaid, and which is still vacant, but the said defendants unjustly hinder her, &c. The Bishop of *Lincoln* by his plea disclaimed except as to the admission, institution and induction of the rectors to the same rectory and parish church, and all such other things as belong to the ordinary as ordinary of that place.   The other defendants pleaded that after the said *Thomas Rennell* had so died without having presented any person to the said rectory of the said parish church, and while the said church was so vacant as aforesaid, to wit on &c., at &c., he, the said defendant *T. H. Mirehouse*, clerk, was lawfully admitted &c. prebendary of the said prebend or canonry with its appurtenances, to which said prebend or canonry the said advowson with its appurtenances then belonged and still belongs, whereby he, the said *T. H. Mirehouse*, then and there became and was seised of and in the said prebend or canonry with its appurtenances, to which &c., in his demesne as of fee in right of the said prebend or canonry, and whereby it then and there belonged to him to present a fit person to the said rectory so being vacant as aforesaid; and that the said *T. H. Mirehouse* presented the said defendant *W. S. Mirehouse*.   Upon the bishop's disclaiming, the plaintiff prayed judgment against him, and demurred to the plea of the other defendants. Joinder in demurrer. The case was first argued in C. P., and judgment given for the defendants, whereupon the plaintiff brought a writ of error. The case was argued in *Michaelmas* term, 1826, by *Patteson* for the plaintiff, and *D'Oyley*, Serjt., for the defendants, when the Court took time for consideration, and there being a difference of opinion on the bench, the learned Judges now delivered judgment *seriatim*.

LITTLEDALE, J.—The question raised upon the defendants' plea, to which there is a demurrer, is, if there be a prebendary of a prebend to which the advowson of a church is appendant, and the church becomes void in the lifetime of the prebendary, and he dies without presenting to the church, whether the successor of the prebendary is entitled to present. But that point need not be decided, because, though if the affirmative of that be true, it would be an answer to the plaintiff's declaration; yet supposing it not to be true, the defendants have a right to shew, that, even though the right be not in the successor, yet it is not in the plaintiff. And, therefore, the point comes more properly to be considered on the plaintiff's declaration, and upon that the question is, " if there be a prebendary of a prebend, to which an advowson is appendant, and the church becomes void in the lifetime of the prebendary, and he dies without presenting to the church, whether the executor or administrator (as the case may be) of the deceased prebendary be entitled to present." For if not, it is quite immaterial to the plaintiff's claim whether the right be in the successor, or in the king, or in the bishop of the diocese in which the prebend is, or in the bishop of the diocese in which the rectory is. I may, however, say that though the question is upon the plaintiff's right, yet the dispute is in effect between the plaintiff and the successor to the prebend; because there does not appear to be any ground for the claim of the crown, except, that if no one can establish a legal right, the presentation would belong to the king, as the head of the church. There seems no ground for the claim either of the Bishop of *Lincoln* or *Salisbury*, as there is no lapse; no such right is set up, and it is not necessary to enter into any discussion to shew that such right could not be supported. It is admitted on both sides, that this is the first case in which the question has come to be decided in a court of justice; and it must be considered in what way presentative benefices have been treated in the decisions which have taken place in cases which have any resemblance to the present, and in the opinions of text writers of authority. There is no doubt that in case of a benefice presentable for institution, if a person in his own right, as contra-distinguished from his corporate rights, be seised in fee or in tail of an advowson appendant to a manor or other estate, or of an advowson in gross, and the church becomes void in the lifetime of the patron, and the patron dies, the church still being void, the executor shall present, and not the heir, *Brooke's Abr.* tit. *Presentacion à l'Esglise*, 34; *Fitz-herbert, Presentment à l'Eglises*, 7; *Fitzherbert's N. B.* 33, 34; *Co. Litt.* 388 a.; *The Queen, Fane*, and the *Arch-bishop of Canterbury's* case (a); *Comyn's Digest, Esglise*, H. 2, where he mentions it as of his own authority; admitted in the case of *Repinton* v. *The Governors of Tamworth School* (b); recognised in the case of *Holt* v. *Bishop of Win-chester* (c), where the case was, that if a man seised in fee of an advowson be parson of the church, and dies, his heir, and not his executor, shall present; for though the advowson doth not descend to the heir till after the death of the ancestor, and by his death the church is become void, so that the avoidance may be said to be severed from the advowson before it descend to the heir and vest in the executor, yet both the avoidance and the descent to the heir happening at the same instant, the title of the heir shall be preferred as the elder. But that recognises the general proposition, though in the particular case the title of the heir is to be preferred. How the presentation came to

(a) 4 Leon. 109.   (b) 2 Wils. 150.   (c) 3 Lev. 47.

belong to the executor, and whether it would not have been
as well if it had been held to belong to the heir, it is now
too late to inquire; the law has been so long settled and
has been so repeatedly admitted, that it would be most dangerous to think of disturbing it. The reason assigned in
Fitz. N. B. 33, for its going to the executor is, that it is a
chattel vested and severed from the manor, and in *Plowd.*
109, it is called a chattel. In *Wentworth's Office of Executors,* 54, it is said that the next presentation before it becomes void is a chattel real, and after, it is a personal
chattel. The language of six judges in *Stephens v. Watts,*
(where the question was whether the present avoidance of
a church could be granted by a subject) is, that the grant of
the present avoidance was void " because it was a mere
personal thing annexed to the person of him who was
patron in expectancy at the time of the vacancy; and also
a thing in right, power, and authority, and a chose in
action; and in effect, the fruit and execution of the advowson, and not any advowson, and yet executors shall have it
by privity of law." The principal case was, whether the
present avoidance of a church could be granted by a subject;
and six of the judges, to whom the above expressions are attributed, held that it could not; but though the other three
judges differed, I do not understand that to be as to what is
there said by six of the judges, but only as to the point itself
in discussion. However the law has since been recognised
according to the decision in *Dyer* as to the principal case;
Co. Litt. 120 a, 3 *Burr.* 1515. The case itself is recognised in *Brokesby v. Wickham and the Bishop of London* (b).
There are other cases also besides these, of executors of
tenants in fee or in tail, where the void turn is treated as a
chattel. If a woman be seised of an advowson and married,
and she and her husband have issue, though the right of
patronage descends to his heir, and though the wife never
presented, and died before the church became vacant, the
right of presenting is vested in the husband during his life;

(a) Dyer, 282.   (b) 1 Leon. 17.

as tenant by the curtesy, though his wife had, but a seisin in law, because he could by no industry obtain any other seisin. And if the church in this case becomes void during the life of the husband, and he dies during the vacancy, the heir shall not present, but the husband's executor; and if, the church being void, the wife dies, not having had issue, so that the husband is not tenant by the curtesy, yet he shall present to the void turn as being a chattel, Co. Litt. 29 a, 120 a, 388 a. Bro. Abr. Present, à l'Esglise, 18—22, Watson, Incumbent, c. 12. And in Fitz. N. B. 34, " If a vicarage happen void, and before the parson present, he is made a bishop, &c., yet he shall present to this turn, because it is a chattel vested in him." This last position of Fitzherbert shews, that in his opinion it was as much a chattel in case of an ecclesiastic as in any other case. The plaintiff therefore contends, that as this is a chattel vested in her, in her quality of administratrix, the right to present is in her. But though the law be not doubted by the defendant to the extent of the cases to which it has been carried, yet he says that it is not founded on principle, and should not be carried beyond the cases already decided. And he says the presentation ought not to go to the executor, because it is not assets; and for this may be cited Co. Litt. 388 a, " Nothing can be taken for a presentation, and therefore it is not assets;" Co. Litt. 120 a, " It is not merely a chose in action;" Fitz. N. B. 33, " And if there be guardian in socage of a manor to which an advowson is appendant, and the church becomes void, the heir shall present and not the guardian, because he cannot account for the same." So Co. Litt. 17 b, guardian in socage shall not present to an advowson, because he can take nothing for it, and cannot account for it, and he shall not meddle with any thing he cannot account for; S. P. in Co. Litt. 89 a: and there the reason given that he can make no benefit of it is, that the law doth abhor simony; and the same reason is given in the Bishop of Lincoln v. Wolfestan (a). But as to this point, the cases

(a) 3 Burr. 1514.

of guardians do not apply, because their duty is to account for what they make, and of course they cannot meddle with what they cannot turn into profit. But it is otherwise in the case of an executor. An advowson is assets in the hands of the heir, and the right of the next presentation to a church which is full, is assets in the hands of an executor; both these are allowed by the law to be sold, but a void presentation is not. The meaning of assets is, that it may be converted into money, which a void presentation cannot be; but the reason of that is, not that it is a chose in action, but because the law against simony prevents its being sold, which otherwise it might be. In 3 *Burr.* 1515, Lord *Mansfield* and Mr. Justice *Wilmot* say, that the true reason why a grant of a fallen presentation is not good is the public utility, and the better to guard against simony; not for the fictitious reason of its having then become a chose in action. In the case of *London* v. *The Collegiate Church of Southwell* (a) it was said, that in a lease by a prebendary, under the words " commodities, emoluments, profits, and advantages to the prebend belonging," the advowson of a vicarage would not pass, because these words imply things gainful, which is contrary to the nature of an advowson. But the report goes on, " yet an advowson may be yielded in value upon a voucher, and may be assets in the hands of an executor." But the case was decided on the particular meaning of the words used, denoting something gainful. No question was made but that if proper words had been used, the advowson would have passed. And there can be no doubt whatever that the next presentation, if the church be full, is of value, and would be saleable by law, and would be assets in the hands of an executor; and the only distinction between a presentation where the church is full or void, is, that in one case it is not simoniacal to sell it, and in the other it is. But though it be not saleable as the subject of profit, it is not the less a chattel, or the less belongs to the executor.

(a) Hob. 303.

An outstanding term to attend the inheritance, or a term in trust for other purposes, cannot be made the subject of sale, or be made available assets in the hands of the termor, but they go to the executor. It is also contended by the defendant, that the rule does not hold universally, even in the case of lay patronage; for that in the case of donatives the right of presentation vests in the heir and not in the executor, as was decided, after two arguments, in the case of *Repington* v. *The Governor of Tamworth School* (a). Though the case must have been very much discussed, the grounds of the decision are not given at length; but it was said, " that before the council of *Lateran* all benefices were like what donatives are now; that no lapse could have occurred in ancient times, and that bishops had no right of institution before the reign of *Richard* 2." " *Ante concilium Lateranense*," says *Bracton*, " *nullum currebat tempus contra præsentantes*."—*Selden's History of Tithes*, c. 12, fol. 390. When *Richard* the Second is mentioned in *Wilson*, it must be a mistake in the reporter; it should be *Richard* the First. It will require some detail of the history of the church in earlier times, and of lay patronage and lay investitures, and the law of lapse, to shew how what is stated in *Wilson* could be any ground for the presentations being adjudged to the heir; but when that is done I think it will appear that the decision is quite proper, and founded upon the original state of church patronage and the law of lapse, and that the short minutes of the reporter, when expanded into a fuller explanation, were really what was the substance of the decision. It will be seen, however, by what I am about to state, that though the law of lapse took place nearly about the same time as the right of institution by the bishops, yet that they were measures wholly unconnected, though both of them are applicable to the right of the heir in the case of donatives. In the early ages of Christianity the bishops had probably the appointment and regulation of the inferior clergy, who were to perform

(a) 2 Wils. 150.

divine service, and to preach in such places as the bishop thought best calculated to promote the cause of religion; and they were to be paid out of the funds which went to the common treasury of the diocese, and over which the bishop had the disposal for himself, his clergy, the poor, and the repairing of churches. But in the early centuries of Christianity there were no compulsory payments; no tithes were paid, and the whole of the funds depended upon voluntary donations and oblations made from time to time, or the produce of lands which had been given to the church. The countries of Christendom were not in the earlier times divided into parishes, as they have since been, and the ministers of the church had neither permanent places in which they were to discharge their ecclesiastical duties, nor had they any permanent funds allotted to their maintenance and support. What are now called ecclesiastical livings were at that time unknown, and the early ages of Christianity will afford no guide in considering the rights of parties to church presentation or appointment. By degrees the funds of the church became increased, territorial possessions were from time to time given to religious houses, or otherwise for the purposes of religion, and about 400 years from the birth of our Saviour tithes began to be paid in some places; and in the seventh century some churches were endowed with the perpetual right to tithes, and some provincial ordinances, but by no means general, were made for their payment. After about eight centuries the payment of them became more frequent, and consecrations of them were made from time to time to churches and religious houses, as is stated in *Selden on Tithes*; and in these centuries there were some provincial constitutions of the clergy directing the payment of tithes; these, however, were probably not much more attended to than the inclination of persons led them to do, but that inclination, no doubt, increased among all classes. In the year 855, there is a charter of *Ethelwolf*, in which, with the consent of his bishops and his princes, he directs some tithes to be given

to the church; but what was the exact language of this
charter and the extent of the ordinance, the older historians
are by no means agreed. Different kings after him, before
the conquest, made different orders for the payment of
tithes, but it is by no means clear that the payment of them
was even then altogether general or compulsory. Soon
after the conquest the payment of them seems to have
become general, though not always, to the churches of the
parishes where they arose. That council of *Lateran* which
was held in 1215, endeavours to alter some usages which
had prevailed to the contrary, and directs all payments in
future to be made to the parish church; but it seems doubtful whether this obligation to pay to the parish church was
fully established till the general council of *Lyons* in the
year 1274. Tithes, however, were not the only possessions
of the church; lands were from time to time given for religious purposes. Some were given to religious houses, that
they might dispose of the profits. The clergy are said at
one time to have had their general residence in the same
place with the bishops, except when they were on their
missions; but by degrees, as devotion increased, the clergy
came to reside more permanently in particular places, and
some persons gave their tithes, and others appropriated
their land, for their support, and others built churches;
and persons would become more willing to endow the
church founded chiefly for the use of themselves and their
families and tenants, if they could have the liberty of giving
the incumbent there resident a special and several maintenance, instead of the former community of the clergy's
revenue remaining. There is no doubt but the bishops
would give their sanction to these foundations, and the
profits of the several churches would be restrained to the
incumbents. It does not very well appear when these lay
foundations began in *England*. It appears from *Selden's*
History of Tithes, c. 9, s. 4, that the first instance that
occurs is about the year 700, and he says, that about the
year 800 many churches founded by laymen are said to

have been appropriated to the Abbey of *Crowland*, and by this time probably lay foundations had become very common, and parochial limits assigned to the incumbents; though from other parts of *Selden's* work it seems that the payment of tithes did not always correspond to the parochial divisions till some centuries afterwards. When gifts were first made to the church, and churches founded by laymen, it does not always appear to have been done through pure devotion; for in some countries of Christendom, at least, the patron sometimes arbitrarily divided part with the incumbent, and what the incumbent did not receive the patron took to his own use, and by different councils of the church lay patrons were forbidden from making such a disposition. The lay patrons, however, in their new created churches, claimed a right of collation or investiture, whereby the incumbent might receive full possession without the aid of the bishop or other churchman; and notwithstanding some imperials were made against this course of proceeding, the lay patrons could not be prevented from claiming the patronage, and they took upon themselves not only the advocation or advowson, that is, the defence or patrociny of the incumbent's title, but also the collation by investiture, without presentation, at any vacancy. And the right of advowson, whereto the right of investiture was in these times annexed, the bishop in some places confirmed to the patron, by putting a robe or some other thing upon him at the dedication. And from this right of collation and patronage reserved by lay patrons the practice came to be, that parish churches, and all the temporalities annexed to them, as the glebe and tithe, were at every vacancy conferred by the patron on the new incumbent by some ceremony of investiture, with these words, " accipe ecclesiam," or the like. Upon these presentations the bishop did not institute, as has been done since. And the incumbent as really, fully, and immediately received the body of his church and his glebe, and such tithes as were joined with it in point of interest, from the patron's hands, as a lessee for life receives his lands by livery of the lessor. These investitures by lay patrons were very objectionable to the church, and in a general council at *Constantinople* in 870, some attempts were made to prevent them; and in the council of *Rome* in 1078, further regulations were endeavoured to be made against them. There is a canon against them, and in the council of *Lateran*, in 1119, many decrees were made to the same effect; and soon after a general council, which was held in 1138, they became less frequent, and institution now and then followed upon presentation. And as the canons acquired force, and the papal power increased, it appears to have been out of use about the year 1200; but till then it was not left off. So also *Selden*, in his *History of Tithes*, c. 12, s. 5, says, " But after such time as the decretals and the increasing authority of the canons, about the year 1200, had settled the universal course here of filling churches by presentation to the bishop, or, as it seems it sometimes was, to the archdeacon, or to the vicar of the bishop, as guardian of the spiritualities, that use of investiture of churches and tithes severally or together, practised by laymen, was left off, and a division of ecclesiastical right from thence hath continued in practice. Neither did the king afterwards, much less common persons, fill their common parochial churches without such presentments to bishops—parochial churches, for of special donative chapels we here speak not—neither were appropriations of churches and tithes afterwards allowed that had not confirmation from the ordinary, immediate or supreme." Up to this time, therefore, benefices were donative. The patrons had the whole of the advowsons in their own hands; they invested the incumbent with the full possession of the church, either severally or together, and the incumbents were in the nature of lessees for life under the patron. There was then no law of lapse, and the investiture of the incumbent might take place wherever it suited the patron, though the patron, by ecclesiastical censures, might be compelled to fill the church. I do not find any

statement that in these times the patrons took the profits
of the benefices to their own use; but there can be no
doubt that it was so, because in the case of donatives, even
now, when the rights of the lay patrons are so much less
than formerly, the patrons are entitled to take them;
though, according to *Selden*, they cannot institute any suit
for the recovery of them if they are refused to be paid.
Some few donatives there are at the present day; whether
they were suffered to continue as they formerly were at the
time when the investiture by lay patrons was discontinued,
or whether they have been since founded by letters-patent
or licence from the crown, or whether there are some of
each, I cannot at all say. In the twelfth century the law
of lapse was introduced. A general council was held at
Lateran in 1175, at which, our *Selden* says, in c. 12, n. 5,
as last cited, four bishops were sent, according to custom,
as agents to the church of *England*. And *Bracton*, lib. 4,
241, says, " ante concilium *Lateranense* nullum currebat
tempus contrà præsentantes." Lord *Coke*, in 2 *Institute*,
273 and 361, notices that *Briton* and *Fleta* describe the
council as having been held at *Lyons*, and not at *Lateran*,
as *Bracton* does; but it is not material where it was held.
Selden, however, says, " by that council, after vacancy of
six months, the chapter is to bestow those churches which
the bishop, being patron, had left so long void, and upon
their default the metropolitan. But no word of lay patron
is in it; yet by reason of the authority of that council, and
a decretal of the same pope, (*Alexander* the Third,) which
speaks of like time, upon default of lay patrons, it hath
been since taken here generally, that after vacancy of six
months, the next ordinary is regularly to collate by lapse."
It appears, therefore, that nearly about the same period of
time the discontinuance of investitures by laymen, the law
of lapse, and the payment of tithes in the parishes where
they arose, were introduced. These measures, however,
were wholly unconnected with each other, though they all
arose from the increasing authority of the church and the

forces of the canons. In the case of donatives, which I consider all benefices of lay patronage to have been, and, as I have before endeavoured to shew, as long as the right of institution was in the patron, the complete dominion remained with the patron. When the church is vacant, he is entitled to take the profits to his own use, but he has no remedy to compel payment; and if a stranger takes them, the patron cannot bring an action for them, but must put in a clerk, who is to sue. It is said by *Popham*, C. J., in *Fairchild* v. *Gaire* (a), that the patron may take the profits, and sue for them in the Spiritual Court; and though the other judges differ with *Popham*, yet I consider their point of difference to apply to his opinion, that if the patron will not collate, there is no remedy to compel him, but he is left to his conscience; for when they are said to be contrà, they say that the ordinary may compel him to collate a clerk, and give their reasons; but as they say nothing about the patron taking the profits, I do not understand them to differ upon that point. The same point was put in argument in *Britton* v. *Wurd* (b), where it is said, that when the church is void, the patron may take the profits to his own use, if the parishioners will pay them, but he has no remedy to compel them to pay their tithes to him. The same case of *Britton* v. *Ward* is reported in *Cro. Jac.* 515, but there called *Britten* v. *Wade*, and there it is also said, " but if any take the profits from him, he cannot maintain the action, but he ought to put in his clerk, and he maintain the action;" but the language there is, that the patron of a donative may *lose* the profits if he will; that is evidently a mistake, it is not proper *English*, and is not consistent with what follows; the mistake seems to arise from the translator taking the French word to be *perdre* instead of *prendre;* it is *prendre* in *Rolle's* Reports; and in *Mallory's Quare Impedit,* 35, where this case is cited, he says the patron may *take* the profits. So also *Burn* in his *Ecclesiastical Law,* title " Vacation," says, that in case of

(a) Yelv. 61.   (b) 2 Roll. Rep. 97.

donatives the patron may take the profits during the time of vacation. Donatives may be resigned by the incumbent to the patron, *Fairchild* v. *Gaire*, as before cited in *Yelverton*, 60, and *Cro. Jac.* 65, where the Court held, that a donative begins only by the erection and foundation of the donor, and he hath the sole visitation and correction, the ordinary nothing to do therewith; and as he comes in by him, so he may restore to him, for unum quodque eodem modo quo colligatum est dissolvitur. And although the presentee, when he is in, hath the freehold, yet he may revest it by his resignation, without any other ceremony, and the ordinary hath nothing to do therein. And in the *Yearbook*, 6 *Hen.* 7, c. 14, *Keble* says, that if the founder ordain that he and his heirs shall present, then the ordinary shall have nothing to do with it; and *Brooke, Presentment d l'Esglise*, in referring to the *Year-book* just cited, says, where a free chapel donative is void, the founder may retake it, and need not appoint any other incumbent. The old history of the church, as well as the more modern cases, treat donatives as being the entire property of the patron; if the church be void, the freehold is in him, though perhaps, upon consideration of all the authorities on both sides, he may be compelled by ecclesiastical censures to fill it, but in the meantime he may enter upon the glebe, and take the profits of that and the tithes; and if he may take them, his heir may take them after his death, as the foundation of the church is on behalf of himself and his heirs; and as there is no lapse in the case of donatives, this taking of the profits may continue till the church is filled; but if the executor could collate to the church, that would be adverse to the right of the heir to take the profits; and I think that, from the whole of the law of donatives, the right to collate is in the heir, and does not at all clash with the right of the executor as to benefices, which are presentative for institution. And though it may be said that the right of presentation is as completely severed from the advowson in case of a donative as in a presentative living,

I do not so consider it, as the nature of a donative is such, that the whole vests in the patron and his heirs, who may take the profits during the vacancy, and, therefore, the executor has nothing to do with it. But the defendant contends that, supposing the case of the donative to be accounted for by any means as constituting a well-founded difference from a benefice presentable for institution, yet that the case of ecclesiastical persons having benefices in right of their church is at all events different, and the first instance that is shewn is the case of a bishop, who, in right of his bishopric, has an advowson, and the church becomes void and he dies, the king shall present. For this are cited 2 *Rolle's Abr.* 345, " If a church of the patronage of the bishop void in the time of the bishop and after the bishop dies, the king shall have the presentment by reason of the temporalities, and not his executor ;" *Brook's Abr. Presentacion à l'Esglise,* 10, " Where the avoidance is of a benefice belonging to the bishop, and he dies before he makes collation, the king shall have it by reason of the temporalities of the bishop, and not the executors of the bishop ;" *Fitzh. N. B.* 33, " If the bishop die, and the advowson happen void before his death, the king shall present to the same by reason of the temporalities, and not the bishop's executors ;" *Co. Litt.* 90 *a,* " If a bishop have an advowson, and the church become void and the bishop die, neither the successor nor the executors shall present, but the king, because it is but a chose in action ;" *Co. Litt.* 388 *a,* " If a church become void in the life of a bishop, and so remain till after his decease, the king shall present thereto, and not the executor or administrator, for nothing can be taken for a presentment, and, therefore, it is no assets." The reason given in *Co. Litt.* 90 *a,* that it does not go to the successor or executors, because it is a chose in action, does not appear at all satisfactory, because choses in action do go to the executors. And there is a note by the writer of the earlier notes to *Co. Litt.* who gives this explanation of the passage, " that in the case of a chose in action, so peculiar as the right of presentation, the law favours the king more than the bishop's executors, and, therefore, gives the king, as having in his custody the temporalities of the vacant bishopric, that presentation which in general executors are entitled to when opposed to an heir." And the writer of these notes, after discussing the reason of the presentation belonging to the king, comes at last to the conclusion, that it is most safe to rely on the right of the king, as settled by authorities and long practice. In none of these authorities is there any mention made of the successors, except in Co. Litt. 90. But they are all, even in Co. Litt. 388 a, as to the king's right as opposed to that of the executors, and, consequently, if the king had not the right, treating it as if it would go to the executors. It is true, that in the Year-books, to which these authorities refer, there is nothing about the executors. If there had been, it would have been stronger; but as it is, there is the statement of Brooke, Rolle, Fitzherbert, and Coke, as to the claimants, and, therefore, their opinions, that the law was that, except for the right of the king, it would go to the executors. But indeed the right of the king is so strong that in 2 Roll's Abr. 345, it is said, if a church, of the patronage of a bishop, abbot, or prior, voids, and the bishop, abbot, or prior, presents and afterwards dies before institution, the king shall have this presentment by his prerogative, The Prior of Bermondsey's case; and so in the same book and page, " if the bishop, abbot, or prior, dies after institution of the clerk, and before induction, the king shall have this presentment by his prerogative." It seems from the next placitum in Rolle as if the contrary had been held in one case, but there seems no reason to doubt the position; for in F. N. B. 34, K. it is said, if a bishop make a collation, and before induction or installation dieth, and the king seizes the temporalities, he shall have the presentment, because that the church is not full against the king until the parson or prebend be installed or inducted. And the same point seems admitted in Fitzherbert, N. B. 36, K, though there the king did not prevail, because he ought not to have given the prebend to his own clerk, but should have removed the clerk collated by the bishop by quare impedit. And the same point is in *Bro. Presentment à l'Esglise* in one part of *pl.* 13. The instance of the bishop dying before presentation, after the right had vested in him, is not the only one where the king's prerogative gives him the right to present. For if the tenant of the king has an advowson, and an avoidance happens, and after the tenant dies, his heir in ward to the king, the king shall have the presentation and not the executor of the father, though the heir be of full age, 2 *Rolle's Abr.* 345, pl. 1; and in *Co. Litt.* 388. a, if the king's tenant by knight's service in capite be seised of a manor, whereunto an advowson is appendant, and the church become void, the tenant dieth, his heir within age, the king shall present to the church, and not the executor or administrator, but if the lands be holden of a common person, in that case the executor shall present and not the guardian. So in *Co. Litt.* 90 b, in speaking of the king's right he says, so it is, in case where the king hath wardship, but that is a prerogative that belongeth to the king, to provide for the church being void; for where the tenure by knight's service is of a common person, the executors of the tenant shall present where the avoidance fell in the life of the tenant. And so if the tenant of the king has an advowson and an avoidance happens, and the tenant presents and his clerk is admitted and instituted and before induction the patron dies, and the advowson comes by wardship to the king, he shall present, for the church is not full against him before induction, 2 *Rolle's Abr.* 345. Other cases may be put, though not applicable to the case of executors, where the king's prerogative gives him a right to present where a subject would not. As if the youngest daughter, coparcener, be in ward to the king, and the church becomes void, the king shall have the presentment alone, and not the other coparceners, 2 *Rolle's Abr.* 344, pl. 8. These cases, therefore, which are excepted out of the rule, that executors shall present where the chattel is vested, must be confined to those cases where the king, by his prerogative, has a right to present either in the instance of his being guardian of the temporalities in the cases of bishops, abbots, and priors, or in the instances of the king's tenants in capite, where he has the wardship. In all these instances, the question has been between the king and the executors; and in case of the bishop, no surmise (except that in one of the cases there mentioned) was ever made that the successor would have the presentation in case the king had not been entitled by his prerogative. Another exception to the rule is alleged, that in case of a person holding an office, in the right of which he presents to another office, and that other office becomes void in the lifetime of the patron, and the patron dies, his successor and not his executor, shall appoint to the office; and the case of exigenter is put as reported in *Scroggs* v. *Coleshill; Dyer*, p. 175. To that case I entirely agree; but the reason of that is, that it is a personal thing annexed to the judge of the court who is to appoint the officers of the court; and if the office becomes vacant, and the judge dies, his executor can have nothing to do with the appointment, for it belongs to the judge to appoint the officers of the court. The office of judge is not like an advowson, which is a thing which descends and is capable of being conveyed from one person to another, and the presentation of which is the fruit of the advowson. But if an advowson be annexed to an office and the church becomes void, and then the person holding the office dies, I think the right to present would be in the executor and not the successor, because it would be a fruit fallen, a chose in action personally vested in the officer. If the principle be established, that a vacant presentation is a chose in action, and is like a fruit fallen, and goes to the executor of a private person, I do not see why it should not go to the executor of a prebendary patron. He is seised of the advowson itself in right of his prebend in his corporate capacity, and as long as the prebend remains in

1827.

BENNELL
v.
BISHOP OF
LINCOLN.

him, he has it in his corporate character. But it is only the prebend itself and the advowson which he has as such; the proceeds of a prebend stand upon a different ground. These proceeds do not belong to him in his corporate character, for if they did, they could only be enjoyed by him while he exercises that character. The produce of the lands, such as corn, hay, fruits, and vegetables, come to him to be eaten, consumed, or sold at his pleasure. So the rents of the lands of the prebend, when they fall due, are to be received by him for his own private use, and not to be laid out on his prebend, but at his own pleasure. In the case of death, such of these issues and profits as remain fallen or due, but have not actually come into the hands of the prebendary, do not go to the successor, or the king, or the ordinary, but go to his executors, as any other part of his personal property. The reason is, because these things, by being severed from the prebend, become chattels, and are no longer parcel of the prebend; and no persons, who afterwards have any interest in the prebend, either direct or incidental, can claim what has thus been severed from it. The same rule holds as to the issues and profits of any thing which is appurtenant to the prebend, and which become chattels, such as proceeds of fisheries, common of turbary, housebotes, and other things which have been taken and remain in specie at the death of the prebendary; for things appurtenant to the prebend are as much parcel of it as if they were of the actual corpus of it. The general principle of such manual chattels and choses in action as I have mentioned being admitted, it is to be considered, whether the right of presentation to a church is to be considered in the same light. In the case of a private individual, if for *prebend* you substitute *manor*, there is no doubt upon the current of all the authorities. The species of property is the same: in the one case, it is an advowson appendant to a manor, in the other it is an advowson appendant to a prebend in right of the prebend. But in both cases it is an advowson, and being an advowson, it must partake of the qualities applicable to an advowson. In the case of lay patronage the vacant presentation becomes severed from the inheritance; but if that be the nature of an advowson, that a right to a presentation becomes severed from the inheritance, it must have that quality throughout, to whomsoever the advowson belongs, or in whatever right it is held; for otherwise great confusion would ensue. And if it be a chattel it must go, as all other chattels do. A chattel does not go to the successor of a corporation sole, except in the case of the king, Co. Litt. 90, a. But the king is altogether upon a different footing from other corporations sole. If then this be a chattel and should go to the successor, it would be quite an anomaly, and an exception to the general rule. But there is one very important instance where the right of presentation is transmissible to the personal representatives, and does not go to the successor. I mean the option of the archbishop, which is founded on a grant made to the archbishop; and upon the death of the archbishop during the continuance of the bishop in his see, it will devolve on his executors or administrators; that being a personal grant to the archbishop, is different from the present; but it proves that in the highest ecclesiastical dignity in the church, the principle, in one instance at least, is recognised, that it is transmissible to the personal representatives. It has been said that this is a trust to be exercised for the benefit of the church, and that it is more proper that a spiritual person should exercise it; but it is also an important trust if it be exercised by a layman, he, also, has a duty to perform in the selection he makes. The ordinary, both in the case of ecclesiastical and lay patronage, is to examine into the fitness of the clerk, and the only thing that can be said in favour of the ecclesiastic is, that he will make a better choice; but that is not a principle upon which the legal rights of parties can be decided. The state of patronage is as much diversified in *England* as it is possible to be; all classes in the community that can be enumerated have a patronage belonging to them, and their rights are to be

TRINITY TERM, VIII GEO. IV.

841

1828.

RENNELL
v.
BISHOP OF
LINCOLN.

determined by legal principles; and where there has been no decision or practice or received opinion, then by analogy, as far as can be collected; but the question, what class of patrons are likely to make the best choice, cannot, I think, be taken into consideration. In the course of the argument it has been said, that this prebend has been appropriate to the church of *Salisbury*, and also that the will and intention of the founder is to be considered. As to that we know nothing upon this record; all we know is, that the advowson is appendant to the prebend; but how it became so does not appear, or who was the founder, or what were the terms of the foundation, or by what statutes it is governed; if there were any terms or statutes they might have been shewn: if there were none, the case must be governed by the general rules of law. Neither can we look to the constitutions of the church of *Salisbury*, they are not stated in the record; and in the absence of any thing particular in them the rules of law, as applicable to all churches in general, must prevail. The statute of the 28 *Hen.* 8, c. 11, has been adverted to. It states what things are to go to the successor of an archdeacon, dean, prebendary, parson, &c. &c., but the enumeration is of things growing, arising, or coming during the time of vacation; no allusion is made to any thing which fell during the time of the predecessor. This statute has been said to be only declaratory of the common law: whether it be so or not cannot be material, because if it was, it would be a declaration of what the successor would take by the common law, which is only of things falling in the vacation. But as the statute directs these things to go to the successor towards payment of the first fruits to the king, it would not enumerate things which could not be converted into money, and, therefore, would not include a vacant presentation, and the statute consequently does not affect the question. For the reasons I have already mentioned, I think that the plaintiff is entitled to present in the present case, and that the judgment of the Court of *Common Pleas* should be reversed.

HOLROYD, J.—The question is on the right of the plaintiff, though the demurrer is to the claim of right in the defendants, set forth in the plea. The question is whether the plaintiff as administratrix of the deceased prebendary is entitled to present. It is admitted that if the advowson had been in lay hands, the right would have been in the administratrix, and not in the heir; but it is contended that as it was in the prebendary (a person having an ecclesiastical station or office derived from the bishop) and in right of his prebend, ergo, as a body corporate, that it is in him as a confidential trust reposed in the body corporate, or person holding the office, and not as an individual, and that it does not, therefore, vest in any person who is his personal representative as an individual, but though a fruit fallen, that it belongs to his successor. If that were so, we might expect to find that the right to present would have been deemed so much a confidential trust, in whoever is the prebendary, as to be, therefore, inseparable from the office or station: But this I think is not so, as will, as it seems to me, appear by what follows. Even in the case of a bishop, where it goes not to his personal representative, it goes not to his successor but vests in the king, as guardian of the temporalities by his prerogative. In the case of a common person, by the vacancy, the right to present on that turn becomes separated from the advowson as a fruit fallen, it becomes a personal chattel in the person entitled; though he has the advowson in fee, it descends not with the advowson to his heir in case of his death, but goes to his personal representative; and in case the right was in such common person before and until the vacancy by a grant of the next presentation, in which case the right would, until the vacancy had happened, be in him as a chattel real, the vacancy turns it into a chattel personal. *Vin. Exor.* (Z.) pl.

4, cites *Wentw. Exor.* 54 & 73, for this; like rent due, which on death goes to the executor, though the land or reversion goes to the successor, or heir, or devisee, according to *Digby* v. *Fitch*(a). So a termor shall present, though after the term is expired, to a vacancy which happened during the term. *Fitz. N. B., Quare impedit*, 33 *A.* It is a chattel vested, and not merely a chose in action, and, therefore, the husband shall present to a turn after his wife's death, on a vacancy happening in her life in her advowson, although he could not sue after her death on a bond to her, because that is merely in action. *Co. Litt.* 120 *a.* The nature of the right to present on a vacancy having fallen, is not changed by its being vested in a prebendary in right of his prebend; but the rules of law (such as its being a fruit fallen separated from the advowson, a right vested, a chattel personal and transmissible to executors, &c.) applicable to it from its nature, must in like manner still be applicable to it, unless we find some rule or principle of law established, such as the king's prerogative in the case of bishops (and the prerogative is the sole ground on which the king's case is varied, as will appear from a case I shall state hereafter) unless we find some rule or principle of law, I say, to prevent their being so applied, or to vary this right in the case of a prebendary from the same right in the case of a lay patron. And I think there is no such rule or principle of law to prevent their being so applied, or to vary the case of a prebendary from that of a lay patron. In the case of a bishop, the nature of the right to present is not at all changed from what it would be in the case of a lay patron; but notwithstanding the nature of the right in each of those cases be the same, the established rule of law to be found in our books as to the king's prerogative intervenes and applies in the one case, the bishop's, to deprive his executors, &c. of the right to present, which but for the prerogative applicable to the bishop's case, the executor would have in the one case as well as in the other. But I do not

(a) Brownl. & Gouldsb. 167.

find any where in our books any rule or principle of law
applicable to the case of a prebendary who is patron in
right of his prebend to vary it from the case of a lay patron,
more especially as a prebendary might formerly have been
a layman, according to *Bland* v. *Maddox* (a) and other authorities.   Suppose an advowson of a representative rectory
to be conveyed by a lay patron to a prebendary and his
successors in right of the prebend in fee, or to be conveyed to a lay patron in fee by a prebendary who has it
in right of his prebend, concurrentibus iis qui de jure re-
quiruntur; which conveyance, in former times, before the
restraining statutes, would have been good even against his
successors, and would now be good against the individual
prebendary himself, unless the advowson or right of presentation of a prebendary in right of his prebend can be
shewn to be wholly inalienable, either on account of its
being vested in him as a personal trust and confidence in
the person who may be the prebendary, or otherwise.
Would the nature of the right to present be varied when a
vacancy has happened?   Would it not be equally a fruit
fallen and separated from the advowson, a right vested a
chattel personal, whether the patron be ecclesiastical or lay,
and, consequently, transmissible to executors, &c. in one
case as well as in the other? unless there be found some
established rule or principle of law to intercept it, as in the
case of a bishop; and it does not appear to me that there
is any such rule or principle of law established, applicable
to the case of a prebendary.   None such is any where that
I know of, to be found.   That an advowson or right of
presentation of a prebendary in right of his prebend is not
at common law wholly inalienable or inseparable either on
account of a personal trust and confidence in the person
who may be the prebendary, or otherwise, appears, I think,
by our books.   His being an ecclesiastical corporation
does not render it inseparable, for *F. N. B.* 34 Q. shews
that the vacant turn is not inseparable from the station or

(a) Cro. Eliz. 79.

office of a prior, though an ecclesiastical and corporate office, so as where a vacancy has happened to vest in his successor. For there it appears that the founder of a priory shall have a quare impedit against a sub-prior and the convent, if they disturb him to present to an advowson which belongeth to the house, if void during the vacation, where the founder ought to have the temporalities during the vacation. So in *Poyner* v. *Chorleton, Dyer,* 135 a, (cited also in 3 *Wils.* 327), it appears that the grantee of abbot, and convent, of the next avoidance, recovered in quare impedit. *Winch's, Coke's,* and other entries, shew that ecclesiastical bodies and persons have been in the habit of granting away their spiritual preferment as well as lay persons, and that their grantees have been in the habit of suing in their own names. In the *Dean and Chapter of Hereford* v. *The Bishop of Hereford*(a) a grant of the next presentation by dean and chapter was held not good against the successor, but that was only by reason of the statute 13 *Eliz.*, and no doubt that it was good against the dean, the grantor himself, and his chapter. So in *Armiger* v. *The Bishop of Norwich* (b) a grant of advowson for twenty-one years by a bishop, which he had in right of his bishopric, was held good against himself, but not against his successor, or against the king during vacancy, though confirmed by dean and chapter, but it is void against them only by reason of statute 1 *Eliz.* c. 19. In *Smallwood* v. *The Bishop of Coventry* (c) there was a grant of the advowson of an arch-deaconry by a bishop to *A. B.* for 21 years, who assigned to *C. D.* the vacancy in *C. D.'s* life and disturbance of him in his life, his executors sued. By the report of that case in *Latw.* 1, and also in *Sav.* 94 & 118, though the writ was quashed as informal, the right to sue was decided in their favour, and afterwards, in an action reported in *Cro. Eliz.* 807, the grant was held good against the bishop that made it, though not against his successor by reason of the statute, and the executors had judgment. Why then is such a right

(a) Cro. Eliz. 440.   (b) Cro. Eliz. 690.   (c) Cro. Eliz. 807; 4 Leon. 15.

not equally grantable by a prebendary, and separable from the office either in deed or by act or operation of law upon death, &c.? It is no more a matter of trust and confidence in him, than in the other cases of ecclesiastical bodies or persons. But an estate or interest, though coupled with a confidence and trust, is still in law assignable and grantable, and such assignment or grant will pass the estate or interest for so long time as the same continues to subsist in the assignee or grantee, and the creator of the confidence or trust cannot by law deprive the estate or interest (even by express words and declaration) of such assignable or grantable quality. It is so in conveyances of lands or tenements to trustees in fee, or for terms of years, and the estates will, if not assigned or granted away by them, vest by law in heirs, or executors, &c., as long as their respective estates continue to exist, whatever the conveyance or conveyor may declare shall be the contrary. So *Com. Dig. Grant* (C), says, " A present estate or interest may be granted, though it be accompanied with a trust, as guardian in chivalry or socage may grant his guardianship," and cites 2 *Roll. Abr.* 46 H. So as to archbishop's options, which may be disposed of by his will, and will pass to his executors, as appears in *Potter* v. *Chapman* (a). The case of a donative, supposing it to be a settled case, is to be considered as an exception ; at least the rule of law in that respect not only has never been applied to a presentative right, but the very contrary. But there may be also this distinction, that according to the cases above referred to, a right of presentation, when a vacancy has happened in a presentative living, is not a mere right or chose in action, but is a chattel personal and vested. But it does not, that I am aware of, appear that the right of nomination is so in the case of a donative. It may not be a separate thing or right from the advowson itself of a donative, when a vacancy has arisen, as in the case of a presentative living, but may, instead of becoming in law a right separated from such donative advowson, and a chattel per-

(a) Ambl. 98.

sonal vested, continue a right, part of the advowson, unseparated from and merged in the general right to the advowson, and to be exercised only by him who has that general right, unless where it has been expressly separated from such general right to the advowson itself by a grant or conveyance of the right of nomination on such next vacancy. This consideration alone would be sufficient to account for its not going to the bishop by lapse, although its not going to the bishop by lapse, I admit, is otherwise accounted for in our books. But it has been urged that (besides that this is to be considered as a confidence and trust to be exercised only by such person as holds the prebend), the prebendary is a body corporate, and, therefore, that the right of presentation for that turn, though the vacancy arise in his life time, has vested in his successor, and not in his administratrix, who represents him only in his natural character as an individual, and not as a body corporate, but there is no authority or principle of law to support this position ; on the contrary, the authority and principle of law appear to me to be directly in opposition to it. For in *Co. Litt.* 90 *a*, Lord *Coke* states this case :
" A tenant holdeth land of a bishop by knight's service, which seignorie the bishop hath in the right of his bishopric, the tenant dieth, his heir within age, the bishop, either before or after seizure, dieth, neither the king nor the successor of the bishop shall have the wardship, but his executors. For albeit the bishop hath the seignorie en autre droit, yet the wardship being but a chattel he hath in his own right, and a chattel cannot go in succession of a sole corporation, unless it be in the case of the king." So that a chattel could go in succession in the case of the king, though it could not in the case of the bishop ; and although the seigniory was in the bishop in autre droit, yet neither the king nor the succeeding bishop should have the wardship, because it was a *chattel*, and, therefore, the former bishop had the wardship as a chattel in his own right, and his executors shall have it, though the seignorie was in him as a bishop ; and Lord

Coke, in p. 46 *b* of *Co. Litt.* says, " If a lease for years be made to *a bishop and his successors*, yet his executors or administrators shall have it in auter droit, for regularly no chattel can go in succession in case of a sole corporation, no more than if a lease be made to a man and his heirs, it can go to his heirs." So that the rule extends to chattels, whether real or personal. And in 4 *Co.* 65 *a*, and 1 *Rolle's Abr.* 515 L, the rule of law as laid down by Lord Chief Baron *Comyns* in his *Digest, Biens,* C., from those authorities appears to be, that all chattels of a corporation sole, as a bishop, parson, &c., go to his executors or administrators, and not to his successor, and this according to Lord *Coke*, and as laid down by *Comyns,* extends to chattels in action as well as in possession. As the right now in question, therefore, was a fruit fallen, separated from the advowson, and a right and *chattel vested* in the deceased prebendary, I think that after his death it went to his administratrix, as it would have done if he had had the advowson in his own right as a mere individual, and not in his corporate character, and that it has not vested in his successor. It stands on the same footing, as it appears to me, with rent due to the deceased as prebendary, and remaining in arrear at his death, which would go to his administratrix, and not to his successor. I think, therefore, that the judgment of the Court of Common Pleas should be reversed.

BAYLEY, J.—This was a writ of error from C. B. in a case of quare impedit. The declaration stated, that *William Dodwell,* D. D. was seised of the prebend or canonry of *South Grantham,* founded in the cathedral church of *Salisbury,* to which prebend or canonry the advowson of the rectory of the parish church of *Welby* (the church in question) belonged in his demesne as of fee, in right of the said prebend or canonry; that he presented *William Dodwell,* and died; that *Price* succeeded Dr. *Dodwell,* and died; that *Rennell* succeeded *Price,* and died; that the church became vacant by Dr. *Dodwell's* death, whereby it belonged to *Rennell* to present; that he died intestate, without presenting; that administration was granted to the plaintiff, and that thereupon it belonged to the plaintiff, as administratrix, to present, but that she was hindered by the defendants. She complains, therefore, not of a disturbance in the intestate's time, but of a disturbance in her own; and the question is, whether upon an advowson, circumstanced as this advowson is, if a right of presentation accrue in the lifetime of the prebendary, and he dies without filling it up, that right passes to his personal representative. The declaration does not describe the prebendary as seised of the advowson in right of the prebend or canonry, or indeed as being seised of the advowson at all; but it states him to be seised of the prebend or canonry in his demesne as of fee, in right of the said prebend or canonry, and describes the advowson as belonging to the prebend or canonry. I think it must be taken that it was in right of the prebend and canonry only that Mr. *Rennell* had any seisin of or right in the advowson. But though the title to the advowson be in right of the prebend or canonry, the question is, whether the right of presentation, when a vacancy has happened, is still attached to the prebend and canonry, and to be exercised only in right of the prebend or canonry upon a continuation of the prebendary's estate in the prebend or canonry, or whether it does not become an independent personal right, vesting indeed in him, because he was prebendary when the vacancy happened and the right accrued, but severed altogether from the inheritance and the advowson, and becoming in him a detached personal right, to be exercised by him in his own right, whether he should continue prebendary or not, and in case he should die without exercising it, transmissible by him as a personal right to his executors or administrators. The latter is the right which the declaration states. It does not state that Dr. *Dodwell* presented in right of his prebend or canonry, but simply that Dr. *Dodwell* presented; and upon the vacancy in question, it does not state that it belonged to Mr. *Rennell* in right of his prebend or canonry, but simply that it belonged to Mr. *Rennell* to present; and upon the best consideration I have been able to give this case, I am of opinion that, in the absence of any custom to control it, this is the correct mode of statement; and that though the prebendary acquires the right of presentation because he is prebendary, and in right of his prebend or canonry, the right, when once acquired, becomes his own private personal right, as the right to the underwood he has cut, or the grass he has mown, or the fruit he has gathered from his prebendal lands. I have no difficulty in saying that I came to the argument in this case with a very strong impression upon my mind against the plaintiff's right, but the light which was thrown upon the subject by the powerful argument of Mr. *Patteson*, and the authorities to which I have referred, have induced me to think that my first impressions were erroneous; and though I might think it would be better if the right were to be inseparable from the stall, I cannot find legal principles to carry me to that conclusion. The first point I shall consider is, what is the effect of a vacancy in case of a presentative living; and I take it to be clear that it immediately gives a new personal right, a right arising from property in the advowson, but, from the moment of its creation, ceasing to depend upon or to be influenced by it. Whatever may become of the advowson, though the right to it instantly ceases, the right of presentation continues untouched. In the common case, where a church becomes vacant and the patron dies, the advowson descends upon his heir; but to whom does the right of presentation pass? To his heir? No, but to his personal representative. And why? Because it is no part of the advowson; it is a personal right yielded by the advowson, a fruit created by it, but it is no part of the advowson, it is wholly independent of it. *Fitz. N. B.* 33 *P.* puts the case, and gives his reason. If a man be seised of an advowson in gross or in fee appendant unto a manor, and the church become void, and he die, his executor shall present, and not his heir. Why?

Because it was a chattel vested and severed from the manor.
The same point, without the reason, is put 21 *H.* 7, *pl.* 6.
Bro. Present. à l'Eglise, 34. If *A.* be tenant in tail of an
advowson, and the church become vacant, and *A.* die, *A.'s*
executor shall present, not the issue in tail; *Fitz. N. B.*
34 *B.* If tenant in tail of a manor to which an advowson
is appendant make a lease, (before or not within the statute
of *H.* 8,) which will end with his death, and the church
becomes void, the tenant in tail dies, so that the lease is
become void, the lessee shall nevertheless have the presentment, 10 *Edw.* 3, (*a*). If I grant land, to which an advowson is appendant, to husband and wife in tail, the husband
dies, the widow marries *J. S.*, the church becomes void,
the woman dies without issue, *J. S.* shall present; for
though the right to the land is wholly in me, the right to
present is in him, 38 *H.* 6, 36 B. If a baron be seised of
an advowson in right of his wife, and the church become
void, and the wife die before issue had, still the husband
shall have the presentment, 21 *H.* 6, B.; *Bro. Present. à
l'Eglise*, pl. 22; *Co. Litt.* 120. If a manor, with an advowson appendant, be assigned to a widow for dower, and
she marry again, and the church become void, and she dies,
her second husband shall present, 14 *H.* 4, c. 12. If, whilst
a church is void, the patron be outlawed in trespass, which
works a forfeiture of goods and chattels, the king shall present, *Bro. Present. à l'Eglise*, 22. " If a man have an advowson for a term, and the church, during the term, become
void, and the term expire, the termor shall nevertheless
present, *Fitz. N. B.* 34, B; *Bro. Present. à l'Eglise*, 22.
Lastly, if a vicarage become void, and before the parson
present he be made bishop, he shall nevertheless present,
because *it was a chattel vested in him*, *Fitz. N. B.* 34, N.
These authorities appear to me to prove, beyond all question, that upon a common presentative benefice a vacancy
creates a new right from thenceforth, detached from and

(*a*) Taken from the index to the Year-book—not to be found in the
book itself.

independent of the advowson, and liable to go in a different line from the advowson. And the next point I shall consider is, what is the legal character of this right. I take it to be a chattel, and a chattel only. I am aware that in different books different names are given to it, that it is called a personal thing, annexed to the person of him who is patron in expectancy at the time of the vacancy; (*Dyer*, 283 *a*, *Gibs*. 797); a thing in right, power, and authority, (*Dyer*, 283 *a*, *Gibs*. 797); a chose in action, (*Dyer*, 283 *a*, *Gibs*. 797, *Co. Litt.* 90;) the fruit and execution of the advowson, not the advowson itself, (*Dyer*, 283 *a*, *Gibs*. 797); and a trust in the hands of the patron, by consent of the bishop, for the benefit of the church and religion, (*Gibs*. 796); but notwithstanding all these descriptive and figurative expressions, its legal character seems to me that of a chattel only. I am aware too that in *Rex* v. *The Archbishop of Canterbury* (a), where the question was, whether a grant from the crown of the goods and chattels of felons and outlaws would pass a right to present to the advowson of an outlaw where the church became vacant after the outlawry, *Anderson*, C. J., said, (according to *Owen*,) that an avoidance was no chattel, or right of chattel, which *Periam* denied; but, according to the reports in *Leonard*, *Anderson* considered it as a right, a thing in action, a jus presentandi; but he thought the words " goods and chattels" not proper words to pass it, and that they were confined to household goods, money, and the like personal things, and things in possession; but *Shuttleworth*, Serjt., who argued against its passing by the grant, admitted it was a special chattel capable of being granted; and *Walmsley* and *Periam*, justices, both stated it was a chattel; and though it may be immaterial to the decision of this case what particular species of chattel this may be, which seems there to have been the question, it appears to me, upon other authorities, that it clearly is a chattel of some description. The right to present upon a grant of the next presentation cannot differ in nature from

(a) Owen, 155; 1 Leon. 201; 4 Leon. 107.

the right which devolves upon the patron in case of vacancy, where there has been no grant, and in such case *Brooke* considers the right granted clearly as a chattel. In 34 *H.* 6, c. 27, pl. 38, a grant of the two next presentations was made to *J. N.* and his heirs, and it was alleged upon the first vacancy *J. N.* presented, and upon the second his heir, and per *Moile*, J., the heir had no title to present, for the executors ought to present in this case, and not the heir, notwithstanding the form of the grant. *Brooke* abridges this case, title *Chattels*, pl. 20, and *Estates*, pl. 51; and he has a similar case, title *Chattels*, pl. 6; and in each he gives as the reason, that the right to present in such case is *a chattel*. If one grant the two next presentations of a church to *A.*, these are chattels, and if *A.* die the executors shall have them, not the heir, *Bro. Chattels*, pl. 20. A man grants the next presentation to a church to *A.* and his heirs, or lease for years to him and his heirs, the executor shall have this, and not the heir, for the heir shall not have *chattels*, *Bro. Est.* pl. 51. A man grants to another the next presentation to a benefice, and the grant was to him, his heirs and assigns; and yet it was admitted clearly that it was *but a chattel*, notwithstanding this word *heirs*, for it is but for a term, and where a thing is *but a chattel*, this word *heirs* cannot make it an inheritance. The same law of a lease for twenty years to *A.* and his heirs, *Bro. Chattels*, pl. 20. In the cases I have mentioned from *Fitz. N. B.* 33, P. and 34, N., the right to present, which accrues to the patron upon a vacancy, is called a chattel, and so it must have been considered, *Co. Litt.* 388. Indeed how can an executor or administrator have any right to it, except on the ground of its being a chattel? The statutes relating to administrators use the word "goods" only. By the 13 *Edw.* 1, c. 19, the ordinary shall answer the debts as far as the *goods* of the deceased will extend. By the 33 *Edw.* 3, st. 1, c. 11, the ordinary shall depute the next and most lawful friends of the deceased to administer the *goods* of the deceased; and the 21 *H.* 8, c. 5, speaks of commission of the administration of the *goods* of an intestate. Upon these grounds it appears to me, that upon the vacancy of a presentative advowson, a right and interest independent of the advowson accrues to the patron, and that this is a chattel right and chattel interest. It remains to be seen whether there be any thing particular in this case to take it out of the ordinary rules of chattels. And one ground insisted upon is, that this right accrues to the prebendary in right of his prebend, and that it is commensurate with his continuance as prebendary, and that when he ceases to be prebendary the right is gone. But is there any authority to warrant this conclusion? I agree that the right accrues to him in right of his prebend, because he is prebendary; but when the right has accrued by the vacancy, I deny that it is dependent upon the prebend or to cease with it, but I insist that, like all the instances I have put in the early part of what I have been stating, it is independent of and unconnected with the advowson, and a distinct independent chattel. The case put, *Fitz. N. B.* 34, of the parson who is made a bishop, is upon principle in point, but it is not the only case. *Co. Litt.* 90 *a*, and 388, in the case of a ward, is in point also. The objection is, that the chattel interest is acquired, not in his personal but in his corporate character. The parson in *Fitz. N. B.* acquires his right, the very same species of right, in the same way. In *Co. Litt.* 90 *a*, this case is put: " A tenant holds of a bishop by knight's service, the bishop has the seigniory in right of the bishopric, the tenant dies, his heir within age, the bishop either before or after seizure dies, neither the king nor successor shall have the wardship, but the executors. For albeit the bishop hath the seigniory en auter droit, yet the wardship being but a chattel, he hath *in his own right,* and a chattel cannot go in the succession of a sole corporation unless it be in the case of the king." The same point is put more shortly, *Co. Litt.* 388 *a*: " If a bishop hath a ward fallen and dieth, the king shall not have the ward, nor the successor, but the executor, and the ward shall be assets in his hands.

So it is of a heriot, relief, or the like." Now this, as it
seems to me, bears a strict analogy to the present case;
the bishop there has a seigniory in right of his see; here,
the prebendary has an advowson in right of his prebend;
a chattel accrues from each; a wardship in the one case,
a right of presentation in the other. The wardship goes to
the bishop in his own right. Why shall not the right of
presentation in the other? The former goes to the executor. Why shall not the latter? The only difference between the two cases is, that the wardship is assets; the
right of presentation is not, though the damages for an
obstruction to it would be. But is this difference material?
A right of presentation, though not assets, goes to the executor in ordinary cases. The only recognised exception is
in the case of the king. The constituting assets, therefore,
is not the criterion. But in the very case of bishoprics
there is a difference between the case of wardships and the
case of a right of presentation; the former went to the
executor, the latter to the king. Will this, therefore, furnish a ground upon which the defendant in error can stand
in this case? Can he shew that this is founded upon the
nature of the right, viz. a right of presentation, and that it
extends to all cases of such a right; or will it not appear
that it extends to all cases of the king upon a tenure in
capite, and that it is confined to the king and that peculiar
species of tenure? The case I have already mentioned
from *Fitzherbert,* viz. the case of the parson made bishop,
shews that it is not founded upon the nature of the right,
viz. the right of presentation; and the fact that it extends
to cases of wardship, upon a tenure *in capite* in the king's
case, shews that the peculiarity results from the peculiarity
of tenure and the rights of the crown, and not from the
nature of the right. The general rule is, that a chattel
cannot pass by succession from predecessor to successor.
Co. Litt. 9 *a*, 46 *b*, 90 *a.* But by custom it may; as in the
case of *The Chamberlain of the City of London,* where, by the
custom of the city, a bond to the chamberlain for orphan-

age-money will pass to the successor; *Fulwood's case*(a); *Byrd* v. *Wilford*(b); or it may be the terms and conditions of a tenure. And it is to this I attribute the peculiarity in the case of the bishops, upon which great stress was laid in the argument, rather than to the spiritual right in respect of which they hold their possessions. If, for instance, a living becomes vacant, of which a bishop, in right of his see, is patron, and the bishop dies, the right to fill up that living passes with the other temporal rights of the see to the crown. And though the crown restore the temporalities to the successor, without filling up the vacancy, the right to fill it up remains with the crown. But I do not find this to be the case with respect to advowsons in the patronage of any other corporations sole; and I find that in the case of the crown there is a similar peculiarity in the case of every tenure in capite. If the king's tenant in capite holds an advowson as parcel of his advowson, and the church become void, and the tenant die without presenting, the right of presentation, if the heir be of full age, will be in the tenant's executors; but if the heir be within age, the right will be in the crown. Upon what, then, does this right in the crown depend? Clearly not upon the spiritual nature of the property, because it is a right of presentation; for if the heir was of full age he would have it but upon this, that according to the terms and conditions of the tenure, if the land came to the crown for wardship or otherwise, whilst the church was void, the right of filling up the church should be, not in the executors of the tenant, but of the crown. And in the same way in the case of a bishopric, the right of the crown may be founded upon this, that according to the terms and conditions of a tenancy of the bishop, (for every bishop always held of the crown,) whenever a bishopric became vacant, the right of filling up all vacant churches within the patronage of the see should be, not in the executors of the bishop, but in the crown. This, as it seems to me, accounts satisfactorily for the peculiarity

(a) 4 Co. 64 b.   (b) Cro. Eliz. 464.

of the case of bishops, puts them on the same footing as other tenants in capite (*Co. Litt.* 70 b), and makes the peculiarity of their case inapplicable to the present. The only remaining argument against the plaintiff below (I believe) is founded upon the case of donatives. But when the distinction between donatives and presentative benefices is considered, and attention is paid to the ground upon which *Repington* v. *Tamworth School* (a) was decided, the case of donatives, as it seems, will furnish no argument which can bear upon this case. In case of a presentative benefice there is a duty upon the patron to present. The public is considered as having an interest in there being a prompt and speedy presentment. A neglect is punished by lapse. This is, I apprehend, the foundation of the right the law creates when a vacancy occurs. The right is the consequence and offspring of the duty. But in case of a donative the law recognises no such duty, and the miserable report of the case we have in *Wilson* states, as the ground of the decision, that in the case of a donative there is no lapse. I am aware that it was said arguendo in *Colt* v. *Glover* (b), that it had been argued in *Gaire* ats. *Fairchild* that the ordinary might sequester a donative if the patron would not present; and that, according to the report in *Yelv.* 61, *Gawdy, Fenner, Yelverton,* and *Williams,* (against *Popham,* C.J.) held, that the ordinary might compel the patron to collate some clerk; but this point was not necessary to be decided in that case, for the only points were, whether the incumbent could resign to his patron, and whether his resignation was good. I do not find this point mentioned in the contemporaneous reports, *Cro. Jac.* 63, *Moore,* 765, or *Co. Litt.* 344 a, which contains the substance of this case. I have never heard of any instance of a proceeding in a spiritual court to compel the filling up of a donative, and the case of *Repington* v. *Tamworth School* appears to me to have proceeded on the supposition that there was no power to compel the patron of a donative to fill the

(a) 2 Wils. 150.   (b) 1 Roll. Rep. 453, Hil. 14 Jac.

church, and that the necessity, therefore, of raising a personal right detached from, and independent of, the advowson did not arise. Why should the question of lapse
have been mentioned, except to shew this distinction between a common benefice and a donative, that in the latter
it was optional in the patron to fill the church or not; and
that the law, therefore, did not raise a chattel out of the
inheritance, as in the case of a common benefice, because
until the patron took the step to fill the church it was not
certain he would ever fill it, and until he chose to exercise
his right it would remain in the inheritance as part and
parcel of the estate? Upon these grounds I am of opinion
that the case of a donative is distinguishable from this case,
and that we are not warranted by the case in *Wilson* to take
this out of the ordinary case of presentative benefices. The
point, that a prebendary is a *spiritual* and not a *lay* corporation, I do not particularly notice, because it is clear the
prebendary has no cure of souls; his functions are not of
necessity spiritual; the filling up his church is not a spiritual
function. Until the statute of 13 and 14 *Car.* 2, c. 4, he
might have been a layman, and though spiritual persons
have an advantage over laymen in knowing the merits and
talents of members of their own profession, it is to be presumed that when laymen have the distribution of any church
preferment they will act conscientiously in bestowing it according to the best judgment they can form for themselves,
or can obtain from the opinion of others. Upon the whole,
therefore, I am of opinion that in the case of a presentative
benefice, as this is, a vacancy separates from the inheritance a right of presentation; that that right is a chattel
interest; that it vests in the prebendary, not in his corporate, but in his individual capacity; and that there is
nothing which will justify us in saying that it shall not take
the direction and be subject to all the incidents of an ordinary chattel. Whilst I was considering this case, I thought
it proper to endeavour to get what light I could upon the
position in *Co. Litt.* 90 and 388, that the bishop's ward

would go to his executors, because that is one of the main
grounds upon which my opinion rests, and had that position appeared erroneous my opinion might have been different. In my search I met with two cases, which I think
right to mention; one in 40 *Edw.* 3, 14, and the other in
2 *Hen.* 4, 19. In the first the bishop of *Lincoln* brought
a writ of ward, and counted that the infant's ancestor held
of him by knight's service. *Belknap* pleaded in abatement
that the ancestor died in the lifetime of the preceding
bishop. *Candish*, for the bishop, said he might hold of
us in our own right. *Belknap* thereupon pleaded that
he held of the predecessor as in right of his church, and
died in his time, and said that in such case the plaintiff
should have supposed in his writ that the ancestor held
of the preceding bishop, and he prayed judgment, not in
bar, but of the writ. The plaintiff was driven to maintain
his writ, and then he pleaded that he died after the preceding
bishop. Sed per *Thorpe*, C. J. he might have died whilst
the temporalities were in the king's hands, and then the
ward would belong to the king. You must plead that he
died in your time: which was done, and issue was joined
thereon. Upon this the reporter makes this note: "It
seems to me by the opinion here of this book, that if a ward
fall in the time of a bishop, and the bishop die, and the
king present another bishop, the infant being within age,
the king shall not have the ward, nor the executors of
the former bishop, but the successor. But that if it fall
whilst the temporalities are in the king's hands, the king
shall have it." This certainly is the inference from the defendant's pleading the matter in abatement, and not in bar;
for it assumes that it would have been a better writ had it
stated that the tenant died in the preceding bishop's time.
Brooke notices this case, *Gard.* pl. 9, and adds, quod nota
et videtur, if he die in the life of the predecessor, the executor shall have it, and not the new bishop; and he refers to 2 *Hen.* 4, 16, and 11 *Hen.* 4, 80 (which I cannot
find.) I do not find this case in *Fitzh.* In 2 *Hen.* 4, 19,

the Bishop of *Lincoln* brought a writ of ravishment of ward,
and it was said to have been held for clear law that, if a
bishop's tenant die, his heir within age, and the bishop die
without seizing the ward, the successor may seize him, and
shall have a writ of ravishment of ward against any that
takes him out of his possession; and some said the successor might have a writ of ward.   Quod quære.   And it
was laid down there, as it had been in 2 *Hen.* 4, 14, that
upon ravishment of ward it was not sufficient to impeach
the plaintiff's title, defendant must shew a title to remove
him, for possession is sufficient except against title.   *Fitzh.*
Gard. pl. 73, notices the position, that some said, " successor might have a writ of ward;" and makes no comment
or query.   *Bro.* notices it also, *Gard.* 23, and *Ravishment*
de Gard. 7, and in the former case inserts " Q." and in the
latter " quod quære;" but whether the query is to note his
own doubt, or the query in the Year Book, may perhaps be
inferred from his quod nota, &c. to the case of 40 *Edw.* 2,
but not otherwise.   The latest of these two cases is two
centuries before the time when Lord *Coke* published his
comment upon *Littleton;* and from the decisive manner in
which he states the point, there can be little doubt, but that
what was matter of doubt in the time of *Henry* 4, had
become matter of legal certainty before the time of *James* 1.
The matter would be likely frequently to occur, and therefore was not likely to remain unsettled for two centuries.
I have not relied on the prebendary's case, 24 *Edw.* 3,
26, because he might proceed for damages only and not
for a writ to the bishop.   And yet his right to damages
would be founded upon this, that the right of presentation
was a chattel and part of his personal estate.   Upon the
whole I am of opinion that the plaintiff is entitled to our
judgment, and has a right to a writ to the bishop.

Lord TENTERDEN, C. J.—This was a proceeding in a
quare impedit, brought by the administratrix of the late
prebendary of the prebend or canonry of *South Grantham,*
founded in the cathedral church of *Salisbury,* and to which

prebend the advowson of the rectory of *Welby* is alleged to belong, claiming to be permitted to present a fit person to that rectory, being void. It appears by the pleadings that the rectory became void in the life of the late prebendary, the intestate, and so continued until his death. The question is, whether the administratrix be entitled to present. The Court of *Common Pleas* held that she was not entitled, and gave judgment for the defendants; upon which a writ of error has been brought, and the case has been argued before us with great ability and learning. It does not appear that such a question has ever been presented to a court of law before the present occasion, nor what practice has prevailed in such cases. Some points are settled by many decisions. If a person seised in his natural capacity of an advowson of a presentative benefice, either appendant or in gross, whether seised in fee or for life, dies after the avoidance of the benefice, the presentation for that turn belongs to the executor, and not to the heir or remainder-man. So if a wife seised of an advowson dies after vacancy, the husband shall present, though she die without having had issue, and he does not become tenant of the advowson by the curtesy. For this the 21 *Hen.* 6, 20 *b*, has been quoted. It is clear also that if the next presentation be granted, either by a natural or politic person before avoidance, this is considered in law as the grant of a chattel, and the turn shall go to the executor, and not to the heir of the grantee, even though the grant be made in words to the grantee and his heirs. In this case the thing granted must necessarily be a chattel, it is not for the life of any one or more, nor does it convey an interest in fee or tail, for those are perpetual and this only temporary. In the case of a presentative benefice and a natural person, the void turn in the hands of the owner of the advowson is also called a chattel, and on that account said to pass to the executor. In the time of Queen *Elizabeth* a question arose whether it should pass by a grant of bona et catalla utlagatorum made by King *Edward* the Fourth. The Court of *Common Pleas*, in which the case arose, were not unanimous on the question. It does not appear that any judgment was given. Another point arose, upon which, it should seem, that judgment might have been given for the queen, without deciding this point. The case will be found in *Owen*, 155, and 1 *Leon.* 201, and 4 *Leon.* 107. *Periam, J.* is reported to have said that " the presentation was a chattel, for if the patron dieth, the executor shall present, for it was a chattel vested in the testator." *Anderson, C. J.* appears to have thought otherwise; he says, " A man cannot be said to have a chattel but where he is possessed of it, and here this interest is but jus presentandi." In the case of a donative whereof a natural person dies seised, a contrary rule has been laid down, and it has been decided that the executor is not entitled. 2 *Wils.* 150. I have not, however, found any sufficient reason for a distinction. The reasons of the judgment do not appear in the report. It may have been that the Court thought the rule as to presentative benefices not well founded, and therefore not to be extended. A donative, however, is of so peculiar a nature that it does not seem to furnish any argument of general weight. There is one instance mentioned in the books, which I must own I cannot but consider as an exception to the rule even in the case of a presentative benefice and a natural person. If the king's tenant by knight service in capite died after vacancy, his heir within age, the king presented. It is said that this was a prerogative right, and that therefore no argument can be drawn from it. The king may certainly take a chattel by virtue of his prerogative, but there is no reason for his doing so when there exists another person capable of taking. And if the void turn had been severed from the advowson, and become a chattel, the prerogative right of wardship could not attach upon it, for that could only attach upon what descended to the ward. If the heir were of full age, there is no authority for saying that the nature of the tenure would prevent the executor from presenting as in the case of tenure in socage. If the void turn were not considered as severed from the inheritance, but still remaining parcel of it, the king's right to present would be clear, and the right having once vested in the crown would remain in the crown by virtue of the prerogative, notwithstanding the heir attaining his age; and this upon the general rule, that a matter once vested in the crown cannot pass but by special grant of record. If the case of the tenant in capite be considered as an exception to the general rule, that case, as well as the case of a donative, will shew, that even where a natural person is seised of the advowson, the right of the executor is not universally acknowledged. But the question now before the Court does not arise on the case of a natural person. The intestate was seised of the advowson in his politic, and not in his natural capacity. If he had presented, he would have presented not in his personal right, but in right of his prebend. And the question, therefore, is, whether the rule admitted to prevail generally in the case of natural persons, and so far as regards a presentative benefice, with one exception only, if there be one, is to be extended to a person in a politic capacity: and I must say, I think it is not. I have not found any reason satisfactory to my own mind for considering the void turn as a chattel, on a question between the heir and executor of a natural person. The turn is not assets; nothing can be made of it for the payment of debts; and, therefore, the rule cannot be founded upon any consideration of that kind. I do not think the want of a satisfactory reason to be a sufficient ground for overturning a rule grounded upon the authority of decisions, and of a practice long continued. But when, as at present, a question arises, whether such a rule shall be applied to a new case, I think the want of such a reason authorises me to say that it ought not to be so applied, if any distinction between the cases can be discovered. It is true that a successor in a sole corporation cannot, according to general rules, take a chattel by succession; but it is also true, that a sole corporation cannot in that character take a chattel; and though granted to the corporator and his successors; it will vest in him, not in his politic or corporate, but in his natural capacity, *Arundel's* case (a). And if a sole corporation cannot take a chattel, by grant, how happens it that the void turn shall become a chattel vested in the corporator? Can vacancy so far change the nature of the thing as to vest that right in him, in his natural capacity, which before vacancy he had in his politic capacity? The only authority that I have met with in support of such a doctrine is in *Fitzherbert*, N. B. 34, N. It is there said, "If a vicarage happen void, and before the parson presents, he is made a bishop, yet he shall present to this vicarage, because it was a chattel vested in him." This proposition is not supported by a reference to any decision, and rests therefore upon the authority of *Fitzherbert*, which is certainly entitled to great respect. But if the opinion of that learned judge was grounded only upon the prevalent notion that a void turn was a chattel, and this can be shewn inapplicable to the case of a politic person, it will lose its weight. Standing alone as it does, I cannot think it sufficient to bind the judgment of the Court. In the case itself, however, there is no necessary change in the nature of the right; the presentment would be made by a person in whom the right had at one time vested. The same events might happen on the translation of a bishop, but I have not found by whom the presentation has been made under those circumstances. The presentation of the crown on the death of a bishop appears to me, for the reason that I shall mention hereafter, to be inconsistent with this opinion of *Fitzherbert*. And if this opinion of *Fitzherbert* be law, a presentation by the prebendary himself will not be made in his politic but in his natural capacity, not in right of his prebend, but in his personal right, and he might make his presentation in the same form as a natural person, and without naming himself prebendary, which I apprehend to be contrary to all practice, as it certainly is contrary to the last presentment to this very benifice, of which a copy is quoted at length

(a) Hob. 64.

by the Lord Chief Justice. It is clear that the administratrix cannot present in right of the prebend, because the prebend is not vested in her. If, therefore, she be allowed to present, she must present in a right different from that in which the intestate would have presented, and this will not be conformable to the general rights of an administrator, which are those only that belong to the person or personal property of the intestate. She is the administratrix of the personal rights and property of the intestate, but I find no authority for saying that she is the administratrix of his political rights or property also. It is not necessary in the present case to decide in whom the right is. It is sufficient for the purpose of this judgment to say, that it is not in the plaintiff. My opinion would, however, have been less satisfactory to my own mind if I had not been able also to form an opinion as to the person entitled to present. Whether, with that addition, it will be satisfactory to others, it is not for me to say. In my opinion the right is in the successor. But if the nature of it be such as that, according to any rule of law, it cannot pass to the successor, yet it will not necessarily follow that it should pass to the executor; it may devolve upon the crown for want of title in any other person. If the right be considered as parcel of the inheritance, it will pass with the inheritance to the successor. The only ground for saying that the right will not pass to the successor is, that it has been severed from the inheritance and is become a chattel. I have already intimated that I have found no satisfactory reason for preferring the executor to the heir even of a natural person. The case in *Dyer*, 283 *a*, has been often quoted upon this point. The case was this:—A patron granted the first and next presentation and advowson of a church, and the right of presenting to the same then being vacant, so that the grantee might nominate and present a fit person for that one turn only. Neither party presented within the six months, and the ordinary collated by lapse. The church became void again. Both parties presented;

the clerk of the grantor was admitted. The grantee brought a quare impedit, and judgment was given against him. Six judges appeared to have held that the grant of the present avoidance was void, "for," says the reporter, who was one of the six, "it is a mere personal thing annexed to the person of him who was patron in expectancy at the time of the vacancy; and also a thing in right, power, and authority; and also a chose in action, and in effect, the fruit and execution of the advowson, and not any advowson. And yet the executors shall have it by privity of law." It is to be observed, that this was the case of a natural person. The expression " a mere personal thing" is suited to such a case; the phrase *a mere prebendal thing* would not be less suited to the case of a prebendary. The words, " a thing in right, power, and authority," may be applied to a prebendary, a prebendal right, power, and authority. The words, " the fruit and execution of the advowson, and not the advowson," are applicable to either case. The only phrase that leads to the exclusion of the heir or successor is the expression, " a chose in action;" and this is altogether unnecessary to the judgment, which may be well supported upon the other expressions used by the reporter. In the present times, I apprehend, such a question would be decided upon a more solid and less technical and subtle ground, namely, the prevention of simony. If in the case before the Court it be held that the administratrix is entitled to present, it cannot be denied, that a right generally annexed to a prebend will, in the particular instance, be exercised, not merely by a person who had not the prebend, but by a person claiming as if he, from whom the title is derived, and who had the advowson in his politic capacity, had in fact held it in his natural capacity. A decision to this effect will be contrary to the nature of the right. A decision against the administratrix will be contrary to the general rule by which a void turn is considered as a chattel in the case of a natural person. A choice must be made between these two difficulties. In my opinion the principles of law will be less violated by holding that the void turn is not a chattel in this case of a corporation sole, and thereby giving the presentation to the successor, who will present in right of the prebend to which the advowson belongs, than by holding it to be a chattel, and thereby severing the presentation for this turn from the prebend. If it be said that such a severance takes place under a grant of the next presentation, which, before the restraining statutes, would have been good against the successor of a prebendary or bishop, and may still be good against the grantor himself, (as in the case of the archbishop's options, which take effect under grants of the next avoidance made by the bishops of the province), and that in these cases the right is exercised by a person in whom the politic character to which the right belonged, is not vested, I answer, that in those cases the right of the grantee is derived from the politic character of the grantor, who is capable of making the grant, and does, in fact, make it in his corporate capacity. Whereas an administrator can derive nothing from the politic character of the intestate, not being the representative of that character, but of the person only. And although a right to present on the next avoidance may be made a chattel by the act of a party, it does not follow that it shall become a chattel by operation of law. I am not aware that in any case the nature of a right is changed by the mere operation of the law working by itself without any act of the party. In the case of a natural person the nature of the right is not changed by giving the presentation to the executor. It is only a preference of one representative to another, the heir as well as the executor being a representative of the deceased. I may be asked, how, then, does the executor become entitled to rent due in the life of the prebendary? I think there is a manifest distinction between a rent and a presentation. The rent is intended for the maintenance of the prebendary; it can be enjoyed and used in his personal capacity only, and not in his politic capacity. It is assets in the hands of his executor, and nothing remains to be done to give or to accompany the present right to receive

it; whereas a presentation is an act to be done, and must
be accompanied by a right to do it. Thus far I have
treated the question on principle only, and as if the law
furnished no decision or authority in favour of my opinion.
But the case of a bishop dying after avoidance, and before
presentation, does, as I think, furnish an authority. In
that event the king is entitled to the presentation, Co. Litt.
388 a., as he is if the benefice become void during the
vacancy of the see. This is, however, said to be by virtue
of the prerogative ; and so in one sense it is, but the matter
is open to observations similar to those which I have already
made on the case of the tenant in capite. It seems agreed
that the king's right is by reason of the temporalities vested
in him. A ward, relief, heriot, &c. passed to the executor,
and were assets in his hands. All of these, however, were
considered in law as chattels from the beginning, and came
to the bishop as chattels. Guardian in chivalry may grant,
by deed or without deed, the wardship of the lands or of
the heir, or both, to another, Lit. s. 116. The reason for
the power of assigning without deed given by Lord Coke,
is, that the wardship is an original chattel during the
minority, derived out of no freehold, Co. Litt. 85 a. If
the turn had become a chattel, it must have ceased to be
parcel of the temporalities, and must have vested in the
bishop in his personal or natural character, and so have
passed to his executors, as the void turn in the present case
is alleged to do. The inference to my mind, therefore, is,
that the void turn in that case of a corporation sole has not
been considered as a chattel, but as still remaining parcel
of the inheritance and of the temporalities, and being thus
vested in the crown, the prerogative right would attach
upon it in full force, and it would remain in the crown notwithstanding restitution of the temporalities to the successor,
such restitution not being accompanied with a special grant
of the particular presentation. In Co. Litt. 388 a, the
reason given against the right of the executor of the bishop is,
that nothing can be made of the presentment. It is obvious
that this reason will apply with equal force to the executor

of a natural person, and it seems, therefore, that this reason
cannot have been the foundation of the rule, nor can I
think that the rule is founded upon any other reason,
except that of the presentation remaining and passing as
part of the temporalities. I have hitherto purposely ab-
stained from offering any argument from the presumed
intention of the founder of the prebend. We are not
judicially informed of the foundation of this particular prebend. Speaking of prebends generally, I believe their
foundations to be various, some by the diocesan, some by
the crown, and some by private persons. But whoever may
have been the founder, I conceive the object of the foundation to have been the maintenance of the prebendary, and
that where an advowson formed part of the foundation, it
was at least thought probable by the founder that the prebendary might become the incumbent, and so derive his
maintenance from the benefice, if it was not absolultely
intended that he should do so. This opinion or intention
of the founder will be best carried into effect by holding
the void turn to be parcel of the inheritance, and so to pass
to the successor, because the successor will be thereby
enabled to present himself, which he cannot do if the turn
passes to the executor of his predecessor. And if the an-
nexation of the advowson to the prebend be considered as
a trust intended to be vested in the prebendary, and to be
executed only by the prebendary, this intention will certainly
be defeated by allowing an executor to present. It is true,
that before the statute 13 and 14 *Car.* 2, a prebendary
might have been a layman, and incapable of holding the
benefice; but this was certainly contrary to general practice,
and I apprehend also contrary to the general policy of the
law. And although this fact may diminish the weight of
observations derived from the ecclesiastical character of a
prebendary, yet it does not affect his corporate character, nor
the nature of the supposed trust. My judgment is grounded
upon that character, and it is upon consideration of the
nature of the right, as vested in the politic, and not in the

natural person, and upon the want of any sufficient reason for the rule that has prevailed, and must still prevail, unless altered by an authority superior to that of this Court, in the case of natural persons, that I think that rule ought not to be applied to the case of a corporation sole, and that the void turn must be considered as parcel of the inheritance passing to the successor, and not as a chattel severed from it and passing to the personal representavive of the prebendary.

Judgment reversed.

HANSARD v. ROBINSON.

By the custom of merchants the indorsee of a lost bill of exchange cannot recover at law the amount against the acceptor, although the loss was after the bill became due, and although the acceptor was offered an indemnity.

ASSUMPSIT by indorsee against acceptor of a bill of exchange for 32*l.* dated 10th *October*, 1823, payable 40 days after date, drawn by *Henry Butterworth* upon and accepted by defendant, and indorsed by *Butterworth* to plaintiff. Plea, non assumpsit; and issue thereon. At the trial before *Littledale*, J., at the *Middlesex* sittings after *Michaelmas* term, 1826, the case was this :—The defendant owing *Butterworth* 32*l.*, he, on the 10th *October*, 1823, drew a bill on him for that sum, payable forty days after date, which the defendant accepted. The bill bore the proper stamp. *Butterworth* indorsed the bill in blank, and delivered it in that state to the plaintiff. It became due on the 22d of *November*, 1823, but was not presented for payment till the 1st of *May*, 1824. The defendant then offered another bill, but before that was given the plaintiff's clerk lost the original bill. The plaintiff informed the defendant of the loss, and offered him an indemnity, but he refused to pay unless the bill was delivered up to him. The learned Judge was of opinion that the plaintiff being unable to produce the bill could not recover, and he nonsuited the plaintiff, but gave him leave to move to enter a verdict for 32*l.* A rule nisi having been obtained accordingly,

, Campbell and Patteson, in the course of last term, shewed cause. They cited and relied upon Pierson v. Hutchinson (a), Mayor v. Johnson (b), Poole v. Smith (c), Dangerfield v. Wilby (d), Bevan v. Hill (e), a case mentioned by Lord Eldon in Ex parte Greenway (f), Davis v. Dodd (g), and Champion v. Terry (h); and they endeavoured to distinguish the present case from Williamson v. Clements (i), Long v. Baillie (k), Brown v. Messiter (l), Glover v. Thomson (m), and Hart v. King (n).

Gurney and Chitty, contrà, relied upon the three last-mentioned cases.

Cur. adv. vult.

The judgment of the Court was now delivered by

Lord TENTERDEN, C. J.—This was an action on a bill of exchange, brought by the indorsee against the acceptor. The bill was not produced at the trial, but proof was given of the signature of the parties, and other particulars of the bill, and that it was lost after it had become due, and after payment had been required of the defendant, and he had requested time and promised payment. It is not necessary to say whether any special action could have been framed and maintained upon the particular facts and the defendant's promise, because the declaration in the present cause is not founded upon such facts, but upon the bill itself, in the usual way. We would not, however, be understood to give any encouragement to such an action, and we think the special facts cannot properly be considered as affording

(a) 2 Campb. 211.
(b) 3 Campb. 324.
(c) 1 Holt's N.P.C. 144.
(d) 4 Esp. N.P.C. 159.
(e) 2 Campb. 381.
(f) 6 Ves. jun. 812.
(g) 4 Taunt. 602.

(h) 3 Brod. & Bingh. 295.
(i) 1 Taunt. 523.
(k) 2 Campb. 214.
(l) 3 M. & S. 281.
(m) 1 Ryan & M. 403.
(n) 12 Mod. 310.

a satisfactory ground for decision in this case; but the case must be considered generally, as an action brought upon a lost bill, and introducing the general question, whether such an action can be maintained. Upon this question the opinion of judges, as they are to be found in the cases quoted at the bar, have not been uniform, and cannot be reconciled to each other. It is not necessary to advert again to the cases. Amidst conflicting opinions, the proper course is to revert to the principle of these actions on bills of exchange, and to pronounce such a decision as may best conform thereto. Now the principle upon which all such actions are founded is the custom of merchants. The general rule of the *English* law does not allow a suit by the assignee of a chose in action. The custom of merchants, considered as part of the law, furnishes in this case an exception to the general rule. What then is the custom in this respect? It is that the holder of the bill shall present the instrument at its maturity to the acceptor, demand payment of its amount, and upon receipt of the money deliver up the bill. The acceptor paying the bill has a right to the possession of the instrument for his own security, and as his voucher and discharge *pro tanto* in his account with the drawer. If, upon an offer of payment, the holder should refuse to deliver up the bill, can it be doubted that the acceptor might retract his offer or retain his money? And if this be the right of an acceptor ready to pay at the maturity of the bill, must not his right remain the same if, though not ready at that time, he is ready afterwards; and can his right be varied if the payment is to be made under a compulsory process of law? The foundation of his right, his own security, his voucher, and his discharge toward the drawer, remain unchanged. As far as regards his voucher and discharge toward the drawer, it will be the same thing whether the instrument has been destroyed or mislaid. With respect to his own security against a demand by another holder, there may be a difference. But how is he to be assured of the fact, either of the loss or destruction of the bill? Is he to rely upon the assertion of the holder, or to defend an action at the peril of costs? And if the bill should afterwards appear, and a suit be brought against him by another holder, a fact not absolutely improbable in the case of a lost bill, is he to seek for the witnesses to prove the loss, and to prove that the new plaintiff must have obtained it after it became due? Has the holder a right, by his own negligence or misfortune, to cast this burden upon the acceptor, even as a punishment for not discharging the bill on the day it became due? We think the custom of merchants does not authorise us to say that this is the law. Is the holder then without remedy? Not wholly so. He may tender sufficient indemnity to the acceptor, and if it be refused, he may enforce payment thereupon in a Court of Equity. And this is agreeable to the mercantile law of other countries. In the modern *Code de Commerce of France*, *liv.* 1, *tit.* 9, *art.* 151, 152, this is distinctly provided. And this provision is not new in the law of that country, but is found also in the *Ordonnance de Commerce* of *Lewis* the Fourteenth, *tit.* 5, *art.* 19. The rule for entering a verdict for the plaintiff must therefore be discharged.

Rule discharged.

Sir Oswald Mosley, Bart. v. John Walker.

CASE. The declaration stated, that plaintiff, on 1st of *January*, 1824, and long before, was and from thenceforth had been, and still was lawfully possessed of a certain market holden in the town of *Manchester*, in the county of *Lancaster*, on *Tuesday*, *Thursday*, and *Saturday*, in every week throughout the year, except on *Christmas-day* and *New-year's-day*, when they respectively happened on *Tuesday*, *Thursday*, or *Saturday*, for the buying and selling, among other things, of all manner of fish of such kinds as are usually bought and sold in markets; and of all liberties,

The lord of an ancient fish-market may by law have a right to prevent persons from selling fish in their own houses, within the limits of his franchise.

customs, privileges, tolls, stallages, and all other emoluments belonging thereto; and had during all that time provided proper and sufficient stalls in the market for such persons who needed and required the same for the sale of their fish on *Tuesdays, Thursdays,* and *Saturdays,* being such market-days as aforesaid; and also had, and of right ought to have the correction of the market: and whereas all fishmongers and other persons selling their fish of such kinds as are usually sold in markets on *Tuesdays, Thursdays* or *Saturdays,* or on any of those days, being market-days in the town of *Manchester,* ought to sell the same in the open public market there, and not in any private houses, shops, or buildings in the said town, out of the open public market there, and without the license and authority of plaintiff; and such fishmongers and other persons selling such fish on those days in the same town, upon any stalls placed there, ought to sell, and until &c. had sold the same upon the stalls of plaintiff there, or upon stalls placed there by his permission, paying therefore a reasonable sum of money for every stall placed there for that purpose by plaintiff, or by his permission, and made use of by such persons for the sale of their fish on the market-days aforesaid; and thereby plaintiff had and enjoyed, and ought to have continued to have and enjoy great profit &c.: Yet defendant, intending to prevent plaintiff from enjoying the benefit of his market, on the 1st of *January,* 1824, and on divers other *Tuesdays,* &c., being market-days in the town of *Manchester,* wrongfully exposed to sale and sold divers large quantities of his fish, of such kinds as are usually exposed to sale and sold in markets, and as were on &c. exposed to sale and sold in the market of plaintiff, so holden on *Tuesdays,* &c., as aforesaid, and being of the value of 500l., in certain private houses, shops and buildings in the same town, out of the open public market there, and not upon any of the stalls of plaintiff, or any stalls erected by plaintiff, or by his permission, without the license and against the will of plaintiff, and without any lawful authority.

rity, to the injury of plaintiff, and to the nuisance of the
market, &c. Plea, not guilty; and issue thereon. At the
trial before Hullock, B., at the *Lancashire* summer assizes,
1826, the plaintiff produced the following documentary
evidence in support of his title to the market:—An *inqui-
sitio post mortem* in the reign of *Edw.* 1, A. D. 1282, finding
that the tolls of the market and fair of *Manchester* were
worth 6l. 13s. 4d., and that *Robert Gresley* was seised at
his death of the manor of *Manchester* with its appurtenances, and therein of fairs, markets, tollage, stallage, and
profits of fairs and markets, in his demesne as of fee, as
part of the duchy of *Lancaster;* an indenture, 38 *Eliz.*
A. D. 1597, whereby *John Lacy*, in consideration of 3500l.,
sold to *Nicholas Mosley*, alderman of *London*, and *Robert
Mosley*, his heir apparent, the said manor of *Manchester*,
and all manner of courts, markets, tolls, &c. in fee; the
books of the Court Leet from 1582 to 1687, and from 1734
to the time of the trial, the intervening book being lost.
Entries in these books shewed that inspectors of fish and
flesh had been appointed at every *Michaelmas* session.
Their number varied, but there were never less than twelve
in any one year; and in 1825 there were twenty-one. In
the Court book for *Michaelmas*, 1663, there were amercements for offering for sale unwholesome flesh, stinking
salmon, and unsound herrings. The plaintiff then produced parol evidence as follows:—The plaintiff or his ancestors had exercised the right of supervision of the market
as far back as living memory could go. They had received
rents for stalls in the market, and the inspectors appointed
at the Court Leet had seized unwholesome fish and flesh
out of the market. The manor of *Manchester* is co-extensive with the township. Fish was sold every day except
Sunday and *Christmas-day.* It was exposed to sale in the
old market-place, which was a public street, and in no other
place, by permission of the lord of the market. It was
generally much crowded, persons frequenting it were much
incommoded by carriages, and the stalls were sometimes

knocked down. At one time the fishmongers applied to the plaintiff for more space, when he directed his steward to select some more convenient spot. Within the last few years the plaintiff had expended 20,000*l.* in building a new market-house for flesh and vegetables. The defendant had a stall in the fish-market, which he might occupy exclusively; but in 1825 he hired an old house out of the market-place, but adjoining to it, and opened a shop and sold fish there. The plaintiff told him he could not permit him to sell fish out of the market, but the defendant insisted he had a right to do so. On the part of the defendant it was endeavoured to prove that fish had been sold by retail in shops out of the market-place; but it did not appear that it had ever been so sold with the knowledge of the lord of the market, or that there was any fishmonger's shop in *Manchester* out of the market-place. It was contended for the defendant, that the mere grant of the market could not give the plaintiff the right to prevent any individual from selling fish in his private house out of the market, and even if it could, that the plaintiff had not sufficiently proved that he had that right; and that the plaintiff could not recover, because it appeared that there was not convenient accommodation for the public in the market. The learned Judge told the jury there were two questions for their consideration: first, whether the state of the fish-market afforded the defendant reasonable grounds for leaving his stall, and selling in his own house; upon which his lordship observed, that the defendant, when applied to by the plaintiff, did not plead want of accommodation in the market, but claimed a right to sell out of it; and secondly, whether the plaintiff, as lord of the manor and market, had or had not a right to exact stallage for all fish sold in *Manchester*, though sold out of the market-place: and he directed them to find for the plaintiff if they thought that he had established that right, and that the state of the market did not justify the defendant in leaving it. The jury found for the plaintiff.

A rule nisi for a new trial having in last *Michaelmas* term been obtained on both points,

Scarlett, A. G., *Starkie*, and *Parke*, now shewed cause. First, there was sufficient evidence to establish the plaintiff's exclusive right to compel all fishmongers to sell in the market-place, and not in any private house; and that question was fully and correctly left to the jury. The privilege of holding a market is in its nature exclusive. It is beneficial to the public as well as to the lord of the market; to the public, by means of the supervision exercised by the lord of the market over the articles brought there for sale; to the lord, by means of the tolls, stallages, &c.: but neither the public nor the lord could receive the full benefit of the market, unless the right were exclusive. Where the franchise of a market exists, no individual can sell in a private shop, so as to infringe on the rights of the owner of the market. The king cannot grant that a shop shall be market overt; *Clifton* v. *Chancellor* (a); *Com. Dig. Market*, (E); 2 *Rol. Abr.* 123, l. 30; *Wood's Inst.* 208; *The Prior of Dunstable's case* (b). But the question has been decided in favour of the plaintiff, with reference to this very market, in *Mosley* v. *Chadwick* and others, T. 1782. That was an action brought by an ancestor of the present plaintiff against *Chadwick* and others, for defrauding the plaintiff of the profits of his market by erecting another market near to the plaintiff's, for selling flesh-meat for hire and reward, without the license of the plaintiff. Upon special verdict it was found that the plaintiff was seised of the franchise of the market, and that the defendants erected stalls very near to his market, and took money in the nature of rent for those stalls, and that the profits of the plaintiff's market were thereby diminished: and the Court, after argument, gave judgment for the plaintiff. Secondly, even if there was not sufficient accommodation for the public in the

(a) Moor, 624.   *case of the City of London*, 8 Co.
(b) 11 *H.* 6, 19 *a*, cited in *The*   Rep. 127.

market, that is no answer to this action, because the defendant had a stall in the market-place, and might have occupied it, at the very time when he was selling fish in his shop. *Prince v. Lewis* (a). therefore, does not apply, because there the defendant generally could not find room in the market, and he was not told that there was room for him in the market on the particular occasion out of which the action arose.

Gurney, Patteson and *Wightman,* contrà. The question whether a person, with a reasonable regard to his own safety, could place himself in the market, and sell goods there, was not left to the jury. It was proved that the market was very much crowded, and that the stalls were sometimes knocked down by the carriages. The market-place was not only inconvenient, but dangerous. The defendant being lord of the manor, which is co-extensive with the township, may hold the market in any place within the township. As to the lord's right to prevent a man from selling in his own private house, it seems doubtful whether such a right can exist in point of law. In *The Prior of Dunstable's case* (b), another market was set up; which distinguishes that case from the present. That case only establishes that where there is a grant of a market in one part of a town, the inhabitants of another part cannot erect a new market for the sale of their goods, for that would be to the injury of the lord of the market. In most of the cases the lord was deprived of his toll. It appears to have been so in *The Dorking Market case,* from the observations made upon it by Lord *Ellenborough* in *The Bailiffs of Tewkesbury* v. *Diston* (c). [Lord *Tenterden,* C. J. Lord *Ellenborough* must have meant stallage; it was not necessary for him to distinguish toll from stallage.] Toll is not incident to a market, but the subject of specific grant; stallage is derived from the right to the soil, and so is

(a) 8 D. & R. 121; 5 B. & C. 363.   (c) 6 East, 438.
(b) 11 *Hen.* 6, 19 a.

pickage. In *Com. Dig. Market*, (F), 2, it is said, " The owner of a house next to a fair or market cannot open his shop for selling in a market, *without payment of stallage*; for if he takes the benefit of the market, he ought to pay the duties there." This is said to have been so ruled in *The Newington Fair case*, contrary to the opinion of *Dodderidge*, J. In *Vin. Abr. Market*, it is said, " If a person has a shop near a fair or market, he may sell there on payment of stallage, but not otherwise." In *The Dorking Market case*, referred to in *The Bailiffs of Tewkesbury* v. *Bricknell* (*a*), it appeared that a man had fitted up a room in a public house, and pitched and sold corn there, his own, and that of others. That was setting up another market. The grant of a market by no means gives the right to prevent others from selling in their own private houses in or near the market; and although a private person may have a right to sell in his own house a commodity usually sold in the market, he cannot, therefore, set up another market. It is a great advantage to a grantee to have a right of market in a place where another cannot interfere with him. The plaintiff complains that the defendant sold goods in his own house, not that he set up another market. In *The Prior of Dunstable's case* (*b*), the defendant was charged with procuring other persons to sell in his own house; that was setting up another market, and that case resembled the case of the *Dorking Market* in that respect.

Lord TENTERDEN, C. J.—I am of opinion that this rule ought to be discharged. We are not called upon, on the present occasion, to lay down as a general rule and principle of law, that the grant of a market for the sale of certain things necessarily carries with it an exclusion of the right of sale of similar commodities in a private house, whether the market is convenient or not; because, admitting it to have been a question of fact whether the lord of the market had that exclusive right on the present occasion, the

(*a*) 2 Taunt. 133. (*b*) 11 *Hen.* 6, 19 *a*.

evidence abundantly shews that Sir *Oswald Mosley* had that right: and the verdict of the jury, given upon that evidence, decided the question of fact, which was distinctly left to them. Indeed, it is a most extraordinary circumstance, that in so populous a town as *Manchester*, the defendant should not have been able to prove half a dozen instances of shops having been continually open for the sale of fish. The want of such a convenience in such a place as *Manchester* appears to me abundantly to shew that the exclusive right of the lord must have been known and recognised. Another point made was as to the insufficiency and inconvenience of the market itself, in the place where it is holden. As to the insufficiency, the defendant had no ground of complaint, for he had a stall which he might have used at the time when he sold fish at his private house. As to the inconvenience, it appears that the market is holden in that place where in ancient time it had been holden; not in a place convenient for a market certainly, but in the public street, where most ancient markets were held. In modern times many market places or houses have been built adjoining to, or a little way removed from, the street; but formerly all markets were holden in the public streets. And if the ancient market has been held in the public street, can we say that because population and commerce have increased, and that a greater number of carriages pass through the street in modern times than passed in ancient times, the lord, therefore, is to lose his franchise? If, indeed, it could have been proved that any complaint or remonstrance had been made to the lord on the subject, as he has the power to hold the market in any part of *Manchester*, he being lord of the manor and owner of the soil; and that after complaint and remonstrance on the part of persons frequenting the market, he had persisted to hold the market in this place, when he might have holden it elsewhere, there might have been some foundation for the argument addressed to us on the part of the defendant; but in the absence of any such proof, I think the Court ought to maintain this ancient right, for, as a general rule, I think that all ancient rights and ancient establishments ought to be upheld by us as far as by law they may. For these reasons I am of opinion that the rule must be discharged.

The other Judges concurred.

Rule discharged.

On moving for the rule, *Brougham* intimated that he should also move in arrest of judgment, on the ground that by an old statute, (27 *Hen.* 6, c. 5.) the holding of a market on certain feast days, (*Ascension day* and *Good Friday*) was prohibited ; and that all the counts in this declaration alleged the market to be held on certain specified days in the week, without any exception as to those feasts. But *Patteson* now admitted that the case of *Comyns* v. *Boyer*, Cro. *Eliz.* 485, was an authority to shew that where the law raises the exception, it need not be stated in pleading.

BRIGGS *v.* WILKINSON and three others.

ASSUMPSIT, for goods sold and delivered. The defendant *Wilkinson* pleaded *non assumpsit*, whereupon issue was joined ; the other defendants suffered judgment by default. At the trial before *Hullock*, B. at the *Carlisle Summer* assizes, 1826, the case was this :—Down to *November*, 1823, the defendants, (except *Wilkinson*,) and *H.* and *J. Bowman*, were overseers of the brig *Bolton* of *Maryport*. *H. Bowman* resided at that place, and acted as ship's husband. In that month, the brig being then at sea, the *Bowmans*, by bill of sale reciting the certificate of registry, in consideration of 280*l.* previously advanced to them by *Wilkinson*, assigned their share in the *Bolton* to him and his executors, &c. for ever, in trust, at any time after the 13th *January* then next, with or without their concurrence,

The managing owner of a ship mortgages his share, and the transfer is duly indorsed on the certificate of registry. He continues to manage as before, and the mortgagee never takes possession of, or interferes with the ship:—The mortgagee is not liable for goods supplied to the ship by order of the mortgagor.

to sell the share for the best price that could be obtained,
and with the purchase-money first to pay the expenses of
the sale and of effecting insurances, with all such other
sums as *Wilkinson*, his executors, &c., should thereafter pay
or become liable to as registered owner of the vessel, or
for or on account of the vessel; then to retain the 280*l.* and
interest; and then to pay the surplus, if any, to the *Bowmans*, or their order. The bill of sale was deposited with
the proper officer at *Maryport* on the 19th *December*, 1823.
The *Bolton* returned from sea on the 23d *January*, 1824,
and on the 27th the transfer was indorsed on her certificate
of registry. *H. Bowman* acted as ship's husband after the
transfer as before, and in 1825 ordered the goods for the
price of which the action was brought, and which were
furnished for the use of the *Bolton* by the plaintiff, who did
not know that *Wilkinson* was interested in her, nor had
Wilkinson at that time taken possession of or interfered
with the vessel. In *April*, 1826, *Wilkinson*, in consideration of 656*l.*, executed a bill of sale of his share in the
Bolton to one *Tyson*. The learned judge thought there
was no proof that the goods were furnished upon the credit
of *Wilkinson*, and as the plaintiff's counsel did not desire
that point to be left to the jury, he directed a nonsuit, but
gave the plaintiff leave to move to enter a verdict for the
price of the goods, if the Court should be of opinion that
Wilkinson was liable in the action. A rule *nisi* having in
last *Michaelmas* been obtained accordingly,

Scarlett, A. G., and *Parke*, now shewed cause. The
goods were clearly supplied on the credit of *H. Bowman*,
and not on the credit of *Wilkinson*; therefore *Wilkinson*,
being a mortgagee of the ship not in possession, and having
no credit given to him, is not liable for goods supplied for
her use: *Annett* v. *Carstairs*(a), *Jennings* v. *Griffiths*(b).
In the former, the action was brought by the master of a
ship against a mortgagee, not in possession, for wages, and

(a) 3 Campb. 354.   (b) 1 Ry. & M. 42.

Lord Ellenborough said, "Title has nothing to do with these cases; we must look to the contract between the parties;" and the plaintiff was nonsuited. In the latter, the action was brought against the legal owner of a ship for repairs, and *Abbott*, C. J. told the jury that the question for their consideration was, " Were or were not the repairs done upon the credit of the defendant;" upon which the plaintiff's counsel elected to be nonsuited. These are modern decisions, but they lay down no new principle; they merely follow the rule given in earlier cases: *Jackson* v. *Vernon*(a), *Chinnery* v. *Blackburne*(b), *M'Iver* v. *Humble*(c).

Alderson and *Patteson*, contrà. *Wilkinson* was not a mere mortgagee. He had power to sell the ship, and to repay himself his first advance, and all sums which he might pay as registered owner. The 4 *Geo.* 4, c. 41, s. 43, provides, " that where a transfer is made by way of mortgage, or for the purpose of effecting a sale for the payment of debts, that shall be expressed in the indorsement on the certificate of registry, and then the person to whom such transfer is made shall not by reason thereof be deemed an owner." That was not done in this case, therefore *Wilkinson* became owner, and incurred all the liabilities of an owner. Before the transfer *H. Bowman* was agent for the other owners; after the transfer he became agent for *Wilkinson*, as well as the other owners: therefore the real question in the cause was, whether credit was not given to *H. Bowman* as the agent of *Wilkinson* and the other owners; and if the jury had found that there was, *Wilkinson* could clearly have been liable. *Jackson* v. *Vernon*(a) is much shaken by the observations of Lord *Kenyon* in *Westerdell* v. *Dale*(d), and of *Abbott*, C. J. in *Dowson* v. *Leake*(e); and *Eaton* v. *Juques*(f), upon the authority of which it was decided, was overruled by *Williams* v. *Bosanquet*(g).

(a) 1 H. Bl. 114.
(b) 1 H. Bl. 117, n.
(c) 16 East, 109.
(d) 7 T. R. 306.

(e) D. & R. N. P. C. 52.
(f) 1 Dougl. 455.
(g) 1 Brod. & Bing. 238.

Lord TENTERDEN, C. J.—It seems to me that the only question in this case is, whether the goods were supplied for the ship under the authority of *Wilkinson*, express or implied. Express authority there was clearly none. Do the facts of the case raise an implied authority? I think not. The goods were ordered by *H. Bowman*, who had been an owner, but had transferred his legal interest to *Wilkinson*. That, however, was partly for his own benefit; it was not entirely for the benefit of *Wilkinson*. Although *H. Bowman* had no longer a legal interest in the ship, he still continued interested beyond the sum secured by the bill of sale, and upon repayment of all that was due he might have had his share reconveyed to him. In the mean time he continued to manage the ship as before, and gave the order for the goods as if no such bill of sale had been executed. During this period *Wilkinson* never interfered in the concerns of the ship, and it is impossible for us to say that he gave *H. Bowman* authority to order the goods. There are, undoubtedly, conflicting *dicta* and decisions upon this subject. They have arisen since the passing of the Registry Acts, which appear to have influenced the judgment of the Courts; though I, for one, do not understand how those statutes affect the question. They enable a person to ascertain who are the legal owners of a vessel, but that might have been ascertained *aliunde;* and if a legal owner would not be liable at common law to such a demand as the present merely by reason of his ownership, I cannot think that he is so by reason of any thing in the Registry Acts. I am, therefore, of opinion that the nonsuit in this case was right, and that the rule for entering a verdict for the plaintiff ought to be discharged.

The other Judges concurring,

Rule discharged.

The Duke of DEVONSHIRE *v.* LODGE.

Grouse are not birds of warren.

TRESPASS for breaking and entering the free-chase and free-warren of the plaintiff, and killing and taking away grouse. Plea, not guilty; and issue thereon. At the trial before *Park,* J. at the *Yorkshire* summer assizes 1826, the trespass was proved, but it was contended that grouse were not birds of warren, and that, therefore, the action could not be maintained. The learned judge reserved the point, and the plaintiff had a verdict. In *Michaelmas* term last a rule nisi for entering a nonsuit having been obtained,

Scarlett, A. G., *Tindal,* S. G., and *Brougham,* on a former day in this term, shewed cause. The authorities relied on as shewing that grouse are not birds of warren are *Manwood's Forest Laws* and *Barrington's case,* (a). *Manwood* says (b) that the beasts and fowls of warren are " hare, coney, pheasant and partridge;" and the same list is given in *Barrington's case.* But both these books refer to a passage in the first *Institute,* where it is said (c), " The beasts of parque or chase *properly* extend to the buck, the doe, the fox, the marten, the roe; but in a *common and legal* sense to all the beasts of the forest. There be both beasts and fowls of the warren. Beasts, *as* hares, conies and roes; fowls of two sorts, viz. terrestres and aquatiles; terrestres of two sorts, silvestres and campestres; campestres, *as* partridge, quaile, raile, &c.; silvestres, *as* pheasant, woodcock, &c." Lord *Coke,* it is observable, there distinguishes between such animals as are beasts and birds of warren in the proper sense, and such as are so in a common and legal sense; and the birds which he enumerates are clearly mentioned as examples, for the use of the " as" and the " &c." shews that he considered there were other birds of warren besides those enumerated. *Manwood and Barrington's case,* though they refer to that passage, are not conformable to it,

(a) 8 Co. Rep. 275. (b) 362, 4th ed. (c) 1 Inst. 233.

for they omit the quaile and the raile, which Lord Coke mentions. In very early times grouse are not mentioned; probably because they were not known, for they could not be
taken by either of the modes of sporting then in use,
namely, netting and hawking. But the statute 1 *Jac.* 1, c.
27, which was passed about the time when *Manwood* wrote,
mentions grouse, and treats them as game of the same
nature as pheasant and partridge; for after reciting that
there were good laws inflicting penalties on those who
should spoil or destroy the game of pheasant, partridge,
hearn, mallard, *and such like*, it imposes, in s. 2, a penalty
upon those who shall kill or destroy any pheasant, partridge,
&c., *grouse*, heathcock, *moor-game*, &c.

J. Williams, Alderson, and *Parke*, contrà. *Manwood's*
enumeration seems most likely to be correct. The object
of the reservation of warren was to provide hawking for the
king; and the birds of warren were those usually taken by
means of hawks, which, it is admitted, grouse could not be.
The forest laws being of *Norman* origin would naturally
be silent as to grouse, which were not known out of *Great
Britain. Manwood*, in his first edition, c. 1, s. 3, says, "A
forest is not a privileged place generally for all manner of
wild beasts, nor for all manner of fowls, but only for those
that are of forest, chase and warren;" and he afterwards, in
c. 4, s. 3, adds, " the beasts and fowls of warren are these,
the hare, coney, pheasant, and partridge, and none other are
accounted beasts or fowls of warren:" and he cites the
Register of Writs, 93; the *Book of Entries*, 96; and *Fitzh.
N. B.*, 87. *Manwood* wrote before Lord *Coke*, and therefore could not, in his first edition, refer to the first *Institute;*
and though there is such a reference in subsequent editions
published after his death, that proves nothing against his
accuracy or consistency. The statute of *James* shews that
grouse were then well known and treated as game, therefore if they had been considered birds of warren, they
would doubtless have been mentioned by *Manwood.* Grouse

cannot come even within Lord *Coke*'s description in the first *Institute*, for they are neither campestres nor silvestres.

Cur. adv. vult.

Judgment was now delivered by

Lord TENTERDEN, C. J., who, after recapitulating the facts of the case, thus proceeded:—The franchise of free-warren is of great antiquity, and very singular in its nature; for it gives a property in wild animals on the land of another, and to the exclusion of the owner of the land. Such a right ought not to be extended by argument and inference to animals not clearly proved to have been antiently within it. Now there is no book in the law in which grouse are mentioned as birds of warren. *Manwood* confines his description to two species, pheasants and partridges, and he founds his doctrine upon old writs and entries, and in them birds and beasts of warren are not mentioned generally, but are specially designated. Perhaps it may not be easy at this distance of time to say why one species should be bird of warren and another not. One reason why grouse were not so considered may have been, that they were not birds that could be taken by any of the ordinary modes of sport in use at the time when the franchise had its origin. Another may be, that grouse were not generally known, being found in particular parts of the kingdom only. However that may be, not finding grouse any where mentioned as birds of warren, and, for the reasons given, not thinking it right to extend the franchise, we are of opinion that a non-suit must be entered.

Rule absolute (a).

(a) There were other points discussed upon the argument of the case, but it was thought desirable to confine the report to the single point on which the judgment of the Court proceeded.

ROGERS *v.* JONES.

A person de-
puted to take
affidavits only,
is not a
" deputy"
within 12 Geo.
1, c. 29, s. 2,
which re-
quires, before
arrest in an
inferior Court,
an affidavit of
debt to be
made " before
the officer who
issues the pro-
cess, or his
deputy."*

An admis-
sion of a debt
due, made by
a debtor, after
arrest, but
before an
escape, is evi-
dence against
the marshal in
an action for
the escape.

CASE against the marshal of *K. B.* for an escape. The
declaration stated that one *H. S.*, on &c., at the town and
port of *Dover*, and within the jurisdiction of the Court of
Record of our lord the king holden before the mayor and
jurats of *Dover*, to wit at *Westminster*, was indebted to
plaintiff in 200*l.* in respect of certain causes of action before
then accrued to plaintiff against *H. S.*, within the jurisdiction of the said Court. That such money being unpaid,
and *H. S.* then being a prisoner for debt in the actual
custody of the mayor &c. of *Dover*, at the suit of *H. D.*
plaintiff, for the recovery of his debt on &c., at &c., and
within the jurisdiction of the said Court, duly made an
affidavit before *T. P.*, duly constituted and appointed to
take affidavits in the same Court. (The declaration then
set out the affidavit, plaint, and precept, and alleged a
detainer of *H. S.* thereon.) And *H. S.* being detained, and
remaining a prisoner at the suit of plaintiff for the cause
aforesaid, afterwards, to wit on &c., at &c., was brought
before Sir *G. S. Holroyd*, one of the justices of *K. B.*, by
virtue of a writ of habeas corpus, and was thereupon then
and there duly committed by Sir *G. S. Holroyd* to the
custody of the marshal of the Marshalsea, there to remain
until &c. By virtue of which commitment defendant then
and still being marshal &c., took *H. S.* into his custody,
and detained her until afterwards, to wit on &c., he, defendant, without the license &c., voluntarily suffered her to
escape. Plea, not guilty; and issue thereon. At the trial
before Lord *Tenterden*, C. J., at the *Middlesex* sittings after
last *Hilary* term, it was proved that *H. S.*, a native of *France*,
had given to the plaintiff four promissory notes for 50*l.* each,
dated at *Dover*, but payable at *Calais*. It was not proved
that the consideration for the notes was given at *Dover*.
The town-clerk of *Dover* is the proper officer to issue
process out of the Court of Record holden before the mayor
and jurats, and has been for many years in the habit of

1827.

ROGERS
v.
JONES.

giving to several persons at *Dover* a deputation to take
affidavits of debt. *T. P.*, before whom the affidavit mentioned in the declaration was sworn, had a deputation of
this nature, but was not the deputy of the town-clerk for
general purposes. The arrest of *H. S.*, an acknowledgment
of the debt by her when in custody at *Dover*, the removal
by habeas corpus issued at the suit of the plaintiff, and the
escape, were then proved. It was objected for the defendant, that there was no proof that the debt arose within the
jurisdiction of the Court of Record at *Dover*, and that
T. P. had not sufficient authority to take the affidavit of
debt. The Lord Chief Justice reserved both points, and
the plaintiff had a verdict. A rule nisi for entering a nonsuit having afterwards been granted,

Scarlett, A. G., and *Comyn*, now shewed cause. First,
the affidavit was sworn before a person who had a deputation for that purpose from the town-clerk, according to the
practice followed for many years. He was, therefore, for
that purpose, the deputy of the town-clerk, and his appointment was analogous to the appointment of commissioners
for taking affidavits in the superior Courts. The statute
12 *Geo.* 1, c. 29, does not require that he shall be a deputy
for general purposes. Secondly, the notes were made at
Dover, and that constituted a debt *there;* besides, as the
cause was removed into this Court, the plaintiff was not
bound to prove that the cause of action arose within the
jurisdiction of the Court below. [Lord *Tenterden*, C. J.
The cause was removed by the plaintiff, and it does appear
singular that a party should be able to arrest a debtor by
process out of an inferior Court for a cause not within its
jurisdiction, and have the benefit of that arrest by removing
the cause into a superior Court.] At all events the giving
of the notes to the plaintiff constituted a cause of action,
and that arose at *Dover*.

Gurney and *Campbell*, contrà. First, the affidavit of

debt was made before a person who had no authority to
take it. The statute 12 *Geo.* 1, c. 29, which was passed,
" to prevent frivolous and vexatious arrests," takes a distinction in this very respect between superior and inferior
Courts; for, by section 2, in the former the affidavit may be
made " before any judge or commissioner of the Court out
of which the process issues;" but in the latter it must be
made " before the officer who issues the process, or his
deputy," which must mean his deputy for general purposes,
not his deputy merely for the purpose of taking affidavits.
Secondly, there was no proof that the cause of action arose
within the inferior jurisdiction. The notes being *dated* at
Dover was no evidence that they were *made* or *delivered*
there; and there was no other evidence of either of those
facts. As to the acknowledgment of the debt, that being
made after the arrest, was not evidence against the marshal.
[*Bayley*, J. It would be evidence if made before the escape.]

Lord TENTERDEN, C. J. (after conferring with the other
Judges.)—We are all of opinion that *Pain*, before whom
the affidavit of debt was made, was not a deputy within the
meaning of the statute 12 *Geo.* 1, c. 29, s. 2. That clause
requires that the affidavit shall be made before the officer
who issues the process, or his deputy. It is not necessary
to decide whether that means a deputy appointed generally
for the officer, but at all events it makes it necessary that
he should be deputy for the purpose of issuing process.
Now the only authority delegated to *Pain* was that of
taking affidavits, consequently the arrest was illegal; and as
the party was never legally in custody, no action for the
escape can be maintained against the marshal. The rule
for entering a nonsuit must therefore be made absolute on
this ground; and it becomes unnecessary to give any decision upon the other point. It may, however, be proper to
notice, that in *Melsome* v. *Gardner* (a) it was decided, after
consideration, that a plaintiff having arrested a debtor by

(a) 1 Cowp. 116.

1827.

Rogers
v.
Jones.

process out of an inferior Court, could not, by habeas corpus ad respondendum, remove him into this Court to answer to a new action here for the same debt.

Rule absolute.

TOPE, and NICHOLLS, Assignees of J. FORD, v. W. L. HOCKIN, Gent. one &c.

ASSUMPSIT for money had and received; plea, non assumpsit; and issue thereon. At the trial before *Little-dale*, J. at the *Devonshire* summer assizes, 1826, the plaintiffs had a verdict for £15, subject to the following case for the opinion of this Court as to increasing the damages:—

The plaintiffs were the assignees of *John Ford* under a commission of bankruptcy dated 4th *December*, 1823, which was issued on that day upon the petition of *John Lyndon*, the brother-in-law of *Ford*. The acts of bankruptcy in respect of which *Ford* was adjudged a bankrupt, and which were stated in the proceedings before the commissioners, were committed on the 21st *November* and 1st *December*, 1823. At the trial, the trading, the petitioning creditor's debt, and these acts of bankruptcy, were duly proved, and no question was made thereon; and there was proved, and given in evidence, a certain indenture dated 1st *October*, 1823, made between *Ford* of the first part, and one *H. Mudge* and *J. Lyndon* of the other part, whereby *Ford* granted and conveyed all his goods and chattels in the county of *Devon* to *Mudge* and *Lyndon* upon certain trusts in the deed specified. It did not appear that the bankrupt had, at the date of the deed, any goods or chattels out of the county of *Devon*. The deed was executed by *Ford* on the day of the date. *Lyndon* did not execute, but he was privy to it. Many years before this time, *Ford*, being the owner of a freehold estate at *Brent*, in the county of *Devon*, had mortgaged it at several times to several persons; but in 1823, he, by the intervention of *Smith*, an attorney, who

The assignees of a bankrupt, though neither of them is petitioning creditor, cannot avail themselves of an act of bankruptcy of which the petitioning creditor would be estopped from availing himself.

Money lodged by a bankrupt in the hands of an arbitrator, and paid over by the latter before the commission issued, and in ignorance of an act of bankruptcy, cannot be recovered by the assignees from the arbitrator.

had been for a long time concerned for him as such, contracted to sell the same to a Mr. *Cornish,* and the purchase
was to be completed on the 4th *October* in that year. Accordingly on that day a meeting took place for that purpose
at *Totness,* at which were present *Ford, Cornish* (the purchaser) with his attorney, some of the mortgagees, *Smith,*
who attended there as well on behalf of *Ford* as on behalf
of two of the mortgagees, and *Hockin,* the defendant, who
attended on behalf of a third mortgagee. *Smith* brought
with him the title deeds of the estate which had been in his
possession for several years, and which had first come into
his possession as the attorney for and on behalf of his
clients, two of the mortgagees. The parties being assembled, *Cornish,* the purchaser, drew four checks upon a bank
at *Totness* for the amount of the purchase money, i. e. three
for the separate amounts of the said several claims of the
three mortgagees, payable to them respectively or bearer,
and the fourth for the amount of the residue, being 904*l.*
payable to *Ford* or bearer. The first three checks were
then given to the respective mortgagees, and the fourth
Ford took from the hand of *Cornish,* and put into his pocket,
but *Smith* immediately claimed to have possession of it,
and declared that the business should not be completed if
the check was not given up to him. At this time the first
two mortgagees had executed the deeds of conveyance, and
the third mortgagee was in the act of executing them, but
an altercation ensuing between *Smith* and *Ford* respecting
the check, the business was interrupted and the first three
checks were given back to *Cornish.* It was, however, finally
agreed between *Smith* and *Ford* that the check in question
should be deposited in the hands of the defendant, who was
named by *Ford.* Contradictory evidence was given both as
to the grounds on which *Smith* claimed possession of the
check, and also as to the purpose of the deposit with the
defendant; but the jury found that *Smith* had made his
claim on the ground of a balance due to him for bills of
costs and on a cash account, and also on the ground of the

authority hereinafter mentioned; and the jury also found that the deposit was made for the purpose of the defendant's determining how much was due from *Ford* to *Smith*, and also to Messrs. *Hine* & Co. at that time bankers at *Dartmouth*, after payment of which sums he was to return the residue to *Ford*. The check was thereupon deposited by *Ford* in the hands of the defendant, and the purchase was completed. The defendant deposited this check at his bankers on the 6th *October*, and had credit with them for the amount in a separate account; and on the 18th, *Ford* with one *Fowle*, an accountant, and *Smith*, met at the defendant's office at *Dartmouth*, when *Ford* agreed to a balance of account between himself and *Smith* to the amount of 262*l.* After this, but at the same meeting, Mr. *Hine* came to the defendant's office, and produced an account of the claims of *Hine* & Co. against *Ford*, and *Smith* also produced the paper writing dated 31st *May*, 1823, hereinafter set forth, and *Ford* and *Hine* went through the last mentioned account; and finally, the defendant decided, that the sum of 627*l.* was due from *Ford* to *Hine* & Co. He accordingly drew and delivered to *Smith* a check on his bankers for 889*l.*, whereof 262*l.* was for *Smith* himself, and 627*l.* was to be by him paid to *Hine* & Co. The paper writing so produced by *Smith* was as follows:— " Mr. *J. B. Smith.* Sir, I hereby authorise and request you to retain the deeds of my estate at *Brent*, as security for my debt to Messrs. *Hine* and *Holdsworth*, after satisfying the mortgage, and request you to pay them the balance of my account out of the purchase money, as soon as the property is sold. *John Ford, Dartmouth*, 31st *May*, 1823." This paper was signed by *Ford* at the time of its date; and on signing it he gave it to Mr. *Hine*, and at *Hine*'s request he immediately afterwards delivered it to *Smith*. The paper was stamped only with an agreement stamp of 1*l.* It appeared by the said account of *Hine* & Co. that on the 31st *May*, 1823, there was due from *Ford* to *Hine* & Co. 306*l.* 18*s.* 11*d.* only, and on the 18th *October* following 627*l.* The question for the opinion of the Court was, whether the plaintiffs were entitled to recover the sum of 889*l.*, or any and what part thereof. If the Court should be of opinion that the plaintiffs were entitled to recover the sum of 889*l.*, or any part thereof, the damages were to be increased accordingly, but if otherwise, the damages to remain at the amount of 15*l.* as aforesaid.

Carter, for the plaintiffs. The deed of the 1st *October*, 1823, was clearly an act of bankruptcy, and annulled the payments made on the 18th of *October*. The money came into the defendant's hands on the 6th of *October*, when he had credit for it with his bankers, and so remained until the 18th. It was, therefore, money had and received by him to the use of the assignees, which they are entitled to recover. But it will be said that this was a concerted act of bankruptcy, and, therefore, cannot be rendered available; that although the act in itself may be an act of bankruptcy, yet the petitioning creditor is estopped from saying that it is so. The estoppel, however, is limited to the petitioning creditor; he must establish an act of bankruptcy available by himself to support the commission. The assignees also must shew such an act of bankruptcy in order to originate their jurisdiction. But when that has been done, the creditors at large, represented by the assignees, may take the benefit of another act of bankruptcy, although the petitioning creditor was a consenting party to it. *Tappenden v. Burgess*(a) shews that the estoppel does not apply to assignees, who are mere trustees for the creditors at large, but only to a petitioning creditor who originates the commission.

Coleridge, contrà. The deed of the 1st *October*, 1823, is not available for any purpose under a commission sued out by *Lyndon*, because he was privy to it. He could not have sued out a commission upon that act of bankruptcy, and although a commission has been sued out upon another

(a) 4 East, 230.

act of bankruptcy, the assignees cannot refer to the deed
for the purpose of bringing property into the general fund.
The deed must be fraudulent in order to be an act of bankruptcy; and he who has executed, assented to, or acted
under such a deed is estopped from saying that it is fraudulent.   This estoppel is not confined to the petitioning creditor but extends to the assignees; *Bamford* v. *Baron* (a).
Tappenden v. *Burgess* (b) shews that the estoppel on the
assignees is in virtue of their representative, not their individual character, for there all the assignees except *Tappenden* (the petitioning creditor) were privy to the deed; and
yet it was held that they might, under a commission founded
on that deed, sue for and recover the bankrupt's estate.   It
was not necessary that *Lyndon* should execute the deed;
Back v. *Gooch* (c), *Hicks* v. *Burfitt* (d).   In *Ex parte
Cantwell* (e), the Lord Chancellor said, " If the petitioning
creditor has acted under the deed, although he may not
have executed it, he not only cannot avail himself of it as
an act of bankruptcy, but will be liable to all the costs of
the commission."   But supposing that the assignees may
treat this deed as an act of bankruptcy, still this action is
not maintainable against the present defendant.   He was
a mere arbitrator.   The money was only deposited with
him.   He had no interest in it.   He never mixed it with
his own, and he paid it over without having notice of any
act of bankruptcy or of insolvency.   *Coles* v. *Robins* (f)
and *Coles* v. *Wright* (g) are authorities to shew that under
such circumstances the defendant is not liable.

Cur. adv. vult.

Lord TENTERDEN, C. J. now delivered judgment, and
after recapitulating the facts of the case thus proceeded :—

(a) 2 T. R. 593.
(b) 4 East, 230.
(c) Holt, N. P. C. 13; 4 Camp.
232.
(d) 4 Camp. 235.
(e) 1 Rose, 318.
(f) 3 Camp. 183.
(g) 4 Taunt. 198.

Upon the argument of this case some questions were raised upon the effect of the paper signed by the bankrupt *Ford*, on the 31st *May*, 1823, and the sufficiency of the stamp upon it, as relating to the lien of *Hine* and *Holdsworth* on the title deeds of the estate sold to *Cornish*, and which were in the hands of *Smith*, and also as to the lien of *Smith* himself upon those deeds. But as the payment made by the defendant to *Smith* was of a sum assented and agreed to by the bankrupt, and the payment to *Hine* and *Holdsworth* was made under an authority delegated by him to the defendant, as an arbitrator, to settle and pay their claim, if these payments were made before any act of bankruptcy committed by *Ford*, of which the plaintiffs can avail themselves, all those questions become immaterial. And we think the payments were so made (*a*). They were made on the 18th *October*. The commission issued on acts of bankruptcy committed on the 21st *November* and 1st *December* following. It issued on the petition of *John Lyndon*. The plaintiffs endeavoured to overreach these payments by proof of an act of bankruptcy committed on the 1st *October*. That act of bankruptcy was the execution of a deed conveying all the bankrupt's goods and chattels in *Devonshire*, the county of his residence, to one *Henry Mudge* and this *John Lyndon*, for the purpose of discharging a debt due to them. *Lyndon* was privy to this transaction, and, therefore, taking the deed to be an act of bankruptcy, it is clear by all the authorities that *Lyndon* could not be allowed so to treat it and to take out a commission upon it. But it was argued that although the law might be so as to the suing out a commission, yet if the commission were sued out upon another distinct act of bankruptcy sufficient to sustain it, the creditors represented by the assignees (*Lyndon* not being an assignee) might nevertheless avail themselves of this act of bankruptcy for the purpose of avoiding subsequent acts by force of the relation to this deed. We, how-

(*a*) In concurrence with his lordship's observation, the arguments urged upon those points have been omitted.

ever, think that the reasons upon which the creditors at large are not allowed to avail themselves for the purpose of supporting the commission of an act, which the petitioning creditor is not allowed to call an act of bankruptcy, although another creditor might do so for that purpose, apply equally to the present purpose, for which they rely upon it. One reason must be, that the creditors at large are to be considered as connected with the petitioning creditor and as deriving their rights under the commission from him; for if they were not so considered, they might say, " here is a good act of bankruptcy and a sufficient debt owing to the petitioning creditor. His connection with the act of bankruptcy is immaterial to us; there are many among us to whom debts are owing of sufficient amount to have authorised us to sue out a commission, and, therefore, in our favour the commission shall stand good." Another reason may be, that if a commission sued out by such a petitioning creditor could be available, he would have a right to prove his debt under it and participate in the dividend, and so would derive a benefit from a commission which he ought not to have sued out, and thus take advantage of his own wrong. And this reason also will be applicable to the purpose for which the act of bankruptcy in *October* is insisted on. For if the plaintiffs can avail themselves of that they will increase the fund, and *Lyndon* will participate in that increase. As this objection alone is sufficient to defeat the plaintiffs' claim, it is not necessary to pronounce a judicial opinion upon any other. But adverting to the case of *Coles* v. *Wright* (a), which was quoted by Mr. *Coleridge* in support of his last objection, we think that that objection is also good, and that the money cannot be recovered from the present defendant. It was placed under his control for a special purpose; it was never mixed with his own, but kept separate as a distinct fund to answer that purpose; he was to derive no benefit from it; he afterwards applied it to the intended purpose, in part with the express assent,

(a) 4 Taunt. 198.

and in part under the authority of *Ford.* He was, therefore, as it appears to us, a mere channel of conveyance, and
his situation was the same in effect as that of *F. Wright* in
the case that has been quoted, with this difference in his
favour, that *F. Wright* might have known that the person to
whom he carried the money and who was then in prison
for debt, might be continuing in prison, becomes bankrupt,
from a time antecedent to the transaction, whereas the present defendant had no knowledge of the execution of the
deed, which had been managed altogether in secret. It is
obvious that much inconvenience and obstruction to business might take place, if one who is employed as a mere
gratuitous carrier, or made the gratuitous channel of conveyance or delivery, should be answerable for property passing
through his hands under circumstances which lead to no
suspicion that the transfer may not be made lawfully and
without injury to the right of any third person, and a decision to this effect would be a great hardship on the individual so employed, and give a very harsh (and I may say, as
to him, a very injurious) effect to that relation to the act of
bankruptcy, which, though necessary for many purposes, it
has been the object of the legislature, in modern times, to
narrow and contract within the compass that justice to particular individuals requires. For these reasons, we think
that the damages ought not to be increased, but that the
verdict should stand for 15*l.* only.

Judgment accordingly.

Shaw and others, Assignees of E. Howard and J. Gibbs, 1827.
          v. Woodcock.—In Error.

ASSUMPSIT for money had and received, brought by *Woodcock,* the plaintiff below, to recover from *Shaw* and others, the defendants below, assignees of *Howard* and *Gibbs,* bankrupts, the sum of 715*l.* 3*s.* 7*d.* paid to them by the plaintiff below, in order to obtain possession of certain policies of insurance belonging to him, and upon which the assignees claimed a lien to that amount, and which they refused to deliver up until that sum was paid. The bankrupts acted as the agents of the plaintiff for the purpose of receiving instalments of annuities due to him, and charged him a commission for so doing, and from time to time rendered him accounts of all sums paid or received for him. In the accounts delivered they from time to time gave credit for several instalments of annuities due, but which were not received, and were so described in the accounts, but they paid him the balance of those accounts as if all the instalments had been received. In the succeeding accounts no notice was ever taken of the instalments which in the preceding accounts had been marked as not then received. At the trial in C. P. at the *London* sittings after *Hilary* term, 1825, before *Best,* C. J., the jury, under his direction, (to which a bill of exceptions was tendered,) found a verdict for the plaintiff below. The record, when brought into this Court by writ of error, after setting out the pleadings and continuances, stated, that on a certain day the cause came on to be tried, and that one *J. Hindman* was produced and examined as a witness for the plaintiff, and gave the following evidence:—In the year 1822 he had been and still was the attorney for the plaintiff. The defendants, as assignees of the estate and effects of *Howard* and *Gibbs,* had been in possession of certain policies of insurance belonging to the plaintiff, which had been effected on the joint lives of one *Gowland* and his wife. He the witness, in the early part of the said year, and soon

Money paid, as the only means of recovering possession of property to which the party is entitled, constitutes a compulsory payment, and may be recovered back.

If the agent of the grantee of annuities renders accounts crediting his principal with instalments which he states have not been received, but charging commission and afterwards paying the balance as if they had been received; the jury may infer an agreement by the agent to be responsible for such instalments in case they were not paid by the grantors of the annuities.

after the death of *Gowland*, had applied to the defendants
to deliver up the policies of insurance, but they claimed
from the plaintiff a sum of 715*l.* 5*s.* 7*d.* as assignees of
Howard and *Gibbs*, and claimed a lien upon the policies
for that sum. *Hindman*, as the attorney for and on the
behalf of the plaintiff, paid to the defendants, in order to
get the policies out of their hands, the sum of 715*l.* 5*s.* 7*d.*,
the balance so claimed, but which he the witness denied
to be due. It was a disputed account, and he was obliged
to pay the money before they would deliver the policies.
At the time when he paid the 715*l.* 5*s.* 7*d.* he gave to the
defendants a notice in writing, signed by *Woodcock*, stating
" that he had paid to the assignees 715*l.* 5*s.* 7*d.*, for which
they claimed a lien on the policies, his (*Woodcock's*) property, in order to obtain possession of such policies, and on
no other account; and that by such payment to them he
did not mean to admit that they were entitled to a lien to
such amount, or to any amount, on the said policies; and
that he (*Woodcock*) should bring an action against them to
recover back the said sum of 715*l.* 5*s.* 7*d.*" The witness
then produced certain paper writings in the handwriting of
Gibbs, one of the bankrupts, which writings the witness had
received from *Woodcock*. The first was an account which
contained a statement of transactions between *Woodcock*
and the bankrupts from *December*, 1818, to *March* 17,
1819. *Woodcock* was there debited with various sums of
money paid on his account for insurance on lives, and for
cash paid and for commission on all the annuity instalments
then due, and stamps. He was credited with various sums
due to him on account of annuities, and among others with
" 50*l.*, one half-year's annuity due from *B. Sydenham*, not
yet received," and 14*l.* 5*s.*, another half-year's annuity "due
from *R. S. Gowland*, not received," and the balance due
to *Woodcock* was in the account stated to be 94*l.* 5*s.* 9*d.*
This account was sent to *Woodcock* inclosed in a letter from
Gibbs, dated 17th *March*, 1819, and in which he stated
that he had not received either *Gowland's* or *Sydenham's*

annuity, but that he would accept *Woodcock's* bill at two
months after date for the balance of the account. The
second account was delivered on the 23d *October*, 1819,
and contained statements of money transactions between
the parties from 17th *March*, 1819, to 17th *September.*
Woodcock was debited with various sums paid on his account,
with commission on annuity instalments then due, and he
was credited with several sums received, and with 50*l.*, one
half-year's annuity due from *B. Sydenham*, 9th *September*,
and 83*l.* 10*s.* a half-year's annuity due from one *Cunliff*,
17th *May.* These two instalments were marked as not
received, and the balance due to him was stated to be
107*l.* 16*s.* 3*d.* This account was also inclosed in a letter
from *Gibbs*, in which he stated that he had included all the
annuities though not received, and added, if he (*Woodcock*)
felt the necessity of drawing, he was to let him (*Gibbs*)
know. The third account contained a statement of money
paid and received on account of *Woodcock* from *January*
to 23d *February*, 1820. *Woodcock* was, as before, debited
with various sums of money paid on his account, with commission on the annuity instalments then due, and credited with
83*l.* 10*s.* one half-year's annuity due from one *Cunliff*, but
which was stated to be not yet received, and the balance due
to him upon that account was 56*l.* 4*s.* 7*d.*, and *Gibbs*, in his
letter inclosing the account, stated, that although half a year's
annuity, with which *Woodcock* was credited, was not received, he might draw for the balance. The fourth account
was transmitted on the 25th *November*, 1820, inclosed in a
letter from *Gibbs*. It contained an account of money transactions between the parties from 4th *April* to 24th *November*, 1820. In that account *Woodcock* was debited with
various sums paid on his account, with commission on all
the half-yearly instalments of annuities then due, and credited with several sums due to him on account of half-
yearly payments of annuities; but two of these half-yearly
instalments, viz. one for 100*l.*, due from *B. Sydenham*, 9th
September, and 167*l.*, another due from *Cunliff*, 17th *No-*

vember, were stated to be not yet received. These two instalments were given credit for on the 4th *November*, and the balance due to *Woodcock* was stated to be 56*l.* 4*s.* 7*d.* *Gibbs* transmitted this account to *Woodcock* by a letter dated 23d *February*, 1820. The instalments on the half-yearly annuities, which were stated as not received, were not placed to the credit of *Woodcock* on the days when they respectively became due, but on subsequent days; and in some instances credit was given generally without date. No evidence being produced on the part of the defendants, the Chief Justice delivered his opinion to the jury, that the payment of the sum of 715*l.* 5*s.* 7*d.* by the plaintiff to the defendants, having been made to obtain possession of a paper of great value to the plaintiff, and because he was obliged to make the payment for that purpose, was not a voluntary payment, and that the plaintiff was not concluded from recovering the said sum of 715*l.* 5*s.* 7*d.* from the defendants: and the Chief Justice did further deliver his opinion to the jury, that such sums of money as were stated in the accounts to have been received, the jury might conclude to have been received, as there was no evidence to the contrary; and that with respect to such items as were stated in the accounts to be not received or not yet received, the jury might consider the mode in which the parties dealt together, as evidenced by the letters and accounts; and inasmuch as commission was charged by *Howard* and *Gibbs*, the bankrupts, on all those items, and as successive accounts were rendered still charging commission, and the items stated in a former account not to have been received not being brought forward in subsequent accounts between the parties, or debited to the plaintiff, or any subsequent notice given to the plaintiff of their non-payment, there being in evidence four successive accounts between the parties, they, the jury, might infer an agreement by *Howard* and *Gibbs*, the bankrupts, to take the responsibility for the payment of the said items on themselves; but that it was a question for their consideration and decision, and that upon the aforesaid evidence the jury might lawfully find a verdict for the plaintiff: and with that direction left the same to the jury.

Hill, for the plaintiff in error. There was no proof of any agreement on the part of the bankrupts to pay the instalments of the several annuities in default of payment by the grantors. Such an agreement would be an undertaking to pay the debt of another, and must be in writing. The original agreement, therefore, should have been produced or shewn to have been lost or destroyed. In *Shaw* v. *Dartnell* (a) it was contended that the bankrupts were agents acting under a *del credere* commission, but the Court were of a contrary opinion. If that had been the case here, the bankrupts would have given the grantee of the annuities credit for the instalments on the days when they became due. The entries in the accounts afforded no evidence that the bankrupts had agreed to guarantee the payment of the annuities; they only proved that the bankrupts wished to make the plaintiff believe that the annuities had been paid, to induce him to continue his dealings with them. Secondly, this was a voluntary payment made with full knowledge of all the facts, therefore the money cannot be recovered back. Two circumstances must concur to take a case out of that rule. First, the payment must be made in order to get possession of goods for which the owner has an immediate pressing necessity, *Astley* v. *Reynolds* (b). Secondly, the claim of lien must be clearly void. In *Fulham* v. *Down* (c) Lord *Kenyon* said, where a voluntary payment is made of an illegal demand, (the party knowing the demand to be illegal,) without an immediate and urgent necessity, that is, unless to redeem or preserve his person or goods, it is not the subject of an action for money had and received. Here *Woodcock* had no immediate pressing necessity for the policies, neither was the claim of lien clearly void. This being so, *Woodcock* ought to have brought trover, which is the proper legal remedy in such a case. He must in that

(a) *Ante,* 54; 6 B. & C. 56.   (b) Strange, 915.   (c) 6 Esp. 26.

form of action have tendered the exact amount of the defendant's lien, which in a matter of such complicated account it might be difficult to ascertain, and in default of so doing would have had to pay the costs of the action. By paying the money claimed he makes the assignees defendants, and throws on those who held the security the necessity of making the proper tender.

Parke, contrà. This was a compulsory payment, for the assignees refused to deliver up the policies until the money was paid. The Lord Chief Justice was right in leaving it to the jury to find whether, under the circumstances, *Howward* and *Gibbs* had or had not agreed to make themselves responsible for the annuity instalments for which they gave credit, but which were stated at the time not to have been received. It was a question for the jury with what intent those entries were made. Four accounts were delivered. In all of them credit was given for annuity payments which were not received, and the bankrupts paid the grantee those instalments as if they had been received, and in the later accounts never intimated that they looked to the plaintiff to repay them those sums for which they had given him credit in the former.

Lord TENTERDEN, C. J.—I think that this question was properly submitted to the jury. The bill of exceptions, after setting out the evidence, states that the Lord Chief Justice told the jury, that from the evidence they might infer an agreement by the bankrupts to take on themselves the responsibility as to those items of account for which credit was given to *Woodcock*, the plaintiff below, but which were described as not received, but that it was a question for their consideration upon the evidence. The question now before this Court is, not whether the conclusion come to by the jury was correct, but whether the evidence was such as that the jury might lawfully infer from it such an agreement. It appeared that there had been delivered to

Woodcock by the bankrupts four successive accounts, in each of which the latter took credit for commission on the instalments of the annuities as if they had been received. In the first account they gave him credit for half-yearly instalments of two annuities, and stated a balance of 94*l*. to be due to *Woodcock*. In a letter from one of the bankrupts, accompanying this account, he informs *Woodcock* that those two sums had not been received, but that his bill for the balance would be accepted. At the very time, therefore, when he says he has not received the money for which credit is given, he charges commission as if it had been received, and promises to accept a bill, drawn upon him and his partner, for the balance of the account. The second account is afterwards sent in, in which all the annuity instalments due to *Woodcock* were included, although they were not received, and *Gibbs* desires that when he feels a necessity to draw, he will let him (*Gibbs*) know. So, when the third account is sent, although *Woodcock* is informed by *Gibbs* that the half-yearly instalment of *Cunliffe's* annuity, for which credit was then given, had not been received, he is at the same time told that he may draw for the balance struck in that account. In the fourth account credit is given for two half-yearly instalments which were stated not to have been received, but in the letter accompanying that account the plaintiff is not informed that he may draw for the balance. It must, however, be taken that he did draw for the balance of that as well as all the other accounts, for otherwise there could not have been due to the bankrupts or the assignees the balance claimed and paid to redeem the policies. This being the state of the accounts between the parties, the assignees of the bankrupts insisted that they were entitled to be allowed in account all those sums for which they had authorised *Woodcock* to draw, and which were paid by the bankrupts in respect of those annuity instalments which were stated not to have been received; and they, as assignees, being in possession of certain policies of insurance, and *Woodcock* having occasion for them,

the assignees refused to deliver them up unless he paid
715l. 5s. 7d. The question which arises in this action,
wherein the plaintiff below seeks to recover back the money
which he paid in order to obtain possession of the policies,
is precisely the same as if the assignees had brought an
action to recover back the money paid by them; and it is
clear that such an action would be answered, if the defendant were to shew that the bankrupts had agreed to become
responsible for the instalments of the annuities in default
of payment by the grantors; and that being so, if there was
such an agreement proved in this case, the assignees had
no lien, and consequently cannot retain the money which
they compelled the plaintiff to pay. Now the circumstances of the bankrupts having from time to time given
the grantee credit for the annuity instalments, and having
authorised him to draw for the amount of those instalments,
and having actually paid them although they had not received them, and not having intimated in the later accounts
that they expected to be repaid those sums, and having,
moreover, charged commission upon those sums, were
some evidence for the jury to infer that they had made those
payments in pursuance of some agreement on their part to
do so, whether they received them or not; and if there was
evidence to go to the jury, then I think the question was
properly submitted to their consideration, and consequently
the judgment of the Court of Common Pleas ought to be
affirmed.

The other Judges concurring,

Judgment affirmed.

1827.

ARLETT v. ELLIS, HEWETT, SHEFFORD and MILES.

TRESPASS for breaking and entering plaintiff's close, situate at Yately, in the county of Southampton, and breaking down his fences, &c. Plea, that the close in which, &c., before and at the time when, &c., was and is within and parcel of the manor of Crondall in the county of Southampton; that defendant Shefford was the owner of a certain copyhold messuage and land within the manor, and in right of such messuage and land was at the time when, &c., by custom entitled to common of pasture on plaintiff's close, and that he, and the other defendants as his servants, committed the trespass in the exercise of that right, and because the fences had been wrongfully erected, and were wrongfully standing upon the said close in which, &c., so that without pulling down and destroying the fences defendant Shefford could not use or enjoy his common of pasture in the close in which, &c., he, Shefford, in his own right and the other defendants as his servants, pulled down and a little destroyed the fences, doing no unnecessary damage to plaintiff or the fences. Another plea claimed a right of common of turbary upon the close to cut, dig, and take turf. The replication took issue upon the custom, and new assigned that defendants on other and different occasions, and for other purposes than those in the pleas respectively mentioned, and in a greater degree and to a greater extent, and with more force and violence than was necessary, committed the several trespasses. The defendants joined issue on the replication, and pleaded not guilty to the new assignment. At the trial before Park, J., at the Hampshire spring assizes, 1827, the case was this:—In October, 1825, the dean and chapter of Winchester, lords of the manor, granted to the plaintiff two acres of land, part of the waste of the manor, to hold to him, his heirs and assigns, for ever, according to the custom of the manor, at the yearly rent of 2s. 6d., and all other burdens and services. The plaintiff paid a fine of 8l. and was ad-

Quære, whether the lord of a manor may, in general, make grants of the waste upon which the copyholders have a right of common, provided he leave sufficient for the copyholders.

A special custom that he may, leaving sufficient for the copyholders, would be good.

Semble, that a special custom that he may, without limit, would be bad.

1827.

ABBOTT
v.
EGLIS.

mitted tenant. In *February*, 1826, the plaintiff began to inclose the piece of ground and made an embankment, and before the inclosure was completed the defendants, on the 7th of *March*, entered upon the land and threw down the embankment. There was neither turf, fit for fuel, nor pasture on the land in question, and the defendants had no cattle with them nor any instrument to cut turves. They might have entered upon the common and upon the piece of land in question, and turned on their cattle without throwing down the embankment. The defendants then gave evidence in support of the right of common of pasture and of turbary claimed in the pleas. The plaintiff in reply, in order to prove a custom by the lord to inclose parcels of the waste, produced in evidence the court rolls, containing entries of various grants of parcels of the waste made by the lords of the manor from the year 1669 to the time of the trial. It did not appear on the face of the grants that they were made with the consent of the homage, or that a sufficiency of common remained for the commoners. It was contended by the defendants' counsel that this evidence was not admissible upon the issue joined in this case, that issue being whether the custom stated in the plea existed; and assuming that the evidence was admissible, the custom itself, being without limit or restriction, was void. The plaintiff's counsel then urged, that the plaintiff at all events was entitled to a verdict upon the new assignment, because it appeared clearly upon the evidence that the defendants, by pulling down the bank, had done more than was necessary to assert the right of common. The learned judge left three questions to the jury, first, whether the defendants had established the right of common of pasture and of turbary stated in the pleas—the jury found that they had. Secondly, whether there was within the manor a custom for the lord to make grants of parcels of waste, without limit or restriction—the jury found that there was such a custom. Thirdly, whether the defendants had done more than was necessary for asserting the right of common of pasture and of turbary—the jury found that the defendants did more than was necessary for the purpose of asserting their right of common. The learned judge then directed a verdict to be entered for the plaintiff for 1s. damages, but reserved liberty to the defendants to move to enter a nonsuit if the Court should be of opinion that the evidence of the custom to inclose ought not to have been received, or if that custom was void; and it was agreed that the Court should (as they thought fit) order a verdict to be finally entered for the plaintiff or the defendants on all or any of the issues. Selwyn, in Easter term last, obtained a rule nisi for a new trial, when he cited Hollis v. Proud (a), Duberly v. Page (b), Clarkson v. Woodhouse (c), Shakespeare v. Peppin (d), Grant v. Gunner (e), Badger v. Ford (f), Folkard v. Hemmett (g), and Wilson v. Willes (h).

R. Williams and Follett now shewed cause against the rule. They cited Com. Dig. Pleader, G. 2, Covert's case (i), Durvant v. Child (k), Henchin v. Knight (l), Spooner v. Day (m), Margatroid v. Law (n), Grant v. Gunner (o), Weeks v. Sparke (p), Rotherham v. Green (p), Davison v. Gill (r), Bateson v. Green (s), Cooper v. Marshall (t), Kirby v. Sadgrove (u), Lord Northwick v. Stanway (x), Clarkson v. Woodhouse (y), Folkard v. Hemmett (z), Badger v.

(a) 4 D. & R. 31 ; 1 B. & C. 8.	(n) Carth. 116.
(b) 2 T. R. 391.	(o) 1 Taunt. 435.
(c) 5 T. R. 412.	(p) 1 M. & S. 679.
(d) 6 T. R. 742.	(q) Cro. Eliz. 593.
(e) 1 Taunt. 435.	(r) 1 East, 6.
(f) 3 B. & A. 153.	(s) 5 T. R. 411.
(g) 5 T. R. 417.	(t) 1 Burr. 259.
(h) 7 East, 127.	(u) 6 T. R. 483.
(i) Cro. Eliz. 754.	(x) 3 B. & P. 346.
(k) Yelv. 227.	(y) 5 T. R. 411.
(l) 1 Wils. 253.	(z) Id. 417.
(m) Cro. Car. 432.	

Ford(a), *Rex* v. *Warblington*(b), *Doe* v. *Davidson*(c), *Rex* v. *Wilby*(d), and *Rex* v. *Hornchurch*(e).

E. Lawes, Serjt. and *Selwyn* were heard in support of the rule. They cited *Bracton*, lib. 4, c. 37, *Bro. Abr.* " *Common*," pl. 9, the *Year Book*, 15 *Hen.* 7, 10 b, and 2 *Inst.* 88 a.

BAYLEY, J.—I think this rule ought to be made absolute. The question upon which I have entertained the greatest difficulty during the argument is whether the plaintiff is entitled to retain his verdict upon the new assignment, and upon the whole I think that he is not. The authorities cited from Brooke's Abridgment and the Year Book satisfy my mind that where a fence has been erected upon a common inclosing and separating parts of that common from the residue, and thereby interfering with the rights of the commoners, the latter are not by law restrained in the exercise of those rights to pulling down so much of that fence as it may be necessary for them to remove for the purpose of enabling their cattle to enter and feed upon the residue of the common, but that they are entitled to consider the whole of that fence so erected upon the common as a nuisance, and to remove it accordingly. Those authorities shew that there is an essential distinction between this case and that of *Sadgrove* v. *Kirby* (f). The fences placed upon the common in this case were *primâ facie* as against the commoners wrongfully and illegally placed there, and a nuisance which they might abate; but the trees growing upon the common in *Sadgrove* v. *Kirby* were not *primâ facie* illegally growing there, for the lord, as owner of the soil, had *primâ facie* a right to plant and to have those trees there, and the trees would not become

(a) 3 B. & A. 153.   (d) Id. 504.
(b) 1 T. R. 242.   (e) 2 B. & A. 189.
(c) 2 M. & S. 184.   (f) 6 T. R. 438.

wrongful, as against the commoners, unless it were by injuring their easement, and not leaving them a sufficiency of common for their cattle. The lord, by granting rights of common upon his waste, does not thereby exclude himself or his tenants from all use of the waste on which the right of common is to be exercised, but merely grants to others in common with himself and his tenants certain rights upon that waste. All that the lord has not granted remains in him. He may therefore apply the waste to any purposes not inconsistent with the rights which he has previously granted to the commoners. One mode by which he may make his waste beneficial to himself is by planting trees on it. They may also be beneficial to the commoners by affording shade to the cattle at particular periods of the year. He may also exercise his right by turning in rabbits, provided he leave a sufficiency of common for the commoners. The turning rabbits on the common is an act not *primâ facie injuriosum*. It is *primâ facie* in the exercise of his legal rights as owner of the soil. It was therefore properly decided in *Sadgrove* v. *Kirby* (a) and *Cooper* v. *Marshall* (b) that a commoner in such a case is not to take upon himself to decide that the trees or rabbits on a common are a nuisance, and to cut the trees down or destroy the rabbits, but that he is bound in the first instance to bring his action and to establish to the satisfaction of a jury that they are a nuisance. If that be a sound distinction between those cases and the present, what was the principle upon which the verdict was given for the plaintiff on the new assignment? The jury seem to have been of opinion that the defendants had done more than was necessary for the purpose of asserting the right of common; and if the decision in *Sadgrove* v. *Kirby* were to govern the present case, and the erection of the fence were an act which the lord and his grantee *primâ facie* had a right to do, the defendants would have done more than was necessary for the purpose of using the right of common, if they had

(a) 6 T. R. 483.   (b) 1 Burr. 259.

pulled down any part of the bank or fence, because there
was an opening by which they might have entered upon
the plaintiff's close; but if the whole of that bank or fence
were a *nocumentum injuriosum*, which the defendants in
the exercise of their rights of common were justified in removing, the verdict of the jury, that they had done more
than was necessary for the purpose of asserting their rights,
could not be well founded. It seems to me that the verdict upon the new assignment was founded upon the notion
that the defendants, in pulling down the fence, had done
something more than they had a right to do in asserting
their rights of common. But the authorities shew that
they had not done more than by law they were entitled to
do. I think, therefore, that the jury were not warranted
in coming to the conclusion that the defendants entered the
close for other purposes than those mentioned in the pleas,
and that the verdict for the plaintiff upon the new assignment is not warranted by the evidence.

The next question is whether the plaintiff be entitled to
recover on the ground that he has proved a custom for the
lord to inclose parcels of the waste; and that raises the
great question in this case whether the lord had any such
right. The lord had granted to the plaintiff a particular
spot, parcel of a large waste. The defendants had a right
of common on the waste, including the space of land
granted to the plaintiff, unless that spot had been legally
separated from the residue of the manor by the lord. I
have no difficulty in saying that if it were legally separated,
the plaintiff had a sufficient possession to entitle him to
maintain trespass. The possession of the whole waste,
notwithstanding the right of common, remains in the lord,
and if he, in the manner warranted by the custom, transfers
the possession to the plaintiff, and the latter enters, then
he becomes possessed and acquires a lawful possession as
against the lord, and the right of the commoners to turn
their cattle over that land, as well as the residue of the

waste, is perfectly consistent with the right of possession being vested and perfected in him.

Then as to the right of the lord to inclose the land in question, and to grant a perfect title to the plaintiff, it was insisted, first, that the lord had an unlimited and unrestricted right (founded upon a custom in this particular manor) to abridge the rights of the commoners, and to confer in severalty upon any person, from time to time, such portions of the waste as he in his discretion should think fit. It seems to me that such a right is utterly inconsistent with an existing right of common, for the lord might by degrees inclose the whole of the waste and so annihilate the right of the commoners. *Badger* v. *Ford* (a) is an authority upon that point. But had there been no authority I should have thought that wherever it is once established that a right of common has existed from time immemorial, such privilege or custom in the lord cannot by law be supported, because it would be in destruction of that right of common. All the authorities which have been cited in support of such a right are distinguishable from the present case. The right claimed is to sever and take away permanently from the common a beneficial part of it, so as to deprive the commoner of any power or right over that part. In *Bateson* v. *Green* (b) there had been from time immemorial an usage for the lord to dig clay upon the waste, and that was held to be evidence to shew that when he granted out the right of common to the commoners, he reserved to himself the right of digging clay. The extent to which it had been carried in that case did not appear to be unreasonable. Lord *Kenyon,* in delivering judgment, intimated that there was no evidence to shew that the right had been more exercised of late years than formerly. Now the lord by digging for clay takes from the land a product of a particular species, but the land afterwards remains capable of yielding food fit for the feeding of cattle. Indeed it frequently happens that land, besides the

(a) 3 B. & A. 153.   (b) 5 T. R. 411.

support which it yields for the food of man or of cattle, has within it some valuable product, as marl or limestone, which it is desirable for the owner of the waste to obtain; and it is not unreasonable that the lord of a manor when he grants rights on that land should reserve to himself the right of taking such marl or limestone. But when he takes them, he does not permanently deprive the commoners of that benefit which they are entitled to derive from the surface of that part of the land from which the marl or limestone is so taken. A case of that sort is distinguishable from the present, because the lord still leaves for the benefit of the commoner something capable of yielding food for his cattle. The user of the privilege by the lord from time to time is evidence to shew that he reserved that right to himself, and the nature of the substance which is taken from the earth shews that such reservation was not unreasonable. The exercise of such a right will no doubt interfere with the privilege of the commoners during the time the produce is taken from the earth, and until the surface reproduces pasturage. But the distinction between that case and the present is, that here the consumer is wholly and permanently deprived of the benefit of a quantity of land, whereas in that case the land was only taken away for a certain period. The case of *Clarkson* v. *Woodhouse* is distinguishable from the present. The question in that case was on the record, and came on for argument on motion in arrest of judgment. That was an action of trespass for breaking and entering the plaintiff's close in *Stalmine* in the county of *Lancaster*. The defendant by his pleas claimed, in right of an ancient messuage in *Stalmine*, common of pasture and of turbary. The plaintiff relied upon a grant of parcel of the waste. The right claimed by the defendant would be exercised on those portions of the waste which yielded pasture and turbary respectively. When the grants of common were first made, it is probable the pasturage would be confined to those places which yielded pasture, and that that quantity was deemed sufficient for the cattle of all the commoners. The right stated in the replication was not to withdraw from the commoners any portion of the pasture or turf land, but that the owner should assign to particular individuals a particular portion of moss land, and that they should work upon that and not elsewhere until all the turbary should be exhausted, and then that the owner might inclose. The words are " so long as any turbary remained, or should remain, in such respective moss-dales; and when and so often as the turbary of such moss-dales so assigned, &c. had been got and cleared therefrom by such digging and getting of turves for the purposes aforesaid, the owners of the said waste for the time being for all the time whereof, &c. had inclosed and approved, &c. to themselves all such moss-dales, or parts of the said waste called *Stalmine Moss*, as had been or should be cleared, to hold the same so inclosed at their pleasure in severalty for ever afterwards, freed and discharged from all common of pasture and turbary thereon." The fair meaning of the custom to inclose stated upon that record seems to me to be, that when the land was exhausted and incapable of producing any more turf, the owner of the same might inclose, for until it was so rendered incapable of yielding more turf, it could not be truly said that the turbary was all got and cleared therefrom; and if that be the true meaning of the custom there stated, then it only amounts to this, that when particular portions of the land which have been destined for turbary ceased to have the power of producing turbary, the owner should be at liberty to take that portion to himself. That case, therefore, is distinguishable from the present, because the owner of the waste there did not take away from the commoners any thing which had been originally appropriated to them for the purposes of turbary or pasture. In *Folkard* v. *Hemmett*(a) the grant of the soil was made by the lord, and with the consent of the homage. Now the homage are persons associated together at the lord's court, (at which all the tenants of the manor may attend), to act as between the

(a) 5 T. R. 417.

lord and his tenants. Being tenants themselves it is not very likely that they will lean unfairly towards the lord, and if the homage say therefore that a grant shall be made, (assuming that the lord has a right to grant wherever there is more land than is necessary for the purpose of the commoners,) it may be reasonably presumed that the homage have given their consent to the grant only when satisfied that the land granted may be taken by the grantor, without interfering with the rights of the commoners. And on the other hand it may be fairly presumed that the homage would never consent to any part of the common being taken away from the tenants, unless they were satisfied that sufficient remained for the commoners. The case, therefore, is distinguishable from the present; there the grant was made with the consent of the homage, here it is done by the act of the lord himself. I have no difficulty in saying that in my judgment the lord has rights of his own reserved upon the waste. I do not say subservient to, but concurrent with, the rights of the commoners. He has the right to stock the common, and to every benefit to be derived from the soil not inconsistent with the rights of the commoners. And when it is ascertained that there is more common than is necessary for the cattle of the commoners, the lord, as it seems to me, is entitled to take that for his own purposes. That is the principle upon which the statute of *Merton* is founded. The lord has a right to approve not as lord, but as owner of the soil. *Glover v. Lane* (a) shews that the owner of the soil, whether lord or not, may make such an approvement. It seems to me that the lord's right is this; he may approve, provided he leaves sufficiency of common of pasturage for all the cattle which are entitled to feed upon it. The common may originally have been destined for a definite number of cattle, or for all cattle levant and couchant upon certain lands. Many of these rights may be extinguished, or the common itself may produce so much more herbage, that a smaller portion of that

(a) 3 T. R. 445.

common may be sufficient for depasturing the cattle of the persons entitled than when it was originally destined to that purpose. Now whenever that is the case, I think that the lord has a right to inclose; but in order to justify making the inclosure, it is incumbent upon him or his grantee, when the right to inclose is questioned, to shew that there is sufficiency of common left. In all the cases in which the right of the lord to inclose has been stated on the record, there has been an allegation that he left sufficient common for the commoners. That was so in *Glover* v. *Lane* and in *Grant* v. *Gunner* (a). The commoner has a certain right over the whole of the waste, and when the lord abridges that right, he ought to shew that he has done that which the law requires him to do before he abridges the right of the commoner. And therefore I am of opinion that in this case it ought to have been submitted to the jury, whether there was or was not, at the time when the lord made the grant of the *locus in quo*, a sufficiency of common left for all the persons having rights of common upon the waste in question. The right of the lord to inclose must depend on the finding of the jury on that question. It is impossible for this Court, without knowledge what the fact is, to say whether the verdict ought to be entered for the plaintiff or for the defendants. It is not necessary to give an opinion upon the question whether there can be any approvement against a right of common of turbary. There are undoubtedly authorities to shew that the owners of the soil, generally speaking, cannot approve against such a right. In this manor, however, numerous instances of an exercise of the right have been shewn, and in all those instances persons having the right of common of turbary must have been excluded from the parts inclosed. These instances having been always submitted to, may establish that, at least in this manor, the right to approve does exist; and I think that such right may reasonably exist. Common of

turf to ....

(a) 1 Taunt, 435.

turbary must be enjoyed in respect of ancient messuages. Many of those ancient messuages may be destroyed and others not substituted, and it would be unreasonable that the whole of a waste should remain uninclosed so long as a single commoner, in respect of an ancient messuage, should continue to have a right to cut turves on the common. Without giving any distinct opinion on that point, it seems to me that in this case there was a sufficient evidence of a custom for the lord to inclose, to take this out of the general rule which is laid down with respect to common of turbary; and that, as against the common of turbary in this case, the lord may have a right to inclose. But inasmuch as the question whether a sufficiency of common of turbary or pasture was left for the commoner, and whether the turbary left was sufficiently near and convenient to that messuage in respect of which the right is claimed, has not been submitted to the jury, I think that there ought to be a new trial.

The other judges concurring,

Rule absolute.

Doe on the demise of JAMES PRING and JOHN ROBERTS
v. PEARSEY.

It is a presumption of law that waste land adjoining a road belongs to the owner of the adjoining inclosed land, whether freeholder, leaseholder, or copyholder.

EJECTMENT for a cottage and garden in the parish of *Taunton St. Mary Magdalen*, in the county of *Somerset*. Plea, not guilty. At the trial before *Burrough*, J. at the *Somersetshire* spring assizes, 1827, it appeared that the cottage in question had been built by the defendant's father in 1804 on a slip of waste land (by the side of the turnpike road) adjoining to inclosed land, which was copyhold, belonging to *John Roberts*, one of the lessors of the plaintiff, and which at the time of the serving of the ejectment

1827.

Doe
v.
Pearsey.

was in the occupation of his tenant, *James Pring*. There was no evidence to shew what number of acres the inclosed land contained. It was contended, that as the adjoining land belonged to *Roberts*, the *primâ facie* presumption was, that the waste between his land and the high road belonged also to him. On the other hand it was insisted that that presumption only took effect where the owner of the adjoining lands was a freeholder. The learned judge directed the jury to find for the plaintiff, but reserved liberty to the defendant to move to enter a nonsuit. A rule nisi having been obtained for that purpose,

F. Pollock and *C. F. Williams* now shewed cause, and *Erskine* and *Carter* were heard in support of the rule.

Bayley, J.—It is desirable that there should be one definite rule applicable to all cases of this description. Now it is a *primâ facie* presumption, that waste land on the sides, and the soil to the middle, of a highway, belongs to the owner of the adjoining freehold land. The rule is founded on a supposition that the proprietor of the adjoining land at some former period gave up to the public for passage all the land between his inclosure and the middle of the road. I think that rule applies, not only to freehold, but to copyhold lands also. There was no evidence to shew when the road was first made, but it was a turnpike road. If the road existed at the time when the copyhold was first granted, viz. from time immemorial, the right of property in the road and the waste adjoining, might have remained in the lord. But if the road were taken out of the land after the copyhold was granted, the presumption would be that the property in the road and the waste adjoining was in the copyholder. Now I think we ought not to presume that the road in question was made before the time of legal memory. The probability is that it was made long since. And if the road was made within the time of legal memory, then the *primâ facie* presumption is,

1827.

Doe
v.
Pearsey.

that the waste land adjoining the road belonged to *Roberts*, the copyhold tenant of the land next adjoining, and not to the lord. The rule for entering a nonsuit must therefore be discharged.

The other judges concurring,

Rule discharged.

INDEX

TO THE

PRINCIPAL MATTERS.

ABATEMENT.

See PRACTICE, 5.

Where a *certiorari* was granted on the application of two parties, and one of them died before the matter came on for argument, the Court heard the case notwithstanding. *Rex* v. *Yorkshire, N. R. Justices, H.* 7 & 8 G. 4. **Page 204**

ACCEPTANCE.

See BILL OF EXCHANGE.

ACCEPTOR.

See BILL OF EXCHANGE.

ACT OF BANKRUPTCY.

See ASSIGNEES, 2.

ACTIONABLE WORDS.

See PLEADING, 1.

ADMISSION.

An admission of a debt due, made by a debtor, after arrest, but before an escape, is evidence against the Marshal in an action for the escape. *Rogers* v. *Jones, T.* 8 G. 4. **878**

AD QUOD DAMNUM.

See NAVIGATION, 1.

ADVOWSON.

See CLERGY.

AFFIDAVIT.

See BAIL, 2.—DEPUTY.—INDICT-MENT.—QUO WARRANTO.

Affidavits are not admissible to aggravate punishment upon a conviction for felony, though the record is removed into this Court. *Rex* v. *Ellis, M.* 7 G. 4. **Page 174**

AGENT.

See VENDOR AND VENDEE, 7.

If the agent of the grantee of annuities renders accounts crediting his principal with instalments, which he states have not been received, but charging commission, and afterwards paying the balance, as if they had been received; the jury may infer an agreement by the agent to be responsible for such instalments, in case they were not paid by the grantors of the annuities. *Shaw* v. *Woodcock, T.* 8 G. 4. **889**

AGREEMENT.

See EVIDENCE, 13.—LANDLORD AND TENANT, 1.—LEASE, 2, 3.

1. By writing not under seal *A.* agrees, in consideration of 7000*l.*, to present the nominee of *B.* to the next turn of a rectory, and to furnish an abstract of title to, and execute a conveyance of, the next presentation to *B.*:—Such a writing

is only an agreement, not a conveyance, and does not require an *ad valorem* stamp. *Wilmot* v. *Wilkinson*, *E.* 8 *G.* 4. Page 620

2. Afterwards, *A.*, by consent of *B.*, agrees to sell the next presentation to *C.* for 7,500*l.*, on having such title as *A.* had received, *C.* paying to *B.*, absolutely, on a day certain, the odd 500*l. A.* furnishes an abstract of such title as he had received, which *C.* refuses to accept, and no conveyance is tendered to him. *B.* sues *C.* for the 500*l.* There is a good consideration to support the action, and *A.* having done all that his contract required, it is no answer to the action that no conveyance was tendered to *C. Id.* *ibid.*

ALIEN ENEMY.

See PATENT, 3.

AMENDMENT.

See CERTIORARI—CORONER, 1, 2.

Where a bill was filed against the Marshal for an escape, entitled generally of the term, and alleging the escape to have taken place on the 15th day of the same term, to which there was a special demurrer, that the cause of action had relation to the first day of the term, the Court allowed the plaintiff to amend his bill by specially entitling it, upon payment of costs, although it appeared by affidavit that the prisoner was recaptured before the motion was made for leave to amend. *Brazier* v. *Jones*, *H.* 7 & 8 *G.* 4. 349

ANNUITY.

1. An annuity deed need not be executed before the memorial thereof is inrolled, if the memorial is inrolled within thirty days from the *date* mentioned in the deed. *Buckeridge* v. *Flight*, *M.* 7 *G.* 4. 113

2. In the memorial of an annuity deed, it is sufficient to set forth all the names of the subscribing witnesses, without specifying which party's execution the witnesses respectively attested. *Buckeridge* v. *Flight*, *M.* 7 *G.* 4. Page 113

3. Where a married man, living with his wife, cohabited with a single woman, who knew that he was married, and at the termination of the illicit intercourse, gave her a bond to secure the payment of an annuity for the support of herself and two children, the offspring of their cohabitation:—Held, that an action at law might be maintained on the bond to recover the arrears of the annuity. *Nye* v. *Moseley*, *M.* 7 *G.* 4. 165

4. Where the grantor of an annuity, in pursuance of an agreement with the broker, received the whole consideration money, and immediately afterwards returned 15*l.* per cent. for law expenses and brokerage, and the amount of one year's annuity, which was deposited in a bank and drawn out quarterly to pay the annuitants:—Held, that this was an illegal retainer of part of the consideration money, within the meaning of 53 *G.* 3, c. 141, s. 6, and after the lapse of eight years the Court set aside the annuity on paying principal and interest on the money advanced, together with reasonable expenses, although the annuitants were not directly privy to the retainer, and although one of them was dead before the application made. *Finley* v. *Gardner*, *H.* 7 & 8 *G.* 4. 207

5. An indenture, releasing one annuity and granting another, is well described in the memorial as a "*grant* of an annuity," within 53 *G.* 3, c. 141, s. 2. *Crowther* v. *Wentworth*, *H.* 7 & 8 *G.* 4. 286

6. "Grant of annuity" is a sufficient description in the memorial of an annuity deed containing special covenants. *Browne* v. *Lee*, *E.* 8 *G.* 4. 700

7. A surety may sue a co-surety for payments made by the former on account of an annuity, notwithstanding the bankruptcy and certificate of the latter; a surety not being a creditor within the 49 G. 3, c. 121, s. 17. *Browne* v. *Lee, E.* 8 G. 4. Page 700

8. Where the grantor of an annuity assigned it, together with all the securities, for a valuable consideration, to *A.*, part of which belonged to *B*, one of the co-sureties for the payment of the annuity, and it was agreed by deed between *A.* and *B.* that the former should retain out of the annual payments sufficient to pay him the principal sum advanced, together with interest, and that when he should have been paid principal and interest, the annuity should be for the benefit of *B.*:—Held, that the annuity did not thereby become extinguished, and that the co-sureties still remained liable to contribution to *A.*, although *B.* had assigned stock for further securing the payment of the annuity. *Id.* *ibid.*

9. *A.* purchased and paid for an annuity for his life, which was regularly paid up to the time of his death. No memorial was inrolled:—Held, that his executrix could not recover back any part of the consideration money. *Davis* v. *Bryan, E.* 8 G. 4. 726

APPEAL.
See County Rate.

APPRENTICE.
See Pleading, 6.

ARBITRATOR.
See Award.—Money Paid, 2.

ARREST.
See Constable, 2.—Deputy.—Practice, 2.

1. Where a yeoman warder of the

Tower of *London* was arrested and put in special bail, and thereby obtained his liberation, the Court refused to decide on motion his right to be exempt from arrest, even though the terms of his warrant gave him that privilege. *Bidgood* v. *Davies, M.* 7 G. 4. Page 153

2. In an action for maliciously arresting and imprisoning plaintiff until he gave bail, it was proved that in consequence of a verbal message sent, plaintiff went voluntarily to the bailiff's house, and gave a bail-bond:—Held, that this was not an arrest and imprisonment to sustain an action on the case against the original plaintiff, although the latter had no cause of action. *Berry* v. *Adamson, E.* 8 G. 4. Page 558

ASSIGNEES.
See Bankrupt. — Money Paid.— Set-off.—Sheriff, 1.—Warrant of Attorney.

1. Where assignees, under a second commission of bankrupt, have refused to interfere, and the bankrupt has not paid 15s. in the pound, but has effects whereon to levy, a creditor may take out execution upon a judgment recovered before the second commission. *Austin* v. *Denniford, E.* 8 G. 4. 600

2. The assignees of a bankrupt, though neither of them is petitioning creditor, cannot avail themselves of an act of bankruptcy of which the petitioning creditor would be estopped from availing himself. *Tope* v. *Hockin, T.* 8 G. 4. 881

ASSIGNMENT.
See Annuity, 8.—Landlord and Tenant, 1.—Sale, 1.

ASSUMPSIT.
See Annuity, 9.—Evidence, 10.— Money Paid.—Partners, 3.— Pleading, 4.—Tolls, 1.

ATTORNEY.

See AWARD, 1.—BAIL, 2.—EVIDENCE, 2, 9.—PRACTICE, 7.—TRESPASS.

" To attending defendant to a lock-up-house, filling up a bail-bond, and obtaining his release," is a taxable item in an attorney's bill, as a charge at law, within 2 *G*. 3, c. 23, s. 23. *Fearne* v. *Wilson, M. 7 G. 4.*   *Page* 157

AWARD.

See COSTS, 1.

1. Where all matters in difference between parties to a suit in equity, some of whom were *infants* represented by their next friends, were referred to arbitration by an order of the Vice-Chancellor, " with the consent of *the attornies* of the parties in the *said suit*," and an action was brought upon the award:—Held, in error, that the award was not binding on the infants. *Biddell* v. *Dowse, H. 7 & 8 G. 4.*   404

2. Where an award is sought to be set aside on the ground that the arbitrator has not determined all matters in difference:—Held, that if the affidavit, coupled with a rule nisi, discloses the objections to the award, it is a sufficient compliance with the rule *E. T. 2 G. 4. Rawsthorne* v. *Arnold, E. 8 G. 4.*   556

3. A motion to set aside an award, made under an order of *nisi prius*, must be made within the time allowed for moving for a new trial, unless a sufficient excuse is shewn for the delay. *Id.*   *ibid.*

BAIL.

See ARREST.—PRACTICE, 2, 6.

1. Time allowed to add and justify bail by habeas corpus, where one of the bail, of whom notice had been given, was suddenly taken ill. *Gullbank's Bail, M. 7 G. 4.*   6

2. Where time was applied for to send an affidavit of justification into

the country, to amend a mistake in the jurat, the Court made the attorney pay the costs of the application. *Shillitoe's Bail, M. 7 G. 4.*   *Page* 6

BANKERS.

See PARTNERS, 4.

BANKRUPT.

See ANNUITY, 7.—ASSIGNEES.—MONEY PAID.—PLEADING, 5.—PRACTICE, 7.—SET-OFF.—SHERIFF, 1.

1. A consignee ordered goods to be delivered to him at his own warehouse, and on their arrival at the warehouse of the carrier, took samples of them to his own warehouse, and left the bulk, for his own convenience, at the carrier's, and became bankrupt:—Held, that the transitus was at an end; that the property in the goods had vested in the consignee; and that his assignees were entitled to recover them from the consignor, who had stopped them in the hands of the carrier. *Foster* v. *Frampton, M. 7 G. 4.* 109

2. If a bankrupt is sued upon a cause of action arising before his bankruptcy, and obtains his certificate pending the suit, he must plead it *puis darein continuance;* and if he does not, and judgment is obtained and an action thereon brought against him, he cannot plead his certificate. *Todd* v. *Maxfield, M. 7 G. 4.*   171

3. Where an act of parliament secured to certain persons, for a further term, the benefit arising from a patent for making a machine, with a proviso that it should become void if they should transfer or assign their interest therein to any persons *exceeding the number of five,* and two of the patentees became bankrupt:—Held, that the assignment of their interests to their assignees for the benefit of creditors, though the number exceeded twenty, was

not within the proviso. *Bloxham* v. *Elsee, H. 7 & 8 G. 4.*   *Page* 215

4. A debtor appointing a time and place to meet and pay his creditor, and failing to keep his appointment, must be presumed, in the absence of evidence to the contrary, to have absented himself with intent to delay his creditor, and thereby commits an act of bankruptcy; and in an action by a bankrupt against his assignees to try the validity of the commission, the plaintiff must give evidence to rebut that presumption, or he cannot maintain the action. *Widger* v. *Browning, H. 7 & 8 G. 4.*   306

5. A person having the security of a warrant of attorney for his debt, entered up judgment by *non sum informatus*, and took out execution against the goods of his debtor, and by bill of sale from the sheriff took possession of the same. In a few days afterwards the debtor became bankrupt, and the assignees re-took the goods. In trover, Held, that the plaintiff was not a creditor having security for his debt within 6 G. 4, c. 16, s. 108, and was entitled to recover back the goods. *Weymer* v. *Kemble, E. 8 G. 4.*   511

6. A *general* notice of defendant's intention to dispute the *bankruptcy* in an action by assignees of a bankrupt, is not sufficient under 6 G. 4, c. 16, s. 90. *Trimley* v. *Uwins, E. 8 G. 4.*   548

BASTARD.

One magistrate has no power to commit a single woman for refusing to be examined respecting the father of her bastard child. *Martin, ex parte, M. 7 G. 4.*   65

BATH.

See Trover.

BILL OF EXCHANGE.

See Evidence, 5.

1. If a negotiable instrument for the payment of money is framed in such equivocal terms as to render it ambiguous whether it be a bill of exchange or a promissory note, the holder has the option of treating it as either, as against the maker. *Edis* v. *Bury, E. 8 G. 4. Page* 492

2. If the indorser of a bill is compelled by the holder to pay him part of the amount, he may recover, it back from the acceptor in an action for money paid to his use. *Pownal* v. *Ferrand, E. 8 G. 4.*   603

3. The statute 1 & 2 G. 4, c. 78, embraces *all* bills payable at a particular place, whether made so payable by the drawer or by the acceptor. *Fayle* v. *Bird, E. 8 G. 4.*   639

4. A bill drawn payable in *London*, and accepted payable *there*, without adding "only and not otherwise or elsewhere," is accepted *generally* within the statute, and need not be presented for payment in *London*. *Id.*   *ibid.*

5. By the custom of merchants the indorsee of a lost bill of exchange cannot recover at law the amount against the acceptor, although the loss was after the bill became due, and although the acceptor was offered an indemnity. *Hansard* v. *Robinson, T. 8 G. 4.*   860

BISHOP.

See Execution, 1.

BROKER.

See Annuity, 4. — Evidence, 3. — Frauds, Statute of. — Lien. — Partners, 3.

A sworn broker of the city of *London* is in the nature of a public agent, and, therefore, in an action against him for negligence in making a contract, the Court will, on motion, compel him to produce his books, for the purpose of enabling the plaintiff to inspect them and take a copy of the contract. *Browning* v. *Aylwin, T. 8 G. 4.*   801

CANALS.

See POOR RATE, 5, 6.

In an action by a canal company, bound by act of parliament to keep the banks of the canal in good repair, against the owner of adjoining land for excavating his land, whereby the banks fell in, the plaintiffs cannot recover without shewing that the banks were in good repair when they fell in. *Stafford Canal Co.* v. *Hallen, H.* 7 & 8 *G.* 4. *Page* 266

CARRIER.

See BANKRUPT, 1.

CASE.

See PLEADING, 4.

CERTIORARI.

See ABATEMENT.

A return to a *certiorari* signed by justices, without their descriptions as such, and without their seals, is bad; but the Court will send it back to them for amendment. *Rex* v. *Kenyon, E.* 8 *G.* 4. 694

CLERGY.

See LEASE, 1.—SEQUESTRATION.—TITHES.

A prebendary, who had the advowson of a rectory in right of his prebend, died while the church was vacant:—Held, that his administratrix had the right of presentation for that turn. *Rennell* v. *Bishop of Lincoln, T.* 8 *G.* 4. 810

COAL MINES.

See NAVIGATION.—POOR RATE, 2, 3.

COMMITMENT.

See BASTARD.—JUSTICES, 1.

COMMON.

See COPYHOLD.

COPYHOLD.

COMPULSORY PAYMENT.

See MONEY PAID, 2.

CONSIDERATION.

See AGREEMENT, 2.—ANNUITY, 3, 4. PATENT, 2.

CONSTABLE.

See NOTICE OF ACTION.

1. A constable, having a warrant authorising the seizure of certain specified goods alleged to have been stolen, seized those goods and others not specified in the warrant. The latter goods were not likely to furnish evidence of the identity of the former:—Held, that he was liable in an action of trespass, though a copy of the warrant had not been demanded of him, pursuant to 24 *G.* 2, c. 44, s. 6. *Crozier* v. *Cundy, H.* 7 & 8 *G.* 4. *Page* 224

2. A constable may arrest a person upon a reasonable suspicion of felony, and take him before a magistrate, although no felony has in fact been committed. *Beckwith* v. *Philby, E.* 8 *G.* 4. 487

3. A high constable, by the direction of justices, employed and paid special and ordinary constables to suppress riots at an election:—Held, that the sums so paid were extraordinary expenses incurred by the high constable within 41 *G.* 3, c. 78, s. 2, which the justices might make an order upon the treasurer to reimburse him. *Rex* v. *Leicester Justices, T.* 8 *G.* 4. *Page* 772

CONVERSION.

See VENDOR AND VENDEE, 2.

CONVICTION.

See EXCISE.

COPYHOLD.

See CUSTOM.—EVIDENCE, 12.—HERIOT.—WASTE.

1. *Quære*, whether the lord of a manor

may, in general, make grants of the
waste, upon which the copyholders
have a right of common, provided
he leave sufficient for the copyholders. *Arlett* v. *Ellis*, T. 8 G. 4.
Page 897

2. A special custom that he may,
leaving sufficient for the copyholders, would be good. *Id.* ibid.

3. *Semble*, that a special custom that
he may, without limit, would be
bad. *Id.* ibid.

CORONER.

1. A coroner's inquisition can be
amended in matters of *form only*.
Rex v. *Evett*, H. 7 & 8 G. 4. 237

2. Omitting the name of the place
where the death happened, or the
body was found; omitting the names
of the jurors in the body of the inquisition; inserting their christian
names by initials or abbreviations;
stating the death to have been
caused by horses the property of *A.*,
B. and Co., they being in fact the
property of *A.* and *B.* only; are all
defects of *substance*, which cannot
be supplied by amendment, and for
which an inquisition may be quashed. *Id.* ibid.

3. Trespass will not lie against a coroner for turning a person out of
a room in which he is about to hold
an inquest. *Garnett* v. *Ferrand*, E.
8 G. 4. 657

CORPORATION.

See JUSTICES, 1.—QUO WARRANTO, 1.

1. *Quo warranto* information, for
usurping the office of justice within
the borough of *S.* Plea, that defendant was elected at a corporate
meeting where a majority of the
aldermen and capital burgesses were
present. Replication, that at the
supposed election five capital burgesses (naming them) and no others
were present, and that they were
not the major part of the capital
burgesses. Rejoinder, that at the

election, besides the five capital
burgesses named in the replication,
there were present *K.* and *T.*, then
being capital burgesses, and that the
five capital burgesses named in the
replication, together with *K.* and *T.*,
were the major part of the capital
burgesses. Surrejoinder, that *K.*
and *T.*, before the election of defendant, had been elected, admitted
into, and exercised the office of
alderman, and at the election of defendant were present as aldermen,
and that before defendant's election
two other persons were elected and
admitted as capital burgesses in the
room and stead of *K.* and *T.* Rebutter, that at the election of *K.*
and *T.* as aldermen, the major part
of the aldermen were not assembled,
and that after the election of *K.*
and *T.*, and before the election of
defendant, and while *K.* and *T.*
exercised the office of alderman, *quo
warranto* informations were filed
against them, and judgment of ouster given; with a denial that *K.*
and *T.* were ever aldermen:—Held,
on demurrer, that *K.* and *T.* were
not good capital burgesses, though
they had been ousted from the office
of alderman; and judgment for the
crown. *Rex* v. *Hubball*, M. 7 G. 4.
Page 143

2. A corporator who has voted at an
election of corporate officers, is not
a competent relator to impeach that
election, on the ground of an objection to the presiding officer; at *least*
without shewing that he was ignorant of the objection when he voted
at the election. *Rex* v. *Slythe*, H.
7 & 8 G. 4. 181

3. The like point. *Rex* v. *Lane*, and
Rex v. *Cobbold*, H. 7 & 8 G. 4. 183

4. The title of a person having an
inchoate right to be admitted a free
burgess of a borough, cannot be
impeached on the ground of a defect
of title in the officer by whom he
was admitted. *Rex* v. *Slythe*, H.
7 & 8 G. 4. 226

COSTS.

See AMENDMENT.——ATTORNEY.——
BAIL, 2.—PARTNERS, 2.—PROHI-
BITION.

1. A cause and all matters in difference were referred to an arbitrator,
the costs of the cause *to abide the
event of the award.* The arbitrator
found 45*l.* to be due to the plaintiff
on a balance of accounts, but as the
defendant had been arrested without
reasonable or probable cause for a
larger sum than was due, he awarded
him 20*l.* as a compensation for the
unlawful arrest, and directed a verdict to be entered for the plaintiff
for 25*l.*, the difference:—Held, that
the defendant was not entitled to
costs under 43 *G.* 3, c. 46, s. 3.
Thompson v. *Atkinson, H.* 7 & 8
G. 4.　　　　　　　　*Page* 347
2. The Court, without a judge's certificate, will not enter a suggestion
on the roll to deprive the plaintiff
of his costs under 5 *G.* 4, c. 106,
in an action where the defendant
resided in *Wales* at the time of
serving process, although the sum
recovered is under 50*l.* *Mortimer*
v. *Harris, E.* 8 *G.* 4.　　　534

COUNTY RATE.

Where a county rate is made under a
local act giving a limited right of
appeal, parties aggrieved have still
the unlimited right of appeal given
by the general act, 55 *G.* 3, c. 51,
s. 14. *Rex* v. *Bucks Justices, T.*
8 *G.* 4.　　　　　　　　777

COVENANT.

See PLEADING, 3, 6.

A covenant that defendant has not
permitted or suffered to be done any
act whereby the estate was incum-
bered, is not broken by his *consenting* to an act which he *could not
prevent.* *Hobson* v. *Middleton, H.*
7 & 8 *G.* 4.　　　　　　249

CUSTOM.

See COPYHOLD.—EVIDENCE, 12.

Semble, that a custom to present a surrender of copyhold lands for enrolment within an indefinite time, is
an unreasonable custom. *Doe* v.
Callaway, E. 8 *G.* 4.　　*Page* 518

CUSTOM OF MERCHANTS.

See BILL OF EXCHANGE.

DEED.

See AGREEMENT, 1. — ANNUITY.—
EVIDENCE, 8, 13.—HUSBAND AND
WIFE, 1.

DEPUTY.

A person deputed to *take affidavits only,*
is not a " deputy" within 12 *Geo.* 1,
c. 29, s. 2, which requires, before
arrest in an inferior Court, an affidavit of debt to be made " before the
officer who *issues the process, or his
deputy.*" *Rogers* v. *Jones, T.* 8 *G.* 4.
878

DEVISE.

See DISCLAIMER.

1. *J. L.* devised to his son *J. H. L.*
for life; remainder to trustees to
preserve contingent remainders; remainder to the *second,* third, fourth,
and *all and every other* the son and
sons of his said son *J. H. L.* in tail
male, according to seniority of age
and priority of birth. There was
no limitation to the *first* son of
J. H. L. The declaration of the
trust contained a provision to raise
money for the daughters of *J. H. L.*
on failure of issue male of his body;
and the will also provided that in
case *J. H. L.* should have any child
or children other than and except
an eldest or only son, then *J. H. L.*
might raise money for portions:—
Held, that the *first* son of *J. H. L.*
took no estate under the will. *Langston* v. *Pole, H.* 7 & 8 *G.* 4.　298
2. Testator willed as follows: "I give
and bequeath to my son *W.* 30*l.*

extra more, than any other of my
sons; and likewise unto *A. B.* my
wife the whole of my effects during
her life: also the freehold estate
which I now enjoy I bequeath as
follows: *A. B.* my daughter, *J. B.*
and *I. B.* my sons, likewise *B. B.*
otherwise *N.*, all the last mentioned
names to be all equal sums, whatever it may amount to, except any
of the aforementioned should die,
then their shares to be equally divided among the other that is surviving:"—Held, that the freehold
estate passed to the four devisees
last mentioned, and that *B. B.* otherwise *N.* having been ousted by *A. B.*
might maintain ejectment for one
undivided fourth part. *Roe v. Burn,*
H. 7 & 8 G. 4. *Page* 441

3. Testator being seised in fee of freehold and copyhold lands, and having
also leasehold for lives and for years,
and other personal property, devised
and bequeathed the same to trustees,
their heirs and assigns, habendum
in trust for and during all testator's
right, title, and estate therein, upon
trust, first to pay debts and funeral
expenses, and then to apply the annual income to the use of his two
nieces for their lives; and after their
decease there were devises to their
grandchildren, male and female, in
terms so ambiguous and contradictory, as to make it doubtful what
equitable interest the grandchildren
took:—Held, that the trustees took
an estate in fee in the freehold and
copyhold lands, and an absolute interest in the leasehold for lives and
years, and that the devises over,
though full of difficulties, did not
make the will void for uncertainty.
Houston v. Hughes, *E. 8 G. 4.* 464

4. Testator, after giving some pecuniary legacies, proceeded thus: "All
my property and effects of all claims
I shall have, I give to my brother;
but my mother is at liberty to give
100*l.* of my property where she
pleases:"—Held, that the testator's

real estate passed to his brother.
Doe v. Morgan, *E. 8 G. 4.*
Page 633

DISCLAIMER.

1. *Quære,* Whether a disclaimer of
lands devised can be by parol. *Doe*
v. *Smyth, M. 7 G. 4.* 136
2. A devisee of lands refused to take
them under the will, but claimed to
be entitled to them as heir at law:
—Held, no disclaimer, and that he
might afterwards recover the lands
as devisee. *Id.* *ibid.*

DISTRESS.

See EXCISE.—VARIANCE.

DISTRICT PARISHES.

A parish cannot be legally separated
into districts for the relief and maintenance of the poor, unless it cannot
otherwise reap the full benefit of
the statute 43 *Eliz.* c. 2. *Bastock*
v. *Ridgway, E. 8 G. 4.* 585

DOCKS.

See POOR RATE, 7.

DURHAM.

See EXECUTION.

EJECTMENT.

See DEVISE, 2.—MARRIAGE SETTLE-
MENT.—WASTE.

1. Where *A.* has been tenant of premises, and upon his quitting them
B. takes possession, the legal presumption, until the contrary appear,
is that *B.* came in as assignee of *A.*;
and a notice to quit served upon *B.*
will sustain an ejectment against *A.*
Doe v. Williams, M. 7 G. 4. 30
2. A person who held glebe lands as
tenant to one incumbent, and continued in possession under his successor, without disturbance, must
be presumed to hold as tenant to
the latter, and cannot be dispos-
sessed without a notice to quit.
Doe v. Somerville, M. 7 G. 4. 100

ERROR.

See AWARD, 1.—PRACTICE, 6.

ESCAPE.

See ADMISSION.—AMENDMENT.

EVIDENCE.

See ADMISSION.—AFFIDAVIT.—BANK-
RUPT, 4.—BROKER.—CANALS.—
CORPORATION, 2.—EJECTMENT.—
FRAUDS, STATUTE OF.—LIMITA-
TION OF ACTIONS.—PLEADING, 2.—
POLICY OF INSURANCE.—SHIP, 1.
—STAMP.—TITHES, 1.—VARI-
ANCE.—VENDOR AND VENDEE, 2.
—WASTE.

1. A ship sailing in 1821 for her port
of destination, and never arriving,
but reported a few days after her
departure to have foundered, crew
surviving, may reasonably be presumed to have been lost by perils
of the sea, in absence of proof to
the contrary, and the assured on
goods is not bound to call any of the
crew, assuming them to have survived the loss of the ship.   *Koster
v. Reid, M. 7 G. 4.   Page 2*

2. Attorney for lessor of plaintiff in
ejectment obtained from defendant
an existing lease to him of the premises in question, for the purpose
of preventing defendant from setting
it up as a defence to the action, and
afterwards produced it at the trial,
pursuant to notice from defendant:
—Held, that he thereby admitted
the lease, and that it might be read
in evidence on the part of defendant, without proof of its execution.
Doe v. Hemming, M 7 G. 4.   15

3. The signed entry of a contract in
a broker's book is not, of necessity,
the only evidence to render the contract binding within the Statute of
Frauds. *Goom v. Aftalo, M. 7 G. 4.*
148

4. If several acts of felonious taking
property are so connected as to form
one transaction, evidence of each
taking may be received against the

prisoner, so as to establish the specific
felony charged in the indictment.
Rex v. Ellis, M. 7 G. 4.   Page 174

5. In an action by indorsee against
indorser of a bill of exchange, evidence of an acknowledgment of an
existing debt, and of a promise to
pay by the defendant, is admissible,
and sufficient to support an account
upon an account stated. *Wheatcliffe
v. Boardman, H. 7 & 8 G. 4.   248*

6. On the trial of an action for a malicious prosecution, the defendant
produced a witness to prove reasonable and probable cause for the prosecution, and there being nothing
to contradict his evidence:—Held,
that the judge was warranted in
acting upon it and directing a nonsuit, without leaving his credit to
the jury. *Davis v. Hardy, H. 7 &
8 G. 4.   380*

7. *A.* being possessed of two closes
divided by a fence and gate, sold
one to *B.*, and afterwards the other
to *C. C.* twice repaired the gate at
his own expense, after notice from
B. to do so, under a threat, in one
instance, of impounding his cattle
if he did not:—Held, that this was
some evidence to go to the jury, from
which they might presume a legal
obligation on the part of *B.* to repair the gate. *Boyle v. Tamlyn, H.
7 & 8 G. 4.   430*

8. Such an obligation may be declared
on, as being "in respect of the defendant's occupation," though evidenced by a deed. *Id.   ibid.*

9. On the trial of an action for an
attorney's bill it is not necessary to
prove notice to produce the bill delivered before action brought; it is
sufficient to give an examined copy
in evidence. *Colling v. Treweek,
H. 7 & 8 G. 4.   456*

10. A person having title to land sued
for use and occupation against *A.*,
who had received possession from a
third possession:—Held, that *A.*'s
declaration, "I don't consider the
land as yours, but prove the right,

EXCISE.

EXECUTION.

See SHERIFF.

EXECUTOR.

FACTOR.

FISH-MARKET.

FORFEITURE.

FORGERY.

FRANCHISE.

FRAUDS, *Statute of.*

FREE WARREN.

Grouse are not birds of warren. *Duke of Devonshire* v. *Lodge*, T. 8 G. 4.
Page 875

FREIGHT.

See Ship, 1.

GAME.

See Free Warren.

GRANT.

See Annuity.—Copyhold.

HACKNEY COACHES.

A paving act authorised the commissioners to " direct and regulate" the hackney-coach stands within their district:—Held, that they might remove a stand altogether, if it obstructed a public street. *Rex* v. *Rawlinson*, M. 7 G. 4.
7

HARBOUR.

See Mandamus, 4, 5.

HERIOT.

The creation of a tenancy in common in a copyhold tenement held by heriot custom, entitles the lord to a heriot from each of the tenants in common; but if the several tenancies are reunited in the same person, the lord is entitled to one heriot only. *Holloway* v. *Berkeley*, M. 7 & G. 4.
83

HIGHWAYS.

See Petit Sessions.—Poor Rate, 8.—Sessions, 1.—Waste.

An order for stopping up an unnecessary footway under 55 G. 3, c. 68, s. 2, must state distinctly the parish in which the footway lies, must describe its length and breadth, and, *semble*, must order it to be sold as well as stopped up. *Rex* v. *Kenyon*, E. 8 G. 4.
694

HUSBAND AND WIFE.

See Practice, 5.

1. Where husband and wife agreed by deed to separate immediately and live apart, the former to allow the latter a maintenance, and they did not in fact separate immediately, but lived together several months afterwards, apparently as man and wife:—Held, that the deed was void. *Hindley* v. *Marquis of Westmeath*, H. 7 & 8 G. 4.
Page 851

2. If a wife lives apart from her husband against his wish, and he is willing to maintain her in his own house, he is not liable even for necessaries contracted for by her during the separation. *Id.*
ibid.

INDICTMENT.

See Evidence, 4.

1. In an indictment for perjury it is sufficient to state that the person who administered the oath had competent authority to do so, without setting out the nature of his authority. *Rex* v. *Callanan*, M. 7 G. 4.
97

2. If an indictment assigns perjury upon several parts of an affidavit, and sets them out as continuous, though other matters, not set out, intervene in the affidavit, this is not a fatal variance. *Id.*
ibid.

INFANT.

See Award, 1.

INFERIOR COURT.

See Deputy.

INQUISITION.

See Coroner.

INSOLVENT DEBTOR.

See Warrant of Attorney.

Where a defendant is arrested for a debt in respect of which he has been discharged under an insolvent act, and gives a bail-bond, the Court will order the bail-bond to be delivered up to be cancelled. *Norton* v. *Moseley, M.* 7 *G.* 4.

Page 107

JOINT STOCK COMPANY.

1. By the *Thames Tunnel* Act, 5 *G.* 4, c. 156, s. 23, it was enacted, "that the persons who had *subscribed*, or should thereafter *subscribe or advance money* towards making the tunnel, should pay the sums by them *subscribed* at the time and place, and in the manner directed by the company, and in case any such subscribers should neglect to pay, the company were empowered to sue for and recover the money." By s. 91, reciting that the probable expenses would amount to £160,000, and that more than four fifth parts of such expenses had already been *subscribed* by several persons under a contract, binding them, their heirs, &c. for payment of the sums so *subscribed* by them, it was enacted, that the whole £160,000 should be *subscribed* in like manner, before the act should be put in force:—Held, that the word *subscriber* in the act meant only those who had stipulated to pay, and not those who had paid money, and that a person whose name was inserted in the act, and who had paid a deposit on shares, but who had not signed the contract, was not a SUBSCRIBER within the act, nor liable to be sued by the company. *Thames Tunnel Company* v. *Sheldon, H.* 7 & 8 *G.* 4.

278

2. The deed of settlement of a joint-stock company provided, that the directors should without summons meet at their office once a week, on and at such day and hour as they should from time to time agree upon, and at such other times as they should from time to time be convened in manner hereinafter mentioned, or adjourned, and that three directors should be a board. Another clause authorised any three directors at any time to call a special board, by giving under their hands in writing three days' notice to the other directors, which notices were to be countersigned by the secretary, and to be sent by him two days prior to the time appointed for such meeting:—Held, that to constitute a good weekly meeting without summons, the day and hour must have been previously agreed upon by the directors, and consequently that a meeting of three directors without previous agreement on their part to meet on any fixed day or hour, was not a meeting duly convened within the meaning of the deed of settlement. *Moore* v. *Hammond, E.* 8 *G.* 4.

Page 482

JURISDICTION.

See JUSTICES, 1.—PETIT SESSIONS.—SESSIONS, 3.

JUSTICES.

See BASTARD.—CERTIORARI.—CONSTABLE, 3.—CORPORATION, 1.—HACKNEY COACHES.—HIGHWAYS.—NOTICE OF ACTION.—PETIT SESSIONS.—SESSIONS.

1. Where the justices of a borough had exclusive jurisdiction within the borough, but concurrent jurisdiction with the justices of the county over the liberties of the borough:—Held, that for offences committed within the liberties, they might commit to the county gaol, and try the prisoners at the borough sessions. *Rex* v. *Musson, M.* 7 *G.* 4.

172

2. The 2 *G.* 3, c. 28, which gives additional protection to justices in cases of actions brought against

them for any thing done *in pursu-ance of that act*, but which does not require notice of action, does not deprive them of their right to the notice required by the 24 *G.* 2, c. 44, which requires notice in cases of actions brought against justices for any thing done *in execution of their office*. *Rogers* v. *Broderip*, *H.* 7 *&* 8 *G.* 4. *Page* 194

2. Where in an action against a magistrate, under the 2 *G.* 3, c. 28, the plaintiff proved service of a notice not perfectly conformable with the requisites of the 24 *G.* 2, c. 44, and was thereupon nonsuited :—Held, that the nonsuit was right. *Id.* *ibid.*

LANDLORD AND TENANT.

See EXECUTION.—LEASE.

1. An agreement for the sale and assignment of a term in certain premises contained a stipulation that the vendee should "in the mean time and until the assignment was made, pay and allow to the vendor at the rate of £100 per annum, from the time of taking possession of the premises until the completion of the purchase :"—Held, that this constituted the relation of landlord and tenant, and that a half-yearly payment having become due before the completion of the purchase, the landlord was entitled to be first satisfied out of the proceeds of the tenant's effects sold under a *fi. fa.* *Saunders* v. *Musgrave*, *E.* 8 *G.* 4. 529

2. If the reservation of rent in a lease refers to a subsequent proviso, by which the rent is to be reduced if a certain event happens, the plaintiff, in an action of debt for the rent, must set out the reservation with the proviso in his declaration, although the event has not happened. *Vavasour* v. *Ormrod*, *E.* 8 *G.* 4. 597

LAW AND EQUITY.

See AWARD, 1.

1. An action at law cannot be maintained upon an order of a court of equity. *Biddell* v. *Dowse*, *H.* 7 & 8 *G.* 4. *Page* 404

2. This court will not give any opinion upon a case sent from Chancery containing questions upon equitable estates merely. *Houston* v. *Hughes*, *E.* 8 *G.* 4. 464

LEASE.

See EJECTMENT, 2.—LANDLORD AND TENANT.

1. A lease by a rector of his glebe lands and other rectorial property, made between the years 1803 and 1816, while the 13 *Eliz.* c. 20, continued repealed, is valid. *Doe* v. *Somerville*, *M.* 7 *G.* 4. 100

2. *A.* agrees to grant *B.* a lease of a house as soon as he becomes possessed thereof, to bear date from 21st *December*, 1825, for fourteen or twenty-one years. At the date of the agreement the house was under a lease which would not expire till *Midsummer*, 1827 ; the legal estate being in trustees, first to pay debts, and secondly to pay an annuity to *T.*, and subject thereto, to the use of *A.* if he attained twenty-four. In *June*, 1825, after *A.* had attained twenty-four, but before the outstanding lease had expired, he and the trustees joined in a fresh lease to *C.* for twenty-three years :—Held, that *A.* was liable to an action before the expiration of the lease ; but that the damages would be only the value of a lease for so much of the term as would probably be subsisting when the lease did expire. *Ford* v. *Tiley*, *H.* 7 & 8 *G.* 4. 448

3. A lease contained a proviso, "that if the rent should be in arrear for twenty-one days after demand, or if any of the covenants should be

broken, the term granted, or so much thereof as should be unexpired, should be void, and it should be lawful for the landlord to re-enter :—Held, that the lease was only voidable by breach of the covenant, and that the landlord was bound to make an actual re-entry in order to take advantage of the forfeiture, of which a subsequent receipt of rent was a waiver. *Arnsby* v. *Woodward*, E. 8 G. 4. *Page* 536

4. By agreement of 31st *March*, *A.* agreed to grant *B.* a lease of a public-house for twenty-one years, from 29th *September* then next, in consideration of £1000, of which £10 was paid down, £90 was to be paid on 13th *April*, and the residue on having possession. *B.* being called on to pay the £90 required *A.* to prove his title, which being refused, he gave notice that he would rescind the contract, and brought an action to recover the £10, which he had paid :—Held, that he had a right so to do, and that he was not bound to wait until 29th *September*, from which time the lease was to run. *Roper* v. *Coombes*, E. 8 G. 4. 562

LIBEL.

See PLEADING, 1.

LIEN.

An agreement by a broker that he will sell goods for his principal, and pay over the whole proceeds, without setting off a debt then due to him from his principal, is not binding upon the broker, so as to deprive him of his legal right of lien or set off. *M'Gillivray* v. *Simson*, M. 7 G. 4. 35

LIGHTHOUSE.

See POOR RATE, 1.

LIMITATION OF ACTIONS.

1. One of two joint executors was applied to for payment of a debt of his testator, who had been dead twenty years, and as against whom the debt was barred by the statute of limitations, and said, " I believe the debt is a just one, and has never been paid. I should be happy to serve you in the matter if I could, but I cannot do any thing without the consent of the (testator's) family :"—Held, in an action against both executors, that there was no such acknowledgment of the debt as took the case out of the statute of limitations as against them ; there being no promise, express or implied, to pay the debt. *M'Culloch* v. *Dawes*, M. 7 G. 4. *Page* 40

2. On issue taken of *actio non accrevit infra sex annos*, in an action of assumpsit, it was proved that the defendant said within six years, on being applied to for payment, " I cannot pay the debt at present, but I will pay it as soon as I can :"—Held, that this was not a sufficient acknowledgment to take the case out of the statute of limitations, without proof on the part of the plaintiff of the defendant's ability to pay. *Tanner* v. *Smart*, E. 8 G. 4. 549

3. Where, after the lapse of six years, a defendant, being asked for the payment of a debt, said, " I owed the money, but I have a receipt in full of all demands, I shall search for it, and let you know in the event of my not being able to find it :"—Held, that this was not sufficient to take the case out of the statute of limitations. *Brydges* v. *Plumptre*, T. 8. G. 4. 746

MANDAMUS.

1. *Mandamus* refused to the trustees of the *Rugby Charity* to compel the payment of increased alms to claimants on the funds, although the applicants were at an advanced age, and would probably be dead before relief could be had in Chancery. *Rugby Charity Trustees, ex parte*, H. 7 & 8 G. 4. 214

2. *Mandamus* lies to a minister to restore a parish-clerk removed by him without just cause. And the Court will not judge of the justice of the cause of removal upon the *ex parte* statement of the minister; he must state it in his return to the *mandamus*, and give the clerk an opportunity of answering it. *Rex v. Davies, H. 7 & 8 G. 4. Page* 234

3. The return to a *mandamus*, denying the matters of the writ with a *protestando*, is bad. *Rex v. Bristol Dock Co. H. 7 & 8 G. 4.* 309

4. An 'act of parliament authorised the *Bristol* Dock Co. to make a floating harbour, and required them to make a common sewer in a certain direction, and also to alter and reconstruct all or any of the sewers of *Bristol* at the mouths, so that they might be discharged considerably under the surface of the water in the harbour, and also to make such " *other alterations and amendments*" in the sewers as should be necessary in consequence of the floating harbour. The sewers constructed under the water of the floating harbour became a nuisance to the neighbourhood:—Held, that *mandamus* would lie to compel the company, under the words " other alterations and amendments," to construct a new sewer, without carrying it under the floating harbour, even at the expense of purchasing land adjacent. *Id.* ibid.

5. A *mandamus* " to make such alterations and amendments in the sewers as were necessary in consequence of the floating of the harbour" is sufficiently specific, the mode of remedying the evil being left by parliament to the discretion of the company. *Id.* ibid.

MANOR.
See COPYHOLD.—MARKET.—WASTE.

MARKET.
The lord of an ancient fish-market may by law have a right to prevent persons from selling fish in their own houses, within the limits of his franchise. *Mosley v. Walker, T. 8. G. 4.* Page 863

MARRIAGE SETTLEMENT.
1. By marriage settlement, settlor limited his estate to trustees " to the only proper use and behoof of them, their heirs and assigns for ever," in trust for settlor until his marriage, and from and after his marriage, in trust for husband and wife for life and the longest liver; then in trust for a term to other trustees to raise portions for younger children; then in trust for the first son and the heirs male of the body; then to the second son in like manner, and then to the daughters; and, for default of such issue, then over to the right heirs of the body of the settlor:—Held, that the *first* trustees took the legal estate by common law, and not by the statute of uses, and that the *second* use could not be executed by the statute. *Doe v. Passingham, H. 7 & 8 G. 4.* 416

2. The purposes of the settlement, however, being at an end, in ejectment by the devisee of the person last seised, after the lapse of forty years, it was held, that it might be left to the jury to presume a reconveyance of the legal estate from the trustees. *Id.* ibid.

MARSHAL.
See ADMISSION.

MEMORIAL.
See ANNUITY.

MILITIA.
See SETTLEMENT *by Hiring and Service*, 3.

MINISTER.
See MANDAMUS, 2.

MONEY HAD AND RECEIVED.

See ANNUITY, 9.—MONEY PAID.—PARTNERS, 3.

MONEY PAID.

See ANNUITY, 9.—BILL OF EXCHANGE, 2.

1. Money paid in ignorance of a fact, and without full means of obtaining knowledge of that fact, may be recovered back by the party paying it, in an action for money had and received. *Milnes* v. *Duncan, E.* 8 G. 4. *Page* 731

2. Money lodged by a bankrupt in the hands of an arbitrator, and paid over by the latter before the commission issued, and in ignorance of an act of bankruptcy, cannot be recovered by the assignees from the arbitrator. *Tope* v. *Hockin, T.* 8. G. 4. 881

3. Money paid as the only means of recovering possession of property to which the party is entitled, constitutes a compulsory payment, and may be recovered back. *Shaw* v. *Woodcook, T.* 8 G. 4. 889

MORTGAGEE.
See SHIP, 2.

MORTGAGOR.
See SHIP, 2.

NAVIGATION.

Where staiths were erected in the river *Tyne* for the purpose of loading vessels with coals:—Held, in an indictment against the owners of the staiths for a nuisance, that they were properly acquitted, the jury being of opinion that the abridgment of the right of passage occasioned by the staiths was for a public purpose, that they produced a public benefit, were erected in a reasonable situation, and left a reasonable space for the passage of vessels on the river. Held also, that the jury might properly take into consideration, that by means of the staiths coals were supplied to the public at a cheaper rate, and in a better condition, than they otherwise could be. Held also, that the want of a previous writ of *ad quod damnum* was not conclusive against the defendants. *Rex* v. *Russell, E.* 8 G. 4. *Page* 566

NEGLIGENCE.

See BROKER.—NEW TRIAL.

A motion may be made in this Court for a new trial after judgment and execution in a cause tried in the Courts of Great Sessions in *Wales*, without entering into the recognizance required by 5 G. 4, c. 106, s. 4. *Howell* v. *Howell, E.* 8 G. 4. 477

NOTICE OF ACTION.

See CONSTABLE, 1.—JUSTICES, 2, 3.

Where a statute provides that " no plaintiff shall recover in any action commenced against any person for any thing done in execution or under authority of the act, unless notice in writing shall be given to the person intended to be sued 28 days before such action shall be commenced;" no notice is necessary where the defendant had not any reasonable ground for supposing that he had acted in execution or under authority of the act. *Cooke* v. *Leonard, H.* 7 & 8 G. 4. 339

NOTICE TO QUIT.
See EJECTMENT.

NUISANCE.
See NAVIGATION.

ORDER OF REMOVAL.

An order of removal made by two justices, one of whom appears by the order to be one of the church-wardens making the complaint, is bad. *Res* v. *Great Yarmouth, Inhabitants.* E. 8 G. 4.   *Page* 682

PARISH CLERK.

See MANDAMUS, 2.

PARISH OFFICERS.

See ORDER OF REMOVAL.

PARTNERS.

See JOINT STOCK COMPANY.—POOR RATE, 4.—SALE.

1. Where a partner borrows money on his own private account, and subsequently applies part of it to partnership purposes, the lender cannot sue the partnership for the money so borrowed. *Lloyd* v. *Freshfield, M.* 7 G. 4.   19
2. Several actions will not lie against the different members of a partnership firm for the same identical debt. Therefore, where a plaintiff brought two actions against two joint contractors for the same debt, the Court set aside the proceedings *without* costs in one action, the debt and costs in the other having been paid. *Carne* v. *Legh, M.* 7 G. 4.   126
3. Three ship-brokers agreed in writing with a ship-owner to freight his vessel at a certain commission, dividing profits and commission. One of the brokers alone paid and received money on account of the ship, and delivered to the owner an account charging a liquidated sum for commission. The owner acquiesced in the accuracy of the account, but objected to the charge for commission being too much, but which the broker retained in his hands. There was no adjustment of accounts between the brokers :—Held, that money had and received would not lie by two bro-

kers against the third, for their share of the commission. *Bovill* v. *Hammond, H.* 7 & 8 G. 4. *Page* 186

4. F being one of three co-trustees, proprietors of stock, and also one of three co-partners in a banking-house, forged the names of his co-trustees to a power of attorney, under which he sold the stock, and paid the money into his own banking-house. Neither his co-trustees nor his co-partners were privy to the transaction. F. was executed for another forgery. The surviving trustees sued the surviving partners for the money. On an issue from Chancery, directing that no objection should be taken that F. had been interested both as a trustee and a partner:—Held, that the money constituted a debt from the bankers to the trustees. *Stone* v. *Marsh, E.* 8 G. 4.   643

PATENT.

See BANKRUPT, 3.

1. A patent being granted upon a specification, that the machine was capable of performing all the operations necessary to the perfection of the proposed invention; and it appearing that a second patent was taken out for improvements necessary to the efficient operation of the original machine :—Held, that the consideration for the first patent having failed, both patents were void. *Bloxham* v. *Elsee, H.* 7 & 8 G. 4.   215
2. *Quære,* whether a patent, in which an alien enemy has an interest, can be supported. *Id.*   *ibid.*

PERJURY.

See INDICTMENT.

PETITIONING CREDITOR.

See ASSIGNMENT, 8.

PETIT SESSIONS.

See SESSIONS.

The petit sessions have no jurisdiction to allow the accounts of a surveyor of highways under 13 G. 3, c. 78, s. 48, where the parties have been before one justice, who had not gone into the accounts, but referred the case to the petit sessions. *Rex v. Yorkshire, N. R. Justices,* H. 7 & 8 G. 4.   *Page* 204

PILOT ACT.

1. The master of a vessel having on board a licensed pilot appointed by the Trinity House of *Newcastle-upon-Tyne,* under the local act, 41 G. 3, c. 86, s. 6, is not entitled to the protection of the 55th section of the General Pilot Act, 6 G. 4, c. 125. *Dodds* v. *Embleton,* M. 7 G. 4.   27

2. The master of a vessel laden with wine and fruit, which latter, being stowed above the former, was, by the bill of lading, to be delivered at *Cox's Quay,* which is higher up the river *Thames* than the *London Docks,* where the wine was to be delivered, conveyed her first to the *London Docks,* where he discharged the pilot, but the vessel did not break bulk. The consignees of the fruit refused to let it be landed in the *London Docks,* whereupon the master took on board another pilot to convey the vessel to *Cox's Quay.* In the passage, the vessel ran foul of a barge and sunk it :— Held, that the pilot who had charge of the vessel was alone answerable for the loss under 6 G. 4, c. 125. *M'Intosh* v. *Slade,* T. 8 G. 4.   738

PLEADING.

See BANKRUPT, 2.—CORPORATION, 1. —COVENANT—EVIDENCE, 7, 8, 11. LANDLORD AND TENANT.—TITHES, 1.—VARIANCE.

1. A declaration for a libel concerning plaintiff set out the following

matter :— "Society of Guardians for the Protection of Trade against Swindlers and Sharpers, &c. I (defendant) am directed to inform you that G. (plaintiff) is reported to this Society as improper to be proposed to be balloted for as a member thereof," (meaning that plaintiff was a swindler and sharper, and an improper person to be a member of the said society):—Held, after verdict, that the innuendo was not warranted by the libel, and that the words themselves were not actionable for want of a colloquium. *Goldstein* v. *Foss,* H. 7 & 8 G. 4.
                    Page 197

2. In a declaration in debt for rent, an averment of a demise of " a messuage, lands, and premises, with the appurtenances," is well supported by proof of a demise of " a messuage, &c. together with the furniture, utensils, and implements." *Farewell* v. *Dickenson,* H. 7 & 8 G. 4.   245

3. It is a general rule in pleading that an equivocal expression shall be construed against the party using it; but if the other party pleads over, it shall be construed in that sense which will support the previous pleadings. *Hobson* v. *Middleton,* H. 7 & 8 G. 4.   249

4. A count stating, " that plaintiff, at request of defendant, caused to be delivered to defendant divers pigs, to be taken care of by defendant for plaintiff, *for reward to defendant, and in consideration thereof, defendant undertook and agreed* with plaintiff to take care of the pigs, and to *re-deliver* them on request," is a count in *assumpsit,* and cannot be joined with counts in *case. Corbett* v. *Packington,* H. 7 & 8 G. 4.   258

5. *A.* agreed with *B.* to sell him the stock and goodwill of his business as an apothecary, and to demise to him his house in which the business was carried on, for which *B.*

was to pay 800*l.* and to take the furniture and fixtures at a fair valuation, which were afterwards valued at 170*l.* 4*s.* 400*l.* was paid in hand at the time of executing the agreement, and B. further agreed to accept and pay two bills of exchange, one for 400*l.* payable at twelve months after date, and the other for 170*l.* 4*s.* at two months after date ; and A. agreed not to carry on the like business within five miles of the same house : and for the true performance of the agreement each party bound himself to the other in the *penal* sum of 500*l.*, to be recoverable on breach of the agreement in a Court of law, as and by way of *liquidated damages:*—Held, that this was a *penalty*, and could not be pleaded by way of set-off as *liquidated damages* in an action by B. for a breach of the agreement in carrying on the business within five miles of the house. Held, also, that though B. replied *bankruptcy* to part of A.'s plea, and demurred as to the rest, upon which there was a joinder in demurrer, A. could not avail himself of the bankruptcy to deprive B. of his judgment on demurrer. *Davies* v. *Penton*, H. 7 & 8 G. 4.   *Page* 369

6. Covenant, by the father of an apprentice against the master, for not teaching the apprentice. Plea, that defendant did teach, until the apprentice ran away and never returned. Replication, that on a certain day defendant refused, then or ever, to take back the apprentice, and thereby discharged him. Rejoinder, that the apprentice had previously enlisted as a soldier, and that plaintiff never requested defendant to take back the apprentice at a time when he was able to return. Surrejoinder, that soon after the apprentice had enlisted, defendant refused, then or ever, to take him back, and wholly

discharged him. Demurrer. Held, that the surrejoinder was bad, and no answer to the rejoinder ; and that the plea was good and an answer to the action. *Hughes* v. *Humphreys*, E. 8 G. 4.   *Page* 715

POLICY OF INSURANCE.

Where a policy was effected on goods at and from *Liverpool* to *London*, and on the voyage the vessel deviated to *Southampton*, there to deliver goods shipped for that place at *Liverpool* :—Held, that the policy attached on the goods insured until the point of deviation, and that the underwriters were liable for an average loss upon the goods which had sustained a sea damage before the deviation, the jury having found such a loss to have arisen. *Hare* v. *Trevis*, T. 8 G. 4.   748

POOR RATE.

See DISTRICT PARISHES.—TITHES, 2.

1. A light-house erected on the shore for conveying light to ships at sea, is not rateable in respect of the value of the tolls paid by the shipowners for the benefit so communicated, but simply as a building. *Rex* v. *Fowke*, M. 7 G. 4.   120

2. The *owner* and occupier of a coal mine is rateable at the sum for which the mine would let, without reference to the expense incurred in making the mine productive. *Rex* v. *Attwood*, H. 7 & 8 G. 4.   328

3. The *lessee* and occupier of a coal mine is rateable at the sum which he pays as rent or royalty for it, without reference to the expense incurred in planting or improving the mine. *Id.*   *ibid.*

4. Where one only of several partners was resident in a parish, and a poor rate was made upon him in respect of all the partnership pro-

perty, and not upon his individual share:—Held, that the rate could not be supported. *Rex* v. *Gosse,* *T.* 8 *G.* 4.   *Page* 759

5. The *Regent's* Canal Company are rateable to the poor only in respect of the annual value of the land occupied by their canal *quâ* land, and not in respect of the value of the rates and tolls arising therefrom, which, being made personal property, is not rateable. *Rex* v. *Regent's Canal Company, T.* 8 *G.* 4.   760

6. A slip of land in a natural state, used as a landing-place for goods on the edge of a basin belonging to a canal company, is not a wharf within the meaning of 52 *G.* 3, c. 195, nor rateable as such to the poor. *Id.*   *ibid.*

7. An act of parliament vested a dock and the dues arising therefrom in trustees, and provided that those dues should be applied to paying off the debt incurred in making the dock, and to keeping it in repair, and then that the dues should be lowered:—Held, that the trustees were not rateable to the poor, either for the dock dues, or for the premises purchased or rented for the purposes of the dock, there being no beneficial occupation of either by any person. *Rex* v. *Liverpool, Inhabitants, T.* 8 *G.* 4.   780

8. Trustees are not rateable to the poor in respect of the tolls of a navigation received by them, the surplus of which is by statute made applicable to the repair of public bridges and highways. *Rex* v. *Weaver Trustees, T.* 8 *G.* 4.   788

PRACTICE.

1. Process being returnable in *Easter,* plaintiff in *Trinity* term files common bail for defendant, and delivers a declaration with notice to plead. In *Trinity* vacation judgment is signed for want of a plea. Defendant is not entitled to an imparlance until *Michaelmas* term, for that rule applies only where the defendant himself is properly in Court before the declaration is delivered. *Winter* v. *Barnes, M.* 7 *G.* 4.   *Page* 19

2. A defendant was arrested upon a latitat made returnable in vacation, and after the return-day took out a summons for time to put in bail:—Held, that this waived the irregularity. *Moore* v. *Stockwell, M.* 7 *G.* 4.   124

3. A town cause was entered for trial, and notice given for the sittings after *Easter* term. At those sittings it was made a remanet to the sittings after *Trinity* term, when the plaintiff did not try:—Held, that the defendant was entitled to judgment as in case of a nonsuit. *Ham* v. *Gregg, M.* 7 *G.* 4.   125

4. It is no ground for setting aside serviceable process that the initials instead of the full *Christian* names of a defendant are introduced. *Rolfe* v. *Peckham, H.* 7 & 8 *G.* 4.   214

5. Where husband and wife sue for money lent by the wife while sole, and the wife dies pending the suit, the suit abates, and the defendant cannot have judgment as in case of a nonsuit. *Checchi* v. *Powell, H.* 7 & 8 *G.* 4.   243

6. Where plaintiff in error put in bail in vacation, and defendant in error excepted thereto, and gave a rule for better bail, and plaintiff gave notice for justifying the same bail on the first day of *Michaelmas* term, but they did not justify :—Held, that the bail in error were still liable upon the recognizance for the

costs of the proceedings in error. *Adnam v. Wilkes, H.* 7 & 8 G. 4.
Page 387

7. By the master's allocatur an attorney was ordered, on the 12th *May,* to pay over 15*l.* to his client. On the 26th *June* the attorney became bankrupt, and afterwards obtained his certificate:—Held, that it was then too late to move for an attachment for not paying the money pursuant to the master's allocatur. *Baron v. Martell, H.* 7 & 8 G. 4.
390

PREBENDARY.

See CLERGY.

PRIVILEGE.

See ARREST, 1.

PROHIBITION.

1. In prohibition, a writ of consultation sued out and delivered to the Judge of the Court below, before a writ of error is allowed, is not supersedable by such writ of error; and this Court will not stay the proceedings upon it. *Free v. Burgoyne, M.* 7 G. 4.
14

2. A plaintiff in prohibition obtaining judgment after demurrer is not entitled to costs, except his case is within 8 & 9 W. 3, c. 11, s. 3; and if the judgment he obtains is for a partial prohibition, and a partial consultation, his case is not within that statute. *Free v. Burgoyne, E.* 8 G. 4.
601

PROMISSORY NOTE.

See BILL OF EXCHANGE, 1.

PUIS DAREIN CONTINUANCE.

See BANKRUPT, 2.

QUO WARRANTO.

See CORPORATION.

The affidavit of a relator in a motion for a quo warranto, that "he has been informed and believes" that the defendant exercises the office which he is charged with usurping, is sufficient. *Rex v. Slythe, H.* 7 & 8 G. 4.
Page 226

REPLEVIN.

See VARIANCE.

REQUESTS, COURT OF.

See TROVER.

SALE.

See AGREEMENT — LANDLORD AND TENANT, 1.—PARTNERS, 2.—VENDOR AND VENDEE.

An assignment for money, by one partner to another, of his share of the partnership interest in contracts with government, is not a *sale of property* within 49 G. 3, c. 149, and does not require an *ad valorem* stamp. *Belcher v. Sykes, H.* 7 & 8 G. 4.
231

SEQUESTRATION.

A writ of sequestration need not be published before the return day of the writ of *levari facias,* on which it is founded, nor need a copy of it be affixed on the church door. *Bennett v. Apperley, E.* 8 G. 4.
673

SESSIONS.

See JUSTICES, 1.—PETIT SESSIONS.

1. Notices of holding a special sessions for stopping up a footway were *signed* by the chief constables, and *served* by a person acting under their authority upon the justices:— Held, that the notices were *given* by the chief constables within the meaning of 13 G. 3, c. 78, s. 62, and regular. *Rex v. Suffolk Justices, M.* 7 G. 4.
111

2. Three several appeals, involving

the same facts and the same questions of law, having been entered for hearing at sessions, and the appellants having agreed that the decision of the Court on one should bind the other cases, and the sessions having by a majority of justices decided with the respondent in the first :—Held, that this Court would not compel the sessions to hear the other cases, although the justices had granted a case, but not upon any doubt of their own as to the propriety of their decision. *Rex* v. *Worcestershire, Justices*, H. 7 & 8 G. 4. 　　*Page* 210

3. The 54 G. 3, c. 84, which enacts that the *Michaelmas* Quarter Sessions *shall be* holden in the week next after the 11th of *October*, is merely directory, and those sessions may be legally holden at another time. *Rex* v. *Leicester, Justices*, T. 8 G. 4. 　　772

SET-OFF.

See LIEN.—PLEADING, 5.

1. Assignees may recover from the factor of a bankrupt all monies received by him from the bankrupt within two months of the issuing of the commission: and the factor cannot set off debts incurred by the bankrupt to him within the same time, although the factor has acted *bona fide*, and in ignorance of the act of bankruptcy. *Note*—this applies only to commissions issued prior to 6. G. 4, c. 16; *vide* s. 50 of which. *Kinder* v. *Butterworth*, M. 7 G. 4. 　　47

2. Where the agents for the grantor and grantee of an annuity rendered accounts to the latter, crediting him with instalments upon the annuity as "not yet received," and debiting him with commission and receipt stamps; and also other accounts crediting him with instalments as actually received, and debiting him with commission and receipt

stamps; but afterwards, with the knowledge and consent of the grantee, debited him with the same instalments as not having been paid, which, in fact they had not; and the agent afterwards became bankrupt:—Held, that his assignees were entitled to withdraw those sums from the credit side of the grantee's account with the bankrupt. *Shaw* v. *Dartnall*, M. 7 G. 4. 　　*Page* 54

SETTLEMENT, By *Estate*.

See EVIDENCE, 13.

SETTLEMENT, By *hiring and service*.

1. A hiring for an indefinite period, at six shillings a week for the winter, and nine shillings a week for the summer, is not a yearly hiring, and a year's service under it confers no settlement. *Rex* v. *Warminster, Inhabitants*, M. 7 G. 4. 　　70

2. A shoemaker proposed to the mother of a pauper, a boy, to take him to learn his business. The boy was to serve four years, was to board and lodge with his mother, and was to have half what he earned. The mother consented, and the boy served four years upon those terms. No indentures were executed *on account of the poverty of the mother*, and no premium was paid :—Held, that this was not a contract of hiring and service, but a defective contract of apprenticeship, and that the pauper gained no settlement by service under it. *Rex* v. *St. Margaret's, King's Lynn, Inhabitants*, M. 7 G. 4. 　　160

3. A militia-man hired himself for a year, and served a year under such hiring. It did not appear that at the time of the hiring he told his master that he was a militia-man: —Held, that he gained no settlement. *Rex* v. *Holsworthy, Inhabitants*, H. 8 G. 4. 　　332

SETTLEMENT, *By renting a tenement.*

1. A person coming into a parish *as a servant*, and during his servitude renting a tenement, *without residing thereon*, of 10*l.* value, gains a settlement under 13 & 14 *C.* 2, c. 12. *Rex* v. *Kevardington, Inhabitants, M. 7 G. 4.* Page 72

2. Where a person hired a house at 12*l.* a year for a whole year, and died three days before the year expired, but his corpse remained in the house until after the year had expired, and after his death his widow resided there and paid the year's rent:—Held, that he gained no settlement under 59 *G.* 3, c. 50, which could be communicated to his wife and children. *Rex* v. *Crayford, Inhabitants, M. 7 G. 4.* 80

3. A pauper took a house at the annual rent of 8*l.* from *Lady-day* to *Michaelmas,* 1821, and then took another house from *Michaelmas,* 1821, to *Lady-day,* 1822, at the annual rent of 9*l.,* and during the whole of both periods was the tenant of a piece of garden ground at the annual rent of two guineas, but had agreed with a third person that they should share the expense and profits equally of cultivating the garden ground, and the partner paid half the rent to the pauper, but the latter paid the whole to the landlord:—Held, that no settlement was gained under 59 *G.* 3, c. 50. *Rex* v. *Tonbridge, Inhabitants, M. 7 G. 4.* 128

4. A person hires and occupies a 10*l.* tenement for more than a year, and after his death the rent is paid out of the proceeds of the sale of his effects, no settlement is gained either under 59 *G.* 3, c. 50, or 6 *G.* 4, c. 57. *Rex* v. *Carshalton, Inhabitants, M. 7. G. 4.* 132

5. Under 6 *G.* 4, c. 57, no settlement can be acquired by renting a tenement, unless the entire rent for the term of one whole year at the least, whatever its amount, be actually paid. *Rex* v. *Ramsgate, Inhabitants, E. 8 G. 4.* Page 688

6. Where a shepherd hired himself under an agreement for 12*l.* per week, and to have "twenty-one ewes going:"—Held, that as it was no part of the contract that the sheep should be pasture fed, no settlement was gained; although the feed was worth more than 10*l.* a year, and might have been in fact pasture feeding. *Rex* v. *Thornham, Inhabitants, T. 8 G. 4.* 762

SHERIFF.

See EXECUTION.

1. A bailiff had taken in execution goods of a trader more than sufficient to satisfy the levy. The trader became bankrupt, and his assignees authorised the bailiff to sell all the goods by private contract for a certain sum, which he did, and received the money. The bailiff then satisfied the execution creditor, but never paid over the surplus to the assignees. The assignees sued the sheriff for the surplus:—Held, that they could not recover, because the bailiff in selling goods beyond the amount of the levy was the agent of the assignees and not of the sheriff. *Cook* v. *Pallmer, E. 8 G. 4.* 723

2. Where, under a *fi. fa.,* a judgment creditor was left in possession by the sheriff's officer of a chattel taken in execution, and with the consent of the debtor and creditor, it was delivered to *A.*; and the officer retook it to pay poundage:—Held, that *A.,* who had *bonâ fide* paid the price of the chattel, might maintain trover for it against the sheriff. *Goode* v. *Langley, T. 8 G. 4.* 791

SHIP.

See PARTNERS, 3.—FINAL ACT.— POLICY OF INSURANCE. — POOR RATE, 1.

1. The captain and co-owner of a ship signed bills of lading making the cargo deliverable to the consignee or their assigns, he or they paying freight. He delivered the cargo to the consignees, and took a bill for the freight, which was dishonoured. In an action against the consignors for the freight:—Held, first, that the jury were rightly directed to find for the defendants, if they thought the captain took the bill as a matter of preference and convenience to himself; and secondly, that it lay upon the plaintiffs to prove that he took it from necessity, if the fact were so. *Strong* v. *Hart*, H. 7 & 8 G. 4.   *Page* 189

2. The managing owner of a ship mortgages his share, and the transfer is duly indorsed on the certificate of registry. He continues to manage as before, and the mortgagee never takes possession of, or interferes with the ship:—The mortgagee is not liable for goods supplied to the ship by order of the mortgagor. *Briggs* v. *Wilkinson*, T. 8 G. 4.   871

STAGE-COACH.

See SUNDAY.

STAMP.

See AGREEMENT, 1.—EVIDENCE, 13. SALE.

A memorandum in these words, "Mr. *T.* has left in my hands 200*l.*," may be given in evidence in support of an action for money had and received, without a stamp. *Tomkins* v. *Ashby*, E. 8 G. 4. 543

STATUTE OF LIMITATIONS.

—*See* LIMITATION OF ACTIONS.

STATUTES—CITED OR COMMENTED ON.

STOPPAGE IN TRANSITU.

See BANKRUPT, 1.

1. Where goods are ordered to be delivered up to a consignee at a particular place, the transitus, generally speaking, continues until they are delivered to him there; but if he postpones or changes the place of the delivery, or does any act equivalent to taking possession of the goods, the transitus is at an end. *Foster* v. *Frampton, M. 7 G. 4.* Page 108

2. Goods purchased by an agent at *Manchester,* for the avowed purpose of being sent to his principal at *Lisbon,* are *in transitu* until they arrive at *Lisbon,* and, on the insolvency of the principal, may be stopped by the seller in the warehouse of the agent at *Manchester. Coates* v. *Railton; E. 8 G. 4.* Page 593

SUNDAY.

Where a person booked a place and paid half the fare to go by a common stage-coach from C. to L. on a *Sunday,* and the coach proprietor refused to carry him because there were no other passengers, whereupon the plaintiff hired a post-chaise to go to his destination:— Held, that the coach proprietor was liable for the chaise hire notwithstanding the contract was made on a *Sunday. Sandiman* v. *Breach, T. 8 G. 4.* 796

SURETY.

See ANNUITY, 7, 8.

SURRENDER.

See EVIDENCE, 12.

SURVEYORS' ACCOUNTS.

See PETIT SESSIONS.

TITHES.

See LEASE, 1.

1. In an action for not setting out tithes of hay, an immemorial custom for setting out such tithes was averred to exist " within the parish, and the limits, bounds, and titheable places thereof." It appeared in evidence that one township of the parish was covered by a modus for hay-tithes:— Held, no variance from the custom alleged. *Piggott* v. *Bayley, M. 7 G. 4.* 12

2. A corn rent given to the rector in lieu of tithes, payable " free from all *taxes* and other deductions whatsoever, except the land tax," is exempt from payment of poor rates. *Mitchell* v. *Fordham, H. 7 & 8 G. 4.* 335

3. The rakings of corn are titheable,

where, from the course of husbandry used, their quantity is necessarily considerable, though no fraud is practised or intended. *Glanville v. Stacey, E.* 8 G. 4. Page 626

TOLLS.

See POOR RATE, 1. 5. 8.

Assumpsit lies for fish claimed as toll for the use of a capstan and windlass in drawing fishing boats upon the beach out of the sea. *Earl Falmouth v. Penrose, H.* 7 & 8 G. 4. 452

TRESPASS.

See CONSTABLE, 1.—CORONER, 3.— EVIDENCE, 11.

Where an attorney, at the instance of a creditor, sued out process against a debtor in the county court, and the attorney's agent, after the debt and costs had been paid, but in ignorance of that fact, signed judgment, sued out execution, and levied upon the debtor's goods, though he had never appeared:—Held, that both the creditor and his attorney were liable to the debtor in an action of *trespass. Bates v. Pilling, M.* 7 G. 4. 44

TROVER.

See BANKRUPT, 5.—SHERIFF, 2.— VENDOR AND VENDEE, 2.

Trover is not a cause of action within the operation of the *Bath* Court of Requests' Act, 45 G. 3, c. 67. *Weare v. Calder, E.* 8 G. 4. 546

TRUSTEES.

See PARTNERS, 4.—POOR RATE, 4. 8.

USE AND OCCUPATION.

See EVIDENCE, 10.

VARIANCE.

See INDICTMENT.—PLEADING, 2.— TITHES, 1.

In replevin for illegally distraining

plaintiff's growing corn in *four* closes, defendants avowed for rent in arrear, averring that plaintiff held the closes in which, &c. at certain yearly rent. Plaintiff pleaded, that he did not hold in manner and form alleged. Proof, that plaintiff held the *four* closes, and *two* others, at the rent stated in the avowry. No variance. *Hargrave v. Shewin, M.* 7 G. 4. Page 20

VENDOR AND VENDEE.

See BANKRUPT, 1.—EVIDENCE, 3.— FRAUDS, STATUTE OF.—LANDLORD AND TENANT.—STOPPAGE IN TRANSITU.

1. Vendor contracting to sell to vendee an estate with a good title, when he has only an equitable title himself and is not in possession, and failing in his contract, is liable to more than *nominal damages* for the breach of contract, besides the expenses incurred by the vendee. *Hopkins v. Gracebrook, M.* 7 G. 4. 22

2. Vendor ships by order of vendee goods, which are consigned by bill of lading to a third person at a foreign port. Before the vessel sails, the vendee stops payment, and the vendor thereupon demands the goods of the captain, without tendering freight or expenses of unshipping. The captain refuses to deliver, solely on the ground that he has signed a bill of lading for the consignee:—Held sufficient evidence of a conversion to support trover at the suit of the vendor. *Thompson v. Trail, M.* 7 G. 4. 31

3. Defendant agreed to sell to plaintiff a stack of hay for 145l., to be paid for in one month, and to be allowed to stand on defendant's premises for three months. Plaintiff stipulated that the hay should not be cut till paid for. The hay was accidentally burned on defendant's premises:—Held, that

there was a contract for immediate sale, by which the property in the hay vested immediately in plaintiff, and that he, having paid for the hay, could not recover back the price from defendant. *Tarling* v. *Baxter*, *H*. 7 & 8 *G*. 4. *Page* 272

4. *A.* agreed, *by parol*, to sell to *B.* twenty hogsheads of sugar out of a larger quantity which he had in bulk. *A.* filled four hogsheads, and delivered them to *B.*, who accepted them. *A.* afterwards filled sixteen other hogsheads, and requested *B.* to fetch them away, who promised so to do:—Held, that the property in the sixteen hogsheads thereby passed to *B.*; that his acceptance of the four was an acceptance of part of the twenty, within the exception in 29 *Car.* 2, c. 3, s. 17; and that *A.* might recover the value of the whole from *B.* in an action for goods bargained and sold. *Rohde* v. *Thwaites*, *H.* 7 & 8 *G.* 4. 293

5. Where goods were paid for in country bank notes in the afternoon of a day in the morning of which the bankers had stopped payment, without the knowledge of the vendor and the vendee, and the latter, at the end of a week, offered to return the notes to the former, demanding payment of them:— Held, that the vendee should have promptly presented the notes to the insolvent bankers, and given notice of non-payment to the vendor according to the law - merchant, and that by his neglect to do so he had made the notes his own. *Camidge* v. *Allenby*, *H.* 7 & 8 *G.* 4. 391

6. Where the vendee of a quantity of hops acknowledged by letter to the vendor the receipt of the invoice, but said that the hops were not arrived, and added, " if they do not arrive in a few days I must get some elsewhere:"—Held, that the invoice and the letter taken together did not constitute a note in writing of the contract to satisfy the statute of frauds. *Richards* v. *Porter*, *E.* 8 *G.* 4. *Page* 497

7. An agent for the vendor of goods received from the vendee an order upon his banker for the price to be paid out of funds specifically deposited for that purpose with the banker. The latter offered to pay in cash, deducting discount for the credit given, or by a bill upon a third person. The agent, without the knowledge of the vendee, took the bill, which was dishonoured :— Held, that the vendor could not sue the vendee for the price of the goods. *Smith* v. *Ferrand*, *T.* 8 *G.* 4. 803

WAIVER.

See LEASE, 2.

WALES.

See NEW TRIAL.

WARRANT.

See CONSTABLE, 1.

WARRANT OF ATTORNEY.

See BANKRUPT, 5.

A warrant of attorney subject to a defeazance not written on the same paper, is not void against the assignee of an insolvent debtor, within 3 *G.* 4, c. 39, s. 4. *Morris* v. *Mellin*, *E.* 8 *G.*· 4. 503

WARREN.

See FREE WARREN.

WASTE.

See COPYHOLD.

It is a presumption of law that waste land adjoining a road belongs to the owner of the adjoining inclosed land, whether freeholder, leaseholder, or copyholder. *Doe* v. *Pearsey*, *T.* 8 *G.* 4. 908

WHARF.

See POOR RATE, 6.